COMPUTERS IN URBAN AND REGIONAL GOVERNMENT

Papers from the Fourteenth Annual Conference

of the

URBAN AND REGIONAL INFORMATION

SYSTEMS ASSOCIATION

August 29 - September 2, 1976, Atlanta, Georgia

EDITOR:

ONONEZE M. ANOCHIE

Management Development Center
International City Management
          Association

Computers in Urban and Regional Government

Library of Congress cataloging in Publication Data

Urban and Regional Information Systems Association
    Computers in Urban and Regional Government.

        1. Local government--United States--Data processing--Congresses.
        2. Municipal government--United States--Data processing--Congresses.

    I. Anochie, Ononeze M.   II. Title
    JS344.E4U7 1977   352'.94'810973   77-777876
    ISBN 0-916848-13-2

Printed in the United States of America.

OFFICERS OF URISA

Donald S. Luria, President
George Farnsworth, Past President
Robert T. Aangeenbrug, President-Elect
Joyce Healy, Vice-President
Barry S. Wellar, Vice-President
Agnes D. Livingood, Secretary
Patricia C. Becker, Treasurer

BOARD OF DIRECTORS

Myron E. Weiner
Dani Emery
James R. Verougstraete
Donald F. Cooke
Kenneth J. Dueker
Carolee Bush
Edgar M. Horwood, Board Member Emeritus

1976 CONFERENCE COMMITTEE

Irene Wreen	Bill Sparrowhawk	Carolee Bush
Bob Dunphy	Jim Stevens	Bob Harper
Caby Smith	Regina Glenn	Susan Bresler
Barry Wellar	W. Phil Wynn, Jr.	Beverly Stephens
Herman Lujan	Jim McManama	Victor Davis
Douglas Herman	Joyce Annecillo	Dan Moravec
Ken Dueker	Jon Rickert	Susan Pearson
Mike Kevany	John Wilson	Eloise Coiner
Rick Schweitzer	Curtis Branscome	Adelle Kushner
Judith Odom	Patricia Becker	

Robert Aangeenbrug, Chairman   Brenda Day, Co-Chairwoman

URISA PUBLICATIONS COMMITTEE

Kenneth L. Kraemer, Editor-in-Chief

Ononeze M. Anochie
Managing Editor
Conference Proceedings

Joyce Annecillo
Managing Editor
Newsletter

PREFACE

The Urban and Regional Information Systems Association (URISA) is the largest and oldest professional organization for individuals concerned with the effective use of information systems technology in the public sector. Founded in 1963, URISA has well over 1,000 members in the United States, Canada and several other countries. This membership includes a variety of professionals whose careers and jobs affect and are affected by urban and regional information systems. These include public administrators, urban planners, local government departmental staff, data processing managers and staffs, employees of state, provincial and the national governments, university professors and their graduate students, and employees of hardware, software and other computer service companies.

Computers In Urban and Regional Government is the Proceedings of the Fourteenth Annual URISA Conference held in Atlanta Georgia, August 29 - September 1, 1976. The 54 papers included in this volume represent roughly 36% of all papers presented at the conference. Another 45 papers (30%) had been transmitted by the Papers Committee for publication in a second volume of these Proceedings. However, in March 1977, the URISA Board of Directors decided for financial reasons, to publish only one volume of the 1976 Proceedings. As a result, only those papers which had been received by the Papers Committee by the deadline of August 1, 1976 are included in this publication. For a listing of the 45 papers which did not make the deadline see pages 652 - 655. Copies of any of these papers will be made available on request to URISA members at the cost of reproduction.

The readers attention is called to the list of published Proceedings from earlier URISA conferences which can be ordered from the URISA Secretariat as indicated on the last page. The Association also publishes a very attractive and informative newsletter, URISA NEWS, for distribution to its members. URISA membership information and application forms can also be obtained from the Secretariat.

Finally, I want to commend Ms. Irene Wreen for the outstanding job she did as the Chairperson of the Papers Committee. Were it not for the temporary cash flow problems that URISA experienced in late 1976-early 1977, these Proceedings would have been published in record time - primarily because of the meticulous job that Irene and the Papers Committee had done. I also want to thank Bob Aangeenbrug, our new president and Conference Chairman; Ken Kraemer, Editor-in-Chief and Chairman of the Publications Committee; Rebecca Russum of MFOA and Cora L. Pace of ICMA for their assistance in getting this Proceedings out.

Ononeze M. Anochie
Director, Urban Information Systems
Management Development Center
International City Management Association

Washington, D.C.
April, 1977

TABLE OF CONTENTS

CONTENTS

CONTENTS

CONTENTS

x

CONTENTS

COMPUTERS IN URBAN AND REGIONAL GOVERNMENT

John H. Robinson
DAMES & MOORE
1100 Glendon Avenue
Los Angeles, CA 90024

USE OF AN INFORMATION SYSTEM TO AID CITIZEN PLANNNERS:
A CASE STUDY

One of the recent changes in the planning process is the increased active involvement of citizens.

Parallel with this shift in emphasis in the planning process, a more comprehensive information base on which planning decisions are made has developed. The increase in demand for information has led to a greater involvement by individuals from the scientific and data management disciplines.

Considering the increase of available data and the trend towards more active involvement of the public in the development of new urban and regional plans, a need has developed for an effective interface between the average citizen who seeks to be involved in the planning process and the technical data that is required to adequately understand and respond to the complex problems of the future.

Information scientists or data managers have successfully created this critical interface between a group of citizens and the planning process in a recent General Plan project in Los Angeles County, California. The subject study included the development of a comprehensive General Plan for the northern portion of Los Angeles County which included both rural and urban areas.

Discussion of the planning study will include each of the major elements of the citizen participation program, focusing particularly on: 1) review of the data inventory, 2) development of growth alternatives, 3) a Delphi assessment of environmental factors, 4) land use capability analysis, and 5) development of land use plan alternatives. As each element in the process is described, use of the information system and the concept of data management will be illustrated. In addition, the benefits of using an information system and the resultant impacts on the General Plan will be discussed.

1.0 INTRODUCTION

As the issues of living become more complex, and lifestyles are changing in an ever increasing pace, the people of the society are becoming more involved and more critical of the processes that govern them. One of the processes of governing that is undergoing criticism is the institutions and processes of planning that shape and form our urban environments. Planning, in the broad sense, is the guideline or framework that structures change in the environment as we develop from the present to some future state. The process of planning has traditionally focused primarily on those physical attributes of the urban environment that are most readily definable and easily understood. However, in current times, an increased awareness and desire to understand the processes of social interaction and the relationship between the physical and nonphysical elements of the environment, such as the social and economic structures, has developed. This change in emphasis is easily illustrated by the various types of environmental legislation which have been enacted in the last decade, and the resultant changes in social discussion of, and procedures for, current urban planning.

2.0 GENERAL PLAN REQUIREMENTS

The pressure to more effectively plan for the future has resulted in requirements for comprehensive general plans in several states as well as ongoing discussion of mandating land use planning at the Federal level. Most notable among these is the requirement in California for a comprehensive General Plan for every incorporated and nonincorporated area of the state.[1] This planning requirement, which is part of the state planning legislation which was enacted in 1970, also included requirements that the General Plan must be technically accurate, and that all of its elements must be totally integrated. An additional function of the California legislation was to provide, within the process of adopting and implementing the General Plan, a procedure for public review of the plan through public hearings.

The General Plan requirement in California stipulates in its guidelines that the General Plan must include the following elements: land use, transportation, health and public safety, conservation and resource management, housing, community design, and several others. The planning requirement is very comprehensive in nature, and the plans generated through the impetus of this legislation have required extensive planning efforts.

2.1 Data/Information Requirements for Planning

To develop the General Plan using the State Guidelines, and to effectively respond to the matrix of interrelated problems that a community faces as it develops, a comprehensive set of data must be collected and available for the planners as they develop the General Plan. This data includes such things as resource data, geotechnical data, land use data, economic data, housing data, census data, and many other types of data.

As with all data collection efforts, each of the data topics is collected and stored by different agencies, and must be obtained from different sources. In addition, each type of data has a different degree of reliability, is updated or maintained in different ways, and has different levels of usefulness through the planning process.

2.2 Multidisciplinary Approach

As the requirements for general plans to be more complete and comprehensive have grown, the number of people involved in the planning process have also increased. The time of general plans being a road network design, which is the perview of road engineers, has long passed. In fact, the term planner has now been adopted by a large cross section of the professional and academic community encompassing all those who seek to participate in the definition and solution of urban and resource management problems.

Not only has the desire to be involved in planning, but the increased responsibility to define current problems in more comprehensive terms has necessitated the emergence of multidisciplinary planning methodology. Today, planners include most of the engineering disciplines, natural scientists, social scientists, economists, urban designers and architects, politicians, and a host of other specialized people who are formed together into the "multidisciplinary" planning team. The organization of this large, diverse group of people, each of whom have paradigm-based methods for analysis into an effective team for planning the future, must be founded in the basic element of all planning activity: data and information. It is through the development of an effective and utilitarian data base that the requisite information for making decisions about the future and shaping a responsive general plan can be realized.

2.3 Data Management in Planning

To effectively deal with the great amount of data that is required for the general planning process, and to manage the variety, complexity, and abundance of such data, the planning process must include as one of its elements an effective tool for managing data and creating information for use in the planning process. If the planner is to effectively understand the context of the community or region for which the plan is to be developed, and to respond to the problems of that area, data and information about the area must be available. Further, the planner must have the freedom to manipulate the data such that it reveals the true state of the community and allows effective assessment of the impacts of decisions being made about the future of that community. This means that there must be provision for some sort of dynamic method of handling and managing data within the planning process. Specifically, the method for managing data must include the provision for accessibility, flexibility, and credibility.

If the planner is to have a reasonable opportunity to develop a successful plan, the data and information that is required in developing that plan must be accessible to the planner. That is, while there are usually great quantities of data available, much of that data is not in

a form that is directly applicable to the type of problem being considered by the planner. The data must be stored in a manner that it
can be formed into information that directly applies to the problem
being considered. The ability of stored data to be reformed into
specific types of information can be said to be a measure of the
accessibility of that data.

Flexibility refers to the concept that data must be gathered
and stored for use in such a manner that it can be modified, combined
with other types of data, and useful information created. Many times
data is collected in a format that is designed for a specific use,
which in its design, limits the use of data for other purposes. All
data should be collected and stored in a format that is most generic,
which allows the data to have the greatest utility within the planning
process.

In each case, the data that is collected and used as part of the
planning process should be reviewed to assure that it is the most
current data available and that it has a degree of resolution and
locational accuracy, and that some measure of quality control has
been observed in its collection and storage. The underlying factor
of the credibility of a plan is the source data used in the planning
process.

To effectively handle the great variety of data that is available
for a planning process, the planner must rely on an information management system. Since the advent of computer mapping technology, many
computer-based mapping systems have been developed precisely for this
purpose. These systems provide the planner with a tool to store,
analyze, and display geographically-referenced data in a variety of
ways such that the data has the greatest degree of accessibility and
flexibility for the planning process. In addition, the credibility
of the data can be most easily delineated through the use of the
computer-based mapping system. One of the most important elements
of a computer-based mapping system is the ability of the system to
display the results of the use of the data, and to track the use of
the data within some problem-solving environment. That is, that
through the use of the computer-based mapping system, the requirements for manipulating the data for an analysis must be explicitly
stated to the computer, and as such, they become explicitly documented.

Other benefits of using computer-based mapping systems include the
ability to recall and display large amounts of data at a very inexpensive cost, as well as to modify the types of analyses conducted during
the planning process, and to redisplay the results at a minimal cost.

3.0 CITIZEN PARTICIPATION IN PLANNING

One of the most notable trends within the last decade has been
the rise of the special interest group and the effect these groups
have had upon urban problems through the process of advocacy planning.
This notion, in its more primitive form, focused on the advocacy of
a specific course of action (plan) that would mitigate some critical
problem or need. Advocacy planning as a planning procedure has diminished in prominence. However, the role of the citizen or individual

representing his or her interests has evolved into a new form where active citizen involvement has become an integral and mandatory part of the planning process.[2]

It is an implicit assumption of planning that everyone represents a special interest. Each person belongs, in fact, to a matrix of special interest groups represented by the following concerns: professional or employment, lifestyle, economic, ethnic groups, and a variety of other cross sections of interest that an individual may be involved in or relate to. One role of planning, then, is to facilitate, through a synergistic relationship, all of these special interests into a statement of a desired future through either a process (administrative code) or product (general plan) that will best serve all special interests.

3.1 Traditional Citizen Participation

The current or traditional method of citizen involvement as institutionalized in the planning process is the requirement for open public hearings as a review function at the end of the planning process. The framework for the plan and for the future desired state of the community is effectively established during the development of the plan. However, the ability of the public to freely criticize and effect change in the plan is operationally limited in the public hearing process. Therefore, it can be concluded that the instutionalized method for active involvement of citizens in the planning process is not true participation at all. This is not to neglect the establishment of citizen participation councils as mandated by law, but again, these councils serve only as a review function and are not necessarily actively involved in the development of the plan under legal mandate. In addition, traditionally, the planner, because of the limitation of resources available for planning, and limitations on mechanisms for processing information, has not had an opportunity to effectively involve citizens in the planning process. Therefore, traditional "citizen participation programs" have primarily been manifested as public information-type meetings where information about the plan is distributed to the public, but no effective feedback through participation is formed.[3]

3.2 Active Participation of Citizens in the Planning Process

One of the keys then to active participation is the ability of the planner to make data and information available in a form such that a member of the public can effectively understand and deal with that information in the context of the General Plan. Again, the tools of flexibility, accessibility, and credibility in an information system can be applied to the environment of involving citizens in the planning process.

To create this synapse between the complexity of planning and true participation in the planning process, a new type of planner must come forward and assume a leadership role. This planner must have available to him the information processing tools, such as computer-based mapping systems, and the comprehensive understanding of the planning process such that he can extent the use of information management tools and the planning process to citizens so they can create their own plans.

At this point, a definition of citizen participation should be stated. One could offer the definition that citizen participation truly means the involvement of citizens in developing the plans such that the citizens create the plans and that planners become facilitators in the development of that plan. This nontraditional role for the planner is, in fact, one of the newly identified critical roles in planning.

4.0 CASE STUDY - NORTH LOS ANGELES COUNTY GENERAL PLAN

The key to the planning process and the effective participation of the community is the ability of the community to "understand the problem", that is, the forces that affect their community, and to make decisions concerning their desired future. These decisions, of course, must be based on an understanding of the problem through information that is available to describe various alternatives for the future, and the impacts of selecting one alternative in preference to another. At the base of the problem is information, and providing information is a meaningful form such that individual citizens who are not broad based generalists, but rather have specific expertise and interests, can understand that information and evaluate it to make meaningful decisions. To understand the impact of information in the decisionmaking and planning processes, and to explore methodology for facilitating that process for citizen planners, a case study project was used. It should be noted that this project was part of an ongoing planning effort, and not developed specifically to test new methods for citizen participation; however, this does not detract from the activities that were undertaken and the results of these experiments.

The case study was developed as part of a general planning program instituted by the County of Los Angeles in California. The County, in association with several other local jurisdictions that had planning authority,[4] selected a planning consultant to take the leadership role in the development of the plan and all associated citizen participation programs. The consultant, in concert with the staff of the County's planning agency, developed the plan in its entirety and conducted the citizen participation program.

The planning program took place over a two-year period starting in the fall of 1973. The first year of the planning effort was devoted to the development of a regional scale plan, and the second year focused on the development of more specific community plans.

4.1 Study Area Definition

The planning area encompassed the northern portion of Los Angeles County in California. This region of approximately 2,600 square miles includes two major population centers and an existing population of approximately 142,000 people. It is primarily a rural region adjacent to the major metropolitan region of Los Angeles partially blocked by a barrier of mountains from the metropolitan area.

The region is geophysically divided into two distinct areas; one is the Antelope Valley, which is a desert region totally separated from the rest of the county by a range of mountains. This subregion is primarily rural in nature and has historically been so. The second predominant area is the Santa Clarita Valley, which is an extension of the suburban regions of the Los Angeles metropolitan area. This area has undergone historical growth pressure from the spillover effect of suburban development, and is closely associated with the metropolitan region. In addition, there are other very small settlements on the fringes of the two predominant areas.

4.2 Historical Background

At the point of departure for the planning project, a countywide general plan, as mandated by the State of California land use planning legislation, had been stricken down by the courts due to major inadequacies in the plan. Therefore, at the time that the planning project was undertaken, no currently developed plan was in effect, and a moratorium on all activity had been instituted such that most development activity had to undergo an interim judicial review.

The economic base of the region is primarily aerospace and has also historically had a component of agriculture. The region is under implicit growth pressure due to the proposed development of a major airport (Palmdale Intercontinental Airport), which will be designed as a major West Coast air terminal for both domestic and international air travel. This airport is proposed to be larger at its full development than all of the existing regional metropolitan airports in existence at this point. Because of the proposal for the intercontinental airport, the speculation on land has become a critical problem in this region as well as the zoning practices that had been historically observed.

4.3 Planning Approach - Citizen Participation

The planning program that was defined for developing a General Plan for the northern portion of Los Angeles County is a two-step process. In the first portion of the planning program, a regional plan, including all mandated elements by California law, would be developed. The second portion of the program would include the development of local plans, including all mandated elements, for each of the local communities. The development of citizen participation strategies in the planning process were undertaken as part of the regional planning effort. They were successful in this effort and were used again in the community planning effort. However, only the case study program developed during the regional plan program will be reported here.

As the major mechanism for citizen participation within the planning process, a Citizens Planning Council (CPC) was formed. This council was derived from an existing communitywide standing committee. The CPC has no planning authority, and minimal political power in the region; however, within the local study area, that is the north Los Angeles County planning study area, this committee became an effective and implicitly powerful body. The CPC was officially recognized by the County government and was operated within the institutionalized structure of the County's planning organization.

The planning program developed to produce the regional plan was based on the simple concept of an economic model; that is, that there is demand for land and resources based on projections of growth and change in the future, and these demands must be satisfied by the supply of land and resources as it exists now and will in the future. The purpose of the plan, then, is to achieve an interaction of supply and demand to develop an equilibrium state in the community as the present becomes the future.

4.4 Citizens Planning Council

The CPC was selected so that a broad based representation of the communities included in the study was realized. A matrix was established listing as many specific interests as could be identified. These included public interests as well as private interests. Recommendations for nomination to the CPC were elicited from community groups, community leaders, and local government officials (specifically, the representative supervisoral office). Each nominee was listed on the matrix and cross referenced to the special interest groups listed. Those individuals that were able to represent more than one interest were considered more desirable as potential candidates for CPC membership than individuals that could only represent one interest. The CPC membership was limited to approximately 30 persons due to the logistical support necessary for such a group. It should be noted, however, that all the activities of the CPC were publicized and open to the public, and, in fact, most of the meetings had significant attendance from the general public.

After review of the candidates, the planning consultant, in concert with the county planning staff, recommended to the Board of Supervisors (the local legislative body) nominations for appointment to the CPC. These appointments were subsequently made, and the North Los Angeles County Citizens Planning Council was formed.

5.0 CITIZEN PARTICIPATION OBJECTIVES

At the onset of the planning program, a specific effort was made to establish a set of objectives around which the participation program could be designed. It was felt that the specific activities in which the citizen group were going to be involved would only yield meaningful results for the participants as well as the planning team if these activities were formed within a framework of objectives. This was further supported by the participation of many individuals from the planning team staff at different points in the process, but few who would be involved and have responsibility throughout the program. The stated objectives allowed a background against which those who did not participate throughout could define their own activities. The major objectives defined prior to the design of the citizen participation objective included the following items.

5.1 Involvement in Development of the Plan

As previously described, the traditional mode of participation of citizens in the planning process is at the end, when the plan has been formed and public hearings are held to elicit "public input". It is most difficult to have effective input to something that has already been completed. Those who have formed the plan will be defensive about it, if for no other reason than the impact changes may have on the budget available to produce the plan. Therefore, to "input" effectively, the public must participate in the development of the plan.

One of the often heard criticisms of the public by planners is that "they don't understand how complex the problem is, and what we went through to solve it." This attitude, which illustrates an important problem, would be solved in the proposed participation program by actively involving the CPC in all major elements of the planning process. In this way, not only would the participants have effective input to the process of developing the plan, but they would understand the process by which the plan is created.

5.2 Determine True Community Goals

To develop a successful plan, the planning team had to find the real community attitudes toward growth in the community, the size the communities wish to maintain, the image the local citizens had of themselves in their community, and the problems and attitudes they had toward self government versus regional government.

All of these general issues are an aggregation of many specific local concerns that have historically been identified, as well as illustrated by a questionnaire distributed to citizens in the study area. It was immediately felt by the professional planning team, however, that while community attitude surveys serve a useful purpose in identifying general trends, they cannot seek to effectively explore an issue once it has been defined.

5.3 Assure the Plan is Implementable

The viability of a plan and its process centers on implementability. This means that while the plan can be described as a desired future state for some future time, the plan actually takes shape in the process of implementation as the existing state becomes the futures state. One of the most notable problems in creating a plan that is implementable is to develop or elicit community support for that plan. This is one of the failings of planning and planners; that they are charged with creating a plan document that describes in graphic and text form a desired future state, but are not involved in the process of implementation of that plan over a period of 10 to 15 years, and so, never develop a feedback loop to critique their concept of implementation, and secondly, have no actual experience with implementing or administering a plan. Citizens who have lived with a plan and its administration can provide insight into how that plan can best be administered, and therefore, increase its ability to be implemented.

6.0 CITIZEN PARTICIPATION PROCESS

Recognizing the objectives for participation by representatives of the community in the development of a general plan for the future of the north Los Angeles County, a process was designed that attempted to integrate the citizens as an active part of the planning process. This process was formed around five areas of involvement in the actual generation of the plan, and was then supported by a supplementary process of criticism and reformulation. For purposes of illustrating the process and the interaction of the planning activities and support of the information system, only the five basic plan development activities will be reported. These activities included:

1) Data inventory
2) Assess growth alternatives
3) Assess environmental factors
4) Land use capability analysis
5) Land use plan alternatives

6.1 Data Inventory

The act of planning is recognized to depend significantly on the availability of data describing the natural and manmade environments as well as interactions between various sectors of the environment. As an initial activity for introduction of the CPC to the planning process, the rigors of selecting data sources, collection and mapping of data, and the initiation of a computer-based system for storage, analysis, and display of the data required for the development of a general plan were explained.

The discussion and activity of inventory of the requisite data was initiated with a session that dealt with the various issues to be explored during the course of the planning process. This included data and information required to conduct the land use suitability analysis, the assessment of growth of population, and the resultant impact on land use requirements, transportation, housing, employment, etc. The data topics were listed, and each topic explained in terms of it's content and usefulness. In addition to describing the data, all those data topics which were defined in geographic terms and had been entered into the computer's data base, were displayed using computer display techniques, and presented to the CPC. The participants then had an opportunity to critically review the maps to be used in the planning process and comment on their content and method of description.

At this point in the process, the citizens were seeing for the first time one of the benefits of using a computer-based mapping system. That is, all of the data maps presented to the citizens were presented at the same scale, and in the same format. It was easy for a participant to find a geographic location on one data map and refer to the same location on the map of another data topic. This clarity and consistency of presentation was to become one of the more important features of the information system as a tool for facilitating the planning process.

At the conclusion of the data inventory and review, several of the data topics were revised in response to requests by the citizen group, and new map display generated.

6.2 Assess Growth Alternatives

At the most gross level of allocation of future growth (in a predictive sense), the two subregions were considered. The total growth predicted to occur in the next 20 years (the planning period) was divided between the Antelope Valley and the Santa Clarita Valley. In no case was the allocated share of growth less than the projected employment that was locally centered or focused. That is, growth that would only logically occur in the Santa Clarita Valley from exogenous employment in the greater metropolitan area was not allocated to Antelope Valley, which is outside effective commuting distance for those jobs. A third segment of the growth was allocated to those areas that are not specifically within the two subregional valleys, but in the mountainous area between, and populated sparsely. The shares of growth allocated to each of the subregions was examined using the following general considerations:

1. Past trends of growth--specific types of employment generators were examined, and the preferences for commuting as well as the availability of housing (housing patterns) were used as indicators of the likely distribution of people employed by different industries. Also, the general growth trends for each of the communities in the planning area were examined and aggregated to the subregional level.

2. Adjacency to metropolitan area--the distance to employment opportunities in the Los Angeles metropolitan region (which is considered as exogenous employment), and the required commuting distances were considered in allocating growth induced by exogenous employment.

3. Community attitudes--a cross sectional attitudinal survey was conducted to discern the basic community attitudes towards additional population growth.

     One of the most predominant subjects of discussion as a result of the attitude survey was the desire for growth and development which was viewed by many as a conflict with the expressed desire to maintain a rural style of life in existing communities. In the Antelope Valley, which was the site of the greatest increase in employment due to the Palmdale Airport, the community attitude was split between those who sought to maintain the rural character of the community and those who saw the development of the airport as a growth and development opportunity. The Santa Clarita Valley, in contrast, viewed growth as an undesirable change in the existing character of the many small communities that populate that subregion.

As an initial assumption for allocation of growth, approximately 30 percent was allocated to the Santa Clarita Valley, approximately 60 percent to the Antelope Valley, and that remaining was assumed to occur in the small peripheral communities. This initial allocation was to serve as the basis for the development of alternative future land use plans. The development of each alternative and the assumptions made to develop each alternative altered the original assumed allocation of growth shares.

At this point in the planning process, the citizens have been exposed to the inexact science of predicting future growth, the assumption of growth, and a rigorous discussion had ensued concerning the gross allocation of shares of that growth within the two major subregional areas.

6.3 Assessment of Environmental Factors

To establish an estimate of the available land for specific types of land use, the quantity of land available was determined, and its geographic location defined. This estimate was derived through a land use suitability analysis where the various environmental factors that determine suitability for each type of land use were mapped for the entire study region, and then using a weighted overlay analysis (where one factor could be assigned numerically greater importance than other factors) for each land use type, a series of suitability maps were created. These maps show, for each specific type of land use considered, the most suitable, second most suitable, and third most suitable, etc. areas for development. The areas that are least suitable for development (or most sensitive to development) could still be developed, but have the greatest environmental cost if developed. A further classification of suitability exists; those areas that should be restricted from development because they are flood channels, steep hillsides, potential landslide areas, etc., and are shown on the suitability map as restricted.

To assess the importance of each of the environmental factors considered in determining suitability for the various land uses, the CPC used a formatted group discussion technique similar to the Delphi[5] technique. In this discussion process, the computer-based information system played two important roles. It provided feedback to the participants in the form of group-based statistics about the group's assessment of the importance of various environmental factors (data topics). It also provided map displays of those same factors to provide a contextural base for the citizen evaluation. The assessment was iterative, where the CPC, which was divided into small working groups, submitted assessments of importance for each of the environmental factors that were considered as a locational characteristic for a specific type of land use. These values, termed importance ratios, were then submitted to a statistical summary computer program which determined the normalized values for each working group, and then computed the group average and standard deviation. These values were reported to the CPC in the form of individual computer printouts. Using the group average value as a reference, each working group offered arguments for the entire group's consideration in an attempt to change the group average opinion (value). After each group had the opportunity to present arguments on all factors, the working groups submitted revised values for further processing. At the conclusion of several iterations of discussion and reassessment, it was found that group average opinion for each factor was changing insignificantly. At this point, the group had reached a concensus opinion and the assessment was complete.

6.4 Land Capability Analysis

Using the importance ratios developed by the citizens through the group-based decision process, suitability maps were produced and displayed by the computer.[6] These maps were presented to the CPC illustrating the results of their analysis of environmental factors in geographic form. In review of the suitability maps, the citizens were able to assess the impact of the assessment in terms of the importance they assigned to some of the environmental factors. For example, the factor of slope was not considered to have relatively great importance for residential land use suitability in the group's average opinion as a result of the assessment of environmental factors. However, review of the resultant suitability maps produced by the computer, using the values derived from the group average, revealed a pattern of suitability that was questioned by the citizens. It was shown that those areas the citizens intuitively observed to be unsuitable for development were shown as suitable even though they exhibited steep slope conditions, because the slope factor had been weighted lower relative to other factors. In several cases the group requested changes in the importance values be submitted to the computer, and that new suitability maps should be computed and displayed. Through the availability of the computer and the ability of the computer to quickly reprocess the suitability analysis, the planning process was demonstrated to be responsive to the needs of the participants as a planning tool.

6.5 Land Use Plan Alternatives

The active involvement of the CPC in development of the land use plan was accomplished through the use of a land use simulation model. This simulation model took the form of a plexiglass model board on which a transparent base map of the study region had been laid. The model board was designed so that information maps such as the land use suitability maps or any of the source data maps could be slipped beneath the model board to provide information in geographic form about the implications of a specific land use plan.

During the course of the land use plan simulation, the CPC was divided into working groups so that each group included members of the CPC that represented both geographic subregions in the study area. It was the intent of the land use simulation to develop several alternative land use plans using the simulation technique, and to involve CPC members for the two subregions in a geographically interactive activity. The simulation included the following steps:

1. Definition of Urban Form--to initiate the simulation, each working group was required to articulate some desired concept of the two-dimensional physical form of the urban environment. Alternative urban forms, such as cluster or dispersed development, were illustrated for the citizens through the use of small models. These models included prototype examples of the pattern that residential, commercial, industrial, recreational, and public facilities land use might assume to meet a specific set of land use objectives. For example, one form concept was titled, "The Dispersed Urban Form." In the dispersed urban form, residential development was dispersed at a very low density and in proximity to an extension of existing strip commercial development. It was pointed out to members of the planning council that this concept of urban form fostered an increased reliance on the automobile for transportation within the community, and that this type of dispersion did not support the desire for public transportation that was not subsidized because of the lack of concentrations of origins and destinations. This type of discussion was carried out for each of several basic concepts for urban form offered as urban form alternatives.

At the conclusion of the discussion of urban form illustrations, each group articulated their own desired concept of urban form, which could include elements of several of the models presented to the group. One element that was discussed in each group's articulation of its concept of urban form was the relationship between the suitability maps and the existing pattern of land use. This was particularly important because it illustrated to the CPC that while the computer-generated environmental suitability analysis shows in geographic form those areas that are most suitable for specific types of development, that in fact, in the current form of existing land use, many land use areas exist in areas that are not environmentally suitable.

2. Representation of Land Use--each working group was given a number of small square plastic elements that were color coded to represent specific amounts of land use. For example, a single "chip" (coded yellow) represented for residential land use 90 acres of residential development at an average density of 6 units per acre, which considering average household size, represented approximately 900 persons. The participants were allowed to stack the chips on top of each other, thereby representing increases in density. For example, if two chips of residential development were stacked on top of each other, this doubled the density from 6 units per acre to 12 units per acre, or represented approximately 1,800 persons in 90 acres. A similar equivalent of activity per chip was defined for the other types of land use, which were coded as follows: residential, yellow; commercial, red; industrial, blue; recreation, green; and public facilities, grey.

3. Allocation of Scenario One Growth--Scenario One represented the land use demand required to support the amount of population the group predicted for the first 5-year time period of the plan. The amount of chips of each type of land use were equal to the land use demand required to support the projected population growth. The participants allocated the chips, or placed them on the model board in any sequence and location that they felt was appropriate. They were urged to remember that the impacts of allocation of one land use in proximity to another could be severe, or that locating in areas that were shown on the suitability map to be unsuitable also incur a public cost.

The suitability maps were used as a guide for location of different types of land use. The citizens were able to insert different suitability maps for different types of land use in and out from beneath the model board, thereby allowing them to consider suitability for residential land use at one time, and suitability for industrial land use at another time, etc. During the allocation sequence, the citizens quite actively used the different suitability maps in making their location decisions.

4. Review--after all land use chips had been located, each participant group documented the reasons for the development of the specific land use pattern that resulted from their activities. In each case, they were required to articulate the reasons why they may have located land use in areas that were environmentally unsuitable, but conformed to the concept of urban form they had established. In other cases, they departed from their concept of urban form in order to conform to the pattern of land use suitability established by the computer-generated maps. In situations where capricious locations of land use were made, these were noted and allowed to exist. During the review process, each working group found that the pattern they had developed in some cases did not satisfy the objectives of their urban form concept due to the pattern of environmental suitability represented on the suitability map. In cases where they departed from the pattern of suitability, it was recognized that this would require public expenditure of funds to mitigate the environmental problems represented by the suitability map. In those cases where they chose to leave allocations of land use in unsuitable areas, this cost was recognized by the group as a statement that environmental cost would be incurred in order to conform to other objectives represented by the land use plan.

Other discussions that occurred during the course of the review portion of the simulation sequence centered on the impact on public transportation, the impact on housing, the impact on public services, and changes in urban form that were illustrated by their particular allocation of the Scenario One land use.

5. Allocation of Scenario Two--at the conclusion of the review, each working group then allocated the chips representing land use demand to satisfy population growth for the second 5-year time period of the plan. This allocation was made in recognition of the impacts generated through the discussion at the conclusion of Scenario One. During the allocation sequence of Scenario Two, each citizen working group was allowed to change their urban form objective and to alter their land use policies concerning environmental impacts. Any change was allowed as long as it was clearly stated and documented by each working group.

At the conclusion of the allocation of all Scenario Two land use, a review was conducted, and discussions were documented. This sequence was also continued for the allocation of Scenario Three growth, which represented the population growth projected to occur in the third time period of the plan.

At the end of the allocation steps in the simulation, each of the participant groups had formed a low growth alternative, represented by Scenario One, a moderate growth alternative shown in Scenario Two, and a high growth alternative represented by Scenario Three. Because these scenarios were presented in a time phased sequence, the planning team was able to observe the response of the participants to growth pressure in terms of land use patterns and density.

6. Summary of Citizen-Generated Land Use Plans—at the conclusion of the allocation sequence for each of the three scenarios, the citizen working groups each had developed a final land use plan that showed a desired land use plan allocation for the planning horizon year, 1995. Each of these land use plans, of which there were four (one from each group), had gone through a simulated growth sequence, and the factors shaping the growth of each pattern had been documented. At this point, the results of each working group were compared to determine similarities and differences between the alternative plans. It should be remembered that each of the working groups started with the same basic information, that is, several alternative concepts of urban form, the land use suitability maps, and projected demand for each type of land use for three different time periods of the future.

7.0 CONCLUSIONS

The citizen participation program, coupled with the use of a computer-based planning information system, proved to be an integral and important part of the general planning program. Further, it demonstrated that the involvement of the public in planning is a realizable and meaningful goal. It was demonstrated, however, that for citizens to participate to a level other than tokenism requires a specific commitment on the part of the planning team to budget sufficient resources, and to develop attitudes that will include the citizens in the planning process rather than view them as an adjunct to that process.

7.1 Successful Citizen Participation Program

The benefits of providing effective support for the Citizens Planning Council in the completion of the participation program are best defined in terms of the overall planning objectives. The planning team, through the CPC program, were able to develop a comprehensive understanding of the significant issues facing the north Los Angeles County communities. This understanding was not only developed in discussion, but was documented by the specific activities undertaken by the CPC. While the planning consultant had initiated an attitudinal survey at the inception of the planning program to determine community attitudes, it was only through the citizen participation program and the activities undertaken as part of that program, that the planning team was able to effectively understand and define the issues of concern of the community.

This was particularly apparent in assessment of environmental factors and suitability analysis where the information system provided the feedback mechanism and the framework for discussion of these various issues. The simulation sequence also provided an important structure for discussion and debate of community-based issues.

In addition to exploring community concerns, the citizens demonstrated their ability to understand the planning process. Specifically, each of the members of the CPC was able to assimilate, through the course of the participation program, the major elements undertaken in the course of developing the General Plan, and to deal with the basic concepts of planning. This was manifested through their ability to actively participate in the review of data, assessment of growth alternatives and environmental factors, the land use capability analysis, and the land use simulation. In addition, during the course of the participation program many situations occurred in which the members of the general public attending the meetings asked questions of the Council. While answering these questions, it became apparent to those in the audience that the members of the Council had, in fact, taken an active role in developing the plan, and understood the basic tenants of the plan. While this did not wholly justify to the public the credibility of the plan, it did serve to illustrate the level to which the members of the community were participating in the planning process.

Finally, through the citizen participation program, and the commensurate level of understanding of the planning process developed by the participants, the Citizens Planning Council became an active advocate in the community for the draft General Plan developed by the consultant. The citizen participants of the Planning Council recognized the complexity of the planning process and were willing to accept judgments made by the consultant planner in developing the final draft General Plan. While the final proposed draft of the Plan[7] did not include all of the thoughts and ideas created by the CPC, the participants had developed respect for the planning team, and were then willing to accept the planning team's judgment in specific areas. It should also be noted that many of the participants became valuable critics for the planning team during the course of the project. Through gaining an understanding of the planning process, individual participants were able to critique many of the proposals offered by the planning team in a meaningful way from the community's viewpoint, yet articulating their critique within the vocabulary and methodological framework of the planners.

7.2 Support of Participation by the Planning Information System

The computer-based planning information system played a critical role in the citizen participation program. The first reaction of the CPC to the spectra of a computer and the use of computer-generated maps in the planning process was to be guardedly suspicious. The computer presents a highly technical image that further supported the general belief that the real technical issues of generating the plan would be kept from the citizens because of the difficulty of presenting these complex issues to the lay public. The use of the information system in the course of the project had the opposite effect. At the beginning of the project during the data inventory stage, the demands of the information system to rigorously document and process the source data upon entry to the computer, provided a stable base for discussion of that data with the citizen participants. In addition, the consistent format of the presentation of all computer-generated maps allowed the participants to more easily read and assimilate the data and information presented.

In addition to rigorous attention to the data, the information system allowed the planning team to quickly respond to information requests of the participants as well as to respond to changes and criticisms offered by the citizens. This facilitation of the planning process to the extent of refocusing the process from control by the technical limitations of mapping and analysis, to the discussion and development of the planning issues, resulted in a more successful planning effort.

The use of the computer-based planning information system in the case study has served to facilitate a cumbersome, if not impossible, task based on previous experiences in citizen participation. The question then must be asked what other applications of the information process technology now in use or under development could further open the process of governing to those who are governed. What other situations now exist that are institutionalized in a manner that shuts out the public because of the inability of the institution to process and present information to the public in a manner that is clear and can be understood? It is clear that many of these situations exist. The burden of identifying them and searching for new solutions belongs to the planner and information scientist.

NOTES:

[1] California Government Code Section 65302

[2] For a discussion of strategies for citizen participation programs, see: Burke, Edmund M., "Citizen Participation Strategies", Journal of the American Institute of Planners, September 1968.

[3] For a discussion on the merits of participation, and a critique of participation strategies, see: Arnstein, Sherry R., "A Ladder of Citizen Participation", Journal of the American Institute of Planners", July 1969.

[4] The consortium of planning agencies included in the planning study included: 1) County of Los Angeles Board of Supervisors, 2) City of Los Angeles Department of Airports, 3) City of Palmdale, and 4) Southern California Association of Governments. The County Department of Planning was responsible for supervision of the contract with the planning consultant who executed the project.

[5] For a discussion of the Delphi method, see: Linstone, Harold A., and Turoff, Murray (editors), "The Delphi Method, Techniques and Applications", 1975.

[6] Unpublished technical report, Quinton-Redgate, Los Angeles, "Data Aggregation Weighting Structure", (15 217.01).

[7] County of Los Angeles Planning Department, North Los Angeles County General Plan - Draft, November 1974, Land Use Vol. 2.

Dr. Stephen C. Sunderland
Dean, College for Human Services
201 Varick St.
New York City, N.Y.   10014

INFORMATION AND JUDGEMENT FOR THE
CITIZEN-PROFESSIONAL IN THE HUMAN SERVICES

ABSTRACT: The empowering of citizens in the human
services is one of the major goals of the 1970s. Through
changing both the role expectations and the quality of information received by the citizen, the judgements of the citizen
can be expected to become increasingly effective and humane.
In effect, a new professional responsibility for respecting
the citizen's own professional capacity needs to be demonstrated in the dynamics of the relationship between all human
service practitioners and citizen-professionals. This talk
describes five major conditions for improving both professional
and citizen-professional relationships toward the goal of
citizen empowerment. The successful performance of improving
a) purposes, b) values, c) knowledge of self and others,
d) systems know-how, and e) skills will bring into being a
more interdependent and caring relationship

INTRODUCTION

The shrouding of obedience to immediate necessity,
The mask of "What do I care?" to cover "What can I do?"
One half-real face put on to hide a more real face under,
The waiting of the hope of the inner face while the outer face

-20-

Holds to its look and says yes to immediate necessity,
Says yes to whatever is for the immediate moment --
This is the pokerface of the populace never read till long afterward.

- Carl Sandburg, The People, Yes

The subject appreciates that his environment will create an impression on
the observer, and so attempts to set the stage beforehand. Aware that his
actions, expressions, and words will provide information to the observer,
the subject incorporates into the initial phases of this activity a consideration of the informing aspects of its later phases, so that the definition of the situation he eventually provides for the observer hopefully
will be one he feels from the beginning would be profitable to evoke. To
this end the subject turns on himself, and from the point of view of the
observer perceives his own activity in order to exert control over it...
the observer "takes" the viewpoint of the subject, but does not "identify"
his interests within it.

- Irving Goffman, "Expression Games," Strategic Interaction,
(Ballantine, 1969) p. 26

It is now all too clear that the fundamental relationship between
the provider of professional services and the recipient is being called
into question by professional groups, legislatures demanding quality
control, citizens demanding better and safer practice, and educational
and service organizations that are emphasizing alternative approaches to
providing training for services. For the citizen the time has come to
expect a different approach to the information that is most critically
related to service. The importance of this information to the citizen
as a major factor in sharing in judgements surrounding service needs
discussion, especially since there is such widespread skepticism
surrounding the present methods of making judgements in the human services.

"Information" may mean anything which contributes to the capacity
of the citizen to tell whether or not the services provided to him or her
are satisfactory, unsatisfactory, or unknown. This broad definition is
an invitation to examine the many impacts the citizen experiences on the
route toward, during the execution of, and in the leaving of the service
interaction. It is the assumption of this paper that the present method
of training professional human service workers rarely includes the
training in the assumptions and experiences of the recipient in relationship to the critical information surrounding the service interaction. In
fact, the present human service approach is thought about strictly
within professional terms. Irrespective of whether the sub-area is social
services, teaching, drug and alcohol rehabilitation, day care, foster
care, etc., the dominant source of information on the appropriate methods
of understanding comes from a judgement perspective that is attunded
to the professional role. [1]

The omission of the citizen as a source of information of importance is neither new nor unexplainable. It is not the intent of this paper to review the history of the professions and the place of the citizen other than to note that the tradition of devaluing the citizen's status has been a major element in the institutional development of service elites from the Middle Ages to the present.[2] Rather, this paper wishes to emphasize that the context for giving and receiving information, as well as deciding upon the usefulness of information, is constantly a context of highly-charged emotions, especially when citizen judgement is in disagreement with the professional. Citizen information stands outside the realm of important information, almost by definition. The professional in the human services "professes" from a role position of honor, stability, and tradition. The citizen, oftentimes called client, patient, or student, is in the degrading, passive, and unknowledgable role position which has been created to sharpen the boundary between those who are authorized to help and the recipient. To alter these boundaries is to confuse the worthiness of the information by confusing the authority of the traditional sender and recipient of the information. The strength of the professions resides in large part in the ability to continue to protect the boundary between the honored and the degraded.[3]

The citizen's vulnerability to those with degrees, coupled with the development of information that is transmitted through an instrument (the practitioner) that serves to heal and confuse, has often prevented an examination of the citizen's information, while emphasizing information related to honor.[4] By introducing a fee for service as a major transaction symbol in the relationship, the citizen's purpose -- particularly for the largest proportion of uses of service -- is further deflected and confused. One major message that citizens must send is that they can pay, even if the information they receive is useless -- or worse, harmful. Without this message, or the potentiality of sending this message on the part of the citizen, the transmission of other vital information, indeed the apparent reason for seeking the service, is not even permitted.[5]

This paper attempts to stand this current and traditional system upon its head. By assuming that the citizen is within an honored role, a role which permits and encourages the sending of information previously considered to be the possession of the professional role, the citizen can become a major co-provider of services, as well as self-sufficient to provide services to others; or, more importantly, to become the major resource of self-helping.[6] By improving the status of the citizen, there is the possibility of an improvement in the informational processes that are related to determining the quality of services delivered. As the judgement of the citizen improves, as competence in decision-making is accompanied by further competence in performance, the citizen will become behaviorally more informative and wise. The informational model necessary for establishing a process of competent self-and-other services can be described and implemented in such a way that the qualitative improvement in "constructive actions" for service by the citizen can be documented.[7]

Moreover, it is also possible to describe the conditions which will
influence the improvement of wider information sharing and judgement
between citizens as they become new professionals and upon traditional
professionals as they become more self-developed.

THE TWIN MESSAGES OF KNOWLEDGE AND ACCOUNTABILITY FOR THE CITIZEN-PROFESSIONAL.

Technical changes make quality control possible; social changes make it
necessary. But quality control cannot be instituted or improved...unless
we face two related problems. One is that physicians tend to see quality
control as a punitive measure threatening their professional standing
or dignity. The other is that quality control...appears to be in direct
conflict with the individual physician's control of the care of his
individual patient.

> - Dr. Paul Ellwood, quoted in Dr. Robert McCleery's One Life,
>   One Physician, (Public Affairs Press, 1971), p. 12

Another thing -- doctors want to be in power all the time; when you visit
them in their office, they will not listen to your ideas about something
you are certainly more familiar with than they, such as your own body,
or what the effect of certain medicines are for you. They are great
believers in sedatives for any and almost every ailment, especially if you
are older. One does not want to be a sedated zombie -- it does not help
you or your condition, but simply prolongs it. I tried to tell my doctor
that getting out among people, even ones I do not know so well, and
talking about my problems is very helpful; that exercise and walking and
riding a bike is more helpful than the sedatives; that all this gives me
a restful night's sleep. His response was, if I did not want to listen
to him, I should not come back. I am now lying to him, and saying I take
the drugs, and he tells me: "See how much better you are feeling!"

> - A citizen, 1976

For the remainder of the paper, the citizen will be described as
the citizen-professional. This term signifies an individual assuming
the responsibility for co-providing human service according to the
standards of practice to be described as minimal for caring and thorough
practice. The term is not meant to denote a pre- or para-professional
person or approach. The citizen-professional is fully capable of meeting
the on-going professional conditions for performance within the context
of knowledge and accountability. By "knowledge" is meant the message
of a) knowledge in the self, b) knowledge in the resources of experience as codified according to the guidelines of science, and c) knowledge in practice. Each of these messages communicates to the citizen-
professional a legitimate source of information to be used as part of the
training and development of the citizen-professional perspective. Knowledge is to be used to increase the options available to the one being
served and serving.

The uses of knowledge in the very core of practice send off a signal to the user and the recipient, a signal of wariness as well as of interest in the relationship of any form of knowledge to the actual improvement of the judgement of the recipient. Knowledge moves to a public condition for communication, for weighing of alternatives, for planning between the human service practitioner and the citizen-professional; it provides, if truly communicated, a substantial anchor for further transactions about the uses of service.

This form of knowledge is both different in substance and method from the traditional approaches to knowledge and its utilization. Traditional professions within the human service area assume knowledge to be a unique province of the professional alone, to be studied in specially-prepared processes, for an agreed-upon period of time held to be equally critical. These elements of knowledge acquisition are held up to be of more importance than the knowledge itself, as the professional must be prepared to receive the knowledge as if knowledge, like the apple in the garden, contains explosive elements dangerous to those who inadvertantly touch it. By making the message of knowledge so fraught with danger, the professional reinforces the separation of knowledgable information from the judgement process. Self-knowledge of the citizen becomes less worthy, knowledge in practice is only noted for the professional and not the citizen, and further resources for scientifically adducing the causes or understanding of the problem are relegated to the professional alone, and not to the citizen.

The citizen-professional has a framework for knowledge acquisition that is both more rich informationally and more open to the problems of discrimination amongst a larger set of alternatives. By freeing the information system to be inclusive, the citizen-professional sharply reduces the likelihood of distortion of meanings, of wrongfully accepting knowledge without looking at the range of consequences, and avoids the possibility of side-stepping the memory and educative function of information. Through encouraging sharing in judgement by a self-case approach, as well as supplementing this with the knowledge brought from other resources, the citizen-professional triggers preventative messages and a process for incorporating these varied elements of information into an ongoing process of preventative education.[8]

Knowledge, even knowledge freed of the ritualistic and purposely confusing elements, is not enough of a base for the citizen-professional. Added to this is the condition of accountability. Knowledge and practice combine in performance. The acceptance of standards for acceptable performance in service is a second informational message needing to be delimited for the sender and receiver of the service. By the message "accountability" is meant a public discussion of the effects of the service rendered and of establishing the conditions for further self-learning on the part of the recipient. For the citizen-professional the information gained from review of each element of the service rendered provides the basis for communicating an experience of competence. The omission of a lived experience between the served and the servicer where the factors of choice and risk are discussed, where the self is drawn in and tested, where other knowledge is brought into consideration, and where doubts and fears are placed in perspective communicates to the relationship an experience of mystery and vulnerability.[9] Through accountability the citizen-professional creates a formal bedrock of rational messages, each examined from the respective positions of co-provider and co-recipient. The consequences of such an accountability are to be seen in the improvement of the information shared by both members of the service network, but especially in the lived experience of the recipient to provide to themselves an important self-dialogue of effectiveness. The communication of competence to the self-concept, undertaken within the educative context of looking at one's own case as a departure point for learning and effectiveness, are the twin factors which imbed the idea of effectiveness into the linkage between the service partners.

For traditional professionals, such a process of accountability is seen as a major intrusion upon the informational and judgement contexts of their select professions. Depending on the sub-speciality, the traditional professional is reluctant to communicate information concerning the procedures that are to be undertaken or that effected the judgement of the practitioner. This reluctance to communicate underlying assumptions extends to both members of the profession as well as the so-called "lay" public. In general, the present approach to accountability within the caring professions is more characterized by its absence than by any model of peer review, citizen assessment, or any serious auditing procedure. The obvious consequences of this condition are to proscribe the judgement context for those encountering the professional, and for the professional as well. Correct judgements are assumed to be occuring even when there is countervailing evidence, even death.[10] Judgement and the information relevant to service are placed within a context where the informational symbol of power is more highly protected than the substantive information.

The citizen-professional's acceptance of the twin conditions of knowledge and accountability establishes a commitment to an informational and judgement context that can be assessed in the performance of both the sender and the receiver of the service. By increasing the information for both parties, the opportunities of increasing the effectiveness of the performance of both parties is also enhanced. Mutual feedback loops connecting within honored and open contexts raise the possibility of establishing a standard for performance that can be measured in terms of the quality of the interpersonal relations, as it contributed to actual service improvement and reeducation. Such an emphasis encourages a focus on the standards of information which will improve service and decrease the necessity for ritualistic subservience and its attendant conditions of deafness and blindness.[11]

<u>FIVE CONDITIONS FOR IMPROVING THE INFORMATION AND JUDGEMENT CONTEXT FOR
CITIZEN-PROFESSIONALS.</u>

Experimentation with the citizen-professional paradigm has been in
process for the last ten years at the College for Human Services. The
College has developed a major new modality for training and assessing the
work of professionals within the generic area of the human services.
All student-practitioners in the College's program are examined in eight
major competency Crystals which make up the entire curriculum of the
College.** All of the student-practitioners are drawn from the low-
income strata, are highly-motivated citizens with a strong self-concept
aimed at service improvement, are adults, and come with a wide traditional
and non-traditional educational and service background. Their education
in the Crystals is done within the College and a service agency, where the
crystals are worked with directly under the supervision of agency staff
and citizen-professionals who are in need of service. Student-practitioners
who successfully complete the program are eligible for a combined bacca-
laureate and masters degree in the human services.[12]

At the heart of the College's approach to performance is a commitment
to empower the citizen, to raise the competence of the recipient to a
level where the citizen can become an active partner in service delivery
and improve his or her self-sufficiency. All of the College's student-
practitioners are assessed on eight Crystals for their ability to raise
the competence of citizens along dimensions of performance. It is our
belief that the mutual judgement of the citizen-professional can only be
prized if the citizen-professional and the human service practitioner
are trained to understand and to use similar information concerning the

---

** The Eight Competency Crystals are:
1. Assume responsibility for lifelong development of professional competence.
2. Establish professional relationships at the worksite with co-workers
and citizens (pupils).
3. Work with people in groups, helping to establish clear goals and
achieve optimum results.
4. Function as a teacher, helping citizens (pupils) to define and
achieve appropriate learning goals.
5. Function as a counselor, helping citizens (pupils) resolve problems in
a manner that promotes their growth and independence.
6. Function as a supervisor, teaching, encouraging and enabling other
workers to make best use of their abilities on behalf of the other
citizens.
7. Function as a community liaison, working with sections of the
community to identify community needs and deliver services that meet
those needs.
8. Act as a change agent, planning, researching, and promoting programs
to improve human service delivery.

improvement of the human services. The opportunity for this mutual
education occurs best during the time when the citizen is seeking service
rather than during a theoretical time or through a simulation. Through
understanding the actual self-case study, both the citizen-professional
and the human service practitioner in training can begin to meet the
fullest definition of information and judgement. Prior to actual service
delivery, the student-practitioner is trained in the informational
attitudes necessary for successful citizen empowerment. This occurs
during the first two crystals, where the importance of learning and professional relationships are established and assessed. The remainder of the
six Crystals are functional approaches to major service themes that
continually overlap and appear within the generic area of the human
services. The College expects that performance, education, and assessment will provide the fullest opportunity for a) examining the ongoing
competence of the human service practitioner to send and receive information, and b) make collaborative judgements of performance competence
based on successfully educating the citizen professional along similar
lines. The criteria for education, assessment, and collaboration are:

Criteria One: All service must be purposeful for the service recipient.
        Both the sender and the receiver of the service have to agree on
the major purposes of the expected service. This means being able to set
long- and short-range goals of meaning based on a holistic approach to the
citizen. The citizen therefore leaves the relationship being able to
demonstrate both an awareness and the skill in setting his or her own
goals, and in understanding the importance of clarifying purpose. The
accomplishment of this condition establishes a communication linkage between
the sender and receiver of service that is open to discovering the deepest
purposes of the recipient, of finding ways of accepting the limits of
service, or of opening ways to finding resources. In learning to set
purposes with a human service professional, the citizen-professional
improves the likelihood of using such an approval in the future. This
methodology, then, becomes a major skill that can be reused and taught to
others.

Criteria Two: All service must include the clarification of the values
of the service sender as well as the receiver.
        The introduction of the value element permits the partners in
service to examine the underlying beliefs that are effected by service
strategies, and to clarify which attitudes or ideas are of critical importance. The message this process sends is one of humaneness, of trusting
that the sharing of feelings and ideas of value will strengthen and en-
large the capacities of both members of the relationship. The citizen
and the citizen-professional leave the relationship being able to demonstrate an awareness of this skill in using the values held or discovered
as a critical part of the service relationship.

<u>Criteria Three</u>: All service must strengthen the self-and-other con-
cept between the service partners.

   Providing and receiving service directly interacts with concepts
of the self, of feelings of importance and identity. The acceptance of
the possibility and actuality of resources flowing back and forth between
the relationship is both an area of knowledge and skill that will need
exploration and experience. The citizen will leave the relationship with
a greater understanding of how his or her own self-concept affected the
citizen-professional, and ultimately related to the successful completion
of the service. Moreover, the citizen will be able to describe and
use this experience as a part of other service experiences.

<u>Criteria Four</u>: All service must include a knowledge of the systems
involved in gaining resources and the ways in which these systems can be
worked with to provide the resources.

   The citizen seeks service within an institutional context that will
need description from the perspectives of gaining and providing resources.
Knowledge of how to use the systems of service can be shared with the
concomitant improvement in the judgement as to whether all possible and
probable resources were tapped. The citizen will need to leave the
relationship with an understanding of the ways systems operate for and
against the service seeker, and be able to demonstrate that this system
can be reentered more efficiently and effectively for the completion of
this or other service needs.

<u>Criteria Five</u>: All service must be skilled, and improve the skills of
the provider and the recipient.

   This message communicates to the recipient that he or she is to be
involved in a thorough understanding and demonstration of the communication, problem solving, and knowledge acquisition skills necessary for
providing service. These skills are understood from the perspective of
opportunities for improving the understanding and the performance of
both partners. Such information may continually improve the judgement
context for both partners, as it provides a question of performance on the
part of both persons for the reasons underlying skills, and the actual
use of the skills themselves. The service recipient leaves the relationship with a curriculum aimed at improving skills, as well as an understanding of how these skills helped in the formation of a successful
or unsuccessful service conclusion.

   All five of these criteria provide a very different stage for
sharing information about service, and for making decisions about the
quality of the service rendered. These criteria provide for an environment where the citizen is honored in that his or her own competence to
be self-sustaining is respected. This attitude communicates to both
partners that the approach and evaluation of service and service delivery
will need to be more marked by messages of collaboration than dependence.
By shifting the judgement context as well to more interdependence, the
citizen is catapulted into an examination of both contemporary and future

planning and development resources. Judgements about self and service are not made in private; rather, the very public nature of the interaction and context permits the partners in the service process to remove all the traditional conditions which reduce information and force a totalistic acceptance or rejection of the judgement of the citizen or the professional.

CONCLUSION

The elimination of the expectation of dependence has the far-reaching effect of liberating both partners to be more effective in their performance, to share both the successes and failures through an educative and public performance process.

For the professional human service worker, this can have the dramatic effect of increasing his or her productivity. Able to now extend and deepen his or her effectiveness through greater knowledge and accountability, the human service professional can enjoy the implications of service delivery and education. This combination can provide new solutions to human service problems that were previously thought unworkable. Examples of this kind of practitioner breakthrough are occuring in the areas of the mentally retarded, drug rehabilitation, and in education and counseling.[13] In each case, the major characteristics appear to be the public recognition of the talent and worthiness of the citizen to co-participate in the entire service relationship.

For the citizen, the implications of greater involvement bring a rush of previously undertapped resources into greater play and, equally important, provide for the dramatic improvement in the actual services expected and received. Examples of citizen-professionals joining professional practitioners as allies in the fight for service improvement, budget increases, and in the management of service centers from this perspective are now becoming more evident. As the citizen's role, information and judgement has increased, the very definition of service has become transformed in the areas of mental health, community service to the aged, and for all those who are seeking services from within the human service perspective.[14]

For the service agency and the educational institutions that are training the professional, the consequences of these changes are beginning to be felt in the demands of the agency, staff, and students for more relevant performance-focused methods of assessment and education. One example of this is provided by the spread of the College's approach to over fifty different kind of agencies within the New York and Philadelphia areas, as well as the beginning adaptation of the College's curriculum to major professional schools around the country. Other examples of citizen-professional influence are appearing and being documented as a part of the massive self-help movement that already has over half a million adherents.[15]

The pressures for professional reform are already in process. What this paper has described is the kind of information and criteria for information that are needed by citizen-professionals and human service practitioners. Through systematically building upon the experience of citizen-professional groups from around the country, the movement for better service delivery and education will continue to gain adherents for a new kind of professional and citizen relationship process and product.[16]

FOOTNOTES

1. For a review of the central issues in professional domination, see: Stephen Sunderland, "Creating the New Profession," Education and Urban Society, Volume 7, No. 2, February 1975, pp. 141-171.

2. See especially Max Weber, "Bureaucracy," and "The Social Psychology of World Religions," in H.H. Gerth and C. Wright Mills' From Max Weber, (Oxford University Press, 1958).

3. See especially Jethro Lieberman, The Tyranny of the Experts, (Walker, 1970) and Eveing Goffman, Frame Analysis, (Harper, 1974), especially chs. 2 and 10 .

4. E. Goffman, Ibid., p. 35.

5. Eva J. Salber, Caring and Curing, (Prodist, 1975). Also see Howard Waitzkin and Barbara Waterman, The Exploitation of Illness in Capitalist Society, (Bobbs-Merrill, 1975).

6. Leonard D. Borman, "Barn-Raising Revisited: The Upsurge in Self-Help Groups," Center Report, June, 1976, pp. 16-17.

7. Stephen Sunderland, Evaluating the Citizen-Professional's Performance: The Constructive Action Paradigm. Paper delivered at the American Society of Public Administration, 20 April 1976 .

8. See David Bakan, Disease, Pain, and Sacrifice, (Beacon, 1968), especially chs. 1 and 2.

9. William R. Torbert, Learning from Experience (Columbia University, 1972).

10. Diana Crane, The Sanctity of Social Life: Physicians' Treatment of Critically-Ill Patients, (Russell Sage, 1975), pp. 17 - 34.

11. Harold H. Weissman, Overcoming Mismanagement in the Human Services, (Jossey-Bass, 1973), p. 48.

12. The College is accredited in the State of New York by the State Department of Education, and is seeking authority to award a combined baccalaureate/masters degree. For more information on the College curriculum, write: College for Human Services, 201 Varick St., New York City, N.Y. 10014.

13. S. Sunderland, Op. Cit, P. 30. See also Gerald Hunt, A Guide for the Effective Functioning of Citizen Health and Mental Health Advisory Groups, (Maryland Mental Health Department, 1973).

14. Ibid., p. 30. See also the Citizen Empowerment Manual, College for Human Services, 1976.

15. Leonard D. Borman, Op. Cit., p. 16.

16. Audrey C. Cohen, "The Third Alternative," forthcoming in Change. Also see Boyce Rensburger, "Michigan State: Young Medical School Becomes College of Bedside Manner," The New York Times, 8 June 1976. Also Hans Jonas, "Responsibility Today: The Ethics of an Endangered Future," Social Research, Vol. 43, No. 1, Spring, 1976. Also Bertram Brown, Involving the Public in Federal Decision-Making, speech given 2 April 1976.

ACKNOWLEDGEMENTS

Support for the investigation of the modality of citizen empowerment has been provided through the Fund for the Improvement of Post-Secondary Education. The author also wishes to thank in particular for their services Elizabeth Schneewind, Deborah Allen, Ruth Messinger, and the staff, students, and citizens of the College for Human Services.

Mary Lynne Markus
2450 Overlook Rd., #310
Cleveland Heights, Ohio   44106

Nathan D. Grundstein
Professor
2872 Washington Blvd.
Cleveland Heights, Ohio   44118

A SOCIO-TECHNOLOGICAL ASSESSMENT OF INTERACTIVE MEDIA

Recently, a number of communications technologies have appeared which promote increased participation and accelerated feedback in group discussions. These technologies combine the information processing and storage capacity of electronic computers with the audio-visual information transfer capabilities of telephone, radio and Cable TV. The interactive media represent an entirely new medium of communication and information processing because they significantly increase the speed and range of two-way communications among groups of people.

The interactive media are socio-technical systems because, in them, human users interact with technology to process information. Four examples of interactive media are discussed in this paper: the MIT Community Dialog Project, MINERVA, visual-telephone conference systems and CB Radio. A socio-technical analysis assesses the impact of the interactive media according to the probable social consequences of their wide-spread use and the uses to which they can be put. Analysis and discussion beforehand is crucial for our ability to control and to cope with the consequences of the interactive media.

A SOCIO-TECHNOLOGICAL ASSESSMENT OF INTERACTIVE MEDIA

Recently, a number of communication technologies have appeared which promote increased participation and accelerated feedback in group discussions. These technologies combine the information processing and storage capacity of electronic computers with the audio-visual information transfer capabilities of telephone, radio and Cable TV. Some of the techologies focus on information sharing within a group assembled in one or two locations. Others are designed to facilitate dialogue among geographically dispersed citizens. All of the interactive media, however, share a crucial characteristic: they increase the speed and range of two-way communication among groups of people.

It is my belief that this characteristic distinguishes the interactive media from other communications technology. Newspapers, opinion polls, TV, telephone, elections, computerized MIS and radio are all information systems. Yet none of these has the capacity for real-time interaction among groups of people. The interactive media, in my opinion, represent an entirely new medium of information processing.

It is not hardware or technology which gives the interactive media their status as a new medium. For the most part, there are few major technological innovations involved in interactive media systems. They all use combinations of existing media such as telephone, radio, video-tape or TV. Some have added special switching, computational facilities or computers. The tendency has been to build upon existing communications technology. I am not trying to disparage the engineering part in the development of interactive media, nor to deny the possibility of future technical innovations. My point is that the essential feature of the interactive media is not the technology but the social consequences of the technology.

New media always have profound consequences for the social systems which give rise to them. McLuhan has traced the effects of roads, phoenetic alphabets, movable type and TV on the societies that used them. A similar analysis must be performed for the society which is developing interactive media. It may already be too late for Americans to choose not to accept the probable consequences of the use of interaction media: acceleration of change and disruption of existing social patterns. Other countries, however, should be able to examine our experiences and choose. Perhaps there is still time for Americans to limit and control the uses to which the new medium is applied. In any case, our chances for successfully coping with the consequences of interactive media will be greater if analysis and discussion take place beforehand.

An analysis of the probable consequences of interactive media cannot be merely an analysis of technology or program content. As I have already stated, the technology of the new medium does not differ greatly from that of other existing media forms. An analysis of the possible content of interactive media forums would likewise not contribute much to an understanding of probable social consequences. McLuhan has shown that a medium can have effects apart from the content it transmits. Just as the major effects of TV are independent of the content of TV shows, the effects of the new medium will occur through a wide range of program content. The Community Dialog technology alone has already been used with such diverse content as: canned consciousness raising pack-ages on patriotism, sexism, etc., citizen meetings on transportation problems, a meeting between school principles and state officials, high school class materials, professional society meetings, and so forth.

More important than the content transmitted by the interactive media are the uses to which they can be put. Since all the interactive media are designed with the capacity for two-way dialogue, they possess inherently the capacity for one-directional communication. As instruments of dialogue, the interactive media may be used to facilitate mutual education, community problem solving, participatory democracy and issue balloting. By blocking feedback channels, however, nearly one-way communication can be achieved. A few of the more obvious examples of this are: information referral systems, opinion polling, propagandizing, community organizing and campaigning. These almost one-way information processing systems may be used for purposes either "good" or "bad" depending upon one's social position and perspective. The interactive media are potentially an extremely powerful political tool capable of being applied to maintaining the status quo or to promoting rapid change. This implies that analysis of the interactive media must go far beyond a description of technology or content.

Media analysis usually focuses on technology and content rather than on form and social consequences because media are commonly thought of as technologies. They are not. Instead, they are socio-technical systems. That is, media are composed to two subsystems, one social, the other technological. The technological subsystem consists of the knowledge, skills or machinery needed to carry out a task. The social system is composed of the people who carry out the tasks and the social interrelationships among them. An example of a simple information system is "me and a dictionary." Notice that I do not define the dictionary as the system. The task of this socio-technical system is to obtain proper spellings, pronunciations, definitions and syntactic uses of words. The social component of this system is "me" since I am the only user. The technology consists of the dictionary and my know-ledge that words are arranged in alphabetical order, that keywords are located at the tops of pages, etc. The major advantage of this way of looking at information systems is that it enables exploration of the impact of technology on social systems. This does not occur when the technology is examined by itself. Socio-technological assessment of information systems encourages the asking of unusual questions. To return to my example, analysis using a socio-technical perspective would reveal my difficulty finding definitions for words I cannot spell. This prompts the question: "Could the words be organized in phoenetic rather than alphabetic sequence?"

The interactive media are socio-technical systems because, in them, human users interact with technology and hardware to complete the tasks of generating, processing, storing and transferring information. Four examples of interactive media will be examined briefly in this paper: the MIT Community Dialog Project, MINERVA, visual-telephone conference systems and CB Radio. This will be followed by a socio-technical analysis of the probable consequences of interactive media.

Community Dialog

The purpose of this project, headed by Thomas B. Sheridan at the Massachusetts Institute of Technology is "to develop and evaluate techniques for improving interpersonal communication and participation in group meetings using electronic polling, computation and display technology." The voting machine invented by Thomas Edison forms the core of the hardware in this project. Participants in group meetings hold ten-position switches to signal responses to statements. A mini-computer tallies and stores the "votes." These can be displayed on a board to the total group simultaneously, at a later time, or continuously. This technology allows for considerable flexibility in group meeting procedures. Questions posed by a moderator may be answered by group members. Groups may control the content of the discussion by constructing an agenda with the help of a moderator. Group members may use the response switches to signal quantitative judgements or to give continuous feedback to speakers concerning the clarity and pace of the presentation or agreement with the issues raised. This system gives each of a large group of people in one location an opportunity to participate in a group discussion, even those not verbally fluent. Immediate feedback on the discussion is available to all and anonymity is preserved. Evaluation of the technology has indicated a fairly high degree of acceptance. It is seen as an improvement over one-way, top-down communications structures. Sheridan asserts "with some confidence, that the general process can produce increased sense of involvement, more rapid confrontation of the 'real issues' bothering the participants, more satisfaction in the direction of the discussion, more efficient use of meeting time." These advantages are contingent, however, on adequate preparation and appropriate moderator behavior. The moderator must be able to keep the meeting alive without resorting to the speech-making of many TV and radio personalities. Community Dialog technology is spatially limited. Participants must be assembled in the same room. Thus, Sheridan sees the Dialog project as a "simulation of critical group interactions [that] will help plan for expanded citizen participation through two-way cable TV," rather than the final form of an interactive medium.

MINERVA

The MINERVA project, under the direction of Amitai Etzioni at Columbia University, is less limited than the MIT project by the spatial locations of the interactors. MINERVA grew out of research on the group meetings of an apartment house community network (Ball). The meetings were telephone-based and involved issue balloting. MINERVA is an electronic system to "allow people dispersed in space to conduct a dialogue with each other in groups and to register their views as a group, in the same way a group is able to do when meeting face-to-face perhaps in a townhall." The project is difficult to summarize because it comprises four stages of increasing complexity. The first stage was contained in one building for trial runs and development of access rules. In the second phase, citizens are linked with a county government through existing radio broadcasting and telephone facilities with the addition of MINERVA switching hardware. In the next stage, the system is enlarged to allow for dialogue between two geographically distant communities. Visual as well as audio transmission is involved. The full MINERVA links members of a community to one another and communities to each other. This stage requires replacing the intracommunity radio broadcasts of the second stage with Cable TV transmission and adding satellite hookups for intercommunity forums. Etzioni lists three main shortcomings of today's radio and TV broadcasts with listener phone-ins:
"(a) a lack of interaction among listeners,
(b) access rules that encourage mass democracy because each citizen who has the ear of the total audience speaks only for himself, and
(c) lack of assessment of audience sentiments, and their feeding

back into the discussion." MINERVA was designed to overcome those difficulties. During the design process a number of technological choices were made. Etzioni discusses these choices in a paper on collaboration between engineers and social scientists. I would like to mention them briefly, because I believe they illustrate the social choices involved in the use of interactive media. Not the least of the technological choices was the decision to use existing radio, telephone and TV systems with only minor modifications instead of developing a new technology. This decision decreased the probable cost and increased the population of potential users of a MINERVA system. Sequentially, the first strategy choice described by Etzioni was to seek electronic equivalents rather than to simulate natural group processes. Another choice centered around the option of continuous feedback. Continuous feedback is often absent even from face-to-face discussions. When continuous feedback is provided by electronic signalling, it greatly accelerates social processes. Etzioni and his colleagues chose to add a moderator with the ability to control the timing and amount of feedback available to the total group in order to prevent too great an acceleration. The remaining choices concerned the form and functions of the moderator. Human or automated, moderators use certain rules for allowing discussants access to "the mike." MINERVA designers have experimented with both "harsh" and "meek" access rules.

Visual-Telephone Conference Systems

Visual-telephone conference systems, as well as phones with visual capacity (e.g., picturephone) to which they are related, are finding most of their applications in the business world. This is due to currently prohibitive cost and technological problems of transmitting visual data along telephone wires. Optical fibers may solve both problems. The New York Times (7/9/76) reported recently on the first working use of glass fibers in Cable TV transmission. Bells Labs has been developing optical fiber technology for some time. Widespread use of optical fibers may produce a low-cost conference system available as an interactive medium for the ordinary citizen. Thrower has described a number of the conference systems currently marketed. British Columbia Telephone's Confravision is a two-way visual system. To confer, participants must assemble in special rooms in two cities. Each group is able to see the other on a receiver and to monitor its own appearance to the other group. Visual data such as charts and graphs may also be transmitted. Facsimile transmission of "hard copy" is possible, as is access to a computer. In addition to intracity picturephone service, AT & T is experimenting with "Intercity Visual Conferencing" in a few locations. The system is similar to Confravisison except that voice-activated circuitry transmits the picture of the speaker only, not of the entire group. Special rooms on phone company premises are also required in this system. Western Telecommunication has installed a slow-scan video conference system between two cities. It takes up to 25 seconds to transmit a single picture on the assumption that charts and graphs are more important than the faces of and gestures of the conferees. The cost of slow scan is lower than real-time visual conferencing a little higher than regular long-distance telephoning. Interest in visual-telephone conference systems has increased with rising fuel prices. Some telephone analysts believe that Americans are increasingly choosing to call rather than to travel, a tendency which counters our excessive mobility. Low cost audio-visual conference systems may increase this trend by providing for real-time interaction among groups of people.

CB Radio

According to Jane Woolman, " . . . the very fact that the Citizens' Band is available to everyone has caused the service to be hailed on the one hand as 'the greatest tool the government has ever given us, the most democratic activity in the United States, and criticized, on the other, as a potential threat to privacy, as an aid to organized crime, and, used recklessly, as an instrument for destruction." Everyone must be aware of the enormous interest in CB Radio. 1976 sales of sets and accessories are expected to reach one billion dollars. A manual of CB jargon has achieved a position on the New York Times best selling paperbacks list. The FCC is expected almost to double the number of channels available to CB users in August, 1976 (N.Y.T., 7/10/76). The consequences of the CB boom are, however, still unclear. Citizen participation in reporting highway safety hazards and in fighting crime appears to make it easier to violate the law, as when it is used to warn speeding motorists of highway patrolmen. The interference problem from CB sets has prompted a bill before Congress to give the F.C.C. regulatory authority over all electronic equipment (N.Y.T., 7/10/76). One thing did become clear during the nationwide truckers' strike in 1974. CB Radio is an interactive medium, because it allows for real-time interaction among groups of people. Such interaction can produce rapid formation or strengthening of social groups.

ASSESSMENT

The interactive media art set apart as a new medium from other citizen information systems by the real-time interactions these media provide among groups of people. The most likely consequences of widespread use of interactive media are: acceleration in the rate of social change and disruption of existing social structures and processes. McLuhan has stated that acceleration and disruption are the principal factors in the impact of any mediums. I believe that there are reasons for believing this to be especially true for the interactive media.

Use of the interactive media creates new social groups. These groups may be temporary, as when a forum is called over an issue like street fighting in a community. Sometimes, however, access to interactive media will allow a group to coalesce more permanently. Groups are defined as collections of individuals that possess both shared values or beliefs and defined norms or roles. Geographically dispersed individuals without the means to interact may have similar values but no way to develop shared norms and roles. Real-time interaction makes possible this aspect of becoming a group. CB Radio may have been the critical factor which made the truckers' strike possible and successful.

In other words, an interactive medium can make group action possible for a collection of previously dispersed individuals.

Other media, such as roads, letters and movies can also provide the impetus needed for forming new groups. Yet these media are relatively slow, it takes time to interact with someone through letters. There is a gap from the time someone has the idea for a film and the time when others see it. This gap is closed by the interactive media. Interaction becomes instantaneous, real-time. With TV, it is possible to watch news as it happens. Within the interactive media, it is possible for people to share with each other their reactions to news as it happens. This can only accelerate even more the currently rapid rate of social change.

Not only will new groups be formed much more rapidly through use of the interactive media but these groups will be more complex. Most currently used media do not allow for interaction among people, e.g., movies or TV. Even the electric media of interaction, like the telephone, do not permit interaction among more than two people without the addition of extensions, amplifiers, etc. Computerized information systems require user-machine interaction or client-service provider interaction but do not usually involve interactions among users. Use of interactive media means that groups of users will be interacting. Relationships among users will become more richly patterned, in a word, more complex, through the frequent and in-depth interactions provided by the new medium.

The rapid formation of new social groupings with complex internal relationships will have profound consequences for our society. The new groups may challenge existing ones and established social processes. The interactive media may become a weapon in the struggle among groups. Though designed for two-way communication, the interactive media can be used for propaganditing and organizing by blocking the feedback channels. These media would be pivotal in any take-over or cooptation strategy.

I am by no means stating that struggles and misuse of the new medium are inevitable. Interactive media are, in fact, likely to be the key to cooperation among groups. Ball has mentioned that a violent conflict in Newfoundland was damped down through the use of video taped messages between parties. McLuhan has noted the tendency of TV to cool down emotions and to increase participation. And Etzioni has stated that " . . . group pressures and tensions are not as fervent in electronic meetings as they might be if the participants came together in person [because] the media carry only part of the nonverbal aggressive cues emitted by agitated people." Even as an instrument of intergroup cooperation, the interactive media will change or bypass the existing social processes for dealing with conflict and cooperation. This may mean radical change in governmental structures and processes.

My point is that the interactive media will have profound social consequences. Some of these consequences are beginning to be felt: the impacts of the CB boom, for example. Analysis and discussion beforehand is, in my opinion, crucial to our ability as a society to control and to cope with the consequences of the interactive media.

References

Ball, Geoffrey H., "Action Research Needs in Citizen Information," unpublished mineo; 1973.

Etzioni, Amitai, "An Engineer-Social Science Team at Work," Technology Review; Jan., 1975.

Leonard, Etzioni, et. al., "MINERVA: A Participatory Technology System," Bulletin of the Atomic Scientists; Nov., 1971.

McLuhan, Marshall, Understanding Media: The Extension of Man, The New American Library, Inc; 1964.

Sheridan, Thomas B., "Progress Report of the MIT Community Dialog Project," Massachusetts Institutute of Technology; July, 1973.

Thrower, Ray D., "Alexander Graham Bell, You Ain't Seen Nothin Yet," Sky (Delta Air Lines); August, 1974.

Wollman, Jane, "Get Your Ears on, Good Buddy; This is CB Radio," Ms. Magazine; May, 1976.

Drew Hyman, Director
Citizen's Advocacy and Governmental
    Responsiveness Organization
Center for Human Services Development
The Pennsylvania State University
University Park, Pennsylvania   16802

Robert Frymoyer, Director
Research and Information Systems
The Governor's Action Center
The Office of the Governor
Harrisburg, Pennsylvania   17101

EVALUATIVE FEEDBACK ON PUBLIC PROGRAMS: CITIZEN COMPLAINTS AS ERROR SIGNALS

Citizen demands on an executive ombudsman are a source of evaluative feedback on public programs. The Pennsylvania Governor's Action Center Information and Evaluation System provides computerized data on a number of variables which are used to provide "error signals" regarding a wide variety of programs. A detailed example is presented, along with a discussion of some of the successes and disappointments to date. It is suggested that this system can make government more accessible and responsive to citizens by enhancing the evaluation and control functions of elected officials.

In 1974 we outlined an approach to utilizing citizen's complaints as social indicators in a paper to the Twelfth Annual Conference of URISA.[1] We suggested that citizen's complaints to an executive ombudsman contain valuable information on the performance of public programs. The paper described a management information and evaluation system designed to utilize citizen complaints as social and organizational indicators. We now want to report on our experience in utilizing the Pennsylvania Governor's Action Center Information and Evaluation System. The rationale for the system, and its primary components are reviewed first, followed by a detailed example and discussion of how it has (and has not) been used.

---

[1] Drew Hyman, Robert Frymoyer, R. C. Moyer and Catherine Powanda, "The Use of Citizen's Complaints as Social and Organizational Indicators," in Urban and Regional Information Systems: Resources and Results, Vol. II, eds. C. F. Davis, Jr., and J. E. Rickert, (URISA 1975), pp. 230-246.

THE OPERATIONAL SETTING

Pennsylvania's executive ombudsman, the Governor's Action Center (GAC), was established in June 1973 by Governor Milton J. Shapp to provide the citizens of Pennsylvania with a source of access to services throughout the state, and a channel for investigation of their problems and complaints. Utilizing a centralized, toll-free telephone network and mailed requests, the action center receives problems and complaints from individual citizens. In response to these requests, the action center staff provides a spectrum of case advocacy services including information and referral, mediation, red-tape cutting, and complaint-handling.[2]

Each case is documented fully from initial contact through final resolution. The PGAC Information and Evaluation System aggregates this data on several input and output variables for all cases. There are now over 150,000 cases on the system. The number and variety of cases allows for delineation of problems and trends in a wide spectrum of community agencies. Furthermore, the information can be broken down by variables such as agency, sector, geographic area, date, time-in-process and outcome. In addition to its use in internal program management, this data provides a large pool of information about the responsiveness of agencies, and contains instances of specific cases where problems exist in law, policy or regulation. Our job is to develop methods and perform analyses of the data so that the resulting "error signals" can be brought to the attention of appropriate decision-makers. This program of "class advocacy"[3] provides citizens a direct role in evaluating public programs, and increases bureaucratic accountability to the elected chief executive.

CITIZEN'S COMPLAINTS AS ERROR SIGNALS

The rationale behind our approach is as follows. Public laws and policies can be considered as statements of community goals. They set out agreed upon quantity and quality of life in specific areas. When existing policies or regulations are out of step with citizen interests, or when service delivery systems fail or are inadequate in their operations, citizens affected are the first to know. In many instances, however, citizens have no way to communicate this information to responsible decision-makers except through the very structures which are giving them problems. And these structures, when dealing with

---

[2]Drew Hyman and Dan Griffiths, An Advocate for the People: The Pennsylvania Governor's Action Center, University Park, Pennsylvania: The Center for Human Services Development, (Report No. 89), May 1976, describes the program.

[3]Alfred J. Kahn, Social Policy and Social Services (New York: Random House, 1973) distinguishes between case and class advocacy. Class advocacy involves identification of problems in law, policy, procedural or regulation and precipitation of change action toward assuring more effective public systems.

citizens often exhibit self-serving interests inimical to resolving the problem. Furthermore, these agencies are often the only source of evaluative information about such issues available to elected officials. It is true that interest groups and political parties identify many major issues, but insofar as the average citizen is concerned, many problems are effectively kept out of the decision-making process. In this regard, our approach says explicitly: "Let the system operate as long as it is working fairly well. We'll listen to the people who pay for it (taxpayers), and those who need to use it (consumers), when they find the system fails them."

The resulting citizen complaints and problems are evaluative judgments that discrepancies exist between the goals established in public policy and the current operation of the system. Thus the demands on an executive ombudsman like the action center are a form of negative feedback, analysis of which can provide specific "error signals" about where community goals and aspirations are not effectively carried out. Furthermore, the action center is typically an advocate of last resort-- a place to appeal to when other organizations fail. And because it is open to the general public, the action center does not control the nature of its input. Little opportunity exists for biasing by political elites and organized interest groups, or for bureaucratic obfuscation-- the character of demands is determined by individual citizens.[4]

As depicted in table one, the demands on the action center span the entire spectrum of community service systems. Moreover, the problems are not restricted to state government: they reflect demands about both public and private sectors, and at local, county, state, and federal levels. The action center's data can therefore reveal many specific areas wherein all levels of government can be made more responsive to citizens, and it enhances the capability of the chief executive to exercise his evaluation and control function. The Governor has described it as providing him the "worm's eye view of the bird." (The taxpayer's view of the system.)

------

[4]Studies by the Citizen's Advocacy and Governmental Responsiveness Organization at Penn State find that over 96.5 percent of the demands on the action center are from individual citizens. Of the remaining, 1.8 percent are profit agency (business) representatives, 0.9 percent are state or local officials, 0.4 percent are interest group representatives, and 0.3 percent nonprofit agency representatives. Data also indicate that callers represent a cross-section of the state's population on demographic variables such as age, income, social class, household size, urban/rural distribution, political efficacy, and trust in government. There is a slight underrepresentation of black people and people over 65 years. Thus, our conclusion that demands on the action center reflect the desires of "the people."

TABLE I

ANNUAL VOLUME OF GAC ACTIVITY
BY MAJOR PROBLEM INDICATORS

(July 1973 - December 1975)

Problem Area	FY 1974	FY 1975	FY 1976 (6 mo.)	Total
Income maintenance	3,221	10,912	8,070	22,203
Transportation	7,647	8,894	3,868	20,409
Social services and individual health	1,913	2,845	1,558	6,316
Housing and living conditions	1,243	2,717	1,889	5,849
Administrative, regulatory and consumer protection	2,540	7,911	2,654	13,105
Education	2,514	2,015	1,120	5,649
Environmental, community health and safety	3,151	3,019	1,776	7,946
Revenue and community fiscal matters	2,365	4,097	1,583	8,045
Justice	1,047	1,831	992	3,870
Public issues:				
Legislative, gubernatorial, and others	5,840	11,991	6,540	24,371
Total all cases	31,481	56,132	30,050	117,663

ERROR SIGNAL INDICATORS

Here's how our system works. First, each incoming contact with GAC is categorized in terms of several major input variables:

1. Primary Problem Indicator: a summary problem classification according to major community functions or "subsystems." e.g., income maintenance, transportation, education, social services, health, revenue, etc. They are problem or function-oriented, and are not restricted by agency or jurisdictional factors.

2. Sub-Problem Indicator: A specification of the major problem indicators. There are over four hundred such subcategories. e.g., income maintenance is sub-divided into public assistance, social security, unemployment compensation, etc. These categories are open to revision and are derived entirely from the character and volume of citizen demands.

3. Type-of-Demand Descriptors: a classification of all demands into categories of service request, inform-ation request, complaint, or opinions about public issues.

4. System-level indicators: defines the problem according to public, private or voluntary sector, and also identifies the level of jurisdiction (local, county, regional, state, or federal). They indicate the structural components of the system.

5. Organization Descriptors: identification of the specific agency or organization (or type) that is involved. (There are over five hundred sub-divisions.)

6. Several other input variables like geographical source of the demand, date, zip code, and demographic character-istics of users are also available.

In addition, three major output variables provide evaluative information on the resolution of the problem and speed of handling:

7. Response-time Measure: a calculation of the length of time required to act on a demand (irrespective of whether the resolution is successful or not.) This measure is directed toward a judgment of efficiency.

8. Resolution Measure: an evaluation of whether or not the case is resolved successfully in terms of the citi-zen's perspective. This measure is directed toward a judgment of system effectiveness.

9. Citizen Satisfaction Measure: a judgment as to whether the citizen and/or the action center were satisfied with the entire process.

Potential error signals are generated in several ways. (1) Regular and special analyses identify patterns or trends in particular areas. (2) Case evaluators spot specific instances where an "unreasonable" or "ineffective" law, policy, or procedure prevents successful resolution of citizen's requests. (3) Case advocates or their supervisors bring suspected problems or patterns to the attention of management. (4) Or, ad-hoc interest groups call about a problem (a large, unorgan-ized number of citizens) in a short period. The information system is utilized to provide further specification and documentation of suspected problems, and for data to support requests that agencies consider changes in their operations or policies. The following extended example shows how the system works.

FROM INDICATOR TO ERROR SIGNAL TO POLICY CHANGE

Trends in two major problem indicators are depicted in Figure 1. Compared to the trend in overall GAC demands (Figure 2), income maintenance exhibits a dramatic surge in 1975. This was viewed as an indicator of potential problems. In fact, by the middle of 1975, income maintenance calls clearly became the largest volume major problem category for all GAC calls. (See also Table 1.)

FIGURE 1

INCOME MAINTENANCE AND SOCIAL SERVICES TRENDS

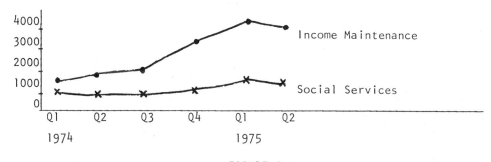

FIGURE 2

OVERALL GAC DEMANDS

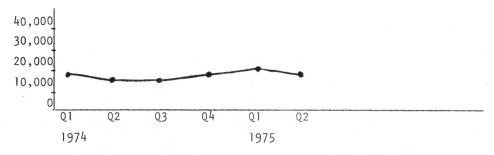

The decision-makers in the operating agencies brushed off these first indicators of possible problems with the comment that the rapid rise simply reflected an increased demand for services. Such an increase for income maintenance (I.M.) services might be expected since the nation was in recession. Action center assertions of internal problems were pushed aside.

Sub-Problem Indicators. Analysis of the data by sub-problem indicators within I.M., however, revealed that the overwhelming source of the increase was not in service requests, but in complaints about agency administration, specifically in unemployment compensation. Table 2 shows the volume of complaints of the dominant sub-problem areas within I.M.

The dramatic rise is clearly due to unemployment compensation (U.C.).[5]
(Complaints in U.C. rose gradually from 69 in the first quarter of
1974, to 175 in the third quarter. The fourth quarter increased to
over 300 complaints, almost doubled the prior figure. The first two
quarters of 1975 each registered over 800 complaints.) Analysis
showed that the complaint rate, in fact, rose many times faster than
the statewide unemployment rate.

TABLE 2

COMPLAINTS VOLUME: SELECTED SUB-PROBLEM INDICATORS
WITHIN INCOME MAINTENANCE

(January 1974 - June 1975)

Sub-Problem Indicator	1974 Q1	Q2	Quarter Q3	Q4	1975 Q1	Q2
Social Security	18	51	116	182	156	156
Public Assistance	142	156	150	329	301	236
Unemployment Compensation	69	81	175	319	843	824

Type of Demand and Organization Descriptors. Table 3 further pinpoints the source of problems by indicating that the increase is, in
fact, due to the rise in complaints about agency unresponsiveness, not
requests for service. (Information and referral, in fact, shows a
dramatic decrease).

TABLE 3

U.C. BY TYPE OF DEMAND DESCRIPTORS (1974-75)

	1974 Q1	Q2	Q3	Q4	1975 Q1	Q2	Q3	Q4
I & R	42.3%	43.8%	45.2%	40.9%	27.8%	23.6%	15.4%	10.6%
Complaints	53.1	56.2	52.4	55.8	69.2	73.4	75.3	85.8
Other	4.6	0	2.4	3.3	3.0	3.0	9.3	3.6

The average quarterly proportion of complaint calls in 1974 is 54%--
just over half the calls made. In 1975 a dramatic change begins in the
first quarter, and the average quarterly proportion of complaint calls

[5]More detailed analysis for the agency is contained in: Richard
Wunderlich, "Unemployment Compensation Cases Handled by the Action
Center During 1975," University Park, Pennsylvania: Governor's Action
Center Project, (March 1976), unpublished report. Several of the
following tables are drawn from the report.

for the year rises to 76 percent--over three-quarters of all calls made.
Organizational descriptors pointed overwhelmingly to the state-
administered Bureau of Economic Security (BES). (Table 4) Regular
monitoring began, and U.C. complaints exceeded 1,400 and 1,300 respectively in the last two quarters of 1975.

TABLE 4

STATE OFFICE U.C. COMPLAINTS AS A PERCENTAGE OF
TOTAL COMPLAINTS, BY QUARTER (1975)

	Q1	Q2	Q3	Q4
% State Office	99.5%	99.4%	98.3%	99.7%
All Other	0.5	0.6	1.7	0.3

Agency Obfuscation. While the action center viewed this data as
convincing evidence of the need for action, agency officials again
brushed aside the idea that there were major problems in their operations. They suggested that the complaints were due to "cranks" upset
by being denied compensation.

In most political systems action would have ended at this point.
Chief executives typically must rely on their administrative agency
executives for information and explanations of bureaucratic operations.
Thus, further action would normally have had to await pressure by a
major interest group, or the emergence of a crisis situation of adequate
proportions to precipitate a major investigation. Such was not the case
here, however.

Because it was clear at this point that the agency head would not
consider acknowledging the existence of problems, a confrontation was
arranged in the presence of a special assistant to the Governor. The
agency head was again presented the data along with seventy specific
cases--complaints about issues other than denial of benefits. This time
he responded to suggestions of major problems in the agency by offering
to set up a procedure to handle such complaints more quickly. The
Action Center perceived this as a "cooling mechanism," and argued that
some systemic problem was generating the complaints, and would continue
to do so--and that this was the issue which should be addressed.

Response-time and Resolution. The action center turned again to
its information system to pinpoint specific areas where problems might
exist. Evaluative output data on resolution and response-time suggested
that U.C. cases were taking longer to handle and resolution was increasingly less successful.

TABLE 5

U.C. COMPLAINTS: PERCENTAGE DISTRIBUTION OF RESPONSE TIME (1975)

Quarter	Up to 1 Week	8 Days- 2 Weeks	15 Days- 3 Weeks	22 Days- 4 Weeks	1 Month and Longer
Q1	35.2%	22.1%	13.2%	7.4%	22.1%
Q2	31.7%	17.8%	12.0%	12.1%	26.4%
Q3	21.5%	16.5%	15.5%	11.8%	34.7%

Table 5 indicates that the percentage of U.C. cases resolved in one week declined from 35.2% to 21.5% during the first three quarters of 1975. Moreover, the percentage of complaints taking longer than one month rose from 22.1 percent to 34.7 percent. Table 6 compares rates of successful resolution by type-of-demand for 1975 with information and referral requests. This information, too, suggested that BES was becoming increasingly unable to handle the demand. Agency unresponsiveness was the issue.

TABLE 6

U.C. RESOLUTION RATES (PERCENT SUCCESSFUL: 1975)

	Q1	Q2	Q3	Q4
Total U.C.	85.7%	79.8%	78.6%	83.0%
Complaints	85.2	76.3	76.1	80.3
I & R	87.0	90.8	89.0	93.7

Geographic Breakdowns. Computer mapping of problems per 10,000 population by county suggested that complaints were not distributed uniformly throughout the state (Figure 3): the problems might be

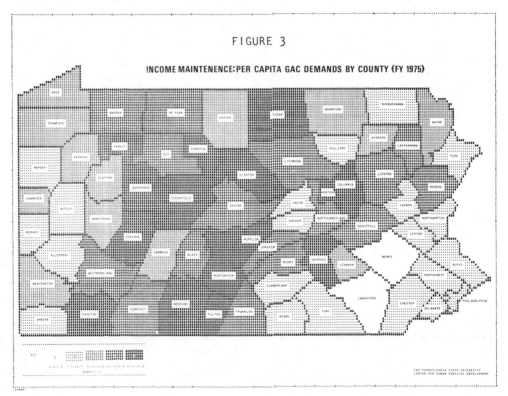

FIGURE 3

INCOME MAINTENENCE: PER CAPITA GAC DEMANDS BY COUNTY (FY 1975)

manifest in specific county offices. Data on changing county complaint rates compared to the county labor force provided further indication on which offices might be more problematic. (Table 7)

TABLE 7

U.C. COMPLAINT RATES FOR SELECTED COUNTIES COMPARED
TO SIZE OF LABOR FORCE

County Population 25,000 to 50,000	1975 Projected Labor Force	Mean Q1+Q2	Mean Q3+Q4	% Change	4 Quarter Mean
. . .					
Columbia	25,172	5.4	4.0	-26%	4.7
Armstrong	27,473	2.7	3.6	+34%	3.2
Clearfield	28,676	6.6	6.4	- 2%	6.5
. . .					
Lycoming	47,902	3.1	1.8	-43%	2.4
Mercer	48,638	1.3	6.9	+414%	4.1
Butler	49,835	2.7	4.6	+71%	3.7
. . .					
County Population Greater than 250,000					
Delaware	258,982	.8	.8	- 2%	.8
Montgomery	285,764	.6	.8	+19%	.7
Allegheny	634,055	.9	1.8	+99%	1.3
Philadelphia	811,894	1.3	2.8	+121%	2.0

Individual Case Reviews. Finally, individual cases which could not
be resolved because of agency procedure or problems in rules were isolated and reviewed. In addition to general patterns of delay and
unresponsiveness outlined above, many specific problems were revealed.
Among other things, it was discovered that the Board of Review had a
whole month's backlog in transcript typing--which in itself prevented
any timely consideration of appeals. Referees, it was suggested, often
refused to hear out the citizens, relying on employer information.
Communication was sufficiently poor between some local offices and the
central processing unit that the local workers, frustrated by their
inability to act, frequently referred people to the action center to
straighten out delays. Many people were not notified of the status of
their case during long delays; this led to frequent inquiries which
further increased the demand on local workers. People were often
required to live for months without benefits, sometimes up to a year,
because of blockages in the appeals process. Misunderstandings about
regular unemployment compensation and supplemental unemployment benefits (SUA) compounded the confusion.

Results. Presentation of information of this specificity finally persuaded the agency to begin to examine and revise its procedures and policies. Action is now in process, and analysis of data similar to that above will be utilized to monitor implementation and to provide a continuing check on the effectiveness of the revisions.

This example suggests how this form of evaluative feedback can be employed to identify and document a policy or organizational problem. The case example found (1) that the trend in this social problem paralleled a national trend; (2) that where the system for public policy implementation was inadequate the problems could be pinpointed; and (3) that data was available which could support the interests of citizens when otherwise the agency view could have prevailed and no action would have been forthcoming; and (4) that the transition from indicator to policy change led to the persuasion of authority. We think this a pretty powerful indicator of the utility of this approach.

PROGRAM EVALUATION IN THE 1970'S

The widespread adoption of program evaluation was a significant social policy innovation of the late 1960's. This occurred because the failure of public programs to achieve the lofty goals set forth in legislation became a major issue in both political and professional arenas. Program evaluation was believed capable of utilizing "hard" social science research techniques to determine whether a program was meeting its objectives. Information systems would provide data for program management and guidance on a continuing basis. Legislators, chief executives and the public would be assured that programs were accountable to legislative goals; those which did not would be identified through the use of evaluative data and brought into conformance with the public interest. Thus, evaluations were required by law or regulation for a large number of programs.[6]

Despite the high hopes of academics, professionals and politicians, disillusionment over the failure of evaluation to significantly affect social programs is a keynote of the early 1970's. Evaluative research failed either because it did not provide information on programs' objectives, (outputs and/or impact), or by failure to produce the data in a manner conducive to ongoing program guidance.

> Current indications are that evaluation research
> has so far failed to deliver. Assessments of program
> evaluation research work at the federal level are in
> general agreement not only that most of the work has
> been unsuccessful, but also that even the uncommon

---

[6]See, for example, Walter Williams, Social Policy Research and Analysis, (New York: Elsevier Press, 1971); and Yehezkel Dror, Ventures in Policy Sciences, (New York: Elsevier Press, 1971). Peter H. Rossi and Walter Williams (eds.), Evaluating Social Programs, New York: Seminar Press, 1972; and Carol H. Weiss, Evaluation Research, Englewood Cliffs, New Jersey: Prentice-Hall, 1972.

> instances of technically "successful" evalu-
> ation research have failed to affect program
> policy making or administration in any signifi-
> cant way.[7]

The requirement to provide information on results, or "output," has proven to both the key and the enigma of evaluative research. Post-mortem assessments suggest that we failed to produce feasible systems for measurement of program effects on a widespread, ongoing basis. Favored methods utilizing experimental and survey-research approaches tend to be both time-consuming and too expensive for continuous operation.[8] It is also difficult to control for all of the many variables in the typical social action program; thus, to the chagrin of managers, hard data researchers often settle on a few items which can be measured. As a result, these evaluations are often relegated to demonstration projects or small areas within broader programs. Moreover, problems of design and analysis continue to plague such evaluations. Process designs, on the other hand, can encompass many variables, cover wide program areas, and provide timely data of a character which administrators and managers are open to utilizing. They do not, however, indicate program effects and degrees of goal-achievement. Moreover, descriptive and subjective studies are always subject to interpretation and challenge by others[9] bringing us full-circle to the original problem of interpretation--which generated the need for evaluation in the first place. The failure of evaluation to achieve its objectives of informing public policy has led to a general assessment of its role in public policy, and a search for more feasible models for evaluative systems.[10]

---

[7]Thomas A. Morehouse, "Program Evaluation: Social Research Versus Public Policy," Public Administration Review, 32 (November/December 1972), pp. 868-874.

[8]Donald T. Campbell, and J. Stanley, Experimental and Quasi-experimental Designs for Research, Chicago: Rand McNally Co., 1963; Alice Rivlin, Systematic Thinking for Social Action, Washington, D. C.: The Brookings Institution, (1971); and Noralou P. Roos, "Proposed Guidelines for Evaluation Research," Policy Studies Journal, Vol. 3 (Autumn 1974), pp. 107-111.

[9]Robert S. Weiss, and Martin Rein, "The Evaluation of Broad-Aim Programs: Experimental Design, Its Difficulties, and an Alternative," Administrative Science Quarterly, Vol. 15, 1970, pp. 97-109; and Donald T. Campbell, "Considering the Case Against Experimental Evaluations of Social Innovations," ibid., pp. 110-113.

[10]Morehouse, ibid. Also, National Science Foundation, The Nation's Use of the Social Sciences, Report of the Special Commission on the Social Sciences of the National Science Board, (Washington, D. C.: U.S. Government Printing Office, 1969); and Joseph S. Wholey, et al., Federal Evaluation Policy: Analyzing the Effects of Public Programs, Washington, D. C.: The Urban Institute, (1970).

THE NEGATIVE FEEDBACK MODEL OF EVALUATION

While we do not suggest that the negative feedback system we have described meets the objectives of the program evaluation movement, we think it capable of providing some useful evaluative information on an ongoing cost-feasible basis. The aggregation of tens-of-thousands of individual judgments about the operation of community systems has been shown to be capable of producing a wide range of data about programs which are unresponsive and/or are not meeting their goals. In this regard it has several qualities which approximate the purposes of program evaluation.

Output-Oriented. The character of demands on Pennsylvania's executive ombudsman is essentially output-oriented--but in an inverse manner. People complain when programs are perceived to be operating improperly or are not achieving their goals. Most evaluation systems would take a positive feedback approach--to document how well agencies are operating. While this is perhaps the optimal approach (for it tells decision-makers what is, and is not, being done), where large-scale social programs are concerned such evaluations are expensive and time consuming. And in the present fiscal situation, "research and development," and "consulting" are typically the last funded and first cut. Thus, the dearth of evaluative information which presently exists.

The negative feedback approach can provide a wealth of evaluative information about problems of bureaucracies. It pinpoints some of the areas where "the system" is going awry. Moreover, this system operates through an external, open communications channel and is thus especially valuable as a medium for citizen input to top administrators and elected officials who otherwise must rely on the very bureaucrats whose interest is often to obscure information on their shortcomings.

Continuing Evaluation. The data from the negative feedback model is also available on a continuous basis. As long as the executive ombudsman (or other complaint-handling mechanism) operates, the data continues to accumulate. This means that information is provided with an immediacy and specificity appropriate to ongoing program management and policy making. The I.M. example above suggests that the specificity of information and timing was such that the error signals were apparent to the executive ombudsman (and thus the chief executive's office) some time before agency managers would even admit that something might be amiss.

Quantified and Operationalized. The classification of individual demands into a number of salient variables provides a data base which is readily available and quantified. The PGAC Information and Evaluation System provides a continuous flow of data in an on-line mode. There are at most two weeks from citizen demand to on-line availability for aggregate analysis. In fact, error signals are often generated more quickly when case advocates bring matters of policy and program to the attention of agency staff in the course of resolution of citizen problems.

Reliable and Valid. Data on input variables is primarily objective and requires little translation from initial citizen statement to information-system codes. The possibility of biasing by the case advocates is easily controlled by a systematic quality control system. Pennsylvania performs this function through the externally-based Citizen's Advocacy and Governmental Responsiveness Organization at The Pennsylvania State University. The quality control system provides for individual reviews of all cases for completeness of data and quality of advocacy. A continuing sample survey to citizens provides an additional check on the data items. Thus, the entire data base takes on an "objective" character.

Government and University Collaboration. An interesting aspect to Pennsylvania's system is the ongoing relationship between the Governor's Office and the state University. From the University's perspective, the activity provides an opportunity for a "real world" laboratory for the development and testing of new ideas. The agency views the relationship as an opportunity to benefit from new knowledge and technology to provide continuous program evaluation and improvement. As the action center interacts with bureaucratic officials, it must continually defend its citizen-oriented stance, and support its role as an oversight office. (State capitol environments by definition are intensely political places.) The fact that the data base is developed and maintained by the University tends to provide an external legitimization to the data.

Cost-Feasible. A major selling point of the system is its operation as a spinoff of another ongoing program. The establishment of citizen's advocacy and complaint-handling programs is almost a universal phenomenon today. Programs are being established at all levels of government and in both public and private sectors.[11] Pennsylvania's computer-based information and evaluation system represents a relatively small increment to the budget of the main program. (An additional benefit is the fact that the information system also provides data for internal program management and reporting.)

In a Manner Conducive to Program Guidance and Control. The association of the negative feedback evaluation system with an operating program also carries the benefit of providing continuous information of a highly specific character. The time from citizen complaint to availability to the program manager is simply the period required for data preparation and analysis. The richness of data on both inputs and outputs allows for a wide variety of cross-classifications and breakdowns of data. The capability to shift focus from a suspected general problem to a more specific error signal provides managers and decision-makers with data for decisions regarding program monitoring and improvement.

Impacts: Large and Small. Changes in specific rules, regulations, and procedures to assure greater efficiency in the administration of programs is the stated objective of the system. Negative feedback assists decision-makers by providing alternative sources of information to the usual channels. The considerable number of such changes already initiated by the action center is the best measure of the effectiveness

---

[11]See, for example, the International Bar Association, Ombudsman Committee, Development Report, (July 1973 - June 1974), Bernard Frank, Chairman, 832 Hamilton Mall, Allentown, Pennsylvania 18105; and Bernard Frank, "State Ombudsman Legislation in the United States,"

of this endeavor. Furthermore, an indirect impact results from the implication to agency officials that they may be "found out" if their organizations continue to be unresponsive. While this latter quantity is difficult to measure, a gradual increase in requests for information on their programs by agency heads is viewed as a positive development.

   Limitations. We are also aware of a number of potential limitations to the negative feedback system. (1) It does not identify all problems. Agency information systems, legislative oversight, interest groups and the press all must continue their role. This system can add to the list of oversight mechanisms a capability to receive problems directly from citizens in all walks of life and to translate some of their demands into issues for consideration of higher authority, but it does not aspire to be a comprehensive evaluation system. (2) Not everyone may view the executive ombudsman as the place to take their problems and complaints. Thus, the effectiveness of the system depends on a participant citizenry who feels the program can help them with their individual problems. Should this not be the case, few errors would be detected. (The use of the information and evaluation system to assure internal program effectiveness is important here.) (3) The character of people who call will determine whose interests are represented. If wealthy, middle-class people, organized interest groups or other minorities are predominant, the message will be biased in their direction. If, on the other hand, users represent a cross-section of the population (as is the case in Pennsylvania), it might be inferred that the system represents the messages of "the people" about where attention is required. (4) We are also aware that the most "important" problems may not be presented. Many of the findings of Pennsylvania's action center are relatively minor and affect only the fringes of bureaucratic behavior. Action on these little things, however, can "fine tune" government making it more responsive and effective in the long-run. It is also true that some major defects will show up which might not get attention until a breakdown occurs. External documentation of these issues and support for changes can serve to correct problems as they develop. In this way, it might be possible to work out of the "crisis management" syndrome which pervades so many bureaucracies today.

   There is also the problem of gaining the "attentive interest" of the appropriate decision-makers. The executive ombudsman is, in effect, "external" to the bureaucracies. The predominant reaction of bureaucrats to the action center's error signals has been first of all to defend their programs; secondly, to obfuscate, and only when pushed to consider remedial action. Thus, in the first year, the predominance of motor vehicle license delays and errors required an eventual confrontation in the presence of the Governor between the Secretary, and the Director of the Action Center to precipitate action. Only later could

University of Miami Law Review, Vol. 29, No. 3, (Spring 1975), pp. 397-445; and Stanley V. Anderson, Ombudsman Papers: American Experience and Proposals, Berkeley, California: Institute of Governmental Studies, (1969).

action be pursued at lower levels--and even now can be termed only reluctant cooperation. It took several meetings with the Secretary of Education, and considerable data presentation, to convince him that his department should take an active role in dealing with local school board arbitrariness and unresponsiveness to citizens. (Rates for successful resolution for education demands jumped from a very low 33.7 percent in FY 1974 to 76.4 percent and 68.6 percent in the subsequent years.) Similar experiences occurred with many other issues.

The problem is that the typical bureaucratic reaction to suggestions that something may be wrong in their agency is to defend. Rather than asking "Is this, in fact, a problem in my organization?" And, if so, "How can I make changes so that we are more effective?" (like an over-protective parent coming to the defense of an errant child), the usual reaction is defense of present practice or policy. Thus, there is the need to present data in a non-threatening manner to the non-technical user and to establish relationships so every issue does not become an interorganizational struggle.

On the other hand, it was the action center and the evidence it could present which gained the attentive interest of higher authorities in a considerable number of situations in Pennsylvania. The fact that the Governor and his appointed assistants had an alternate source of feedback allowed them to become aware of problems which would have been obscured in bureaucratic machinations. In turn, the availability of hard data to support action center findings was a crucial factor in overcoming bureaucratic defense-reactions. There are now some officials who frequently request information on their programs--a positive development and an indication of the growing effectiveness of the system.

CONCLUSION

Finally, there are several ways to view the data itself. One, typically the bureaucratic perspective, would suggest that the number of demands in specific areas are miniscule in comparison with the overall caseload of their agencies; thus, this feedback on agency operations would be dismissed. Others would say that their agencies have been aware of problems--that present policy is adequate--but they have other, "important" things to attend to.

Another approach, that of the executive ombudsman, suggests that citizen inputs, freely given, can be considered as observations of discrepancies between public goals and bureaucratic performance. And, if it can be shown that there is a degree of representativeness in the overall population (as is the case with GAC users), these citizen-generated "error signals" should be considered as indicators of areas for the attention of decision makers.

The negative feedback system takes the latter perspective. Citizens' problems and complaints are viewed not only as requests for aid in individual situations but constitute negative feedback about the operation of government. In this way the executive ombudsman can precipitate increased responsiveness of government on the part of individuals and in the domain of program and policy.

This is not to say that the problems so identified are otherwise unknown, nor are they the only problems which exist. What we do
assert is that citizens have problems with "the system" everyday, but
typically have no way to communicate their concerns to the appropriate
decision makers. We also expect that many lower- and mid-level bureaucrats who are aware of problems are either prevented from communicating
them by the vertical and downward thrust of bureaucratic communications, or are obscured by conscious decisions of higher-ups who have
an interest in other issues or do not wish to reveal problems in their
organization. Thus, we suggest that citizen demands on a generalized
citizen's advocate can (1) reveal general trends in some social problems
as they develop and can pinpoint sources of dysfunction before breakdown occurs, (2) provide a way around the bureaucratic hierarchy for
demand which otherwise would be submerged in agency affairs, (3)
identify many issues which would not come through other channels of
demand (e.g., interest groups or political parties), except as problems
affect specific elites or a crisis develops, and (4) establish a
queueing phenomenon which places citizen-generated demand in higher
priority.

Deborah K. Polivy
Community Council of the Capitol Region
999 Asylum Avenue
Hartford, Connecticut 06005

Tony Salvatore
Health and Welfare Council
Seven Benjamin Franklin Parkway
Philadelphia, Pa. 19103

CONSTRAINTS ON EFFECTIVE INFORMATION SYSTEM
DEVELOPMENT AND USE
IN THE VOLUNTARY HUMAN SERVICES SECTOR

ABSTRACT: The social welfare field,
which is responsible for the provision of
social services to youth, adults, families,
and the elderly, is very heavily dependent
upon information storage, analysis and re-
rieval for purposes of administration, program planning, and the delivery of services
to clients. The oldest group of social service providers are the voluntary agencies
which are comprised of a large variety of
non-profit, non-governmental organizations
offering an even larger variety of services,
from infant daycare to meals-on-wheels for
the aged. A majority of these voluntary
agencies receive funding from the United Way
or Community Chest. (The extent of funding
differs from agency to agency.) In many
communities, Health and Welfare Councils
have been established to coordinate the operations of the specialized direct service
agencies, to carry out community planning
and needs assessments, and to supply consultation and evaluations to the United Way
in relation to the allocation of United Way
contributions to member, provider agencies.
Recently, these Health and Welfare Councils
have begun to stimulate and assist in an
effort to "systematize" information processing on the part of United Way and other
community agencies. Most of these efforts
have been toward the establishment of management information systems, to aid in administration and making agencies "more accountable," and the establishment of resource
data banks to facilitate the retrieval of information about what services are offered by
other community agencies to aid in the proper
referral or placement of clients. (This is
commonly referred to as information and referral.) The information system activities
of the Health and Welfare Councils are critically assessed and found to be ineffective

and sometimes wasteful of all too scarce
community resources. It is argued that in
the voluntary sector, human service information systems fail for largely the same
reasons as those in business and government --
they are planned and designed without proper
definition of the purpose for the system and
without proper recognition of the impact of
individual and organizational behavior on the
performance of the operating system. Alternative uses of data are suggested which take
into account the needs of the Health and
Welfare Countil as well as its interorganizational environment.

Introduction

Social Welfare agencies are mandated to help people solve
or at least ameliorate personal, family or community problems.
The areas they are engaged in run the gambit of America's social
problems -- alcoholism, drug abuse, poverty, poor housing, marital
and family discord, social isolation, mental illness, child neglect,
delinquency, and so forth. Social Welfare agencies endeavor to
overcome these problems on an individual, family, group, or community
level   They enlist an array of techniques in the course of this
confrontation including counseling or casework; financial assistance;
social services, e.g. daycare and homemakers; the provision of goods
and commodities e.g., clothing and meals; residential care and
shelter; institutional services; and community organization which
can include planning, research, mobilization of people and or
agencies; etc.

These social agencies are usually non-profit and can be under
public or private auspices. Those in the latter category are usually
referred to as "voluntary agencies." In social welfare they manifest themselves in the form of agencies which offer their services
on a voluntary basis to the community and are administered by citizen volunteers who serve as uncompensated members of the Board of
Directors. Most are either charities or dependent upon organized
charities, such as the United Way, or the contributions of individual citizens. They are "outside the private, profit-seeking sector
and outside the public sector."[1]

Social Welfare agencies in recent years have been increasingly
preoccupied with the installation and operation of automated computerized information systems to aid in their mission of meeting
human needs. Perhaps the most extensive development has occurred
in the "public sector" under the auspices of federal, state, or
local government. However, the voluntary sector has also been

---

[1]   Burton A. Weisbrod, "Toward a Theory of the Voluntary Non-Profit
   Sector in a Three Sector Economy." Reprint Series (#52). Institute for Research on Poverty University of Wisconsin, Madison. 1975.

-58-

drawn into this activity, especially that part of it which relates to the United Way and Health and Welfare Councils; and the latter have been at the vanguard of this movement.

Health and Welfare Councils have encouraged two types of information systems:

1. Management Information Systems which would report data on the provision of services for the purpose of improved administration, program planning, and resource allocation.

2. Resource Information Systems which would permit the storage and retrieval of indexed information about community services for use in response to consumer inquiries in the Information and Referral (I & R) Process.[1]

It is our contention that in the voluntary social welfare system, the adaptation of such information systems has not "paid off" in terms of benefits that equal or exceed their developmental and operating costs, and the "opportunity costs" derived from misplaced initiatives and investments. This is because the fundamental problem is, and continues to be, a lack of clear definition of the problem in terms of service delivery or service systems rather than a lack of information per se. In addition, if the problem is not defined clearly or correctly, then the proposed solution - the development of information systems - will have little effective impact.

In addition to the lack of proper problem definition, there are other reasons that information systems have not worked in the voluntary sector. These are primarily linked to the federative nature of the voluntary system as well as to the mechanics of creating and using a mechanized system.

It is our conclusion that the voluntary sector has not developed information systems aligned to its needs, but rather has too closely followed the approaches of better endowed (financially) government and business sectors. Similarly, the nature of the interorganizational structure of the voluntary sector has not figured sufficiently in the considerations of implementing such systems.

It is our contention that the solution to this problem is to be more self-conscious of the role, mission and constraints of the voluntary sector in meeting human needs. We shall pose some specific design strategies which take into account the limitations inherent to the voluntary sector.

The Nature of a Voluntary Health and Welfare Council

Health and Welfare Councils are legitimated to plan in the voluntary social service sector - an admittedly small arena in

---

[1] For a general discussion of Information and Referral Systems, see Nicholas Long, "Information and Referral Services: A Short History and Some Recommendations" Social Service Review, March, 1973.

-59-

comparison to the public sector. These councils are usually linked to the United Way in some fashion - either as a department of the United Way or as a separate organization. They may be what Warren calls a "unitary structure," i.e. the planning council is located within the United Way structure, as a department of it; decision-making is common with the United Way structure in that the Board and Executive Director are the same for both; and the Council only reflects a division of labor within the structure - in this case for planning. (Other divisions would be for fund-raising; public relations; etc.) The Council may be a separate organization, and at the same time, a part of a "federative" struc-ture in which each organizational unit has "disparate goals" from the United Way, but also has a formal link and shares some "in-clusive goals." Decision-making is separate in that the Council has its own Board and Executive Director, and there is a "division of labor" in that the planning for the United Way is carried out by the Council, in return for which the United Way provides the Council with financial resources which are usually ongoing.[1] In either case, as a department of or separate organization from the United Way, the primary focus of endeavor for the Council is the voluntary health and social welfare field. The Council often takes on certain projects in the public arena, but usually on a contract basis. Therefore, legitimation in the public arena is usually transitory and dependent on the assignment. The amount of "clout" available to the Health and Welfare Council is dependent upon the strength of its linkage to the United Way, and on the amount of resources it can amass and have at its disposal for allocative purposes from both the public and private arenas. For example, in Hartford, the local Health and Welfare Council is one of the State Area Agencies on Aging, and in this capacity it has amassed over a quarter of a million dollars for which it has allocative responsi-bilities. Therefore, in the particular area of aging, the Council has amassed some clout. Similarly, in Philadelphia, the Council participated in a multi-year project with the Pennsylvania Depart-ment of Public Welfare and was able to realize many of its objec-tives for public social services.

Councils, whether as departments of the United Way or as separate organizations, are still very much federations of agencies themselves. Being federations, they are dependent upon the con-sensus of other agencies for their legitimacy. Furthermore, by their very self-definition as citizen-based agencies they are also dependent upon the consent of citizens for their continuation, and these citizens are often the powerful, or "semi-powerful" citizens in the Community. (The literature points to the fact that the most powerful citizens are represented on the allocative committees of the United Way, and the next echelon of power on the Committees of the Health and Welfare Council.) In summary, the ability of a Council to plan is often proscribed by its tenuous linkage to re-sources, limited amount of clout, and need for consensus for its continued legitimacy.

---

[1] Roland Warren, "The Interorganizational Field As a Focus For Investigation," Administrative Science Quarterly, 12, No. 3 (December 1967): 396-419.

Definition of Social Problems By Health and Welfare Councils

Given the legitimacy of such Councils to plan for the delivery of social services in the private sector, the Councils must identify certain problems within that field. If social services are not "working" to solve the major problems of our times, i.e. poverty, unemployment delinquency, etc., then there must be a reason social services are still maintained as a way to solve these problems. The dilemma then resides in how they are being delivered. A frequent diagnosis for the lack of effectiveness of social srrvices is "duplication of services," and the remedy most often proposed for "duplication of services" is "coordination of services." By the way, this diagnosis and remedy are not at all confined to the voluntary sector. As Warren et al describe in their new book, The Structure of Urban Reform, in the 1960's this diagnosis was applied to the urban problems, by the federal government and the strategy for dealing with the problems was promulgated in the Model Cities legislation. Warren, et al write,

"This supplement to the services strategy (i.e. problems can be solved thru the provision of social services) provides both an implicit diagnosis for its past failures and a promise for its future success. Lack of effectiveness in improving social conditions is attributed to the circumstance that organizations - whether governmental or non-governmental - are working independent of each other; or worse yet, at cross purposes, and so their combined efforts do not achieve their full potential .....

The remedy is implicit in the diagnosis: comprehensive planning and coordination."

It is our contention that a new diagnosis is now at hand. The new diagnosis for the lack of effectiveness in improving social conditions is that information is lacking, or that information is available, but it is unorganized and non-comparable. This rationale maintains that if information were to be organized and made comparable, then better decisions could be made; solutions to social problems might be found, but in any case, social services would be thereby improved. Thus, the solution is to develop new, computerized data systems. In other words, a new diagnosis has come into vogue. What is worse - the old diagnoses have yet to be thrown out. The social welfare councils are not facing up to the structural problems inherent in our society, or if they are - they are not directing their planning to those places where they might have an impact. Instead, they are extending the sham of diagnosing the problem and finding the remedy in terms of what are seen as "manageable" and "innovative" solutions. The depressing part of this activity is that, as we shall proceed to demonstrate, the development of electronic, information systems has been no more manageable for the voluntary sector as was coordination for Model Cities.

This is not a critique that has its origins with us. In the final chapter of The Structure of Urban Reform, Warren et al write:

"More recently, the direction of liberal reform has been modified, largely as a result of the essential failure of these earlier efforts. The new efforts are focused on mechanisms that will give the local municipal government more power vis a vis such relatively independent .... organizations as the boards of education and the various independent local authorities. They emphasize the need to strengthen the local chief executive's technical ability in the field of planning and service coordination, especially through such hardware as computers and through such technologies as systems analyses." Warren concludes, "While it hopefully will result in some economies of administration and planning, nothing in its substantive content promises more."[1]

Management Information Systems: Their Intended Use and Inherent Problems.

Given this background, Management Information Systems were proposed for the collection of up-to-date, comparable data on service providers, and users or beneficiaries. The rationale for such systems is that once data is obtained on service users and service providers, certain baseline data will then become available upon which decisions could be made. There is a certain amount of presumption in such claims. Although such systems were proposed to extend beyond the United Way system of agencies, the United Way system would be the starting point. The presumption resides in the limited scope of United Way agencies and therefore the implied leap that the data provided would be sufficient to reveal gaps and needs in services.

However, beside sheer presumption in terms of what such data might "indicate" in terms of need, as good planners, we do believe in starting small, even with demonstrations, of course assuming that our claims as to what we are trying to accomplish are based in at least a fairly accurate problem definition. The United Way system is a small, well boundaried system that may have served as a good starting, controllable demonstration if the very nature of the federative system did not work against such a demonstration.

OVERVIEW OF FAILURE FACTORS

In addition to the lack of proper problem definition, there are other reasons that information systems have not worked in the voluntary sector. These are primarily linked to the federative nature of the voluntary system as well as to the mechanics of creating and using a mechanized system. It is our opinion that management information systems have not been effective in the voluntary sector for reasons such as:

1. Voluntary fund allocations are not made in terms of need.
2. There has been insufficient user involvement, orientation, and support.
3. Accountability and reporting requirements are overly demanding and in constant state of flux.

---

[1] Roland Warren, Stephen M. Rose, and Ann F. Bergunder, The Structure of Urban Reform, (Lexington, Massachusetts: Lexington Books, 1974).

4. Illusion that information systems are panaceas makes them part of the problem, not the solution.
5. Human service planning tends to be opportunistic; program objectives are determined by funding availability rather than need.

Resource information systems have failed because:

1. People want direct help, not information.
2. Human service professionals do not understand the mechanics of indexing, storage, and retrieval.
3. No need for computerized, I & R data has been identified by those currently operating the systems.

Information systems of both varieties have fallen short of their promise in the voluntary sector because:

1. The systems became ends in themselves rather than means.
2. Manual and semi-automated systems had never been used to full potential. Human routines were programmed rather than redesigned for machine capacities.
3. Pre-system information practices were poor and under-developed.
4. Quantity of data and information took precedent over quality. As Ackoff predicted, the pool of information has become a tidal wave that can be remedied only by filtration and condensation.[1]
5. Terms and measures were never operationally defined and standardized.
6. Systems were promoted to make agencies more "business-like" when the objective should have been to employ a system as a tool which would eventually result in the enhancement of service delivery and render agencies more "social welfare-like."[2]

MIS FAILURE FACTORS

Voluntary Fund Allocations Are Not Made in Terms of Need.

The United Way is a federated system, which in order to ensure its continuation, is dependent upon the continued consensus to the federation of those organizations of which it is formed, as well as the community upon which it is dependent for resources. Member agencies expect to receive resources from the United Way in order to ensure the continued viability of their own organizations. Therefore, "rules" or "norms" exist to protect the status quo, and these have been well documented. "(1.) Fund allocations are expected to be about the same as they were in the previous fiscal year. (2.) 'Unrealistic' requests

---

[1] Russell L. Ackoff, A Concept of Corporate Planning (N.Y.: Wiley-Interscience, (1970) pp. 113-116.

[2] This point is made in Peter F. Drucker, "Managing the Public Service Institution," The Public Interest, (Fall, 1973, pp.43-60.)

may reflect unfavorably on the member agency and its leadership...(3.) It is better for everyone to get a piece of the pie than for some agencies to get cut out and create the possibility of debilitating conflict."[1] In short, the claim for implementing a M.I.S. in the voluntary sector, i.e., to help in decision-making about the allocation of funds in order to better reflect need - is completely contradictory to the rationale for federation which is the raison d'etre of the United Way system.

There Has Been Insufficient User Involvement, Orientation, and Support.

In order for a M.I.S. to be successful in the voluntary system, it must be used by the member agencies, as well as the allocative and planning branches of the United Way. Agencies, in particular, must see some advantages to having such a system since they must be the providers of the information. However, unless some advantages can be demonstrated for these agencies, such a system might not only have no attraction for them in terms of what it might do for them, but it also could be threatening to the very core of the member agencies - their mainstay - their allocation which they have grown to expect without serious question from the United Way every year. Further, the citizens on the allocation committee and the staff of the United Way may have, and rightly so, no desire to threaten these agencies since the former are responsible for the maintenance of the federation which in turn means keeping conflict at a low level. Therefore, unless users - agencies, citizens, and United Way staff - can be oriented to the advantages of such a system and involved in designing it so they are not threatened, the system can be impeded from the very start.

Accountability and Reporting Requirements Are Overly Demanding And In Constant State of Flux.

The constant changes in reporting systems, especially under federal, state, and city regulations, almost make a system outdated before it is established. From another viewpoint, since it takes so long to set up a system (sometimes years), the reporting requirements upon which a system may have been fashioned might become obsolete before a system is completed.

Illusion That Information Systems are Panaceas Makes Them Part of The Problem, Not The Solution.

This point has been alluded to in the discussion of problem definition. Moreover, if it is assumed that such

---

[1] Stanley Wenocur, "Political View of The United Way," Social Work, May 1975.

-64-

systems will provide the "answers" to problems in the
field of social welfare, then nothing might ever get
solved! Such thinking and the effort needed to make
such systems work can be so absorbing and for such a
long period of time, that the real problems inherent
in the structure and delivery of social services could
be avoided for a long time - and that is a problem!

Human Service Planning Tends to Be Opportunistic; Program Objectives Are Determined by Funding Availability Rather Than Need.

Anyone who has been in the business of social service delivery
will acknowledge that many programs are planned according to what
the "trend-setters" in Washington promulgate as the new style.
Since their promulgations are made with the added carrot of dollars
for those who will adopt the new fashion, those of us in the planning sector who want to attract resources, i.e., most of us, plan
accordingly. The nature of the field therefore, once again, is
contradictory to the rationale for a M.I.S.

RESOURCE INFORMATION SYSTEM FAILURE FACTORS

People Want Direct Help Not Information

Although I & R systems are established on the fact that
people want information, a majority of consumers call for help, not
information. In fact, social workers often pass over information
giving and concentrate on "referral" or connecting the inquirer
with a resource. Practive has built a "mystique" about this activity and rendered it a complicated "helping process".[1] Information giving thus becomes secondary and almost obviates the need
for present I & R systems to have large, computerized information
systems.

Ignorance of Mechanics

Social welfare workers usually have no grasp of accepted
storage and retrieval practices. The main reason is not lack of
exposure, but the fact that they are specialists and often have
an intimate personal knowledge of a large number of agencies.
When they receive a request, they can deal with it based on their
own knowledge base. A worker need only turn to a more elaborate
system upon receipt of an unusual request, and then there is
question as to whether a computerized system would actually be
used.

However, as Information and Referral Systems are expanding their geographic coverage, especially with new Title XX funds,
better file organization and management will be necessary since
workers will not have intimate knowledge of all agencies in these
larger areas. At that time, collaboration between social welfare
and information service professional might be necessary.[2]

---

[1] Joseph L. Vigilante, "Back to the Old Neighborhood" Social Service
Review, June 1976. p. 202.

[2] See especially Harvey A. Licht, "The Information Professional and
the Neighborhood Information Service" Special Libraries.
March 1976.

No Recognized Need for Computerized Retrieval Systems.

I & R service providers are not seriously dissatisfied with the validity, scope, and retrievability of their current base of human service resource information. As a result of experience and personal relationships, I & R staffs direct callers to sources of service that they are sure will respond and sometimes even ignore accurate data bases. They are comfortable with the printed directories and card files that they have customarily used, and the Philadelphia experience has demonstrated that they resist the use of video displays or microfilms. Furthermore, there may even be among I & R workers, a serious conviction that someday machines will do it all and there will be nothing left for the professional to do.

Planning experience has taught us that unless there is a recognized need and openness to change, efforts in such directions are usually fruitless and not worth the effort given the constraints.

STRATEGIES FOR CHANGE

Data is a tool which when used appropriately can help, along with other tools in most cases, to effect change. The key is in defining the problem and the proposed solution, and then identifying the type of data which will be useful in helping to bring about the particular solution. The questions that are appropriately asked are - how much data and to what degree are information systems needed in the processing of that data? Another important factor to consider is the scope and constraints of the voluntary sector in determining a desirable change; the strategy for bringing it about; and the data processing capability. There are several strategies available for effecting change and each use data to some degree.

Documentation

A time-worn strategy of change is the documentation of fact which supports the desired change. Such documentation could make use of either primary or secondary data. Computer systems could be used for the analysis of data. In addition, information systems housed outside of the United Way could be tapped for the information which they hold, such as census data or other special studies. The key is to avoid maintenance of storage facilities in-house because of the costs and to make use of data stored on other systems; or in collecting primary data, to use systems when manual analysis is too cumbersome and difficult.

Demonstration Projects

Demonstration projects are another "old" strategy for effecting change.[1] The use of a demonstration project is particularly

---

[1] The rationale for using demonstration projects as a strategy for change is well discussed in Rothman, Jack, John L. Erlich and Joseph G. Theresa, Promoting Innovation and Changes in Organizations and Communities: A Planning Manual (N.Y.: John Wiley & Sons, Inc., 1976).

effective for the voluntary sector since it is small and
controllable, but if successful in its demonstration, it can
be replicated at a "macro" level. The demonstration project
is a method for influencing change in both the public and private sectors. Information systems might be used for the collection and analysis of data on the demonstration project. However,
an inherent problem of all demonstrations is the lack of clarity
about how the results will actually be transferred from the trial
setting to the field at large. This is a serious failing and one
that is recognized by those who are not anxious to bring about
change. As small-scale experiments demonstrations are not serious
threats, they can be readily endorsed because immediate change is
not compulsory or even advisable in the light of a permanent uncertainty in regard to the validity of the methods and the reliability of the outcome. To be effective demonstrations must not
be undertaken only on the fact that they will lead to change, but
must be structured to expedite if not induce change. Who is to
be influenced by the results must be determined in advance and a
research design drawn to facilitate acceptance of the results.
Findings can only be conclusive when we know who is to draw the
final policy conclusions.

Collection of Data From Agencies

If the object of change is the way in which the United
Way is allocating funds, even in a marginal way, then collecting
data from agencies might be one tool for use in demonstrating
need or new patterns of client use. The collection might be made
by fields of service in order that units of service be comparable
without much work in trying to define comparability across such
diverse categories as recreation, meals-on-wheels, homemaker
services, and court appearances of Legal Aid attorneys. The
processing of such data might be accomplished manually. The key,
again, is in defining the scope of the change. Changes at the
margins of agency programs may not need a major effort in data
analysis; it might be limited to data provided in response to
very specific questions - as opposed to fishing exhibitions.

Another strategy for effecting change in allocations in
United Ways is by collecting data from clients themselves. This
precludes defining comparable units of service and can focus in
on facets of service delivery that may need changing. For example, a client reaction survey on mini-buses for the elderly
asked questions of riders on comfortability, punctuality, scheduling, etc. This method is limited to obtaining data on present programs as opposed to need for new programs. However,
primary data collected at the agency level for the purpose of
effecting change in allocations is appropriate to the change goal.

CONCLUSIONS

Three major conclusions can be drawn from our review:

(1) Inasmuch as information systems are established to
    support decision-making, their effectiveness in terms
    of design and operation is largely dependent on the
    clarity of understanding about the decision processes to

be supported. The voluntary social welfare sector has evidenced much misunderstanding and indecisiveness in regard to what it expects of its information systems. The social welfare field tends to be reactive rather than proactive but has neither designed systems to accommodate this fact or changed the style of decision-making, planning, and administration so that management information systems could be of greater utility.

(2) Computerized systems are very costly, and the voluntary sector, which has such limited resources, must be very certain of purpose and expected results before entering into such undertakings.

(3) "The major reason that social welfare information systems have failed is the same reason most systems fail: ... We have ignored organizational behavior problems in the design and operation of computer-based systems. If steps are not taken to understand and solve these organizational behavior problems, systems will continue to fail."[1]

In short, social welfare system failures are not atypical and can be amenable to rehabilitation given changes in the perception of what they are to do vis à vis the problems at hand.

---

[1] Henry C. Lucas, Jr., Why Information Systems Fail (N.Y.: Columbia University Press, 1975) p.6

Jeffrey D. Wynne, Acting Chief
Division of Alcohol Programs, County of San Diego
2870 Fourth Avenue
San Diego, Ca 92103

Michael M. Collins, Ph.D.
General Research Corporation
5383 Hollister Avenue
Santa Barbara, Ca 93105

A FUTURE-ORIENTED APPLICATION OF A DATA
SYSTEM TO ALCOHOLISM PROGRAM MANAGEMENT*

ABSTRACT: This paper describes the Management
Information Indicator System (MIIS) developed specifically for alcoholism programs in San Diego
County, California. It further details the methodology used to provide information on the estimated
need for services as well as information on the
identified need for services.

INTRODUCTION

San Diego County, having one of the higher rates of
alcoholism of California's 58 counties, pioneered in the development of publicly-funded alcoholism services during the
first half of this decade. As treatment and rehabilitation
services expanded to provide over 1,200 treatment admissions
monthly, and as operating costs mushroomed to over $2 million
annually, demands developed to demonstrate the impact of
services on the community's alcoholism problem.
Anticipating the need to evaluate the impact of services,
the County's Department of Substance Abuse sought and obtained, in 1975, a $78,149 grant from the State Office of Alco-
holism to develop an alcoholism program - specific Management
Information Indicator System (MIIS). Ten months were utilized to design and develop the system and it was implemented in
January, 1976. Six months after implementation, the system
has proven successful and has been utilized in the decision
making leading to substantive programmatic changes.

---

*This paper was prepared as part of work under a grant from
the California State Office of Alcoholism.

Currently, fifteen alcohol programs are using MIIS as their primary data collection/retrieval system.

AN OVERVIEW OF THE SYSTEM OBJECTIVES

The primary purpose of MIIS is to provide information to County and alcohol program personnel which can be useful in decision-making.

The MIIS objectives at the County level are oriented toward three major planning issues:

o   The identification of service needs in various county regions;

o   The allocation of limited resources in response to these needs; and

o   The selection of service delivery organizations (programs) which, based upon past performance, most likely will meet those needs effectively and efficiently.

At the local program level, the MIIS is directed towards:

o   The monitoring of service delivery and the retrospective assessment of the quality of those services; and

o   The presentation of such evaluation data in a format which is appropriate to an important planning question--how can the quality of services be improved.

CONCEPTS IMPORTANT TO THE SYSTEM DESIGN

Defining Geographical Boundaries in the Community

MIIS can identify service needs in various parts of the County by providing detailed summaries of the identified level of need and treatment activity within each of six health catchment regions; these regions correspond to the major sub-regional census boundaries as defined in the 1970 census. Clients are assigned to a planning area on the basis of their area of residence.

Defining Alcohol Service Categories/Intensity

MIIS uses five major service categories or intensity levels and twenty different program types. Clients are categorized by service category on the basis of the type of program most appropriate to their treatment needs. This decision is basically subjective on the part of the person interviewing the client at the time of contact. MIIS also generates a recommendation based on the Screening form.

The five levels and twenty program types are:

Level A--Prevention:

1. Information/Referral   4. Follow-up
2. Alcohol Education   5. DWI
3. Outreach   6. PSI
                         7. Occupational
                            Programs

Level B--Detoxification:

8. Social Detoxification
9. Medical Detoxification

Level C--Non-Residential Services

10. Self-help Groups   12. Day Treatment
11. Outpatient Services 13. Drop-in Services

Level D--Residential Services

14. Residential Treatment
15. Recovery Home Services

Level E--Other Services

16. Emergency Medical   19. Ancillary Services
17. Other Hospital   20. Other
18. Vocational Rehab-
    ilitation

Defining Need in the Community

Two categories of need for services are referred to in MIIS: (1) estimated need--the need for services of the population that would be reached given intensified outreach and casefinding efforts; and (2) identified need for services of clients actually admitted into the service delivery system based upon an initial diagnostic evaluation.

The technique utilized by MIIS to determine the estimated prevalence of alcohol abuse is called "capture-recapture." In its most usual application for alcohol prevalence estimates it involves correlation of data based on such indicators as drunk driving arrests with data on hospital admissions for alcoholism. Most often, this technique calls for the correlation of data from two sources, one of which "captures" a large number of "cases" and one of which "recaptures" some smaller number of "cases."

When applying this technique, it is important to understand that the relevant population for planning purposes is not persons with identified alcohol problems. Instead, it is persons who might be identified and induced into treatment given more intensive outreach. Thus, MIIS uses a statistical sampling of existing and potential outreach resources within the community to develop a "capture" roster. This is the reason why the MIIS needs input from a number of community agencies, programs and individuals.

During one week out of every calendar quarter, a sample of professionals (e.g., doctors, ministers, school counselors, probation officers, welfare workers, present outreach workers, etc.) can be solicited to participate in the development of a capture sample to include a contact form for any individuals whom they are currently seeing who have an alcohol-related problem. It is also mandatory that a unique client identifier which protects confidentiality be submitted with the contact data.

Since the "recaptures" will be actual admissions into the existing treatment system, it will be important that "capture" not significantly alter the probability of "recapture." Thus, those potential outreach and casefinding sources participating (viz., doctors, counselors, etc.) should be asked to complete the necessary forms without altering or modifying whatever services they are presently providing.

The identified need for services methodology used by MIIS is described in the section of this paper on output reports.

THE MIIS SYSTEM DESIGN

The MIIS design is based on a design to simplify the collection and dissemination of information within the County alcohol service delivery system while at the same time satisfying all program, County and State information requirements, and improving the level of services provided to alcohol clients.

The MIIS system design is quite simple. There are six basic types of forms: Contact, Screening, Admission, Discharge, Follow-up, and Program Activity. There is also a Progress Worksheet, which is for program use only. These six forms are completed based on client activities and indirect services data, and are batched and forwarded to County Data Processing for keypunching into the computer. Each month output reports are generated by the computer for use by the Department of Substance Abuse, the programs, and the State. The system can be described most easily from two facets: the output reports and the data collection forms.

MIIS Output Reports

Four categories of reports are generated by MIIS:

Countywide Reports

o   Identified Need for Services Report

o Estimated Need for Services Reports
o Impact of Services Reports
o Location of Existing Services
o Client Survey Report

Program Specific Reports

o Client Survey Report
o Quarterly Admission Reports
o Admission Trend Reports
o Program Impact Reports
o Time to Successful Completion Differential Reports
o Time to Unsuccessful Completion Differential Reports
o Service Delivery Comparison Reports

State Required Reports

o Monthly Core Data Reports
o Monthly Program Data Report
o Quarterly Core Data Report
o Quarterly Information and Referral Core Data Report
o Yearly Person Data Tape
o Edit and Validate Reports

Countywide Reports

These reports are produced for each major geographical area and service delivery intensity level in the County. A summary countywide report is also produced.

Estimated Need for Services Reports

These reports provide an estimate of the number of people in each area in the County in need of each level of service. These reports can assist in answering the following kinds of questions: (1) is there a growing trend in alcohol abuse, (2) which services in which area would be responsive to the greatest need, (3) what will be the future demand for services.

Current Demand for Services Reports

These reports show the number of admissions each quarter by the client's area of residence and client's level of treatment need. Area codes are:

1. Central   4. East Suburban
2. North City   5. North County
3. South Suburban   6. East County

Treatment Need Codes are:

1. Prevention
2. Detoxification
3. Non-residential Services

4. Residential Services
5. Other Services

These reports identify current treatment demand and provide some indication of the future demand for services if current outreach and related activities remain the same and the current trend in demand continues.

These reports can be used to assist in determining:

--where certain services should be located
--what kinds of services are in demand
--seasonal variation in demand for various types
  of services by area

Impact of Services Reports

These reports present admission and follow-up behavioral and situation data on clients in treatment by areas of the County, treatment category and program. Uses include (1) measuring and comparing program impact, (2) identifying need for ancillary services, (3) understanding characteristics and needs of clients in treatment.

Location of Existing Services Reports

These reports show the number of clients in treatment programs, by type of program, in each area of the County. This can assist in assessing the impact of a new program, and determining whether current programs are located in the areas of the County where the greatest need exists.

Client Survey Reports

These reports summarize demographic client flow and hours per client of services delivered. Provide a quick overview of client service delivery activity by program and Countywide.

Program Specific Reports

Six types of quarterly reports describing different aspects of the activities of individual alcohol programs in the County. These reports include the following:

Quarterly Admission Bar Chart and Trend Reports

These reports show the number of clients in a program by treatment need. They also show the percent of admissions during each of the last ten quarters who require the same

category of treatment as that provided by the program. These
reports are useful in identifying changes in admission policy
or types of clients seeking treatment.

Program Impact Reports

These reports show characteristics of clients at admission
and follow-up and comparison with similar clients in similar
programs. Reveal differences in program admission policy and
extremely useful in assessing program impact.

Outcome Indicators Report

This report is similar to the Impact of Services Report.
It compares follow-up data on clients requiring a certain
level of services in a program with outcome data on all
clients in the program and other similar clients in similar
programs.

Completion and Service Delivery Reports

These reports display the percent of discharges during
the previous quarter by type of discharge and client characteristics. They can be useful in identifying differences
in services delivery to different clients and attrition
rates and patterns of various types of clients.

Time to Unsuccessful Completion Differential Reports

These reports graph the cumulative percent of discharges
during the quarter by time to unsuccessful completion (discharge because of three months inactivity; discharged, did
not complete treatment, but left with staff approval; discharged, did not complete treatment, left without staff approval, etc.) A display is also presented for subsets of the
discharge population if requested. The subsets available
include:

>   Age categories
>   Sex
>   Ethnicity
>   Source of Referral at Contact
>   Service Intensity Required
>   Employment Status
>   Arrests in Previous Six Months
>   Alcohol-related Arrests in Previous Six Months
>   Education Level
>   Marital Status

This report could indicate if a program is having a
problem with a particular type of client.

Service Delivery Comparison Reports

The last set of program specific reports are those which show the average number of hours per week of a particular type of service provided to clients discharged during the previous quarter, by time in treatment. These reports can be requested on the following types of services:

o   Individual Counseling
o   Group Counseling
o   Family Counseling
o   Vocational Training
o   Schooling
o   Medical
o   Detoxification
o   Antabuse or other medications
o   Alcoholics Anonymous
o   Formal recreational and social activities
o   Other

The reports will also display data on subsets of clients:

Age
Sex
Ethnicity
Source of Referral at first contact
Alcohol program services required
Employment status
Arrests
Alcohol-related arrests
Education level
Marital status

These reports can be used to further understand why some clients might choose differential attrition. It can also indicate if a program is responding differently to different types of clients.

It is important to note that in all of these reports, no attempt is made to explain the phenomena. Instead, programs are asked to examine the data and explain them if necessary.

State Office of Alcoholism Reports

The California State Office of Alcoholism, which sponsored the development of this system, requires four output reports and two tapes to be produced for their use.

o   Monthly Core Data Report
o   Monthly Program Data Report
o   Quarterly Core Data Report
o   Quarterly Information and Referral Core Data Report
o   Yearly Admission Data Tape
o   Yearly Follow-up Data Tape

This section describes these reports and tapes in terms of interpreting the data and its possible use by the Department of Substance Abuse. In general the reports provide general monitoring and documentation of services.

Monthly Core Data Report

This report presents the number of intakes and discharges in the County during the month and the open caseload at the end of the month. An Intake is defined to be an admission to the treatment system. It does not include clients who were admitted to a program within three months after being discharged and referred by another program. The intent is to measure the client flow into and out of the treatment system. Similarly, a discharge does not include a client who was referred to further treatment at the time of discharge from a program and was later admitted for further treatment within three months of discharge. An open case is any case for which there is an admission record but no discharge record. Programs are instructed to discharge a case that has been inactive for three months. Therefore, these discharges are not counted in the monthly open caseload figures. The open caseload figure is the number of clients in the treatment system at the end of the month.

These figures are useful for a very general summary of the treatment activity in the County. They could be combined with budget figures to get an estimate of cost per client and, if displayed over time, might indicate changes in treatment activity in the County.

Monthly Program Data Report

This report is designed to collect information about the indirect, outreach, and information and referral services provided in the County during the previous month. This data is a simple tabulation of the data submitted monthly by each program using the Program Monthly Activity Form. This information may have some use when studies in conjunction with the Current Demand for Services Reports to determine the possible impact of alcoholism education on future treatment demand.

Quarterly Core Items

Once each quarter, MIIS generates an output report that displays cases dropped due to inactivity in the County during the previous quarter and the number of each type of services provided during the quarter.

Quarterly Information and Referral Core Data Report

This report is generated quarterly summarizing information and referral activities of those programs participating in this aspect of MIIS.

Yearly Admission Data Tape

Once each year, a unique identifiable core item record is submitted for each new admission for the previous year. As with monthly core data, an admission is defined to exclude admissions who had been discharged and referred previously from other programs within three months prior to the date of admission. The record presents the following data:

o Month of Admission Date
o Year of Admission Date
o Sequence Number (Program ID, Client ID)
o County Code (37)
o Sex
o Age
o Race, Ethnicity
o Marital Status
o Number of Dependents
o Monthly Earned Income
o Other Earned Income
o Source of Other Income
o Years in Community
o Years of Education
o Occupation
o Employment Status
o Drinking Level
o Binge Drinking
o Years of Heavy Drinking
o Source of Referral at First Contact
o Referred to at First Contact
o Visit Status

These data items will be on computer tape which will be sent to the State each year.

Yearly Follow-Up Data Tape

Using a procedure yet to be developed by the State, a six-month follow-up from date of admission will be conducted on a sample of new admissions reported on the Yearly Admission Data Tape. The follow-up data will be collected using the follow-up form. It will be included as part of the Client Master Record and transcribed onto computer tape.

Edit and Validate Reports

Five basic types of data validation and file maintenance reports are generated by MIIS. These are designed to inform the County and the individual programs of the results of the computer's attempt to add, correct or delete data from one of the three master files: the Client Master File, the Program Master File, and the Code File. These reports will not be described in detail in this paper.

Audit Report

Also each month, the MIIS produces an Audit Report, showing the status of all clients in the Master File. This printout should be reviewed for completeness and any missing
forms should be requested from the program.

FORMS UTILIZED IN DATA COLLECTION

The forms utilized by program staff in collecting information for MIIS include:
The Contact form--initiated whenever a request for assistance is made. It establishes a unique client identification
number based on a coded last name at birth, birthdate, and
ethnicity and provides demographic and referral data on potential clients, without compromising the confidentiality of the
client records.
The Screening form--completed on each client or potential
client for whom a treatment plan will be prepared. It is
designed to focus on major factors which are important in
determining a client's need for services. It includes such
questions as (1) the status of the client's health; (2)
current social situation including family, vocation and perr
relationships (3) past and current alcohol use activity; and
(4) motivation for treatment.
The Admission form--filled out on every client admitted
to a program. It collects simple objective economic, vocational and alcohol-related behavior data useful for identifying
possible need for ancillary services and available resources
and for measuring program impact.
The Discharge form--completed on every client who leaves
a program. It records what services were received, when they
were received, discharge status and referral recommendations.
The Follow-up form--collects data useful in measuring
long-term program impact and indicating possible need for
timely intervention. Follow-up is an important aspect of the
MIIS and will be conducted on a sample of clients.
The Program Activity form--documents indirect services
provided by each program monthly as well as basic program resource information.

APPLICATIONS AND SUMMARY

Applications of MIIS, to date, have focused primarily upon
the uses of monthly reports by County and program personnel.
The recent implementation of MIIS has prevented the development
of conclusive quarterly reports, however it is expected that
the quarterly reports will become available with highly useful
information within six months.
Programs participating in MIIS initially expressed concern

that completing the MIIS input forms on clients would be too
time consuming, however recent experience suggests that the
input forms can be completed quickly and can be of value in
assisting therapists in screening and evaluating clients.
A degree of resistance to MIIS has remained with selected
alcoholism programs as such programs have not used MIIS to
replace their other data collection instruments.

The MIIS program designed to provide data on estimated
need has not yet been fully implemented due to the amount
of time required to recruit and train personnel in hundreds
of potential "capture" centers. It is anticipated that such
training can be accomplished during the next year.

The utilization of MIIS in San Diego County suggests
that an alcoholism-specific management information system
can be helpful in evaluating such programs and in providing the comparative program data needed to make major decisions on alcoholism services.

MARILYN K. JAMES
PROGRAM EVALUATOR
OFFICE OF PROGRAM EVALUATION
COUNTY OF SAN DIEGO
1600 PACIFIC HIGHWAY ROOM 272
SAN DIEGO, CALIFORNIA 92101

DETERMINING FOOD STAMP PROGRAM PARTICIPATION RATES FOR SAN DIEGO COUNTY

In late 1974, the Board of Supervisors of the County of San Diego charged the Office of Program Evaluation (OPE) with the task of evaluating the County's Food Stamp Program. With this directive, OPE conducted an evaluation of both the efficiency of the operation of the County's program in providing services to applicants and clients and the effectiveness of the program in "reaching" those households who were eligible for food stamps. By employing a lengthy yet conceptually uncomplicated methodology, food stamp participation rates were calculated through a comparison of the number of households who had participated in the program since its inception in July of 1974 to estimates of the number of households who had been eligible for the program. These participation rates were calculated for each of the County's six major statistical areas, for the County as a whole, and for the County's senior citizen population.

INTRODUCTION

In July 1974, the County of San Diego replaced its Food Commodity Distribution Program with the Food Stamp Program.[1] After several months of the program's operation, the County's Board of Supervisors assigned to the newly formed Office of Program Evaluation (OPE) the task of evaluating the efficiency and effectiveness of the Food Stamp Program at the local level. As part of the effectiveness portion of the evaluation,[2] a study was undertaken to examine the participation level of eligible San Diego

---

[1] The County of San Diego SMSA has a population of over 1.6 million and covers approximately 4,300 square miles.
[2] Also included in the effectiveness portion was a summary of the research available on the nutritional benefits of the FS Program-see bibliography for citations concerning topic.

County households in the program. At the time the study was being conducted, the State of California Department of Benefit Payments was considering the possibility of mandating an outreach program to ensure that eligible households were aware of the program.

The purpose of this paper is to present the basic methodology used to determine participation levels or rates, as well as to aquaint the reader with the type of population statistics required to derive this data and the limitations of the data. The methodology and data requirements presented in this paper can generally be applied to any Standard Metropolitan Statistical Area (SMSA), since the basic source of population statistics is the U.S. Census. The type of participation data that was derived can be used for a variety of purposes, such as for implementation of outreach programs, for locating possible sites for welfare offices that serve FS clients, and for use as a socio-economic indicator.[3]

METHODOLOGY

For the purposes of this study, a Food Stamp (FS) Program has been defined to be effective if it "reaches" those components of the population that are eligible for the services the program can provide, i.e., food stamps for households whose income limits their food purchasing capacity below United States Department of Agriculture (U.S.D.A.) established levels.[4] The measure of program effectiveness used in this study is a FS participation rate - a comparison of the number of households who have participated in the FS program to estimates of the number of eligible households. If a household had been certified to receive FS during a certain time frame, then the program was successful in "reaching" that household regardless of whether the household did not continue to participate in the program.[5]

---

[3] The data derived in this study was used as an index for determining the geographic areas of the County most in need of Federal Community Services Administration (CSA) grant monies - see Fair Share Formula, a joint venture of the Economic Opportunity Commission of San Diego County and the County Human Resources Agency, 1975.
[4] The Food Stamp Program allotment amount is currently based on the U.S.D.A. thrifty diet plan.
[5] Analyses of San Diego County data showed that there is a high turnover of households participating in the program; during the first eight months of the program, nearly 17,000 households had participated in the program and dropped out. This figure reqresents 43% of the total households who had or were still participating in the program during those eight months.

In this study, household participation rates were calculated on a countywide basis, for each of the County's six major statistical areas (MSA's) and for certain age brackets of the heads of households. The basic methodology used to calculate the rates is described below:

1. Data Requirements

    Three basic sets of data were essential for the calculation of FS participation rates, as follows:

    A. A 1974 count of all FS-eligible households in San Diego County, by household size, annual gross income, and MSA of residence. The Comprehensive Planning Organization provided OPE with gross tabulations of 1970 U.S. Census of Housing counts.

    B. The number of households certified to receive FS since the program inception in July, 1974. The San Diego County Welfare Department provided OPE with a count of households who had been certified to receive FS aid, by MSA of residence, during the program's first eight months of operation.

    C. An estimate of the annual gross income limits used for determination of FS eligibility, for each household size (one through six or more members). Gross income limits were derived from a sample of households currently certified to receive FS aid.

2. Adjustments to 1970 Census Data

    In order to derive data requirement #1 as described above, the following adjustments to the Census data were made:

    A. Household Count Adjustment
        1974 MSA population counts (person counts) were compared to 1970 counts and population growth factors for the four-year period were derived for each MSA. These factors were then applied to 1970 Census household counts to obtain 1974 household counts.

B. Income Level Adjustments
    Income level brackets for the 1970 Census
    data (e.g., < $2,000, $2,000 - 2,999,
    $3,000 - $4,999,etc.) were converted to
    1974 dollars using the Consumer Price
    Index, with 1969 = 100.0 and 1974 = 134.6.
    It was also necessary to subdivide the
    larger household income levels into smaller
    $1,000 intervals and then assign household
    counts to those intervals based on house-
    hold income distribution data available
    from Table P-4 of the Census of Housing.

By applying the adjustments cited above to the 1970
Census data, matrices were derived for each of the
County's six major statistical areas to show house-
hold counts by household size and income level.
(See sample matrix in Exhibit 1).

3. Calculation of FS Gross Income Limits

    Federal FS regulations establish household monthly
    net income limits that are used to determine a
    household's eligibility for FS. A household's
    monthly net income is derived by subtracting al-
    lowable deductions from the household's monthly
    gross income.[6] Since the household income reported
    in the Census is annual gross income, adjustments
    were necessary to convert FS monthly net income
    limits to estimates of annual gross income limits.
    The gross income limits were derived by sampling
    active FS cases to determine the average dollar
    amount of deductions taken by each household size.
    This amount was then added to FS net income limits
    and converted to an annual income level for each
    household size (See Exhibit 2).

4. Identification and Count of FS-Eligible
    Households by MSA

    For each MSA household size and income matrix, the
    1974 Census income brackets which each of the
    derived FS gross income limits fell within was
    identified and defined as the "critical income
    bracket" for each household size. A linear
    approximation was then made to determine the
    percentage and subsequently the number of households
    in that income bracket that fell below the FS gross

---

[6] Allowable deductions include such items as medical payments, child support, tuition, shelter expenses, mandatory
salary deductions, etc.

EXHIBIT 1

COUNTS OF 1974 HOUSEHOLDS BY SIZE, BY INCOME LEVEL

MAJOR STATISTICAL AREA (MSA):

NORTH CITY (1)

Annual 1974 Household Income (CPI adjusted from 1969 levels)

Household Size	< $2,692	$2,692-4,037	$4,038-5,383	$5,384-6,729	$6,730-8,075	$8,076-9,421	$9,422-10,767	$10,768-12,113	$12,114-13,459
1	3,434	2,205	1,485	1,611	1,404	1,378	1,075	1,102	1,067
2	327	48	140	154	292	288	546	560	544
3	2,013	1,362	1,706	1,852	2,061	2,024	1,943	1,992	1,926
4	1,198	472	622	675	901	887	1,064	1,090	1,056
5	816	246	336	366	683	672	1,069	1,097	1,061
6+	466	158	197	215	362	356	663	680	659
TOTAL	8,254	4,491	4,486	4,873	5,703	5,605	6,360	6,521	6,313

EXHIBIT 2

ESTIMATE OF FOOD STAMP (FS) PROGRAM GROSS INCOME LIMITS
BY HOUSEHOLD SIZE

Household Size	FS Monthly Maximum Net Income Limit	Average Dollar Deductions[1] (Household Gross Minus Net Income)	Estimated Monthly FS Maximum Gross Income Limit	Annual FS Maximum Gross Income Limit
1	$194	$ 85	$279	$3,348
2	280	149	429	5,148
3	406	150	556	6,672
4	513	178	691	8,292
5	606	201	807	9,684
6 or more[2]	793	173[3]	966	11,592

1 Estimated through a 10% sample of current food stamp households. (This sample size assured results at a 95% level of confidence). The use of nonstudent household income tends to make this estimate conservative. If student households had been included, higher deductions would have resulted from allowable tuition and fee payments.

2 The FS net income limit for a 7-member household has been used here. Of the size "6 or more" households sampled, 64% had at least 7 members. Therefore, the use of the FS monthly net income for a 7-member household should be considered a conservative FS net income limit.

3 This drop in average dollar deductions could be representative of many things, including changes in shelter deductions allowed for higher income levels.

income limit. The count of all households falling below the critical income bracket was then added to the count of FS eligible households falling within the critical income bracket. This was done for all household sizes, and the total (of all household sizes) is the base for determining the number of households eligible for FS on the basis of household income requirements only. However, several additional adjustments, as described below, must be applied to these base figures to derive a more "realistic" count of eligible households.

5. Adjustment for Household Excess Assets

In addition to the maximum income limits used to determine FS eligibility, federal regulations also limit the amount of assets, beyond income, that a household may possess. These assets generally do not include a home and a car, and the following asset limits for determining FS eligibility have been established:

A. If all household members are under 60 years of age, household assets cannot exceed $1,500.

B. If one member of a household is over 60 years of age, household assets cannot exceed $3,000.

Since the Census does not provide information on household assets, it was necessary to explore alternative sources for this type of data. A study of household assets was identified that stated nationally, about 20% of the households falling in the FS eligible income categories had assets which would make them ineligible for FS.[7] Therefore, counts of households eligible for FS on the basis of income alone were reduced by 20% to reflect households ineligible due to excess assets.

6. Adjustment for "Income Accounting Effect"

A study that was conducted on FS participation rates by state has indicated that when a household's annual income level is used to determine eligibility based on monthly income, an undercount of eligible

---

7 Dorthy Projector and Gertrude Weiss, Survey of Financial Characteristics of Consumers, Federal Reserve Technical Paper, August, 1966, Table A-39.

households results in the magnitudes of 40% to 60%,[8]
e.g., it is conceivable that a household with an
annual income of $12,000 experienced months with
little or no income and would have been eligible
for FS during those months. In order to compensate
for this undercounting, which Bickel and MacDonald
refer to as an "income accounting effect" (see footnote 6), the number of FS eligible households
derived from the Census counts and adjusted for
excess assets, was then adjusted upwards by 40%
(Note: the County's FS program had been in
operation for about two thirds of a year).

7.   Other Adjustments

Special adjustments in the counts of FS-eligible
households were made at the countywide level (Note:
data was not available at the MSA level) to exclude
certain military families living off base who would
not likely be eligible to participate in the FS
Program due to significant military pay increases
which occurred since the 1970 household income data
was reported in the Census. Additional adjustments
were made using data supplied by the Social Security
Administration to exclude SSI/SSP recipients who
are not eligible to participate in the FS Program
in California.[9]

8.   Calculation of FS Participation Rates

In order to calculate FS participation rates for
each MSA and the entire County, the number of
households eligible to participate in the program
(which was derived through the steps previously
described) was compared to the counts of households

---

8   Gary Bickel and Maurice MacDonald, "Participation Rates
in the Food Stamp Program: Estimated Levels, By State," a
preliminary version of an Institute for Research on Poverty
Discussion Paper (IRPDP), University of Wisconsin, p. 10;
see also, Jodie T. Allen, "Designing Income Maintenance
Systems: The Income Accounting Problem," in Studies in
Public Welfare, Paper No. 5, Part III, Issues in Welfare
Administration: Implications of the Income Maintenance
Experiments, prepared for the Fiscal Policy Subcommittee
of the Joint Economic Committee of Congress, March 12, 1973,
pp. 69-97.
9   SSI/SSP recipients in California are "cashed out"; that
is, $10 is added to the basic SSI/SSP allotment to compen-
sate for the approximate value of the bonus stamps the
individual would otherwise be entitled to receive.

who had participated in the program (supplied by
the Welfare Department). Counts of eligible households with and without the 40% "income accounting
effect" adjustment were used to derive a range of
participation.

9. Basic Assumptions Underlying Household Eligibility
    Counts

    U.S. Census of Housing data is the only source of
    income data available at the level of detail re-
    quired for this study. However, certain assumptions
    are implicit in the use of this data to estimate
    household eligibility counts and are described, as
    follows:

    A. 1974 Household Count Distribution is the Same
        as in 1970
        The 1974 counts of households derived from
        the 1970 Census exhibit the same household
        income and size distributions as the 1970
        household counts.

    B. Effects of Census Undercounting of Household
        Income and Low Income Households Serve to
        Net Each Other Out
        A recent study of FS participation rates
        reports that the Census undercounts house-
        hold incomes of most types.[10] This state-
        ment was based on data presented in The
        Current Population Reports which indicate
        that an overall 10% income undercounting
        by the Census exists.[11] However, no data
        is currently available to determine how
        severe the undercounting is in the ranks
        of the low income households. On the
        other side of the incoming reporting
        problem, studies have indicated that the
        Census undercounts low income households.[12]
        These two factors, the undercount of house-
        hold income and the undercount of low income
        families, would tend to balance each other.

---

10 Bickel and MacDonald, op. cit., p. 10.
11 "Characteristics of the Low-Income Population, 1970."
Comsumer Income, Current Population Reports, p. 60, No. 81,
November, 1971, p. 19.
12 "Counting the Forgotten: The 1970 Census of Persons of
Spanish speaking Background in the United States," U.S.
Civil Rights Commission, April, 1974.

For this reason, and the difficulty of trying to quantify these problems, no special adjustments have been made for these potential Census biases.

C. Effect of San Diego County's Unemployment
    Rate on Household Eligibility Counts
    The County's average unemployment rate rose from 6.3% in 1969 to over 9% in 1974. Many people filing for unemployment benefits may have had incomes below FS limits even while employed, and therefore were included in eligibility counts. Others were originally from income levels above FS gross income limits, and would have been designated ineligible for FS using historical income data. Although these factors cannot be quantified for this evaluation, it is possible that higher unemployment rates have the potential to increase household eligibility counts beyond the levels presented in this study.[13]

RESULTS

Results of the countywide participation rate analyses showed that between 31% and 46% of the eligible households have participated in the program. Results of the major statistical area (MSA) participation rate analyses showed that participation levels ranged from a low of 16% - 23% for the East County MSA to a high of 32% - 45% for the Central MSA. While the results of the participation rate analyses cited above serve to identify the areas of the County with the lowest and highest participation rates, it is also important for outreach purposes to identify the areas of the County that have the highest number of non-participants in order to place the data in proper perspective. What this means is that even though an MSA might have a high participation rate, it might also have a relatively high number of eligible non-participants. This type of analysis was conducted on the participation data developed in the study, and results indicated that the MSA

---

13 The full impact of unemployed households on the FS program is unknown. However, according to a Rand Study on Seattle's Adaptation to Recession, only 7% of the unemployed went on public assistance (other than unemployment compensation). It is possible that many of the unemployed from higher income brackets would be FS ineligible due to excess assets.

with the highest participation rate also had the highest number of eligible households who had not participated in the program. The MSA with the lowest participation rate had the lowest number of eligible but non-participating households.

In addition to MSA participation rate analyses, the study also examined the participation of senior citizens in the program through the use of U.S. Census of Housing data adjusted to 1974 levels, with appropriate reductions for excess assets[14] and reductions for senior citizens participating in the SSI/SSP program and therefore not eligible for FS. Based on this data, it was estimated that less that 6% of the eligible senior citizen households have participated in the program.

CONCLUSIONS

At the time this study was conducted, little research was available in the area of FS participation analysis, and as this paper points out, several basic assumptions must be made when conducting a study of this type due to the detailed nature of the data that is required. However, in spite of these limitations, the data that was derived can be useful in attempting to recognize the needs of the populace. For instance, low FS participation rates, as identified through a demographic study of this type, could be attributed to a number of reasons, such as:

1. An accessibility problem, particularly for rural households, in getting to welfare offices to apply for FS or to stores approved for FS coupon redemption.

2. An unawareness of either the existence of the FS program or its eligibility requirements.

3. A disinterest in participation because of a high FS purchase requirement or because of the welfare stigma attached to receiving assistance.

Although it is unlikely that a public welfare agency could or would want to address the reason for low participation cited in #3 above, the reasons for low participation as cited in #1 and #2 are certainly addressable and to some extent correctable. Through the conduct of participation

---

14 Dorthy Projector and Gertrude Weiss, op. cit., Table A-35 - Nationally, below poverty level families with heads of households aged 65 or older had more assets than those with younger heads of households.

analyses of the type presented in this study, policy makers can be provided with a statistical basis for making decisions concerning the most effective use of their resources, e.g., the establishment of welfare offices to serve a potential FS clientele and direction of outreach efforts in areas that will benefit most from the program.

BIBLIOGRAPHY

Allen, Jodie T., "Designing Income Maintenance Systems: The Income Accounting Problem," in Studies in Public Welfare, Paper No. 5, Part III, Issues in Welfare Administration: Implications of the Income Maintenance Experiments, prepared for the Joint Economic Committee of Congress, March 12, 1973.

Bickel, Gary and MacDonald, Maurice, "Participation Rates in the Food Stamp Program: Estimated Levels by State," Institute for Research on Poverty Discussion Paper, University of Wisconsin, Preliminary Version (Received January, 1975).

Comprehensive Planning Organization (CPO)
- July 1974 Population Estimated (Computer Runs)
- 1970 Census Tracts with Predominant Group Quarters Population
- Info 74, Number 2, October 1974, Table 4: "Detailed Forecasts of Population by Age and Sex."

Feaster, J. Gerald and Perkins, Garey B., "Families in the Expanded Food and Nutrition Education Program: Comparison of Food Stamp and Food Distribution Program Participants and Non-Participants," Agricultural Economic Report No. 246, Economic Research Service, U.S. Department of Agriculture, September, 1973.

Lane, Sylvia, Food Distribution and Food Stamp Program Effects on Nutritional Achievement, University of California-Davis, Preliminary Report (Received January, 1975).

Madden, J. Patrick and Yoder, Marion D., Program Evaluation: Food Stamps and Commodity Distribution in Rural Areas of Central Pennsylvania, Bulletin 780, Department of Agriculture Economics and Rural Sociology, Pennsylvania State University, June 1972.

Projector, Dorothy and Weiss, Gertrude, Survey of Financial Characteristics of Consumers, Federal Reserve Technical Paper, August 1966.

Rand Corporation, <u>Seattle's Adaptation to Recession</u>,
Prepared for the National Science Foundation, September
1973.

San Diego County EDP Services (through County Welfare
Department).
Computer runs for:
    Food Stamp User Age Distribution
    All Households Ever Certified for FS

Social Security Administration, SSI/SSP Data, Office of
Research and Statistics, Baltimore, Maryland; also:
San Diego District Office.

U.S. Bureau of the Census, "Census Tracts - San Diego,
California," <u>U.S. Census of Population and Housing</u>,
PMC (1)-188.

_____ <u>Current Population Reports - Consumer Income Series</u>
P-60, No. 95, "Supplementary Report on the Low Income
Population: 1966 to 1972," July 1974.

_____ "Poverty Thresholds in 1969, by Size of Family and
Sex of Head," May 1972.

Kenneth D. Mai
Data Processing Coordinator
One Civic Plaza
Kansas City, Kansas 66101

PROCEDURES AND PITFALLS IN MONITORING CETA CLIENTS

ABSTRACT: The Comprehensive Employment and
Training Act (CETA) Client Monitoring System
developed in Kansas City, Kansas is a computerized
information system that provides the information
necessary both for top-level management decisions
as well as day-to-day administrative activities.
In addition, through the use of the Geographic
Base File for Wyandotte County, Kansas various
types of computer-generated maps can be produced
from the system quite easily.
The programs in the system were written in
Cobol with the consideration that other CETA prime
sponsors might find transferring the system to their
own sites desirable. It is likely that the problems
encountered in developing this system would be common to other prime sponsors and the solutions and
techniques used could save them a significant amount
of time and money. Transferring of the entire system if it meets the needs of another prime sponsor
is a possibility. This paper will describe how the
system works, the data collection forms, the reports
produced, problems encountered, and the possibilities of transferring all or part of the system to
another site.

INTRODUCTION

Design of the Kansas City/Wyandotte County CETA Client Monitoring
system was begun in the City Planning Department in June of 1974. In
late 1974, the Manpower division of the Planning Department was created.
The Manpower division then became a user of the services of the Information and Research Division of the Planning Department. This relationship has continued to the present, with Manpower now being a separate
City department. The Information and Research Division of the Department of Planning and Development is responsible for the mechanics of
processing the data and providing technical resources for developing
and maintaining the system, while the Manpower department is responsible
for collecting the data, correcting any errors found, and notifying
Information and Research when any technical difficulties arise.
A client begins the process of receiving training and job references by applying at an enrollment site. Initially, there were two main
enrollment sites. The enrollment site assigns a Program Liaison Person

(PLP) to work with the client. The Program Liaison Person then aids the client in filling out the application form. Information collected on the application form includes basic information such as name, address, age, race, and sex; past employment history; prior education and vocational training; and any conditions that may cause problems in getting a job or keeping it.

By working with the client, the Program Liaison Person determines whether the client can be placed directly in a job or if he should first receive some training. If it is decided that the client should receive training, he is entered into one or several program activities and manpower services. The system will allow up to nine "entries" for each client. The program activities available are:

(1) Classroom prime sponsor
(2) Classroom vocational education
(3) On-the-job training
(4) Public service employment
(5) Work experience
(6) Other activities

The manpower services available include the following:

(1) Pre-training
(2) Job Readiness
(3) Basic Education
(4) GED Preparation
(5) English as a Second Language
(6) Occupational Training
(7) Work Experience - Youth
(8) Work Experience - Other
(9) On-The-Job Training
(10) College
(11) Individual Referral
(12) Remedial Education

This information is recorded on the "entry" form. Other data on the entry form are the entry date, expected exit date, and the code for the subcontractor providing the services.

After the client completes the activities indicated on the entry form, he "exits" from that program activity and manpower service. The exit may be due to one of several reasons; the full course may have been completed, he may have voluntarily or involuntarily dropped out, or he may not have shown up. The exit form records the exit date, how many days and hours were attended, how many days he was absent, and the nature of the completion (full course, etc.).

When the client has exits for all of his entries (the average is two or three), he may be placed in a job and terminated from the program. The termination form is used to collect information about the termination. Of particular interest on the termination form is the termination code. This code indicates the reason why the client was terminated from the program. A termination is classified as a termination to employment, positive, or non-positive. Termination to employment includes direct, indirect, and self placements.

A direct placement is when the client is placed into a job as soon as he enrolls. An indirect placement is one that occurs after he has received some training. A self placement occurs when a client finds a job for himself (or through another agency) after he has enrolled in the CETA program. If the client has a job at the time he is terminated, the employer's name and address and supervisor's name are recorded.

Follow-up information is collected and input thirty days and six months after the date of termination. The same form is used for both follow-ups. The purpose of the follow-ups is to determine whether the job training and placement resulted in a long-lasting job or if the help from CETA was only temporary. The primary data on the follow-up is whether the client is still working at his CETA placement, and if not, the reason why.

Another concept that it is important to understand is that of the "pending applicant." A pending applicant is one who has applied to the CETA program but has not entered a program activity or terminated. Pending applicants are identified by the fact that no forms have been processed for them other than the application form. Each week a list of pending applicants is produced. For all other reports and listings the pending applicants are first deleted from the file. This is because a pending applicant has received no services, he has only filled out an application form.

HOW THE SYSTEM WORKS

Most of the input to the system originates at the subcontractor. During the week the subcontracted agencies complete the various forms as necessary to reflect the clients' current status. On Friday the forms are turned in to the prime sponsor, who at that time distributes the new program listings from the previous week's data.

CETA employees then check over the forms to find and correct any obvious errors. If necessary, a form may be returned to the subcontractor to clarify or correct part or all of it. On Tuesday all of the forms are sent to the Department of Planning and Development for processing.

Planning then keypunches the data and runs the computer programs to produce the reports for that week. All of the computer output, including errors from the edit and update programs, is returned to the CETA prime sponsor on Thursday. The prime sponsor then distributes the new listings to the subcontractors when they bring in their new forms on Friday. The prime sponsor is also responsible for making corrections based on the errors found by the edit and update programs.

There are two different groups of listing programs that are run from the CETA data. The first group is a set of programs that are run each week as administrative listings. These give lists of current enrollees by subcontractor, liaison person, and the CETA program overall. The second group of programs is run monthly and are mostly summaries to be used for management and evaluation purposes. On the average, it takes less than one hour of computer time each week to run the CETA system in Kansas City, Kansas.

The primary output from the CETA Client Monitoring system is the weekly and monthly reports prepared by computer. Some of these reports list current enrollees by subcontractor, program liaison person, or all enrollees for the prime sponsor. Other reports are summaries that are used to evaluate the performance of a particular subcontractor, manpower service, or the CETA program as a whole.

The following is a list of those reports that are run each week:

(1) Alphabetic Listing of All Past and Current Enrollees

(2) Liaison Person Alphabetic Listing of Current Enrollees

(3) Subcontractor Alphabetic Listing of Current Enrollees

(4) Numeric Listing of All Past and Current Enrollees

(5) Program Activity Entries and Exits of All Past and Current Enrollees

(6) List of Pending Applicants By Enrollment Site

Several reports are run on a monthly cycle. These listings are:

(1) Quarterly Report and Summary of Client Characteristics

(2) Program Activity Entries, Exits, and Current Participation

(3) Enrollments Received By Enrollment Site

(4) Number of Terminations By Reason and Enrollment Site

(5) Follow-ups Due By Liaison Person

(6) Follow-ups Completed By Enrollment Site and Labor Force Status

(7) Reason For Termination By Job Readiness Class

(8) Nature of Completion By Manpower Service

(9) Reason For Termination By D.O.T. Code

(10)   Overdue Exits By Subcontractor and Enrollment
        Site

(11)   Labor Force Status At Follow-up By Reason For
        Termination

(12)   List of Overdue Follow-ups

(13)   List of Preprocessor Rejects

(14)   List of Matcher Rejects

Copies of the Liaison Person and subcontractor listings are distributed each week so that they can be used as a reference list. This
also serves as a double check in case a termination form or exit form
was misplaced since the client will remain on the listing until the
proper form is processed. Any errors that are found by the liaison persons or subcontractors are brought to the attention of the prime sponsor
and the correction is made the following week.

In many cases, it is important to know the geographic distribution
of the CETA clients. For this reason, geocoding of clients' addresses
is done on a monthly basis. The geocoding is done by the use of the
Census Bureau's ADMATCH program and the DIME file for Wyandotte County.
The normal match rate is about 85 to 90 percent. Those addresses that
cannot be geocoded by computer are then listed and the tract and block
codes are determined manually.

The census tract codes were used to determine elibility when Title
II money was made available for those clients living in certain areas of
the City. It was very easy to identify the eligible enrollees from the
total number that were being served after the area was defined in terms
of census tracts. The alternative would have been to check each address
manually to see if it was in the Title II area.

It is also possible to determine if the areas being served, as indicated by the clients' home address, is that area that needs the CETA
services most. The 1970 Census of Population and Housing is an abundant
source of information about the social, economic, and demographic characteristics of census tracts. Data elements such as unemployment rate,
income below poverty level, and education level can be drawn on maps to
indicate the areas that are most in need of services. These areas
should then be the ones that are actually receiving the CETA services.
Three maps are included with this paper to illustrate this point. The
first map shows the unemployment rate from the 1970 Census for the census tracts in Wyandotte County. The second is a dot map showing the
actual distribution of CETA clients in May of 1975. The third map shows
the percent of persons in each tract being served by CETA. All three
maps are computer-generated plots produced with software developed
locally.

In 1976, it was necessary to reduce the number of primary enrollment agencies from two to one. One of the considerations in this process was how well each served the population in need. Dot maps were
generated by computer to show the home addresses of the clients from
each enrollment agency. A comparison of the two maps clearly showed

that one of the enrollment agencies was doing a better job of serving
the entire area in need than the other. This information was taken into
account when the choice between the two was made.

PROBLEMS ENCOUNTERED IN THE SYSTEM

As would be expected with any new large-scale system, several problems have been encountered in using the CETA client monitoring system.
These can generally be divided into two categories: procedural and
technical.

Procedural problems are those that are the result of the process of
using the system. It was discovered quite early that some of the subcontractors were better at following instructions than others, especially
when it came to filling out forms. Although an edit was the first program developed for the system, many changes were made later to check
for errors that could not be anticipated. The screening of all input
forms by an experienced CETA employee was found to be essential.

Another problem was found with the way edit and update errors were
handled. The design of the system specified that it should be able to
run even if the input was completely wrong. Any forms that have fatal
errors are just written to a reject file and the system continues without them. The intention is that all of these errors be corrected each
week. In practice, it was found that the error file was allowed to
build up until it was rejecting about 400 forms each week, with the
previous week's errors being added together with the new ones from the
current week. The only solution was to set a high priority on correcting errors and to make sure that sufficient resources were available to
do it each week. After the initial effort of correcting all the old
errors was completed, it has been a relatively easy task to fix new
errors each week as they are found.

Some of the technical problems originated in procedures but were
corrected by adding logic to some of the programs. It was found that
quite often the subcontractors were terminating clients from the system
without first completing "exit" forms for all of the client's "entries".
This was solved by rejecting any attempted terminations if the client
still had outstanding entries. Similarly, a termination is required
before a follow-up will be accepted. Some important information was
being lost because of the missing forms until these changes were made.

TRANSFERABILITY AND AVAILABILITY

The CETA client monitoring system developed in Kansas City, Kansas
has been productional for over a year and a half. The weekly and monthly reports have been used during that time as administrative and management aids, and have been refined as time passes. We feel that this
system may be useful to other prime sponsors in need of a CETA management information system. In 1975 representatives of the Department of
Labor visited Kansas City, Kansas to study the CETA system. They con-

sidered it to be one of the best computerized systems they had found in the country. Some documentation is expected to be made available by the Department of Labor in the future.

The Kansas City/Wyandotte County CETA Client Monitoring system is a batch computer system designed to require a minimum of computer resources. The system is a set of about thirty Cobol programs developed and implemented on an IBM 370/145 with DOS/VS and POWER/VS. All programming was done with transferability in mind. Only sequential files are used and it should be possible to transfer the system to any computer that has Cobol, with only a few modifications necessary. The four input forms are included to show what data is being collected for the system. Any changes made to the forms would naturally require program changes.

This paper was written primarily with the hope that other prime sponsors would find the system useful and could save themselves several thousand dollars in development costs by transferring the system implemented in Kansas City, Kansas. The system is available at the cost of reproduction and handling. Examples of the system outputs are also available. Any further information about the system is available from the author or from the Office of Manpower Planning and Coordination. Interested persons are also invited to visit Kansas City, Kansas to see the system on-site.

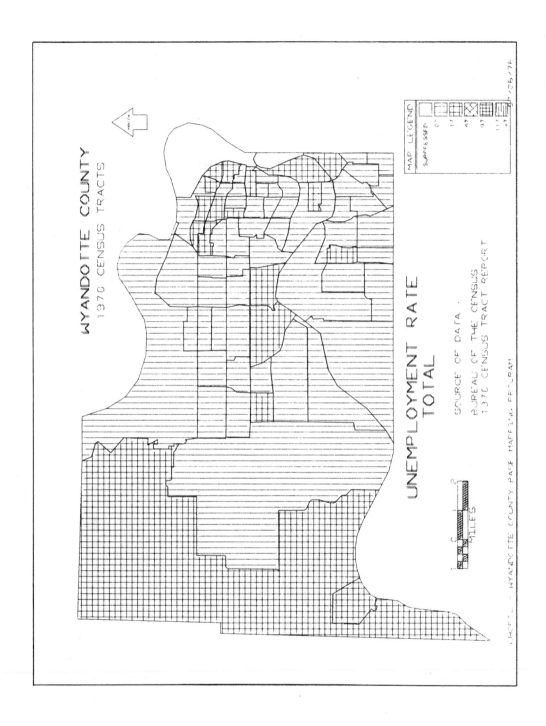

CHOROPLETH MAP OF 1970 UNEMPLOYMENT RATE

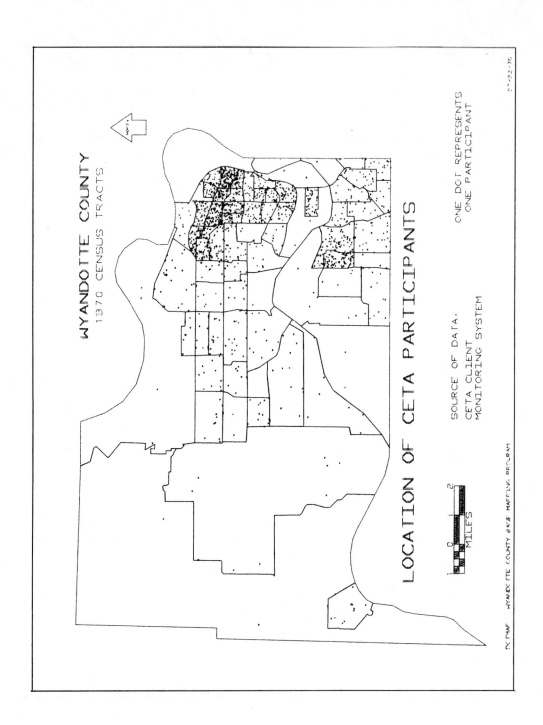

WYANDOTTE COUNTY
1970 CENSUS TRACTS

LOCATION OF CETA PARTICIPANTS

SOURCE OF DATA:
CETA CLIENT
MONITORING SYSTEM

ONE DOT REPRESENTS
ONE PARTICIPANT

MILES

DOT MAP OF CLIENTS' HOME ADDRESS

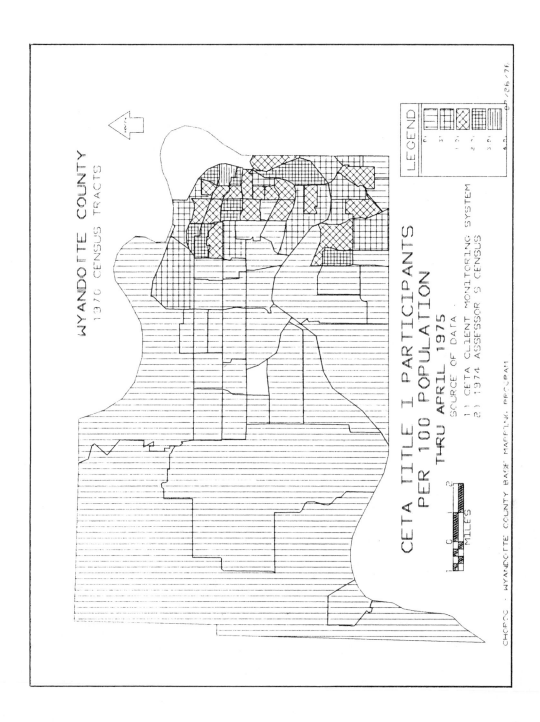

CHOROPLETH MAP OF PARTICIPATION RATE

Instructions: Applicant complete upper portion of this page. Interviewer complete bottom of this page. Coder code center portion of this page. Applicant also completes a Work History.	KANSAS CITY/WYANDOTTE COUNTY CETA PROGRAM APPLICATION **16428** Application No.	Planned Action by Core Service:	Distribution for Eligibles 1 Enrollment File 1 MIS 1 P.L.P. 1 Program Activity

1. Date Mo/Day/Yr	2. Social Security No.	3. Name (Last, First, Middle initial)	4. Phone No.	5. Date of Birth (mo/day/yr)

6. Address (Number, Street, City, State, Zip Code)	7. County of Residence	8. Sex 1. ___ Male 2. ___ Female

9. Circle Highest Grade of School Completed Grade School High School College BA MA PhD. 0 1 2 3 4 5 6 7 8 9 10 11 12 13 14 15 16 17 18 19	10. Number in Family	11. Number of Dependents - Excluding Self	12. Public Assistance Recipient 1. ___ AFDC 2. ___ S.S.I. 3. ___ No	13. Estimated Family Income Last 12 Months $	14. Veteran 1. ___ Non-Veteran 2. ___ Vietnam 3. ___ Other Veteran 4. ___

15. Previous Job Training 1. ___ Yes (If yes, give Occupation) 2. ___ No _____	16 A. Title of Job Desired 16 B. Title of Last Full-Time Job	17. Estimated Average Hourly Earnings on Last Full-Time Job $	18. Years of Gainful Employment	19. Last day of Employment mo day yr	20. Veteran's Discharge Date mo day yr

DO NOT WRITE BELOW THIS LINE. COMPLETE THE REVERSE SIDE OF THIS APPLICATION.

1. Application No.   Card   [0 1]   2. Social Security No.   3. Last Name   First Name   MI
1   6   8   9   17   18   31   32   39   40

4. Phone   5. Birth (mo/yr)   6. Address Number   H/R   Dir.   Street
41   47   48   51   52   56   57   58   60   77

Application No.   Card   [0 2]   Street Type   Apt.   City   State   Zip Code   7. County   8. Sex
1   6   8   9   12   13   15   16   27   28   30   34   35   37   38

9. Grade   10. Family   11. Depts.   12. PA   13. Income   14. Vet.   15. Tr.   16 A. DOT   16 B. DOT   17. Earnings   18. Yr.
41   43   45   46   50   51   52   53   58   59   64   65   68   69 70

19. Last day Employed   20. Discharge (4 yrs.)   1. Yes   2. No   Application No.   Card   [0 3]
71   76   77   1   6   8

21. Labor Force Status at time interviewed (Check only one) 1. Employed 2. Underemployed 3. Unemployed 4. Full-time student 5. Not in Labor Force 6. CETA Enrollee 9	22. Weeks unemployed Current Spell 10 12	23. U.I. Eligible 1. Yes, filed and eligible 2. No, did not file or is not eligible 3. Exhausted benefits 13	24. Farm 1. Migrant Farm Worker 2. Seasonal Farm Worker 3. None of the above 14	25. Offender 1. Yes 2. No 15	26. Primary Wage Earner 1. Yes 2. No 16	27. Head of Household 1. Yes 2. No 17

28. Economically Disadvantaged 1. Yes 2. No 18	29. Referred by: 1. CETA Agency 2. Employer 3. Union 4. Welfare 5. Self 6. Other 7. E.S. 19	30. Ethnic 1. White 2. Black 3. Asian 4. Am. Indian 5. Alaskan 6. INA 20	31. Spanish 1. Yes 2. No 21	32. Limited English Speaking Ability 1. Yes 2. No 22	33. Handicapped a. Physical b. Emotional c. Mental d. Chronic Illness e. Disabled Veteran f. Vet Retired Disabled a b c d e f 23	1. Yes 2. No 28	34. Barriers to Employment a. Lacks education, skill, or experience b. School Dropout c. Transportation Problems d. Child Care Problem e. Care of other family member a b c d e 29 1. Yes 2. No 33

35. Disposition 1. Eligible 2. Not eligible 34	36. Date of Application mo day yr 35 40	37. CETA Program 1. Title I 2. Title II 3. Title III 4. Title VI 41	38. Agency Responsible For Enrollment 42	39. Previously Enrolled and Terminated 1. Yes 2. No 44	40. Application is For 1. Enrollment 2. Correcting Previous Application 45	41. Enrollee assigned to Program Liaison Person Name _____ PLP Code 46 49

42. Previous Application Number 50 55	43. Applicant interviewed by: Name _____	Additional Information and Notes 19 - 003 - 01 Revised Sept. 75

APPLICATION FORM

Instructions: PLP complete Part A.
Subcontractor complete Part B.

Distribution A	Distribution B
1 Enrollment File	1 PLP - File
1 MIS	1 PLP - MIS
1 Sub-contractor	1 Sub-contractor

Application No.

1   6

Assignment

A

7   9

Enrollee's Name

Entry Date
mo   day   yr

10   15

ENTRY INFORMATION

Expected Exit
mo   day   yr

16   21

Sub-Contractor Codes		
01 Black Motivation	11 OIC	17 Wyandotte Sheriff
03 Donnelly College	12 OJT/UL	18 Community Service Center
04 EOF	13 SER	19 U.A.W.
06 K.C. Plan	14 Turner House	20 Turner USD 202
09 M.L.K. Urban Center	15 USD No. 500 Inschool	99 Not listed above
10 MTSC	16 USD No. 500 Summer	

Sub-Contractor

22   23

Program Activity

24

Program Activity Codes					
1 Classroom Prime Sponsor	2. Classroom Voc. Ed.	3. On the Job Training	4. Public Service Employment	5. Work Experience	6. Other Activities

Manpower Service

25   26

Manpower Service Codes		
01 Pre-Training	05 English Second Lang.	09 On the Job Training
02 Job Readiness	06 Occupational Training	10 College
03 Basic Ed.	07 Work Experience - Youth	11 Individual Referral
04 GED Prep.	08 Work Experience - Other	12 Remedial Ed.

DOT*

27   32

Complete only for Occupational Training, Work Experience, OJT

Occupational title_____

WIN?   1. Yes
          2. No

33

Program Liaison Person: Name _____

Sub-Contractor Representative: Name _____

EXIT INFORMATION

Application No.		Assignment	Exit Date			Occupation, if any
		B	mo	day	yr	
1	6	7 9	10		15	16 21

Days Attended	Days Absent	Total Hours Attended	Nature of Completion	Nature of Completion Codes	
				Completed Objective	Non-Completed Objective
				1. Full Course	3. Involuntary drop
				2. Early Complete	4. Voluntary drop
22 24	25 27	28 31	32		5. No show

Comments:

Certification By Training Facility

This is to certify that the circumstances of termination for the trainee to whom this report refers are:

1		For Good Cause	2		Not for Good Cause

a. Facility Name and Address

b. Name and Title of Authorized Official

c. Signature

d. Date

Review by Facility or Department Head

I have reviewed the circumstances surrounding the exit of the Trainee to which this report refers and have found them to be accurately described

a. Agency Name and Address

b. Name and Title of Authorized Official

c. Signature

d. Date

Revised 5/27/75

ENTRY/EXIT FORM

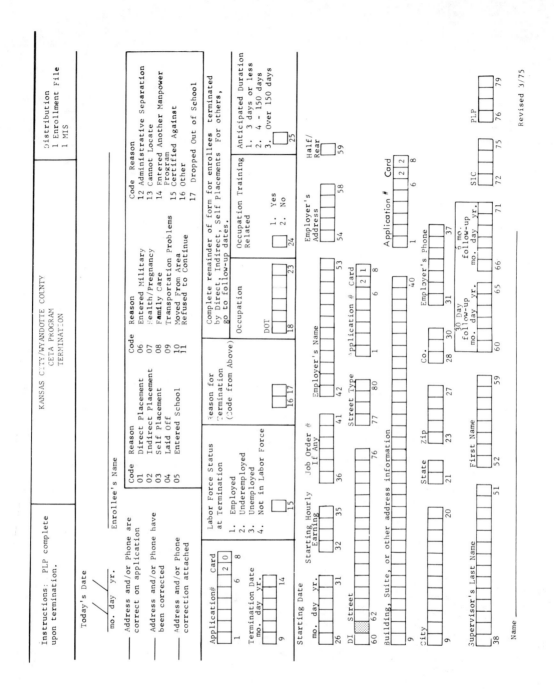

TERMINATION FORM

-106-

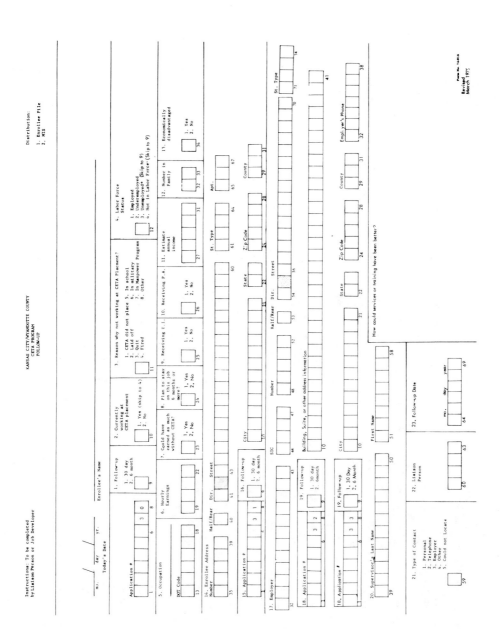

FOLLOW-UP FORM

Jeanne M. Schaaf
Office for Computing Activities
University of Dayton
Dayton, Ohio 45469

"INFORMATION ISN'T EVERYTHING"

ABSTRACT - The expansion of computerized data
processing techniques to the field of human services
extended the horizon of information science professionals and created new challenges for data personnel.
In many cases, information scientists invaded the
human service market and developed elaborate information systems which were awesome both in terms
of cost and data output. Quite often the Federal
government paid, or rather, is paying, the bill. As
with most Federally financed programs, however, the
fate of these systems can probably be predicted when
the government withdraws its generous support. In
all likelihood, human service personnel will be left
holding the proverbial bag since few communities are
able to assume the support of large scale, high cost
information systems. In these cases, information
science has merely confounded the problems of human
service delivery.
Although the benefits of electronic data processing
have been proven in other professional disciplines, the
advantages accrued human service professionals are
questionable. As information scientists then, we have
failed to meet the human service challenge. Consequently, this paper serves to outline (1) the social
issues encountered in the application of EDP techniques
to the field of human services, (2) the problems created
by overly enthusiastic information scientists, and (3) a
reasonable solution to the human service information
dilemma.

Whereas Information Science and Accounting form a marriage
made in heaven, the combination of Electronic Data Processing and
Human Services is best described as The Taming of the Shrew. The
human service delivery system has some very serious problems
which information scientists generally do not recognize. Information

science is, after all, a very logical, precise, scientific discipline. Human services is everything BUT logical, precise, or scientific. In fact, human service personnel do not concur on the definition of the term. The human service delivery system is fragmented, erratic, inefficient, and, as most taxpayers believe, ineffective. Information processing was introduced into human services to remedy this chaos. EDP failed. It is not, however, EDP methodology which was faulty, but its application to the field of human services. Let's examine, then, the human service system, information processing in human services, and finally, one simple solution to the information dilemma.

Most people perceive human services to be either public welfare give-away programs, such as food stamps and ADC, or privately funded United Way activities such as counseling and adoption services. For persons outside the system, few perspectives differ from these. Unfortunately, the vision of persons working within the system is even more astounding. Those of us employed in the voluntary service sector are painfully ignorant of public assistance programs; as proof, consider the service havoc wreaked by the introduction of Title XX. On the other hand, welfare workers view private sector employees as "extras" on a movie set. Municipal administrators look askance at both service groups and pray that between us we can get our program together so that urban government can avoid having to assign the public works or finance director the task of social programming.

Quite seriously, urban governments are in a very precarious position in regard to human services since an increasing proportion of the recipients of service programs are city and not suburban residents. We find in our cities a rising number of the elderly, of job seekers without skills, of unemployed youth, and of single parent households. Needless to say, these persons generally are not tax payers. As a consequence, however, the demand for city services, especially social services for city residents, intensifies as potential billpayers flee to the suburbs. This reality has proliferated the number of human service providers so that no longer are human services solely the baliwick of the Welfare Departments or the United Way. Human service programs in Dayton fall under the auspices of Municipal and Common Pleas Court, the County Prosecutor's Office, the Ombudsman, the Board of Mental Health and Mental Retardation, the Combined Health District, local Boards of Education, the Community Action Agency, and city and county government. Rarely, however, does a human service information system take these into account.

In addition to fragmentation, human welfare services are also erratic. Where business has a share of the market and where government has corporation limits, in human services we merely have "turf." In the scramble for dollars and clients we abandon youth drug centers when the Federal government does and substitute rape victimization or child abuse services instead. As a result, social programs are generally temporary in nature, addressing problems or concerns which are in vogue at the national level. Few social problems are actually resolved. Yet, social service personnel have been hoodwinked into believing that information is the solution to these problems; and, when the Federal government is picking up the tab, we're fairly easy to convince. At the same time, the bleeding hearts among us see dollars after dimes pouring into data systems while HEW service programs appear to be always on the Congressional carpet for a cutback. The accountability craze of the last few years has only served to fuel this fire. Consequently we find ourselves collecting more data about more problems with little or no impact. There are no obvious results at any rate. From this standpoint, it appears ludicrous to invest hundreds of thousands of dollars in human service information systems which are frequently temporary and of questionable benefit.

When the United States government was endeavoring to complete a continental communications network, Henry David Thoreau commented that "we seem to be in a great hurry to build a magnetic telegraph between Maine and Texas, but it may well be that Maine and Texas have nothing to say to each other." So it is in human services. We plan and build magnificent information systems which are awesome both in terms of cost and data output. However, judging from the results, when we speak of "Information Systems as Services to Citizens," we generally fall short of servicing either the taxpayer or the client by the application of electronic data processing to the field of human services. An experienced mountain climber was asked one time why he desired to climb Mt. Everest. His reply: "Because it was there." Often in human service information processing the same rationale prevails. This is not to say that information processing in human services is useless - just that information isn't everything.

The information explosion and our obsession with data stems from the development of computers and computer related equipment. The alleged "thinking" machines can process, assemble, and store data faster, more patiently, more accurately, and more completely than any other means either human or artificial. This is indeed their crowning glory. Computers were never designed to make decisions for us nor are they capable of it. In a roundabout way, however, computers can be used to alleviate social distress at a cost we can afford.

As information professionals, we attend our annual conference and applaud the wonders of EDP. We are familiar with client tracking systems, human service administrative accounting systems, and information and referral systems. Let's examine the advantages and disadvantages of each.

Client tracking systems are designed to follow a client through the referral process. It is possible to determine obstacles to service delivery or to document the tenacity of the client. Generally client tracking information systems incorporate resource files to aid in referral and, due to the number of computer communications required among agencies, clients, and data processing centers, tracking systems are often expensive. Moreover, a tracking system which has the cooperation of less than 100% of all service providers is questionable in terms of effectiveness. Additionally, although reams of data are generated, no combination of hardware or software is sufficiently sophisticated to affect client motivation in the least. This, perhaps, is the crux of the service issue. Lastly, the question of confidentiality has never been quite settled. Saul Feldman in <u>Administration in Mental Health</u> states a concern which most of the crusaders among us would support. "Despite the reassurance of colleagues more knowledgeable than I about the security of computer files, I still find myself concerned about the potential for misuse of all those mountains of highly personal information in patient data banks. I cannot help but wonder how many of us would be quite so sanguine if the most intimate details of our lives were equally secure." ("The Equal Right to Privacy" <u>Administration in Mental Health,</u> Fall '73)

As a second option, we often institute human service information systems which count heads, compute unite service costs, and otherwise add to the administrative library of data as a precaution against irate taxpayers. If these systems do not benefit the recipient of services, we've lost sight of our purpose. We are not in social services simply to justify our employment, but, at least in theory, to alleviate social problems. Systems created solely for administrators cannot be rationalized.

A third variety of human service information systems is known as information and referral. While I&R generally connotes a very specific service function, information and referral systems are increasingly valuable to the extent that they can supersede simple I&R expectations. The resource file, which is an integral part of every information and referral system, is the key.

Although the computer is basically an information storage and retrieval instrument, those of us in information sciences frequently promote the mystique of the whirling thinking machines by devising dazzling data generating systems which can spew forth charts, diagrams, maps and Mona Lisas in addition to being unbeatable and indefatigable at chess and tic tac toe. In human service data processing, the development of service resource files is really quite simple. This lack of fanfare often tempts us to develop supplementary processes that can add a little pizazz to our data processing. Fortunately, at the University of Dayton, our aspirations for information grandeur were nipped early due to funding constraints. We have developed, as a consequence, an information system based on a resource file which is low cost and useful. In our experience, information and referral systems, therefore, make good sense.

Resource files generally connote automated referral functions. Although nothing spectacular, this is a significant asset to the service delivery system. In theory, the accuracy of the data is assured and the volume of information which is immediately accessible is immeasurable. Moreover, the efficiency of the caseworker is enhanced in "matching" the client to a service by employing an on-line terminal with search capacities. Even without the immediate access capability, however, printed desk top directories can be easily updated at short term intervals via EDP. Automated resource files further have the potential of "customizing" data since simple SORT commands can tailor the quantity, format, or frequency of the data output to any user's requirements.

Over and above the referral process, resource files can be employed in program planning, service evaluation, mass citizen education programs, and administrative accounting simply by reorganizing data items. Moreover, since resource files are frequently system wide, the issue of fragmentation and duplication of services can be rationally examined. Program planning, as a result, need not be reactionary or erratic. An Information and Referral system, therefore, can be a sound investment. The cost is reasonable. The system assures efficiency and effectiveness in service delivery, provides administrative personnel with data for program planning and resource allocation, and assures the bill payer positive social benefits.

In constructing our resource file at the University of Dayton, we have employed the data base management system (DBMS) of record keeping in order to ensure complete flexibility of component data bits. As opposed to traditional file construction, the data base system allows for data linkages and inter-relationships regardless of how the data is physically stored on a mass storage device. The process of updating service data is also facilitated since one need only be concerned with selected data items rather than the entire file. The flexibility assured by employing the DBMS in human service resource files guarantees a broader application and increased utilization of the service data without increasing costs. In fact, storage costs can be minimized since the DBMS only "saves" space that is being utilized rather than holding uniform amounts of EDP space regardless of whether or not it is completely filled.

The resource file which has been developed at the University of Dayton further eliminates duplication of data collection and update across the service system since data changes made once at the computer center are "automatically" shared with all users of the system.

Moreover, as the number of participants in the system increases, the cost per agency decreases. "Turf," therefore, is not a problem and the concept of "share of the (client) market" surfaces.

Data items included in the Community Resource File are not unlike most directory items, i.e., agency name, location, telephone, hours, fees, eligibility requirements, service area, and programs. In addition, fee policy, funding sources, auspices, facilities for the handicapped, access via public transportation, program budget, percent of total budget, funding period, number of staff, and necessity of parental consent are included in the data base. Moreover, service information is organized both by sponsoring agency and by service provided regardless of the sponsor so that certain data items, for example eligibility or fees, are not generalized for all services of any single agency.

Although the base of information for the resource file is composed of United Way services, the Community Resource File also incorporates human services provided by municipal, township, and county governments, Municipal and Common Pleas Courts, all school districts within the county, and independent not-for-profit service agencies. Members of the staff of the University computer center do not collect the data for the resource file (except initially in the case of municipal and school district information), nor do we publish the data. These functions remain with the local agencies which have traditionally provided that service. The University is responsible for the design of the system. We have introduced uniformity across the human service system in program, fee, eligibility, and service area descriptions. We have potentially augmented the usefulness of the data by incorporating a service rather than the traditional provider orientation in the construction of the data base. Lastly we have developed the foundation for community information sharing and system wide problem solving.

Lest I lead you to believe that all that glitters is gold, may I emphasize that our costs are low because the agencies retain responsibility and financial support for both data gathering and publication so that, at times, progress becomes impeded by cooperation. Further, at this time, complete data input is dependent upon a future broad scale data collection effort since initial data collection activities preceded the system design. Lastly, to avoid the classic reinvention of the wheel, we have employed the United Way Services Identification System (UWASIS) in coding service programs. Since UWASIS II, a classification update, is expected in October of this year, we will undoubtedly face some problems in the transition from the earlier version of UWASIS. Nonetheless, the Community Resource File system developed at the University of Dayton, in our judgment, is indeed an information system which services citizens.

In Dayton, Ohio the potential employment of electronic data processing in helping to alleviate human social problems is a reality. Although information isn't everything, we've found it to be quite significant.

Rick Holloway
Program Development Specialist
One Civic Plaza
Kansas City, Kansas 66101

POLICE DISPATCH REPORTING AND ANALYSIS SYSTEM

ABSTRACT: A computer-based productional system has been implemented to more fully exploit the
information potential of police calls-for-service
data. The system produces three types of output:

    (1)   printed reports of patrol and beat
         workload and individual officer
         activity,

    (2)   computer-generated thematic maps
         showing frequency and frequency
         change of particular crime types
         by census tract,

    (3)   computer-generated street maps
         of sections of the city displaying
         each occurrence of particular types
         of crime for a given time period.

This output provides the police command staff with
a comprehensive body of information which is expected to be of great utility in making decisions
on manpower allocation, beat alignment and crime
trend analysis. The street maps are also used to
keep the patrol officer informed of recent criminal activity in his beat.

INTRODUCTION

The system described in this presentation is being developed by the
Kansas City, Kansas Department of Planning and Development for the
Kansas City, Kansas Police Department (KCKPD) to utilize the rich information potential of police dispatch, or "calls-for-service" data. The
objectives of this system are several. Some have been met; others are
in the development phase. These objectives are as follows:

    1.   To provide a device to measure the impact of
        the Department's community programs;

    2.   To produce summary reports on patrol activity
        and responsiveness by officer, unit, beat,

shift, and census tract by time of day and
day of week;

3. To provide information organized to facilitate the identification of trends or patterns
in crime activity;

4. To monitor the effectiveness of beat alignment and manpower allocation techniques;

5. To provide the officer in the field with
clear, comprehensive, and timely information
on criminal activity in his area of patrol;

6. To provide special reports on a demand basis
addressing particular types of patrol activity within an arbitrarily defined time period
and geographic area.

The data is organized geographically by the use of the DIME geographic
base file. Standard outputs presently consist of periodic report programs, thematic maps of the choropleth type, and street maps which
display individual occurrences of crime. Virtually all processing of
the data is in batch mode.

THE PROBLEM

The potential utility of dispatch data has long been recognized
by KCKPD. The processing of this data was one of several services provided in KCKPD's participation in Kansas City, Missouri's ALERT II system. Unfortunately, the detail of the reports produced from this data
was seriously deficient in two respects.

First, reports could not be produced for a single shift. The
Kansas City, Missouri Police Department (KCMOPD) uses a four-digit
system to number their patrol units; these four digits identify patrol
shift, zone, sector (or beat), and unit respectively. A simple sort
on this data was used to organize the data for input to their patrol
workload programs. The numbering system used by KCKPD did not contain
a shift designation. Further, KCKPD's numbering scheme did not reflect
a beat-within-zone patrol structure. Therefore, though reports were
generated for each patrol unit, the reports were of all three shifts.

Second, KCMOPD does not maintain a geographic base file of Kansas
City, Kansas. Such a file requires considerable resources to maintain,
and could not be expected as a part of the ALERT II service package.
The absence of such a file, however, meant that reports could not be
produced for an area smaller than the patrol beat, which was entered on
each record. Understandably, such data was of little use in realigning
beat boundaries, monitoring activity within a neighborhood, etc.

ALERT II produced monthly reports from this data, which were usually received fifteen to eighteen days after the end of the report period.

More frequent and timely reports were needed to make adequate use of the information.

KCKPD's annual assessment for ALERT II services is computed on the basis of transaction volume. The on-line entry of dispatch data accounted for almost 17% of these transactions. After weighing the cost of the reports against their use, KCKPD decided to discontinue the processing of this particular body of data through ALERT II, and to look for an alternative which would offer a better return on their data processing dollar.

THE SOLUTION

Approximately the same time this decision was being made, KCKPD and the City Planning Department were conducting a study of data processing needs in the Police Department. Because computer support was already provided by ALERT II for KCKPD field operations, the study addressed itself primarily to administrative applications. The problems mentioned above, however, soon made a "calls-for-service" system one of the prime subjects of the study.

Since 1971 the Planning Department's Division of Information and Research has been virtually the sole source of data processing support for municipal government in Kansas City, Kansas. In the past five years this support has grown to include a wide variety of applications serving almost every department in city government. Probably the most significant factor contributing to the success of our data processing effort has been an early and continuing commitment to the development and maintenance of the DIME geographic base file and to geographic processing in general. The value to a local government of being able to readily manipulate and compare a variety of data in a spacial context cannot be overemphasized.

It was decided that the application of this geographic processing capability to police dispatch data would be the most effective initial application of the Planning Department's data processing resources in support of KCKPD. The objectives of such a system (as stated in the introduction) were delineated, and subsequent analysis and design led to a body of software which would organize the data at several levels of aggregation. Computer graphics, cross-tabulation, and simple display techniques were combined to provide police administrators, field personnel, and planners with the proper information at a level of detail appropriate to their task.

ENTRY INTO THE SYSTEM

It was decided that for the sake of procedural consistency, the on-line method used to enter this data on the ALERT II system would be retained. Because the new system was to be installed on the Wyandotte County machine, an IBM 370/145 running a CICS transaction system, it was necessary to write a new transaction module to accomplish this task.

We realized early in the design of the system that because of the volume of input data which would be produced we should avoid handling the physical document more than once. It would be very difficult and time-consuming to retrieve and re-enter records which the necessary edit programs found to be in error. The best solution to this problem was to build the edits into the transaction itself.

The program does three basic kinds of checks -- single field checks, table look-ups, and field interdependency checks. Single field checks assure that required fields are present; that entered data is of the right type; and that certain values, such as times, are valid and in the proper range. Table look-ups are performed to check such items as beat numbers, "type-of-call" codes, and street names and type spellings. Field interdependency checks test the presence or value of one or more fields based on the presence or value of another. For example, if the disposition of the call is entered as a "1", which indicates that an offense or traffic report was written, the program checks for the presence of a case report number and the number of the reporting unit.

These edits are performed immediately after the terminal operator enters a full record. If any of the edits fail, the record is returned to the terminal screen with the errors lighlighted. The operator then corrects and re-enters the record. If the document itself is in error, the operator may delete the record on the screen and lay the card aside for correction. Correct records are written to tape for later processing.

SOURCE OF DATA

A single input record may be thought of as representing a single activity by a patrol unit. Ideally, the sum of these records should represent the total workload of the patrol force except routine patrol. An activity may be initiated by a call for service by the public, by an officer in the field (e.g., a traffic stop), or by police administration. Types of activities may vary from a robbery call to a trip to the police garage.

The data is recorded by radio dispatchers as each call occurs. Several items of information are recorded for each call, including dispatched unit, beat of occurrence, address of occurrence, dispatcher number and shift, case report number, and the times at which the call is received, the unit is sent, the unit arrives, and the call is cleared. The times are recorded using an automatic time clock. The type of call is also recorded using a coding system of 172 types grouped into 24 major categories.

One type of record requires special mention here. Each time a unit goes into service at the beginning of a tour of duty or out of service at the end of a tour, and each time an officer goes in or out of service during a tour of duty, a duty status record is completed which indicates the unit, shift, and officer or officers involved, and the time of occurrence. The unit, shift, and officer information is later automatically appended to each dispatch record involving that unit and shift, thus saving the dispatchers the added time required to record this information on each record.

PROCESSING THE DATA

After the entered records have been accumulated on tape, the file is processed against the corresponding file of duty status records, at which time unit, shift, and officer information is added. The program which does this task also calculates the response time and clear time for each call and adds them to the record.

The data must then be geocoded; that is, the address must be examined, and appropriate census tract and block codes and X-Y coordinates must be assigned to each record. There are two possible address types, which require different methods of processing; thus the file must be split by address type. Street addresses (e.g., 1234 N 5TH ST) are geocoded using the ADMATCH program from the Bureau of the Census. Intersection addresses (N 5TH ST & ANN AV) are processed by a matching program developed locally.

Records with street addresses require one more processing step before the two geocoded files can be merged. In the matching process, each address is actually tested for membership in a set of addresses, represented by an address range on a block face. This kind of match cannot provide the geographic coordinates of the address itself. Instead, the coordinates of the "from" and "to" nodes (the two end points of the block face), the left or right block face indicator, and the address range, are retrieved. This information is then used to calculate the correct point by interpolation.

After the interpolation step the street address and intersection records are merged. At this point, the file is ready for input to the report and mapping routines.

OUTPUTS

The system in its present state of development produces output of two general types -- printed reports and computer-generated maps. In combination the reports and maps provide police administrators with a broad body of information by which to evaluate the performance of the patrol force. In addition, a subset of these reports is of particular interest to the individual patrol officer, giving him a summary of recent activity in his area, and helping him to monitor his own performance.

THE PRINTED REPORTS

The system presently generates the following reports:

    1. Patrol Unit Workload

PROGRAM I.D. - CTYPPDSB
VERSION - 01-01
COST ACCT # - 10-082
REPORT DATE - 07/29/76

K A N S A S   C I T Y ,   K A N S A S   P O L I C E   D E P A R T M E N T

DEPARTMENT OF PLANNING
AND DEVELOPMENT
701 N SEVENTH ST
KANSAS CITY, KANSAS

PATROL SERVICE WORKLOAD

PAGE 1

05/30/76 THRU 06/05/76

UNIT 211   SHIFT 1

------- TYPE OF CALL -------	TOTAL FREQUENCY	TOTAL TIME SPENT	MEAN TIME SPENT	MEAN RESPONSE TIME	MEAN CLEAR TIME
0101 - HOMICIDE	2	0.98	0.49	0.16	0.33
0102 - SUICIDE OR ATTEMPT	1	0.75	0.75	0.25	0.50
0103 - DEAD BODY	1	0.16	0.16	0.08	0.08
0201 - RAPE OR ATTEMPTED RAPE	1	0.34	0.34	0.26	0.08
0301 - ARMED ROBBERY OR ATTEMPT	1	0.44	0.44	0.28	0.16
0401 - ASSAULT - SHOOTING	1	0.43	0.43	0.30	0.13
0403 - OTHER AGGRAVATED ASSAULT	1	0.49	0.49	0.31	0.18
0404 - NON-AGGRAVATED ASSAULT	1	0.43	0.43	0.33	0.10
0405 - SHOOTING ASLT ON OFFICER	1	0.46	0.46	0.35	0.11
0406 - CUTTING ASLT ON OFFICER	3	1.47	0.49	0.36	0.13
0407 - AGGRV ASSAULT ON OFFICER	1	0.53	0.53	0.38	0.15
0601 - LARCENY OR ATTEMPT	1	0.56	0.56	0.40	0.16
0604 - LARCENY - CB RADIO	1	0.59	0.59	0.41	0.18
0701 - STOLEN AUTO OR ATTEMPT	2	0.93	0.46	0.26	0.20
0703 - RECOVERED STOLEN AUTO	1	0.66	0.66	0.45	0.21
0801 - ANIMAL BITE REPORT	1	0.69	0.69	0.46	0.23
0804 - VANDALISM	1	0.73	0.73	0.48	0.25
0809 - OBSCENE PHONE CALL	1	0.76	0.76	0.50	0.26
0810 - MISSING PERSON REPORT	1	0.79	0.79	0.51	0.28
0901 - INTOXICATED PERSON	1	0.83	0.83	0.53	0.30
0902 - INTOXICATED DRIVER	1	0.86	0.86	0.55	0.31
1002 - ARMED DISTURBANCE	1	0.89	0.89	0.56	0.33
1003 - MENTAL DISTURBANCE	1	0.93	0.93	0.58	0.35
1005 - TAVERN DISTURBANCE	1	0.96	0.96	0.60	0.36
1201 - TRAFFIC CONTROL	1	0.99	0.99	0.61	0.38
1203 - OBSTRUCTION IN STREET	1	1.03	1.03	0.63	0.40
1204 - ILLEGALLY PARKED CAR	1	1.06	1.06	0.65	0.41
1301 - NON-INJURY TRFC ACCIDENT	1	1.09	1.09	0.66	0.43
1302 - INJURY TRAFFIC ACCIDENT	1	1.13	1.13	0.68	0.45
1303 - FATAL TRAFFIC ACCIDENT	1	1.16	1.16	0.70	0.46
1304 - HIT AND RUN ACCIDENT	1	1.19	1.19	0.71	0.48
1501 - CALL	1	1.23	1.23	0.73	0.50
1504 - MEET AN OFFICER	1	1.26	1.26	0.75	0.51
1508 - MEAL	1	1.29	1.29	0.76	0.53
1511 - ERRANDS	1	1.33	1.33	0.76	0.55
1512 - WARRANT OR SUBPOENA	1	1.36	1.36	0.80	0.56
1601 - SUSPICIOUS PERSON	1	1.39	1.39	0.81	0.58
1602 - PROWLER	1	1.43	1.43	0.83	0.60
1603 - CAR PROWLER	1	1.46	1.46	0.85	0.61
1604 - OCCUPANT - PARKED CAR	1	1.49	1.49	0.86	0.63

FIGURE 1.   PATROL UNIT WORKLOAD REPORT

NOTE: This report does not represent real data.

2. Officer Workload
3. Beat Workload
4. Census Tract Workload
5. Automatic Alarm Listing

The Patrol Unit Workload Report, which is produced weekly, summarizes all activity in which the unit was engaged during the report period. Each type of call to which the unit responded is listed. For each type of call the frequency, total and mean time spent, mean response time and mean clear time are given. (See Figure 1.) Three listings are provided for each unit -- one for each of three shifts across the report period. Division summary reports are also produced for each shift and across shifts. (For purposes of reporting there are nine divisions: three uniform divisions, tactical, investigative, traffic, outside units, helicopter, and school district divisions. Division membership is indicated by the first digit of the unit number.)

The Officer Workload Report is of the same format as the Patrol Workload Report. Because the production of reports for all officers would result in an unmanageable volume of output, they are run only on a special request basis. Officer activity may be retrived by officer serial number, unit number, or division. If retrieved by unit number or division, only activity related to that unit or division is reported.

The Beat Workload and Census Tract Workload Reports are identical in format. They differ only in that they summarize activity in different geographic areas, and have different report periods. The Beat Report is produced weekly, the Tract Report monthly. A report is produced for each area for each of three eight-hour periods across the report period. Within a single report, frequencies for each type of call are given by hour of day and by day of week (see Figure 2).

The Automatic Alarm Listing, as the name implies, is a listing of each automatic alarm responded to by a patrol unit. For each alarm, name of business, address, time, date, beat, alarm company, and disposition are reported. If the alarm is found to be the result of an offense, the case report number is referenced.

THE MAPS

Probably the most exciting aspect of this system from a technical standpoint was the computer graphics applications that were developed to display the data. The Information and Research Division had been involved in computer graphics for some time, but we had rarely encountered a body of data whose information value could be so greatly enhanced by graphic display.

In the context of "calls-for-service" data, mapping techniques are most helpful in displaying occurrences which tend toward geographic patterns. Residential burglaries, for example, may be found to concentrate in a particular neighborhood, or may move across the city in some systematic fashion. The experienced police officer is sensitive to such patterns and exploits them in the performance of his duties. We therefore rely heavily on the knowledge and intuition of law enforcement personnel in selecting the types of incidents to map.

PROGRAM I.D. - CTYPPDSA   KANSAS CITY, KANSAS POLICE DEPARTMENT   DEPARTMENT OF PLANNING
VERSION   - 01-01   AND DEVELOPMENT
COST ACCT # - 10-032   701 N SEVENTH ST
REPORT DATE - 07/29/76   BEAT SERVICE WORKLOAD   KANSAS CITY, KANSAS

05/30/76 THRU 06/05/76   BEAT 222 FROM 0001 TO 0300   PAGE 1

| | | | | BY HOUR OF DAY | | | | | | BY DAY OF WEEK | | | | | |
TYPE OF CALL	TOTAL	0001-0100	0101-0200	0201-0300	0301-0400	0401-0500	0501-0600	0601-0700	0701-0800	SUN	MON	TUE	WED	THU	FRI	SAT
0101 - HOMICIDE	1															
0201 - RAPE OR ATTEMPTED RAPE	1															
0302 - STRONGARM RBBRY OR ATMPT	1															
0401 - ASSAULT - SHOOTING	1															
0402 - ASSAULT - CUTTING	1															
0602 - SHOPLIFTING	1															
0701 - STOLEN AUTO OR ATTEMPT	1															
0801 - ANIMAL BITE REPORT	1															
0803 - RECOVERED PROPERTY RPT	1															
0804 - VANDALISM	1															
0805 - OTHER PROPERTY DSTRCTN	1															
0806 - OPEN DOOR OR WINDOW RPT	1															
0901 - INTOXICATED PERSON	1															
1002 - ARMED DISTURBANCE	1															
1008 - OTHER DISTURBANCES	1															
1201 - TRAFFIC CONTROL	1															
1202 - CHECK LIGHTS,BARRICADES	1															
1203 - OBSTRUCTION IN STREET	1															
1204 - ILLEGALLY PARKED CAR	1															
1301 - NON-INJURY TRFC ACCIDENT	1															
1302 - INJURY TRAFFIC ACCIDENT	1															
1303 - FATAL TRAFFIC ACCIDENT	1															
1304 - HIT AND RUN ACCIDENT	1															
1402 - BURGLAR ALARM	1															
1403 - FIRE ALARM	1															
1501 - CALL	1															
1503 - GO TO STATION OR BUREAU	1															
1506 - RADIO REPAIR	1															
1508 - MEAL	1															
1510 - COURT	1															
1511 - ERRANDS	1															
1602 - PROWLER	1															
1603 - CAR PROWLER	1															
1702 - AMBULANCE ON THE WAY	1															
1801 - BUILDING FIRE	1															
1803 - GRASS FIRE	1															
1804 - PLANE CRASH	1															
1805 - WEATHER WATCH	1															
1806 - EXPLOSION	1															
1904 - APPREHENSION OF JUVENILE	1															

FIGURE 2.   BEAT WORKLOAD REPORT

NOTE: This report does not represent real data.

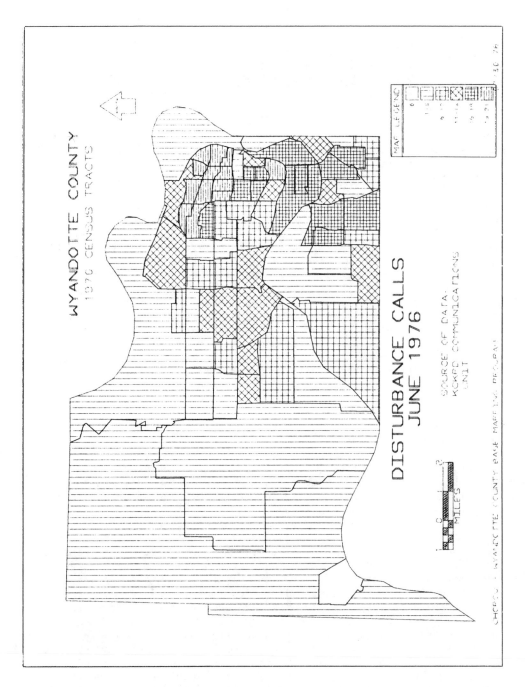

FIGURE 3.   CHOROPLETH MAP   NOTE: This map
does not represent
real data.

Two basic mapping techniques are currently being used to display this data. The first, which for the purpose of this paper will be referred to as statistical mapping, compares frequency of occurrence and change in frequency among rather large geographic areas (see Figure 3). Thematic mapping has been used by the Planning Department for a number of years to display a variety of demographic indicators on a city-wide basis. A choropleth display technique is most often used, with shadings of different colors and patterns used to represent ranges of values. Gross frequency is sometimes represented by the random placement of dots or other symbols within each area, each symbol representing a set number of occurrences. These statistical maps are most helpful in identifying large problem areas and in monitoring the impact of trial reactive measures.

The second mapping technique was developed specifically for this system. It was mentioned earlier that an important function of the address matching process was the retrieval of geographic coordinates for each address. Those coordinates are used to plot individual occurrences by location. This is accomplished by graphically representing the street network, with street names, for a specified portion of the city. Symbols of different colors and shapes are then superimposed on this street network in their proper geographic location (see Figure 4). Each unique color/slope combination represents a different type of call. The result is an easily assimilated graphic portrayal of selected police activity in the specified report period within that subject area. These maps were intended to be of particular utility to the police officer who patrols that area. On a larger scale, however, they may be quite useful in monitoring the effectiveness of patrol deployment, as well as identifying problem areas for the tactical and investigative units.

FUTURE PLANS

This system is still in its infancy. It is expected that as the Police Department becomes better acquainted with the information potential of the data and the capabilities of the system, desirable changes and enhancements will be suggested.

Certain improvements are already being considered. First, we in Information and Research are anticipating an improved method of deriving the actual location of a call. The presently used method of interpolation from address, address range, and segment length is truly accurate only when the addresses are evenly incremented along the segment and when the parcels are of equal width. Accuracy of address coordinates can be assured only by the use of a reference file which contains all addresses in the city and the centroids of the parcels described by those addresses. Such a file, the Wyandotte County Parcel File, is being constructed now, and we hope to be able to use it within the year.

An addition to the body of report programs is also proposed. This program, which will detail the activity of a district patrol unit outside its own beat, will provide another perspective from which to view the effectiveness of the deployment of patrol forces.

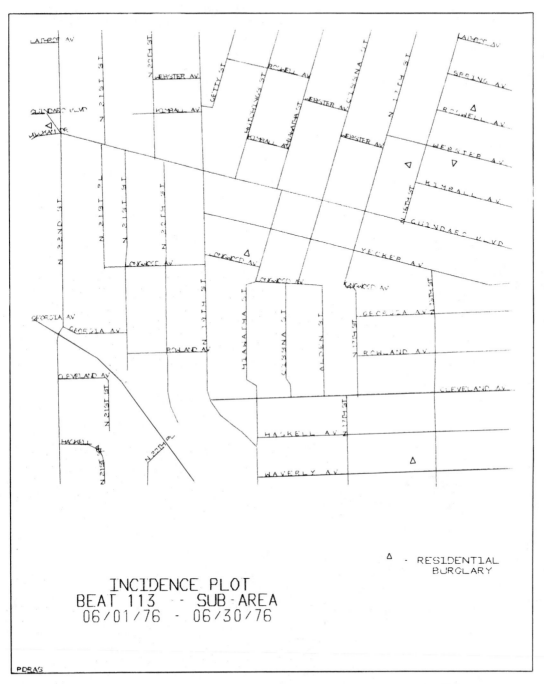

INCIDENCE PLOT
BEAT 113 - SUB-AREA
06/01/76 - 06/30/76

Δ - RESIDENTIAL
BURGLARY

FIGURE 4. INCIDENCE MAP

NOTE: This map
does not represent
real data.

-125-

We are very optimistic about the developmental possibilities of this
system. It is hoped that the information it provides will help KCKPD
to better serve the Kansas City, Kansas community.

Theodore R. Lyman, Policy Analyst
Center for the Analysis of Public Services
Stanford Research Institute
Menlo Park, California 94025

THE COMPREHENSIVE CRIMINAL JUSTICE INFORMATION
SYSTEM: A POLICY EVALUATION

ABSTRACT: A highly complex computer-based information system serving crimimal justice functions
in a California county presented extraordinary evaluation difficulties. The lack of comparative data and
the policy orientation of the supervisor clients precluded a traditional evaluation design. SRI desired
techniques to give objectivity to relevant subjective
information, using a scoring system in conjunction
with interviews. For each of the ten original objectives of the system, evaluation criteria were established. The system was found to be achieving, to
some extent, eight of the objectives, and recommendations were made for further achievement. We believe
that the evaluation technique is transferable to
similar situations.

OVERVIEW

Since 1969, more than $100 million has been spent by the federal
government for complex computer-based information systems serving federal, state, and local criminal justice functions. With few exceptions,
the development costs of the local systems have been covered by the federal government. Local investment for implementation has, more often
than not, been limited to a small cash outlay or a contribution of personnel costs. After the federal funds have run out (grant funds seldom
last more than three years), local jurisdictions have had to assume the
full cost of system operation. With the local assumption of large operating costs has come wide-ranging criticism of the cost-benefit trade-
offs provided by large-scale, multijurisdiction information systems.

127

This paper explores the history of one such system, serving a California county and 17 jurisdictions within the county, and describes an evaluation of the system. It is a fundamental assumption that the availability of federal funds made the decision to implement this system easier than it would otherwise have been. In the discussion of the evaluation of the system, the need for an evaluation of every information system so implemented is implied.

HISTORY

Late in 1969 the Board of Supervisors of Santa Clara County, California, resolved to solicit, from the newly formed Law Enforcement Assistance Administration, funds to develop and implement a comprehensive criminal justice information system. The action of this Board of Supervisors was in recognition of conditions existing in most large urban counties at that time; Santa Clara County, 50 miles south of San Francisco, fifth largest county in the state with a population of 1.1 million, was faced with such problems as an increasing crime rate, unemployment, and drug abuse, and a thoroughly fragmented system of justice was struggling to keep abreast of the situation. The criminal justice agencies of the County and the cities within the County agreed that they faced common problems but recognized that they were unable to pool information and jointly access it. While information was constrained by jurisdictional boundaries, the criminal was not. Clearly, a great deal of effort was being expended by each agency or jurisdiction to determine an individual's present status in, or prior involvement with, the County's justice system. An integrated approach to information handling was needed--an approach crossing organizational lines.

The County adopted the policy of developing, by using federal funds, a single computer-based information system that would store, process, and disseminate information relating to adults arrested and booked anywhere in the County. The system, termed the Criminal Justice Information Control System (CJIC, pronounced "See-jic") was to become one of the nation's first subject-in-process or defendent-tracking systems.

The objectives of the Board of Supervisors' policy and of the resulting system were tenfold. CJIC was to:

- Be an integrated intergovernmental information system.

- Support daily criminal justice operation.

- Support comprehensive criminal justice planning.

- Use modern data-processing technology.

- Use or initiate modern administrative techniques.

- Promote system transferability.

- Establish and maintain effective relations among criminal justice agencies.

- Provide improved management skills and tools.

- Support related criminal justice projects that require or share CJIC data.

- Safeguard security and privacy.

The system, similar to systems in Alameda County, California (the CORPUS system), Portland-Multinoman County, Oregon (the CRISS system), Hamilton County, Ohio (the CLEAR system), and Kansas City, Missouri (the ALERT system), was designed to serve many jurisdictions and nearly all criminal justice functions. As with these other systems, CJIC policy was to be the responsibility of user committees representative of participating agencies and jurisdictions. Because of the Countywide nature of the project, it was an implied decision of the County to assume full operating costs (i.e., for cities and County agencies) after federal funding ceased.

CURRENT STATUS

In Santa Clara County, CJIC serves ten law enforcement agencies representing nine separate political jurisdictions, and eleven agencies of the County government. CJIC operates on the County's central data processing facility (dual IBM 370/158s and a VS operating system), but policy and management are the sole responsibility of user committees.

The developmental costs of CJIC approached $4.5 million. The total annual cost of CJIC is now approximately $1.3 million and annual costs appear to be stabilizing. The County continues to assume all costs except those of the lines, terminals, and modems used by noncounty agencies (cities). CJIC handles approximately 16,000 transactions each working day, and use of the system is increasing rapidly.

NEED FOR A POLICY-ORIENTED EVALUATION

Early in 1975, three years after the system became operational, the County Executive recommended to the Board of Supervisors that revenue-sharing funds be earmarked for an evaluation of CJIC. While evaluations had been attempted previously, none had been entirely successful, and pressures were building for some objective assessment of the system. Recent events included:

- A juvenile subsystem that had been fully designed at a cost of $250,000 but had not been implemented because of the Board of Supervisors' concern with the pressing security and privacy issue.

- An escalation of CJIC costs in the face of the County's first significant budget deficit.

- Continuing complaints, in varying degrees, regarding CJIC performance from nearly every participating agency.

Because CJIC was an integral part of the justice system, the evaluation would have to answer a very difficult but basic question: Should the Board of Supervisors continue to fund CJIC? If so, at what level? If not, could CJIC be discontinued without catastrophic results in the operation of the justice system.

It was clear that the evaluation could not be performed by one of the stakeholder agencies if the evaluation were to be considered credible by other stakeholders. Accordingly, Stanford Research Institute (SRI) was retained under contract to recommend an appropriate evaluation design, to carry out the evaluation, and to make totally independent and thus objective recommendations to the Board of Supervisors.

EVALUATION DESIGN

Previous evaluations had failed principally because of the lack of objective data on which to judge system performance. This was an overwhelming obstacle to a traditional evaluation design. To oversimplify, in a traditional design, presystem data are compared with postsystem data, and changes that have occurred over time are judged as being either "good" or "bad." The second major obstacle was the complexity of CJIC. Literally hundreds of operational procedures were altered with the intervention of CJIC. In sum, nearly everything about criminal justice in the County had changed since implementation of the system in 1972, and no "snapshot" of the pre-CJIC situation was available against which to judge the post-CJIC situation.

SRI adopted three principles of public policy evaluation in its evaluation design:[1]

- Evaluation results that are with high certainty approximately correct are more valuable than results that, although more elegantly derived, may be grossly incorrect.

---

[1] J. S. Coleman, "Problems of Conceptualization and Measurement in Studying Policy Impacts," in Public Policy Evaluation, K. M. Dolbeare, ed. (Sage Publications, Beverly Hills, California 1975).

- Partial information that is available at the time an action must be taken is more useful than complete information after that time.

- The ultimate evaluation product should be not simply a "contribution to existing knowledge" but rather research results intended as a basis for modification of a public policy.

The SRI design took account of the fact that, except for the small amount of objective data available, subjective data such as observations and the opinions of users and experts would have to be the foundation for the evaluation. It was clear that reliance on such information would have the inherent danger of analysis based on, and conclusions drawn from, an inaccurate foundation (the opinions of users might simply reflect "sour grapes"). To overcome this problem, a technique was used to give objectivity to relevant subjective data.

A quantitative scoring scheme was chosen for use in conjunction with interviews. The intention was to interview a relatively large sample of CJIC "stakeholders." It was felt that the resulting "quantified" data base would thus be representative of a wide distribution of subjective data.

First, to aid in organizing the evaluation, the ten system objectives noted earlier in this paper were grouped into four performance dimensions:

- Intergovernmental, organizational, and administrative performance.

- Operational performance.

- Technical performance.

- Security and privacy performance.

Additionally, even though no cost-related objective had been formally stated, a fifth dimension, termed cost performance, was established; it was felt that the existing fiscal environment, of both the County and the cities, warranted special consideration of CJIC cost performance.

Second, for each of the ten objectives, evaluation criteria were established. The intention was to identify a set of criteria against which CJIC could be rated that considered in sum--not individually-- would yield an accurate determination of the extent to which CJIC had achieved its system objectives. Approximately 60 criteria were established, and approximately 70 CJIC "stakeholders" were interviewed. Each interviewee was asked to rate CJIC against each criterion in terms of the following scale:

Rating	Definition

5   <u>Superior/Excellent</u>--No improvements necessary--exemplary--
outstanding.

4   <u>Good/Above Average</u>--Minor improvements would make CJIC superior
in this area--commendable--well done.

3   <u>Acceptable/Average</u>--Some improvements would be desirable--
satisfactory performance--sufficient.

2   <u>Deficient/Below Average</u>--Major improvements necessary--
mediocre performance--insufficient.

1   <u>Unacceptable/Very Poor</u>--Complete overhaul required or recon-
sideration of the need--generally ineffective--unsatisfactory.

0   <u>Not Applicable</u>

During the interviews, the interviewee ratings were noted on an
interview guide, as were any comments that tended to substantiate the
ratings. From the ratings, arithmetic means were then derived. The
means, it was felt, would act to filter out extreme opinions of stakeholders that were more descriptive of the reactions of individual personalities (e.g., cynicism or excessive enthusiasm) than of the information
system, per se. Each criterion, therefore, had associated with it a
single user rating or score. The SRI evaluation team then, on the basis
of the interview data, their observations, and their experience in other
criminal justice information system environments, independently rated
CJIC against the 60 criteria. These ratings too were averaged, thus
providing an assessment somewhat independent of the stakeholder ratings.

The evaluation team analyzed all the ratings and comments and then
developed a number of recommendations intended to spur further attain-
ment of the system's objectives. For the executive summary of the final
report to the Board of Supervisors, the ratings, comments, and recommendations were organized by performance objective. Figures 1 through 4
are examples of these summaries.

EVALUATION RESULTS

As we interviewed the various agencies, we found mildly enthusiastic
users of CJIC and other users who could only articulate complaints about
the system. Indeed, some users expressed the opinion that the system
was a total waste of time, effort, and money. Our most pertinent findings, however, were: the importance of interdependency in multiagency
systems and the importance of user expectations.

The first of these findings was that of those systems the interdependency characterizing the system constitutes both its best aspect

FIGURE 1 INTERGOVERNMENTAL, ORGANIZATIONAL, ADMINISTRATIVE PERFORMANCE SUMMARY

Objective/Criteria	Objective Being Marginally Achieved *		Objective Being Achieved *			Comments	First-Order Recommendations
	1 Unacceptable	2 Deficient	3 Acceptable	4 Above Average	5 Superior		
CJIC WILL BE AN INTEGRATED INTER-GOVERNMENTAL INFORMATION SYSTEM						• Most CJIC awareness is at Management Committee level. • CJIC is clearly perceived as a good discusion forum for entire criminal justice community. • CJIC committee structure and commitment to CJIC are exemplary.	• Increase Policy Committee involve-ment and awareness by thoroughly review-ing this evaluation. • Hold seminars and encourage increased participation of the judiciary.
1. Policy-making structure							
2. Breadth of service							
3. Linkage							
4. Responsiveness to policy change requests							

* These are subjective categorizations. The ratings are averages for all user agencies.

Interviewee Rating   SRI Rating

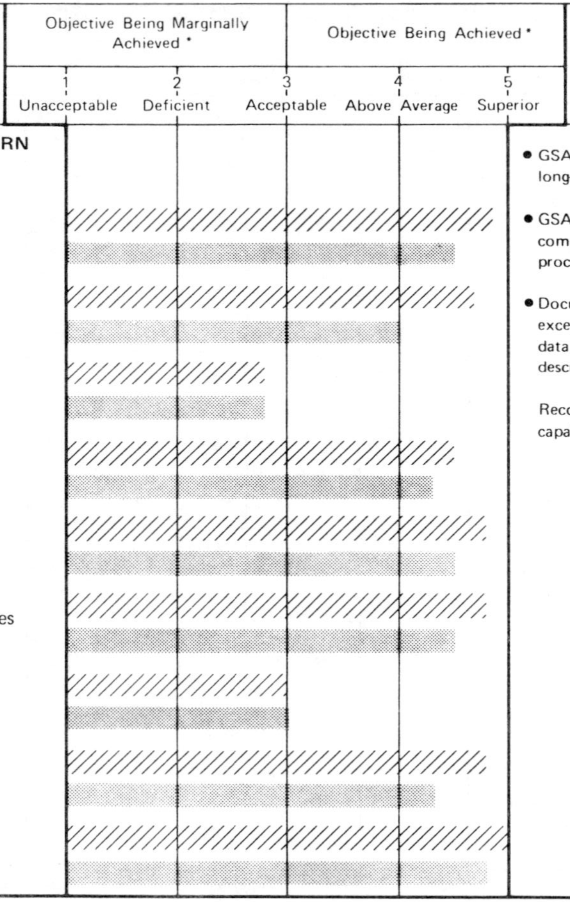
Objective Being Marginally Achieved *
Objective Being Achieved *
1 Unacceptable
2 Deficient
3 Acceptable
4 Above Average
5 Superior

Objective/Criteria	Comments	First-Order Recommendations
CJIC WILL USE MODERN DATA PROCESSING TECHNOLOGY.	• GSA-DP has an exemplary long-range planning process.	• Initiate study of the feasibility of using a DBMS package.
1. Software development	• GSA-DP uses exemplary comprehensive testing procedures and facilities	• Establish permanently scheduled liaison with representatives of data-processing departments of neighboring counties.
2. Documentation	• Documentation is excellent except for an overview and data base architecture description.	
3. File handling	Recovery and backup capability is exemplary.	
4. Teleprocessing		
5. Shared operations		
6. Modification techniques		
7. Interfaces		
8. Hardware/software		
9. Recovery and backup		

* These are subjective categorizations. The ratings are averages for all user agencies.

▨ Interviewee Rating ▒ SRI Rating

FIGURE 2 TECHNICAL PERFORMANCE SUMMARY

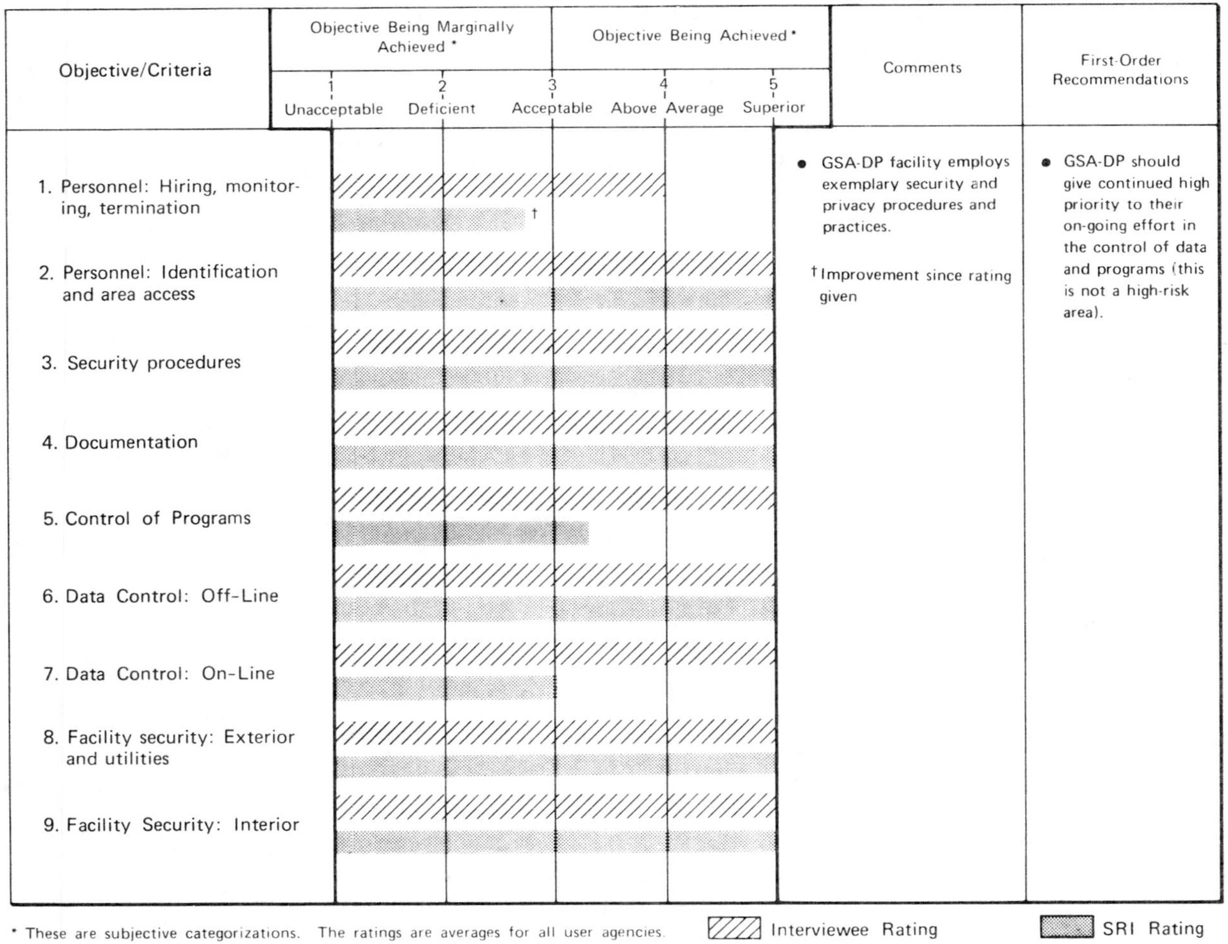

FIGURE 3 SECURITY AND PRIVACY PERFORMANCE SUMMARY (User Facilities)

Objective/Criteria:

1. Personnel: Hiring, monitoring, termination
2. Personnel: Identification and area access
3. Security procedures
4. Documentation
5. Control of Programs
6. Data Control: Off-Line
7. Data Control: On-Line
8. Facility security: Exterior and utilities
9. Facility Security: Interior

Objective Being Marginally Achieved *
1 Unacceptable | 2 Deficient | 3 Acceptable

Objective Being Achieved *
3 Acceptable | 4 Above Average | 5 Superior

Comments:
- GSA-DP facility employs exemplary security and privacy procedures and practices.

† Improvement since rating given

First-Order Recommendations:
- GSA-DP should give continued high priority to their on-going effort in the control of data and programs (this is not a high-risk area).

* These are subjective categorizations. The ratings are averages for all user agencies.

⊞ Interviewee Rating   ⧄ SRI Rating

CJIC WILL SAFEGUARD SECURITY AND PRIVACY.

Objective/Criteria	Objective Being Marginally Achieved*			Objective Being Achieved*		Comments	First-Order Recommendations
	1 Unacceptable	2 Deficient	3 Acceptable	4 Above Average	5 Superior		
1. Personnel practices: hiring, monitoring, and termination						• There has been significant improvement in the past year.	• CJIC Security Subcommittee should be given an immediate and expanded role undertaking full consideration of all CJIC security and privacy aspects. No second-order recommendation should be implemented without full study by this subcommittee.
2. Personnel practices: identification and area access						• New legislation and regulations are continually being considered at the state and federal levels. Many will affect CJIC.	
3. Security procedures						↑ Improvement since rating given.	
4. Documentation							
5. Data Control: off-line							
6. Data Control: on-line							
7. Facility security: exterior and utilities							
8. Facility security: interior							

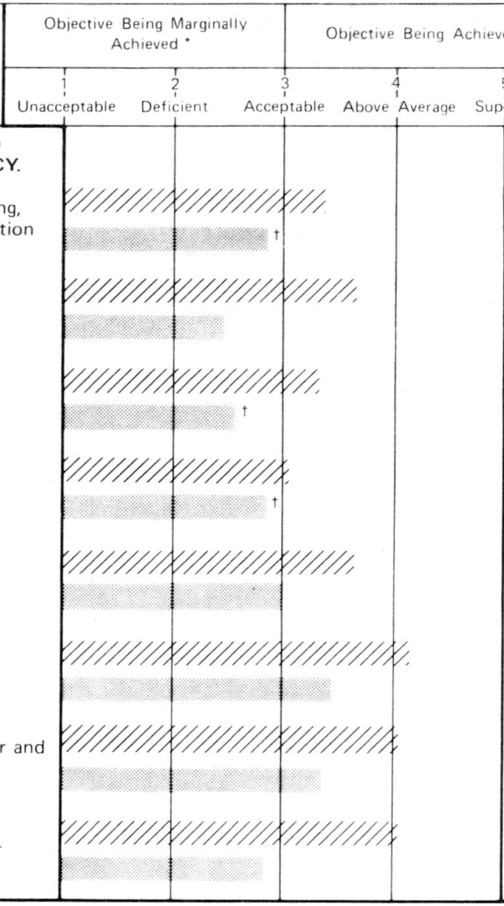

* These are subjective categorizations. The ratings are averages for all user agencies.

Legend: ⧄ Interviewee Rating   ▨ SRI Rating

FIGURE 4   SECURITY AND PRIVACY PERFORMANCE SUMMARY (Central Facility — GSA-DP)

and the root of its perceived problems. To state that timely and accurate output is totally dependent on timely and accurate input is not earthshaking. However, input is largely a function of one set of agencies (the Sheriff and the Municipal Courts), while output is largely relied upon by a second set of agencies (especially the police departments and the District Attorney). Complaints were more often heard from those responsible for input than from those responsible for output, because the input agencies could not readily realize the benefits of their labor. Therefore it was the agencies responsible for input that more often than not expressed a need for major system improvements. Agencies that relied on system output more often than not saw a need for only minor improvements. The significant point is that the cost-sharing formula for the County user agencies did not explicitly balance the value of CJIC to an agency against the effort expended by the agency.

Although ultimately CJIC is paid for out of general County revenue for County accounting purposes, each agency is "billed" for its use of the system. Only from a very high level can a multiagency system be evaluated--a level above agency-by-agency perceptions. It is only from this high level that the interdependency aspect can be properly integrated into the evaluation.

The second pertinent finding, the importance of user expectations, takes on an almost philosophic tone. Where users find CJIC to be, in reality, exactly what they expected it to be, they are more likely to trust the system and to build the operation of their agency around it. Where users have been oversold, and CJIC in reality is not at all what they expected it to be, they more commonly view the system as a hindrance--as something that has to be put up with. Their complaints are then often heard.

The expectation that CJIC would be a management information system (MIS) (as two of its original objectives implied) has probably had the most effect on the perception of users. CJIC was never intended to meet the MIS requirements of every agency. Yet, almost to a manager, CJIC was felt to be somewhat deficient because it did not do anything for the managers. Some viewed CJIC as an overly expensive clerical aid. The evaluation, at its higher level, was able to incorporate these individual and function-specific perceptions into a more objective assessment of how well CJIC was meeting its total set of objectives.

In sum, we judged that, to varying degrees, CJIC was achieving eight of its ten objectives. The other two objectives, that CJIC would support comprehensive criminal justice planning and that CJIC would use or initiate modern administrative techniques, were judged to be only marginally achieved. The evidence did not suggest that CJIC was being a significant contributor to either criminal justice planning or improved administrative techniques.

In terms of cost performance, our assessment of CJIC performance was largely inconclusive. The identifiable cost-offsets fell far short of the $1,300,000 annual system cost. We surmised, however, that, if a realistic value could be associated with each CJIC benefit (admittedly impossible for each benefit could never be identified), the system would be marginally cost-effective. Our most important cost-related conclusions are shown in Figure 5, which indicates a stabilized operating cost, a rapid increase in the use of CJIC, and a correspondingly rapid decrease in the cost per system transaction. This clear indication that the more the system is used the less each transaction will cost played a significant role in the Board of Supervisors' ultimate decision to continue to fund the system.

The Board's decision to fund at roughly a status quo level, rather than at an increased level, may have been based on our observation regarding city participation in system operating costs: The cities had been getting what amounted to a "free ride". In our interviews with city chiefs of police it became clear that they judged CJIC as acceptable given the fact that they were not expected to participate in the cost of operation. Almost to a chief, they said that they would seriously reconsider any participation in the system if the County raised the price of participation. The message was clear: If they had to pay for more than lines, terminals, and modems, they would break away from CJIC.

LESSONS LEARNED

In sum, the complexity of CJIC, a truly comprehensive information system, presented extraordinary evaluation difficulties. Although it was clear that, given the policy orientation of the clients, a traditional evaluation design would be inappropriate, it was not clear what kind of evaluation would serve the interests of policy-makers. By using a technique specifically developed to give objectivity to input that was, in fact, subjective, the opinions and attitudes of system users—which were important to the policy-maker—could be merged into the evaluation.

The most serious problem that developed when the evaluation was presented to the "stakeholders" was a misunderstanding of the arithmetic means. Readers of the report began thinking that there was a significant difference between a mean rating of 3.2 and one of 3.5. In fact, little distinction could be made between arithmetic means that were within 10% or so of each other, and therefore such a difference was no basis for conclusions. This is a common problem associated with quantifying anything, a sense that the numbers themselves are telling a story rather than the interpretation of the numbers. In fact, each rating (that is, arithmetic mean or value) had to be interpreted in light of the specific definition of the value (for example, a mean of 4.0 related to the definition we gave to the value of 4: "above average, minor improvements would make the system superior in this area"). The difference

-138-

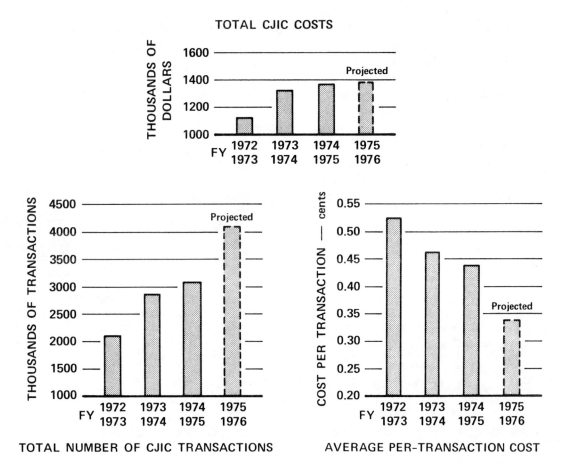

FIGURE 5   CJIC COST DATA

between the values of 3 (average--some improvements would be desirable) and 4 is a subtle difference, and the differences between intervening values of (for example, 3.2 versus 3.6) are more subtle yet. In future use of this technique, care should be taken to avoid making values appear to be unduly precise. Such seeming precision invites misunderstanding (or misuse).

There is little doubt that the evaluation techniques used in the Santa Clara County environment are transferable to other system environments. It is also clear that there are few major information systems that do not currently require a policy-oriented evaluation and perhaps such an evaluation every two years or so. Millions are spent annually on large-scale systems, and the recommendations resulting from such an evaluation can provide top-level administrators and elected officials with an impartial assessment of system performance, in many dimensions and in a language (that is, without technical jargon) enabling policy-relevant decisions to be made.

Dr. Richard C. Larson
Dr. Kent W. Colton
Mr. Gilbert C. Larson

Public Systems Evaluation, Inc.
929 Massachusetts Avenue
Cambridge, Massachusetts 02139

EVALUATION OF AN IMPLEMENTED POLICE AVM SYSTEM:
THE ST. LOUIS EXPERIENCE (PHASE I)[1]

The St. Louis Metropolitan Police Department is the first major police department to implement an automatic vehicle monitoring (AVM) system. Implemented as a Phase I prototype in one police district early in 1975, a revised system is scheduled to be installed city-wide later in 1976. Manufactured by the Boeing Company and called FLAIR (Fleet Location and Information Reporting), the system utilizes a computer-assisted dead-reckoning technology, and tracks the location of the various police cars in the Department. The system also includes digital communication and a special emergency button for police officers.

This paper is an evaluation of the Phase I system and utilizes a three-pronged approach to examine 1) technology, 2) police operations, and 3) attitudes and organizational impact. The analysis

---

[1]The evaluation research reported herein was supported by Grant No. 75NI-99-0014 to Public Systems Evaluation, Inc. from the National Institute of Law Enforcement and Criminal Justice, Law Enforcement Assistance Administration, U.S. Department of Justice. Points of view or opinions stated in this document are those of the authors and do not necessarily represent the official position or policies of the U.S. Department of Justice.

The authors of the paper served as the co-project directors of the evaluation project. Others were especially instrumental in preparing the paper. Mark McKnew was the principal researcher and spent numerous hours working on the project. Others who contributed valuable work include Jim Williamson, Jim Simon, and David Weilmuenster.

The authors would like to thank the following for cooperation in this evaluation effort: the St. Louis Metropolitan Police Department, the St. Louis Commission on Crime and Law Enforcement, the Boeing Company, and the Office of Evaluation of the National Institute of Law Enforcement and Criminal Justice, Law Enforcement Assistance Administration, U.S. Department of Justice.

reports on before and after response time data, answers of
police officers to attitudinal surveys, and field tests
examining the technology. Attention is given to operational
performance in Phase I, to ameliorative action for Phase II,
and to the affects of AVM on response time, officer safety,
voice-band congestion and command and control.

I. INTRODUCTION

In 1971 39% of the police departments in the United States were using
computers; by 1974, the percentage had risen to 56%.[2] This growth is
reflective of an overall increase in the application of technology and
information systems in the law enforcement field. In fact, in a recent
survey of municipal computer usage, it was found that of all computer
applications, police applications were third in overall use (only behind
accounting and revenue collection applications). Further, police applications
were the most intensively developed with the highest percentage of planned
usage for the future.[3]
Information technology, then, receives a wide variety of use within
police departments, ranging from real time computer systems to provide rapid
retrieval of data to the "officer in the street" concerning stolen cars,
outstanding warrants, parking violations, etc. to more complex applications
intended to assist the overall management and command and control of law
enforcement resources.[4] One of the critical issues that must be addressed,
though, is whether the benefits of this technology justify the costs. This
paper will be devoted to examining one of the police innovations which has
received increased attention in recent years--automatic vehicle monitoring (AVM)
systems to keep track of the location of police vehicles.
The potential police uses of AVM systems were first highlighted by the
President's Commission on Law Enforcement and Administration of Justice in
1967.[5] Studies at that time suggested that such systems might achieve cost-

-----

[2] Kent W. Colton, "Computers and the Police: Police Departments and the
New Information Technology," Urban Data Service Report, Washington, D.C.:
International City Management Association, Vol. 6, No. 11, November, 1974.

[3] Kenneth L. Kraemer, William H. Dutton, and Joseph R. Matthews, "Municipal
Computers: Growth, Usage and Management," Washington, D.C.: International
City Management Association, Vol. 7, No. 11, November, 1975.

[4] For a full description of the use of computers by the police, see
references listed in footnotes 2 and 3 above.

[5] President's Commission on Law Enforcement and Administration of Justice,
Task Force Report, Science and Technology, U.S. Government Printing Office,
Washington, D.C., 1967.

effective reductions in police response time. Some hypothesized that AVM would improve apprehension rates and thus serve as a deterrent to crime. Eight years after the President's Commission report, the first full-scale implementation of an AVM system by a major urban police department began with the installation of the FLAIR System[6] by the St. Louis Metropolitan Police Department (MPD). As of early 1976, a Phase I prototype system had been implemented and tested for approximately one year in District 3 of the St. Louis MPD. A Phase II production system, incorporating improvements derived from the Phase I experience, will be implemented city-wide later in 1976.[7] This paper presents a summary of an 18-month evaluation of the Phase I implementation.[8]

FLAIR is a computer-assisted dead-reckoning system. Given that a vehicle's initial position is known, frequent "updating" of distance and direction data from the vehicle make it possible to track its movement. Additionally, the FLAIR computer usually constrains a vehicle's estimated position to be on a street (through a map-matching process), and corrects for accumulated distance errors when the vehicle turns onto another street. This mode of tracking is called "closed loop"; a vehicle estimated to be driving on other than a mapped street will be tracked in "open loop" mode, utilizing only raw distance and heading data. Vehicle location information is presented to the dispatcher on a computer-driven map displayed on a television type screen, utilizing various colors, magnification scales, and a dispatcher-controlled cursor for indicating locations of incidents and vehicles. Using this information, the dispatcher can dispatch the closest car(s) to the scene of the incident and perform certain command and control functions heretofor infeasible without real-time vehicle location information. Among other features, the system utilizes car-to-base station "canned" messages (e.g., "officer-in-trouble" emergency alarm, "arrived at scene") to be transmitted digitally to the dispatcher without using the voice channel; this allows immediate communication to the dispatcher with minimal channel occupancy time.

In a police context, the four major objectives of an AVM system with the capabilities of FLAIR are:

1) Reduction in response time

2) Improvement in officer safety (utilizing the "officer-in-trouble" emergency alarm)

3) Reduction in voice-band congestion (utilizing digital communications)

4) Enhancement of command and control capabilities.

---

[6] FLAIR is a registered trademark of the Boeing Company signifying Fleet Location And Information Reporting.

[7] For Boeing's description of FLAIR and the Phase I implementation results, see Boeing's Carnahan Conference Presentation, Tenth Annual Carnahan Conference on Crime Countermeasures, May, 1976.

[8] For a detailed evaluation of the Phase I experience, see R.C. Larson, K.W. Colton, G.C. Larson, Evaluating an Implemented AVM System, Public Systems Evaluation, Inc., Cambridge, Massachusetts. This document is the full report and will become available through the Office of Evaluation, National Institute of Law Enforcement and Criminal Justice of the Law Enforcement Assistance Administration, U.S. Department of Justice, Washington, D.C., 1976.

In a broader framework, each of these primary objectives, plus others, is supposed to improve the productivity of police departments. (Considering that typically over 90 percent of a police department's budget is consumed by salaries, fringe benefits and pensions, that each round-the-clock two-person patrol car costs between $120,000 and $350,000 per year to operate, that many cities are unable to increase budgets of their urban services, and that demands for urban services keep rising--sometimes by over 10 percent per year--the need for productively improving systems and procedures is apparent.)

In conducting the Phase I review an effort was made to examine each of these objectives. Such evaluation must go beyond the purely technological features of the system, though, so a three-pronged analysis was employed to review first the technology, second the impact on the operational performance of the police, and third the influence on the attitudes and behavior of the personnel affected by the technology. An overall outline of the evaluation plan is presented in Figure 1, and the following sections of the paper will discuss the findings in each of these three areas: technology, operations and attitudes. The concluding section of the paper will discuss more general issues including the benefits and costs of AVM.

In carrying out the evaluation, certain products have been developed, such as computer simulation models and survey design instruments, which can be applied in assessing potential benefits of AVM in other cities. Thus the evaluation work specific to St. Louis also provides basic building blocks for a general AVM evaluation methodology.

Finally, in considering the results of this evaluation, it is important to remember that FLAIR implementation in St. Louis is an "experiment in progress," and Phase II (city-wide) results might be quite different from the results of using the early prototype system in District 3. Still, the issues raised in Phase I are likely to be important for Phase II. Moreover, many of the St. Louis Phase I experiences are not unique to a particular city or AVM technology; thus a discussion of these experiences at this time may assist in the consideration and possible implementation of AVM systems and related technologies in other cities.

II. TECHNOLOGICAL EVALUATION

This section highlights the Phase I FLAIR technical performance. Technological problems will be identified along with the corrective actions proposed for Phase II.

A. Overall System Performance

Considering the complexity of the new technology, and that a prototype system was being used, the system performed well and functioned as intended. At the dispatcher interface, the color display terminal showed the map of a selected part of the city with police vehicles traveling on streets, each vehicle identified by number and class. The vehicle status (available for call, on call, etc.), digital code messages, and the four closest vehicles to the cursor location were readily displayed. Operation of the display terminal was reasonably simple, and most of the better dispatchers integrated the FLAIR-supplied information into the dispatching process.

Occasionally, accumulated errors developed which eventually caused the vehicle to become "lost." When the computer recognized that a vehicle might

Figure 1

Overall Evaluation Plan

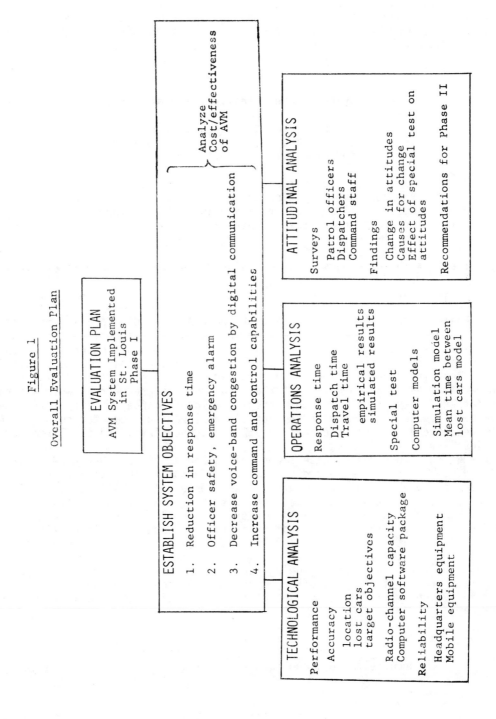

be lost, a V (or W) was displayed with the vehicle number in the status column of the display. This signalled the dispatcher to verify the vehicle's location, and if incorrect, to reinitialize to the proper location.[9]

The principal hardware operating problem during Phase I was accuracy, particularly as it related to the frequency of lost vehicles. Another major system problem was radio-channel capacity wherein the assigned channel (UHF frequency) accommodated only 97 vehicles compared to 200 required by the FCC. These two problems were largely responsible for two major design changes for Phase II:

> 1) An entirely new radio transmission format which provides for an increased number (200) of vehicles per channel, better distance and angular resolution, more precise synchronizing signals, satellite stations and other improvements.

> 2) An entirely new software package that increases computer capacity, includes changes to improve open and closed-loop tracking and provides more information on street widths and off-street areas for improved accuracy.

The effect of these changes will be evaluated during the Phase II evaluation.

B. System Accuracy

Phase I tests showed 95 percent of the FLAIR vehicle location estimates to be within 625 feet of the true location, an average location estimation error of 137 feet (upper bound) to 101 feet (lower bound)--depending on the error distribution assumptions, and 80 percent of the estimates to be within 90 feet of the true location. The computer assistance in constraining vehicles to be on streets and correcting for accumulated distance errors when a corner is turned is responsible for the exceptional performance for 80% of the samples; however, too many of the vehicles escaped the computer hold causing the relatively poor accuracy at the 95% confidence level and the large number of lost vehicles.

During both regular Phase I operations and a special three-week test period, the system experienced an average of about 11 initializations per car per 24-hour day or about 2.2 hours between losses of a FLAIR vehicle. This level of accuracy was unacceptable and resulted in a lack of confidence in the system and a heavy psychological workload for both dispatchers and patrol officers who felt that too much of their time was spent reinitializing vehicles.

Errors that cause loss in location accuracy also cause an increase in the number of lost vehicles. A modeling analysis, coupled with empirical tests, indicated that the following factors all contribute to diminished accuracy and smaller values of the mean time between losses of a FLAIR vehicle (or equivalently, increased values of the number of initializations per vehicle per day):

> 1) Random error. (Due to tire slippage, irregular driving patterns, speed variations (if viewed as uncorrectable), and mapping errors.)

---

[9]The process of relocating a vehicle that has become lost to its proper site is called reinitialization.

2) <u>Quantization in time, distance and angle</u>. (In
Phase I, angular and distance resolution was too
coarse. Also, time quantization was originally
two seconds--i.e., the updating of angular and
distance incremental information at two-second
intervals. To improve accuracy, the update rate
during most of Phase I was at a one-second rate.
Phase II will have an update rate slightly longer
than one second.)

3) <u>Systematic error</u>. (Due to temperature, tire wear
and speed (if viewed as correctable).)

4) <u>Open-loop tracking</u>. (Due to coarse quantization
resolution in Phase I, open-loop driving was a
primary cause of lost vehicles.)

5) <u>Missed or weak signals</u>. (Based on Phase I tests
at least one area within the city was within the
shadow of a hill and a satellite station may be
required to provide reliable signal transfer.)

6) <u>Susceptability to subversion</u>. (Due to acts on the
part of the patrol officers and/or dispatchers
aimed at deliberately reducing system effectiveness,
such as reporting incorrect locations, deliberately
driving near magnetic anomalies which cause the
disruption of the tracking system, etc.)

While some of the error sources described above appear to be of minor
consequence, the cumulative effect of even small errors causes loss of location
accuracy. A number of improvements are planned during Phase II and this is
important if systematic and random errors are to be reduced to the maximum
extent possible. Otherwise it will be very difficult to obtain a mean time
between losses greater than, say, six hours. The inclusion of real-time
speed monitoring in Phase II (made allowable by a finer distance quantization
interval) plus the apparent universal use of steel belted radial tires (to
reduce tire circumference changes due to speed) are steps in the direction of
reducing systematic error. A certain amount of random error will remain,
though, due to the center-line street mapping technique.

As a part of the Phase I evaluation, a model was developed to predict
the mean time between losses of a computer-tracked vehicle location system.[10]
Analysis using this model suggests that reasonably tight tolerances on systematic
and random error could reduce to between one and two per day the number of
losses (per vehicle) due solely to these types of errors. Of course, additional
losses can still occur due to missed signals, open-loop tracking, and system
vulnerability.

---

[10] See R.C. Larson, "Operational Model for Predicting Time Between Losses
of a Vehicle in a Computer-Tracked Vehicle Location System," Appendix B in
the report listed above in footnote 8.

Since system accuracy is such an important factor in the overall operations and acceptance of FLAIR, a level of performance should be achieved in Phase II substantially better than 11 initializations per car per day (as experienced in Phase I). The rate of reinitializations that may be considered acceptable is yet to be determined, and hopefully this will be accomplished during Phase II. The reinitialization process is viewed as an additional workload for both the dispatcher and the patrol officer, and a rate that is too high will cause a loss of confidence in the system.

C. System Reliability

Failures in the base station cause the entire system to be inoperative. During Phase I, the mean time between failure (MTBF) of the base station was 38.9 days, the mean time to repair (MTTR) was 1.32 days--resulting in a total down time per year of 12 days. Most of these failures were computer-related. Phase II will have a standby computer, which should greatly improve this performance. However, the transfer from one computer to the other is a manual operation requiring perhaps a half hour to accomplish--and this does not include the time required to initialize all the cars in the fleet that have moved during this period and those that have not been self-initialized.

For the FLAIR mobile equipment, the mean time between failure was 7.7 days per car, and the mean time to repair was estimated by Boeing at 1.05 hours. The number of repair incidents in Phase I is considered high, but perhaps not unreasonable for a trial system. Phase I service operations were hampered by a lack of service information, service manuals, test equipment, technical experience and spare parts. It is expected that improvements will be made in each of the areas in Phase II and servicing efficiency will improve.

The number of technicians required to service the 200 cars for FLAIR failures during Phase II is estimated at five (minimum), if the service facilities are to be manned seven days a week, 24 hours a day. The number of spare FLAIR-equipped cars required to replace those undergoing repair for FLAIR causes is estimated at three to five cars, assuming 24-hour-a-day repair service. However, the total number of FLAIR-equipped spare cars must also be sufficient to replace those being serviced for non-FLAIR causes, such as for communication or mechanical reasons. Proper provisioning of FLAIR-equipped spare cars is considered particularly important for maintaining a nearly 100% FLAIR presence in the field.

D. Phase II Concerns

Many changes and improvements are scheduled for Phase II that are expected to improve performance and reliability. However, areas of concern still remain:

1) The software is all new, is more sophisticated and has four times the memory and eight times as many cars to track. Some debugging should be expected.

2) The radio transmission digital format is entirely new, employing some state-of-the-art design techniques and it will be operating with much greater loading of the time slots. Effects on performance and reliability must be determined.

3) Signal strengths are weak in at least one area of the city. To correct this, a satellite receiver may be necessary. Such a unit is yet to be tried in the FLAIR system. Also, other areas of weak signal may be discovered during the city-wide implementation.

III. OPERATIONS ANALYSIS

Reduction in response time is often discussed as one of the primary arguments in favor of an AVM system. Thus, a major focus of the Phase I operational evaluation was directed toward response time. To understand the effects of response time due to AVM, it was necessary to examine the entire police response system, both those aspects which were influenced directly by the FLAIR system and those which were not.

A. Response Time Evaluation

Response time is considered to be the total time between a citizen's attempt to contact the police and the arrival of police service at the scene. Response time is comprised of several distinct components:[11]

1) Time until reporting the incident to the police. This includes the time to detect the incident and to make contact with the police.

2) Time for complaint evaluation processing. In St. Louis a citizen's call is transferred from the central operator to a complaint evaluator who either forwards information about the incident to the dispatcher or handles the call in some other manner.

3) Dispatch time. This is the time from dispatcher notification of an incident until dispatch of a vehicle.

4) Travel time. This is the time from dispatch of the police unit until its arrival at the scene of the incident.

Dispatch time and travel time are both "FLAIR-related" components of response time, being directly influenced by the FLAIR system. The various components of the response system will now be discussed.

1. Reporting the incident and complaint evaluation processing. Based on studies by Public Systems Evaluation, an average of about 30 seconds is required to contact a complaint evaluator, and about 90 seconds is required for the

---

[11] For a more complete discussion of the police emergency response system and the potential role of technology in improving system performance, see R.C. Larson, Urban Police Patrol Analysis, MIT Press, Cambridge, Massachusetts, 1972. Chapter 7, "Evaluating Technological Innovations: Automatic Vehicle Location Systems," and the reference in footnote 5 above.

evaluator to record the information and to direct it to a dispatcher. FLAIR
has essentially no influence on these components of response, but if the St.
Louis MPD is particularly concerned about response time, then other improvements might be made that could result in time savings. For example, an estimated
20 seconds might be eliminated by implementing two public telephone numbers in
St. Louis--one for emergencies and one for other calls (mostly administrative).
If the emergency number was the now popular three-digit number 911, additional
reductions might be achieved. Another possibility which requires further evaluation is a Computer-Aided Dispatch (CAD) system.

   2. Dispatch time: empirical results. Proper operation of the FLAIR
system does not require a significant increase in dispatch time. Mean dispatch
time during 1975 (January-November) was 3.62 minutes in District 3, down 1.4%
from 1974. The comparable figures city-wide (less District 3) were 2.55
minutes, down 8.6% from 1974.[12] (See Table 1) The 1975 District 3 dispatch
times were consistently greater than 1974 times during the first half of the
year, but starting in July they dropped noticeably below the 1974 figures.
The initial rise can be attributed to the time required for the dispatchers
to learn the use of the new system. Once the system was mastered, though,
dispatch times for District 3 dropped significantly; in fact, at a rate faster
than the overall city-wide average. Other factors which influenced the city-
wide and District 3 reduction in dispatch time include a drop in call-for-
service workload--a 12% decrease in District 3 and a 10% reduction city-wide,
and perhaps the dispatchers' awareness of the increased attention being given
to this matter as exemplified by the presence of on-scene evaluators.

   3. Limitation of FLAIR dispatch information. On the FLAIR display, the
dispatcher is supposed to be aided by a rank-ordered list of four closest cars
to the scene. Even if the car locations are known with certainty, this list
is of limited value since the "right-angle" distance metric employed in
ranking the cars does not take into account street rotations, barriers to travel,
and one-way streets. Plausible examples have been constructed in which the
travel time estimation errors could exceed one minute. This property of the
FLAIR travel time estimation procedure highlights the importance of the visual
display and motivated dispatchers who can estimate travel time from the street
patterns indicated on the displays.

   4. Travel time: simulated results. Employing a specially developed
simulation model of police patrol and dispatching, mean travel time was estimated
to be reduced by up to 25% by switching from pre-FLAIR dispatching procedures
to closest car dispatching utilized with FLAIR. This figure applied to both
pre-FLAIR and FLAIR sector configurations in District 3. However, a large
fraction of this anticipated reduction in travel time is attributable to the
relatively inefficient (from the perspective of dispatching the closest car)

---

[12] Dispatch time in District 3 has consistently been longer than the rest
of the city. Probable reasons for this include the heavy workload in District 3
and the resulting queuing of dispatches during heavy periods.

Table 1

Average Dispatch Delays*

| | District 3 | | | | City-Wide Less District 3 | | |
	1974	1975	% Change		1974	1975	% Change
	Average Dispatch Delays (in minutes)				Average Dispatch Delays (in minutes)		
JAN	3.22	3.46	+7.4		2.44	1.76	-27.9
FEB	3.02	3.46	+14.6		2.20	1.81	-17.7
MAR	3.25	3.21	-1.2		2.29	1.80	-21.4
APR	2.65	2.93	+10.6		2.19	2.05	-6.4
MAY	2.54	3.66	+44.1		2.12	3.56	+67.9
JUN	3.70	4.38	+18.4		2.93	2.84	-3.1
JUL	5.22	3.62	-30.6		3.41	2.74	-19.6
AUG	4.60	4.06	-11.7		3.85	2.92	-24.2
SEP	4.74	3.81	-19.6		3.52	3.02	-14.2
OCT	3.46	3.34	-0.9		3.03	2.78	-8.2
NOV	3.97	3.77	-5.0		2.75	2.79	+1.4
AVG	3.67	3.62	-1.4		2.79	2.55	-8.6

Table 2

Average Travel Times*

	1974	1975	% Change		1974	1975	% Change
JAN	5.44	5.30	-2.57		5.55	4.83	-12.97
FEB	5.16	4.97	-3.68		4.86	4.62	-4.94
MAR	5.29	4.89	-7.56		4.82	4.60	-4.56
APR	5.18	4.79	-7.53		4.76	4.59	-3.57
MAY	5.37	4.90	-8.75		4.90	4.69	-4.29
JUN	5.32	4.83	-9.21		4.89	4.67	-4.50
JUL	5.46	4.78	-12.45		5.05	4.73	-6.34
AUG	5.59	4.48	-13.42		5.29	4.62	-12.67
SEP	5.58	4.74	-15.05		5.22	4.71	-9.77
OCT	5.31	5.18	-2.45		5.02	4.60	-8.37
NOV	5.18	4.97	-5.41		4.97	4.80	-3.42
AVG	5.35	4.92	-8.00		5.03	4.68	-7.00

* Entries in boxes correspond to months of intensive on-scene evaluation, including stop-watch monitoring, interviewing and special testing.

precinct-oriented dispatch strategy used prior to FLAIR.[13]   Other modeling
analyses indicated that about the most travel time reduction that can be
expected from FLAIR is roughly 11 to 15%, not 25%, when compared to more
conventional non-precinct oriented dispatch policies. The potential benefits
of AVM, then, depend critically on the dispatching policy to which it is
compared.[14]

   5. Travel time: empirical results. Mean travel time in District 3
decreased an average of 8.0% to 4.9 minutes during 1975 (January-November)
compared to the analogous pre-FLAIR period in 1974. However, mean city-wide
travel time decreased 7.0% to 4.7 minutes during this period. (See Table 2)
Due to under-utilization of FLAIR during much of 1975, it is difficult to
draw strong conclusions from these data. During a specially monitored three-
week test, mean travel time in District 3 was down 15% (0.89 minutes) in the
test district as compared to the 12-month earlier (pre-FLAIR) levels, but
city-wide mean travel times were down 11%, suggesting a net 4% decrease due to
FLAIR. Some of these reductions could have arisen from decreased call-for-
service workloads in 1975. Regarding the effect of FLAIR on average travel
times, we must view the results of Phase I as inconclusive. Certainly there is
no indication that FLAIR increases travel time; but the empirical evidence
that it decreases is not very strong. Dispatchers' attitudes, perceptions and
motivations may have played a key role in measured travel time reduction--both
in District 3 and city-wide. (See Section IV on attitudinal and organizational
analysis.)

   6. Overall response system considerations. Mean system response time
in District 3 is roughly 2 minutes for reporting the incident and complaint
evaluation + 3.5 minutes for dispatch time + 5.0 minutes for travel time =
10.5 minutes. So a 30-second reduction in mean travel time corresponds to about
a 5% reduction in overall mean response time. Even if the simulated 25%
reduction in mean FLAIR travel time is found to apply during Phase II, this would
correspond to 1.25 minutes or 75 seconds, about a 12% reduction in overall mean
response time. Recalling that about half of the simulated 25% reduction is due
to precinct-oriented dispatching, only about 37.5 seconds of the travel time
reduction could reasonably be attributed to FLAIR, corresponding to 6% of the
total system response time. One of the conclusions from this is that if the
St. Louis MPD is interested in response time improvements they should also concentrate on other aspects of the police response system which are not directly
related to FLAIR (such as those discussed in Section III A.1. above).

   7. Cross-beat dispatches. Closest-unit dispatching (utilizing AVM)
influences patrol performance since it results in a greater amount of cross-
beat and cross-district dispatching. Such increases in cross-beat dispatches

---

[13] In St. Louis, a precinct is a small collection of contiguous beats,
and each district contains two or more precincts. Dispatch preferences are
given to precinct vehicles, even if a vehicle in the same district but another
precinct is closer.

[14] During the Phase II evaluation, the AVM patrol modeling analysis will
include a new analytical model as well as the simulation model.

should be of particular concern to police departments that desire to maintain (to the extent feasible) the one-man, one-beat concept. For other departments that desire wider overlapping areas of patrol responsibility, this operational consequence of AVM dispatching should cause little or no problem.

B. Special Three-Week Test

A number of operational and accuracy difficulties developed during the Phase I implementation of the FLAIR system in District 3 (see Section II). In addition, on-scene evaluation suggested that dispatchers were not using the FLAIR system as intended during much of Phase I. In one sample, the cursor was used in only about 35% of discretionary dispatches and information from the closest car column influenced the dispatch for only 19% of dispatches. Wide variability of these figures indicated that certain dispatchers were well-motivated and used the system as intended while others bordered on virtually ignoring the system.

In order to examine the operations and influence of the Phase I system under a more favorable set of circumstances, a special test was designed and conducted in District 3 from September 15 to October 5, 1975. The test was needed to study the operation of the system under two important conditions: 1) proper use by dispatchers (a special set of FLAIR dispatchers was selected) and 2) full coverage of the entire district by FLAIR-equipped cars (utilizing "spare" FLAIR vehicles during times of repair). Some of the relevant conclusions are summarized below:

The operations of the system improved significantly. Dispatchers utilized the intended components of the system to dispatch the closest car, and patrol officers seemed more satisfied in overall operations. Although no specific surveys were conducted, on-site evaluators (after talking to patrol officers and riding patrol in police vehicles) reported an increase in confidence in the system.

Trained and motivated dispatchers are essential to the successful use of the system. The way the dispatchers use AVM as an aid to their activities is a major factor in the way officers in the field regard the AVM system, thereby affecting field performance through such activities as voluntary self-initializations.

Spare vehicles and maintenance personnel are essential. As discussed above in Section II C., the special test reconfirmed the importance of spare vehicles in maintaining an acceptable level of system performance.

IV. ANALYSIS OF ATTITUDINAL AND ORGANIZATIONAL IMPACT

The implementation of an AVM system also implies important behavioral and organizational consequences. A number of "successes" have been achieved to date regarding the implementation of "routine" technological innovations in police departments such as establishing real-time computer information systems to provide rapid retrieval of information for the officer in the street. However, when efforts to implement go beyond routine systems to more non-routine innovations, such as transferring modeling or operations research type technologies or implementing an AVM or CAD system, the process has proven to be far more complex

and the success to date has been limited.[15]   One of the reasons that such
efforts have faltered has been a failure to give sufficient consideration to
behavioral and human factors. Several studies have demonstrated that it is often
not technical difficulties which limit long-run implementation, but behavioral
and people-oriented factors.[16] Attitudinal and organizational implications therefore comprise one of the primary components of this evaluation.

A number of attitudinal surveys of dispatchers and patrol officers in
Districts 3 and 5 (a control district) were conducted, both before and after
the implementation of the system. The results of these surveys will first be
summarized, and then their implications for the Phase II implementation of FLAIR
will be outlined.

A. Summary of Findings

General police officer attitudes toward FLAIR shifted significantly during
Phase I. Before using the system, 64.4% of the District 3 officers thought
FLAIR was a "good idea." After the Phase I implementation only 39.8% still felt
this way. A number of factors contributed to this change in attitude:

1) Most important, a crucial link exists between
   attitudes and system performance. Problems with
   the accuracy and reliability of the system seem
   to be the primary cause for the drop in attitudes.

2) The effective operation of FLAIR relies heavily
   on well motivated and trained dispatchers. Since
   the capabilities and motivations of the dispatchers
   who worked with FLAIR were mixed, this uneven
   quality contributed to the shift in attitudes.

3) Attitudes are volatile and a downward trend may
   be reversible if the Phase II system functions
   smoothly. In fact, during the special three-week
   test the careful selection of dispatchers, the
   availability of a full fleet of FLAIR-equipped
   cars, and personal two-way radios all seemed to
   have a positive influence. Still, once a negative
   attitude is established, initial impressions are
   difficult to overcome.

Two other factors were found to be especially important in influencing
attitudes toward FLAIR: level of information about the system and initial source
of information. The pre-implementation training seminar held only in District 3

---

[15] Op. cit., K.W. Colton, "Computers and the Police."

[16] Op. cit., K.W. Colton, and J. Chaiken, J. Crabill, L. Holliday, D. Jacquett,
M. Lawless, E. Quade, Criminal Justice Models: An Overview, the Rand Corporation,
October, 1975, Rand Report #R-1859-DOJ, Santa Monica, California.

seemed instrumental in influencing positive attitudes as compared to District 5. Even after the attitudes of the officers in District 3 dropped, a strong correlation was found to exist between those officers who were favorable toward FLAIR and those who felt well-informed about the system.

The shift in officer attitude during Phase I included a shift in the perceived influence of FLAIR on four areas of police operation:

1) Although officer safety remained as the top area of importance to officers, its overall rating of importance dropped significantly after implementation. (Whereas eight of every ten of the officers surveyed in District 3 before implementation felt that officer safety was very important, after implementation only five out of ten maintained such feelings. Operational difficulties obviously influenced confidence in the system.)

2) The perceived importance of FLAIR in dispatching the nearest officer also dropped significantly in District 3--again showing the influence of technological problems on attitudes.

3) The benefits of the digital communication capability of FLAIR were perceived by both police officers and dispatchers to be one of the most important aspects of the new system.

4) Concern over disciplinary abuses dropped significantly in District 3 since officers felt the system could not track them adequately. (In 1974, 65.1% of the officers expected disciplinary abuses to be the major problem, in 1975 only 27.7% saw such abuses as a major problem.) However, the latent fear that remains on this matter is demonstrated in that disciplinary abuses still remained as the primary concern in District 5.

Responses to surveys indicate that officers feel that FLAIR will have (or has had) little impact on police preventive patrol. However, officers do feel that the AVM system will improve the ability of the department to keep track of where police are located, and in turn, according to survey results, this may diminish their flexibility and force their continued movement on patrol.

B. Implications for Phase II

A number of factors have been identified which contribute to the successful implementation of new technological innovations. After analyzing these influences and relating them to the St. Louis situation, five elements can be pinpointed which seem especially important to the Phase II implementation.

1. Link between attitudes and technology performance. Accuracy and reliability are essential if the new system is to be accepted and made to work over the long run. To avoid the rapid decline in attitudes experienced in District 3 during Phase I, the Phase II system should be tested under

realistic operational field conditions before it is implemented city-wide--
preferably in District 3. Even though the system receives such a test, it
should be realized that problems will still arise and such difficulties should
be anticipated and discussed openly so that people will be prepared.

2. <u>Involvement and training of police personnel</u>. There is a paramount
need for effective training and communication concerning FLAIR. However, this
means more than just an initial training seminar. As pointed out earlier,
feeling informed about the system was one of the most important factors influencing
attitudes toward AVM. An "on-going" dialogue is necessary to answer questions
and to explain problems, and initial training should be supplemented by monthly
or bimonthly visits by St. Louis and/or Boeing personnel to the "roll calls" at
the beginning of each shift in order to answer questions and to discuss problems.
On the other hand, care should be taken not to "oversell" the system. Evidence
indicates that initial expectations were too high in District 3.

3. <u>Man-machine interface</u>. One of the most significant elements in determining
success or failure in implementing new technology is developing the proper
human/technology interface. The point at which this is especially vital with
FLAIR is the link between the dispatcher and the new system. <u>The role of the
dispatcher must receive priority attention in the Phase II implementation</u>.
In addition, procedures for dispatcher-car interactions should be clearly
specified, and special training might be provided. For example, dispatchers
might be provided with specific training in order to simulate how to handle such
"rare events" as responding to officer-in-trouble calls, handling pursuits, or
handling civil disturbances.

4. <u>Involvement of top police supervisors</u>. Experience in other police
departments has shown that new technologies are likely to fail without <u>sustained</u>
commitment from top management. With FLAIR, the Phase I results have demonstrated
that the response time benefits of the system are below initial expectations.
Other potential benefits such as the opportunity for improved command and control
or better management of resources must therefore be examined to determine the
degree to which the benefits may justify the costs. In order to test these
areas, though, the deep involvement of the St. Louis command staff is required.
For example, a new set of computer-prepared operational reports has been designed
for the Phase II FLAIR system. If these reports are to be worthwhile, they
should be modified and perfected by the St. Louis command staff so as to provide
the best information possible from a management perspective. Further, to truly
test the benefits of the system, it may be appropriate to try new command and
control or organizational relationships, at least on a temporary basis, such as
assigning a high-level command person to the dispatch center in order to
supervise command and control situations when they arise.

5. <u>Long-term commitment and continuity of personnel over time</u>. In a recent
study by the Rand Corporation[17] it was found that efforts to implement operations
research modeling projects in criminal justice agencies are often promoted by
a single or small group of advocates. Although such advocates play an important
role in spreading innovation, their presence also leaves the innovation
vulnerable if a shift in personnel occurs and the advocate leaves the agency

---

[17] Op. cit., J. Chaiken, <u>Criminal Justice Models</u>.

or is transferred. In order to assure success of the FLAIR system in St. Louis, a long-term commitment based on a broad base of support is required. To broaden involvement the St. Louis MPD might consider establishing a management users committee of top level command officers to help monitor and oversee change.

V. SYSTEM OBJECTIVES AND COST CONSIDERATIONS

An important question in evaluating an AVM system such as FLAIR is determining whether the objectives of the system have been met and whether the benefits justify the cost. While it is impossible to reach a final conclusion on these issues based soley on the results of the Phase I system, as a means of summarizing our ideas to date it is worthwhile to state our initial conclusions regarding each of the four primary objectives outlined earlier.

A. Response Time Reduction

Phase I tests do not support the expected reduction in response time. Although this question will be examined closely in Phase II, current findings lack evidence to suggest that savings in travel time due soley to AVM will significantly improve police operations or reduce cost.

B. Officer Safety

When the emergency alarm is activated, the dispatcher is alerted visually and audibly, the location of the activating vehicle is known immediately from the display, and the computer-selected closest cars are identified for quick dispatch. However, the effectiveness of the officer safety objective has not been established during Phase I, largely for the following reasons:

1) The high rate of lost cars and system location errors has decreased the confidence of patrol officers as to the dispatcher's ability to locate him accurately and consistently. There appears to be a preference of at least some officers to still announce their situation and location over the voice radio.

2) The emergency alarm has been improperly used by some officers (e.g., activating the alarm to test whether or not the system is operating) and has been accidentally activated at times causing a "false alarm" condition that decreases the urgency in responding to a real alarm.

3) The number of real alarms has been small, making a proper evaluation difficult due to small sample size.

Improvements in the Phase II system and equipment (to increase accuracy), additional training of officers and better emergency knob design (to reduce false alarms), and city-wide implementation (to increase the number of incidents) should establish improved conditions for evaluation during Phase II.

C. Reduction in Voice-Band Congestion

Vehicle-to-base station digital communication in FLAIR allows transmission of 99 "canned" messages, thereby providing an alternative means of interacting with the dispatcher. An original objective was to decrease voice-band congestion by using this new medium. Tests made by the St. Louis MPD during Phase I showed essentially no change in voice-band occupany levels. However, other benefits became apparent, including:

1) High usage of digital communication by the patrol officers involving over 2,000 messages per day or over 100 per day per car. This amounts to an expansion in the capacity of the communications system compared to what could be accommodated by existing voice channels.

2) The patrol officer can communicate a change in status instantly to the dispatcher whereas with voice radio only, he might wait for clear channel status which could involve considerable delay or he may not bother to communicate.

3) The dispatcher can organize work tasks better, permitting some digital inquiries to accumulate before acknowledging if other matters have higher priority.

4) Digital messages are relatively secure and cannot be intercepted by the commonly available "police" monitor radio.

Both officers and dispatchers felt that digital communication provided some of the most important benefits of the Phase I system.

D. Command and Control

In our context, command and control pertains to the ability of the dispatcher to deploy (command) vehicles, especially under extraordinary circumstances, and the ability of patrol administrators to control and modify the manner in which patrol operations are conducted.

Utilizing the FLAIR display, dispatchers had several opportunities during Phase I to incorporate AVM information in their handling of extraordinary events. For instance, in October, 1975, a chase starting in District 3 resulted in the dispatcher commanding patrol cars by voice radio toward locations for possible interception, after the chase left District 3, however, the effectiveness of the dispatcher was greatly reduced because most of the radio time was spent asking for the locations of the various cars involved. Phase II, being city-wide, will provide more opportunities to evaluate the dispatcher-related command and control benefits of the system. It is recommended that dispatchers receive special instructions concerning all aspects of FLAIR usage (not just normal dispatching), and that organizational experiments be conducted such as having an officer experienced in the field of deployment assigned to help oversee the dispatching function for extraordinary incidents, particularly incidents which cross district boundaries.

Few results are available from Phase I regarding the potential of FLAIR for affecting patrol operations. It was our impression that fewer patrol units volunteered for unnecessary back-up assignments and fewer patrol units appeared to congregate for prolonged visits after FLAIR than before. Conversely, the FLAIR-equipped vehicles appeared to be attentive to their assigned duties, whether on assignment or on patrol. This can be observed by viewing the display, and of course the patrol officers are aware of the display. This may result in negative consequences as well, however. For example, in the attitudinal surveys patrol officers indicated that FLAIR had limited their flexibility and their ability to follow up on hunches. If such limits in flexibility result in a reduction of time wasted, good. On the other hand, if officers feel overly restricted in carrying out their law enforcement work this may have a negative impact. Properly used, AVM may be useful in improving the efficiency and effectiveness of the patrol force, but this still must be tested. Moreover, the existence of AVM information provides an important tool for experimental control in possible patrol experiments that may be contemplated.[18]

During Phase II, an attempt will be made to develop measures indicating the extent of improvement of patrol operations. These may include a measure of miles driven per day on preventive patrol as opposed to responding to calls, the number of self-initiated activities, time spent at the District Station, and others. If it can be shown that the force is more effective because of FLAIR, this could be a cost-effective benefit. An improvement of say 10% in one measure of performance should be compared to the amount of additional manpower that would be required to achieve the same 10% improvement. However, it is recognized that a conclusive evaluation based only on quantitative measures may be difficult, and that subjective measures will probably also be necessary.

E. Cost and Related Considerations

The total cost of implementing the Phase II FLAIR system is estimated at $2,700,000.[19] However, these expenses must be placed in the context of overall police operations. By extrapolating probable production costs of FLAIR, we estimate the total system cost to be approximately equal to $9,500 per car (capital investment), or with 10-year life the annual depreciation, about $950 per car per year. The operating/service costs are estimated to exceed this amount, at about $1,000 per car per year. The total of amortized investment

---

[18] For an illustration of such experiments in patrol strategies, see "The Kansas City Preventive Patrol Experiment, a Technical Report," by G.L. Kelling, T. Pate, D. Dieckman and C.E. Brown, published by the Police Foundation, Washington, D.C. 1974.

[19] This amount includes both Phase I and Phase II.

cost and operation/maintenance costs over a ten-year period then approaches $2,000 per car per year.

The average cost of fielding a round-the-clock one-person patrol car usually exceeds $100,000 per year or, for a two-person patrol car, $200,000 per year. The total FLAIR cost at $2,000 per year then represents no more than 2% of the cost for a one-person car (or 1% for a two-person car). Compared to the one-person car, if it can be shown that FLAIR (or any AVM) will increase the efficiency and effectiveness of the force by x% (because of better management of the forces), then FLAIR will provide at least an x:2 return on the investment. If x is equal to 10%, for example, this would produce an impressive 5:1 return on investment.

It should be realized that more than just monetary factors must be considered when evaluating the advantages and disadvantages of AVM. For example, it is important to examine the implications that AVM might have on police policy and approach. To the extent that AVM stresses rapid response to calls for service and dispatching the closest car it may limit or conflict with an alternative approach to policing--the "one-person, one beat" approach which gives a patrol officer responsibility for a particular area (such as with team policing). It will most likely be impossible then, to do a definitive review of costs and benefits that will be applicable to all police departments. The costs and benefits for each city will be different and must be reviewed individually depending on their goals and priorities.

Of interest to all cities, though, is the fact that there have been a number of unknowns and even myths concerning the application of AVM technology. Phase I has been important in answering many of these unknowns, and it is anticipated that the Phase II evaluation will prove extremely useful in providing significant insights into the remaining issues.

Robin J. Milstead, M.S.W.

Milstead Associates
Hill Road
Dresden, Ohio   43821

A PROTOTYPE INFORMATION SYSTEM FOR PLANNING,

MONITORING AND EVALUATING ACTION PROJECTS IN

A METROPOLITAN REGIONAL PLANNING UNIT

ABSTRACT: This paper describes the information system designed for the Regional Planning Unit, RPU, of the Columbus-Franklin County Criminal Justice Coordinating Council in Ohio. The C-FCCJCC is one of six metropolitan planning units for the planning and administration of action projects funded through the Law Enforcement Assistance Administration.
The information system was designed primarily for planning, monitoring and evaluating local action projects in the juvenile and adult judicial, law enforcement and corrections systems. It serves the functions of: 1) monitoring and impact assessment of action projects, 2) generation of community profiles and data bases related to comprehensive planning and policy issue analysis within the RPU's geographic area, and 3) operation of a management information reporting process for continuous feedback to participating criminal justice agencies of the RPU constituency.

INTRODUCTION

The RPU information system was developed by the author, as the RPU Evaluation Consultant, with assistance from the RPU Monitoring Specialist, program planners and a technical advisory committee. The information system emerged as the most feasible vehicle for comprehensive monitoring and evaluation of action projects and coordinating planning among the criminal justice agencies within Franklin County, Ohio.

The monitoring and impact assessment components of the information system are interrelated with the planning functions, project review process and fiscal operations of the RPU in accordance with M7100.1-D OH.20 PARG (4) and (5) as promulgated by Spencer Hendron, Ohio Representatice of Region V, LEAA Chicago Offices. These components were developed through LEAA action project funds in which the RPU served as the implementing agency.

The paper discusses the users of the information system, objectives of the system, three levels of evaluation and the flow of information within the monitoring and impact assessment components of the evaluation system.

USERS OF THE INFORMATION SYSTEM

The RPU information system is designed to serve planners, decision makers and implementers of action projects within the criminal justice systems of Columbus and Franklin County. The primary process for serving these aggregates of users is through the systematic management of information. The information selected for collection, analysis and synthesis is related to the level of evaluation assigned to each action project and the kinds of information needed/requested by users.

There are six types of users of the RPU information system:

1. The RPU Organization
   Program Managers/Planners
   Project Review Board
   Fiscal Officer
   Monitoring Specialist
   Executive Director

2. Columbus-Franklin County Criminal Justice Coordinating Council
   Subcommittees
   Executive Committee
   Council

3. Subgrantee
   Fiscal Accountant
   Administrator

4. Project Management
   Director
   Fiscal Officer
   Programmatic Director

5. Administration of Justice Division (The Ohio State Planning Agency which administers LEAA funds.)
   Monitoring and Evaluation Units
   Planners
   Supervisory Council

6. The Law Enforcement Assistance Administration

The Regional Planning Unit requires detailed data on action projects related to accountability of expenditures of project funds, efficiency of project operations, accomplishments of project objectives and project impact. The subsystems of the RPU require different types of data and levels of detail. The Fiscal Officer is primarily concerned with data on authorized expenditures of funds; program managers are interested in program activities and outcome in accordance with intended project objectives and and program area plans; the Project Review Board requires synthesized status reports on the above data types; the Monitoring Specialist must manage the delivery of all of the above data; and the Executive Director must oversee the efficient coordination and utilization of data among the RPU users of the information system.

The Program Managers/Planners are also interested in data on project performance for use in program area planning and interaction with their respective subcommittee of the C-FCJCC.

The C-FCJCC Subcommittee members require project effectiveness data for their decision making process in selecting new and continuation projects for funding recommendations to the Executive Committee. The Executive Committee seeks data which will enable them to select appropriate projects for inclusion in the annual state plan. Likewise, the entire Council is interested in generic data accross projects as well as discrete data on selected projects. All parts of the RPU and C-FCJCC require timely, accurate data on all projects.

The Subgrantees want assurance (or alerted) that their action projects are operating efficiently - both fiscally and programatically. Directors of action projects can benefit from in-progress feedback of monitoring data for on-going operation of projects and impact assessment data related to continuation of their project.

The Administration of Justice Division must comply with LEAA requirements and rely on the RPU to provide appropriate data related to monitoring and evaluation. These data are also used indirectly by the AJD planners in compiling the Annual Ohio Plan as well as by AJD reviewers of the RPU Annual Plan.

While the LEAA transferred its responsibility for monitoring and evaluating action projects to AJD, LEAA retains an interest in data on projects within Level III (intensive evaluation) of the RPU information system.

The data needs of the above users are addressed by the objectives of the RPU information system.

OBJECTIVES OF THE INFORMATION SYSTEM

There are three levels of objectives of the RPU information system:

    The primary objective
    Three component objectives
    Fourteen functional objectives

The objectives are as follows:

Primary System Objective:	To assess on-going performance and impact of action projects.
Component Objectives:	To obtain/manage information related to implementation, operation and immediate outcome of action projects (Monitoring Component).
	To determine the impact of an action project on target population, criminal justice agency, community agency or program area (Impact Assessment Component).
	To interface/synthesize data appropriate to the level of evaluation assigned to an action project (Both Components).

Functional Objectives: To collect/provide accurate fiscal data on expenditures of project funds.

To collect/provide standardized data on efficiency in project administration.

To collect/provide standardized data on program effectiveness of projects.

To provide in-progress feedback for quality control of projects.

To facilitate continuation of projects.

To maintain a systematic reporting process for project directors.

To maintain a timely flow of information within the RPU organization.

To forward required information to AJD.

To forward useful information to subgrantees.

To identify fiscal/programmatic areas requiring technical assistance/reactive site visits to action projects.

To prevent problem areas in project operation.

To collect standardized data for comparison of process/results within and across projects.

To document the approach/results of projects having potential replicability.

To conduct scheduled site visits to supplement/verify reported data from projects.

DESCRIPTION OF THE RPU INFORMATION SYSTEM

The RPU information system is an orderly arrangement of activities directed toward assessing on-going performances of an action project and its impact. Levels of evaluation range from minimum efforts of descriptive evaluation (basic monitoring) through medium levels of effectiveness evaluation (assessing project outcome) to intensive evaluation of project impact.

The RPU information system has two primary components: Monitoring and Impact Assessment. The Monitoring Component encompassess minimum and medium levels of evaluation in that projects are fiscally and programmatically monitored intensively. The Impact Assessment Component builds upon data of the Monitoring Component as well as data from non-project sources for purposes of determining the affect of the project upon specific groups, agencies, programs and systems related to the respective project.

The RPU information system is premised on three levels of evaluation effort:

Level I   Descriptive Evaluation

Level II   Effectiveness Evaluation

Level III   Intensive Evaluation.

Figure 1 shows the relationship of the three levels of evaluation effort to the two evaluation components of Monitoring and Impact Assessment.

Level I   Descriptive Evaluation

Level I represents the minimum level of RPU evaluation efforts. In Level I, the emphasis is placed on accomplishment of project objectives and accountability of project activities and expenditures of grant funds. The Monitoring Specialist is the primary person responsible for coordinating data collection tasks and management of information flow for Level I evaluations.

Data Sources
The data sources for Level I evaluations are:

Basic-shared monitoring instruments including the AJD monthly financial statement and a number of AJD and RPU modules for Quarterly Progress Reports.

One scheduled site visit per year of funding.

Other sources as appropriate, e.g., reactive site visit reports, project-acquired consultant's reports, etc.....

The Monitoring Specialist synthesizes data from the above sources into Quarterly Status I Reports for projects receiving Level I evaluations.

Level II   Effectiveness Evaluation

Level II represents the medium level of RPU evaluation efforts. In Level II, the emphasis is placed on a project's apparent impact as well as accomplishment of project objectives and accountability of project activities and expenditures of grant funds.

Both the Monitoring Specialist and an Evaluation Specialist/Consultant have key roles in coordinating data collection tasks and management of information flow for Level II evaluations. The Monitoring Specialist retains primary responsibility for data available from project sources, while the Evaluation Specialist/Consultant assumes primary responsibility for data available from non-project sources. Non-project data sources are discussed in Level III evaluations.

Data Sources
The data sources for Level II evaluations are:

Basic-shared monitoring instruments including the AJD monthly financial statements and a number of AJD and RPU modules for Quarterly Progress Reports.

Two scheduled site visits per year of funding.

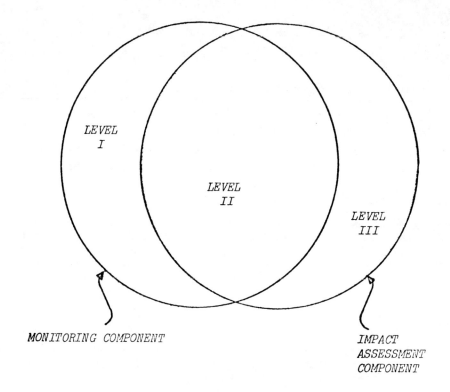

FIGURE 1. RELATIONSHIP OF THE RPU INFORMATION SYSTEM COMPONENTS
AND THE LEVELS OF EVALUATION EFFORTS

Discrete data instruments related to project objectives, work plan and budget. (These data are obtained from both project and non-project sources.)

Other sources as appropriate, e.g., reactive site visit reports, project-acquired consultant's reports, etc.....

The Monitoring Specialist, with assistance from the Evaluation Specialist/ Consultant, synthesizes the data from the above sources into Quarterly Status II Reports for projects receiving Level II evaluations. The Monitoring Specialist also provides a Status I Report for each project receiving Level II evaluations for purposes of maintaining a comprehensive flow of monitoring information to the Project Review Board, which is comparable and standardized across all RPU action projects.

Figure 2 shows the data sources of an action project file in the RPU Monitoring Component.

Level III   Intensive Evaluation

Level III represents the maximum level of RPU evaluation efforts. In Level III, the emphasis is placed on intensively evaluating the actual impact of an action project. This involves utilization of data sources beyond the specific action project files. The data structure of Figure 3 shows the relationships among the data sources of the RPU information system.

While the Monitoring Specialist manages most of the project related data sources, the Evaluation Specialist/Consultant is the primary person responsibile for carrying out data collection tasks and management of information flow for Level III evaluations. Most non-project data are obtained from the data files of the RPU planning unit. However, those projects involving a rigorous analytical research design will require additional data collection tasks beyond the scope of the RPU planning unit.

Data Sources
The data sources for Level III evaluations are:

Basis-shared monitoring instruments including the AJD monthly financial statements and a number of AJD and RPU modules for Quarterly Progress Reports.

Quarterly scheduled site visits per year of funding.

Discrete data instruments related to the projectives, work plan and budget. (These data are obtained from project sources.)

Discrete data instruments related to the methodological design developed to intensively assess the actual impact of an action project. (These data are obtained from non-project sources including related criminal justice agencies, community agencies and other sources including the Census.)

Other sources as appropriate, e.g., reactive site visit reports, project-acquired consultant's reports, etc.....

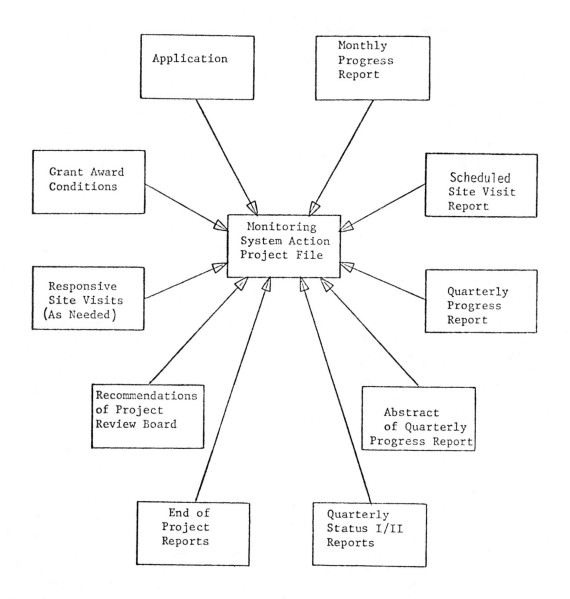

FIGURE 2 DATA SOURCES OF AN ACTION PROJECT FILE IN THE RPU INFORMATION SYSTEM (MONITORING COMPONENT)

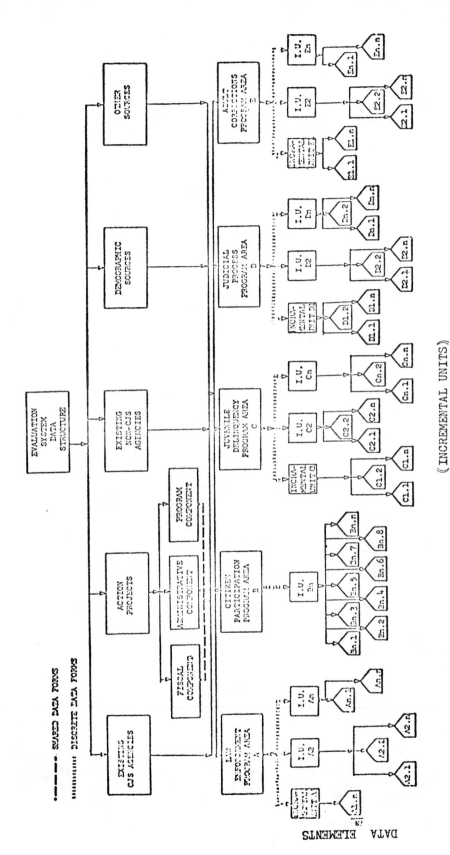

((INCREMENTAL UNITS))

FIGURE 3. DATA STRUCTURE OF THE RPU INFORMATION SYSTEM

-169-

The Evaluation Specialist/Consultant, with assistance from the Monitoring Specialist, synthesizes data from the above sources into Quarterly Status III Reports for projects receiving Level III evaluations. The Monitoring Specialist retains the primary responsibility for providing Status I and II Reports on the projects receiving Level III evaluations for purposes of maintaining the comprehensive flow of monitoring information.

Figure 4 shows the information sources of an action project file in the RPU Impact Assessment Component. Table 1 summarizes the data sources for action projects in both information system components by level of evaluation effort.

APPLICATION OF THE RPU INFORMATION SYSTEM TO ACTION PROJECTS

There are four stages in the life of an action project to which the RPU information system relates:

1. Pre-application Stage
2. Application/Grant Award Stage
3. Operation Stage
4. End of Project Stage.

Pre-application Stage

Assignment of an evaluation level at the pre-application stage provides the opportunity for improvement (if needed) in project objectives, work plan, budget and evaluation designs during the interium period between inclusion in the RPU Annual Plan and notification to proceed to application stage. This activity facilitates 1) the evaluability of projects, 2) preliminary planning time for projects assigned to Level III (for development of methodological designs), 3) allocations of RPU staff time for the site visits and collection of non-project data (Level III), and 4) possible inclusion in the Annual Plan of sufficient funds (possibly new grant pre-applications) for the Level III evaluations.

Application/Grant Award Stage

An action project formally enters the monitoring process at time of grant award. The Monitoring Specialist, Fiscal Officer and Program Planner/Manager of the RPU staff work together in establishing the information system's jacket (folder or file) of the action project.

Operation Stage

In this stage, the Monitoring Specialist (and Evaluation Specialist/Consultant for Level III projects) meet with the project director to negotiate the use of selected shared and discrete data modules.

End of Project Stage

An action project is formally terminated from the Monitoring Component of the RPU information system during this stage. However, Level III action projects remain in the Impact Assessment Component for the length of time appropriate to completion of the intensive evaluation of the project's impact.

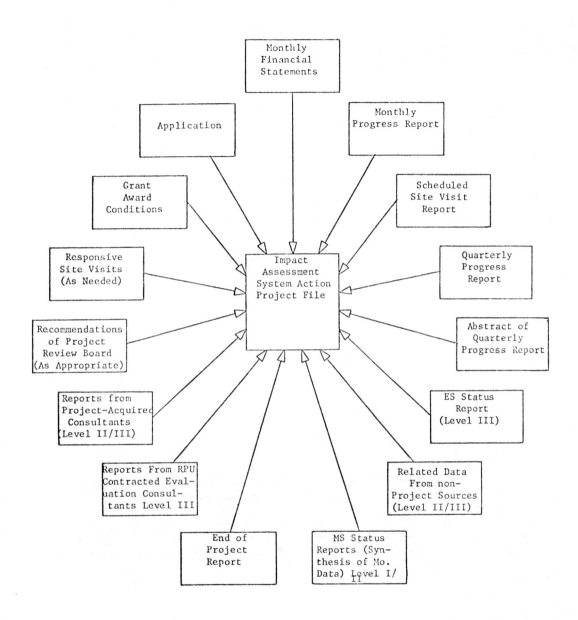

FIGURE 4. INFORMATION SOURCES OF AN ACTION PROJECT FILE IN THE RPU
INFORMATION SYSTEM (IMPACT ASSESSMENT COMPONENT)

LEVELS OF EVALUATION EFFORTS	DATA SOURCES						
	SHARED AND DISCRETE MONITORING INSTRUMENTS			SITE VISITS			OTHER SOURCES AS APPROPRIATE
	BASIC-SHARED DATA FORMS*	DISCRETE DATA FORMS BASED ON PROJECT SOURCES	DISCRETE DATA FORMS BASED ON NON-PROJ. SOURCES	ANNUAL	SEMI-ANNUAL	QUARTERLY	
LEVEL I Descriptive Evaluation	X			X			X
LEVEL II Effectiveness Eval.	X	X	X		X		X
LEVEL III Intensive Evaluation	X	X	X			X	X

*Basic-Shared Data Forms include the AJD Monthly Financial Statements and a number of AJD and RPU Modules for Quarterly Progress Reports.

TABLE 1. SUMMARY OF DATA SOURCES BY LEVELS OF RPU EVALUATION EFFORTS

SUMMARY

The RPU information system consists of Monitoring and Impact Assessment Components of a comprehensive evaluation structure. It is designed as a systematic process which is feasible and pragmatic. Effective utilization of such a system will yield benefits to program planners, staff and clientele of action projects, project monitors and funding agency administrators. It will not solve the problems of crime and delinquency; but it will contribute to the quality control of and enlightened planning for action projects directed toward crime and delinquency.

Caesar Hill and Chester Bowie
Survey Statisticians
Business Division
Bureau of the Census
Washington, D.C.   20233

A SURVEY OF COMMERCIAL BURGLARY AND
ROBBERY IN COMPTON, CALIFORNIA - 1974

This is an abridged version of a paper that provides
a detailed description of the methodology used for the
special commercial victimization survey conducted by
the Bureau of the Census for the Law Enforcement
Assistance Administration (LEAA) in Compton,
California during the latter part of the summer of 1974.
The paper's usefulness lies not only in the fact that it
presents a summarization of the technical and operational aspects of the Compton endeavor but it is indicative
of the kinds of special efforts that can be undertaken in
selected areas where the mechanics, materials, and
expertise already exist in a larger surveying framework; such as the one maintained by the Census Bureau
for conducting the current monthly National Crime Survey.

INTRODUCTION

In recent years there has been an increasing interest in crime
in the United States as the population has become wary of being
victimized. Daily media accounts of murders, robberies, thefts,
burglaries, and assaults perpetually add to this climate.

The Law Enforcement Assistance Administration (LEAA) of
the U.S. Department of Justice has, as one of its roles, the
authority to provide timely data on crime and its impact on
society through reliable statistical programs. However, administrative statistics are not enough since many crimes are not
reported to the police. In addition, administrative statistics
cannot provide the demographic and socioeconomic framework
necessary to the understanding of the broad impact of crime.
Therefore, original and special type efforts must be employed
to produce viable quantifications of crime victimization as it
pertains to the general public. One of these initial special
efforts took place in September of 1974. The Bureau of the
Census conducted for LEAA a victimization survey of businesses
in Compton, California to gather information about the commercial crimes of burglary and robbery in that city.

For a city of its size, Compton, California is perhaps a most engaging and logical choice for a special crime victimization survey mainly because there had been some national attention drawn to its relatively high crime rate, reportedly the highest of any city of its size or larger in the country.

In California, Compton is called the "Hub" City because it is situated geographically in the center of the general area most commonly known as Southern California. Compton is a chartered city with a council-city manager form of government. However, it is also a city struggling to overcome a number of socioeconomic drawbacks, of which unemployment and adverse publicity concerning crime and the local government seem to be main contributors.

This survey was planned as a baseline measure of common crime (burglary and robbery) prior to the implementation of major efforts to reduce crime in that general locale. The Compton program is intended to serve as a model effort by LEAA to explore various citizen initiatives aimed at the crime problem and its solutions.

The data from the victimization survey will thus be definitively analyzed for purposes of understanding the character and distribution of crime in Compton as part of the planning task for targeting specific crime reduction efforts.

The data will further be used by LEAA to establish a "before" measure of the volume and rate of victimization. A follow-up survey in Compton to establish an "after" measure, will likely be conducted, though the exact timing and other details have not been decided as of this writing. The National Commission on Criminal Justice Standards and Goals has recommended this approach--i.e., victim surveys using general population samples conducted prior to and following the implementation of action programs to reduce crime -- as the only valid approach for measuring whether, indeed, common crime rose or fell during the action program period.

In addition, the data are intended to be used by the local law enforcement, judicial, and correctional agencies in conjunction with existing crime reporting methods to determine which kinds of crimes are being committed against which segments of the Compton business population, thereby enabling these agencies to put their resources where they will be more effective.

The Commercial Crime Victimization Survey conducted in Compton focused on measuring robbery and burglary incidents relating to the business operation during a 12-month reference period preceding the interview (September 1, 1973 thru August 31, 1974). Measurement of other important types of commercial crime (employee theft, shoplifting, vandalism, etc.) were not included in the survey because these types of crimes were deemed not subject to accurate statistical measurement using the Bureau's surveying techniques which have been developed to date.

In order for a business establishment to be enumerated, the operations had to be at a permanent facility, such as a permanent building or a permanent vending stand. All business establishments (listable) within the corporate limits of Compton were interviewed except for the following (nonlistable):

1. Establishments engaged in Agricultural Production
2. Foreign, Federal, State, and Local Government, except government owned liquor stores and transportation establishments.
3. Unrecognizable Businesses conducted in Private Homes
4. Construction Sites
5. Unattended Coin Operated Machines (Vending Machines)
6. No - Charge (free) Facilities

The original estimate of total cost for conducting the Compton project was $39,645. A summary of the actual expenditures at the completion of the survey amounted to $41,501.

SAMPLE DESIGN

The results from the current Commercial Victimization Survey programs for selected large cities are based on the area sample surveying techniques as commonly used in the current business programs of the Bureau. Normally the establishments in a pre-determined group of designated land segments located within the particular city boundaries would be surveyed and appropriately weighted to arrive at aggregate estimates for the city. However, because of the manageable size of the commercial universe in Compton (about 1250 business establishments), the accessibility of surveying material and experience, and the available funds, it was decided to conduct a complete canvass of all commercial establishments located within the city limits.

An up-to-date map was obtained from the Compton Chamber of Commerce showing the official boundaries. This map was divided into 15 workable enumeration districts or assignments by the Field Division. The respective enumeration districts were further divided into 4, 5, or 6 working segments depending upon the expected number of interviews in each. The Statistical Methods Branch of the Business Division then assigned a pseudo-segment number to each segment parcel for tabulation purposes. Overall, the city of Compton contained a total of 74 segment parcels.

REPORT FORMS

The Law Enforcement Assistance Administration requested that the Business Division begin planning for the Compton Survey in June 1974, with summary results to be ready as quickly thereafter as possible, preferably by the end of the year 1974.

Therefore, in order to meet LEAA's schedule for conducting the survey, it was decided that the survey questionnaire (CVS-101) that was presently being used for the current Commercial Crime Victimization Survey - City Sample would also suffice for the Compton effort. Since the existing Office of Management and Budget (OMB) clearance for the CVS-101 covered the Commercial Victimization Surveys of all selected cities and had not yet expired, additional requests to OMB were unnecessary and the report form could be used immediately in the Compton survey.

For the actual collection phase of the survey, three basic forms were used.

1. The CVS-101 Questionnaire

   The CVS-101 was the basic questionnaire used in the interview. This form contained the questions asked of the respondent, and spaces were provided for recording the answers directly on the form. A separate questionnaire was used for each establishment interviewed. The questionnaire covered a 12-month survey period. The main parts of the questionnaire with an explanation of their intent and use are as follows:

   A. Part I -- Business Characteristics
      This section contained questions which enabled the interviewers to classify the business establishment as Retail, Wholesale, Manufacturing, Real Estate, Services, or Others.

   B. Interviewer Use Only Item
      This item was designed and used as a record of interview or the reason for any noninterview.

   C. Part II -- Screening
      These questions were used to find out whether any incident of burglary or robbery had occured at the business establishment during the 12-month reference period; if so, how many had occurred; whether there was insurance coverage for burglary and for robbery; and what security measures were used by the establishment.

   D. Incident Report
      This section was used to obtain detailed information about any burglary, attempted burglary, robbery or attempted robbery that occurred at the establishment during the survey reference period.

2. <u>CVS-110, Segment Folder</u>

The CVS-110 Segment Folder was used primarily as a device to list and identify all listable businesses in each of the special segments. The segment folder contained a map of the segment, pages on which to list establishments located in the segment, and space for recording other pertinent information about the segment.

Section V of the segment folder provided space to list and record identifying information for any "listable" commercial establishments the interviewer encountered as the segment was canvassed.

3. <u>CVS-120 Sales/Receipts Flash Card</u>

The flash card which contained annual sales or receipts size categories was given to the respondent when question eight of the CVS-101 questionnaire was asked by the interviewer. The respondent was to indicate the sales interval category into which his particular business should be placed.

The flash card procedure minimized the necessity for the respondent to verbally announce information about his total business sales or receipts. This information would normally be considered confidential or sensitive.

<u>DATA COLLECTION PROCESS</u>

1. <u>The Area Office</u>

In order to collect data for the Compton Commercial Victimization Survey, a temporary area office was established in the city for the duration of the program. The entire office operation was under the direction of the permanent Census Regional Office responsible for the area (Los Angeles). The organization and operations here were patterned after those which were used for enumerating the other cities in the National Crime Panel Program.

The Compton office was staffed with one area supervisory clerk, an office clerk who also served as an edit clerk and one reinterview clerk. The field or "outside" staff consisted of three crew leaders and 15 interviewers. Free space for office quarters was obtained at the Willowbrook Branch of the Post Office in downtown Compton.

The Compton Area Office Organization Chart

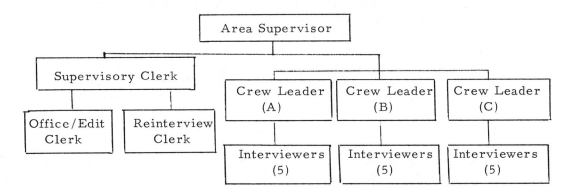

For purposes of establishing and operating the area office and training field personnel, the manuals, training guides, and control forms which were designed and developed by the Cross Surveys Branch of the Business Division and the Field Division's Staff for use with the City survey programs, were utilized. These included the following.

A. Interviewer's Initial Self Study -- a home-study program designed to introduce interviewers to the survey's basic concepts, forms, and interviewing techniques. The interviewers received this self-study about one week prior to the scheduled classroom training.

B. Interviewer's Manual -- A reference book that explained interviewing procedures, definitions and forms, and generally used as a guide for field enumerating.

C. Crew Leader's Manual -- a reference manual compiled to familiarize the crew leaders with job tasks and responsibilities, survey concepts and interviewing procedures.

D. Area Office Manual -- This manual gave instructions on how to establish the area office, and specified the job duties and responsibilities of the area supervisor as well as the rest of the office personnel.

E. Training Guides -- special training instructions were provided for all levels of the training operation.

As in other cities, the Compton interviewers and crew leaders were local people recruited through various community sources. The most frequently used sources included newspapers, unemployment offices and, to a minor extent, referrals. As a final test of acceptance, each interviewer and crew leader had to pass the Standard Field Employee Selection Aid (FESA) test - a written profile type examination composed of 35 basic knowledge questions. Twenty-three, or 65.7 percent correct responses were considered a passing score. Since

there is a significant number of Spanish speaking business enterprises in Compton, it was necessary to assure that some of the
interviewers and at least one of the crew leaders were able to
converse in the Spanish language.

The training of personnel for Compton was conducted during
August of 1974 either in the Regional Office or in temporary free
space acquired in the city of Compton. The Area Supervisor
completed the Interviewer Self Study and made himself familiar
with the Area Office Manual for his training. Each crew leader
completed the Interviewer Self Study before attending the crew
leader training session. This training consisted of two-day
sessions conducted by the Area Supervisor.

Interviewers completed the home-study package before they
attended classroom training. They attended a one-day classroom
training session. Each crew leader trained his crew of interviewers
using a verbatim training guide supplied by the Washington office.
Additional training was conducted for replacement interviewers
throughout the enumeration period.

Most of the office clerk's training was of the "on-the-job"
variety. In preparation for editing, however, the clerk also attended
the interviewer classroom training session.

For the enumeration process, each interviewer was assigned
about 100 establishments to interview in one or more segments as
close as possible to his own residence. The entire enumeration
task was scheduled to be completed within 15 days after the initial
training. With this intended acceleration, the rapid completion of
small assignments and interviewer turnover caused a continual
shuffle of assignments. Competent interviewers who finished their
assignments quickly either helped slower interviewers or completed
assignments of interviewers who had resigned or just plain stopped
work.

In an operation such as this one which is at best temporary and
of short duration, the work force control requires the utmost in
supervisory and crew leader effort. This is essential for the sake
of quality of results.

Throughout the enumeration period, the interviewers were subjected to the following quality checks of their operations and work
submitted:

A. Reconciliation of Interviewer's and Crew Leader's Listings --
    Crew leaders prelisted a portion of each interviewer's assign-
    ment prior to the interviewer's training. When the interviewers
    began their work, they first listed the segment which the crew
    leader had prelisted. A reconciliation of the two lists was then
    used to determine if the interviewer was qualified to continue
    on the job.

B. Observation on the job followed initial training and the prelist reconciliation. Each interviewer was observed for at least a half day by the crew leader. All observation was completed within a week of training.

C. Review of Work by Crew Leader -- Each crew leader met with interviewers at least four times during the survey period, or more frequently as required to pick up completed work. She performed an extensive review of the questionnaires and segment folders before turning them in to the area office.

D. Area Office Edit -- All questionnaires returned from the interviewers were edited for completeness and accuracy according to detailed clerical edit specifications. Any item which could not be corrected or resolved was circled in red pencil for follow-up.

E. Recheck/Reinterview -- As another measure of quality control, a recheck/reinterview program was instituted. This procedure was necessary to evaluate the interviewer's performance in listing and interviewing. Ten percent of the segments were selected for recheck/reinterview. This selection rate included all of the interviews contained in the segment. However, a maximum of only one segment for any one interviewer was rechecked/reinterviewed. Crew leaders performed the recheck/reinterview near the end of the enumeration period. Segments were selected by the Business Division after the initial assignment had been made in the area office. The determination of which segments and which interviewers were to be included in the recheck-reinterview procedure was made by the Washington office. Selected segments were further subsampled by the area office to determine which listings were to be reinterviewed. This selection rate represented about 20 percent of the listings contained in the selected segments. Recheck/reinterview was not conducted if the selected segment had been previously prelisted or observed by the crew leader, since this would have been a duplication of effort and would have resulted in unnecessary additional respondent burden.

Materials were furnished to the crew leader for the recheck of all listings in the selected segment and the reinterview of selected establishments within the segment. After each reinterview, answers differing from the original and reinterview questionnaires were reconciled with the respondent. The listing and interviewing errors were summarized, and the interviewer was rated on overall performance.

INTERVIEWS

For Compton, the owner or manager of the establishment was the person primarily sought to be interviewed and every attempt was made to get to that person on initial contact. If the owner or manager was temporarily absent for the interview period, or if the interviewer was unable to see the owner or manager during the interview period because of his illness or for some other reason, an interview was conducted with the assistant manager, an accountant who handled the company business, the senior sales clerk, or some other employee who was most knowledgeable about the business.

It was often difficult to arrange for an interview with certain types of owners, such as doctors, dentists, or lawyers. If an interviewer was unable to interview this type of owner, she was instructed to complete the questionnaire by interviewing the nurse, secretary, receptionist, or other employee who was most knowledgeable about the business. If the establishment was vacant when the interviewer canvassed the segment, it was accounted for by completing a report form describing the situation. Compton had a high ratio of vacant establishments, about one in four. There were usually very few noninterview cases where the business location was occupied. Generally, commercial establishments are actually easier to interview than private homes in terms of finding someone on the premises to interview. However, there were occasions when an establishment was closed for a month or two while the owner was on vacation. This was an unfortunate result of the survey coinciding with the peak vacation period of the summer. Then again, the business establishment could have been vacant, the owner could have refused to be interviewed, or the interviewer could not obtain a completed interview for some other reason. These cases, few in number as previously stated, were classified as noninterviews and the appropriate box was checked in Part I of the questionnaire.

Commercial noninterviews were classified into three goups -- types A, B, and C.

1. Type A noninterviews were those businesses for which information could have been obtained if an interview were possible. These noninterviews resulted from the following circumstances:
   A. The owner refused to give any information.
   B. The owner was in business at the end of the survey period, but could not be contacted.
2. Type B noninterviews resulted if a business was not in operation at the address at the time an interview could have been conducted. Reasons for these noninterviews were:
   A. The present occupant was not in business at the end of the survey period.
   B. The unit was vacant.
3. Type C noninterviews resulted if the address was no longer used for business. Reasons for Type C noninterviews were:
   A. The business had been converted to residential use.
   B. The unit was occupied by a nonlistable establishment.

C. The business structure had been demolished.

When an establishment was classified as a noninterview, only a few items (mainly for identification purposes) were filled on the questionnaire. For Type A noninterviews, items 1, 4, 6a, 6b, and 9b in Part I were completed. For Type B and C noninterviews, items 1 and 9b in Part I of the report form were completed.

Noninterview rates for the Compton survey were as follows:

Total Schedules	Completed Schedules	Type A		Type B		Type C		Total A, B, C	
		No.	%	No.	%	No.	%	No.	%
1,696	1,206	37	2	444	26	9	1	490	29

PROCESSING OF DATA

1. Clerical

The purpose of the clerical processing was to prepare the data for further computer tabulation and edit. This procedure consisted of two major operations: (1) clerical editing and (2) the keying of the data for transfer to magnetic tape. The primary purpose of the clerical edit was to locate and correct any interviewer errors. Such errors could only be identified by a clerical review of the questionnaires.

As a double check, the clerical review was done both in the field office and later in Washington.

The first step of the clerical edit was the check-in. The check-in was a control operation to insure the following:

A. That all questionnaires listed on the transmittal sheet were received and that each shipment was complete.

B. That the PSU and Segment numbers were correct.

The second step of the clerical edit was to sort the questionnaires into three groups based on incidents reported in Identification Code 1, g.1., page 1 of the questionnaires.

A. With incidents (1, g.1., greater than zero).

B. Without incidents (1, g.1., equal to zero).

C. Item 1, g.1. is blank.

The third step in the clerical edit was to check that all identification codes were complete.

The fourth step was to examine each page on the questionnaire for certain types of entries. Where these types of entries occurred, they were edited as necessary, using the established rules for the general edit. Some of the most common of these types of clerical entries are given below.

A. Numeric entries were made keyable (i.e., monetary entries were rounded to whole dollars; any zeros to the right of the decimal were deleted; where a range had been entered by the interviewer

($60-$70), the range was deleted and the average entered; etc.).

    B.   Write-in entries in "Other-specify" categories were examined to determine if they could be reclassified into a prelisted category.

    C.   If the interviewer had made a notation that the respondent answered, "Don't know", the "Don't know" category was checked for the item and the note was obliterated.

    D.   If multiple entries occurred where only a single entry was acceptable, the entries were edited according to instructions provided for them.

In addition, particular items were examined and edited as necessary. The most important of these are the two listed below:

    (1)   All identification codes must be completed for each questionnaire with incidents.

    (2)   Total numbers reported in Items 10-15 (screening questions) had to agree with the number in Identification Code 1, g.l., page 1 of the questionnaire.

    During clerical edit, special cases as well as any unusual situations identified by the clerks were referred for resolution to the professional analysts directly responsible for the survey review.

2. <u>Mechanical</u>

    Schedules were transmitted from the Business Division to Jeffersonville, Indiana (the Census Bureau's Data Preparation Division) on a flow basis for keying after the clerical edits. They were separated into two groups, those having incidents and those not having incidents. Schedules without incidents were transmitted in lots of approximately 200 and those with incidents in lots of approximately 75.

    The data were keyed on a key-to-tape device. A one-hundred percent verification plan was employed in order to assure an acceptable level of quality of keying.

    Following the clerical processing of the data, the computer processing was initiated. The processing began upon receipt of the tape file of keyed questionnaires. The major parts of the computer processing and analysis tools included in the output of data are indicated below.

    A.   <u>The edit, correction, and imputation program</u> - The general requirements and proper coding were specified for each question contained in the questionnaires. Tolerances were set for dollar value and the number volume questions. Those tolerances were determined according to the averages computed for questions from past experience of similar questions on the CVS National Survey. Control matches were done to insure complete coverage of the Compton area and that all reported incidents of burglary and robbery were indicated in the detail file.

    B.   Included in the computer processing were the procedures for the handling of <u>duplicate records</u> and the logical progression of answers determined by skip patterns on the report form (duplicate records occurred when two questionnaires had identical numbers).

C. The criteria essential for the classification of incidents were also included in the computer processing. There were seven categories, three of which were for burglaries and the other four for robberies, into which the incidents could be classified. The burglary classifications were forcible entry, attempted forcible entry, and unlawful entry. Robberies were classified as either strongarm robbery, attempted strongarm robbery, armed robbery, or attempted armed robbery. These reported incidents were classified according to certain key questions in the Incident Report which determined whether the incident was either burglary or robbery. For a burglary, these key questions ascertained whether there was an illegal entry, whether the offender actually got in or just tried to get in, and by what means the offender was able to obtain illegal entry. The answers to whether someone was present while the incident was occuring, whether the offender had a weapon on his person, and if any money and/or merchandise had been taken because of the incident, were the characteristics used to classify the reported incident as robbery.

D. Edit Cycles - Data tapes created in the Census Bureau's Data Processing Division in Jeffersonville, Ind., were received in Washington and computer processed so that the schedule records could be sorted, matched and edited. Cycle One (I) contained a listing of the input, a listing of all schedules in sequence; a reject listing of all cases that had failed edit, and a listing of the output of the computer edit. The reject listing contained the cases that had failed edit, such as; incorrect or missing segment or line numbers, items that exceeded tolerance limits, and inconsistencies in skip patterns. Also received in the Cycle I run was a list of duplicate records and a list of schedules with unmatched incidents.

Cycle Two (II) was a correction cycle with outputs that indicated where missing data were inserted or inaccurate data were corrected. Cycle Three (III) was the final correction cycle. By the time the data reached this cycle, all schedules were corrected. The imputation factors were compiled during this run.

After the final cycle was run and all corrections to the schedules were made, the output of the imputation subroutine and the final detailed listing obtained from running through the programs were used as the input to the tally program. This detailed file contained a listing of all usable reports. The data were then tallied using prescribed table formats, and finally printed in tabular form.

ESTIMATION PROCEDURES

The data records from the Compton survey were assigned composite weights, computed as discussed below. The weights consisted of the product of some or all of the following three components: (1) sample weight, (2) imputation factor, (3) part year imputation factor.

1. Sample Weight

The sample weight is the inverse of the probability of selection. Since a complete census of commercial establishments in the city was used, the sample weight for each establishment was one ("1").

2. Imputation Factor (Missing Reports)

The imputation factor was the total number of reports required for the imputation class (a kind-of-business) divided by the number of usable reports (schedules containing all "must" information for tabulation) in the class. The total number of cases required for a kind-of-business class was the sum of those eligible cases determined from the listing of the establishment in a particular segment.

3. Part Year Imputation Factor

The part-year imputation factor (12/N) was used for estimating 12 months of incident based upon part-year reports. The denominator (N) represents the number of months the establishment was in operation during the reference period. Thus, the part-year imputation factor would have a value of 4 if the establishment had been in operation for 3 months during the reference period. This factor was applied only to the incident reports, since an overstatement of the establishment count would result if it were applied to the establishment number (1). Therefore, the factor was used only to estimate full-year burglary and robbery incidents for part-year establishments with usable reports. The amount of incident creation depended on N, the number of months the establishment was in business. For example:

If N for the establishment was:	Number of additional incidents created
0-1	11
2	5
3	3
4	2
5, 6, 7, 8	1
9, 10, 11 or 12	0

The general assumption in this procedure is that the part-year rate of incidents is indicative of the entire-year pattern in addition to representing the contribution of those establishments that went out of business during the year.

4. Imputation for Missing Reports

Some schedules did not contain all of the "must" information, and were labeled missing or unusable reports. In
these cases, an imputation was used to adjust for the missing
information. Imputation for the Compton survey was accomplished by making adjustments to the weights of usable
reports. The weights used were the products of the sample
weights and the imputation adjustment factors. The sample
weights were all constant ("1"). The imputation adjustment
factors were computed by the following procedures:

Multiplying the sample weight by a factor equal to the
total number of reports required for a class divided by the
number of usable reports in the class.

This resulting composite factor was applied to the weights
of all usable reports in the designated class. No further use
was made of the unusable reports after this factor had been
computed. In order for this procedure to be applied, it was
necessary to define the class within which the computation was
made, and to determine how the numerator and denominator of
the imputation ratio were to be developed.

The class within which these computations were made were
kind-of-businesses classes at the Compton segment level. The
imputation factors were computed within each of the numbered
groups. However, it was necessary that the denominator of
each imputation ratio be nonzero (i.e., that there was at least
one usable report in the segment-KB class). If, for any
numbered group, there were no usable reports, then the group
was collapsed with other numbered groups in the same bracket
and the same type of computation was made for the collapsed
group.

The kind-of-business computation classes defined for
imputation purposes are as follows:

Retail Major Groups

1. Food
2. Eating and Drinking
3. General Merchandise
4. Apparel
5. Furniture
6. Lumber, Building, Hardware
7. Automotive
8. Drug
9. Liquor
10. Gas
11. Other Retail

Wholesale Major Groups

12. Durable
13. Nondurable

Manufacturing Major Groups

14. Durable
15. Nondurable

Real Estate

16. Apartments
17. Other Real Estate

Other

18. Service
19. Banks
20. Transportation
21. All Other

SUMMARY

Victimization surveys, such as the one described in this paper, are useful in supplying criminal justice officials with new insights into crime and its victims, complementing data resources already at hand for purposes of planning, evaluation, and analysis. The surveys subsume many of the so-called hidden crimes that for a variety of reasons, are never brought to police attention. They also furnish a means for developing victim typologies and, for identifiable sectors of society, yield information necessary to compute the relative risk of being victimized. Victimization surveys can also tally some of the costs of crime in terms of injury or economic loss substained, and they can provide greater understanding as to why certain criminal acts are not reported to police authorities. Conducted periodically in the same area, victimization surveys provide the inputs necessary for developing indicators sensitive to fluctuations in the levels of crime; conducted under the same procedures in different locales, they provide a basis for comparing the crime situation between two or more cities or other geographic areas.

Victimization surveys, whether localized, regional, or national in scope, are extremely useful as statistical tools. Though a victim survey can go a long way toward providing much-needed data for the criminal justice system, there are limitations to its use and practicality. An obvious limitation is the time required to plan and prepare for the development of a well-designed and well-executed victim survey, even at an accelerated pace as the attached operations flow chart points out.

Another inhibiting factor is the expense of a bonafide victim survey. Crime-specific victimization remains a fairly low incidence phenomenon so that statistically large samples must be selected and interviewed to produce reliable measurement.

In the case of Compton, however, because a complete canvass of all commercial establishments located within the city limits was conducted, and the full cooperation and receptiveness that was given to our efforts by the business community, we are more than certain that the results obtained in this survey give an accurate measurement of commercial burglary and robbery in that city for the period September 1973 thru August 1974.

* * *

Time-Operations Overview Flow Chart for Compton, California

Period
6/74 — Request from LEAA to conduct Survey

6/74 — Planning of Approach

7/74 — Preparation of Computer and Clerical Specs | Compile Survey Training Material for Field Personnel | Map Segmentation of Compton Area → Assignment of Segment Numbers → Reproduction of Field Work Copies of Maps

8/1 - 8/16/74 — Selection of Crew Leaders & Interviewers

8/10 - 8/19/74 — Establish Area Office

8/19 - 8/29/74 — Training of Crew Leaders & Interviewers

9/3 - 9/20/74 — Field Enumeration of Establishments

9/23 - 10/4/74 — Recheck Reinterview

9/11 - 10/18/74 — Transmittal of Report Forms to Washington

9/18 - 10/24/74 — Clerical Edit of Report Forms

10/25/74 — Keying of Report Forms

10/26 - 11/6/74 — Cycle I Edit | Cycle II Corrections | Cycle III Imputation

11/15/74 — Table Preparation

12/2/74 — Review and Transmittal of Tables to LEAA

-189-

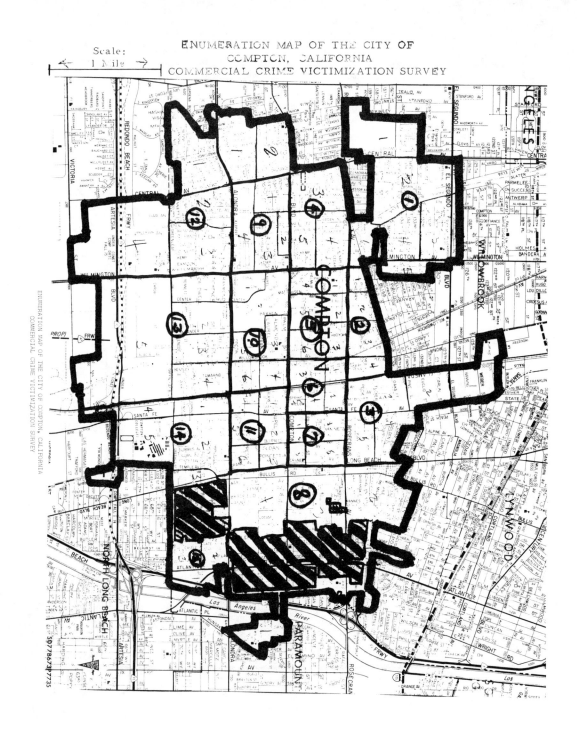

ENUMERATION MAP OF THE CITY OF
COMPTON, CALIFORNIA
COMMERCIAL CRIME VICTIMIZATION SURVEY

Scale:
1 Mile

Bill Sterling
Program Development Specialist I
N. J. Department of Community Affairs
363 West State Street
Trenton, New Jersey 08625

A MANAGEMENT INFORMATION SYSTEM FOR STATEWIDE HOUSING

CODE ENFORCEMENT IN NEW JERSEY

ABSTRACT: A unique approach to Housing Code Enforcement has been followed by the State of New Jersey, which has mandated State level housing code administration. By contractual arrangements with the State, the ability of local governments (94 municipalities) to perform inspections and solve code enforcement problems has been preserved and enhanced. This task is ideal for the application of integrated data processing technology to generate legal notices and to produce the nation's only statewide housing information base that is updated by on site inspections. This report presents an overview of New Jersey's recently designed system of statewide code enforcement. It is written for designers and users of computer assisted code enforcement systems, and covers: 1. Legal parameters, 2. Systems design, 3. File design, 4. Forms design, 5. Reports, 6. Operations, and 7. A look into the future of wide scale code enforcement.

INTRODUCTION

Housing code enforcement is normally performed only by the municipal level of government. Historically, cities alone have regulated the living conditions of their citizens, and generally they have found that this is a complex task. To do it well requires sophisticated managerial, technical, and legal abilities. Although several cities have done rather well at this task,[1] the general record of expertise that cities have gained at housing code enforcement is not high.[2] The critical problems a code enforcement agency must solve are:

1. Legal: It is difficult to prove on the witness stand that a housing violation exists. Most municipal code enforcement systems find housing inspectors on the stand facing sophisticated defense attorneys, as Levi points out in his monograph. (Note 2)

---

[1]See Journal of Housing, January 1975, for a look at the city of Cincinnati's Housing Code Enforcement System. Some other cities that appear to us to have exemplary code enforcement systems are Baltimore, Chicago, and Philadelphia.

[2]See Levi, Focal Leverage Points in Problems Relating To Real Property 1966, Columbia Law Review, pages 275 through 285. See also Teitz and Rosenthal, Housing Code Enforcement in New York City, pages 48 through 55, 57 through 58, Rand Institute, April 1971.

A MANAGEMENT INFORMATION SYSTEM FOR

STATEWIDE HOUSING CODE ENFORCEMENT

IN NEW JERSEY

A paper presented at the 1976 Urban and Regional
Information Systems Association Convention in
Atlanta, Georgia, on August 31, 1976.

By

Bill Sterling

2. Technical: Interpreting, updating and implementing code provisions requires significant training and analytical abilities in the fields of architecture and engineering.

3. Managerial: Training, motivating, deploying, and monitoring an inspection staff is a significant managerial task.

4. Informational: Recording, updating, integrating, and generating the vast amount of data relevant to a building's performance and the performance of the agency regulating these buildings requires the ability to manage information accurately and well.

The State of New Jersey has recognized that the resources to do this job are often lacking at the municipal level. In 1967, the legislature passed the New Jersey Hotel and Multiple Dwelling Health and Safety Law, which made housing code enforcement the clear responsibility of state government. Under the administrative system of the New Jersey Department of Community Affairs, which enforces to law, municipalities are given the option to participate with the state in a cooperative program wherein the municipalities are reimbursed for inspections they perform, and legal enforcement of the violations is done directly by the State.

Before designing the comprehensive data processing system which is the subject of this paper, the Department had seven years of experience in administering the statewide code enforcement law using only the most rudimentary data processing - essentially a manual system using a computer to type violation notices. Results were encouraging, but the sheer scope of the task (there are 100,000 buildings and almost a million dwelling units in the State that fall within the act) made comprehensive data processing essential. In addition, the Hotel and Multiple Dwelling Law sets up an iterative process, in which a building is revisited up to four (4) times in one inspection cycle to insure compliance. This very much strengthens the case for integrated date processing, for the continual management and updating of thousands of cases at a time.

In 1973 the Department of Community Affairs received an Urban Systems Engineering Grant from HUD to study statewide code enforcement in New Jersey. The results of that study will soon be available from HUD as a research report written by the Department of Community Affairs. We are presently in the process of implementing the study team's recommendation for a comprehensive integrated data processing system for code enforcement. The manual system is still in operation and is gradually being phased from its rudimentary status to a much more elaborate design which is described below.

NEW JERSEY SYSTEMS DESIGN

The Legal Parameters[3]

The Hotel and Multiple Dwelling Law requires the state to register all hotels and multiple dwellings in New Jersey, and to inspect all the hotels every three years and the multiple dwellings every five years. As mentioned earlier, most municipal code enforcement systems require the enforcement agency to establish in court the existence of violations in a building. The credibility of the inspector and the inspection agency are at issue from the first moment. The New Jersey law avoids this pitfall. It makes the compliance process an administrative one, not a judicial one, except against the

----

[3]For an overview of code enforcement in New Jersey viewed from a legal perspective see Sol A. Metzger, "Statewide Code Enforcement - New Jersey, The Test Case" Rutgers Law Review, Volume 27, Spring 1974, No. 4.

most intractable and sophisticated landlords, (where more advanced legal remedies provided in the law may indeed be required). Under the Hotel and Multiple Dwelling Law there is an escalating series of administrative fines levied against an owner, based on inspections and reinspections conducted by the State.

Each inspection causes a legal notice of violations to be generated and mailed to the owner containing the results of that inspection. After each such notice, the landlord has the right to a hearing before an impartial officer in the Department to protest the citations of violations. If the owner does not request such a hearing, the existence of violations is established as a matter of law.

To produce and manage this administrative compliance process, a mass of data must be manipulated. Following is a discussion of how we have organized information in the system.

GENERAL INFORMATION REQUIREMENTS FOR INSPECTION SYSTEM

It is useful to distinguish between two basic types of information necessary in a housing inspection system.

1. Identifying information about the building, information which changes little: the building's street address, the name and address of the owner, the type of construction, the number of dwelling units, etc. This information can be called "physical" information, because it directly describes the physical structure itself.

2. Information about the inspection and enforcement process that the code agency is conducting on the building: dates of inspection and reinspection, the name of the inspector, the amount of inspection fees, the dates of notice of violations and amounts of penalties assessed, a list of the open violations themselves, etc. This information changes relatively quickly and must be updated frequently. It may be called "process" information, because it describes the inspection process of the agency.

In our inspection system, both of these types of information are stored in the same place, on the Hotel and Multiple Dwelling Building Master file. This is the largest file in the system. Each record represents an individual building, with 1,000 characters per record, and there are approximately 100,000 records on the file. But the physical and process information are retrieved differently because they describe different areas of interest to management. The physical building information is printed four times a year on Computer Output Microfilm in a Building Master File report. This report lists the 100 or so items of information that are considered important to know about each building. This information is used constantly for reference by the inspection staff. The process information is printed weekly, but only for all buildings with active cases running. It appears on a Status of Open Cases Report, which gives the user the essential information on each open case without searching the manual property file where source documents are stored. (See Figure 2 for a sample of this report)

Thus, by using these two reports, the inspection staff has a complete look at all the physical description and inspection process data on a building. The section of the Bureau that is concerned with registering a building and getting it into the inspection process uses the first report; the section of the Bureau that manages the legal compliance process uses the second report.

With reference to information, we have found that there are several things a housing inspection system must do if it is to operate effectively:

1. The system must provide for unique address identification of each building. There must be an unambiguous set of rules for inspectors to follow in addressing each building (i.e., how to address corner properties), so that the building can be easily located and reinspected, and so that the office staff can easily distinguish among buildings in their records.

2. The system must be able to show when a building is part of a project (such as an apartment complex) for the purpose of deploying inspectors and conducting legal enforcement. We have handled this requirement by assigning to each building a 9 digit registration number, with the last three digits giving the number each building is in a project. A five building project has the same first six digits, and consecutive numbering in the last three. For example:

        123456-001
        123456-002
        123456-003
        123456-004
        123456-005

    If a building is not part of a project, the last three digits are zeroes. This keeps projects together and makes it easy to treat them as whole physical and legal entities. Failure to do this in the old inspection system resulted in considerable problems for the registration and inspection of buildings.

To summarize, in the information requirements of our inspection system, we have distinguished between information that is descriptive of a building, and information that is about the inspection process. In the area of physical information, we have found it necessary to take particular care to insure that each building address be unique and that projects be clearly identified.

THE STATE - LOCAL COOPERATIVE HOUSING INSPECTION PROGRAM:

SPECIAL INFORMATION AND ADMINISTRATIVE REQUIREMENTS

The State has designed its code enforcement program so that it does not preempt local control. Where local code enforcement programs exist, they are encouraged to join a cooperative housing inspection program with the State. Under this program, the municipality contracts to perform housing inspections under the State code, for which they are reimbursed at a set amount for inspections and reinspections. The inspection reports are sent to the State which process violations and penalty notices, and conducts the legal compliance process. As reinspections become due, reinspection documents are sent to the municipality to be performed.

This program, while it benefits both the State and the municipalities (there are presently 94 enrolled in the program) in many ways, also imposes special management and information requirements:

1. Keeping the municipalities advised of the status of each case in the administrative process has not been possible without a comprehensive information system. Under the new system, the Status Report of Open Cases is given to each municipality in the cooperative program. This serves to keep them up to date on administrative actions and enables them to answer questions from local owners and tenant groups.

2. Productivity gains in the cooperative program have been difficult to achieve because:

   A. A level of bureaucracy intervenes between the State and local inspectors;

   B. Inspector performance has not been directly measurable.

The Activity Report by Inspector*will be a valuable tool for achieving management control in this program. We feel that just by making the information available to municipalities we will cause a significant increase in cooperative program productivity. As we gain experience in the new system, productivity and performance standards will be written into cooperative contracts.

3. Quick updating of the Bureau's building information is essential to give munici- palities confidence in the State data base. By contract, municipalities are re- quired to inform the Bureau of changes in building status. The new system pro- vides file maintenance forms that make the update function quick and reliable.

4. Standardized input format. With so many municipalities providing violation data to the system, it is essential to have a single, standardized method for reporting violations. This has been achieved in the new system through a coherent set of violation report forms. (See section on violation reporting)

Essentially the new system provides for a much higher quality of information flowing between the State and its contract municipalities. Input to the system is standardized and rapid. Output reports provide a wealth of data with which to monitor system pro- ductivity, performance, and to make this vast program efficient.

The Three Main System Functions

The system performs three main functions: automatic processing of notices and orders, a management information system, and a housing information system.

Automatic Notice Processing

The system automatically generates four types of documents:

A. registration notices

B. inspection violation notices

C. inspection fee notices

D. inspection and reinspection reports for the inspection staff.

Following is a summary of each of the above four processing sequences.

A. Registration

   When an unregistered building or a transfer of ownership is discovered, the system automatically notifies the owner of the requirement to register the building and follows up with two subsequent notices. If the owner still does not register, a Certificate of Judgment is generated which, when sent to the

*See Figure 3.

Superior Court, automatically gives the Bureau a lien on the building until the Judgment for registration fee and penalty is satisfied.

B. Inspection Violation Notices*

The schedule of violation notices is as follows:

Inspection --▷ First Notice: Notice of Violation and Order to Terminate

|
| 60 days to comply
|
▽

1st Reinspection --▷ Second Notice: Notice of Continuing Violations and Order to Terminate. Order to Pay Penalty for Failure to Terminate

|
| 30 days to comply
|
▽

2nd Reinspection ──▷ Third Notice: Notice of Continuing Violations and Order to Terminate, Notice of Daily Penalty Assessment

|
| 30 days to comply
|
▽

3rd Reinspection ──▷Final Notice; Final Notice of Continuing Violations and Order to Terminate. Order to Pay Penalty for Failure to Terminate

After the Final Notice, penalties continue to accrue daily, even though they are aggregated for collection at this point. When the final notice is printed, simultaneously a notification to the Deputy Attorney General is generated. The DAG serves as the Bureau's collection agent and this computer generated document gives him the facts he needs to prosecute under the New Jersey Penalty Enforcement Law to collect the amount due. While the Bureau's ultimate aim is termination of housing violations, the monetary penalties assessed are a powerful tool to win compliance.

C. Inspection Fee System

The New Jersey Law requires landlords to pay for maintenance inspections every five or three years. When an inspection report enters the system, an accounts payable record is set up for the amount of the inspection fee. The inspection fee is computed according to the number of dwelling units and a formula to modify the fee in the case of projects. The system generates a bill for the inspection fee and follows up with two reminder notices, including a penalty for failure to pay the fee. At the conclusion of this series, if payment has not been received, a notice is postponed if violations are open on the case until the violation notice sequence is completed for that case.

---

*A flowchart of this processing sequence appears as Figure 1.

VIOLATION NOTICES OUTPUT PROGRAM

FIGURE 1

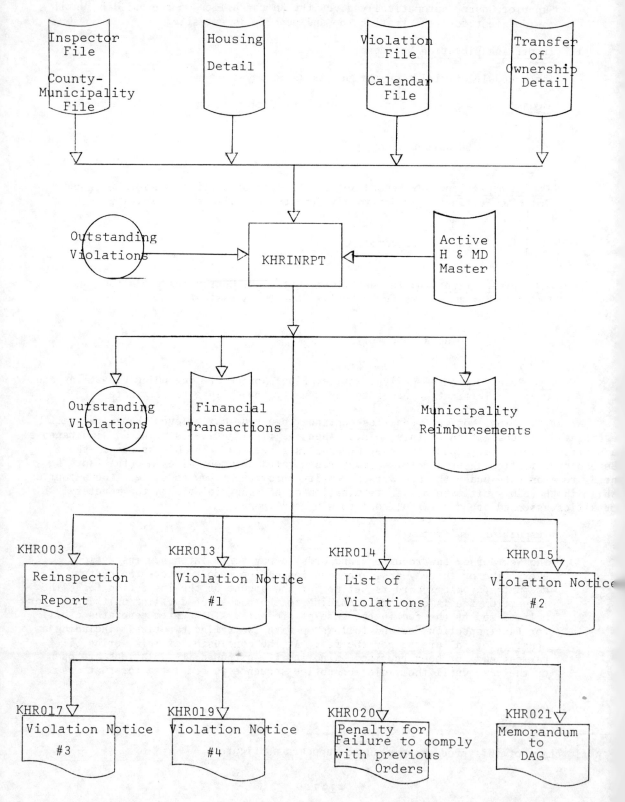

D. Inspection and Reinspection Reports

The first inspection in each 5 or 3 year cycle is generated from the Building Master File. If the completed inspection report does not return to the system in three months, a reminder message is produced on a monthly overdue cyclical inspection report. When the inspection does return, the first notice of violation is generated, and sixty days later the system produces a first reinspection report to the field.[4] This reinspection report is due in thirty days, and if it does not return on time a reminder message appears on an overdue inspection report. When the inspection returns, the system generates the next notice and waits thirty days before producing the next reinspection notice, which lists only the violations reported open at the last reinspection. This process is repeated for a maximum of three reinspections, after which the case goes to court if all violations have not been terminated. It is important to note that the above four sequences of system activity are integrated. The Building Master File is constantly referenced and updated, keeping all these processing sequences up to date. In the previous manual system, registration and inspection operations were carried on independently, creating separate data bases and difficulty in identifying buildings. Some examples of the integrated processing in the new system are outlined in the following sections.

Change of Ownership

When a new owner is found on a case in progress, the system is notified via file maintenance or an inspection report. The new owner is posted to the Building Master File with a subdigit to the registration number indicating that he is a new owner. The violation sequence stops wherever it is and reissues a new first notice of violations to the new owner containing all violations then open, and in sixty days another first reinspection is generated and the case continues. If inspection fees and/or violation penalties are owed by the old owner, the system continues to bill him for those and generates a separate form with an explanation of the previous owner's obligation. This collection case also goes to the Attorney General if necessary.

Upon discovery of a new owner the system also generates a Notice of Failure to Register to the new owner and pursues that registration sequence to its conclusion in court if the new owner fails to register. Thus, it can be seen that all four processing areas are involved in a change of ownership: violation processing, registration sequence, inspection fee sequence, and reinspection generation. Following are a few other unique capabilities that the system has.

Multiple Case Capability

Because the nature of housing inspection is to investigate and abate a deteriorating situation, (compare building inspection, which deals with a growing phenomenum) it is sometimes necessary on a reinspection to cite new violation which may not have been present at the previous inspection. Under the New Jersey law such violations become a wholly new case with independent notification and due process requirements. The system handles such violations as "Addenda Inspections." The inspector fills out a separate inspection report form after completing his reinspection document, and he codes it as an

---

[4]The capability for various "holds" is built into the system to be used when necessary to inhibit production of a reinspection report. See below.

addendum inspection. The system issues a first violation notice for the addendum inspection, and a second, third, or final notice, whichever is required, for the reinspection. The new case is timed independently of the first, but the system cross-references the cases automatically on reinspection and violation notice documents. It can handle up to four cases at a time in this fashion, including one or more complaint inspections.

System Holds

The New Jersey law requires that notices and orders be served upon owners by certified mail, return receipt requested. The signed receipt, in the event that court action is required, is the Bureau's proof that these notices and orders are legally served. It is our experience that roughly 5% of the Bureau's notices do not produce return receipts because of changes of ownership, post office error, or inaccuracy in our address record. Whenever proof of service is not obtained, it is necessary to obtain a correct owner name and address and re-serve the notice on him. It is also necessary to update the timing sequence for reinspection and subsequent notices, since owners receive fixed time periods in the Hotel and Multiple Dwelling law after legal notification of violations in which to repair these violations before the Bureau reinspects.

Therefore, the new system has the capability to put a case on "hold" whenever service is not effected on a notice - or for any other good reason. (Failure to have this ability in the previous manual system resulted in many reinspections which had to be redone.) By file maintenance, the system is notified to hold up a case while we research the problem in a special clerical sub-routine called "Owner verification." When the correct information is obtained (about 20% of the time a new owner is found) the new data is input and the system proceeds to count down for the next reinspection. If a notice has been lost, it can be reconstructed through a special program to reprint any violation form. If we fail to take a case off hold in thirty days, a reminder message comes out on an overdue hold report.

As can be seen, the automated processing system generates a large amount of information for its own use. Our experience with the previous system showed us that the most effective control of such a system comes from using the information required in the processing of work to report on work done, rather than in having separate work reports from operating people. The next section describes how this is achieved in our system.

MANAGEMENT INFORMATION SYSTEM

The scale and complexity of code enforcement in New Jersey makes it essential to have a large amount of management information readily available on a timely basis for the control of operations and for use in long range planning. There are seven reports in the system that provide this capability for us by making use of the process control information on the Building Master File that was mentioned in the first section of this paper.

1. Status report of open cases - Weekly

    This report tells where a case is in the administrative system at any given time. Figure 2 is an example of this report. The number of days between inspection date and notice allows us to monitor the turnaround time of field documents. Total days open is the time between the inspection date and the date of the report, to show how efficiently the case is being handled. The status field tells if the case is running or on hold. Examples of possible "last actions" are: cyclical inspections assigned, first notice sent, first reinspection assigned, second notice sent, etc. Examples of possible "next

FIGURE 2

Status Report of Open Cases with Violations

Region Municipality

X   XXXXXXXXXXXXXXX

Registration #	Building Name & Address	Total # Units	Insp. Date	# Days Between Inspt. Date & Notice	Type Insp.	Total Days Open
XXXXXX-XXX		XXXX	XX/XX/XX	XXX	X	XXXX

Status of Case	Last Action	Date Last Action	Next Action	Date Next Action	Days Since Last Action
XXXXXXXXXXXXXXXXXXXXXXXXXXXXXXXXXXXX		XX/XX/XX		XX/XX/XX	XXX

Penalty Points

	Total	Per/Unit Average
Original	XXXX	XXXX
Present	XXXX	XXXX

Statistics at End of Report:

Average # Days between Inspection/Reinspection & Notice Issuance

Cases Hearing Hold _____ % of Total _____   # Cases Registration Appl. Sent _____ % of Total _____
Cases Service of Process Hold _____ % of Total _____   # Cases No Jurisdiction _____ % of Total _____
Cases Administrative Hold _____ % of Total _____   # Cases Demolished _____ % of Total _____
1st, 2nd, 3rd, & 4th Notices _____ % of Total _____   # Cases Vacant _____ % of Total _____
Cases Violations Terminated _____ % of Total _____   # Cases Error Document _____ % of Total _____
Cases Certificate of Insp. Sent _____ % of Total _____ # Cases Legal Disposition _____ % of Total _____

actions" are: generate first notice, compliance date (date on which the owner must repair violations - also the date <u>after</u> which the Bureau will reinspect), generate second notice, etc. The panalty points field original and/present, tells us how we are proceeding in getting the building repaired from reinspection to reinspection. This amount should lessen as the case proceeds to conclusion. The average penalty points per unit is a field which tells us how bad the building is relative to the Standard Housing Code used throughout New Jersey. We see it as a numeric index of housing condition, something that has been deeply needed in housing policy planning for many years (see section on the Housing Information System).

2. <u>Case Disposition Report</u> - Monthly

When a case is closed, it is removed from the open cases report, and it appears on the case disposition report. There are six possible reasons for closing a case:

A. no jurisdiction - owner may convert his premises and no longer be within the definition of the act. Case is recycled for one year to check for reconversion.

B. building demolished - removed from Bureau's master file.

C. building vacant - recycled one year to check for re-occupancy.

D. closed for legal disposition - case is sent to court and recycled for next cyclical inspection.

E. administratively closed - compliance officer must sign source document and insert in file with reason for closing.

F. certificate of inspection sent - all violations are removed and fees and penalties are paid.

3. <u>Bureau Effectiveness Report</u> - Monthly

This report gives statistics on the Bureau's operation of the past year in three month increments. It includes: number of cases started, number of cases where no violations were reported, number of cases terminated at third reinspection, number of cases no jurisdiction, number of cases building demolished, number of cases building vacant, number of cases inspection certificate issued, number of cases legal disposition, number of cases remaining open. All of the possible case actions are listed here, and by looking at this report it is possible to determine how cases are being administered over time, and whether the Bureau is being effective at its main task, termination of housing violations.

4. <u>Activity Report by Municipality</u> - Monthly

This report enables us to monitor the effectiveness of the municipalities under contract to the Bureau to do inspection work (see the section on the State Local Cooperative Housing Inspection Program). It enables us to tell how many inspections and reinspections a municipality has performed, how many violations are cited in total and per dwelling unit, how many inspections the municipality makes where no violations are reported, the number of violations terminated at each reinspection, the percentage of overdue work, (work assigned by the Bureau but not yet returned) and how accurate the owner information given to us by the municipality is in permitting service of process. This report gives all the information needed for the State to effectively manage a municipality's contractual responsibilities. It allows identification of trouble spots in comparison with other municipalities and with the Bureau's own record. (Buildings not in cooperative municipalities are inspected directly by the State, for which this report is also generated as a means of measuring the State's operating effectiveness.)

5. Activity Report by Inspector - Monthly

There are 45 State inspectors and 300 municipal inspectors in the system. We feel that this report helps a great deal in planning, directing, controlling and coordinating their activities. (Figure 3) Without any additional reporting by the inspector other than his violations report, the system will show a significant amount of information about each inspector's activity. The reports can be used for comparison among inspectors, and most importantly, to develop work standards as we gain experience in the operation of the new system.

6. Overdue Reports - Monthly

As mentioned earlier, the system monitors all activity due dates and generates reminder messages when work has not been received. There are overdue reports for:

      scheduled cyclical inspections - 90 days
      reinspections - 30 days
      system holds - 30 days
      scheduled hearings - 90 days

The information in the above reports is designed to allow the Bureau to manage itself, its municipalities, and its inspectors effectively and efficiently. There is also data in the system on New Jersey's housing stock which can be useful to planners and policymakers if it can be retrieved in a form that is useful to them. We feel that our inspection system offers the beginning stages of a realistic housing information system for the state.

HOUSING INFORMATION SYSTEM

It is generally conceded that there is a serious lack of high quality information on housing in the United States. The report of the President's Committee on Urban Housing, published in 1968, commented,[5] "Virtually all of the consultants to the committee report that they were severely limited in their efforts by the primitive state of construction and housing statistics in the United States."

There are two main types of information that policy makers seem to need about

---

[5]U. S. President's Committee on Urban Housing, A Decent Home, page 203, 1968.

FIGURE 4

Monthly Activity Report By Inspector

Inspector Name _____

Inspector #   XXXXXXXX_____

Total # Cases Active _____

Total # 1st Inspections Month____YTD____/Units Month____YTD____

                         Total Units in Buildings____

Total # 1st Reinspections Month____YTD____

Total # 2nd Reinspections Month____YTD____

Total # 3rd Reinspections Month____YTD____

Total # Inspections, No Violations____%____

Total # Violations cited Month____YTD____

Average # Violations cited per Dwelling Unit____

# of Violations Terminated at 1st Reinspection____/ % of open____

# of Violations Terminated at 2nd Reinspection____/ % of open____

# of Violations Terminated at 3rd Reinspection____/ % of open____

housing.[6] They need data on general housing characteristics: age of the housing stock, type of construction, available services like maintenance personnel, information on rents, vacancy rates, presence of elevators and the like. Secondly, they need reliable data on the quality of the housing, How good is it? How well maintained, safe, and sanitary is it?

Housing Quality

Attempts by the Bureau of the Census to measure housing quality have been disappointing. Their attempt to classify all housing units into 3 categories of sound, deteriorating, or dilapidated has been judged by many, including the Bureau itself, to be inadequate.[7] HUD's classification of units into standard and substandard merely redefines the Census' classification, and as Aaron points out, HUD's classification essentially provides plumbing statistics. Since 1960 the Census Bureau has only estimated housing quality, extrapolating from 1960 housing data by using correlations with demographic data.[8] Therefore, even today, policy analysts find themselves in the uncomfortable position of performing elaborate calculations on old data of very questionable accuracy - but in many cases it is all they have.

It appears that the main ingredient that has been missing from attempts to measure housing quality is a set of objective and measurable standards. We feel that in New Jersey we have such a standard in the statewide housing maintenance code under which inspections are performed. Under the State's new system, violations are derived directly from this housing code, and inspectors are given a manual that explains how to evaluate each situation objectively and how to assign clear severity levels to each violation. Thus, inspections may be conducted in a standardized, easily replicated way.

As mentioned above in the section on reports, the severity code in the system provides a quantitative method for evaluating housing condition. Total penalty points may be aggregated in many ways: by dwelling unit, by building, by municipality, by county, or statewide. We look forward in time to the establishment of a "Housing Quality Index" for the state of New Jersey as a primary social indicator of progress in the quality of housing. With this index it should be possible to tell how "bad" or "good" housing units, buildings, neighborhoods or municipalities are relative to a standardized statewide code. The level of detail in this analysis will be extremely fine, much finer than the sound - deteriorated - dilapidated evaluation of the Census. Trained housing inspectors are required to enter and inspect every multiple dwelling and hotel and check carefully every aspect of the dwelling unit that relates to the safe and sanitary condition of the residence. And none of the information in the data base will be older than 5 years; over 20% of it will be no older than 1 year.

Other Housing Characteristics

Policymakers also need to know about other characteristics of the housing stock. Typical questions are: how old are buildings, what are the types of construction

---

[6]See Jerry L. McGregor, Toward Improved Local Housing Assistance Plans, in Vol. I of the 1975 URISA conference proceedings, pp. 109-125 for an excellent list of variables.

[7]See Henry Aaron, Shelter and Subsidies, Brookings Institution, 1972, page 25 and page 200 through 201. See also Bureau of the Census, Measuring the Quality of Housing, working paper no. 25, 1967 for an extensive treatment of the subject.

[8]Aaron, Op. Cit., page 200 through 201.

materials, how many buildings have elevators, how many stories are they? What are average rents for each given type of structure? What is the vacancy rate per geographic area? Are units overcrowded, and how much? Much of the above information is in our system as a by-product of the inspection process, and it can be retrieved in any desirable form. Items like rents and vacancy rates (by units) are not presently available, but we are presently studying the feasibility of including them.

Thus, we look forward to building a significant housing data base for policy planning in the State, one that relies on primary source data from the State Housing Inspection Program.

The next section shows how violations are standardized and how they are reported.

VIOLATION REPORTING

Cyclical inspections are scheduled by the system automatically as each inspection date comes due based on its 5 or 3 year cycle. When a building's inspection is due, the system prints an inspection report form on which is listed all the relevant information that the inspector needs to know from the Hotel and Multiple Dwelling Building Master File. This form is shown in Figure 4. This is a continuous form generated by the computer. It also has "snap-set" construction permitting the inspector to send an original copy of each inspection to the central office and retain a carbon copy for his own records. The inspector is instructed to cross out any information that is incorrect on this form and write in the corrections. Corrections submitted by the inspector in this way will update the building master, and discrepancies in certain key fields generate a re-registration form to the owner. After the inspection report has been generated by the computer, it must return to the system in 90 days or an error message is generated on an overdue cyclical inspection report.

When the inspector completes this form, if there are violations to be reported on the building, he selects a violations report form for exterior and interior areas, reproduced here as Figure 5. This report is not computer generated but is available to the inspector as a snap-set form. To report a violation, the inspector makes a check mark in the appropriate severity code alongside the violation he is reporting. This both reports the violation and enters a severity into the system; he then checks the appropriate location codes alongside the violation, according to the manual of standard location codes with which he is provided. In printing a violation notice, the system references the violation and location files. Notice that some violations permit the inspector to record three possible severities and some permit him to record only one.

This form is designed in the order in which an inspector inspects a building. When he has completed his inspection of the exterior areas and the interior hallways and common areas, he selects a similar form for use in reporting violations in dwelling units. This form contains a place for the inspector to describe each dwelling unit in a unique manner such as "second floor front" or "apartment C." It also provides for a consecutive dwelling unit sequence number to be entered by the inspector for each dwelling unit in a building, which keeps violations together for reporting purposes.

There are some violations which may occur often enough to be coded, but which do not appear on either of these two printed forms. These violations are present on the file of violations in the system's memory, and the inspector may report them by taking another form designed for this purpose and entering their code number in the locations in which they occur. Furthermore, it is possible that the inspector may feel the need to write out his own violation to accommodate a situation that is not covered by any of the coded violations. Space has been provided on the above mentioned form for him to do this by writing in a violation with a special code number followed by a description of the violation up to 300 characters in length. In these cases, the exact data

PHH 001

NEW JERSEY BUREAU OF HOUSING INSPECTION
INSPECTION REPORT

FIGURE 4

Phase XXKHRW01

Card _____ of _____

Registration # |__|__|__|__|__|__|__|

Date Inspection Performed |__|__|__|__|__|

Date Inspection Scheduled |__|__|__|__|__|

Type Inspection

1 Cyclical
2 Addendum
3 Complaint
4 Registration

Track # (0-3) |__| |__|

Co-op Municipality |__|

Building # _____ of _____

Inspector Signature X _____

INSTRUCTIONS: FILL IN ITEMS THAT ARE BLANK, CROSS OUT INFORMATION THAT IS INCORRECT, AND MAKE CORRECTIONS DIRECTLY UNDERNEATH. PRINT CLEARLY WITH BALL POINT PEN.

Inspector # |__|__|__|

Supervisor Initial X _____

Project Name _____

Building Name _____

Building Address _____

State _____ Zip _____

Agent Name _____

Agent Address _____

State _____ Zip _____

Agent Telephone No. _____

Owner Name _____

Owner Address _____

State _____ Zip _____

Telephone No. _____

Operator Name _____

Operator Address _____

State _____ Zip _____

Operator Telephone No. _____

Region |__|

Municipality Code |__|__|

Block |__|__| Lot |__|__|

Use
1 Hotel
2 Seasonal Hotel
3 Multiple Dwelling

Owner Occupied Yes |__| No |__|

Ownership Transferred Yes |__| No |__|

Date Transferred |__|__|__|

Status
J No Jurisdiction
K Vacant
L Demolished

Type Construction
1 Concrete & Masonry
2 Steel & Masonry
3 Masonry Wall & Frame
4 Frame

Date Constructed
1 Before 1939
2 Between 1940-1949
3 Between 1950-1959
4 Between 1960-1969
5 After 1970

Number Stories |__|__|

Elevator Yes |__| No |__|

Units Inspected |__|__|

Units Total |__|__|

GENERAL VIOLATIONS

000 No Violations
101 Register Building
102 Provide Required Full Time Maintenance Personnel
103 Post Maintenance Personnel Sign
104 Seal Vacant Premises
105 Resecure Vacant Premises
106 Cease Occupancy — Deconversion
107 Occupancy Change Without Plan
108 Entry Refused — Building
Write-In Violations Attached

OFFICE

|__|__|__|__|__|__|
|__|__|__|__|__|__|

|__|__|__|__|__|__|

-207-

BUILDING ADDRESS

CARD # _____ OF _____

FIGURE 5

-R-005

REGISTRATION # _____

TRACK # (0-3) ☐

INSPECTION DATE _____

INSPECTOR SIG. X _____

INSPECTOR # _____

EXTERIOR AREAS

CARD CODE V2

VIOL.#	CHECK	DESCRIPTION	LOCATION
		NO VIOLATIONS	EB
		REMOVE DEBRIS	YD, RF
		REPAIR EXTERIOR STEPS	YD, PK, RF
		PROVIDE RAILS	ES, SW, PK
		REPAIR RAILS	ES, SW, PK
		WASTE RECEPTACLES	RF
		COVERS AT WASTE RECEPTACLES	RF
		4 FOOT POOL FENCE	YD
		REPAIR VENTS	BM, CE, RO
		REPAIR STRUCTURAL SUPPORT	PO, BL, RO
		PAINT EXTERIOR TRIM	EB, FR, RS, LS, RR
		POINT AND SEAL MASONRY	EB, FR, RS, LS, RR
		REPAIR SIDING	EB, FR, RS, LS, RR
		REPAIR MASONRY	EB, FR, RS, LS, RR
		REPAIR EXTERIOR TRIM	EB, FR, RS, LS, RR
		REPAIR GUTTERS AND LEADERS	EB, FR, RS, LS, RR
		PAINT FIRE ESCAPES	EB, FR, RS, LS, RR
		REPAIR FIRE ESCAPES	EB, FR, RS, LS, RR
		EXTERIOR DOOR LOCKS	EB, FR, RS, LS, RR
		REPAIR ELEC. SVC ENTRANCE	EB, FR, RS, LS, RR

INTERIOR COMMON AREAS

CARD CODE V3

VIOL.#	CHECK	DESCRIPTION	LOCATION
		NO VIOLATIONS	
		REPAIR FOUND. WALLS - STRUCT.	BM, CE, LO, CR, ST, CU
		REPAIR VENTS	BM, CE, LO, CR, ST, CU
		REPLACE WINDOW GLASS	BM, CE, LO, CR, ST, CU
		REPLACE DOOR GLASS	BM, CE, LO, CR, ST, CU
		PROVIDE ARTIFICIAL LIGHTING	BM, CE, LO, CR, ST, CU
		REMOVE RUBBISH	BM, CE, LO, CR, ST, CU
		INSTALL FIRE RESIST. CEILING	BM, CE, LO, CR, ST, CU
		REPAIR FIRE RESIST. CEILING	BM, CE, LO, CR, ST, CU
		PROVIDE FIRE RESIST. ENTRY	EB, CE, LO, CR, ST
		SEAL CRAWL SPACE	EB
		REMOVE INFESTATION	EB
		FLOOR NUMBER SIGNS	EB
		UNIT IDENTIFICATION	SR, LO, CR, BL
		INSTALL HANDRAILS	SR, 2F, 3F, 4F, 5F
		REPAIR RAILS	1F, 2F, 3F, 4F, 5F
		FIRE RETARD. OPENINGS - SHAFTS	1F, 2F, 3F, 4F, 5F, AF

INTERIOR COMMON AREAS

CARD CODE V3

VIOL.#	CHECK	DESCRIPTION	LOCATION
604		EXIT DOORS OPENABLE	1F, 2F, 3F, 4F, 5F, AF
620		EXIT SIGNS - MD	SR, CR, LO, CR, CU
621		CLOSET UNDER STAIR - PUBLIC	1F, 2F, 3F, 4F, 5F, AF
623		SELF-CLSNG. DISP. SHFT. DR. 1½	1F, 2F, 3F, 4F, 5F, AF
818		REPAIR DISP. SHAFT DOOR	1F, 2F, 3F, 4F, 5F, AF
502		POST EL INSP. CERTIFICATE	EL
503		ADJUST ELEVATOR STOP	EL
504		ELEVATOR MIRRORS	EL
218		PROVIDE UNIT SECURITY - MD	BM, SR, LO, CR, CU
314		MAKE WINDOWS OPERABLE	BM, CE, LO, CR, CU
315		PROVIDE SCREENS	ED, CE, LO, CR, CU
316		REPAIR SCREENS	EB, CE, LO, CR, CU
427		REPAIR DAMAGED FLOORING	SR, CE, BM, CR, CU
428		REPAIR DAMAGED WALLS	SR, CE, BM, CR, CU
429		REPAIR DAMAGED CEILING	SR, CE, BM, CR, CU
430		PAINT OR PAPER WALLS	SR, CE, BM, CR, CU
431		PAINT OR PAPER CEILINGS	SR, CE, BM, CR, CU
432		REPAIR DOORS	EB, LO, CR, ST, CU
433		REPAIR TRIM	EB, LO, CR, ST, CU
434		PAINT TRIM	EB, LO, CR, ST, CU
806		REMOVE DEAD WIRES AND FITTINGS	EB, CE, BM, CR, CU
808		PROVIDE HOUSE GROUND	BM, SR, LO, CR, CU
811		COVERS - JUNCTION BOXES	EB, CE, LO, CR, CU
812		ELEC. PANEL COVERS	EB, CE, LO, CR, CU
813		SWITCH AND OUTLET COVERS	EB, CE, LO, CR, CU
817		OVERCURRENT PROT. BRANCH CRT.	EB, CE, LO, CR, CU
818		REPLACE BROKEN ELECT. FIXT.	EB, CE, LO, CR, CU
819		REPAIR IMPROP. WIRING - FIXT.	EB, CE, LO, CR, CU
820		REPLACE BRKN. SWITCH OR OUTLET	EB, CE, BM, CR, CU
822		ELEC. INSPECTION	CE
505		OIL BURNER SWITCH	CE, BM
511		REPAIR HEATING PLANT	EB, LO, CR, ST, CU
512		POST BOILER INSP. CERT.	EB
514		REPAIR LEAKING PIPES	EB, CE, BM, CR, CU
516		HOT WATER HEATER PRESSURE VALVE	BM
707		PROVIDE BATH (ROOMING UNITS)	2F, 3F, 4F, 5F

INTERIOR COMMON AREAS - HOTELS ONLY

VIOL.#	CHECK	DESCRIPTION	LOCATION
624		EXIT SIGNS HOTEL	SR, CR, LO
625		PROVIDE DETEC./SPRNKLR/WATCHMAN	EB, CR, LO, AS
626		INTERIOR FIRE ALARM	EB
219		PROVIDE UNIT SECURITY - HOTEL	EB
		PROVIDE HOUSEKEEPING SERV. - HOTEL	

EXTRA VIOLATIONS ATTACHED CARD # _____ OF _____

entered by the inspector on this form appears on the violation notice for the owner.

For all of the coded violations, the inspector is provided with a manual which lists the code number of the violation, its long description and its short description, the citation from the Housing Maintenance Code from which it is taken, and an explanatory section of how and where to report each violation. Thus, by reference to the violations reporting forms, and the inspector's violations manual, it is possible for an inspector to inspect each building in a standardized way, while still retaining the flexibility to report unusual violations if he feels it should be necessary. We feel that this is an optimum way to compromise between the machine speed produced by standardization, and human judgment which is capable of taking into account a larger number of variables.

FILE DESIGN

Following is a description of the computer files in the system and how they function.

Hotel and Multiple Dwelling Master File

This file is the heart of the system and has been described earlier. Everything that happens to a building goes on this file, including registration, inspection fee, and inspection violation data. It can accommodate data on up to four cases (called "tracks" in the system).

County - Municipality File

Every municipality in New Jersey has been given a four digit code number, the first two digits of which represent the County in which the municipality is found. Inspection and violation data is stored on this file by county - municipality code number for use in generating the Activity Report by Municipality.

Municipality Reimbursement File

As explained earlier, cooperative program municipalities are reimbursed by the State for building inspections and reinspections and also for attendance at hearings given in the Department of Community Affairs. When an inspection comes into the system, reimbursement "credits" are added to this file to be drawn on by the municipality at a later date. If the Bureau finds that the inspection was not of acceptable quality, these credits may also be deducted.

Housing Detail

This file contains all abated violations in the system carried by registration number of the building they represent. It is a tape file, for use in generating year-end statistical reports, and also for regenerating any lost notices that may be required.

Financial Transaction File

All financial payments and credits and outstanding judgments relative to owners are carried on this file by registration number of the building concerned. The file is used in generating financial reports in the system.

Project File

This is a file of registration numbers of buildings which are part of a project indicating the total number of buildings in the project. It is used in generating output reports to the inspectors to inform them of how many buildings they should inspect for each project.

Transfer of Ownership File

Any transfer of ownership in the system sets up a record on this file indicating the new owner's name, the registration number of the building, and the case ("track") on which the transfer took place. This is a working file for the system's own use.

Cross Reference File

Since there are so many forms in the system (21 total) this file is used to create a report which is generated at every run of the computer to indicate by registration number the number of forms printed for each building in each computer run, so that they all may be mailed in the same envelope.

Outstanding Violations File

This file contains all open violations for every building in the system.

Violation File

This file contains a numerically coded list of all standard violations which can be reported by an inspector on a building. Every violation has: a code number; a list of possible severities (2, 5, or 9); a list of possible locations at which the violation could occur; a long description of the violation, which is printed for the owner giving him an explanation of the violation and what must be done to fix it; and a short description of the violation for the inspector's use on the reinspection document.

Location File

This file is a list of all the coded locations which can be used by the inspector in reporting a violation location.

Inspector File

The inspector file contains every inspector's name and a code number assigned to him. It also contains his supervisor's code number and performance data on each inspector for use in generating the Activity Report By Inspector.

OPERATIONS

The system is being implemented in a phased way, municipality by municipality. The first municipalities to transfer from the old system to the new one are non-cooperative program municipalities, which are inspected by state inspection teams. This gives us the ability to keep maximum control over the input during the test period. As a municipality goes on the system, all of its records and processing are done by the new system; the old system continues to run for municipalities not yet entered into the system.

For municipalities still on the old system, provision has been made to update information for the new master file, and the master file is being built municipality by municipality.

The system is run on a batch basis with keypunch card input for violations and file maintenance. Large output reports such as the Building Master File Report are produced on COM with a paper option for municipalities that do not have microfiche reading equipment. In the not too distant future, as more and more larger municipalities are phased on to the system, we anticipate going to an on-line system with a CRT display in the Bureau's administrative office, first for data retrieval, and then for file maintenance data entry. We will continue to enter violations, however, through a batch mode. The necessity for an interactive system is based on 3 factors; first, the output reports are large, and even on microfilm do not bear frequent replacement. Secondly, when the enforcement process is fully automated as it is under the new system, the necessity for information to be up-dated in real time will be felt. Finally, we envision the day in which the larger municipalities in New Jersey who are members of the cooperative program (such as Jersey City, Paterson, Newark) may be given on-line access to the data base through their own CRT facility, if they so desire. This step would represent the ultimate evolution of this EDP assisted code enforcement system, providing a network of up to date, integrated code enforcement facilities throughout the state.

CONCLUSIONS

In 1967 the State of New Jersey took the first step in producing the nation's first statewide code enforcement system by passing the Hotel and Multiple Dwelling Health and Safety Law. The realization of the administrative system called for in the law, has required the design and implementation of a comprehensive EDP administrative processing system with a strong MIS component. Critical pieces in the design of the above system were the development of a simple but comprehensive violation reporting mechanism, a data base in which all elements relative to a building are collected, a system of output forms permitting legal notification of an owner concerning violations in his building, and effective and detailed output reports which permit a monitoring of system activity. We feel that this is a state-of-the-art code enforcement system. It appears to represent the forfront of thinking in housing code enforcement both from legal and information technology perspectives. Most judicial commentators have agreed that an administratively based system of enforcement is required to come to grips with the decay of our urban centers; and clearly the kind of data processing utilized in our system has been called for by experts in the field for many years.

Because the problems and complexities of conducting code enforcement in our society are so great, we expect that other states will express an interest in raising the housing code enforcement function to the state level. We hope that our system will show the directions in which such systems should profitably move, and as we gain experience in this task we look forward to sharing it with all interested persons.

ACKNOWLEDGEMENTS

The system described in this paper results from the efforts of many persons. Much of the original system's design was done by Messrs. Jim Bydolek and Sol Metzger of the HUD funded Urban Systems Engineering Study team. The file design and programming were done by the systems and programming staff of the New Jersey Department of Transportation Data Center under the guidance of Messrs. Jim White and Mike Fitzpatrick. The staff of the Bureau of Housing Inspection were most patient and helpful under lengthy "study"; and finally, the system would not exist at all without the continued guidance, work, and detailed understanding of the Administrator of the Bureau, Mr. William Connolly.

Dr. Jeffrey P. Osleeb
Dr. Harold Moellering
Department of Geography
Ohio State University
Columbus, Ohio 43210

TRANPLAN: AN INTERACTIVE GEOGRAPHIC
INFORMATION SYSTEM FOR THE DESIGN AND
ANALYSIS OF URBAN TRANSIT SYSTEMS

ABSTRACT

A number of interactive graphic transit
planning systems have been proposed over
the past few years that rely on highly
aggregated data as input. TRANPLAN makes
the conceptual departure of utilizing
individual household locations and characteristics to determine viable transit
stop locations with the ultimate objective of designing and evaluating present
and proposed transit routes. Variously
defined individual sample populations
such as the disadvantaged, elderly,
university students, university employees,
etc. can be inputed into the system in
order to design transit routes to serve
the targeted population. Individuals are
assigned to potential transit stops on
the basis of the minimization of their
total walking distance subject to a
maximum walking distance constraint.
The operation of TRANPLAN is demonstrated through the use of a test data
set collected in Columbus, Ohio. The
basic operations of the system: node
allocation, node edit, and route design
are shown via figures generated by actual
operation of the system.

I. INTRODUCTION

During the past few years a growing number of cities,
recognizing their responsibility to move people cheaply
within their domain, have made an effort to revitalize their
existing mass transit systems or totally develop new ones.
Several analytical techniques presently exist to aid the
mass transit planner to systematically evaluate the necessary

decisions required to design or redesign urban mass transit systems. However, these techniques such as UTPS (1972) and RUCUS (Nussbaum, Kebibo and Wilhelm, 1975) are batch oriented producing voluminous printed output making them difficult to use or are interactive computer graphic laboratory experiments such as UTRANS (Gehner, 1973) that only handle limited problems and are expensive to use. Schneider (1974) provides a general overview of the latter approach to solving the problem. This paper describes an interactive computer graphic system, TRANPLAN, that has been developed to enable the transit planner to easily and cheaply simulate transit problems in order to effectively evaluate changes to an existing transit system or the design of a totally new one. For a discussion of an earlier batch oriented example see Osleeb, Moellering and Cromley (1975).

An objective of TRANPLAN is to aid in the development of an urban transit system to accomodate a moderate sized city of 50,000 to one million inhabitants. The expectation is that this transit system serves a maximum number of the potential riders who are willing to walk a maximum specified distance in order to be served. Additionally, a minimum number of transit stops are located to permit fastest movement along a route with minimal interference with existing traffic and the minimization of routes to provide a cost effective transit system that minimizes capital and manpower outlays.

This planning technique makes the fundamental departure of using individual household unit observations as its basic building block rather than aggregate traffic zones as have been used by other systems of this type. Starting with the individual permits the planner considerable flexibility in choosing his problem as well as the information and the type of parameters that can be inputed into the model. For example, a maximum walking distance between the individual's household or work place location and a transit stop location can be used in assigning individuals to their closest transit stop. Transit stops can be located to serve a targeted percentage of the population, however population is defined for the problem being solved. Routes can eventually be designed to include these transit stops in the transit system. That is, through the use of individuals, such characteristics of the population as origin and destination for their trip, trip type, age, sex, economic status, etc. can be specifically accounted for and used to design and evaluate mass transit routes.

Imbedded within TRANPLAN are a set of mathematical models that are essentially transparent to the user. These models allocate individuals to their best transit stop through the use of a linear programming technique, reallocates passengers to best alternative transit stops in the eventuality that the planner makes the decision to add a stop to or delete a stop from the system and provides graphic and numerical output to aid in the evaluation of a decision. The user need only interactively initiate a command to accomplish any of these types of operations. Additionally, the user can experiment with various route designs and evaluate each in a similar manner. All that the system requires of the user is to supply the necessary data, specify a set of parameters and make transit design decisions. The results of these decisions are almost instantaneously presented in a graphic and/or numerical analysis on the screen of the cathode ray tube terminal (CRT). The user then has the option of continuing the operation with this set of decisions, operating with a subset of these decisions or inputing a new set of decisions.

The data required for TRANPLAN are the origin and destination of a sample population of individual household trips and any demographic information concerning this sample population the user feels is necessary to solve his problem. For example, if the problem is to route buses to transport high school students to and from school, the household location of a sample of high school students who would potentially utilize such a transit system and their assigned school would be required.

Parameters the user can adjust include a tolerable maximum walking distance to a transit stop, the maximum number of individuals that are permitted to be assigned to a transit stop (to reflect, for example, park and ride limitations), and the percentage of the population that the transit system must accomodate. Once these data and parameters are supplied and the parameters specified, TRANPLAN is ready to accept the planning decisions to aid in solving the transit route design and evaluation problem.

II. COMPUTING ENVIRONMENT

TRANPLAN was developed on the Ohio State University IBM 370/168 which runs under OS and has a TSO partition size of 176k bytes. The system, with 3 megabytes of core storage, is capable of processing a number of batch jobs and supporting about 40 terminals under TSO simultaneously.

The CRT terminal chosen is a storage tube type due to the large amount of data to be displayed, relatively low cost and compatibility with standard I/O interface and terminal support routines. The current implementation of TRANPLAN is for the Tektronix family of graphic CRT terminals. Currently the terminals are interfaced with the mainframe computer via leased telephone lines operating at 1200 baud.

III. SYSTEM ORGANIZATION

TRANPLAN is a research oriented geographical information system which incorporates a number of analytical mathematical procedures for assigning individuals to transit stops and subsequently aid in transit route design. In order to allow the program operator/planner maximum flexibility in the choice of the sequence of commands specified, the system is designed as an interactive geographic information system. Such an interactive approach allows for an efficient division of labor between the decision making ability of the operator/planner and the numerical analytical capability of the computer. Therefore great care has been expended in designing an efficient and convenient man-machine communication (Foley and Wallace, 1974; Newman and Sproull, 1973). The man-machine communication is implemented here by use of a graphic cursor menu selection approach to give the planner direct control over the operation of the program. At appropriate places the planner can also enter numeric inputs as well.

The primary program output to the planner is a cartographic display image (virtual map) (Moellering, 1975a, 1975b) which graphically represents to the planner the numerical status of the internal data structure underlying the mathematical programming. These CRT map images are immediately available to the planner who has direct control over what information is displayed cartographically at any one time. Similarly, the planner has several additional output options available to him, which have a somewhat larger time lag to availability. The first is a printout command which at any time will produce a hard copy print of the complete numerical status of the system. He also has the option of requesting the system to generate plot instructions for producing hard copy plots of an image which is currently appearing on the CRT tube face. Both of these capabilities are useful for further analysis and report generation.

As mentioned above the data inputs for the system are actually rather straightforward: a point set of potential transit passengers, a point set of potential transit stops and a geographical base file (GBF) of cartographic drawing information. From these intital inputs a preprocessing program generates a distance matrix of all individuals to all stops and other internal files. A base Euclidean coordinate system must be chosen for recoding the x,y locations of the information in the above initial data inputs. The specific coordinate system is initially chosen by the planner when the problem to be solved is originally specified. The problem is simplified if all coordinates are in the upper right hand quadrant relative to the origin (i.e. positive). The potential transit passengers are a statistical sample of the target population to be served by the transit system and can be as diverse as an entire SMSA population, the disadvantaged, a university community, the elderly, or some other population of interest. Naturally the absolute size of the target population will directly influence the statistical sampling fraction. The potential transit stops can be defined by criteria specified in light of the problem to be solved. Generally a set of potential stops along primary and secondary arteries in the urban area can be defined for the input data. As the planner begins to solve the problem, potential transit stops can be added and deleted as required. The GBF is a skeletal set of transportation arteries in the urban area to provide the planner viewing the CRT screen with a geographical frame of reference, especially for working with windows. In the initial data collection the planner can choose any density of traffic arteries to be displayed, depending on the context of the problem. It can be seen that TRANPLAN is purposely designed to be very flexible and to accept a wide variety of data inputs, as suggested by the particular problem to be solved.

IV. A WORKED EXAMPLE

TRANPLAN has been used to design a bus transit system to serve the faculty and staff of The Ohio State University in Columbus, Ohio. A simplified example of the way in which this particular transit system was designed follows.

First, an employment tape from the Ohio State University with addresses as well as other demographic information was sampled to reduce the population to a more managable size, 516 individuals. This sample was geocoded to obtain x,y coordinates of individual household locations. Each x,y coordinate represents the origin of a potential passenger while the univeristy, designated by the letter U in the figures to follow, in each case represents the destination.

Next an initial set of 203 potential bus stops were located by their x,y coordinates. Traffic light locations on all primary roads were selected as the initial set of bus stops. A plus designates the location of these bus stops in Figure 1. In addition to locating the stops, a capacity constraint of 40 people was placed on the number of potential passengers that could be assigned to any stop.

Finally, a maximum walk distance constraint of two kilometers was imposed. The walking distance between each individual and each potential bus stop falling within the individual's walking distance constraint was stored. The individuals of the sample population were allocated to their closest potential bus stop so long as neither the bus stop capacity constraint nor the walking distance were violated. Figure 2 shows these allocations with a line representing an allocation to a potential bus stop and an x indicating those individuals that could not be allocated due to the violation of at least one of the constraints.

The immediate goal of the user is to add bus stops in order to serve a greater proportion of the population and to decrease the number of redundant bus stops to meet objectives

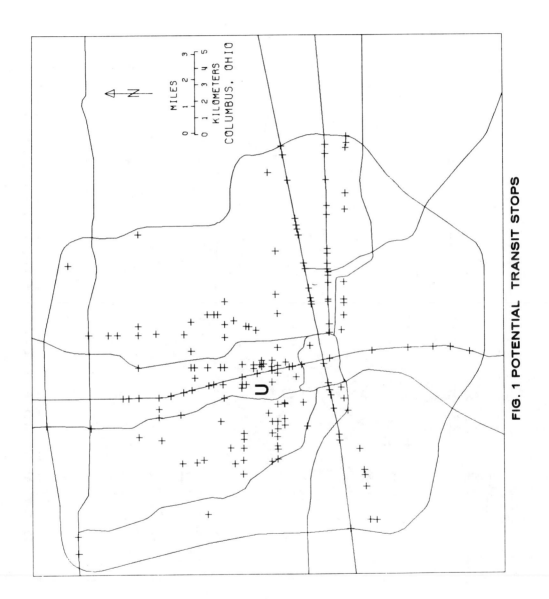

FIG. 1 POTENTIAL TRANSIT STOPS

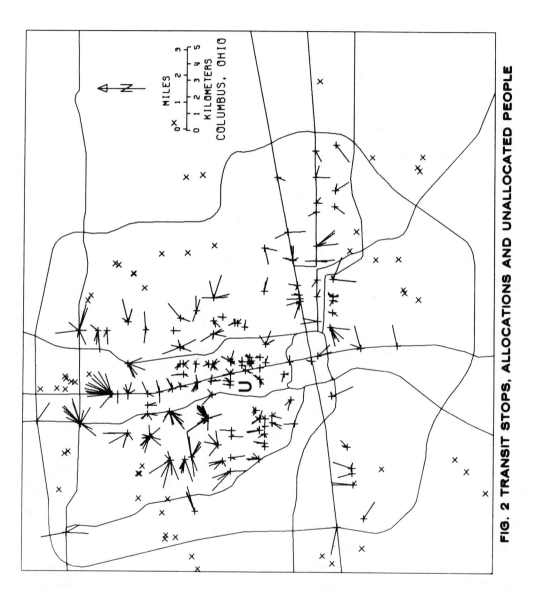

FIG. 2 TRANSIT STOPS, ALLOCATIONS AND UNALLOCATED PEOPLE

as stated in previous sections of this paper. To facilitate these operations, the city was arbitrarily divided into areas with each being operated upon separately. Figure 3 represents one of these areas, the northwest quadrant of Columbus, before any additions or deletions were carried out. Figure 4 shows this same area modified by new bus stops and passenger allocations. It should be noted that almost all of the unallocated individuals appearing in Figure 3 are now being served in Figure 4. Several diagnostics appear on the tube face to aid the user in making the necessary decisions as to where new bus stops should be located. When a new potential bus stop is tried, the number of previously unallocated individuals that are assigned to this stop is shown as well as the total walking distance for those people assigned to that stop. In this way by trying several configurations, the best set of bus stop additions can be chosen.

Next the total set of bus stops were reduced. Once again to facilitate operation a smaller area was used as shown in Figure 5, the near northwest area before the deletions were made. Again a set of diagnostics were presented to the user to help evaluate decisions. In this case the number of individuals who could not be assigned to an alternative stop after a bus stop deletion is provided as is the increase in total walking distance associated with those individuals who have been reassigned. Deletions were made to the bus stop set so as to minimize the number of bus stops while maximizing the number of individuals allocated to a bus stop. The results of this operation for the near northwest area are shown in Figure 6.

Similar operations were performed for all the areas of the city. The results of these operations for the entire city are shown in Figure 7. The bus stops shown in this figure represent the candidates for stops along the bus routes. At this point the proportion of the population being served by the bus stop set is presented. If this proportion is less than the targeted proportion, the above operations can be repeated conceivably with different geographic areas being defined to avoid boundary problems. In this case 95 percent of the sample population was served and was well within the targeted level.

Finally, the bus stops were connected into routes with the orientation of these routes being the university. The connections were determined according to the user's discretion with terminations being made to reflect standard bus operations. The set of bus routes for this problem are shown in Figure 8. To ensure that the routes actually follow the street network, an additional set of points is provided to indicate curves in the street system as well as the location of major street intersections.

This bus route configuration should be viewed as being only one of many possible configurations. The advantage of

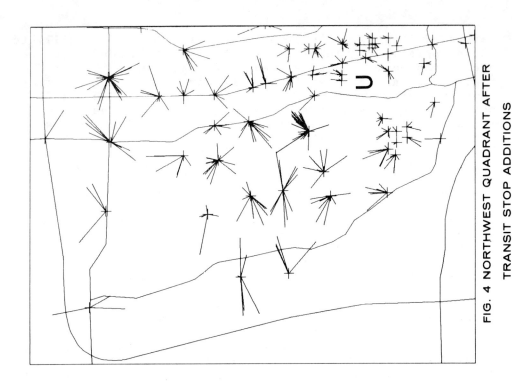

FIG. 4 NORTHWEST QUADRANT AFTER
TRANSIT STOP ADDITIONS

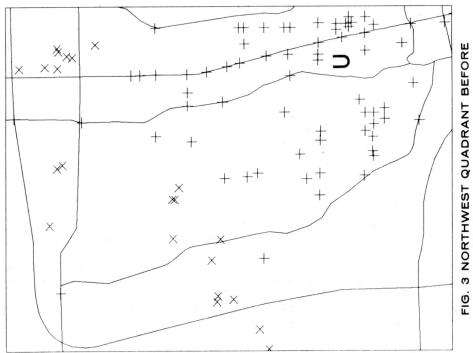

FIG. 3 NORTHWEST QUADRANT BEFORE
TRANSIT STOP EDITING

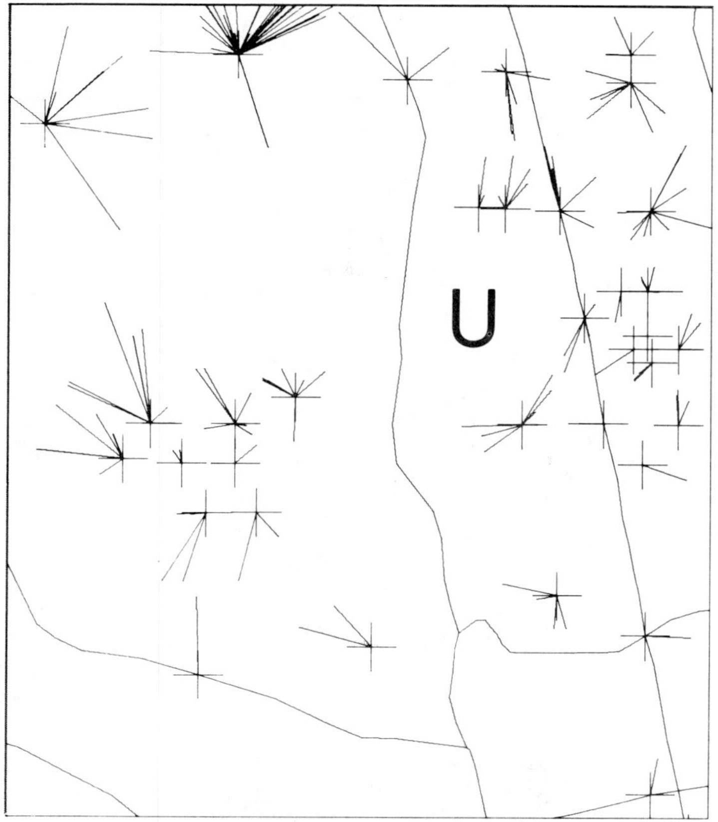

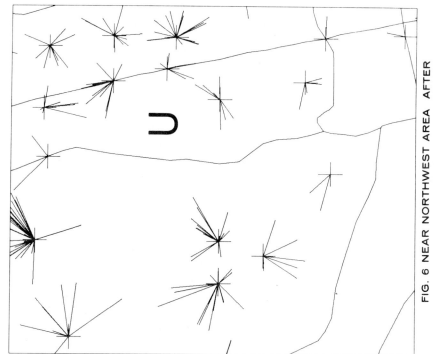

FIG. 6 NEAR NORTHWEST AREA AFTER TRANSIT STOP DELETIONS

FIG. 5 NEAR NORTHWEST AREA BEFORE TRANSIT STOP DELETIONS

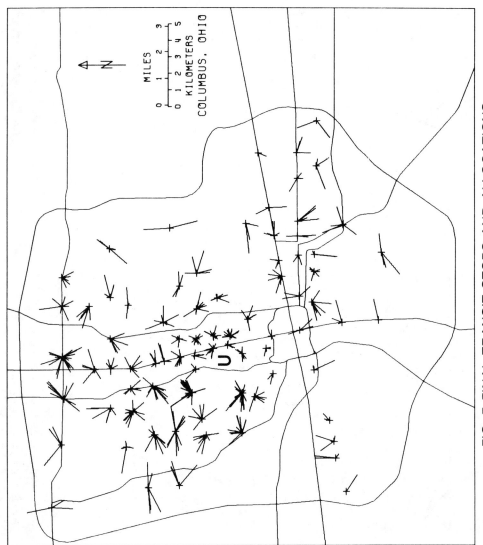

FIG. 7 FINAL TRANSIT STOPS AND ALLOCATIONS

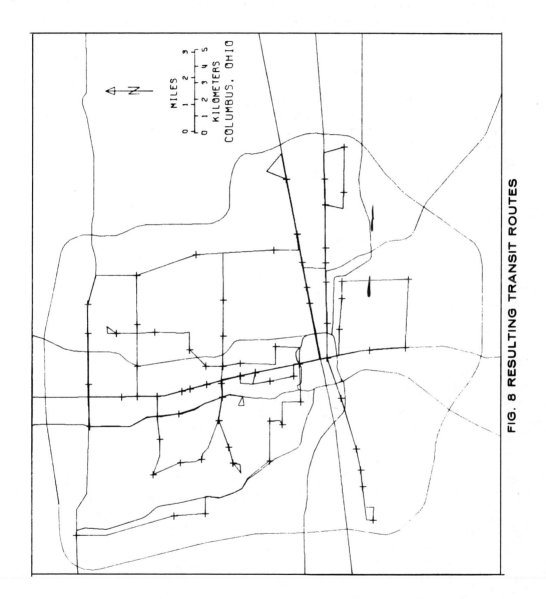

FIG. 8 RESULTING TRANSIT ROUTES

MILES
0 1 2 3
KILOMETERS
0 1 2 3 4 5
COLUMBUS, OHIO

this method is that the entire process only took two hours and clearly many options could be tried and compared in a relatively short time. Additionally, these configurations will always account for transit user characteristics which represent a significant advantage over other existing techniques aimed at solving a similar problem.

ACKNOWLEDGEMENTS

The authors recognize the contribution of R. Cromley and C. Jones as research assistants in this project. This work has been partially funded by an Ohio State University Research Grant.

REFERENCES

Foley, J. and V. Wallace, 1974, "The Art of Natural Graphic Man-Machine Conversation," Proc. IEEE, 62(4), pp. 462-711.

Gehner, Claus D., 1973, The Urban-Region Transit Analysis System (UTRANS), Vol. I and II, Urban Transportation Program, Research Report 72-2, University of Washington, Seattle.

Moellering, H., 1975a, "At the Interface of Cartography and Computer Graphics," Proc. SIGGRAPH '75, in Computer Graphics, 9(1), pp. 256-9.

_____, 1975b, "Interactive Cartography," Proceedings of the International Symposium on Computer-Assisted Cartography, forthcoming.

Newman, W. and R. Sproull, Principles of Interactive Computer Graphics, New York: McGraw-Hill.

Nussbaum, Ernest, Kathy K. Rebibo and Eugene Wilhelm, 1975, RUCUS (Run Cutting and Scheduling) Implementation Manual, Washington, D.C., UMTA.

Osleeb, Jeffrey P., Harold Moellering and Robert Cromley, 1975, A Geographical Analysis for Bus Stop Location for Route Design: Method and Case Study, Discussion Paper No. 48, Department of Geography, Ohio State University.

Schneider, Jerry, 1974, Interactive Graphics in Transportation Systems Planning and Design, Report DOT-TST-74-10.

UMTA Transportation Planning System, 1972, Network Development Manual, Washington, D.C., U.S. Department of Transportation, Urban Mass Transportation Administration.

John W. Nolen, Metropolitan Dade County Fire Department
Malcolm H. Gotterer, Florida International University
Anthony C. Shershin, Florida International University
Henry Kunce, Metropolitan Dade County Fire Department

DISPATCHING EMERGENCY VEHICLES

This paper deals with the problem of responding to a request for emergency vehicles by a citizen. A selection of which type of vehicles should be sent, the number and the point from which they should be dispatched. After the vehicles are sent in response to the request it is then necessary to evaluate the entire protection network to determine if a redeployment of resources is necessary. The computer model described in this paper performs these necessary functions. It has the unique feature of deploying vehicles, called "move-up". The mathematical foundation for the dispatching and move-up are described in the paper and a typical dispatcher-computer dialogue is included.

Introduction

The 1.4 million people in Dade County, Florida will produce over 90,000 alarms requesting emergency fire and medical rescue services in 1976. Population and alarms will continue to increase with a 1980 projection of 1.7 million people and 120,000 alarms.

The Metro-Dade County Fire Department is planning to handle this increase in fire alarm activity by improving the present system. Research on fire prevention, fire fighting techniques, emergency rescue, and other emergencies is being conducted.

Building fires, medical rescue and other types of alarm reported to the fire department all have one thing in common. They all demand immediate service. In order to ensure that the best service possible is offered to the public a better dispatching system is required to handle the alarms especially during high frequency periods.

Mathematical models have been used in the study of the deployment and location of emergency vehicles in various metropolitan areas. Among the models that have been designed and are being used today include the Rand models in New York City and the National Bureau of Standards (NBS) station location computer model, developed for Dade County. Many of these models can be applied with some modifications to work in areas other than originally designed. The models which could be best be used by the Metro-Dade County Fire Department for the location and dispatching of emergency vehicles can only be answered with careful study and testing of the various new models on hand and the possible development of new models based upon the present state of the art.

Models which involve the location of emergency vehicles have been used by the Metro-Dade County Fire Department with the help of Florida International University. Therefore, this report deals with the tactical deployment of fire-fighting units in response to a fire. However, this program can be easily modified to include medical rescue vehicles.

The task of keeping the status of emergency vehicles and men during high alarm activity becomes quite a problem. Usually the nearest units are sent to an alarm, but after a few dispatches it is not easy to determine the closest unit to the next alarm. This is especially true after a few move-ups have been performed.

An on-line computer aided dispatching system set up properly could handle the problems which arise during busy times so as to ensure prompt service. The system must be capable of handling any type of alarm at any given instance. No preset procedure on who to send or move-up can be used by the program because no one knows where the location of the next fire will be or the status or location of the fire-fighting units. The system must be capable of analyzing the immediate situation and making the decision on what to do at that particular moment.

Basically, there are three main criteria which the computer aided dispatching system must meet so as to tactically deploy emergency vehicles. They are:
1. which units and men should be dispatched to any particular fire at any time if all companies are in-house or if there are empty stations;
2. do empty stations, if vacated for a given amount of time, create a deficiency in the fire protection offered;
3. which fire-fighting units should be moved and where during a move-up phase to provide better protection.

A mathematical model which can meet the above criteria is capable of providing information useful in the computer aided dispatching of emergency vehicles. Unlike some so-called CAD systems which only maintain the status of units, a true CAD must assist in sophisticated decision making, such as that required in move-up deployments. The program of this paper accomplishes this significant task.

Allocating Units For Alarms

Currently the Metro-Dade County Fire Department uses a 550 traffic zone map. These traffice zones are called Fire Demand Zones (FDZ) and are combined into 100 sections for the dispatching of emergency vehicles to fire incidents. When an alarm is reported to the alarm office the Officer In Charge (OIC) locates the position of the alarm on the map and sees what units are currently serving that section. The appropriate assignment of men and equipment are dispatched to the incident and their status is kept on a large magnetic board.

Usually the closest available units are sent. The number of units dispatched to an alarm very by the type of alarm reported; e.g., building fire, vehicle fire, grass fire. However, the closest units which are sent to a fire incident may not always be the best policy during high alarm periods. The final decision on this policy is often determined by political and social constraints. The dispatching program described in this paper is not concerned with these socio-economic aspects and accepts the policy that the closest units are sent if available; however, policy constraints could be developed in an expanded model.

The policy of dispatching the nearest unit was chosen because of the fire-fighter goal to suppress the fire in the shortest amount of

time in order to save the loss of life and property. Therefore the
closest units to a fire incident should be the ones to respond. Because
of this policy, the travel times from any station to any particular fire
is an important factor in the decision of what units to send.

It would be impractical to have all the times from every station to
any particular address and therefore the existing 550 FDZ are
used by this program as follows:

When a fire is in a particular zone the units which are closest to
the centroid of that zone are sent. (The centroid of a zone is used because of the odd shapes and areas of the 550 FDZ.)

The program meets the critera of who should be sent to a fire by
the above procedure thus ensuring that the fire-fighters goal is met.
The program assumes that a prescribed number of each type of fire unit
(such as ladders, engines, etc.) have been assigned for different types
of alarms. Such numbers-of-vehicles-needed can be set by the fire chiefs
from their past experiences with the fire activity in the county or they
can be set after doing a careful queuing study.

It is noted that these values which are set must take in consideration the resources available at any particular time. It is recommended
that a resource parameter be build into the dispatching program so as to
dispatch fewer vehicles to some types of alarms during periods of high
alarm activity. Presently, such a parameter is not included in the Dade
County model.

An electronic lighted display of the status of each vehicle is recommended so that the dispatcher has a complete view of the status of each
vehicle at all times. This would enable the dispatcher to view how the
program was internally keeping track of the units and, possibly, allow him
to override the program's proposed deployment. While such a status display
is highly desireable, current technological and economic considerations may
delay its implementation.

Protection Offered

The problem, after a number of units have been dispatched to a fire,
is to provide optimal protection to the area with the remaining available
units. Presently, the Officer in Charge makes the decision on personal
knowledge and upon tactical fire-fighting policies and social and political
commitments.

The algorithm used in computer aided dispatching must be able to
calculate when a dificiency occurs using numerical data. What data would
be best for the model must be studied and carefully selected. Using the
incorrect data or mis-use of correct data can lead to the wrong decision.

The algorithm chosen for this model uses the fact that when a particular area does not meet the requirements for being 'safe' a rearrangement
of the vehicles may be necessary. This differs from the usual algorithms
which trigger rearrangements based upon what stations are not filled.

The 550 FDZ vary from each other in several aspects. Some are large
areas of little population composed mostly of grasslands. Other areas are
relatively small with high rise apartments containing a large population.
The alarm rate for one zone may be only 25 alarms per year where the zone
next to it may have 500 alarms per year. Because of these vast differences
a means of comparing the zones was developed.

One way of comparing the 550 FDZ as to level of protection is by
looking at the travel times to each zone from the stations. We could say

that if a zone can be reached by a unit in a specified amount of time then that zone is protected. One might ask if that is really true in many situations because the demand for fire vehicles may very largely. Some FDZ having very few fires reported each year may show that they need protection because the travel time to them does not meet the required time standard. Realistically, on the other hand, when only a few engines are available one may wish to locate them in a position to best serve the high frequency areas. In other words, frequency of alarms and travel times are both legitimate concerns. Therefore, some means of combining the travel times to a zone and the alarm frequency of that zone is needed for comparison. The leads to the concept of an exposure number which is a weighted alarm frequency.

An exposure number is calculated by the following equation:

$$\text{Exposure number}_{i,j} = \frac{(\text{actual time} - \text{desired time}) \times (\text{frequency})}{(\text{desired time})}$$

Where: Actual time = the time it takes a unit at "station"
j to travel to "zone" i

Desired time = the time which is considered to be a
good response time for any unit to arrive
in "zone" i

Frequency = the number of alarms reported per year
for "zone" i

The concepts of exposure numbers, first introduced in the NBS model, was used in the dispatch model to determine at any given time if the level of protection was adequate according to fire department management. An exposure number is calculated for each station to all FDZ.

One should set the exposure level as low as possible. If one of two stations had to be filled to protect a zone, the station which could protect the zone with the lowest exposure level would ordinarily be filled; however, one can not look at only one zone at a time. One must look at all 550 FDZ so as to give optimal coverage countywide.

If an exposure level were set at a given amount, that is, considered acceptable, and a zone had no stations with a unit in house with an exposure number lower or equal to that level, then that zone is not protected as compared to the other zones which have at least one unit at a station which has met the required exposure level. As an example, see Table 1: if both Stations 1 and 2 have a unit in house and the exposure level was set at 24.0, then Zone 100 could be protected by Station 1 and not by Station 2. But Station 2 could protect zones 101 and 102 whereas Station 1 cannot. If the exposure level was to be set at 30.0, then either Station 1 or Station 2 could protect all three zones.

Management must decide on what level to set the exposure at. One should always start at the lowest possible exposure level in which all zones are covered when all stations have at least one unit in house available for service. Having calculated the exposure numbers which used the frequency of the fires reported, one can see the uncovered zones at various exposure levels in Map 1. When the level reaches approximately 200.0, all zones are covered by the arrangement of stations. The exposure level for all stations could be lowered if stations were located near those zones which are uncovered when the exposure level is high. Since it would be costly to build new stations a temporary site might be the solution to this problem.

Variations of the exposure numbers discussed in this section are possible. For example, one may wish to use:

1. Frequencies which only apply to certain type of incidents; For example, one may calculate exposure numbers using the frequency of high rise building fires;
2. Fluctuations in alarm activity due to tourism, times of year, etc.
3. Other factors such as time of day, day of week, etc.

It is noted that exposure number are an input for the dispatching program and not generated by it. In other words, this particular dispatching program is designed to use any type of exposure numbers.

TABLE 1

Exposure Number Table

Zone	Station 1	Station 2
100	22.5	30.0
101	26.8	18.5
102	29.1	21.0

Re-Location of Vehicles (Move-Up)

Probably the most difficult criteria to meet of any dispatching system is the move-up phase, the relocation of men and vehicles during high alarm periods in order to provide adequate protection to the community. Part of the problem of the move-up phase is constraints involved. Constraints concerning social commitments to incorporated communities, keeping operational costs at a minimum, placing certain units which never leave a presigned area, and others have to be considered. Since these constraints are a managerial decision they were left out of this dispatching program, but they can be added with some modification to the program.

The approach taken in the solution to the move-up problem is basically a station "relocation" model. Actually, the station sites never change location, only their status changes: Either the station is filled by having at least one unit available for service or the station is considered empty when no units are available. Station location models generally take too long to run and, consequently, on-line use is infeasible or impractical. As an alternative, the main idea of the algorithm used in this model is to find one of the best possible arrangements, of the remaining units in the fire stations, which makes all zones covered at the least exposure level.

The approach taken in this program for the move-up phase is quite simple. After a move-up has been recommended because of the number of uncovered zones, one must first decide what stations should be filled and at what exposure level, so as to give maximum coverage. Once the empty stations which need to be filled have been chosen, the program looks to find stations which can lend a unit without creating any uncovered zones and to find stations which can be left without a unit at that exposure level.

After the program determines the number of units needed to fill the empty stations at an acceptable exposure level, then the actual decision of what units to send to what stations needs to be made. Choosing what is the best policy for the actual move-up can be quite a complicated and confusing process. First, one must decide what is the maximum amount of time a vacated station, which should be filled, can be left vacant. If a unit which is eligible for a move-up can travel there in an acceptable amount of time, then it should be sent to that station. If the unit can not do so, one must decide if a "bumping" process should occur whereby several intermediate units are moved in such a manner that one replaces another in sequential fashion. For example, in Figure 1 there are four stations. Station 1 needs to be filled and the unit which must fill it is at Station 4. It has been decided that the longest time that Station 1 can be empty is 10 minutes. There are three possible routes; a) direct route from Station 4 to Station 1; b) send unit from Station 4 to Station 2 and at the same time send unit at Station 2 to Station 1; or c) send the unit from Station 3 to Station 1 and refill Station 3 with the unit from Station 4. The various travel times are shown between stations in the figure. It is obvious that route 1 will not fill Station 1 before 10 minutes have elapsed and so it is ruled out.

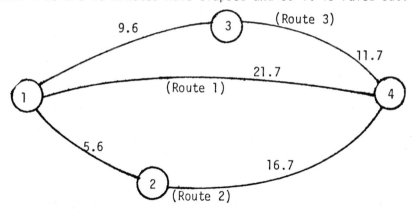

Figure 1   Travel Time in Minutes Between Stations

Route 2 can fill Station 1 in 5.6 minutes but leaves Station 2 vacated for 15.7 minutes. Route 3 can have a unit at Station 1 in 9.6 minutes but leaves Station 3 vacated for 11.7. Which route should one choose between the two is a managerial decision but one would suspect that route 3 would be choosen because it meets the required time to fill Station 1 and minimizes the time the replacement station is vacated, even though Route 2 fills Station 1 quicker.

As one sees from this example the decision on the actual move-up must take quite a few facts into consideration. Therefore, this report only deals with making sure that the stations which need to be filled receive a unit from one of the giving stations. This means that, in terms of the preceding example, the unit in 4 is sent to Station 1. However, it is anticipated that a bumping process could be incorporated into the program.

The algorithm developed for this model creates a "n x m" matrix which is dimensioned by "n", the number of stations which need a unit, and by "m", the number of stations which can be left without a unit. The entries of the matrix are the travel times from each station to every other station. These are named FROM STATIONS (those sending vehicles) and FILL STATIONS (those needing vehicles). A time parameter is given an initial value and another matrix of the same size is created whose entries are 1 if the travel times between those stations are less than or equal to the time parameter and 0 if greater. Having completed making the entries in the second matrix, the rows and columns are summed. Two vectors, A and B, are created. Let vector A represent how many FROM STATIONS are close enough to each FILL STATIONS in a set time and vector B represent how many FILL STATION each FROM STATION can reach in the set time. When vector A has all non-zero entries and vector B has at least "n" non-zeros entries, where the value of "n" is the number of stations which need to be filled, then the actual move-up can be performed. If the above criteria is not met, then the time parameter is incremented and the above process is repeated until the criteria is met.

Once the above criteria is met, the program proceeds to pick out all entries which have a value of 1 in the A vector. It searches the matrix filled with zeros and ones and finds what FROM STATION makes that value appear in that position in vector A. This is done until all 1's in vector A have associated with it a FROM STATION for that particular FILL STATION. At this point the remaining FROM STATIONS and FILL STATIONS form a new smaller matrix for which the process, described in this paragraph and the last, is repeated until all FILL STATIONS are filled. All stations are now filled and move-up can efficiently be carried out in minimal travel time.

One could then use a "bumping" process to do the actual move-up or make the assignments that resulted from the above process. The algorithm developed for this model used the straight assignments and did not take into account any "bumping" process. It was not taken into account in this program because it is not clear yet if bumping is desired. For one thing bumping may place firemen in unfamiliar territory which could degrade their performance. It is noted that the bumping process can be incorporated into this particular dispatching system if and when it is deemed feasible.

Results

Any mathematical model may make logical sense but real world appliciaton of the model may be impractical or impossible. Testing and putting the model to actual use gives a better insight of the concepts which are the basis of the model. Possible improvements may be suggested by its actual use.

To check the algorithms in this report, the computer aided dispatching system was tested to show the feasibility of its usefulness and its ability to run on-line in a minimal amount of time. The test assumed that all stations were in the locations shown in Map 2 and the zones shown in Map 4 were used as the area which needed protection by these stations. Initially, each station had one engine unit and the last two numbers in the unit identification number is the same as the stations which it is usually assigned; for example: Engine 214 is stationed usually at Station 14. No social or political constraints were considered and all units were assumed available for service if in the station.

Looking at Map 2 one sees that 2 fires have been reported, one in Zone 464 and the other in Zone 113. The dispatcher gives the information to the program and three units were sent to each building fire in the zones. The solid arrows show the path of the units which were sent. Units 205, 204, and 224 were sent to the fire in Zone 464. Units 202, 230, and 227 were sent to the fire in Zone 113. After they were dispatched the command was given to see how many zones were uncovered at exposure level 200.0 with Stations 2, 4, 5, 24, 27 and 30 empty.

The uncovered zones can be located on Map 2 by the areas which are shaded. As one sees Station 4 and Station 2 have nearby areas which are not covered. A move-up is decided and the algorithm decided that Station 14 could send its Engine 214 to Station 4, Engine 207 at Station 7 could be moved to Station 2, Station 9 should send Engine 209 to Station 24, Station 5 should receive Engine 206 from Station 6, and Engine 208 could be moved up to Station 27 from Station 8. This move-up can be seen on the map by the dashed arrows.

Most systems developed so far have a tendency to break down after a few dispatches or move-ups; therefore, another fire was reported to test the program on how well it would handle the situation.

The new fire is located in Zone 433 as seen in Map 3. The present stations which have a unit are shown and stations which are empty are not shown. The algorithm again chooses the three closest units to the fire in Zone 433 which are from Station 3, 4 and 13. Units 203, 214 and 213 are sent to the fire and one notes that Unit 214 was sent from Station 4 because it had been relocated after the two previous fires. Again the uncovered zones marked in shaded areas appear on Map 3 at exposure level 200.0. A move-up is performed and Station 1 sends its Engine 201 to Station 3, Engine 229 moves to Station 13 and Engine 209 at Station 24 goes to Station 4 in order to provide better protection to the County. This move-up phase is tested for proper response in the last fire by a second alarm being reported in the same zone, 433. This time Station 4 sent unit 229 to the incident, see Map 4. This unit was at one time at another station but was relocated during a prior move-up phase to service the community better. A partial computer printout of the dispatching for the four fires is seen in Appendix 1.

Conclusions

The dispatching system described demonstrates the feasibility of a computer aided dispatching system for emergency vehicles. This first basic model can have many features added to it. Features such as a command to tell the dispatcher the location of all engine and ladder units in-house has already been added so as to show the expandability of this model. A program to manually place units "in" or "out" of service has also been added in case a unit may have a mechanical breakdown or for some other reason needs a status change. A recall command should be designed to recall units that are sent to an alarm when the alarm is false or the number of units sent is too large.

It is hoped that this paper has given an idea of some of the problems which may arise and concepts that need to be incorporated into a computer aided dispatching system for a large Metropolitan Fire Department. This study and the model developed has demonstrated a feasible alternative to the present manual dispatch system used by the Metropolitan Dade County Fire Department. It is anticipated that such a computer aided on-line dispatch system will assist a fire department in providing a more productive level of service in an expanding environment of people and their requests for emergency service.

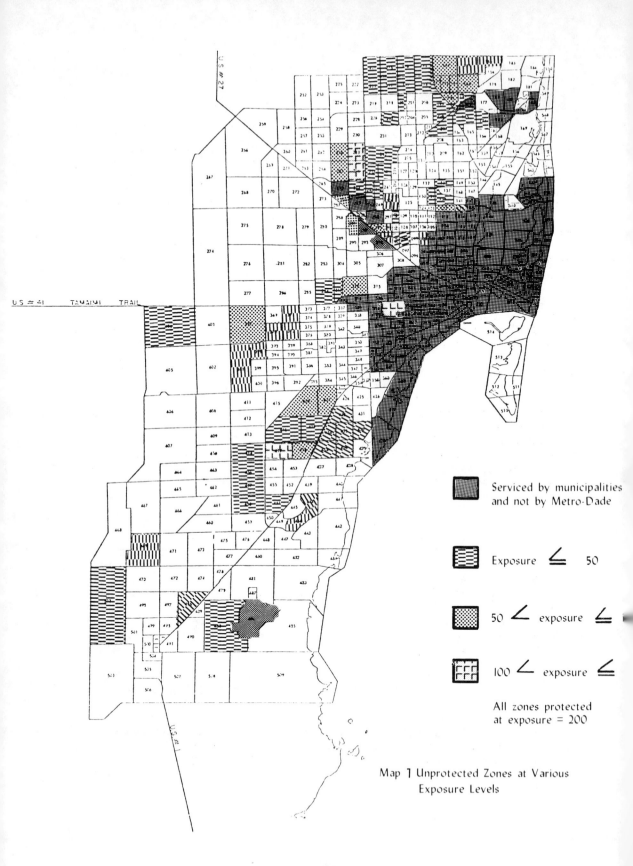

Map 1 Unprotected Zones at Various
Exposure Levels

Legend:

Serviced by municipalities and not by Metro-Dade

Exposure ≤ 50

50 ≤ exposure ≤

100 ≤ exposure ≤

All zones protected at exposure = 200

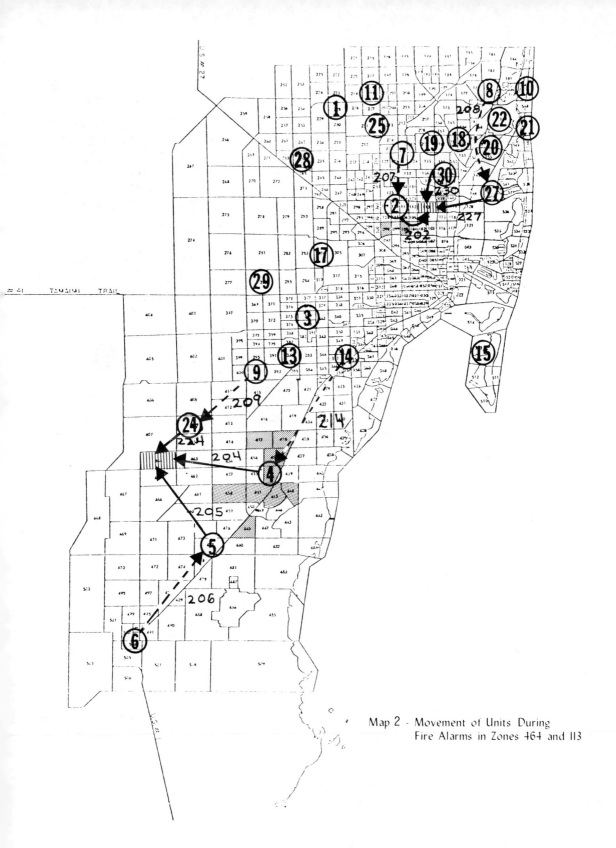

Map 2 - Movement of Units During
Fire Alarms in Zones 464 and 113

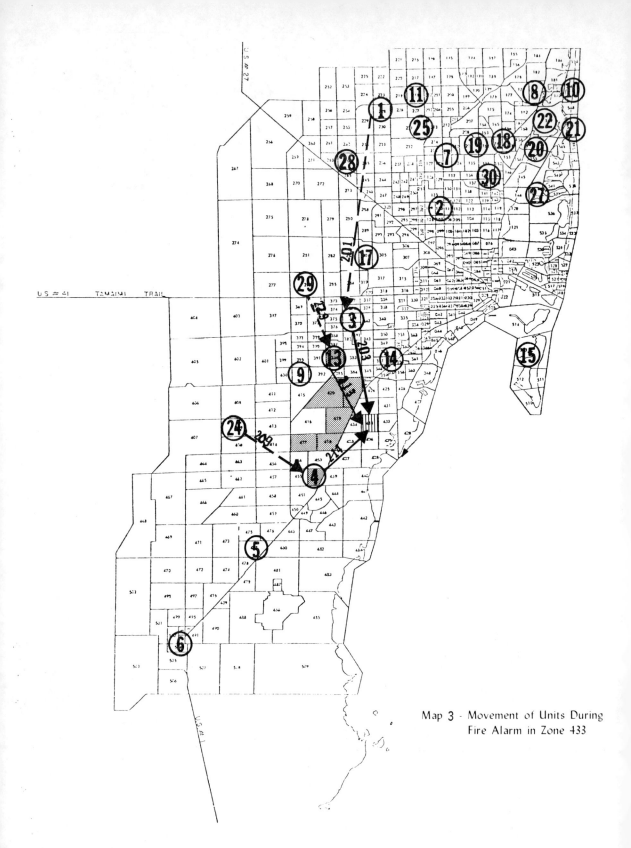

Map 3 - Movement of Units During
Fire Alarm in Zone 433

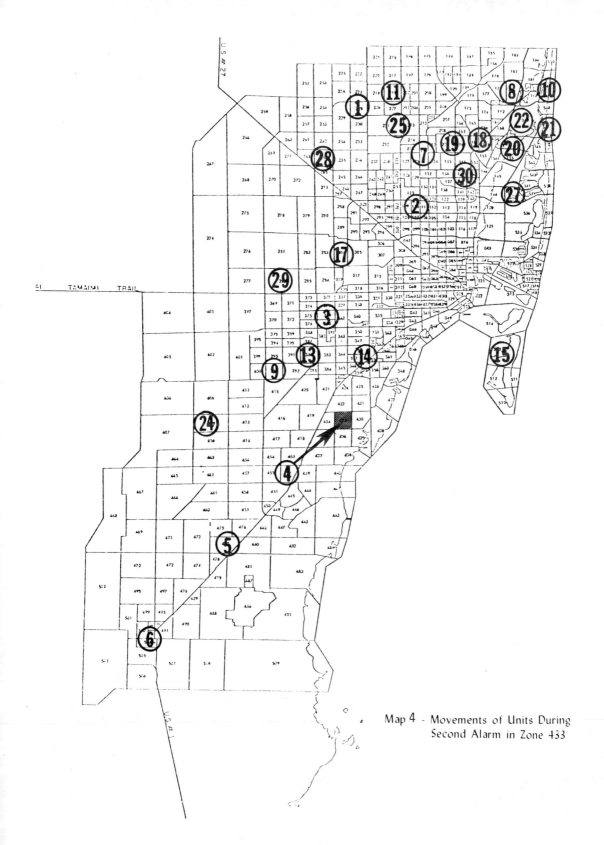

Map 4 - Movements of Units During
Second Alarm in Zone 433

```
>@XQT ISF.JWN.FIRE
```

COMPUTER-DISPATCHER DIALOGUE


```
 WHAT ZONE IS THE FIRE LOCATED IN?
>433

 WHAT TYPE OF FIRE IS IT? (1 FOR BUILDING, 2 FOR HIGH-RISE)
>1

  WHAT ALARM NUMBER IS IT? (1,2,OR 3)
>1

  DISPATCH THE FOLLOWING ENGINES TO FIRE IN ZONE 433

            ENGINE  214

            ENGINE  213

            ENGINE  203

  DISPATCH THE FOLLOWING LADDER(S) TO FIRE IN ZONE 433

            LADDER  301

  TYPE 1 FOR ANTOHER FIRE, 2 FOR EXIT FROM THIS STAGE
>2

  YOU ARE NOW OUT OF THE FIRE STAGE
>@XQT ISF.JWN.STATUS

   WHAT EXPOSURE DO YOU WANT TO START AT?
>200.0

  ***WARNING*** THE FOLLOWING   8 ZONES ARE NOT COVERED   BY ENGINES

            ZONE  354

            ZONE  386

            ZONE  417

            ZONE  418

            ZONE  419

            ZONE  420

            ZONE  421

            ZONE  452

   YOU ARE NOW OUT OF THE STATUS STAGE
>@XQT ISF.JWN.RELOCATE
```

```
ENGINE 211 IS AT STATION 11

ENGINE 213 IS AT A FIRE IN ZONE 433

ENGINE 214 IS AT A FIRE IN ZONE 433

ENGINE 215 IS AT STATION 15

ENGINE 217 IS AT STATION 17

ENGINE 218 IS AT STATION 18

ENGINE 219 IS AT STATION 19

ENGINE 220 IS AT STATION 20

ENGINE 221 IS AT STATION 21

ENGINE 222 IS AT STATION 22

ENGINE 224 IS AT A FIRE IN ZONE 464

ENGINE 225 IS AT STATION 25

ENGINE 227 IS AT A FIRE IN ZONE 113

ENGINE 228 IS AT STATION 28

ENGINE 229 IS AT A FIRE IN ZONE 433

ENGINE 230 IS AT A FIRE IN ZONE 113

LADDER 301 IS AT FIRE IN ZONE 433

LADDER 302 IS AT FIRE IN ZONE 433

LADDER 303 IS AT FIRE IN ZONE 464
LADDER 304 IS AT STATION 10

STATION  1 HAS NO ENGINES!

STATION  4 HAS NO ENGINES!

STATION  6 HAS NO ENGINES!

STATION  7 HAS NO ENGINES!

STATION  8 HAS NO ENGINES!

STATION  9 HAS NO ENGINES!

STATION 14 HAS NO ENGINES!

STATION 24 HAS NO ENGINES!

STATION 29 HAS NO ENGINES!

STATION 30 HAS NO ENGINES!
```

EXPOSURE IS NOW UP TO 200.0

SEND ENGINE 201 FROM STATION 1 TO STATION 3

SEND ENGINE 209 FROM STATION 24 TO STATION 4

SEND ENGINE 229 FROM STATION 29 TO STATION 13

LONGEST TIME FOR RELOCATION FOR UNITS WILL BE 26.0 MINUTES.

YOU ARE NOW OUT OF THE RELOCATION STAGE
>
>@XQT ISP.JWN.FIRE

WHAT ZONE IS THE FIRE LOCATED IN?
>433

WHAT TYPE OF FIRE IS IT? (1 FOR BUILDING, 2 FOR HIGH-RISE)
>1

WHAT ALARM NUMBER IS IT? (1,2,OR 3)
>2

DISPATCH THE FOLLOWING ENGINES TO FIRE IN ZONE 433

              ENGINE 209

DISPATCH THE FOLLOWING LADDER(S) TO FIRE IN ZONE 433

              LADDER 302

TYPE 1 FOR ANOTHER FIRE, 2 FOR EXIT FROM THIS STAGE
>2

YOU ARE NOW OUT OF THE FIRE STAGE
@XQT ISP.JWN.LOCATION

ENGINE 201 IS AT STATION 3

ENGINE 202 IS AT A FIRE IN ZONE 113

ENGINE 203 IS AT A FIRE IN ZONE 433

ENGINE 204 IS AT A FIRE IN ZONE 464

ENGINE 205 IS AT A FIRE IN ZONE 464

ENGINE 206 IS AT STATION 5

ENGINE 207 IS AT STATION 2

ENGINE 208 IS AT STATION 27

ENGINE 209 IS AT STATION 13

ENGINE 210 IS AT STATION 10

-240-

Robert J. Haskell
Program Manager
Westinghouse Urban Systems Center
1911 Jefferson Davis Highway
Arlington, Virginia 22202

COMPUTERIZED PAYROLL/PERSONNEL SYSTEMS FOR THE SMALL JURISDICTION

A National Science Foundation sponsored study on
Decision-Related Research on Technology Utilized by Local
Governments - Computer Programs for Personnel Management
and Payroll is being conducted by a consortium headed by
the Urban Systems Center of the Westinghouse Electric
Corporation; and including the Municipal Finance Officers
Association (MFOA) and the International Personnel Management Association (IPMA). This NSF RANN (Research Applied
to National Needs) project is being monitored by the NSF
Office of Advanced Productivity Research and Technology.
The project has as its end goal the development of transferable computerized payroll/personnel systems specifically designed for the small to mid-sized community.
The project is being conducted in two phases. During
Phase I of the program, the need for two computerized
payroll/personnel systems was identified. One system,
coded in RPG-II, will require a minimum hardware configuration, and is being designed for small jurisdictions.
The other, coded in ANSI-COBOL, is being designed for
jurisdictions with greater support requirements and
capabilities. During Phase II, now in progress, two
recipient sites will participate in the initial transfer
and finalization of the computerized systems being
developed. After completion of the project, both systems
will be in the public domain and will be available at no
cost to jurisdictions requesting them.

INTRODUCTION

The use of a computer is now almost universal within the public
sector. Starting with the larger jurisdictions in the 1960's, its use
has increased as equipment and processing costs have decreased while
personnel costs have skyrockated. Today, an estimated 90 percent of
all U.S. jurisdictions, over 25,000 in population, use a computer for
one or more of their support functions.

As the use of the computer has increased, so has the demand for an
increase in the types of support it can provide. This is certainly
true in the payroll and personnel areas. Nearly all jurisdictions have
a computerized system to produce their payroll; some have also computerized some personnel functions. Few have an integrated payroll/

personnel systems or one which can support the management functions of control and forecasting. Such systems are, however, available. They make use of a common data base and produce all necessary payroll/personnel reports as well as data necessary to control and project personnel requirements. While possessing greatly increased capabilities, they have unfortunately been designed for specific jurisdictions and situations rather than for transferability.

Even knowing of these systems capabilities and even after deciding that their own system needs enhancement, local jurisdictions have been faced with the problem of deciding whether to develop or upgrade a system of their own, to attempt to adopt the system of another jurisdiction, or to contract for use of a proprietary system. Complicating this decision has been the lack of detailed information in the form of technical documentation on systems in the public domain, as well as the need to adapt any system selected to the jurisdiction's own administration procedures and requirements. A further complication has been the difficulty of transfering any but the simplest systems.

In recognition of these problems, the National Science Foundation sponsored in 1974 a program solicitation entitled 'Decision-Related Research on Technology Utilized by Local Governments', in which proposals were requested to develop transferable payroll systems and personnel systems for local governments. The solicitation was sponsored by the Research Applied to National Needs (RANN) Program of the National Science Foundation. A consortium headed by the Urban Systems Center of the Westinghouse Electric Corporation responded to and was awarded the solicitation. This consortium included the Municipal Finance Officers Association (MFOA) and the International Personnel Management Association (IPMA). The Payroll and Personnel systems were integrated on the recommendation of the consortium. This recommendation, later substantiated during the research phase, was based upon the perceived commonality of many of the data elements. Cost savings and increased flexibility are achieved by use of a common data bank.

This program is designed to satisfy the requirements of small to mid-sized jurisdictions, to reflect the projected needs of the communities and to develop systems designed for maximum transferability. Once completed, the computer systems developed for the program will be in the public domain and will be available at no cost to applicant jurisdictions through an NSF-sponsored clearinghouse.

PROJECT PLAN
_____

The Payroll/Personnel program is being completed in two phases. The first, an exploratory phase, had two objectives. One, to define payroll/personnel system requirements of local administrators, based upon a national sample of present practices and future plans; and, two, to identify existing payroll/personnel systems that might serve as model or standard (i.e., exemplary or donor) systems for adoption by other jurisdictions.

Phase I objectives were met by completion of the following tasks:

1. A User Requirements Committee was formed, drawing upon practitioners from a variety of jurisdictions, to over-see the project and ensure the practicality of recommen-dations developed.

2. A payroll/personnel information systems survey was pre-pared and distributed to more than 2,800 jurisdictions nationwide; 1,100 jurisdictions responded.

3. A thorough review was conducted of published literature on payroll/personnel systems and software.

4. The findings of the literature review and the survey were consolidated and reconciled to support identifica-tion of payroll/personnel system requirements.

5. The system design criteria were used as a screening mechanism for survey responses to identify existing systems suitable for use as donors for other jurisdic-tions.

6. The most promising candidate sites were visited, and more complete system descriptions were obtained.

7. Continuing comparative analysis was conducted to reduce the number of jurisdictions proposed as donor systems to four.

8. Consent was obtained from the final four jurisdictions to be used as donor sites for the second phase of the project.

The second developmental phase has three objectives. One, to develop, drawing upon existing public domain software, payroll/person-nel system packages with general applicability in smaller jurisdic-tions; two, to prove the general utility of the developed systems through their implementation at selected recipient sites; and, three, to support establishment of clearinghouse and dissemination activities under the sponsorship and guidance of such professional organizations as the Municipal Finance Officers Association and the International Personnel Management Association.

Phase II is now underway and final negotiations with the two selected recipient sites are proceeding. One will receive the RPG-II coded system designed for use of smaller communities at a minimum cost. The other site will receive a system coded in COBOL and designed for more sizeable communities where the magnitude of their data banks justifies a larger hardware configuration and the use of a more flex-ible programming language.

SYSTEMS CAPABILITIES

Although the actual reports produced by the RPG-II and ANSI-COBOL coded systems will differ in format, both systems are being developed based upon the same functional descriptions and priorities. These

functions and priorities are listed in Table 1. They were identified
and prioritized based upon the experience of the members of the User
Requirements Committee, and the responses to the questionnaires received.

Seventy-three functions were identified - 35 for payroll and 38
for personnel. The functions were then prioritized based upon three
priority ratings. Priority 1 functions were to be accomplished,
priority 2 were highly desirable, and priority 3 were potential capabilities. They form a prescriptive package, and the systems are so
designed that not all need be implemented at one time. This concept
allows recipient sites to quickly implement a basic payroll/personnel
system while retaining the capability to expand the system at a later
date. This extreme capability and flexibility of the systems is
largely due to the use of two basic data files: one for each position,
the other for each individual. While both systems make use of this
concept, they are being designed for two different classes of potential recipients.

The RPG-II Coded System

The RPG-II coded system is being developed for jurisdictions in
the population range of 25,000 to 60,000. However, the system's
capabilities are such that it can be used by both larger and smaller
jurisdictions. The major considerations for its adoption are the capabilities of the computer equipment to be used and the current programming language in use.

The RPG-II system will be a positive time-reporting system as
this is more suitable for use by smaller communities. A general
description of the system installation and operational requirements
is shown in the following tabulation:

Donor Sites:

        Concord, California
        Elgin, Illinois

Recipient Characteristics:

        Jurisdiction - Cities, Counties, Special Jurisdiction
        Population - 25,000 to 60,000
        Hardware - CPU (with 16K memory)
                 2 Disc Drives
                 1 Printer
                 1 Card Reader
        Personnel - 1-2 Technical Support (e.g., one analyst/
                 programmer plus administrative support)

The COBOL Coded System

The ANSI-COBOL system is designed for use by jurisdictions having

PAYROLL PRIORITIES   PERSONNEL PRIORITIES

Priority 1   Priority 1

Time Cards   Vacancy Listing
Time Sheets   Vacancy Analysis
Exception Payroll   Pay Plan Preparation (Pay Schedule
Gross Wages Extended and Calculated   Adjustment)
Supplemental Wages Based Upon Total Hours   Salary Cost Projections
   Worked   Fringe Cost Projections
Withhold Fixed Amounts   Lost Time Nonproductive Time Analysis
Withhold Variable Amounts   Employee Employment History Records
Withhold Mandatory Deductions   Employee Leave History
Withhold Voluntary Deductions   Minority Statistical Reports
Prepare Checks With Detail Gross to Net   EEO-4 Reports
   Deductions   Turnover Statistics
Prepare Check Register   Seniority Rosters
Prepare Deduction Register   Work Force Distribution Statistics
Prepare Quarter-To-Date Earnings Register   Advance Notification for:
Prepare Year-To-Date Earnings Register
Prepare 941-Tax Form   Step Increases
Prepare Workmen's Compensation Reports   Performance Evaluation Review
Prepare W-2 Forms
Have Ability to Prepare Other State or   Fringe Benefit Detail on Check Stub
   Federal Special Reports   Leave Detail on Check Stub
Distribute Gross Payroll by Department   Annual Individual Fringe Benefit Statement
Distribute Gross Payroll by Fund   Position Control
Have Capability for Performing the Following:
   Payroll Bank Reconcilliation   Priority 2
   Overtime Analysis by Reason Worked
   Payroll Cost Forecasts   Salary Survey
   Retroactive Pay Conditions   Retirement Actuarial Projections
   Predicting Termination Pay Costs   OSHA Accident Reports
                                                Annual Reports of Employee Fringe Benefit
Priority 2   Cost for Each Employee

Gross Wages Precalculated   Priority 3
Supplemental Wages Based on Nature of
   Position Held   Manpower Forecasting
Preparation of a Prepayroll Register   Preparing Exam Notices
Preparation of State Unemployment Reports   Scoring Tests
Distribution of Gross Payroll Costs by Program Preparing Eligible Lists
Distribution of Gross Payroll by Object   Position Requirements Analysis
Capability for Making Automatic Bank Deposits   Job Analysis
   to Employee Checking   Employee Performance Evaluation
                                                Man/Job Matching
                                                Skills Inventory
                                                Item Analysis
Priority 3   Reliability and Validation Study
                                                Tailored Testing
Exact Amount Entry of Supplemental Wages   Greivance Analysis
Preparation of Checks Without Detail   Provisions of Contract Analysis
   Gross-To-Net Deductions   Training Records

                   TABLE 1.   SYSTEM FUNCTIONS

populations from 60,000 to 150,000. As with the RPG-II system, this target range is not based upon the capabilities of the system, but rather upon implementation requirements. The COBOL system requires a larger computer memory and more file maintenance overhead. It provides greater flexibility and capacity. Since it is being developed for larger communities, the COBOL system will utilize exception time reporting, which can decrease card punch requirements per month by some 40 percent.

A brief technical description of the ASNI-COBOL system's installation and operational requirements appears in the following tabulation:

Donor Sites:

      Genesee County, Michigan
      Kern County, California

Recipient Characteristics:

      Jurisdiction - Cities, Counties, Special Jurisdictions
      Population - 60,000 to 150,000
      Hardware - CPU w/64K memory
                2 Disc Drives
                2 Tape Drives
                1 Printer
                1 Card Reader
      Personnel - 2-4 Technical Support* (e.g., one analyst/ programmer; one payroll specialist; one personnel specialist, etc.)

PROJECTED SCHEDULE

The two recipient sites have been selected and transfer and enhancement of the donor systems is progressing. Both systems are scheduled for operation by January 1977. Final documentation of the systems will be completed by June 1977, and it is hoped that both systems will be available through a clearinghouse facility under the cognizance of the Municipal Finance Officers Association and the International Personnel Management Association by mid-1977.

Additional information as to the project can be obtained by writing or calling: Westinghouse Urban Systems Center, P.O. Box 457, Mid City Station, Dayton, Ohio 45402. Telephone: (513) 228-9677.

---

*Will vary depending on jurisdiction's requirements.

Dr. George G. Clucas
Professor, Public Administration
California Polytechnic State University
San Luis Obispo, California   93407

THE COMPARATIVE CITIES FINANCE PROJECT

ABSTRACT. A critical question needs to be addressed. Can annual financial reports local governments prepare for the State, and which reports are reviewed and key-punched to meet a State reporting need, be re-programmed to meet needs in local government?
The Comparative Cities Finance Project believes the answer is "Yes!" As evidence, this year over 150 California City Managers/ Administrative Officers again subscribed to sets of comparative revenue and comparative expenditure data tailor-made for the recipient city.
The Project has also produced two statewide reports on Federal Revenue Sharing to the 412 California cities, and other comparative studies are underway.
A similar approach can be used for other local governmental segments such as counties, school districts and special districts.

INTRODUCTION

Each year, local governments throughout the country go through the process of preparing and submitting annual financial reports to the State. Under Federalism, local governments are creatures of the State, and by necessity, the States do require annual reports of local government on a State-prescribed form. The details and totals in various forms are aggregated by each State, and the results are published. The information is also used for national reporting purposes. Both a State and a National need have been met to an acceptable degree.

However, there is a large unmet need in this annual reporting system insofar as local government is concerned. Local government devotes a considerable amount of man hours and expertise in the development of the annual report for the State, and the information feedback is of minimal value in the decision-making processes of local government. The challenge is one of utilizing this wealth of detailed, financial data in a timely and meaningful manner for busy local government administrators, elected officials, and citizens alike.

In a large nation such as ours in which Federalism is a reality, nationwide reporting and studies of local government serve only to remind us that we do have agencies and people in them that are living proof of the well-known qualities of being both pragmatic and ingenious. Because of Federalism, there must be some quantum-like advantage to utilizing intrastate data for comparative purposes involving local governments, and I shall confine myself to the State of California and hope that reporting from one State will have value to you.

LOCAL GOVERNMENT IN CALIFORNIA

California has exercised its prerogative under Federalism by structurally defining local government to consist of:[1]

1. 58 counties
2. 407 cities
3. 1,132 school districts
4. 2,223 special districts

The structural arrangement by itself makes each State unique. In addition to the structural differentiation that exists, the assignment and degree of functions performed by the State and the local units of government vary greatly. For example, unlike the situation in many states, the California cities do not administer schools or welfare. The counties are the administrative arms of the State for welfare purposes, and school districts are a separate governmental entity operating with a combination of local and State funding.

Finally, the widespread usage of special districts in California can obscure the costs of certain functions in the counties and the cities. The following table identifies the major functional areas subject to significant overlapping responsibilities.

---

[1] Bureau of the Census, 1972 Census of Governments, Vol. 1, Governmental Organization, p. 322. The number of governmental units as of January 1, 1972.

TABLE 1

California Local Government Expenditures -
Percentage Sharing of Functions in Which Special
Districts are Significantly Involved[2]

Function	Counties	Cities	Special Districts
Water Transport	--	70.1	29.9
Sewerage	5.7	59.1	35.2
Hospitals	68.4	6.8	24.8

The situation in California can undoubtedly be replicated by each of the other States. This highlights the problem
of interstate comparisons of local government and directs
attention to intrastate studies instead.

THE COMPARATIVE CITIES FINANCE PROJECT

Fortunately, the State of California has an annual
reporting system for local governments to which local government is accustomed. The data is key-punched at the State
level for the preparation and publication of the Annual
Reports.[3] It is these state-produced magnetic tapes which
can be utilized to develop comparative information for use
by local administrators, elected officials and citizens.

Our earliest attempt with the cities was to publish in
both book and booklet form selected revenues and expenditures
of all the California cities. The 398 cities were divided
into Urbanized Area cities and Non-Urbanized Area cities and
arranged by population size. Statewide patterns were provided for groupings of cities by size and type, and the
information included both dollar totals and per capita
amounts.[4] This initial approach did not succeed, and it was
discontinued. Not only were the costs higher, but the information was not tailor-made for the individual city.

Beginning with the 1971-72 data, comparative general
city revenue and expenditure information has been made available to the cities in a form the cities have found to be

[2] U.S. Bureau of the Census, 1972 Census of Governments,
Vol. 4, Government Finance No. 5, Compendium of Government
Finances (Governmental Finances) No. 4, 1974, Table 48,
p. 141.
[3] The State Controller's Office publishes Annual Reports for
counties, cities, schools and special districts.
[4] Clucas, George G., The California Cities: Comparative
Finance 1966-67, Sage Publications, Beverley Hills, 1968.

useful. Exhibit A illustrates the 1974-75 revenue format,
and Exhibit B, the 1974-75 expenditure format for each of
the 412 cities. The Comparative Cities Finance Project
provides the recipient city with a 21-city set that includes
20 other California cities. The set can be either: (1) the
10 next largest and the 10 next smallest urbanized or non-
urbanized area cities, or (2) any 20 other cities chosen by
the recipient city. A set of comparative cities is furnished
at a cost of only $12.00, as the Project utilizes only student
labor, except for the initial programming cost.

The cities use the comparative per capita data for
identifying similarities and differences with other California
cities of similar size and type. Staff studies can be directed
within the context of the comparative information. It has also
proved to be useful when used in conjunction with comparative
information furnished by the League of California Cities on
positions and salary ranges of selected positions.

A CRITIQUE OF AN ARGUMENT FOR USING INTRASTATE COMPARATIVE DATA

Many of the well known limitations to interstate comparative data on local government are overcome by using the intrastate comparative approach. Even with the intrastate
approach, however, there are some problems in the California
situation:

1. Special District operations affect the cities in
   certain functional areas.
2. While cities and counties generally perform
   distinct functions, there are exceptions. Cities
   may contract for certain services to be performed
   by the county, or cities may provide a service
   generally relinquished to the counties.
3. Cities may be deeply involved with programs that
   are not reflected in general revenue and general
   expenditure accounts.
4. Per capita figures do not reflect certain important
   socio-economic variables.
5. Comparative expenditures do not reflect the quality
   of the programs.
6. Accounting practices vary from city to city. The
   interpolation of city accounts to meet State
   reporting needs are not always consistent.

Despite the above problems, and the problems are real,
there is much value to current and timely comparative data:

1. Cities are cities--they are not the State, the
   county, schools or special districts. Cities
   operate within a State-prescribed sphere.
2. There are common sources of general revenues and
   common general expenditures for cities. These can

be set forth for groups of cities by population size and type (i.e., Urbanized Area or Non-Urbanized Area cities).

3. Revenue items have a high degree of reliability in reporting. Property taxes, sales taxes, Federal Revenue Sharing don't suffer from accounting and interpolation differences among cities.

4. City Managers/City Administrative Officers have expertise. With an array of 412 California cities to choose from, it is no good reason why their comparative set of cities should have major differences. The differences that do appear can be subjected to staff analysis.

USES OF THE STATEWIDE COMPARATIVE DATA

1. Each year, the cities can be arranged by the latest June 30 population estimates. Urbanized Area cities and Non-Urbanized Area cities can be isolated. Population groupings can be made.

2. The format described above was used to identify Federal Revenue fund distribution to the cities. Both the per capita range and mean was developed for each grouping of cities. Cities receiving minimal and maximal amounts were identified.

3. Revenue and Expenditure Profiles for groups of cities for 1974-75 have been superimposed on 1971-72 profiles. This technique provides some generalized clues as to how Federal Revenue Sharing affects California cities by size and type (See Exhibit C).

4. Statistical analysis clearly indicates that there was a marked difference in the flow of Federal Revenue Sharing Funds to Urbanized Area cities compared to Non-Urbanized Area cities.

5. Certain socio-economic variables appear to have an explanatory power in regard to expenditure categories. By using regression analysis techniques, formulas are being developed to provide a predicted figure for each major expenditure category by city. The actual per capita expenditure can then be contrasted with the predicted figure for a city of that size and type in California.

SUMMARY

The Comparative Cities Finance Project is an effort to utilize a large mass of city-produced financial data in a comparative manner that will be useful to city managers, city officials and citizens.

Data produced to meet State needs can be reprogrammed and put to good use at the local level providing it is timely and has comparative validity. The Project has taken a beginning step that has an appeal to City Managers/City Administrative Officers. As the work progresses it should also appeal to elected city officials and citizens.

EXHIBIT A

PROPERTY TAXES

CURRENT YEAR -- SECURED	$	27.70
CURRENT YEAR -- UNSECURED		2.26
PRIOR YEARS SECURED & UNSECURED		0.30
OTHER PROPERTY TAXES		0.01
INTEREST & PENALTIES		

TOTAL PROPERTY TAXES   30.27

OTHER TAXES

SALES & USE TAXES	$	40.20
TRANSIENT LODGING TAXES		6.19
FRANCHISES		2.86
BUSINESS LICENSE TAXES		3.91
REAL PROPERTY TRANSFER TAXES		0.43
OTHER NON-PROPERTY TAXES		15.20

TOTAL OTHER TAXES   68.81

LICENSES & PERMITS

ANIMAL LICENSES	$	0.01
BICYCLE LICENSES		
CONSTRUCTION PERMITS		0.96
PARKING		
STREET & CURB PERMITS		0.02
OTHER LICENSES & PERMITS		

TOTAL LICENSES & PERMITS   1.02

FINES, FORFEITS & PENALTIES

VEHICLE CODE FINES -- NET	$	3.15
OTHER FINES -- NET		0.14
OTHER FORFEITS & PENALTIES		0.01

TOTAL FINES, FORFEITS & PENALTIES   3.31

REVENUE FROM USE OF MONEY & PROPERTY

INVESTMENT EARNINGS	$	7.13
RENTS & CONCESSIONS		
ROYALTIES		
OTHER		

TOTAL REVENUE MONEY & PROPERTY   7.13

REVENUE FROM OTHER AGENCIES

STATE ALCOHOLIC BEVERAGE LIC FEES	$	0.81
STATE MOTOT VEHICLE IN LIEU TAXES		8.51
STATE GASOLINE TAXES		8.10
STATE HOMEOWNERS PROPERTY TAX RELIEF		2.79
STATE BUS INVENTORY PROP TAX RELIEF		1.16
STATE TRAILER COACH IN LIEU TAXES		1.24
STATE CIGARETTE TAXES		4.00
OTHER STATE GRANTS		1.38
COUNTY GRANTS OF STATE GAS TAXES		4.01
OTHER COUNTY GRANTS		
FEDERAL -- REVENUE SHARING		11.55
OTHER FEDERAL GRANTS		0.79
OTHER TAXES IN LIEU		0.22

TOTAL REVENUE FROM OTHER AGENCIES   44.61

EXHIBIT A (Continued)

```
       SAN LUIS OBISPO      CITY REVENUES      - NONURBANIZED AREA
              6/30/75 POPULATION ESTIMATE       34,550
                        1974-75  FISCAL  YEAR
CHARGES FROM CURRENT SERVICES
-----------------------------
     ZONING FEES                             $        0.03
     SUBDIVISION FEES                                 0.01
     SALE OF MAPS & PUBLICATIONS                      0.08
     OTHER FILING & CERTIFICATION FEES
     SPECIAL POLICE DEPARTMENT SERVICES              0.09
     SPECIAL FIRE DEPARTMENT SERVICES
     PLAN CHECKING FEES                              0.28
     ANIMAL SHELTER FEES & CHARGES
     ENGINEERING FEES, INSPECTION                    0.20
     STREET, SIDEWALK & CURB REPAIRS                 0.18
     STREET LIGHTING ASSESSMENTS
     WEED & LOT CLEANING                             0.11
     SEWER SERVICE CHARGES
     REFUSE COLLECTION & DUMP CHARGES
     SALE OF REFUSE
     VITAL STATISTICS
     FIRST AID STATION & AMBULANCE SER
     HEALTH INSPECTION FEES
     LIBRARY FINES & FEES
     PARK & RECREATION INCOME                        1.53
     OTHER CURRENT SERVICE CHARGES                   0.73
                                                ===========
          TOTAL CHARGES FOR CURRENT SERVICES                 3.28
OTHER REVENUES
--------------
     SALE OF REAL & PERSONAL PROP            $
     SEWER CONNECTION FEES
     CONTRIBUTIONS MUNI OWNED ENTERPRISES            5.73
     CONTRIBUTIONS NON-GOV SOURCES                   0.04
     OTHER REVENUES                                  0.37
                                                ===========
          TOTAL OTHER REVENUES                               6.15


                                                ===========
     TOTAL CITY REVENUES                          $      164.61
```

EXHIBIT B

SAN LUIS OBISPO   CITY EXPENDITURES - NONURBANIZED AREA

6/30/75 POPULATION ESTIMATE   34,550

1974-75 FISCAL YEAR

	EXPENSE	OUTLAYS	
GENERAL GOVERNMENT - DEPARTMENTAL			
CITY COUNCIL	0.68		
CITY MANAGER OR ADMIN OFFICER	2.01		
CITY CLERK	1.40		
CITY FINANCE OFFICER OR CONTROLLER	2.25	1.03	
CITY TREASURER			
CITY ATTORNEY	1.18	0.02	
PLANNING	6.07		
PERSONNEL ADMINISTRATION	0.13		
GENERAL GOVERNMENT BUILDINGS	0.39	12.05	
OTHER			
	===========	===========	
TOTAL GENERAL GOVT - DEPARTMENTAL	14.65	13.12	27.78
GENERAL GOVERNMENT - NONDEPARTMENTAL			
GENERAL OBLIGATION BONDS -- INT	3.56		
GENERAL OBLIGATION BONDS -- PRIN	2.17		
OTHER BONDS INTEREST			
OTHER BONDS PRINCIPAL			
OTHER LONG TERM INDEBTEDNESS -- INT			
OTHER LONG TERM INDEBTEDNESS -- PRIN			
RETIREMENT AND O.A.S.D.I.			
INSURANCE OR DAMAGE SETTLEMENTS	1.76		
COMMUNITY PROMOTION	3.11		
ELECTIONS	0.43		
OTHER	1.54		
	===========	===========	
TOTAL GEN GOVRN-NONDEPARTMENTAL	12.60		12.60
PUBLIC SAFETY			
POLICE PROTECTION	26.13	1.56	
FIRE PROTECTION	18.48	0.83	
BUILDING REGULATION	2.37		
ANIMAL REGULATION	0.13		
CIVIL DEFENSE	0.06		
	===========	===========	
TOTAL PUBLIC SAFETY	47.19	2.39	49.58
PUBLIC WORKS			
ENGINEERING & ADMINISTRATION	5.22	0.05	
STREETS, STORM DRAINS & STREET LIGHT	26.92	1.07	
PARKING FACILITIES			
SEWAGE COLLECTION & DISPOSAL			
WASTE COLLECTION & DISPOSAL			
UNALLOCATED COSTS - SHOPS & YARDS	2.09	0.44	
	===========	===========	
TOTAL PUBLIC WORKS	34.24	1.57	35.81

EXHIBIT B (Continued)

```
SAN LUIS OBISPO      CITY EXPENDITURES   - NONURBANIZED AREA
            6/30/75 POPULATION ESTIMATE       34,550
                  1974-75  FISCAL  YEAR
                                 EXPENSE       OUTLAYS

HEALTH
------
                            =========== ===========

        HEALTH
LIBRARIES
---------
                            =========== ===========

        LIBRARIES
PARKS, RECREATION & CULTURAL
----------------------------
                            =========== ===========

        PARKS, RECREATION & CURTURAL       10.99        13.57          24.56
CONTRIBUTIONS OTHER GOVT FUNDS & UNITS
-------------------------------------
        CONTRIBUTIONS MUNI OWNED ENTERPRISES
        OTHER
                            =========== ===========

        TOTAL CNTRBTNS OTHER GOVT FUNDS


                            =========== =========== ===========

TOTAL CITY EXPENDITURES                                    $     150.37
```

EXHIBIT C

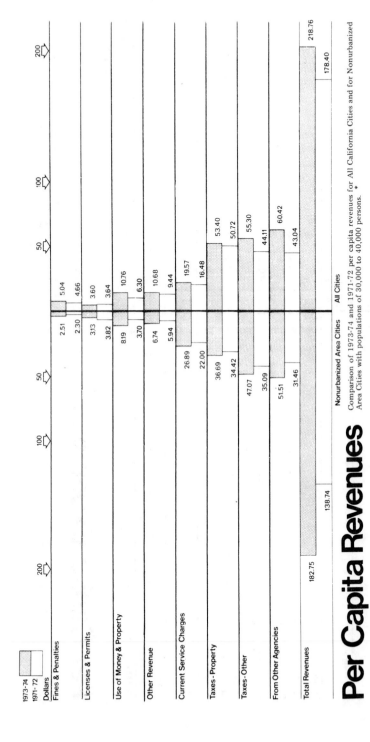

Per Capita Revenues

Comparison of 1973-74 and 1971-72 per capita revenues for All California Cities and for Nonurbanized Area Cities with populations of 30,000 to 40,000 persons. *

* Information compiled from data included in the *Annual Report of Financial Transactions Concerning Cities of California*. State Controller. The Nonorganized Area Cities include Pleasanton, Petaluma, Antioch, San Luis Obispo, Visalia, Santa Maria and Santa Cruz.

EXHIBIT C (Continued)

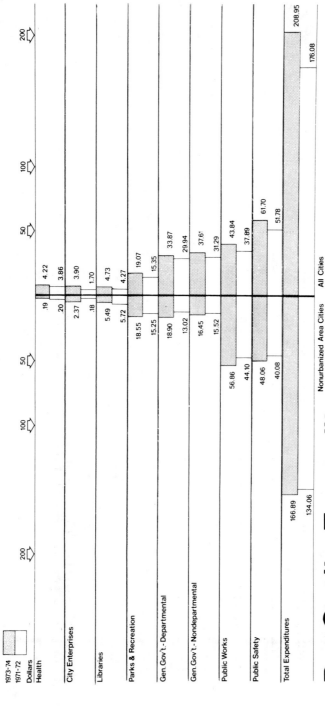

Per Capita Expenditure

Nonurbanized Area Cities   All Cities

Comparison of 1973-74 and 1971-72 per capita expenditures for All California Cities and for Nonurbanized Area Cities with populations of 30,000 to 40,000 persons. *

* Information compiled from data included in the *Annual Report of Financial Transactions Concerning Cities of California*. State Controller. The Nonurbanized Area Cities include Pleasanton, Petaluma, Antioch, San Luis Obispo, Visalia, Santa Maria and Santa Cruz.

Frank W. Prince 3
Computer Operations Consultant
2121 Harriett Drive
Tallahassee, Florida 32303

CONSIDERATIONS FOR FISCAL IMPACT

This paper is concerned with three aspects of fiscal impact fee research and analysis. First, what groups are interested in supporting it and why? Second, what are some of the methodological and organizational concerns associated with it? And lastly, in what kind of a political environment does it exist?

In the second section a rule of thumb for estimating relative resource commitments necessary to carrying out fiscal impact research is presented. It is followed by a description of an organizational structure that has facilitated an existing fiscal impact study.

INTRODUCTION

The Fiscal Impact Study Project with Dr. James Frank as its Principal Investigator was organized in the last half of 1974. It was supported by state level funding and was mandated to answer two basic questions: First, does a judicially defensible method of fiscal impact fee calculation exist? Second, can a useable technique for carrying out that method of calculation be devised?

The study results document that such a method of calculation does exist and that it can be successfully implemented. The results include not only the rationale for such a positive answer, but a working fiscal impact analysis system which considers the effect of new development on thirteen governmental expenditure categories and on nineteen governmental revenue sources. A significant portion of the study effort has been directed toward investigation of three areas which have an effect on fiscal impact research and on the use of fiscal impact analysis techniques. Those three areas are 1) the area of persons and organizations interested in funding or participating in the research 2) the area of the organizational and methodological considerations which are important to carrying out the research or to making the analysis system work and 3) the area of the political environment in which a working fiscal impact analysis system must operate. These are the portions of the study results which we will explore in some detail in this paper.

The Fiscal Impact Research Study has gone, in a single step, from basic research in the field of fiscal impact analysis to an end product useful to several levels of government. Two consequences of that situation are that all three of the areas defined above were being evaluated at the same time and that new information about all three areas was gathered throughout the study's life. In this paper's discussion, the simultaneous nature of our three main themes should be kept in mind so that confusion over chronology might be avoided.

The "one step" nature of the study pointed out above has led to another consequence which is worthy of note. Because the implementation of the analysis system overlapped parts of the research which defined the way in which the analysis was to be carried out, many false starts and poor decisions about the implementation were made. In the section of the paper which describes some cautions and restrictions which were imposed on the final implementation, we concentrate on those characteristics of the analysis method which had the greatest effect on the fiscal impact analysis system implementation.

Throughout the paper we refer to "the development", "governmental jurisdictions", "the models", and "service subsystems". As an example of the use of these terms in context we will outline the fiscal impact analysis procedure. First, a model of a governmental jurisdiction is constructed. The state of operation of each of that jurisdiction's service subsystems is simulated by the model. A development is defined and from that definition, an estimate is made of the physical impact of the development on each service subsystem. The cost of that impact is then estimated. In this scheme, governmental jurisdictions are defined as cities and counties in Florida. The developments of which we speak are conceived to be discrete construction projects which may take place within a jurisdiction. Housing developments, shopping centers and new industry are examples of discrete developments. The service subsystems are parts of a governmental jurisdiction which provide particular services to the jurisdiction's residents. The water or recreation departments of a city (as they are defined in an administrative and accounting sense) constitute service subsystems. Finally, the models are the computerized analysis techniques which produce a fiscal impact estimate as their end product.

ORIGINS OF THE RESEARCH

Generally, three groups have shown interest in giving support to the Fiscal Impact Study. Academicians like Dr. Frank, the Principal Investigator, have shown interest in the new information which the models can generate. Legislators whose constituencies are interested in using impact fees to offset the costs of supplying services to new developments have shown an interest in funding the study. Lastly, state agencies who see the products of the study as useful tools have shown interest in funding the study and in aiding with the research. In this first portion of the paper we will explore these interests more fully.

The interest of Dr. Frank has more dimensions than those of an isolated academic. He has studied governmental fiscal policy for more than ten years. Because of his work as a local planner and planning consultant, he has long been aware that cities and counties are largely unable to answer certain basic questions about the impact of new development on their fiscal systems.

Unfortunately, when Dr. Frank began his work most government agencies were not even asking the questions which he felt were so important to successful planning practice. Would a development cost a city more than it brought in? Do existing planning techniques take into account the full range of a development's impacts? Are existing techniques as accurate as technically possible? The people didn't ask those questions, and as a result, neither did government. But by 1970 that had changed.

It changed first in the high growth states like California and Florida. In these areas, the specter of depleted resources, together with the escalation in resource costs, began to force local and state officials to seriously address the question of growth management. In Florida, some cities and counties were considering the possibility of levying a fee to offset the cost of maintaining their services under the impact of continuing new development.

Legislative interest followed local interest and it happened that a legislator in whose district the fiscal impact fee movement was strong was also Chairman of the Supervisory Committee for the State's Department of Community Affairs. He generated in that department an interest in obtaining research in the appropriateness and legality of fiscal impact fees. The Department of Community Affairs, coincidentally, had identity problems. Originally mandated as a state agency in support of community operations, most of its specific tasks were duplicated in other departments of government. In the period of austerity during the early 70's, Community Affairs needed to find projects which seemed to be legitimately within its perview and in which no other government agency had a stake.

In this manner the stage was set in Florida for the funding of research into fiscal impact analysis. A grant from the Department of Community Affairs (initiated by legislative interest) began the research. That grant was followed by a cooperative grant from Community Affairs and the State University System, again with legislative support.

At this point we can see how three major interest groups were represented in the initiation of the Fiscal Impact Research Study. The goals of the study reflected these interests. The Legislature and the Department of Community Affairs wanted three rather specific questions answered.

1. Was a regularized system of fiscal impact analysis technically possible?
2. Were the results obtained from such an analysis judicially defensible?
3. Could the resulting system be used by state and local government?

Dr. Frank was asking somewhat more academic questions:

1. How is fiscal impact related to development location?
2. How is it related to the income of development residents?
3. What are the relative impacts of the various subsystems?

In the following section we will examine how the study went about answering those questions.

ORGANIZATIONAL AND METHODOLOGICAL CONSIDERATIONS

In this section we will present some of the methodological questions which were raised during the study and the decisions which were made with respect to them. Following that, we will submit certain lessons which we have learned concerning project management and organization as being of general interest.

First Considerations

In the past, when the potential impact of a new development was in question, a combination of per-capita estimates and the calculations of experienced personnel were called upon to provide the answer. If the subsystem managers who carried out the analysis knew their business these estimates were quite accurate. But there were drawbacks to this procedure.

Most jurisdictions couldn't justify the expense of special fiscal impact analyses except in the case of the largest developments. Then, charges of inconsistency and conflict of interest were brought by developers against jurisdictions. In order to overcome that, per-capita estimators were heavily used. Developers then argued that these techniques were insensitive to local conditions, the economics of scale and to the capacities of existing systems. If a private consultant was hired to carry out the analysis, the chances were good that the cost would be high and the accuracy no better than in-house work.

Research into the question indicated that an alternative method might serve better. If an analysis was based on the physical impacts of a development and then costs were proportioned accordingly, a measure of both the physical and fiscal impacts of a development might be obtained. To accomplish this, a static model of a jurisdiction's subsystems in their current condition would be produced. The estimated load from a particular development would then be impressed upon the various subsystems. The change in subsystem operating characteristics would be measured and the cost of bringing the system back to its original condition computed. The ratio of development usage to total capacity would be used to proportion costs and estimate fiscal impact. Costs would be reported in three categories:

1) Remaining value of the existing system.
2) Capital expenditures for new system components.
3) Operation and maintenance cost per year.

Methodological Questions

Let us organize our discussion into two themes. The first is that of decisions made in response to possible questions about our adherence to project goals. The second theme is that of responses to questions raised concerning the allocation of our limited resources. We will present three topics concerning project goals.

In order that we might remain true to the goal of judicial defensibility, it is felt that we cannot justify charging a development with upgrading a service subsystem's operation. As a result, when the design of additions to a subsystem is undertaken, the system is expanded only enough to offset the degrading effects of the development's load. Where the nature of the addition is such that an exact match with increased load cannot be made, the development is charged with only a portion of the new construction cost. That proportion is based on the part of the added capacity which the development actually uses.

In a slightly different vein, only common practice, not academic ideal, is modeled. The analyses have a land use orientation which reflects one trend in organizing information about urban areas. Similarly, throughout the models, the decision rules and analytic techniques used are the ones most common among field personnel working with the various systems evaluated. The decision rules in the models reflect the way these people do things, not some unrealistic academic standard.

Since we are constructing the models for use by local government, the models are straight forward in their presentation of results. The analyses take place at a discrete point in time; the time when all elements of a proposed development are active. Except for the revenue model, no model deals with the changes in the development's character over time. O and M is reported as a yearly amount. New capital expenditures are reported as a lump sum. Therefore, operation and maintenance costs, which are naturally time based and capital expenditures, which can be conceived of as a single value, are not manipulated by the models. This allows the user to consider alternative funding schemes as an analytic factor. For any further use of the results, he is not hampered by a complex reporting scheme.

Turning now to constraints placed on the analyses because of resource limitations, we will show that technological limitations acted in concert with human limitations to restrict the comprehensiveness of the analyses.

In order to avoid the analysis of existing utilization of the land on which a development will stand, the development is considered to be on undeveloped ground. As it turned out, addition of the capability to evaluate existing usage would, in most cases, be quite simple. At the time this decision was made, however, that was not thought to be the case. A more difficult problem to overcome is evidenced in some of the costing procedures.

Constants based on a subsystem's past history are sometimes used in predicting costs. The underlying assumption of this process is that the development being analyzed is small in comparison to the total of subsystem users. That is to say that the development will not change the established configuration of the system. This places limitations on the analysis of very large developments.

The analysis has other restraints on development size. Developments cannot spread across more than one city and one county. Since the calibration data for one jurisdiction is in many ways distinct from that of others, to accommodate more than two jurisdictions simultaneously would require more operating overhead than we are willing to accept.

We note lastly that individual subsystem evaluations were limited in their scope by the size and speed of the computing equipment available. As a result, the concept of 'analysis area' is defined to reference a section of a large system split off and skeletonized to make it small enough to handle.

Analysis of Need

Early in the study, it became apparent that a considerable research effort would be needed before the true complexity of the models could be appreciated. Nonetheless, guidelines for implementation had to be laid down. Six requirements were set: 1) Interactivity 2) Shared data base 3) A central executive 4) Simplicity in operation 5) Consistency of operation 6) and Minimization of resources necessary for operation.

What Worked - What Didn't

Of the objectives set for the implementation, some worked and some didn't.

Interactivity didn't.

We can attribute this failure to a lack of information about the tasks the analysis system was eventually required to perform. Not knowing that caused us to misjudge several other development parameters. We didn't anticipate:

a. The complexity of the task from a programming standpoint in view of the goal of keeping the entire system simple.
b. The response time of the equipment available in a heavily used time-sharing environment.
c. The optimization problems associated with higher level languages for this application.
d. The complex nature of the analysis programs and input requirements.

With other goals we came closer to the mark.

The shared data base almost worked.

Lack of information about the tasks to be performed can be identified as a major problem for the development of the shared data base as well as for the development of the interactive capability. Research was changing the specifications of the tasks to be performed at the same time that the implementing programs were being designed. This situation made definition of an efficient data base organization scheme difficult. The ability to be flexible and to remain calm in the face of frustration is essential for personnel working in this environment. An attempt to be too comprehensive, which grew out of the indefinite nature of the task specification, led to another problem.

The data entry and update programs which were developed, while easy to use, were too large to operate in other than a batch environment.

One of the repercussions of this was that all of the concessions that had been made to interactivity turned out to be useless overhead. In an alternative data structure, implemented for the revenue model, it was seen that a data related paging algorithm in virtual storage would have served our needs better. Update of information in such a structure would be accomplished by reentry of page-size blocks of data from off-line sources (i.e., cards or key tape). If the study's resources had been greater and our path a little more clearly defined, the acquisition of a vendor's data base system might have been justified.

The consistent input format technique was a success.

A liberal input routine complete with a standardized card identification format was much preferred by users over the standard Cobol or Fortran formating procedures. We found further that a rigid field definition was more successful than free formating. This concern for utility was rewarded in another area.

Simple operation of the models was well received by the users.

After the data base has been established, most models can be invoked for a particular development with less than six punched cards. The reactions of users to this capability indicates that it was worth the effort. The expenditure of development effort was somewhat less worthwhile in our resource conservation attempts.

Minimization of machine resources was only a qualified success.

While basic configurations were the design goal, it became quickly apparent that for size and speed constraints to be met many specialized functions (and occasionally less than straight forward solutions) were necessary. The end product was a series of generally small, fast programs which are largely equipment specific. Modularity has acted to moderate potential conversion costs. However, the programs were to be developed within the financial resources of the project. That meant that the overhead of higher operating costs and longer development time which is associated with a concerted effort to make programs portable was unacceptable.

Organizational Considerations

We deal here with the way the Fiscal Impact Study Project is organized. Three elements of its organization are of general interest; an organizing convention, a heuristic for estimating project resource needs and an outline of its organizational structure.

One of the organizing conventions adopted by the study was the development of separate models of the various service subsystems. This allowed for considerable flexibility in allocation of development resources during the project.

A heuristic for estimating how much of the study's resources should be allocated to a particular model was formulated. It was based on the characteristics of the subsystem being modeled. The estimation is only grossly quantitative, but our experience with its application has shown it to be useful as a predictor of resource needs. The three characteristics of the subsystem to be considered are: its complexity, its certainty and the level of analysis applied to it. This is to say that a simple subsystem takes fewer resources than a complex one. A subsystem which can be successfully modeled by taking into account only its aggregate characteristics takes fewer resources than one which requires finer detail (a lower level of analysis) for successful modeling. A subsystem whose structure is largely undefined or whose structure is precisely defined requires fewer resources than one where there are several equally likely structures in competition for the final form of the analysis. We have found that the design phase of model construction was most sensitive to the certainty of the subsystem analysis techniques available. The programming and testing phases were most sensitive to the complexity of the subsystem being modeled. The calibration and utilization of the models were most sensitive to the level of analysis chosen. For example, the water model, which involves a flow analysis of the water supply system, was produced in about nine man months with the majority of the time spent in programming and testing. The general services model, which was a per-capita model, took about one and one half man months.

An organizational structure for medium-sized research projects was formed to facilitate the fiscal impact analysis system development while holding down costs. In this structure the Principal Investigator of the project acts as arbiter and administrator. He defines two lines of authority; programming and model development. The programming line consists of an analyst/programmer and several support programmers. The model development line consists of a research director and several researchers. For models where the development investment is predicted to be low, a researcher/programmer team is assigned to develop the model and its implementing computer program. They work under the general supervision of the research director. For those models where the development investment is predicted to be high, a development team consisting of the research director and one or more researchers and the analyst/programmer and one or more programmers is formed. Usually, the programmers can be involved with one small model or, under the direction of the analyst/programmer, with two large ones. The researchers can usually deal with only one model at a time. Supervision of four models or active participation in one and supervision of two seems an appropriate guideline for the analyst/programmer's workload. The research director may be limited similarly, though estimation of his position's load is much more uncertain than that of the other positions. The heaviest staff configuration in the study's two year effort was three full-time and five half-time personnel. The study costs were modest. For the same period, direct funding of about $125,000.00 was required. Miscellaneous support of about $25,000.00 (computer time, administrative support, etc.) was also received.

POLITICAL ENVIRONMENT

Whenever one embarks upon a research project the support of which is politically motivated and which has, as its end product, both a policy statement and a working utility, it is important to ask what parties are interested in the results of the work. We have done that. And we've also made some notes about the reactions of various persons and agencies to our work as they became aware of it.

We were generally able to anticipate who would be interested in our work. But while our expectations about the nature of that interest were fulfilled for most groups, we failed miserably in predicting the reaction of one very significant interested party.

Concerning our successes: Legislators in high growth areas where resource allocation and growth management were a concern were interested in the policy aspect of the work. They wanted to know whether a modeling technique would serve as the basis for estimation of fiscal impact fees. Those state level government agencies who felt that the information dissemination and analysis functions represented by the models could be used to further their missions were interested in lending financial or moral support to the project. The district level agencies which exist mostly as service agencies to local government (i.e., regional planning organizations) were interested in the models as tools to aid them in their work.

Among these supporters, both personal and organizational motivations for support varied considerably. When we spoke to government agency personnel, we were usually faced with the same sequence of reactions. First, they considered how use of these models would affect their work load. Then, they considered what effect supporting the models would have on their political position in the organization. And lastly, they questioned whether the use of these models would serve their organization's mission.

The only state level agency which seemed primarily concerned with serving the interests of their constituency was one regional planning council. This may be because regional planning councils in Florida survive only when they can maintain the support of their member cities and counties.

Land developers and the legislators who agreed with them were cautious in their reactions to the study. Even though they may have felt threatened by the possibility of fiscal impact fees, there was little hostility. That they were no more vocal may be due to the court's stand in Florida concerning fiscal impact fees. Generally, these fees were found unconstitutional. But recently, a Florida Supreme Court decision supported fiscal impact by defining judicially acceptable fiscal impact fee standards in the Dunedin Decision of February, 1976. The Court held that, in order to be constitutional, a fiscal impact fee must take into account existing subsystem capacity and the fee must charge to a development only those expenses directly attributable to the development. The set of models developed by the Fiscal Impact Research Study meets both these requirements. Further, it anticipates the argument that the revenues produced by the development must also be considered in the calculation of the fee.

In view of this decision, it is our expectation that more organized opposition to fiscal impact fee legislation will develop. This will make the task of the fiscal impact analysis system designer more challenging. He will have to be certain that his work is basically sound and that he can modify the techniques he uses to keep them in line with changing requirements.

The most surprising reaction to the project was that of the cities and counties which were originally intended to be the users of the finished product. We completely misjudged their reaction. They were almost uniformly underwhelmed. The majority of those whom we contacted saw little or no need for fiscal impact analysis at the level of detail we offered. When they admitted to a need, they were very skeptical about the cost effectiveness of the model calibration procedures and the subsequent data maintenance operations.

Examining this phenomenon more closely, we note that as a general rule, the higher up organizationally an administrator is, the more receptive he seems to be toward a mechanized fiscal impact evaluation technique. But it is important to point out that at all levels, a fairly small number of common objections to the procedures were raised. The legitimacy of these objections varied somewhat according to the condition of the jurisdiction that was under consideration. They are, however, basically valid and they must be considered by those wishing to adopt a fiscal impact analysis procedure. We present them here along with our responses. Six objections were raised:

First: We don't need to know what the analysis tells us.

Clearly, if this is true there is no point in going further. But usually this objection means that the uses to which the information produced by the analysis can be put have not been fully explored.

Second: We can't afford to assemble the original base of data.

Even if this effort (we estimate its cost at $15,000 per 100,000 population) is not justified by the fiscal impact analysis alone, the utility of the information in other area may support it.

Third: We can't afford to maintain the data.

The fixed costs of the impact analysis capability should be about $1,000 per month. Some preliminary studies indicate that, if fiscal impact fees are actually adopted, the savings from their application would easily offset this magnitude of cost for most medium-sized jurisdictions.

Fourth: The political environment in the area is wrong for this kind of operation.

If this is true, only the ability to effect the jurisdiction's political climate can overcome this objection.

Fifth: We can't get the various operating departments to support us.

In this case, one should be talking to the person's boss.

Sixth: We already do it another way.

Here, we may be dealing with a turf battle. If the alternative technique is really better, then it would be foolish to force a less worthy procedure on an organization. But the recent advances in these analysis methods and the strength of a comprehensive approach make the likelihood of a more effective unstructured method relatively small.

Anyone who has ever presented a new idea to a government agency will recognize the pattern outlined above. We do not suppose that it is novel. However, we feel that it is important to show its application to fiscal impact analysis.

CONCLUSION

A physically based fiscal impact analysis technique is, by its nature, comprehensive. Any comprehensive analysis requires a great deal of information to drive it. In the context of an established urban information system many of the initial cost barriers to implementing a useful fiscal impact analysis system are already overcome. If no urban information system now exists in an area, the commitment to fiscal impact fees by the involved jurisdiction could have two highly beneficial effects. One, the impact fee process could save considerable money. Two, the information system designed to drive the fiscal impact analysis procedure could act as the basis for a more generally used system.

We have seen that support exists for the development of fiscal impact analysis systems. It is not, in our experience, support at the local level. When local interests are approached, even if they agree that the information they could gain from fiscal impact analysis would benefit them, they are reluctant to allocate limited current resources against the possibility of future gain. They want a completed system that they can put into operation at little risk and at small cost. As more and more state and local governments develop and utilize fiscal impact techniques, those expectations are more likely to be met. After spending several years watching the growth of the technology of fiscal impact analysis, we believe that it will soon become an essential local growth management tool.

Robert Earickson
Plugging the Property Assessment Information Gap
University of Maryland Baltimore County
Baltimore, Maryland 21228

PLUGGING THE PROPERTY ASSESSMENT INFORMATION GAP

ABSTRACT: From the property owner's point of view,
the interrelated problems of fragmented urban governmental jurisdictions and the often haphazard basis of
property valuation result in a credibility gap between
the household and the taxing authority. We would argue
that property assessment should be a primary function
of an urban regional authority and that the geographic
and other bases of property valuation ought to be known
to the taxpayer. The objective of this paper is to
demonstrate a method of computer mapping of assessed
valuation of land and improvements. Printed copies of
all or part of such maps could be mailed to taxpayers
along with their annual tax bills, enabling households
to follow assessment policy trends over time and space.
For demonstration purposes, we have analyzed assessment
data provided by The British Columbia (Canada) Assessment Authority on The Victoria Metropolitan Area, and
have produced computer maps illustrating the land and
improvement valuation "surfaces" for that region. In
addition, maps of the area were produced to illustrate
the valuation surface based on, 1) the assumption that
land assessment for commercial purposes was a function
of accessibility with respect to the Victoria central
business district and major transportation arterials,
and 2) the assumption that residential land assessment
was a function of the amenity value of sites, as determined by a specified set of criteria. Maps at both
regional and neighborhood scale are illustrated.

INTRODUCTION

The typical North American property owner receives his or her property assessment annually. This assessment is normally divided into the
land and the improvements. Changes in the assessment or the rate paid
on properties characteristically occur--usually in the direction of
higher payments to the urban property owner. Whereas one can see the
magnitude of such changes, the basis for a higher or lower tax base is
usually unknown to the property owner. It is another one of those
intangible products of our urban bureaucracies.
The issue this paper is dealing with is that of providing the taxpayer with information as to 1) how his or her property assessment differs

from others in that "community," and 2) how the basis of the assessment was arrived at.

In a metropolitan area that is composed of several independent municipalities, the philosophy and methodology underlying property assessment can vary markedly, resulting in, from the taxpayer's point of view, some glaring disparaties. This situation can be exacerbated if assessment procedures <u>within</u> a municipality are not standardized.[1]   We leave to others the issue of fragmented municipal governments <u>vs</u>. county or regional government of metropolitan areas in order that we can move on to the subject at hand--except that we should like to put in a plug for some measure of metropolitan regional property tax control to relieve the abysmal inequalities that exist between central cities and their suburbs throughout the continent.[2]   If the reader accepts the proposition that some form of metropolitan restructuring is possible, expecially in the realm of raising funds (taxation), then it will soften the admittedly radical notion that we are about to put forth.

COMPUTER MAPPING

Assessor's maps have been hand-drawn since their inception, there being no faster or easier method available to do the job. While adequate for their time, they contain errors and inconsistencies. They are also quite expensive to reproduce. This fact, coupled with the necessity to continually update the original, means that most copies of the master are out of date to some degree.

A computerized mapping system is just one result of the sophisticated application of current computer-graphic technology. Computer graphics have been in existence since the 1960's. The state of this art is well enough known to our colleagues in Census Bureaus and the Geoprocessing Special Interest Group. By 1965 digitizing machines had been developed and were being used to translate existing maps electronically into machine-readable form for computer assimilation and subsequent reconstruction by automated plotting devices. Since that time, new and more sophisticated peripheral equipment, software, and minicomputers have been developed which have made computer-graphic applications even more diversified and cost-effective.[3]

---

[1]See, for example, Fellmeth, Robert C., <u>Politics of Land</u> (New York: Grossman Publishers, 1973), pp. 356-362.

[2]For a concurring opinion, see Mogulof, Melvin B., "A Modest Proposal for the Governance of America's Metropolitan Areas," <u>Journal of the American Institute of Planners</u>, Vol. XLI (1975), 250-257.

[3]Hutchinson, Don J., "A Computerized Mapping System," <u>Assessors Journal</u>, Vol. X (1975), 19-29; Easton, C. H., "The Land Records Information System in Forsyth County, North Carolina," <u>Proceedings</u>, <u>International Property Assessors Administration</u>, Vol. VII (1974), 261-267.

Metropolitan maps, which undergo frequent change and are required at different scales, are a natural application for computerization. We harbor no doubts that computerization is feasible in any sense of the term. It allows mapmakers a flexibility never before possible. No longer are we limited by the many problems that were inherent in manual production. It hardly seems necessary to further sell this notion to any of you. Many urban government agencies are now employing or preparing to purchase equipment which will enable them to take advantage of computer mapping technology.

In the short run, computerization is not inexpensive. The initial cost is high. But, the primary reasons why computerization is an obvious alternative to manual processes are the benefits. Besides the above mentioned capabilities of random scaling and frequent updating, speedy metric conversion and geocoding must be taken into consideration as ultimate legal and logical benefits.

One well-known computer mapping program is that known as Synagraphic Mapping, or SYMAP. Developed at the Laboratory for Computer Graphics and Spatial Analysis at Harvard University, it enables production of a broad range of maps and diagrams which graphically depict spatially disposed quantitative and qualitative information.

This mapping program produces maps by means of either a standard printing device (such as are shown below), or a continuous line plotting device. Geographic data which must be input to the mapping program are most easily prepared through use of a digitizer. Printer or plotter drawn maps convey all of the information that is provided by those manually drawn, and in a fraction of the time and cost.

THE ASSESSMENT APPLICATION

The assessment of property is not a simple task. It can be complicated and time consuming. Assessor's manuals which detail the criteria and procedures for rating land and improvements in cities may consist of two hefty volumes. All of this is public information which any taxpayer may read if he or she wishes to spend some time in the tax records office or public library.

Despite the lengthy guidelines available to the people who are hired to assess property, the assessment of real property is difficult, and calls for a considerable amount of judgment. In many cases, the qualifications for the job are nebulous or have not been insisted upon. In the province of New Brunswick (Canada), for instance, practice is the main qualification, if not the whole of the assessor's training. "Virtually confined to an office in which his colleagues are similarly lacking in any formal training for the difficult work they have to do; observing only standards of practice which are usually low; denied any opportunity of adequate training and perhaps without the general education which would be prerequisite, the assessor must stumble on as best he may. One can readily sympathize with his predicament, but it is impossible to have confidence in the results of this system."[4]

----

[4]White, Philip H. and Stanley W. Hamilton, The Real Property Tax in British Columbia--an Analysis (Vancouver: B.C. School Trustees Association, 1972), p. 28.

It is certainly not our intention to cast general suspicion on the assessment profession and its qualifications and ability to make fair and realistic judgments as to the worth of property. Besides, many assessors now have the aid of statistical experts. In the Province of British Columbia, for example, the Provincial Assessment Authority employs a statistician with a Ph.D., whose current task is to model the property assessment process to determine what factors explain the variation in assessed valuation. Such a model can be used to settle disputed cases, or to provide projections of the income from property assessments for future budgets.

What we would argue is that the taxpayer would be considerably assured of his local government's interest in his welfare if he were to be informed how his property assessment compared with those in his community, or how his neighborhood's tax level compared with that of surrounding neighborhoods. Further, a small amount of information explaining changes in this assessment from one year to the next would go a long way towards fulfilling the urban government's obligation to keep its taxpayers informed.

One way that this might be done is to employ the relatively inexpensive computer mapping capability discussed above. Figures 1, 2 and 3 illustrate hypothetical maps of standardized (for parcel size) land assessment. Figure 1 shows part of the Victoria (B.C.) metropolitan area. A random sample of per-square-foot land assessment figures were drawn from B.C. Assessment Authority records and were entered into the SYMAP program.[5] A choropleth map was produced which showed sample tax values at selected points. The "+" symbol shows areas in which land is assessed at greater than $3.00 per-square-foot. Remaining areas, shown with the "." symbol, are taxed below $3.00. Figure 2 illustrates a hypothetical case where assessment zones might be defined and the standardized assessed values illustrated with different overprint symbols. The value attached to each symbol appears near the center of the respective zone. Figure 3 is a "neighborhood" map which illustrates the assessed value of properties along hypothetical streets in an urban community.

Depending on the scale of the maps produced, a varying number of maps would have to be produced by the computer to cover the entire urban jurisdiction involved. But, once originals were available, copies could be quickly printed on an offset press for each and every property taxpayer, along with a short assessor's report on any change in the assessment over the past year. The property owner would then have much more complete information on which to appeal his or her assessment, should that action be desired.

We are fully aware of the political implications of this scheme. It is a threat to the autonomy of assessors, and in some cases, to the municipal government which employ them. But, in an age of rapidly increasing

---

[5]We wish to express our appreciation to the British Columbia Assessment Authority for providing us with data on individual property assessments for the Victoria Metropolitan Area. The help of the staff and facilities of the Department of Geography and the Computing Center at the University of Victoria are also gratefully acknowledged.

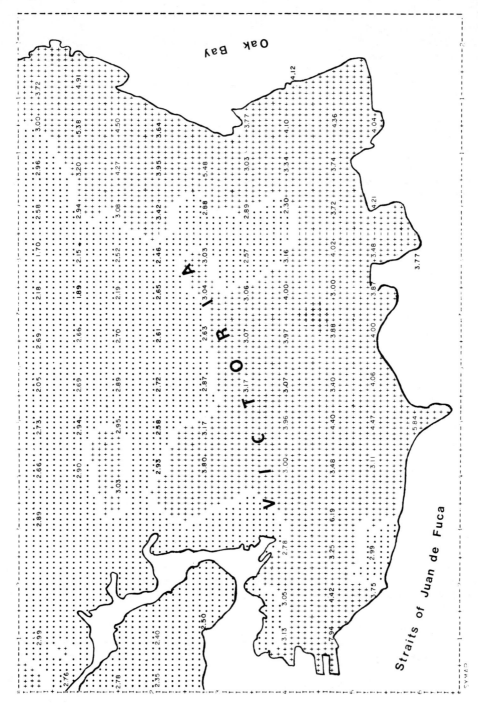

Figure 1. Standardized land assessments for part of the Victoria (B.C.) Metropolitan Area. For explanation, see text.

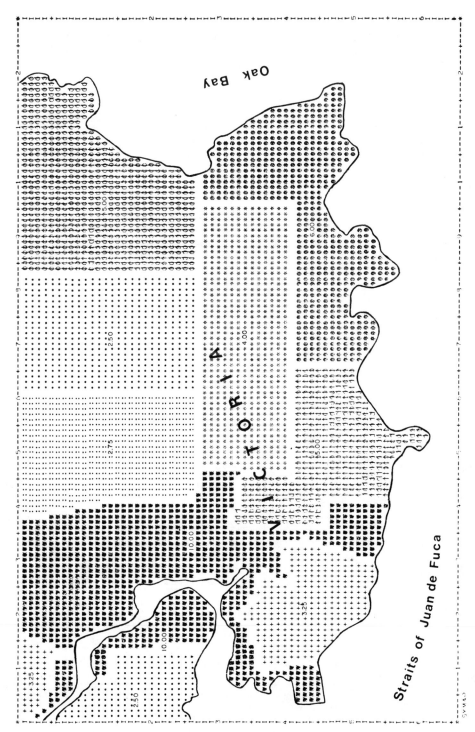

Figure 2. Hypothetical standardized assessments by zone. For explanation, see text.

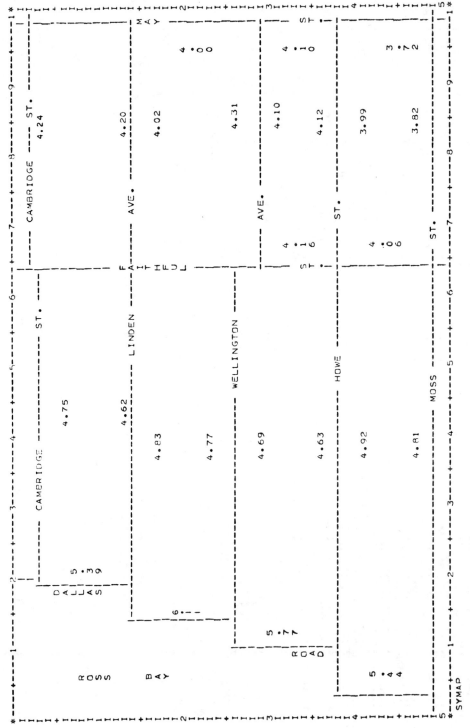

Figure 3. Hypothetical average assessments for properties along streets in a typical urban neighborhood.

costs of everything, the consumer-taxpayer is no longer content to accept rises in costs without a challenge to the basis for the increase. Already neighborhood and community organizations are assailing their municipal representatives with disputes over tax increases. Bond issues are regularly defeated by the taxpaying electorate partly because they do not understand why their property taxes continue to rise. Urban governments can and should keep their constituents informed as to the necessity and justification for tax increases. This paper has suggested one step in that direction.

Charles P. Kindleberger
Director, Planning and
  Programming Division
Community Development Agency
1015 Locust Street
St. Louis, Missouri 63101

THE SCHOOL FACILITY PLANNING SYSTEM: A LONG-RANGE
CAPITAL PLANNING AND BUDGETING TECHNIQUE

ABSTRACT: Capital improvement planning for public
schools requires several activities -- the projection of
students, the determination of space needs, the projection
of fiscal costs and resources, and the selection of construction or closing sites. A system has been developed to assist
planners in conducting these activities in both small and large
school districts. Many of the techniques presented may be
useful in other capital planning and budgeting situations.

INTRODUCTION

The American public spends billions of dollars annually for the
construction and modernization of public school facilities. In recent
years, the form of these capital expenditures has begun to change as
school closings have become as prevalent as openings and school remodeling has competed with new school construction. Many districts
that until recently were growing in both population and assessed valuation have leveled off. Others that stabilized in the late 1960's are in
the midst of a significant enrollment decline. Alternative approaches
to local public education continue to be explored with emphasis on new
curricula, instruction techniques, and forms of school organization.
All of these factors have direct implications for school facilities.
Thus, capital planning and budgeting for school systems in the years
ahead will continue to be characterized by uncertainty.

The School Facility Planning System is a method for helping
school administrators work in an environment of uncertainty. Developed under a National Science Foundation grant, this system
represents the effort of a research consortium, consisting of a local

planning agency, a computer-oriented consulting firm, the departments of urban studies and education at a university, and an architectural firm.* The project began in June, 1974, and continued into the spring of 1976, with the goal of evaluating and improving existing capital planning techniques so as to increase their utility for program administrators. As a result of this work, a planning system has been prepared that provides a basis for assisting not just school administrators, but individuals engaged in a diversity of long-range planning situations.

As indicated in Figure 1, a series of distinct components has been developed, each requiring certain information inputs and producing certain information outputs. Some of the components are further broken into specific system modules. Once a project is identified, most users will develop enrollment projections, followed by facility, fiscal, and geographic analysis. However, the system has been designed so that a component may be skipped which is of no interest, or for which information has been acquired from an independent source.

In keeping with the research directives, two sets of procedures have been developed and documented: one oriented to users with access to a computer, the other requiring only a hand calculator.** Each approach has certain drawbacks. The manual approach will be laborious for most medium and large school districts. Alternatively, use of the computer version may require a longer organizational effort, especially when it is to be used on a non-IBM machine. Each component has been documented in terms that provide a general description of its purpose and design, followed by specific instructions. Examples for all forms (manual version) and input cards (computer version) are provided.

---

*N.S.F. Grant Number APR 74-14195 was awarded to St. Louis County, Missouri, in May, 1974, in response to N.S.F. Program Solicitation Number 73-27. Intech, Incorporated, St. Louis University, Wm. B. Ittner, Incorporated, and a nineteen member review committee assisted the St. Louis County Department of Planning in performing the assignment. The author served as Project Director while employed as Chief of the Department of Planning's Governmental Assistance Division.
**Documentation of the School Facility Planning System is available on a limited basis from the Council of Educational Facility Planners (29 West Woodruff Avenue, Columbus, Ohio, 43210) in three volumes: User's Handbook: Manual Version, User's Handbook: Computer Version, and the Final Report. A tape containing the computer programs is also available.

Figure 1: School Facility Planning System

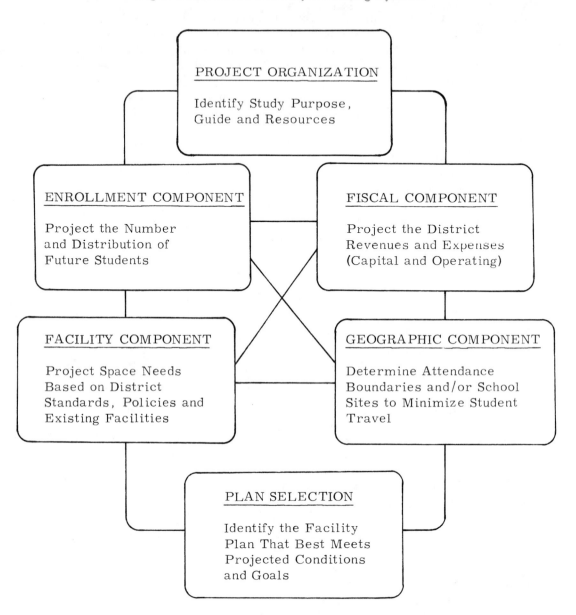

Neither version of the School Facility Planning System replaces the User. The system's primary use will be in testing facility plans, not creating them. It will not replace the data collection requirements, the judgement and the creativity that have traditionally gone into capital planning activities. Therefore, to effectively use the system, the school district will be required to do considerable work. Historical information must be collected, educational standards and policies examined, and alternative solutions to a space problem devised. Given these conditions, the system does provide a structure and format in which to conduct long-range planning. It will enable the combination of intuitively derived standards and empirical information. It will speed up necessary calculations, permitting many "iterations" under different assumptions. It will help a district to appreciate the impact likely to result from alternative school policies or community conditions.

CAPITAL PLANNING AND BUDGETING CONSIDERATIONS

The process of preparing a long-range capital improvements plan involves, in theory, a set of common tasks which must be undertaken independent of the subject matter or institutional setting. As illustrated in Figure 2, the tasks may be thought of as "transformations" which should be carried out by the planner.

Figure 2: Capital Planning Transformations

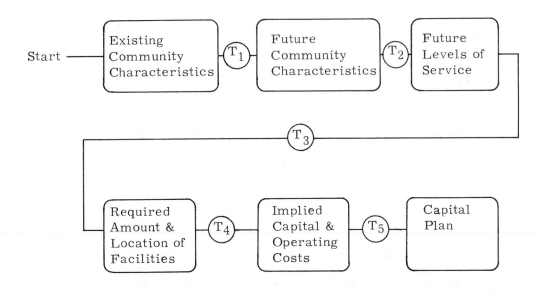

The capital planning activity begins with a review of existing supply and demand conditions. The demand for automobiles, parks, public education, or any other commodity is examined in relation to the available facilities for supplying that commodity. The capital planner must consider potential gaps between demand and supply in the future, as well as the present. Therefore, the first transformation (T_1) requires a projection of future demand and supply conditions. The automobile manufacturer must project the future demand for cars and the future ability of existing plants to build them. The number, wealth, location, and tastes of individuals must be projected, as well as the probable deterioration and obsolescence of currently available factories. Or, to use a public sector example, the city's traffic engineer must consider the expected, as well as current utilization of streets and bridges, and their existing and projected characteristics. Because many future community characteristics will depend upon factors that are beyond the control of the planner, they must be considered carefully, with attention to the probability of alternative futures.

The second step in the process requires that the future community characteristics be translated into their service requirements. The community must be analyzed in terms of its projected need and desire for specific goods. In the case of public goods, this second transformation (T_2) will require the establishment or identification of goals. Decisions must be made as to the desirable amount of open space, refuse collection, or fire protection versus a lower tax bill. Every potential service level will imply a set of facilities, staff, and equipment necessary to provide it.

A comparison of the facilities necessary to meet future community goals with currently available facilities (which can be expected to deteriorate) reveals the extent of the planning problem. The third transformation (T_3) involves the identification of required facilities and the consideration of alternative plans that could satisfy this current and projected need. The problem has aspects both of quantity and geography. The number and the location of parks, clinics, or schools must be analyzed.

Every potential configuration of new facilities will have a price. Transformation four (T_4) "costs out" the fiscal implications of each proposal. The final transformation (T_5) requires that one of the alternative plans be selected, presumably that which comes closest to achieving the desired level of services within acceptable cost guidelines.

The actual capital planning process is, of course, rarely as neat as the diagram in Figure 2. The outputs resulting from a given transformation will often cause a re-examination of the assumptions that led to that conclusion. A plan that appears too expensive (transformation 4) will cause the planner to consider alternative plans (transformation 3). However, the alternative plan options need not be limited to the consideration of smaller or cheaper facilities. Policies that would reduce required service levels during peak hours (transformation 2) may be feasible. Thus, a ban on lawn watering, an incentive for car pools, or an extra charge for electricity use in the evening hours may be reasonable alternatives to a larger water plant, highway, or generator. Similarly, the future community characteristics (transformation 1) need not be regarded as preordained. In recent years many suburban communities have discovered, through the use of zoning and subdivision regulations, the ease with which the number and kinds of people moving into a community may be controlled.

THE SCHOOL PLANNING PROCESS

For the most part, the capital planning and budgeting function for public schools may be conceived within the above framework. School planning in the United States takes many forms. With approximately 18,000 independent school districts across the country, it is understandable that much of the facility planning is characterized by relatively unsophisticated methods and narrow scope. A survey of more than one hundred school districts during the project revealed that 68.9 percent used "professional judgement" to forecast enrollment, and that 61.1 percent used it to forecast fiscal needs.

Educational capital planning requires the analysis of students, finances, and the existing school plant. Student enrollment must be forecast in light of the number and kind of people expected to live within the district. The future number of children within the district will, like most other demographic forecasts, reflect the combined effects of births, deaths, and migration. However, a more complicated aspect must be addressed: all school age children do not attend the public school system. Depending upon wealth, religion, and other family characteristics, some proportion of the children will attend private or parochial school, repeat grades, or drop out.

Fiscal resources must be projected recognizing that they will fluctuate with community development trends, taxation decisions and economic conditions. The physical adequacy of school buildings must be examined given their age and design characteristics.

The service level implications associated with a projected student body will depend upon the educational goals of the community as expressed by school board and superintendent policy, and state legislation. The grade organization, pupil-space and pupil-teacher ratios, curriculum offerings, recreational facilities, and transportation program are established either consciously or unconsciously. Each of these standards and policies must then be translated into its facility implications. Thus the decision to offer an automotive mechanics class, provide a hot lunch, have a football or tennis team, or allow students to drive to school will present a facility requirement which may or may not be possible within the existing facility capacity. A comparison of required facilities with the existing school plant will yield a measure of needed or excess space.

Numerous solutions will typically be feasible for resolving a space problem. Non-structural solutions in the form of grade reorganization, grade relocation, work-study programs, or an open school environment may be appropriate. Structural possibilities will include creating "found space" either within or outside existing facilities; converting unnecessary space to student, administrative, or community quarters; and, of course, constructing or closing a school. Each of these facility solutions can be evaluated in terms of its direct operating and capital costs, as well as its educational benefits. Each may also be examined in terms of its geographic costs as measured in student travel time or distance, and/or student bussing expenses.

The consideration of alternative plans is usually an iterative process. In some instances, none of the alternatives will be found capable of meeting the desired educational goals and financial constraints, in which case additional alternatives must be formulated. In other cases, several alternatives may appear feasible. The trade-offs associated with each must then be evaluated, so that the optimal plan is selected.

The ultimate decision to close or build a school will usually depend on the school district's approach to risk, and particularly its perception of the dangers of over-estimating or under-estimating projected trends. In a situation where nothing can be absolutely certain as to the number of future students, the standards which will apply to their education, or expected revenues and expenses, the school board must evaluate the cost of making a poor capital planning decision versus making a decision to postpone constructing or closing a facility. These costs will vary with the situation. In a growing district the decision to build a school sooner than necessary (i.e., based on a higher than realistic enrollment forecast) may prove wise if the facility ultimately would be necessary. Such a decision would minimize crowding and would save funds that might otherwise be lost to inflation if the district had waited on its decision. However, if after the decision to build, the enrollment trends actually peaked, stabilized, or declined, an unneeded school would have been constructed.

Similarly, in a district with declining enrollment, the costs of a bad estimate must be considered. The decision to sell an unnecessary school may prove wise if enrollments continue to decline. On the other hand, should future enrollment levels stabilize and begin to climb again, a much wiser decision would have been to lease or mothball the unnecessary school until it was required again.

The School Facility Planning System cannot determine the school administrator's or school board's position on such unquantifiable issues. Such positions must be adopted subjectively. The system can, however, provide an administrator with a range of likely future conditions based on selected assumptions. It also provides a mechanism for evaluating policies designed to address such conditions.

THE SYSTEM COMPONENTS

The National Science Foundation's guidelines requiring the development of procedures useable by many school districts with widely divergent sizes, administrative structures and access to data have influenced the resulting product. This focus has precluded development of a model that would assume the presence of an accurate geographic base file or specific state allocation formula. Instead, as described below, a flexible, open-ended system has been formulated that permits use of many traditional analytical techniques. The user is presented with the opportunity to select a manual or computer-based approach, a medium or long-term planning horizon and a general (e.g., district-wide) or detailed (e.g., specific subjects) level of analysis.

Enrollment Component. The system recommends that several techniques be considered when projecting future enrollments. The traditional cohort survival or grade progression technique is suggested for those districts needing specific forecasts for grades over a short- or medium-range time span. This is the most popular projection technique, and, particularly in relatively stable districts, sufficiently accurate in the short run. (Wasik, 1971)

An extrapolation technique may also be appropriate for extending time series data on a linear or non-linear basis. There is evidence that regression techniques yield superior projections in comparison to the cohort survival method (Webster, 1970). The School Facility Planning System provides the following time series forecasting capability:

* Linear Projections
* Exponential Projections
* Modified Exponential Projections (with or without user supplied asymptote)
* Logistics Projection (with or without user supplied asymptote)
* Gompertz Projection (with or without user supplied asymptote, available only in computer version)

Without knowing a district's characteristics, it is, of course, not possible to say which of the time trend techniques are most reasonable. Some, such as the exponential curve, are likely to be unreasonable in a long-range forecasting situation. The use of a curvilinear technique appears more acceptable in a long-range situation, especially since the user can specify an approximate holding capacity (asymptote) which the extrapolation should not exceed. None of the extrapolation techniques can actually shift the direction of the forecast. Thus, a forecast of continued growth (or decline) leveling off, and then actual decline (or growth) would have to be made using one of the other forecasting techniques.

A third technique is the familiar approach to most planners of projecting a population by determining a ratio between that population and a larger population for which an acceptable forecast exists (Jaffe, 1969). This approach is recommended for use in conjunction with another technique, especially when a long-range or small area forecast is contemplated.

Communities characterized by rapid expansion or reduction of their housing stock may want to consider a fourth technique -- the dwelling unit method. This approach requires forecasts of future numbers of dwellings and future students per dwelling. As such, the technique has substantial data requirements. It, as well as the other techniques, may be supported by a district-wide census or enumeration.

In addition to the district-wide projections, sub-area forecasts may be desired by certain school districts. A method is presented for projecting "regional" enrollments and then allocating those to smaller "grids" or "areas" within each region. This geographic dimension will enable the attendance boundary adjustment and site selection procedures that are described in the Geographic Component. Techniques for projecting racial composition and adjusting projections for unique events within a district also are presented.

The Enrollment Component contains the software in the computer version necessary to construct a forecasting model based on multiple regression. However, the absence in most districts of historic data and valid projections for the independent variables limits the applicability of such an approach.

Facility Component. In most facility planning situations, the next step after analyzing future enrollment is to determine the ability of the school district given its existing and expected school plant, to house the projected students. The Facility Component is used to translate projected students into the actual space required to serve them. This needed space can be measured in square feet, teaching spaces, or both. When compared to the district's existing space, an indication is given of the projected shortage or excess of facilities.

The amount of space necessary to accommodate a given number of students varies directly with the policies and standards adopted by the school board. The variation is substantial, especially when a district is willing to consider double sessions, a twelve-month school year and other major policy shifts.

Required space can be defined in terms of teaching stations (e.g., classrooms) or square feet necessary for any subject area which in turn may be defined as one course, a group of courses (with similar space characteristics) or all courses. Required teaching stations (TS) would be calculated as follows:

$$TS = \frac{N \times W}{A \times P \times U}$$

Course Enrollment (N) - The number of students that sign up for a subject area will fluctuate with student tastes, state legislation (e.g., requirements that all students take state history or gymnasium, etc.) and school board policy.

Course Periods Per Week (W) - Many courses meet daily or five times per week. Others meet two or three times per week. When a subject area is defined to include both kinds of courses, the average number of periods per course is likely to be a number such as 4.73. The product of N x W is projected student periods per week for a given subject area.

Desired Students Per Teaching Station (A) - The school administration may consider a variety of alternative standards as to the desired students per room. N x W/A yields projected class periods per week.

Number.of Periods Per Week (P) - Most schools typically have five or six periods per day and are in session five days per week. Those districts on staggered or double sessions or with a work study program would have a number different from the typical 25 or 30 periods per week. Dividing the projected class periods by the available periods in a week during which classes can be taught yields the minimum teaching station requirement.

Utilization Rate (U) - Teaching space may be used for study halls, extracurricular activities, storage, and many additional activities. The utilization rate

is a factor, usually set between .8 and .95, that
can be modified to vary the number of classrooms
available for such flexible uses. The higher the
utilization rate (i.e., the closer to one) the less
uncommitted, hence flexible, space will be required.

Once the required teaching space has been calculated, it may be
compared with existing space to determine the extent of the district's
space deficit or surplus. The system's major benefit will derive
when the user experiments with alternative policies and standards
to explore ways of reducing that deficit or surplus.

Fiscal Component. The third component addresses perhaps the most
complex element of school facility planning. The Facility and Geographic Components involve complicated calculations, but relatively
little uncertainty. They essentially translate one set of projected
conditions into a second set. Projected students are translated into
required space (Facility Component) and expected "transportation
costs" (Geographic Component). The Enrollment Component involves
substantially more uncertainty, but because demographic trends are
usually gradual, historic data often serves as a useful guide to the
future. Fiscal trends are substantially more erratic.

No analytical technique can accurately predict the impact of
inflation, the teacher's union, the local electorate, or state representatives. Judgements regarding next year's effect of these and
other forces on the school budget are extremely difficult, let alone
the effect over a ten- or twenty-year planning period. Therefore,
the Fiscal Component exists primarily to explore the probable impact
of alternative conditions. The user is helped in understanding what
would happen if a bond issue was floated, the tax rate was cut, the
legislature changed its allocation formula, or if any of numerous
other contingencies materialized.

Three elements of the district's financial situation can be explored with the system:

Capital Resources - The user is provided with the
ability to calculate current and future bonding
capacity in light of projected changes in assessed
valuation and possible new bond issue efforts.

Future Revenues - The user is provided with the
ability to forecast revenues from different levels
of government that will be available for both
operating and capital requirements.

> Future Expenditures - The user is provided with the
> ability to project the future costs associated with any
> building program and to evaluate those costs in light
> of expected revenue.

It will be particularly necessary to tailor this component to specific district situations. The instructions for calculating net bonding
capacity can be disregarded by those districts that foresee little need
for new debt or that are not restricted by debt limitations. Similarly,
building costs forecasts and selected revenue or expenditure forecasts will be inappropriate in some areas. Some users will want to
consider redefining the revenue and expenditure categories so that
they coincide with their district's set of accounts.

The model is more open-ended regarding specific forecasting
techniques in the Fiscal Component than in the other components.
Many expenditure categories can be projected as a function of an
independent forecast of students, teacher salaries, or physical
space. Experimentation within a given district will be necessary to
determine which of these, or perhaps other independent variables,
has the most predictive power. In revenue forecasting situations,
users are encouraged to apply the exact local and state formulas
which impact their community, rather than the general approaches
outlined in the handbooks.

Geographic Component. The final component addresses the question
of location. Previous analysis has considered the need for more or
fewer schools and the district's ability to pay, but not important
questions such as where a school should be opened or closed and who
should attend that school. The system has been designed to assist in
the examination of two important locational issues:

> Attendance Boundaries - The user is provided with
> a technique for designating the attendance boundaries
> of existing schools so as to minimize transportation
> costs and improve racial balance.

> Site Selection - The user is provided with a technique
> for determining the general location of school sites
> within a district that would minimize transportation
> costs in light of long-range enrollment projections.

A linear programming approach was selected as most applicable
to these issues. Models requiring a DIME File (Urban Decision
Systems, 1975) were judged to require too much data, and to be
inappropriate when working with long-range enrollment projections.

Models requiring substantial computer resources such as that necessary to support integer programming (Hall, 1974) were similarly rejected.

The linear programming approach assigns students, projected by geographic grid, to schools in a manner such that the total distance commuted is minimized. This information can then be used to delineate attendance zones or to determine the student transportation "costs" of alternative closing or construction options.

The Stepping-Stone or Distribution method is used in the manual version. The Simplex method is used in the computer version. Two programs, BOUND and RBOUND, have been written to provide input and receive output from a previously written subroutine entitled SIMPLX (McMillan and Gonzalez, 1968). RBOUND is a variation designed to permit the identification of attendance boundaries capable of achieving racial balance.

SUMMARY

Developing a generalized system capable of meeting the needs of both small and large institutions is a severe challenge, especially if given a modest budget ($120,000) and limited time (fifteen months, stretched to twenty-two). Major problems during the project included the adoption of a format and analytical techniques suitable to both ordinary and sophisticated users; the conduct of a "state-of-the-art" survey in the face of an interminable OMB review of questionnaires; establishing productive dialogue between planners, computer-oriented professionals, educators, architects and politicians; evaluating a product still in evolution; and editing, typing, proofing and printing approximately 500 pages of documentation.

The ultimate value of the system must await further testing and evaluation conducted over time in a variety of environments. That kind of intensive review has not yet been possible. However, most initial reactions have been positive. Perhaps the pervading characteristic of the School Facility Planning System is flexibility. The user is presented with the ability to measure space requirements in terms of either teaching stations or square feet, depending upon preference. The ability is presented to conduct analysis at different levels of detail, on a district-wide basis, a school-by-school basis, or facility space type basis. Above all, the ability is provided to conduct impact analysis. School districts may examine the probable effect of conditions over which they have no control, such as a shift in migration patterns or in the rate of assessed valuation growth. Similarly, they can examine the impact of changes in school policy or standards. Solutions of both a structural character (e.g., building or closing a school) and non-structural character (e.g., changing the desired students per classroom standard, sessions policy or utilization rate) can be examined with equal ease.

The main purpose of this kind of system is to provide the planner with a means for examining the consequences of his assumptions and observations in a quantitative fashion. It has been said that human beings have great intuitive capability, but that their ability to integrate a large number of sound intuitive notions into correct decisions is often poor. Hopefully, the School Facility Planning Process will facilitate this integration, thereby improving the quality of educational capital planning and budgeting.

REFERENCES

Hall, Fred L., A Preliminary Evaluation of an Optimizing Technique for Use in Selecting New School Locations, Chicago: Chicago Board of Education, Illinois, 1974

Jaffe, A.J., Handbook of Statistical Procedures for Long-Range Projections of Public School Enrollment, Technical Monograph, Washington, D.C.: Department of Health, Education, and Welfare, Office of Education, 1969.

McMillan, Claude and Gonzalez, Richard, Systems Analysis: A Computer Approach to Decision Models, Homewood, Illinois: Richard D. Irwin, 1968.

Urban Decision Systems, Inc., Computer-Assisted School Facility Planning with ONPASS, Los Angeles, California: Urban Decision Systems, Inc., 1975.

Wasik, John L., A Review and Critical Analysis of Mathematical Models Used for Estimating Enrollments in Educational Systems, Raleigh, North Carolina: North Carolina State University, Center for Occupational Education, 1971, ED 059 545.

Webster, John J., "The Cohort-Survival Ratio Method in the Projection of School Attendance," Journal of Experimental Education, Vol. 39, No. 1, Fall 1970, pp. 89-96.

Stephen J. Ondrejas
Director of Planning
City of Wichita Falls
P. O. Box 1431
Wichita Falls, Texas 76307

Stephen R. Morath
Senior Planner
City of Wichita Falls
P. O. Box 1431
Wichita Falls, Texas 76307

URBAN PLANNING IN WICHITA FALLS, TEXAS:

ONE YEAR AFTER USAC

ABSTRACT: In March of 1970, the City of Wichita Falls and the U. S. Department of Housing and Urban Development executed a contract for a cost-shared project in which the city was to research, design, and implement a prototype, totally integrated municipal information system. The contract expired on August 31, 1975 and since that date, the city has maintained and operated the implemented applications.

This paper reports on the effect and utilization of the implemented applications on the urban planning activities of the city since the expiration of the project contract. It also discusses the anticipated future effect and utilization of the implemented applications. The paper concludes that it was possible to implement urban planning applications as part of a totally integrated municipal information system and that the implemented applications offer a great potential for transfer to other municipalities.

INTRODUCTION

In March of 1970, the City of Wichita Falls and the U. S. Department of Housing and Urban Development executed a contract for a cost-shared project in which the city was to research, design, and implement a prototype, totally integrated municipal information system. The contract expired on August 31, 1975 and since that date, the city has maintained and operated the implemented applications.

Two contract specifications are of importance to an understanding of this paper. First, the system was to collect and organize operational data in ways that provide useful information supporting urban planning. Second, the prototype was to be transferrable to other municipalities.

The purpose of this paper is to report on the effect and utilization of the implemented applications on the urban planning activities of the city since the expiration of the project contract. Emphasis also is placed on the expected future effect and utilization of the implemented applications from which concluding observations are drawn.

It contains 1) a brief general description of the project and applications which were implemented with respect to urban planning, 2) a detailed discussion of how the implemented applications affected and were utilized in the city's urban planning activities since the expiration of the project, 3) a discussion of the expected future effect and utilization of the implemented applications, and 4) concluding observations.

GENERAL DESCRIPTION OF THE PROJECT AND IMPLEMENTED APPLICATIONS

The project was under the sponsorship of a consortium of federal agencies called the Urban Information Systems Inter-Agency Committee (USAC). The Integrated Municipal Information System (IMIS) project in Wichita Falls was a research and development project to learn whether prototype urban information systems could be successfully developed and operated and then be transferred to local jurisdictions elsewhere with a minimum of alteration. The IMIS project was approached through the completion of six technical phases: analysis, conceptualization, design, development, implementation and evaluation.

The two major urban planning applications which were implemented by the expiration of the project were 1) Geographic Base Indexing System (GBIS) and 2) Lot and Network Definition (LAND).

GBIS uses the Census Bureau's Geographic Base File (GBF) addressing technique and Dual Independent Map Encoding (DIME) edit technology. It provides a means for accessing, maintaining, and organizing operational data in the city's integrated data base. Through GBIS, place, event, and person data can be organized by geographic sectors for statistical analysis.

LAND provides the basic definition of each parcel and each building located on a parcel. The operational data of several city departments can only be accessed through pointers contained in LAND.

Both GBIS and LAND must be maintained in harmony. If errors are made, operating departments cannot gain access to their operational data. Thus, a base map series has been developed which serves as an important visual edit of GBIS and LAND. Maintenance of these three applications is the responsibility of the Planning Division's planning systems section. A more thorough description of the implemented applications is presented below.

GBIS is a street segment file with data items for each segment including street name, street type, street direction, "left" and "right" address ranges, "from" and "to" intersection node numbers, and "X" and "Y" node coordinates. Special area designators are also assigned to street segments. They include "left" and "right" tract, block, zip, and traffic zone codes. Operationally, GBIS is first an index designed to produce an access key to operational files using a street address and the geographic coordinates of the associated street segment. Second, GBIS is a geocoding tool which can assign parcel coordinate location codes, aggregate data by special areas, and be used to display data in conjunction with computer mapping routines. The street segment file is maintained by the planning systems section in an on-line environment via a video computer terminal. The file is then computer edited and output documents are produced the next day to insure the integrity of the file.

GBIS can be used as a common index mechanism by all departments to access operational data in an on-line environment and in a form that effectively meets their functional requirements. Data access and maintenance through street address replaces redundant and non-integrated indexes such as tax account number, water billing account number, intersection number, street code and subdivision, block and lot number. It can also be used to create reports related to place, event, and person data by special geographic area. Forecasting and decision-making are supported, especially comprehensive planning, community renewal planning, work programming, and work scheduling.

LAND consists of basic parcel and building definitions. The basic parcel record includes front footage, depth, area, land use, coordinate location, and subdivision, lot and block number or property description. The building record indicates building location and is accessed by address through GBIS and the parcel record. Additional pointers in LAND allow several departments to access operational data. LAND is maintained by the planning systems section in an on-line environment via a video computer terminal. Parcel and building data can be added, changed, or deleted. Each update is computer edited and output documents are generated the next day for verification and to insure integrity and harmony.

LAND can be used to obtain consistent, accurate information on parcel characteristics and building location in an on-line environment. Subdivision, zoning and other development proposals can be processed more quickly. Land acquisition strategies can be better developed as well as cost/benefit and environmental assessment reviews. Developers, real estate brokers, attorneys and the general public can also obtain data useful in preparing abstracts of titles and title insurance policies or in determining adverse possessions, laches, or deed transfers. LAND can also be used as a framework on which to build additional applications.

Base maps consisting of a series of 1":100' scale maps were developed from geographically accurate aerial photographs supplemented by county plat records and by delineation of unplatted property from local tax records. The base maps serve as a visual edit of GBIS and LAND and are updated simultaneously. The base maps are drawn on 22" x 36" sheets of .003" mylar with matte on both sides.

In addition, an overlay series has been designed and partially developed. The overlays will serve as a visual edit for use by operating departments accessing data through GBIS and LAND. The overlay series consists of 22" x 36" sheets of .002" mylar with matte on both sides. Both base maps and overlays are updated using standard leroy templates and rapidograph pens.

EFFECT AND UTILIZATION

Since the expiration of the project contract, GBIS, LAND and the base map series have had a major operational effect on the Planning Division. They have also been utilized in the Division's community renewal planning but have been of limited support to the comprehensive planning process.

The effect of the three applications on the operations of the Planning Division has been both inter and intra-divisional. Major inter-divisional effects resulted from the need to establish a planning systems section within the Planning Division and to coordinate its operational procedures with those of the land resource management section.[1] The planning systems section currently consists of two planners and one full-time and one part-time senior engineering draftsman. The effect of establishing this new section required both planners to be trained in data processing basics such as terminal operations, data processing terminology, systems analysis and systems conceptualization. In addition, operational procedures had to be established which defined the tasks and responsibilities of each position. Creation of the planning systems section also greatly increased the duties of the Assistant Director of Planning who was delegated the responsibility of directing the section.

Other inter-divisional effects resulted from the need to establish operational procedures between the planning systems section and the land resource management section. Personnel in the planning systems section had to be trained in the operations of the land resource management section which is the generator of the operational data on streets, subdivisions, land uses and changes in the corporate limits of the city which must be reflected in GBIS, LAND and the base map series. New operational procedures were established to ensure the proper flow of operational data from the land resource management section to the planning systems section. This involved a shift in some tasks and responsibilities in order to achieve better coordination. For example, the approval of new street names was transferred from the land resource management section to the planning systems section. Administrative duties were also regrouped by making the Assistant Director of Planning responsible for both the land resource management and planning systems sections.

Intra-divisional effects resulted from the need to coordinate data maintenance tasks between the planning systems section and other city departments. New operational procedures had to be established to coordinate the maintenance activities of the three applications of the planning systems section and the IMIS applications of other city departments since the operational data of these departments can only be accessed through pointers contained in LAND. This required personnel from the planning systems section and employees of other city departments to be cross-trained in terminal operations, functional requirements of departmental data items and system linkages between IMIS applications. The operational procedures also redefined the tasks and responsibilities of the personnel in the planning systems section and the employees of other city departments. For example, the Building Inspection Department was relieved of all addressing responsibilities for new buildings. The result of establishing these intra-divisional operational procedures increased the administrative duties of both the Assistant Director and Director of Planning who were required to arbitrate in solving procedural problems which occurred between the planning systems section and other city departments.

---

[1]The land resource management section is responsible for current planning activities which include accepting street dedications, processing subdivision plats, approving parcel dimensions and land uses, abandoning previous right-of-way dedications, annexing properties and counseling developers, brokers, attorneys and citizens.

Finally, interaction between the planning systems section and non-city organizations and citizens concerning addressing caused effects on the Planning Division. Both planners in the planning systems section were trained to assign and/or change addresses based on a recently adopted ordinance formally standardizing address procedures by requiring unique street names, unique address ranges for each street segment, consistent ascent of numbers along the street segment for each parcel and building, and regular odd/even parity for addresses on either side of the street. Since the Tax Department also collected the school district's property tax, addresses had to be assigned to parcels and buildings outside the city limits but within the district in order to enter them on the integrated data base for billing purposes. Thus, the system requirements of GBIS and LAND required that the planning systems section assign official addresses to all parcels and buildings within the corporate limits as well as the school district, and change existing addresses which were not in ascent or parity. Completing these tasks had a tremendous effect on the Planning Division because of misinterpretations in the minds of many citizens. For example, citizens equated address assignments to vacant lots with tax increases, property acquisition through eminent domain and annexation of parcels and buildings outside the city limits but in the school district. Address assignments and changes also required extensive communication between the Planning Division and the post office, utility companies and deliverers of emergency service.

In reference to utilization, GBIS, LAND and the base map series have been of assistance in the urban planning activities of the Planning Division. Since the expiration of the project contract, the utility of the three implemented applications for developing a comprehensive plan has been minimal. However, the cause has not been the capacity of the applications, but one of timing. The Planning Division has just recently begun the development of a revised comprehensive plan which is to be completed in 1979. The information accessible in the integrated data base has served no utility for comprehensive planning up to this time simply because there were no work elements being completed which required the use of this data.

In contrast, the utility of the applications in developing community renewal plans has been high. The availability of consistent, accurate information on parcel characteristics and building location in an on-line environment has been of great assistance in preparing a redevelopment plan (MIDTOWN 2000) for the central city area and in preparing the city's Community Development Block Grant Application.

In developing MIDTOWN 2000, the data accessed through GBIS and LAND allowed the development of alternative land acquisition strategies for the siting of a new highway exchange, convention center, new in-town housing and new off-street parking. Had the data not been on-line and accessible by address, the number of alternatives would have significantly decreased. The applications also assisted in researching and developing a historical preservation district which is now planned as part of MIDTOWN 2000. Operational data on the age, structural quality, and unique structural characteristics of buildings, which was contained in the IMIS files of the Tax Department was quickly accessed via GBIS and LAND.

The city's Community Development Block Grant Application was also of a higher quality because of the implemented applications. Information obtained from the integrated data base was used in cost/benefit studies on street paving, street lighting, and drainage projects. Also, data was used in the preparation of environmental assessment reviews for Block Grant projects.

FUTURE EFFECT AND UTILIZATION

GBIS, LAND and the base map series will continue to have a major operational effect on the Planning Division and they will be much more utilized in developing and monitoring comprehensive and community renewal plans as well as programming and scheduling work phases.

The project's future effect on the operations of the Planning Division will be mostly intra rather than inter-divisional. Future inter-divisional effects will be minimal since the planning systems section is in place and has been coordinating operations with the land resource management section for over a year. One additional planner may be required in the planning systems section as additional applications are built on the basic parcel and building framework of LAND.

However, future intra-divisional effects will be considerable as other city departments, non-city organizations and citizens become more aware of the accessibility of data because of GBIS, LAND, and the base map series. It is anticipated that other departments will request reports of place, event and person data by special geographic areas. Also, as other operational files are linked with the integrated data base, additional base map overlays will need to be designed and developed. Requests from non-city organizations for information is expected to increase. The accessing of operational data by way of the on-line system will be used more and more by personnel from numerous taxing districts, utility companies, development corporations, real estate offices, and legal firms. Also, it is expected that the demand for use of the applications by local citizens will increase. Instead of being required to line up for information in several departments, citizens with questions can come to the Planning Division and obtain full information. Responding to a great number of requests will add considerable work for the planning systems section.

As indicated in the previous section, the Planning Division has recently begun the development of a revised comprehensive plan which will be completed in 1979. The data accessible through GBIS and LAND will be greatly utilized in this project. The data will be organized by GBIS to create special reports related to the physical characteristics of the city at the neighborhood level. Detailed land use data will be organized via GBIS in a format on which to base future land use forecasts. The LAND application in conjunction with the base map series will be used to create existing and future land use maps. The utility of these applications for comprehensive planning will be clearly evident in 1979, some five years after the expiration of the project contract.

Future use of the integrated data base for community renewal planning will also be extremely high. Not only will it be used in developing numerous neighborhood conservation, rehabilitation and redevelopment plans and programs, but it will facilitate monitoring benefits of selected projects. For example, using GBIS, "benefit" zones can quickly be coded and data organized to measure the benefit of a program or project over a selected time span. Whereas the system's greatest utility is currently in decision-making, in the future, it will also be used for monitoring "actual" benefits. As experience is gained in measuring actual benefits, future use in measuring impact by project phase is anticipated. The result of this progress will be the maximization of benefits through work programming and work scheduling.

CONCLUDING OBSERVATIONS

The effect and utilization of the three implemented applications, as part of a totally integrated municipal information system, on the urban planning activities of the City of Wichita Falls have been described. The following points should be noted.

. During the first year of operations, the three implemented applications produced significant inter-divisional effects resulting from the need to establish a planning systems section within the Planning Division and to coordinate its operational procedures with those of the land resource management section. In the future, inter-divisional effects will be minimal since the planning systems section is in place and has been coordinating operations with the land resource management section for over a year.

. During the first year of operations, the three implemented applications produced significant intra-divisional effects resulting from the need to coordinate data maintenance tasks between the planning systems section and other city departments. Additional effects resulted from GBF and DIME technical requirements which mandated interaction between the planning systems section and non-city organizations and citizens concerning addressing. In the future intra-divisional effects will remain considerable as other city departments, non-city organizations and citizens become more aware of the accessability of operational data and request special reports and computer terminal access.

. During the first year of operations, the comprehensive planning process has been assisted very little by GBIS, LAND and the base map series. However, this non-use was a factor of timing, not capacity. In the future, through GBIS, data contained in LAND will be organized by geographic sector for inventorying existing land uses, forecasting land use changes, and developing future land use plans. The utility of the three applications for comprehensive planning will be evident in 1979, some five years after the expiration of the project contract.

. During the first year of operations, the community renewal planning process has been greatly assisted by GBIS, LAND and the base map series. The applications assisted in developing land acquisition strategies and completing cost/benefit studies and environmental assessment reviews. In the future, neighborhood conservation, rehabilitation, and renewal plans and programs will be developed using operational data obtained through GBIS. As experience is gained in the use of such data for monitoring benefits of selected projects further progress is expected toward the maximization of benefits by work phases.

The purpose of this paper was to describe the past and future effects and utilization of the Wichita Falls IMIS project on the urban planning activities of the city. From this description, three concluding points can be drawn.

- The Planning Division has successfully implemented and operated three prototype applications as part of a totally integrated municipal information system, which collects and organizes operational data in ways that provide useful information supporting urban planning.

- The implemented prototype applications offer a great transfer potential to other municipalities since GBIS is, in fact, a slightly modified DIME file which has been integrated with the normal operational information flows of the Planning Division. The LAND and base map applications are also transferrable to local jurisdictions elsewhere with a minimum of alteration because they collect and organize operational data generated in most municipal planning departments.

- Municipal planning departments which transfer these applications will have major inter and intra-divisional effects during the first year of operations. Interaction with citizens concerning addressing may be a problem. The applications will probably be of minimum utility for comprehensive planning but of assistance in community renewal planning. In subsequent years, inter-divisional effects should be minimal while intra-divisional effects continue to be substantial. The applications should have a great future utility for developing and monitoring comprehensive and community renewal plans.

George T. C. Peng
Professor of Planning and Urban Design
Texas Tech University
Lubbock, Texas   79409

A MATRIX SYSTEM FOR A NEW CITY DESIGN

ABSTRACT: This paper presents a matrix system
or model which can be used as a basis for designing
new cities. The model consists of (1) philosophical
theory and (2) mathematical criteria in an attempt
to achieve a balanced system of space and services
in relation to the socio-economic and ecological
patterns. These two elements are interdependent and,
at the same time, complement each other.

The proposed matrix is a theoretical form of
a new city design, not a reality. It is conceptual
in nature and abstract in form, simply a basis for
a design solution. Based on philosophical concepts,
it derives a mathematical model in a graphic presentation dealing with urban form, structure and a
service system as related to space need to make a
good city in terms which can be adapted to guide a
new city design.

The optimum matrix for each entity of the city
is established and the various matrices are interrelated into a mathematical and physical relationship. The matrix system is then interpreted and
analyzed for designing a model of a hypothetical
new city of approximately a half million people.

INTRODUCTION

A city is a living entity with organic growth and balanced development. It requires metabolism to remain functioning. It is composed of
many interrelated and interacting parts which are constantly changing,
developing, and rebuilding. In other words, cities possess all the qualities of life. As small as its basic unit, the family, and as large as
the universe, a city is a peculiar type of life whose form is the human
community and whose basic component is a single person.

A city has many conflicts just as a person does, but this is what
gives purpose to life. If there were no obstacles to over come, there
would be no motivation for living; here lies the understanding of what a
city is. A city is viable, ever changing, imperfect and complex thing,
with its own unique set of problems and solutions. We must accept the

city as this just as we must accept man for what he is despite the shortcomings all people have. One can no more create a perfect city than
create a perfect person. We can, however, strive to improve a city's
virtues and cure its problems. But we must realize the task is never
ending, never solvable, always changing and complex, and this is good.

This paper is intended to develop a matrix system or model for a
new city design which will preserve and enhance the sense of man and his
environment, the order of space, and the efficiency of services. This
model will be based on philosophical concepts dealing with man, nature
and environment, presented in a mathematical and physical form as related
to the spatial patterns and service systems.

PHILOSOPHICAL MODEL

My approach to city design is primarily based on the thoughts of
evolution and balance, which are two separate, yet mutually complementing
philosophies, known as organism and dualism, respectively. A concept
integrating these two thoughts was developed as one philosophy which I
named "Organicdualism".

An Organism is a form of life composed of mutually dependent parts
that maintain various vital processes. An organic body must maintain
living function in its physical structure and play a role in its environment to fulfill its responsibilities as part of the hierarchic whole.
Function and growth are the two basic elements of an organism dealing
with the organic quality of an organic entity. Dualism is a theory of
duality and polarity. The two counterparts of duality are opposite qualitatively, complementary functionally and constant quantitatively. Duality
and polarity are the two basic elements of dualism in testing the balance
of the dualistic entity.

```
                                        ┌ organic
                        ┌ Organism ─────┤
                        │               └ dynamic
   Organicdualism ──────┤
                        │               ┌ dualistic
                        └ Dualism  ─────┤
                                        └ static
```

The City as a Living Organism

A city is a living organism possessing all functional systems of an
organic entity which is thought of as a whole. The mass is in the form
of an organic entity and the network is the function of it. All the components of an organic mass are able to form an organic entity only when
they are set into the right positions in the network. The relationship
of the organic entity with its environment formulates an organic system.
The purpose of an organic system is to perform a living process which is
initiated by the interaction between the organic entity and its environment.

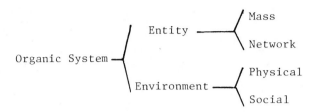

A city, like a person, has a life cycle with its own character and function. It is composed of body, mind and soul. The body of the city is its physical structure; its mind is that thinking part of the city, the government-civic center or the city center, which directs and controls the development of all other parts; and the soul of the city, which is invisible, represents the city's character, identity and image. The city sould may be defined as "city image". The human organism has specific organs to perform specific functions. So does the city. Human organs or parts dealing with special functions are under the skin. The city equivalent of organs - utility lines, rapid transit, etc. - should also be put under the ground. Cities grow when they are young and face the prospects of decline when they become old. A healthy city is full of life and full of human intention. When it gets old, it can be renewed and revitalized.

MAN - CITY MODEL

MAN	CITY	FUNCTION
Head/Mind	Government/Civic Center	Administrative, decision-making, Cultural
Heart	CBD or Downtown	Social, Economic, Entertainment
Limbs	Residential	Living Area
Digestive System	Industrial	Productive
Circulatory System	Traffic Network	Movement of goods and people
Excretory System	Utilities & Maintenance	Disposal
Skeleton	Streets	Framework
Skin	Surface of the Earth	Appearance

The city should provide flexible space for future growth. When the city reaches a maximum size in population and area, the plan should limit its growth through various means, such as greenbelts and traffic ways as buffer zones. Urban growth should be guided by organic systems.

The City as a Balanced Dualism

A healthy city exhibits harmony and unity in a balanced relationship. Each element is dependent on the other in that one can not survive without the other. However, it is possible for the elements to become unbalanced, for one to become dominant. In any city design it is important to include both elements and preserve their balance.

The city is a community of people. A sense of community is a perception of unity between people and the city. Ideally, people come together socially to make life more fruitful and functional. The design of a city should promote a balanced relationship between people and their community.

Physically, a city is comprised of built-up areas and open spaces. Each supplements and enhances the quality of the other. Urban areas are man-made reflecting human activities and technology. Open spaces, on the other hand, are collections of natural elements which together form a natural environment. Both should be given equal emphasis on the balanced relationship in their integrated planning and design.

When bringing city and nature together, the design of city form and structure should respect and cooperate with nature, because human life is bound up with nature's forces. Human adaptation to the environment is that the environment be fit for man, that the adaptation harmonize with the environment, and that this adaptation be expressed in form. Rather than resisted, nature must be treated as an ally and must be understood, because although the city is an artifact in nature, it is also an integral part of nature. Combining the eastern and western philosophies in landscape design, the city is in nature, and nature is in the city.

The City as an Organicdualism

According to the concept of Organicdualism, a city is thought of as an organic whole with its parts in a dualistic balance. The organic whole is composed of two basic parts, the biotic and the cultural. The biotic can be interpreted as the community, defined here as the physical aspect of a city. The cultural can be interpreted as the society, or the spiritual aspect of a city. These two are interdependent and interrelated. Community produces society, and then society shapes community. The interaction between them is ever-recurring. They have reciprocal causation. A person is defined by his physical body and spiritual personality. Similarly, a city is defined by its community, or biotic entity, and its society, or cultural system. A city can not exist or be reduced to either community or society.

A community is visible. It is the physical body of a city. In the development of a community, competition serves as the guiding process. Plants are in competition for nutrition and space; animals for food and shelter. Similarly, the competitive struggle exists also within the city. The result of the competition is reflected by the structure of the community by the land use pattern and the service system. The land use pattern is reflected by the service system; at the same time, the service system is also affected by the land use patterns. Neither should override the other.

Society is invisible. It is the product of the interaction of the

people within it. The formation of society is a result of the diverse
capabilities and shared objectives of its members. Shared objectives of
a society can be attained only when its members are diverse in their capabilities. For example, economic progress results from the division of
the work force, and the division of work force results from the diversity
in individual capabilities.

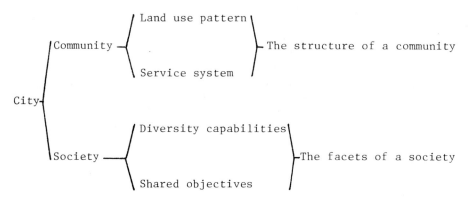

MATHEMATICAL MODEL

A model or matrix as a guide for designing a new city is, in general,
a spatial and/or mathematical framework developed as a tool for developing
an optimum human settlement. It is generally in the form of plans with
the standards of spatial relationships determined by applying theoretical
principles and refined through experienced applications. The model, thus
achieved, guides the design of urban form and structure of a new city.
In planning and designing new cities, no two situations and sites are the
same; they generally differ considerably in size, in location, and in
physiographic and socio-economic conditions. For these reasons, a model
should never be conceived as a standard plan or ready-made solution.
Rather, a model is a flexible framework which should be altered to suit
local conditions and goals.

In designing a new city, it is essential to consider and determine
the city's socio-economic structure. Based on all aspects of urban development, an ideal city population as I think should be between 100,000
and 500,000 people. When a city falls in this range it has reached a
point where the social benefits, community facilities, transportation,
and employment are the highest and the social costs, crime, taxes, and
congestion are the lowest. In addition, urban development and urban
problems can be controlled. Thus, the population size of the model city
is assumed to be 500,000 people. A city of this size should be independent, and self-contained. When a city reaches a population of 100,000,
it must have a self-supporting economic base. If the city is to support
itself, it must have enough industrial development in order to provide
employment opportunity for its residents.

City Form and Structure

In relation to the city, form denotes the overall visual appearance. It is primarily determined by land form and land use patterns. The structure of the city consists of service systems and their organic or functional relationships, usually delineated by the systems of transportation, facilities and utilities. Many factors or forces mold the city into its particular form. Among them are the topography and watersheds, socio-economic base, and politico-cultural conditions. These forces tend to push and pull various city parts, structuring them in a manner that expresses the nature and image of a city.

The land in the United States is generally subdivided into sections of square miles, bounded by county roads or state highways running north to south and east to west. Based on this system, the backbone of the new city matrix is formed. The city location is generally dependent on hte selection of the two axial roads as the major arterial streets. Their intersection is the location of the city center. The four coordinators are the sections for residential developments. Thus, the city is shaped by a central service core that tends to pull residents and competing services toward the center. In an attempt to locate all area development as close to the core as possible, a circular city form is created. This factor is referred to as centripetal force which guides the city growth in a concentric form. When the city development reaches an ultimate size as planned, further urban growth can take place in the form of satellite town systems, and/or linear city developments. The land use patterns as indicated in the study model are classified into residential communities, central places or community centers, industry, and greenbelts which are suitably located in relation to land use functions and circulation systems.

The city structure is defined by the transport system and service networks which are coordinated with city form and land use functions. All public facilities and services are located within community centers based on their design system. City-wide facilities are concentrated in the city center and facilities needed daily are distributed in local communities. Residential areas and community centers are separated by greenbelts or landscaped open spaces, which are used as buffer zones and also provide flexible space for future growth.

Transportation is as important to the life of the city as the blood circulation is to the human body. However, transportation designed improperly can strangle the city, restrict its growth and ultimately create many urban problems as existing in our cities today. In order to achieve utmost efficiency and safety for the movement of people and goods, a well organized transport system should be adopted. Different types of traffic should be separated. Major transport systems should run underground where possible, particularly the rapid transit and through traffic ways.

The arterial traffic ways above ground are classified into five categories: (1) major arterial, (2) secondary arterial, (3) collector arterial, (4) minor arterial and (5) ring arterial. The major arterials, with 1,000-foot right-of-ways, carry high-speed through traffic to and from the city and serve as inter-city freeways. The secondary arterials, with 300-foot right-of-ways carry medium-speed city traffic entering the town centers from major arterials and are the daily-used major roads from home to work and to the major arterials. The collector arterials are 200·foot right-of-ways used as inter-city-and-town freeways. The minor arterials are 150·foot right-of-ways between two towns only carrying local traffic. The ring arterial is a multi-purpose parkway with a right-of-way of 500 feet. As the city limits or buffer zone, the ring arterial separates the rural areas from urban development. Rapid transit is provided inside the ring arterial under, on, or above the right-of-ways of the five arterials. Local streets leading to residential homes and individual buildings are separated into vehicle and pedestrians, as well as bicycle ways. Full segregation of private automobile and pedestrian movement is provided in the city center area and its surrounding park-like open lands inside the four collector arterials. Within the central areas there is no automobile traffic except city provided public transport, walkways, ramps, etc., for transversing short distances. Heavy vehicles and private automobiles entering the central areas are underground. This model of public transport shall be referred to hereafter as the Personal Transportation Device (PTD) which may be any form of comfortable transport, but should be restricted to the central areas. All through traffic entering the city from the four major arterials are underground when they reach the intersections at the collector arterials.

City Composition

The model city is divided and classified into different sizes of communities based on population and geographic patterns. As a matrix system the entire city is classified as Community V, which is composed of four sectors and one cnetral area. The four sectors are called Communities IV, confined between the northsouth and eastwest arterial roads or major arterials. The central area is the city center, or the center of the city or downtown, consisting of all city-wide activities of government, civic, cultural, commerce and entertainment, as well as high density and high-rise housing. Each Community IV, which may be termed a "town", has an enclosed area of about 10,000 acres to serve a population of some 100,000 people. It is self-contained and self-supported, with its own center and employment opportunities offered in public, business and industrial establishments.

Each sector is dubdivided into four smaller communities of class III and one sector cneter or twon center, which contains all types of business and civic activities and medium density housing. Each Community III, which may be termed a "village", has a population of about 20,000 persons. It is further sub-divided into four communities of Class II and one village center. Each Community II is similar in nature to a "neighborhood". This is the basic planning unit of a population size of some 5,000 inhabitants. The neighborhood center provides basic facilities of education, shopping, and recreation. Community I is a "city block" which is the basic design unit with an average population of 50 persons.

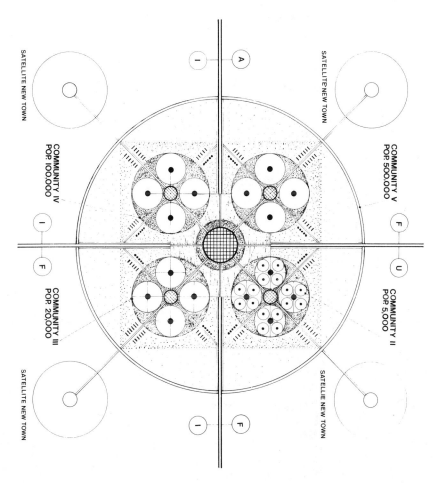

THE MATRIX OF A NEW CITY DESIGN

GEORGE T.C. PENG 1976

○ RESIDENTIAL COMMUNITY
◯ CITY CENTER
⊕ TOWN CENTER
● VILLAGE CENTER
NEIGHBORHOOD CENTER
INDUSTRIAL PARK
BUSINESS
RESERVED OPEN SPACE
PERMANENT OPEN SPACE
CONTROLLED OPEN SPACE
Ⓐ AGRICULTURE
AIRPORT
Ⓤ UNIVERSITY
Ⓕ FACILITY OR UTILITY
HEAVY INDUSTRY
MAJOR ARTERIAL
RING ARTERIAL
SECONDARY ARTERIAL
COLLECTOR ARTERIAL
MINOR ARTERIAL

THE MATRIX UNIT

COMMUNITY V POP. 500,000
COMMUNITY IV POP. 100,000
COMMUNITY III POP. 20,000
COMMUNITY II POP. 5,000

SATELLITE NEW TOWN

CITY CENTER

BODY HEAD

MIND

SOUL

NATURE

LANDSCAPE

air sunshine and green

HOTELS / hotels

OFFICES / offices

APART.MENTS

HOUSING

COMMERCIAL CENTER

LANDSCAPE

Pedestrian and P.T.D. Traffic only

city hall

municipalfederalstatemunic
nicipalfederalstatemunic
ipalfederalstatemunicipal

GOVERNMENTAL CENTER

LANDSCAPE

CIVIC AND URBAN CULTURE CENTER

auditorium
museum
library etc...

NATURE

UNDERGROUND SHOPS & STORES TRANSPORTATION & SERVICES DISTRIBUTION SYSTEMS

RAPID TRANSIT

Community Centers

The city centers or downtowns of our old cities are dominated by highrise buildings, over-crowded population, traffic congestion, air pollution, lack of open space, vanished and urban growth restriction. As a result, central business districts decline and create urban blight, suburban sprawl and uninhabited environments. In order to solve these and many other urban growth problems, there is a need to provide convenient services and beautify city appearances. This model for guiding future new city design and development should reverse existing city forms, restructure the city functions and unite man and nature in a balanced relationship in the city development.

One of the main objectives of this model is to create an "open heart new city". All proposed community centers are open to nature, surrounded by greenblets with flexible open spaces for future growth, and connected to residential areas through convenient and safe traffic systems.

The City Center is the focal point and central attraction of the city, providing city-wide needed facilities and services including a government complex, a cultural complex, a commercial complex, an office complex, high density residential housing, sport and recreation facilities and transportation centers. Retail business and central transportation facilities are built underground. The residential and office oriented buildings are arranged on and above ground in harmonic relationships with nature. Offices, apartments and hotels/motels are high-rise buildings which connect underground with transportation networks and are surrounded by landscaped open spaces.

A Town Center is the activity center of Community IV and consists of an education-cultural complex which includes a community college, a public library and a social center; a shopping center which includes department stores and other retail and service business shops; one health and safety center which includes clinics and hospitals, police and fire stations, and other public facilities; and one town center park which includes a playfield, a stadium and other recreational facilities.

A Village Center is the activity center of Community III consisting of a senior and junior high schools, one public library, one shopping center with one or two grocery stores, one or two drug stores and several retail business shops, one small hospital, one fire station, and one village park which includes a large playground with various sport and recreation facilities. The Neighborhood Center comprises an elementary school, a kindergarten, a playground and one small shopping center providing the daily needs for the neighborhood's residents.

Housing

A house is the focus of one's family life in society. Housing is the complex of homes representing all types of dwellings which make up the physical body of a city. The arrangement of dwelling types for a large community should provide for a normal cross section of the population. The selection of dwelling types must be related, on the one hand, to the densities of buildings required to distribute total land cost among the families and, on the other hand, to the maximum densities which must be imposed on each dwelling type to protect the fundamentals or livability.

In the design of the model city matrix, it is essential to create a well balanced residential development. Predominantly single family housing is located in outlying areas of each community center unit. Medium density of row or group houses are generally located in the central areas of Communities IV and III. High density and high-rise housing projects are placed in the City Center and surrounded by landscaped open spaces.

The purpose of the philosophical model is to provide the city design with a theoretical background. Dealing with both physical and non-physical aspects of design gives life to the otherwise cold, mathematically related structure of the city. Man's relationship to other men, his relationship to nature, and his relationship to the physical form and pattern of the city are the major concepts of the model.

DESIGN MODEL

In summary, the matrix system for new city design consists of two integrated and interrelated models, the philosophical and the mathematical. The former provides the basis which gives meaning to city design; the latter derives a system which expresses the form and structure of the city design. The Philosophical model guides the design of intangible elements relating man to community and community to nature. It will make the city a place for living and not simply a machine. The mathematical model, on the other hand, set criteria and standards for population, land use and services required for the physical functioning of the city and which gives substance to the form of the city. These two must be combined with the consideration and evaluation of local conditions, planning goals, and development policies to make a complete and balanced system, presented as:

$$\text{New City Design} \left\{ \begin{array}{l} \text{Philosophical model} \\ \\ \text{Mathematical model} \end{array} \right\} \text{design model}$$

The philosophical and mathematical models are general in nature, applicable to all locations of new cities. Standards and guide lines are not intended to be absolute but to be adopted as needed. These two models will be used in forming a design concept from which a design solution can be derived. The resulting forms of new cities which follow the matrix system may be many and varied, not necessarily following the strictly geometric and abstract form as shown in the model and because the form and structure must meet the specific requirements of each individual new city design.

The implementation of this new city can be carried out by stages from time to time. Based on the overall new city design, it starts with one or two minor arterial raods which directly connect with existing major arterial roads. When two villages are completed, a diagonal secondary arterial and then a town center can be built. When two or more towns are completed, then the city center and ring arterial can be started, and the major arterials can be rebuilt, as well as other city wide utilities and facilities.

The material presented here is an introduction to the theory of the matrix. Design criteria and standards are not included. It is hoped that this matrix system will be of some aid in the conceptual design of new cities and that this study will shed some light on new city planning and design.

JOHN BAER, Manager, Planning Support
Department of City Planning
Management Information Systems Section
2 Lafayette Street
New York, New York 10007

N.Y.C. LOCAL AREA PLANNING DATABASE

Abstract.   New York City Department of Planning has built a
              local area planning database. The information
              sources are administrative records pertaining to
              land, buildings, and population. The data is
              geocoded and converted from point-in-time to
              time series files. Closely related files are
              merged.

              With the file creation complete the next problem
              is to diffuse the available information to
              potential users. Four methods will be tried:
              standard reports, training and support for
              selected planners, availability of reports to
              the public, and creation of an "early warning
              system".

One major function of the MIS Section of the New York City

Department of Planning (DCP-MIS) is the development of a

local area database.1/ This database supports the

Department's responsibilities in land use planning and site

evaluation, provides Community Boards and Community Groups

with information about their neighborhoods, and enables City

and State Agencies to obtain local area information from a

single source.

This paper will describe the database and the concepts which guided its creation.2/

The database is made up of independent files. Information is
included in this database when it meets three requirements:

(1) The information must be available on a building,
     lot or block level. These units are the geographic
     locus of urban activity. Information (e.g. births,
     deaths, student transfers) available only for areas
     larger than blocks is given a low priority.

(2) The information must be available annually to
     permit the creation of time-series.

(3) The information must describe the physical or
     socio-economic conditions of an area. Our priority
     is information useful as indicators of activity and
     change such as property sales and tax arrears.
     Information which is primarily useful for
     establishing baselines such as land and building
     area has a lower priority.

The information sources to the database are administrative
records primarily from other agencies which describe New
York City's land, buildings, and people - supplemented by
special surveys contracted to the Sanborn Map Company.
These files are obtained by DCP-MIS and processed into
useable local area information. The processing generally
requires six steps:3/

(1)   Geocoding to associate each record with a physical
      block. A "physical" block, however, is occasionally
      a meta-physical concept. New York City is made up
      of about 40,000 blocks. Each block can be
      identified in four independent ways (tax, census,
      physical and data), and different agencies use
      different definitions. Tax blocks assigned by the
      Finance Administration may include two or more
      physical blocks, Census Blocks assigned by the
      Census Bureau may also include more than one or
      only part of a physical block. Physical blocks
      themselves may be defined as being bounded by
      physical streets, mapped streets, or un-mapped
      streets. Data Blocks are assigned by the
      Department of City Planning to be the lowest common
      denominator of all City "blocks" and can be, and
      often are, smaller than physical bocks.
      Inconvenient and confusing as this is, we quickly
      realized that we had no other choice but to make
      information available by whichever "block"
      simplified our processing. We see the solution in
      creating a building address, lot, block side and
      data block equivalence. This can be accomplished
      by associating every lot with a house number and
      street name and then geocoding these addresses to
      obtain a block side number and a data block number.
      This will give us an address, lot, data block

equivalence.

(2) Editing and reformatting to delete irrelevant and confidential information. We have tried - with mixed success - to handle confidential and irrelevant data by excluding it from our database rather than controlling access to it. However, we have found that our decision not to acquire a file may be superseded by the data requirements of another higher level of government. Deciding what is irrelevant requires a deep knowledge of the specific files of other agencies. Often gaps in one's understanding of the data files is revealed only after the file has been processed and used.

(3) Merging files to link closely related information. We have not integrated all of our files into a total database as there is no one common denominator.

(4) Creating time series files out of a series of point-in-time files. Time-series data is an essential component of the database because a time series suggests trends and signals changes. Besides which, one can almost always discover the current status of an area or parcel by physical inspection, but ascertaining what once existed is more difficult.

(5) Placing processed files into IBM's GIS System.4/ While far from perfect GIS is, at present our

-315-

preferred method of accessing and storing the
database. The report language is simple enough for
non-technical people to use, the system facilitates
standarized reports, and most critically, we can
make files available before we have finished all of
our data processing.

(6) Preparing standardized reports in GIS Language to
make the information intelligible to planners and
administrators. Ideally, standarized reports should
be the product of a team of data processors,
researchers, and planners. However, we have found
this process too consuming of time and staff
relative to the benefits that actually emerge. We
chose instead an informal process of consulting
those most knowledgeable and concerned. Our
priority has been to produce the imperfect rapidly
rather than the more perfect at some far distant
time.

The land use information in the database is available for
individual lots, buildings and blocks. The demographic
information is available in block summaries. Blocks, of
course, may be aggregated to almost any larger geographic
unit.

The information available for lots and buildings is various
and detailed. Information obtained yearly from the Finance
Administration's Assessment Department includes the

-316-

dimensions of the lot, type and dimensions of the principal
building, assessed and taxable value, exemption status
(describing the categories of public, quasi public, and
private ownership), Tax delinquency (describing
dis-investment actions), and In Rem status (anticipatory to
City Ownership). Records of property sales, including sale
price, mortgage amount, buyer and seller are also obtained
from the Finance Administration. Each year the Housing and
Development Administration provides a file of Residential
Multiple Dwellings which includes the building size,
description, number of dwelling units and number of cited
and pending violations on the building. Requests for changes
in Zoning, Mapping, and Landmark designation and the
disposition of City owned property and leases are available
directly from the Department of City Planning. The Sanborn
Map Company annually provides a file of the current stock of
vacant buildings.

Certain information is available only in block summaries
either to maintain confidentiality as in the case of
socio-economic data or as a result of current data
collection procedures. The Human Resources Administration
provides block summaries of the public assistance caseload
by type of program category. DCP-MIS obtains an edited
version of the City Income Tax files which it geocodes and
aggregates to a block level. The Sanborn Map Company
provides block summaries of the change in the number of

-317-

housing units by housing type.

The database has several obvious and significent gaps.
First we are missing "building" applications of various
sorts, for example applications, permits and "completion"
certificates for construction, demolition or alteration of
buildings. These records have not been automated at the
source. Second, we are missing information on business
activity; we are faced with problems of confidentiality of
tax records and the cost of alternative sources of data,
e.g. Dun and Bradstreet files. Third, we have no
satisfactory measure of migration within small areas. In
the future, we will explore student transfer records,
utility connect and disconnect records, and "reverse
telephone directory" records to see if these can be used to
monitor migration.

With almost all of the files in the database in place we are
now focusing our attention on increasing the use of this
available information. As seen from DCP-MIS our database
serves five purposes in the planning process. One, the
database is a source of numbers. The Federal Government in
its Grant programs asks for numbers, which we supply in
return for dollars which they supply. Two, the database
provides the input to statistical tables and computer drawn
maps used to illustrate reports. Three, the database
provides data to advocates of policies who are trying to

butress their case and undermine that of their opponents;
the information in the database usually can be made to
support most sides of any issue. Four, our database
improves the state of knowledge about the City. Five, the
database provides information for the decision-making
process.

Without slighting the contractual and political necessities
met by serving the first three purposes, our primary
professional concern is the last two - improving the state
of knowledge about New York City and making accurate
information available to the decision-making process. To
this end DCP-MIS will try to diffuse the information in four
ways.

(1) We are developing for each file standard reports
which present a local area planning issue. These
reports will be available for any area defined by
Tax Blocks and will focus on trends in key
variables (e.g. public assistance caseload,
property sale prices), investment-disinvestment
patterns (e.g. tax arrears, building violations),
area profiles (e.g. lot and building descriptions).
One of our most interesting reports shows the
pattern on a block level of Tax arrearage for major
building types from 1972 to the present. These
tables and reports are designed to be useful to

analysts; for everyone else we have found maps to be the most effective way of presenting local area information. For this purpose we intend to integrate this database with the blocks generated out of the "super" DIME file development now underway with a Census Bureau grant. The stumbling block in marrying the data to the maps is the present incompatability of different definitions of block.

(2) We will devote a large part of our staff time to support those planners and administrators who are committed to and capable of using the information which we can provide. We hope these individuals by their example will encourage (or embarass) others to use information. These "agents of change" will be taught the expertise to assist others in their section in accessing, interpreting, and presenting information.

(3) We will try to meet any reasonable request from anyone for our standard reports. To the extent that planning is an adversary proceding this will encourage opponents if only for self-defense to be aware of, if not use, accurate information. And to the extent planning is a professional process, this will make accurate information available to those committed to objectivity. We are aware that this approach will present us with painful questions:

Do we tell a potential renter the violation experience of a landlord? Do we tell a potential home owner the trend in Tax Delinquencies on a block? Do we tell a mortgage lender the trend in building abandonments in a neighborhood?

(4) We will try to take the initiative in identifying areas which are in change. We have in mind a kind of an early warning system which will alert planners and decision-makers to physical and socio-economic changes in communities and business areas.

In short, while we can provide accurate and credible information this is only a start. The information must diffuse out of DCP-MIS into the hands of those who need it, when they need it, and in a form quickly understood. Once available, Accurate and credible information may be dangerous; area trends casually identified may become self-fulfilling prophecies. We may be the sorcerer's apprentice, for none of the obvious solutions - denying the existence of a trend, limited the distribution of its knowledge, or stoically accepting the consequences - appears satisfactory.

1/ DCP-MIS staff who have made the major contributions to the database include Joyce Cox, Cheryl Hinton, Alan Prete, Drew Minert, and Martin Smilow. Dr. Barbara Braden, Director of MIS, has provided constant and unflinching support.

2/ A similar and influential approach is described by Joseph
Lewis and Dennis Siglinger. See: Geocoding In Denver:
Administrative Problems and An Application"
Urban and Regional Information System: Perspectives on

Information Systems (Claremont, California) 2974) pp.
315-334

3/ The main frame computer is a 370/145 run under VM-CMS
during the day and VS1 at night.

4/ GIS is a "user oriented system which provides for a
variety of information processing capabilities through an
English-like procedural language". GIS at DCP-MIS is run
batch VS1. Data file access are standard OS tapes.

Joseph Drew, Saadia Greenberg, and Bryan Jones
Department of Political Science and
Wayne State University-University of Michigan Institute of Gerontology
Wayne State University, Detroit, Michigan 48202

THE DEVELOPMENT OF A DATA SYSTEMS TECHNOLOGY FOR ASSESSING
THE GEOGRAPHIC DISTRIBUTION OF URBAN GOVERNMENT SERVICES

This paper describes the development of a data
systems technology for the analysis of the distribution of urban public services. The project merged
data from agency records with Tract level Census data
to form a combined dataset suitable for analysis of the
demographic, socio-economic, and geographic variations
in the provision of services. Seven City of Detroit
agencies have been examined. Data from these agencies was geocoded to Census Tracts using a variety of
methods depending on the nature of the service. After
merging agency records and Census data, the authors
used multivariate statistical techniques to test various hypotheses about the manner in which public bureaucracies distribute their services to different
neighborhoods and groups.

INTRODUCTION

One of the primary functions of urban government is to deliver
services. In order to deliver these services, urban governments engage in complex decision-making about the allocation of their personnel and equipment. In doing so urban governments not only deliver
services but also distribute services. The distinction is crucial.
The concept of service delivery implies that all citizens within a
given urban environment are the beneficiaries of services provided by
that government. The concept of service distribution, on the other
hand, addresses itself to the question of the quality and the level
of the service provided to various segments of the public. Distributional studies examine how governmental resources have been allocated to groups differentiated economically, socially, and geographically. Urban governments (and governments in general) continue to
issue such pious platitudes as : "this government is and will continue
to provide the best possible service for all the people of this city
(or country)". While such statements may be pleasing to the electorate, there is a growing body of literature indicating substantial
variations in the service levels provided to different groups and
areas within urban settings (see Jones, Kaufman, Greenberg and Drew;
Lineberry, Benson and Lund, Welch and Chance, Mladenka). Urban governments have, through their bureaucratic agencies distributed resources across the urban environments. This differential allocation
of these resources and the consequences of these allocation decisions

focuses our attention on the question of who gets what and how much among the various groupings of citizens in the urban context. Broaching these two questions necessitates the analysis of the outputs of the political system, economic costs associated with those outputs and possible biases in the delivery of those outputs. In short, one is able to gain some perspective on the outputs of the political system and ,as such ,have an initial reference point with which to begin the determination of policy in the urban context.

METHODS OF STUDYING SERVICE DISTRIBUTION

Before one can begin an analysis of the distribution of local public service, one must specify an appropriate output unit. In this case, the case of bureaucratic performance, the appropriate units are the basic service units. These basic service units, which we consider a single government-to-citizen contact by the service bureaucracy, in turn may be aggregated to determine the levels of service the bureaucracy provides to a particular geographic area or neighborhood, within a city. Having identified these basic service units one is in a position to study the degree to which geographically differentiated neighborhoods receive differing quantities of service levels. Since the urban area is itself a complex clustering of different population groupings within a finite space, resource allocation may be traced across these differentiated population groupings as well as across spatial territories. Measures must be sought which permit distinctions to be made with regard to populations stratified on the basis of economics, ethnic/racial variation ,and locational components of the urban area. In short, one must identity spatial units of analysis in addition to the basic service units of analysis that are generalizable across the entire urban area. Measures must be found that can disaggregate the urban area into acceptable and easily manipulable component spatial territories and component groupings of populations. It is the union of these spatial units with what we termed basic service units that defines the pattern of service distribution for a particular public service for a particular city. In other words, a data systems technology must be developed that will merge basic service unit data with locational unit data in order to study variations in the distribution of public services to geographically identifiable social, economic, and racial groups.

Basic Service Units

A basic service unit may be defined as a single government-to-citizen contact for service bureaucracies which make such contacts. (In other types of bureaucracies, the service unit has other forms.) Most local service organizations do make such contacts. A police response, fire run, a building inspection, and a garbage pickup are all examples of government contacts with citizens or the property or domiciles of citizens. This interface between government and citizen provides a reference point for defining the level of service which service bureaucracies deliver.

In many cases basic service units may be determined from bureaucratic records kept by individual bureaucracies of their daily operations and procedures. Particularly important are the records kept by
and for those individuals who come directly into contact with the public. We believe that the day-to-day operations of the individual inspectors or those individuals who actually perform the service are the
crux of the public's contact with government and more importantly, for
our analysis, determines where, and to whom, services are being generated. Each individual who comes in contact with citizens is generally
required to keep a record of the work he has done and often to record
the nature of the contact that was made. The quality of such records,
of course, varies from bureaucracy to bureaucracy and from city to
city. If the records on the cantacts the "street level" bureaucracy
has made are of sufficient quality, then aggregating all the <u>actions</u>
an individual performs in his daily routines for a single time period
will yield the sum total of his performance regarding citizen contacts
and response to citizens. Furthermore, if we do this for all individuals who keep these forms of records within the bureaucracy, then we
have a measure of organizational performance for the period of time we
select. The nature of the bureaucratic routines employed in contact-
ing citizens are to a large extent standardized in reports that individuals must make to the bureaucracy (such being the norm). <u>It is</u>
<u>our contention that these standarized routines are synonymous with our</u>
<u>definition of basic service units.</u> As such, we may aggregate these
<u>basic service units</u> upon which records are kept by <u>all</u> individuals who
perform the same tasks. In short, there often exists an amenable and
standardized data reporting procedure for the initial step towards the
assessment of resource allocation. The routine task upon which data
are kept are the basic service units provided by the government bureaucracy.

Basic Locational Units

If we wish to account for geographic distribution of resource
allocation and take into account variation of the population in economic, racial-ethnic and ecological terms, then we must utilize some
standarized geographical unit for these purposes. In our studies, conducted in Detroit, we have utilized the Census Tract for these purposes.
This was done for the following reasons: First and foremost, the census
data, while limited to ten year periods, provides a voluminous amount
of data. Second, this data base permits the standardization of units
spatially in that Census Tracts are set up on the basis of a real size
and density. Third, this spatial standardization incorporates data on
the economic, and racial character of urban areas by those same tracts.
Fourth, census data allows controls for demographic variables and the
inclusion of those variables in any form of analysis. Finally, and
this is by no means insignificant, the census materials are computerized and universally available. The primary problem with using Census
Tracts as units in service distribution analysis is that they do not
correspond to neighborhoods in any meaningful sense. Further, they
may not be appropriate for smaller cities.

Merging Basic Service Units with Basic Locational Units

The next stage in the study of service distribution is merging service data with Census Tracts. The form of the merger is dependent upon: 1) the nature of the service delivery system employed by the bureaucracy under study, and 2) the nature of the record keeping, specifically, whether the records are kept on an individual address or "case" basis or whether they are kept on a service area level. Bureaucracies may be divided into two basic forms in their delivery mechanisms: those that deliver services from fixed sites and those which deliver services directly to neighborhoods. The former, the fixed site form of bureaucracy, necessitates the clientele coming to the bureaucracy to receive the service. Examples of this form of bureaucracy are schools, hospitals, parks and libraries. Non-fixed types of bureaucracies are those in which the service is delivered directly to the clientele's residence. Examples of the neighborhood delivery form are fire and police services, virtually any type of inspection service such as buildings inspection, and refuse collection.

With fixed site bureaucracies, there must be a way to attach the basic service units to the locational units. Since this form of service requires populations for some geographic area to utilize a given facility, some measure of this areal dispersion must be developed to determine the accurate demographic and other figures associated with the basic locational unit data, the Census Tracts. It is only with the development of measures of areal dispersion that an analysis of the distribution of these fixed site services can be effected. For most purposes, the areal dispersion measures may most easily be facilitated by direct radial distance measures of concentric ordering from a standardized point within locational units. These measures are based on the hypothesis that access to fixed site facilities is inversly proportional to distance. Hence we term this measure the radial access measure. The determination of the basic service units of the fixed site facilities may only be accomplished through the development of complete and comprehensive inventories of the composition of the facilities and programs of the facilities. This must be done for all facilities within the city. Following this stage, data reduction techniques may be employed to determine appropriate service units. At this point, for the fixed site facilities one may then merge the basic service unit data with the Census Tract data as determined by the areal dispersion measures, the concentric radii.

For bureaucracies delivering services directly to neighborhoods, the procedure for merging the data takes one of two forms. In the first form, service agencies have collected data for each service contact with citizens. Given that the basic service units are already determined as a function of routine reporting mechanisms, one simply needs a geocoding method whereby addresses of residential locations are translatable into tract data. Taking each basic service unit of each type and aggregating up to tract level permits analysis of the variation in the level of service provided for the entire tract. A second form of data base for the non fixed site form of delivery is that which we shall refer to as "service area". In this instance, the bureaucracy assigns personnel to cover certain geographic areas of the urban complex. For the most part, resources are assigned to some geographical service area and data collected is referred to by the bureaucracy only in the context of that area. In this case, the distributional analysis is dependent upon the compilation of total basic service units for the given "service area". For most service agencies, service areas do not correspond to census tracts, and the investigator must convert the service area data to the tract. To do so it is necessary to disaggregate proportionally the service data to the tract. This can be done by using the block as intermediate unit of analysis. Since both service areas and tracts are composed of blocks, the service data may be apportioned to tracts according to the number of blocks in the tract which are serviced by the service area. Each service area which delivers to some portion of the tract may be similarly treated, and, after appropriate weighing, the data may be summed to the tract level. Clearly it would be simpler to aggregate tract data to the service area, but one then has no common geographic unit for use in analyzing different service agencies which employ different service delivery areas.

Later in this paper, we specifically show the nature of the processes we have used for each of the bureaucratic agencies we have examined over the last three years of research effort. What we wish to develop at this juncture in the paper are the following points: First, one may distinguish service agencies in terms of the form of delivery system a bureaucracy may develop. Delivery can either be of the fixed site or the neighborhood delivery variety. Second, that the nature of the data they collect may vary as well but that this data is not routinely assembled by service agencies. These data may be used to assess the outputs of service agencies. So, whether a bureaucracy delivers its services to fixed sites or not, there is theoretical similarity across the data bases even if they must be handled in a statistically different manner in the assessing basic service units. Third, that areal determination is a significant portion of any analysis of distribution. Since socio-economic groupings of citizens generally also tend to be separate geographically, and local services are delivered in a geographical manner, one may merge demographic data and service data to assess the distribution of local public services.

Table I cross-classifies the method of service delivery with the types of data which may be used to assess patterns of service distribution. Within the cells of the table are entered examples of types of local agencies which fit the classification.

THE DETROIT SERVICE DELIVERY PROJECT

We now turn to a description of the Detroit Service Delivery Project, a study of service distribution in the city of Detroit, Michigan, in order to illustrate the points made in the above discussion. We collected extensive agency data for the following service agencies: Sanitation, Environmental Enforcement, Parks and Recreation, and four divisions of the Building and Safety Engineering Department: Bureau of Buildings, Housing Code Enforcement, Plumbing, and Electrical. All data are for 1973.

TABLE 1: Method of Service Delivery Versus Type of Data
          Available, Local Service Agencies.

METHODS OF DELIVERY

		FIXED SITE	NEIGHBORHOOD DELIVERY
1.	AREAL ACCESS	Parks, Libraries	
2.	SERVICE AREA	Schools	Garbage Collections; agencies which aggregate service contacts to geographical service areas.
3.	INDIVIDUAL ADDRESS (CASE)		Building and Code Enforcement inspections; Police, Fire responses; Environmental Enforcement inspections.

"Case" (Individual Address) Data

Data on services delivered directly to neighborhoods was collected
from six agencies in the Environmental Enforcement Division
(EED), the Sanitation Division, and the Department of Buildings and
Safety. Both EED and Buildings and Safety have quasi-police powers
and deliver their services on a "case" basis. Cases are defined as
aggregates of basic service unit (i.e. administrative actions) and
the input characteristics relating to the origin of the cases. Cases of
possible violations of city ordinances are brought to the attention of
these agencies who must then investigate and can issue violation notices (enforceable through the courts) if conditions warrant. Cases
are generally initiated either by direct citizen complaints to the
agency or by referral from other (usually city) agencies. The referring agencies may come upon these possible violations in the course of
their work or the complaint may have been called in to the City Clerk's
Office (this function is now exercised by the city Ombudsman) or the
Mayor's Office who refer the cases to the appropriate agency for
action.

Where data was available on the individual cases, the data management was relatively straightforward. The researchers were able to
obtain complete data from two major bureaus and one minor bureau of
the Department of Buildings and Safety and partial data from one minor
bureau of the Department of Buildings and Safety. Data was also obtained on the citizen complaints referred by the City Clerk's Office
to the Environmental Enforcement Division. (It should also be noted
that the coding was done by the research team and their student assistants going back to the individual case records in the agency files.)
Two levels of analysis were possible with these datasets. First, the
individual cases were coded and analyzed in terms of what service
units were provided, i.e., what administrative action was taken, and
whether the problem (or alleged problem) was satisfactorily resolved.
Since the agency files contain the street address of the possible violation, the coders could include the Census Tract in which the cases
occurred. This geocoding to the Census Tract was a crucial step in
the data management process without which the analysis would have been
restricted to a much more superficial level. The authors were able to
test for differences in the handling of complaints from different
Census Tracts by merging such characteristics of the Tracts as mean
family income, racial composition, and age of housing structures with
the case level basic service unit data. Furthermore, by merging the
total number of cases in a Census Tract (adjusted for population) back
on to the individual cases dataset, it was also possible to ascertain
whether an agency handled cases differently in Tracts with large
numbers of cases.

The second level at which one can analyze this type of case data
is at the Census Tract level. Most of the variables coded for each
case were suitable for aggregation to the Census Tract level. For example, the number of total cases in each Tract, the number (and proportion) of violation notices issued in each Tract, the number (and

proportion) of cases taken to court, as well as the average response time were calculated for each Tract. Adjustments were made for the number of people in each Tract and these variables and others were correlated with Census Tract characteristics that had been merged into the dataset with the administrative data. Use of the Census Tract as a level of analysis not only gave the research team access to a large number of variables from the U.S. Census but also enabled them to include information from several other sources. The Detroit Department of Planning made available its figures on the age of housing structures which are much are much more detailed than the Census figures. The authors themselves measured (using the Census Tract map) the distance from the center of the Central Business District to the center of each Census Tract. Both of these (highly intercorrelated) variables proved to be extremely valuable, both theoretically and practically. Actually, the original research design did not call for the inclusion of these variables but when certain patterns in the data suggested that they might have significant explanatory power, it was fairly simple to calculate these variables at the Tract level and to merge them into the Tract level dataset.

Service Area Data

Data on a service area basis was available for two of the city agencies studied: the Sanitation Division (garbage collection) and the central records of the Environmental Enforcement Division. As noted above, the City Clerk's Office did keep records on a case basis for citizen complaints referred to EED but EED did not have its own records in this format. The EED central records contained only the weekly totals of each type of action taken by each inspector. (EED uses the Sanitation routes as its service areas and one EED inspector is assigned to each route.) The number of cases handled, broken down into a number of categories, and the number of administrative actions of each type possible were coded for each EED service area. These figures were then apportioned among the blocks in each area and the Census Tract totals were aggregated from these block figures. Census Tract characteristics were then merged into this dataset. While these service area aggregates do not contain the same degree of detailed information about the hanling of each case, a considerable number of interesting findings did emerge from the analysis of the EED central records. The reader will also be relieved to note that, insofar as comparability was possible, the analysis of both the EED central records and the City Clerk referrals to EED showed the same kinds of patterns between the explanatory and dependent variables.

The Sanitation Division data was of an entirely different nature. It consisted of actual service area data, not case data that happened to have been aggregated to a larger geographical level. Fortunately for this project, the Sanitation Division had on its staff a specialist in operations research who had gathered a considerable amount of data (on computer tape) as part of his efforts to reorganize the service areas of the Sanitation crews and increase their efficiency. This dataset included the pounds of garbage collected in each area, the number of paid man-hours, and the number of loads collected in

each service area. The one major problem with this dataset was that
the approximately 1300 Sanitation service areas (each are
by one truck and crew in one day) did not correspond to the 420 Census
Tracts in Detroit. Working jointly with the Sanitation Division, the
project prepared a tape which listed each Census Block in the city
along with its Census Tract and Sanitation service area. The population and number of occupied housing units in each Block was extracted from the Census Third Count Block level data and merged into
this last Block-Tract-service area dataset. Through a series of
aggregations and merges, it was possible to calculate the proportion
of each Sanitation service area within the Census Tract it covered
(some of these areas were wholly within one Tract but some crossed
Tract lines). The various service level variables (pounds of garbage
collected, etc.) were apportioned among these "service area-Tract
pieces" and then aggregated to the Tract level. Also the fractional
number of service areas (or truck-days) was summed for each Tract.
Finally, these variables were adjusted on a per thousand population
and a per one thousand occupied housing units basis (e.g., pounds of
residential garbage collected per one thousand population). This
dataset was merged with the Tract characteristics to make it possible
to analyze the socio-demographic patterns along which the Division
collects the garbage, allocates its personnel, and apportions its service areas.

Area Data (Fixed Site Facilities)

Many public services are not delivered directly to their intended
clientele but are delivered to a number of fixed site facilities to
which the public must go in order to obtain these services. Such
services include parks and recreational programs, libraries, and
hospitals. Each fixed site facility of this type is, of course, intended to serve the residents of the surrounding area. Previous
studies of the distribution of municipal facilities have generally
used linear measures of access. Lineberry, for example, in his study
of the distribution of parks and libraries in San Antonio measured the
distance from six random points in each Census Tract to the nearest
park and the nearest library. Originally this project also utilized
a linear measure of access to study the distribution of parks in
Detroit. The distance from the center of each Census Tract to the
nearest large park, the nearest park of any kind, as well as the nearest playground, playfield, playlot, and golf course. (these are the
official categories of the Recreation Department). The linear distance
measures obtained in this manner were then merged with Tract characteristics and analyzed for variations in the access to recreational
facilities provided to different areas of the city. While the results
of this analysis were quite interesting, several major defects were
noted. First, the linear measurement of access ignored the possibility
that the nearest park may be quite small and poorly equipped. Second,
the official categories of recreational facilities are overlapping in
terms of the size of and equipment on these facilities. This is especially true of the designated "parks" which range in size from under

one half acre to over one thousand acres. The researchers therefore
decided to develop a different type of measure of access which would
more completely measure the total facilities available to the people
residing in different areas of the city.

In order to avoid the weaknesses of the linear method of measuring access, a radial measure of access was developed. A dataset was
assembled from figures supplied by the Recreation Department listing
the acreage, and number of each type of equipment and facilities at
each property. (Actually, the Recreation Department sent its personnel
into the field to check our printout of their initial figures and the
data was edited to correspond to the results of this field survey.)
A factor analysis was then carried out on this dataset to identify
which items of equipment and types of facilities form non-redundant
indicators of quality. The indicators from this recreational property dataset were selected for merger with a Census Tract-based dataset.

The Recreation Department properties were then drawn onto a large
Census Tract map (as was done in the case of the linear measure of
access). A clear plastic overlay was prepared with two concentric
circles drawn on it to the scale of the map. The smaller of the two
circles had a radius which was equivalent to one half mile and the
larger circle had a radius equivalent to one and one half miles. This
overlay was then placed on the Census Tract map with the center of the
circles at the center of one Census Tract. All of the Recreation Department properties within the one half mile radius were noted and all
the properties within the one and one half mile radius were also coded.
This procedure was repeated for all the Census Tracts in the city so
that all the facilities within a one half mile radius of the center of
each Census Tract and all the facilities within a one and one half mile
radius of the center of each Tract were coded.

The last stage of this radial measurement of access involved
aggregation of the indicators of quality at the Census Tract level.
For each of the two radii of each Census, the indicators were summed,
that is, the total acreage, the number of hardball diamonds, etc. that
were in recreational properties within one half mile and one and one
half mile, respectively, of the centers of each Tract was calculated
for each Tract. The result consisted of two sets of indicators of
recreational facilities provided: one measured the facilities within
one half mile and the other measured the facilities within one and one
half miles. Each of the two sets of variables measures different aspects of the quality of facilities provided as suggested by the factor
analysis. The final dataset was merged with the Census Tract characteristics to produce a dataset which enabled the project to analyze
variations in the broad range of recreational facilities available to
areas of differing socio-demographic composition. However, unlike
much of the previous work on the subject, the methodology employed by
this study takes into account the range of facilities accessable to the
population of each Census Tract.

The Software

As a parenthetical note, the reader may be curious about the software used for the data management procedures described above. This
project was fortunate to have available to it a large, extremely versatile, interactive computer system with several statistical software
packages--namely, the Michigan Terminal System (MTS) at Wayne State
University. While the extraction of the Census variables was accomplished by use of the DUALABS CENSUS package, most of the other data
management processing was done using the OSIRIS package which was developed by the Institute for Social Research at the University of
Michigan. OSIRIS is a statistical analysis program package similar in
its statistical capabilities to the somewhat better known SPSS package
(which was also used by the researchers). OSIRIS, however, contains
several excellent programs which enable the non-programmer user to
merge data from different sources (even from different units of analysis), to aggregate data from smaller to large geographical units, and
to merge data from large geographical units back onto smaller components of these units. OSIRIS also has very convenient options for
the handling of missing data, especially when merging two datasets.
OSIRIS has provisions for a wide variety of variable transformations
and, of course, statistical procedures. Finally, the OSIRIS intern-
ally-readable dataset can be read by several other statistical program packages including SPSS so the OSIRIS user is not locked in to
the exclusive use of OSIRIS for statistical analysis. Projects which
involve the kind of data management undertaken here should give serious consideration to the use of OSIRIS.

The Findings: A Brief Synopsis

The initial focus of this research project was to examine the
possible existence of racial or economic inequities in the response of
city agencies to citizen demands for service. The data collected on
the activities of the Environmental Enforcement Division did not not
support the hypothesis of class or racial discrimination. There was
a significant tendency for citizen complaints for EED services to
originate in areas at the middle range of social well-being, rather
than at the upper or lower ends of the well-being scale. These areas
with high demands for service tended to have a longer response time
(although virtually all complaints were investigated) but neither the
response time nor the type of actions taken correlated to the racial
or economic composition of the neighborhood. As the research progressed, it became clear that variations or inequalities in the level of
services provided by the city agencies were caused not by overt racial
or class bias but by the operation of the "service delivery rules" of
the agencies. These regularized procedures for the delivery of services are often formulated with the goal of making service delivery
more "rational" or efficient or to ensure the maximization of some
other organizational objective. Whatever their purpose, service delivery rules have distributional consequences and these effects can
be measured by techniques such as those used in this project.

These distributional effects of service delivery rules were quite apparent in our later analysis. The Sanitation Division had revised its service areas shortly before this research began in order to equalize the amount of garbage collected by each truck. This efficiency-oriented criterion resulted in the allocation of more truck-days and paid man-hours in the neighborhoods that ranked high in terms of social well-being (which produce more garbage). At the same time, there was a definite tendency to place more resources in the central city where management believes its crews do a poorer job (because of the alley pickup system used).

The analysis of the data from four bureaus of the Department of Buildings and Safety and the Department of Recreation is still in progress but some preliminary observations can be offered. The pattern of citizen contacts found in EED is also present in the Department of Buildings and Safety. There is a strong tendency for citizen complaints to Building and Safety to originate in areas that fall in the middle range of social well-being. The response time of the agency to these complaints tends to be higher in these neighborhoods with high rates of complaints but this is not related to the racial composition of the neighborhood.

The radial measurement of access to the facilities of the Department of Recreation has not yet been completed but the linear measures of access did produce some very interesting results. The five largest parks in the city are located in areas of fairly high social well-being although this did not correlate with race. The small playlots which were mostly acquired between 1940 and 1970, (long after most of Detroit's available land was developed) do tend to be located in older, low income, and Black neighborhoods. Of all the agencies studied, the Recreation Department is perhaps the most conscious of the distributional consequences of its allocational decisions. Nonetheless, it is fairly obvious that it is largely prevented from undertaking any major redistribution of resources by the necessity of maintaining its current facilities as well as the cost of acquiring large tracts of land in the central city, even if they were available.

CONCLUDING REMARKS

The potential uses of the data systems technology developed in this project go far beyond the primarily theoretical research described above. This technology can be used to evaluate the efficiency effectiveness, equity, and responsiveness of public agencies. Management Information Systems can be constructed with this type of data. Perhaps the most important use of this data management techniques is to enable public agencies to evaluate the impact of their service delivery rules in terms of their distributional consequences. With this knowledge and with this methodology it is also feasible to predict the distributional effects of proposed alternative policy changes and help agencies to formulate and implement service delivery rules which meet the agency's goals. While the technology cannot define these goals, the inherent dynamic of this system is to promote more responsive and effective administration of public services.

SOURCES

Charles S. Benson and Peter B. Lund, "The Neighborhood Distribution of Local Public Service", The Institute of Government Studies, University of California at Berkeley, 1969.

Bryan D. Jones, Saadia Greenberg, Clifford Kaufman, and Joseph Drew, "Service Delivery Rules and the Distribution of Local Public Services: Three Detroit Bureaucracies", presented at the American Political Science Association Meeting, San Francisco, California, September 2-6, 1975.

Bryan D. Jones, Saadia Greenberg, Joseph Drew, and Clifford Kaufman, "Bureaucratic Response to Citizen-Initiated Contacts: Environmental Enforcement in Detroit", American Political Science Review (Forthcoming, March, 1977). This paper was originally presented at the Southwest Political Science Association Meeting, San Antonio, Texas, March 27-29, 1975.

Robert L. Lineberry, "Equality, Public Policy, and Public Services: the Underclass Hypothesis and the limits to Equality", a paper presented at the Annual Meeting of the American Political Science Association, San Francisco, California, September 2-6, 1975.

Kenneth Mladenka, "The Distribution of Public Services", unpublished Ph. D. dissertation, Rice University, Houston, Texas, 1975.

Robert E. Welch, Jr. and Truett L. Chance, "The Distribution of Urban Public Services: Some Conceptual Considerations and a Preliminary Analysis", a paper delivered at the Annual Meeting of the Southwest Social Science Association, San Antonio, Texas, March 30 - April 1, 1972.

William F. Gayk, Research Analyst
Carolyn S. Harris, Research Analyst
Ronald L. La Porte, Research Analyst

John D. Dedischew, Chief
Program Planning Division
Orange County Administrative Office
515 North Sycamore Street
Santa Ana, California 92701

SOCIAL INDICATORS AND PROGRAM PLANNING:
AN EXAMPLE OF MATERNAL AND INFANT
HEALTH NEEDS ASSESSMENT

ABSTRACT: This paper briefly summarizes a needs
assessment study of maternal and infant health in Orange
County, California. It focuses heavily on the choice of
analytic techniques and their application to a variety
of administrative questions. Within the context of social
indication, this study illustrates the potential of policy
research where the relevant concepts are relatively well-
defined and where a data base exists from which these concepts
can be converted directly into measures for small geographic
areas.

INTRODUCTION

The purpose of this paper is to present an approach employed in the
assessment of maternal and infant health needs in Orange County, California.
This study was conducted to identify geographic areas in the County with
similar types of maternal and infant health problems and to relate
these areas to socio-demographic characteristics which would have particular application for the planning and delivery of services.

This paper was prepared by the Program Planning Division of the
County Administrative Office under the authorization and direction
of the Orange County Board of Supervisors and funded through Social
Revenue Sharing. It is based on work previously published in the
Report on the State of the County 1976 (Orange County Administrative
Office).

This study is felt to be rather exemplary of the "state-of-the-art" in social indication in that it applies advanced analytic procedures to a well-defined, comprehensive data set, in addressing fairly clear administrative decisions. As such, the study as a whole may help to illuminate certain increasingly apparent problems in the social indicators movement, especially the general lack of relevant, well-defined concepts and measures of need, and the lack of current, appropriate, and comprehensive data.

Background

This study was undertaken by the Program Planning Division of the County Administrative Office as part of the Needs Assessment Project funded by the Orange County Board of Supervisors through Social Revenue Sharing monies. Prior to this project, two surveys were conducted to determine the high priority human service needs in Orange County. One of these surveys included a random sample of citizens; the other a panel of professionals and paraprofessionals involved in the planning and delivery of human services. Both groups ranked health as a high priority need. In the development of the needs assessment project, therefore, further analysis into this area of need was included. Maternal and infant health was selected from many potential areas of health primarily for programmatic considerations. In addition to public sector agencies, a number of health agencies, professional and paraprofessional, and voluntary health organizations are addressing maternal and infant health problems: A potential existed, therefore, for broad and immediate applicability.

Methodology

The study consisted of five types of analyses, each type employing a different technique and/or data base:

- Trend analysis of vital statistics related to maternal and infant health.
- Choropleth mapping of nine selected indicators of maternal and infant health by census tract; these indicators were based on all births, fetal deaths and infant deaths (approximately 48,000 records) occurring to residents of Orange County for the two year period from 1973 through 1974.
- Cluster analysis of the nine maternal and infant health indicators.
- Cluster analysis of five selected indicators of socio-economic status associated with maternal and infant health program design.
- Composite mapping of the two cluster analyses included above.

These analyses will be discussed in more detail below.

TREND ANALYSIS OF HEALTH STATISTICS

Graphs were developed from published health statistics related to maternal
and infant health. Depending on the availability of the statistics, the
graphs displayed either five- or ten-year trends. These statistics
included fertility, age-specific birth rates, fetal death rates, infant
death rate, perinatal death rates, neonatal death, post-neonatal and
immaturity rates. (See Figure 1 for the description of the various
categories of infant mortality.) California and United States fetal and
infant death rates were also included in the analysis.

FIGURE 1

INFANT MORTALITY CHART*

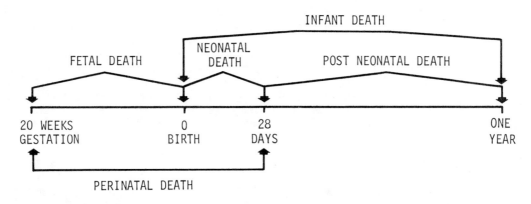

* Adapted from "A Guide for the Study of Perinatal Mortality and Morbidity,"
  Revised Edition 1962, American Medical Association

The value of this type of analysis is that it identifies where impacts have been made and need to be made. In particular, this analysis demonstrated that most infant mortality in Orange County occurs during the fetal and neonatal periods, i.e., perinatal period, and these rates appear to have reached a plateau. Since the major causes of these deaths are conditions surrounding the pregnancy itself, this suggests that programs designed to improve the health of women before and during pregnancy should have an impact in further reducing perinatal death rates.

MAPPING OF MATERNAL AND INFANT HEALTH INDICATORS

For this analysis, nine indicators of maternal and infant health were identified following consultation with the Orange County Health Department and extensive review of pertinent literature.* The selected indicators can be categorized according to whether they represent conditions that surround pregnancy, or whether they represent outcomes of pregnancy. The indicators of conditions surrounding pregnancy generally reflect pregnancy risks, in that when these conditions are present, the outcomes of pregnancy are more likely to be unfavorable, i.e., result in mortality or morbidity. The fertility rate, inadequate prenatal care, pregnancies in women 19 years and under, and pregnancies in women 35 years and over comprise the measures of "conditions surrounding pregnancy" employed in this investigation.

Similarly, the "outcome of pregnancy" indicators consist of infant mortality rates and selected conditions that are generally associated with higher infant mortality: perinatal deaths, post-neonatal deaths, low weight births, high weight births, and congenital malformations.

A computer-generated choropleth map of each indicator was provided which depicted the rate or percent of occurrence for the indicator in 316 census tracts. (Three census tracts were eliminated from this analysis because only two births occurred in those tracts during 1973-1974.) Map 1, Percent of Pregnancies with Inadequate Prenatal Care, provides an example of this type of map.

The nine indicators were mapped individually because many programs and services deal with one particular condition or problem. For example, prenatal care providers may be concerned more with the level of inadequate prenatal care than the fertility rate. Thus, prenatal care program services could be provided in the vicinity of the greatest concentration of inadequate prenatal care.

---

* The assistance and cooperation of the Orange County Health Department is gratefully acknowledged.

MAP 1

PERCENT OF PREGNANCIES WITH INADEQUATE PRENATAL
CARE, 1973-74

	FROM	TO	FREQUENCY
	0	2.0	64
	2	3.5	63
	3.5	4.7	63
	4.7	6.5	63
	6.5	24.3	66

SOURCE: Orange County Health Department

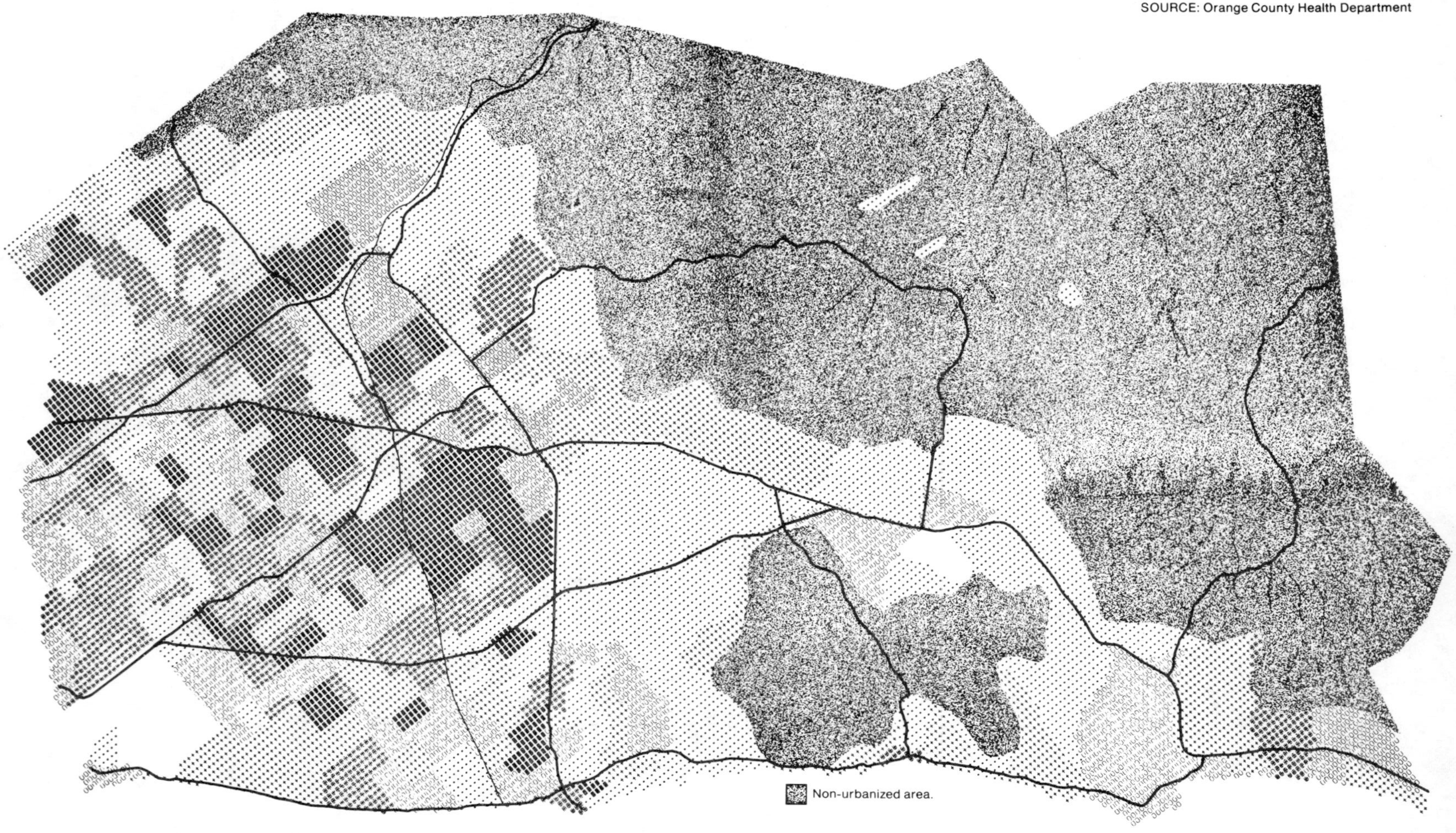

Non-urbanized area.

CLUSTER ANALYSIS OF MATERNAL AND INFANT HEALTH INDICATORS

Cluster analysis is a statistical technique that arranges a group of cases into subgroupings based on the degree of similarity between the cases on measured characteristics. In this study, the "cases" are census tracts; the measured characteristics are the nine maternal and infant health indicators discussed in the preceding section.

Five clusters of census tracts were identified through this analysis. The census tracts that form a particular cluster are more similar based on the nine indicators than the census tracts in the other clusters.

Once the census tracts comprising each cluster were identified, five "cluster maps" were prepared which displayed the tracts in the individual clusters. The data were further processed to determine the indicator values for each cluster, the deviation of the cluster from the County-wide norm, and the contribution of each cluster to the County-wide incidence of each maternal and infant health characteristic. The results of this analysis were presented in both tabular and graphic form. This analysis thus provided information on both the intensity and the magnitude of problems and conditions.

This analysis showed that the clusters were generally arrayed along a continuum of favorable to unfavorable maternal and infant health. In comparison to the other clusters, Cluster 5 exhibited a wide range of maternal and infant health problems. It had the highest fertility rate, highest level of inadequate prenatal care, highest percent pregnancies in women 19 years or less, the highest percent of low weight births, and the lowest percent of high weight births. As can be seen in Figure 2, this cluster accounted for 29.5 percent of the County's total births, yet accounted for 53 percent of the pregnancies with inadequate prenatal care, 45.8 percent of the pregnancies in women 19 years or less, 31.6 percent of all perinatal deaths, 32.9 percent of the County's post-neonatal deaths, 34.2 percent of all the low weight births, and 26.2 percent of the high weight births.

Cluster analysis provides two types of information with highly practical applications. The first application is in the definition of target areas, i.e., those areas that appear to have the greatest problems or most unfavorable conditions based on the selected indicators. The second application is in the determination of appropriate combinations of services that may be provided to address the problem by cluster. For example, Cluster 5 has a high incidence of age-related pregnancy risk, inadequate prenatal care, and low weight births. Thus, a prenatal care program including high risk pregnancy identification, nutrition supplement, and nutrition education may impact a range of maternal and infant health problems in this cluster.

FIGURE 2

PERCENT DISTRIBUTION OF MATERNAL AND INFANT HEALTH INDICATORS BY CLUSTER

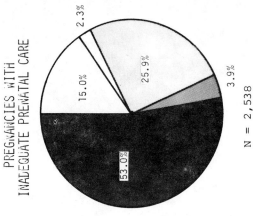
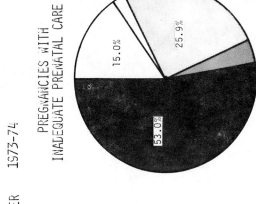
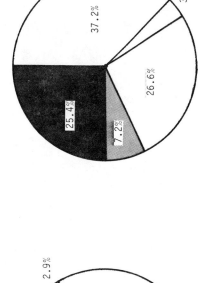
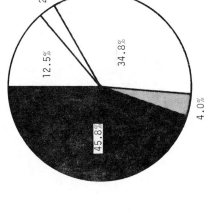
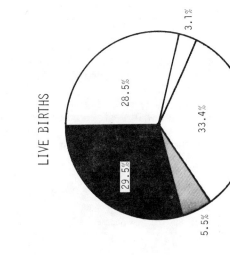

FIGURE 2 CONTINUED

PERCENT DISTRIBUTION OF MATERNAL AND INFANT HEALTH INDICATORS BY CLUSTER   1973-74

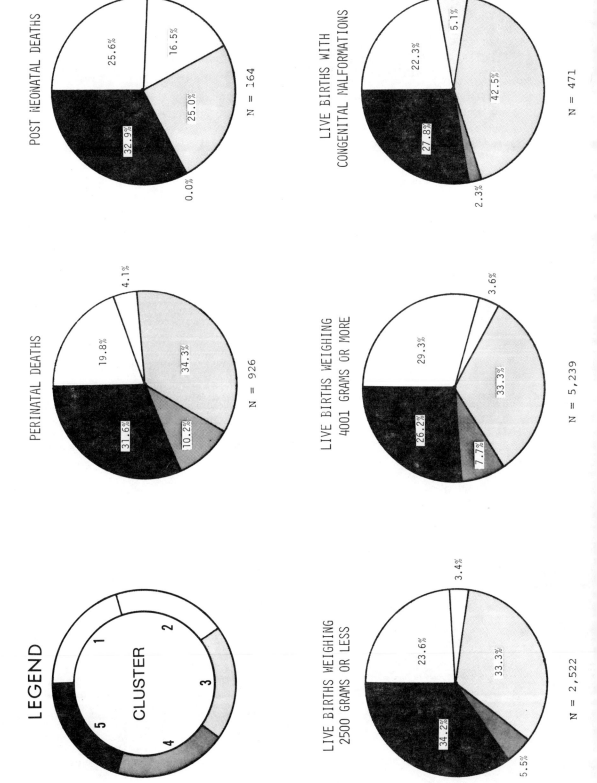

LEGEND

POST NEONATAL DEATHS

N = 164

LIVE BIRTHS WITH
CONGENITAL MALFORMATIONS

N = 471

PERINATAL DEATHS

N = 926

LIVE BIRTHS WEIGHING
4001 GRAMS OR MORE

N = 5,239

LIVE BIRTHS WEIGHING
2500 GRAMS OR LESS

N = 2,522

CLUSTER ANALYSIS OF SELECTED SOCIO-ECONOMIC INDICATORS
ASSOCIATED WITH MATERNAL AND INFANT HEALTH

Previous research has demonstrated that many socio-economic characteristics
are related to maternal and infant health. It was determined that further
analysis employing socio-economic indicators would provide further focus
to the above analyses, especially as related to the identification of
target areas for County-provided services.

Five socio-economic indicators were selected based on their applicability
to such programs: Aid to Families with Dependent Children, 1973;
families below poverty level; population of Spanish language or surname;
Black population; and females 25 years or older with 8 years of education
or less. One or more of these indicators can be used to determine
concentrations of the medically indigent, or areas where eligible clients
may reside, in addition to identifying culture-specific program elements
(e.g., bilingual service practitioners).

Cluster analysis again was employed due to its capability of summarizing
multiple variables. Six clusters of census tracts were identified in
this analysis. As can be seen in Table 1, Cluster 3, 4, 5, and 6 reflect
lower socio-economic status based on the five indicators.

COMPARISON OF CLUSTER ANALYSIS

For the final phase of the assessment of maternal and infant health needs,
a composite mapping technique was employed to provide a comparison of
the two cluster analyses. Clusters 4 and 5 of the maternal and infant
health analysis and Clusters 3, 4, 5, and 6 of the socio-economic analysis
were included in the composite map (see Map 2).

TABLE 1. SOCIOECONOMIC INDICATORS BY CLUSTER

Cluster	AFDC Rate	Percent Black	Percent Spanish Speaking or Surname	Percent Females 25 Years + with 8 Years or Less Education	Percent Families Below Poverty Level
1	19.0	0.2	5.3	5.3	2.6
2	71.0	0.2	8.1	10.5	4.6
3	560.4	32.5	36.3	34.6	13.7
4	334.8	1.9	45.4	37.1	12.0
5	175.2	1.0	24.7	25.0	8.3
6	172.1	0.4	13.2	18.8	6.5
County-wide Average	101.9	0.7	11.5	13.4	5.2

COMPOSITE OF LOW SOCIOECONOMIC STATUS AND MATERNAL AND INFANT HEALTH

ORANGE COUNTY, CALIFORNIA

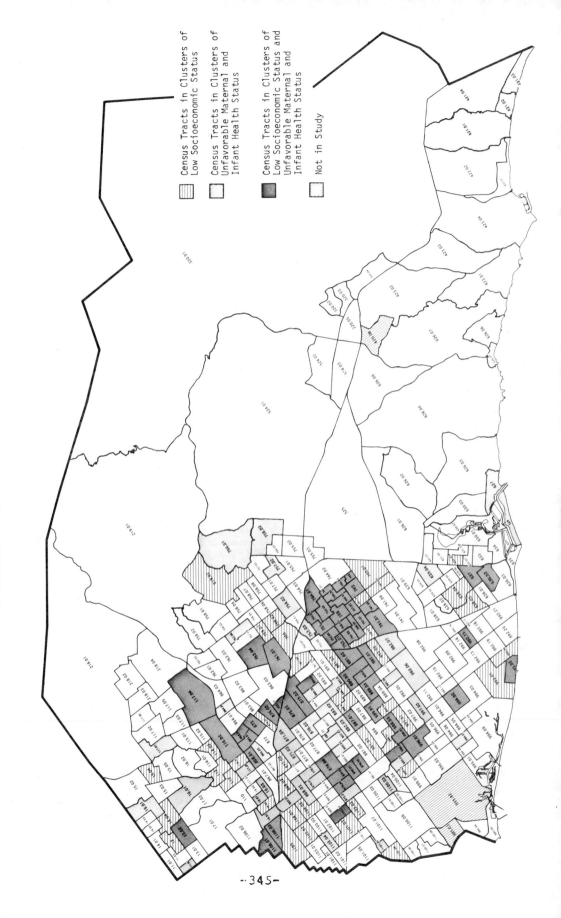

Cluster 5 of the maternal and infant health analysis was included because it exhibited the widest range of maternal and infant health problems. The inclusion of the Cluster 4 was based on its perinatal death rate, which was the highest in the County. The four clusters selected through the socio-economic analysis represented geographic areas of relatively low overall socio-economic status.

This approach was chosen, rather than performing a cluster analysis of all fourteen indicators, because it does not "dilute" the maternal and infant health cluster analysis. This was important because not all service providers are restricted by socio-economic considerations and because the problems cross a broad spectrum of social groups. Where health program planners and service providers are interested in socio-economic considerations, the composite map shows those areas that exhibit both unfavorable maternal and infant health conditions and socio-economic conditions from the perspective of health care.

CONCLUSION

A broad spectrum of human services planners in addition to health planners and service providers could potentially use information on maternal and infant health provided by the five types of analyses utilized in this study. To meet the potential multi-informational needs, a variety of analytic techniques were needed. Depending on the specific data need, the information provided through each technique can be used individually or in combination.

It is instructive to note that the approach employed here was greatly facilitated by certain features, the absence of which constrains its applicability to other kinds of policy questions. Some of the more salient features are the following:

- Maternal and infant health care services focus directly on the widely-shaped and explicit goal of reducing perinatal morbidity and mortality.
- A large body of research also exists which documents medical, social and demographic factors associated with perinatal morbidity and mortality. Thus the indicators of this need are relatively well-defined.
- Geocoded health data were available for this analysis which provided the capability for detailed, small geographic area (census tract) analysis. Further, this data base is remarkably "clean", comprehensive, and self-contained.

A full discussion of these issues is beyond the scope of this report; however, it is apparent that the constraints represented by the absence of the features--that is, the lack of well-defined and measurable goals, appropriately-defined indicators, and available and reliable data--will become increasingly problematic to practitioners in social indicator and policy research.

Reese C. Wilson, Assistant Director
Peter D. Miller, Sociologist
and
Blair C. Burgess, Senior Systems Specialist
Urban and Regional Studies Department
Stanford Research Institute
Menlo Park, California 94025

THE ROLE OF SOCIAL INDICATORS IN
PUBLIC SECTOR PRODUCTIVITY SYSTEMS

ABSTRACT: Evaluation of public sector productivity
and effectiveness can be enhanced by the use of valid
and reliable social indicators. The role of social
indicators in urban and regional productivity improvement programs and information systems is explored, and
the potential for practical application is assessed.
Standards are suggested to determine the validity and
local applicability of social indicators to increase
public sector productivity, responding to political,
economic, environmental, and social pressures for improvement in services delivered to the public.

INTRODUCTION

Public agencies exist primarily to serve the public through regulatory powers and delivery of essential services. Despite (or perhaps
because of) the proliferation of agencies and swelling public employment,
the effectiveness of regulations and services is increasingly questioned
by elected officials and citizens, as the quality of life continues to
deteriorate in numerous urban areas. In an era when many Americans are
alienated from government and many are already dissatisfied with the
quality of public services, economic trends are forcing frustrating
choices between increased taxes and reduced service levels. Clearly,
improved program effectiveness is needed to achieve the best investment
of public resources at the urban and regional levels. The need is intensified by the devolution of decision-making responsibilities through
federal general revenue sharing and block grant programs.
Several jurisdictions have initiated comprehensive programs, usually
with federal financial or technical assistance, designed to improve

regulatory or service-delivery effectiveness. The City of San Diego, for example, is implementing a Comprehensive Management Planning (CMP) system intended to achieve the highest feasible quality of life for all residents through effective city government. The CMP program stresses five major processes:[1]*

- Community Needs Assessment--Identify current and potential community problems and needs to provide the basis for municipal goals and priority setting, using citizen input data where appropriate.
- Planning and Analysis--Define objectives and develop long and midrange plans to realize the objectives, commensurate with established goals, priorities, and policies. Analyze alternative means of achieving stated objectives within revenue and resource constraints.
- Program Budgeting--Allocate resources in a manner that allows their contribution to meeting stated objectives to be measured in terms of program effectiveness.
- Management and Control--Perform operational planning and management to insure efficient utilization of resources within the framework of approved program plans and budgets.
- Program Evaluation--Determine the effectiveness and efficiency of ongoing programs through measurement and evaluation of municipal operations and results achieved within the community.

An urban data bank and supporting information systems are explicitly included in the San Diego approach.

San Diego's approach is representative of approaches initiated by other thoughtful urban and regional organizations striving to increase overall effectiveness. It is important that productivity improvement programs and systems be incorporated within a rational policy and decision-making framework, if social indicator data are to have a real impact on the decision-making process.

Theorists and practitioners increasingly recognize that social indicators are vital to establishing goals, policies, and programs that will satisfy community needs economically. Virginia Canupp has proposed an evaluation method using socioeconomic indicators based on selected economic, health, education, housing, physical environment, and crime measures.[2] The Urban Institute has developed and comparatively measured a number of urban indicators within 18 large metropolitan areas, for several quality of life categories (e.g., unemployment, poverty, public order, transportation, and air quality).[3] More recently, Richard Nathan and his colleagues at the Brookings Institution have developed and measured hardship indices for 55 large cities, based on six measures available from the 1970 census: unemployment, dependency, education,

---

*References are listed at the end of this paper.

-348

income level, crowded housing, and poverty.[4] Dedischew has articulated
the problem of incorporating social indicators into local planning and
management processes as "trying to understand the multidimensional overlays of specific data in such a way as to indicate socioeconomic states
or statuses of any particular geographic area or segment of the population."[5]

These suggestions for the use of social indicators vary in terms of
program purpose, the level of government to which they are addressed, and
the degree to which they have been implemented in decision making. Social
indicators have not been systematically applied in most urban and regional
policy and decision-making processes. Their application to governmental
activities has not been adequately clarified, but a promising field for
their use is the assessment of local government effectiveness. Since
improved social well-being is a major "product" of local government, it
is reasonable that social indicators be linked to measures of productivity.

A TYPOLOGY FOR PRODUCTIVITY INDICATORS

Three Classes of Productivity Indicators

Broadly defined, productivity indicators fall into three general
classes:

- Social Indicators--Measures of community conditions that
  may be affected by governmental regulatory and service
  activities.
- Measures of Effectiveness--Measures of achieved results
  that can be attributed to policies and programs having
  specific output goals and objectives.
- Efficiency Measures--Measures of the amount of service
  output, in proportion to the amount of resource input.

Overlap among the three classes is inevitable, both in concept and
in practice. Social indicators are, in fact, employed to some degree
in measures of effectiveness of programs intended to have a specific
impact on community conditions. Measures of effectiveness and efficiency
both require information about program output. Conceptually, the three
classes form a continuum, as Figure 1 suggests.

Efficiency measures quantity of output derived from a given input,
while effectiveness measures quality of results, and social indicators
allow changes in community conditions to be measured. Social indicators
are the focus of this discussion. They can be employed in measures of
effectiveness for programs to improve community conditions, such as
better water quality or reduced vandalism in schools. They can also be
used, independently of specific programs, to measure the status of community conditions and to assist decision makers in policy choices leading

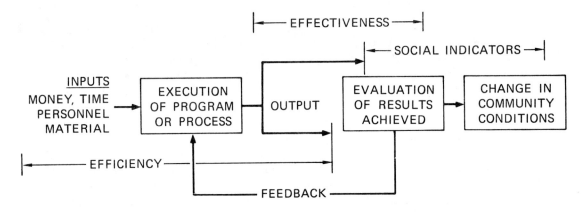

Figure 1   PRODUCTIVITY MEASUREMENT SPECTRUM

to effective programs. A single statistic--for example, the percent of
population below the poverty line (provided the line is revised for
inflation)--by itself provides useful information. The reliability of
the indicator increases if longitudinal data are available because changes
over time are more revealing than "snapshots" taken at only one point.

Measures of Effectiveness Based on Social Indicators

Candidate Axiom 1: If measureable program objectives have not
been established and accepted by management, social indicators
will not fulfill their legitimate role in a productivity
system.

Harry Hatry and his collegues at the Urban Institute have observed
that measures of effectiveness "measure the extent to which goals and
objectives of the service are being met." If the objective deals with
community conditions, such as quality of housing, public transit, or
employment, social indicators are needed to determine the degree to which
objectives are realized.

Social indicators must be directly related to policy goals and objectives. Without clearly articulated objectives that can be measured,
it is pointless to invest resources in the development of social indicators. On the other hand, such development can aid in the articulation
of goals and purposes, suggesting that the specification of objectives
and the development of social indicators may proceed concurrently.

A 1970 Management Information Services Report proposed six tests
for the development of measures of effectiveness for municipal services,
similar to the measures termed "productivity indicators" in this paper.[7]
They are:

- Validity--Does the productivity indicator really measure societal conditions, or effectiveness or efficiency of the service-delivery activity?
- Quantifiability--Is the indicator in a ready-to-use quantifiable format?
- Availability--Are the requisite data available without special research?
- Simplicity--Is the indicator intuitively meaningful?
- Acceptability--Will people accept the indicator as a valid measure of productivity?
- Timeliness--Will the productivity indicator show problems soon enough to permit corrective action before significant loss or degradation of service occurs?

Candidate Axiom 2: If high quality measurement data cannot be acquired and analyzed in time to influence the decision for which information is needed, social indicators will not fulfill their legitimate role in a productivity system.

Valid indicators for which reliable data can be economically and readily obtained are rare. The national census--a rich source of socioeconomic and demographic data--comes but once every 10 years. Although other sources of data are published on a more regular basis, many problems faced by urban and regional decision makers require data and information that must be specially collected.

Candidate Axiom 3: If data cannot be transformed into information that has a direct bearing on policy, social indicators will not fulfill their legitimate role in a productivity system.

A recent Southern California Association of Governments report differentiates between data and social indicators.[8] Data "enumerate the prevalence of a condition or the number of transactions, events or activities occurring within a defined space and a specified time," and social indicators are "the result of analysis and interpretation of data and other information in the context of a particular question. Social indicators are information derived from various data to provide knowledge about conditions in society." These definitions distinguish descriptive statistics from policy analysis, highlighting the fact that data usually need some sort of processing and analysis to yield useful information. All too often raw data are presented to policy management in the form of voluminus computer printouts or in other semi-processed form, thus burying potentially useful information in a mass of irrelevant data.

In sum, the utility of each class of productivity indicator will be enhanced by defining measurable objectives, acquiring reliable data, and producing concise, usable information.

Responsibilities and Functions

The third dimension for the productivity indicator typology is based on the responsibilities and functions of urban and regional organizations. The complications arising from the extreme diversity of local governmental responsibilities was highlighted in a recent study of formula alternatives for general revenue sharing:[9]

> Because local governments are creatures of the State, and are empowered, regulated, and often financed by the State, and because there are real differences of opinion about what a Federal grant-in-aid program should reward local governments for doing, measuring government responsibilities is not a clear-cut issue. Inevitably, normative judgments become necessary, and when coupled with the considerable operational difficulties, any measure of government responsibilities and functions becomes less than ideal.

A successful national strategy to provide federal financial or technical assistance for social indicators will have to take some account of the great variety in American local governments.

If the responsibility for determining local priorities is to be exercised at the local level, then local officials will need to establish goals and objectives, develop useful measures of effectiveness incorporating social indicators, and be careful to consider the three candidate axioms in their plans for implementing a productivity system.

USE OF SOCIAL INDICATORS IN PRODUCTIVITY SYSTEMS

Seven Steps to Increased Government Effectiveness

A paper presented recently at the First Western States Municipal Productivity Conference suggested seven steps to increased local government effectiveness:[10]

(1) Identify community needs and priorities
(2) Establish goals and objectives
(3) Develop effective policies, plans, and programs
(4) Develop effective support systems and management and staff capacity (including an urban data bank)
(5) Allocate needed resources
(6) Manage and control service activities
(7) Evaluate program results.

The steps are circular in the sense that the evaluation of program results (Step 7) usually contributes to the baseline needed for the identification of community needs and priorities (Step 1), especially if the approach incorporates social indicators.

This planning and management framework is used to construct an example of how one might go about using social indicators in a comprehensive productivity system. Emphasis is placed on Steps 1, 4, and 7.

Practical Considerations in Realizing the Seven Steps

Urban and regional needs are usually identified through the political process, relying on both original (primary) and published (secondary) data. Primary data may be collected through citizen surveys designed to sample attitudes and perceptions,[11] by direct observation and monitoring, and by community profiling. A quicker and less expensive way to secure data may be to contact a local interest group, for example, the League of Women Voters. Or the acquisition of primary data can occur as a spinoff of on-going activities. The amount of solid waste collected, for instance, can be used to develop projections for sanitary fills that will be needed. Secondary data are often available at almost no cost, through such usual published sources as the decennial Census of Population and Housing. An analysis of four data elements available from the 1970 Census--number of women in labor force, children under five years, families with female heads, families with low income--could yield information on the need for day care facilities, as suggested by the SCAG report cited earlier.

Some local governments, for example, the City of Los Angeles' Community Analysis Bureau, have developed sophisticated systems for the analysis of community needs. There is no point, however, in collecting data without reference to a particular goal, policy, or program. It would be futile to commit resources to a data bank on day care needs if the resources for day care facilities are unavailable. Thus the needs and priorities established by the political process will suggest directions appropriate for data-gathering efforts.

Social indicators, especially changes in community conditions over time, can provide extremely important information to decision makers and interest groups in formulating and influencing goals and objectives. Several precautions should be observed however.

Tracing the linkages between a regulation, policy, or program and the related societal condition or status can be difficult. For example, local law enforcement agencies may claim credit for a reduced crime rate, when the real reason may be more closely related to the reduced number of 14- to 24-year-old males in the population. Or several levels of government may be involved in a program, and they may be working at cross purposes. Constraints imposed by higher levels of government can greatly inhibit the effectiveness of programs initiated by lower levels. The negative effect of federal policies on depreciation of urban rental housing units, for example, may outweigh any positive effects to be gained through local urban renewal programs. (This example also highlights the

-353-

fact that contradictory goals and effects are embedded in various federal
programs.) Goals and objectives, in short, must be established in the
context of the specific jurisdiction or jurisdictions having responsibility for the policy or program.

Few urban and regional agencies have the support systems and capacity
to adequately develop and employ social indicators in their planning and
management processes. However, general revenue sharing and block grant
programs are beginning to provide resources to build the needed systems
and capacity. The perilous financial condition of many jurisdictions
provides additional incentive for increased productivity.

Program evaluation, the final step of the seven-step process, has
perhaps the most important implications for social indicators and productivity systems. It is here that the actual impact of regulations and
service-delivery programs on the community is assessed.

Implementing a Productivity System

Keep It Simple

The history of ambitious productivity improvement programs in the
public sector (e.g., PPBS, MIS, MBO) does not inspire confidence. Although the temptation to recommend comprehensive approaches seems
inescapable, it is more prudent to begin with only one planning and
management function (usually resource allocation) and one service-delivery
function (often solid waste or police protection) at a time. If measurable objectives can be included in the annual budget document, and data
collected for a few basic productivity indicators within one service-
delivery function, experience can be gained at reasonable cost. Measurable objectives, measures, and measurement systems can then be expanded
into other functional areas over time.

Development of a Program Structure and Productivity Indicators

The quality of planning and management directly influence the effectiveness of service-delivery systems. Though the initial production
improvement program is kept simple, it should be planned within a program
structure, to provide a framework for objectives and indicators. Most
social indicators are related to one or more functions (e.g., housing,
health, public safety), and a program structure is preferably defined
along functional lines. Table 1 illustrates one such framework, developed
by the City of San Diego.

Given some kind of programmatic framework, candidate social indicators
and other productivity indicators can be evaluated as to the six tests
mentioned earlier: validity, quantifiability, availability, simplicity,

Table 1

PROGRAM STRUCTURE

Life support
  Air
  Potable water
  Food
  Housing
  Health
  Coordinate and support the Life Support Program category

Security of persons and property
  Security from crime
  Security from fire
  Security from accidents
  Security from elements and environment
  Security from disasters
  Civil remedies
  Coordinate and support the Security of Persons and Property Program
   category

Economic security
  Employment
  Vocational training
  Economic subsistence
  Economic conservation
  Coordinate and support the Economic Security Program category

Transportation and utilities development
  Transportation
  Communications
  Energy
  Coordinate and support the Transportation and Utilities Development
   Program category

Environmental development
  Natural resources--preservation and enhancement
  Urban development
  Coordinate and support the Environmental Development Program category

Individual development
  Education
  Recreation
  Culture
  Social development
  Coordinate and support the Individual Development Program category

Effective government
  Legislative
  Administrative
  Coordinate and support the Effective Government Program category

acceptability, and timeliness. A sample evaluation form is shown in Figure 2. Low ratings in one or more of the parameters would diminish the likelihood of immediate use of a potential indicator.

Development of Productivity Measurement Systems

Productivity measurement systems are primarily concerned with collecting and processing data into values for social indicators, measures of effectiveness, and efficiency measures. Although automated support is not indispensable, the sheer volume of data often creates a data management problem that can be eased with automation. In any case, it is usually a good idea to pilot test data collection and processing procedures in a manual mode, prior to automating them.

As data and productivity indicator measurement values accumulate, organizing them for ready access becomes important. Productivity indicator data or measurement values can be organized along several dimensions:

- Functional--A well-developed program structure specifies how productivity measurement data should be organized among and within major program categories, programs, subprograms, program elements, and so on.
- Organizational--The value for each productivity indicator may be linked to the responsible organizational unit.
- Geographical--Social indicators may apply to such specific geographical areas within a jurisdiction as blocks, block groups, or census tracts. Then a geographic base file can interrelate varying geographical systems employed for various functions (e.g., police beats to fire prevention districts).
- Temporal--Productivity statistics apply to a time period which they purport to represent (fiscal year 1970, first quarter of calendar year 1976). It is necessary to store historical data as more current data are being developed.

With proper attention to the dimensions suggested above, it is possible to design an urban data bank that will support comparisons of current versus past performance (longitudinal analyses) as well as comparison among various functions or geographical areas (cross-sectional analyses). Forecasts can also be developed from various time series data.

CONCLUSIONS AND RECOMMENDATIONS

Social indicators can contribute vitally to public sector productivity if they are properly incorporated into measures of the effectiveness of policies or programs having an impact on community conditions. To

PRODUCTIVITY INDICATOR RATING

	Activity:
Program Category:	
Program:	Prepared by _____ Date _____
Sub program:	
Program element:	Approved by _____ Date _____

INSTRUCTIONS	RATINGS							
1. List productivity indicators. 2. Rate: E(excellent); G(good); P(poor) 3. Rank the measures: 1,2,3. . . . . 4. Indicate in last column the decision on whether to use.	Validity	Quantifiability	Availability	Simplicity	Acceptability	Timeliness	Ranking	Use
POTENTIAL SOCIAL INDICATORS								
POTENTIAL MEASURES OF EFFECTIVENESS								
POTENTIAL EFFICIENCY MEASURES								

Figure 2   PRODUCTIVITY INDICATOR EVALUATION FORM

ensure that social indicators fulfill their potential role, three axioms
should be carefully observed:

(1) Measurable program objectives must be established and
accepted by management.

(2) High quality measurement data must be acquired and
analyzed in time to influence the decision for which
information is needed.

(3) Data must be transformable into information that has
a direct bearing on social policy.

Since valid social indicators for which reliable data can be readily obtained are rare, candidate indicators should be tested for the six qualities, validity, quantifiability, availability, simplicity, acceptability,
and timeliness, before making a final decision as to their utility. Care
should also be taken in the organization of a data bank to support policy
makers, with initial system implementation efforts restricted to a single
planning and management function and a single program.

In spite of the practical difficulties, it appears that increased
emphasis must be placed on social indicators in urban and regional productivity systems. Most public policies and programs cannot be effectively planned or accurately evaluated without measuring social conditions
within a community.

REFERENCES

1. "Comprehensive Management Planning System," CMP staff, City of San
Diego, California, and Stanford Research Institute, Menlo Park,
California (June 1973).

2. V. P. Canupp, "An Evaluation Method: Socio-Economic Indicators,"
Community Development Department, Gainesville, Georgia (August 1975).

3. M. J. Flax, "A Study in Comparative Urban Indicators: Conditions in
18 Large Metropolitan Areas," The Urban Institute, Washington, D.C.
(April 1972).

4. R. P. Nathan and C. Adams, "Understanding Central City Hardship,"
Political Science Quarterly, Vol. 91, No. 1 (Spring 1976).

5. "Public Policy Decision-Making and Social Indicators," Urban and
Regional Information Systems Association, Municipal Systems
Research, Claremont Men's College, Claremont, California.

6. H. P. Hatry and D. M. Fisk, directors, "The Challenge of Productivity Diversity: Improving Local Government Productivity Measurement and Evaluation. Part I: Overall Summary and Recommendations," The Urban Institute and The International City Management Association, Washington, D.C. (1971-1972).

7. "Measuring Effectiveness of Municipal Services," Management Information Service, Vol. 2, LS-8, International City Management Association, Washington, D.C. (August 1970).

8. A Guide to Social Indicators for Local Government or How to Improve Your Policy Decisions with Information You Didn't Know You Had, The Southern California Association of Government (October 1975).

9. R. C. Wilson et al., "General Revenue Sharing Formula Alternatives," SRI Project 9300, Stanford Research Institute, Menlo Park, California (June 1975).

10. R. C. Wilson, "Urban Priority Number 1: Increased Local Government Effectiveness," Stanford Research Institute, Menlo Park, California (February 1976).

11. R. C. Wilson et al., "Applications of Consumer Analysis in the Public Sector," prepared for the National Center for Productivity and Quality of Working Life, Stanford Research Institute, Menlo Park, California (July 1976).

Kitty B. Herrin
Systems Development Group
Center for Urban Affairs
  and Community Services
North Carolina State University

SOCIAL AREA ANALYSIS VIA FACTOR ANALYSIS:
A REVIEW AND EVALUATION OF TECHNIQUES
USED IN IDENTIFYING URBAN SOCIAL AREAS

Analyses of the socio-economic structure of residential areas have been handled largely by sociologists using the neighborhood concept or social area analysis as a framework. Social area analysis is designed to provide a systematic classification of residential areas within large cities. As originally conceived, social area analysis depended upon the somewhat arbitrary grouping of a series of census characteristics into three indexes, economic status (social rank), family status (urbanization) and ethnic status (segregation). Factor analytic studies of census tract data for a large number of U. S. cities, using a wide range of socio-economic characteristics, have consistently identified these same three basic factors of differentiation. Analysis of the spatial distribution of the index or factor scores of census tracts on these three dimensions may be used to test the concentric and sectorial models of urban structure and growth. Results from the studies of a limited number of cities suggest that economic status is primarily distributed sectorially, family status is a concentric phenomenon, and ethnic status is associated with the existence of ghettoes or similar clusterings of people with common cultural backgrounds.

This paper presents a very brief sketch of the theoretical and empirical background of comparative urban ecology and a look at studies in social area analysis using multivariate techniques. Following this review is a brief discussion of the problems that are associated with the field and finally an evaluation of factor analysis as a technique for identifying urban social areas.

The location and socio-economic characteristics of residential areas within large American cities have been studied for many years by sociologists, economists, geographers, and others. Attempts to explain the location of residential areas within cities have emphasized a wide range of social and economic factors such as accessibility to the city center and to work places within the city, the social relations which exist among community subgroups, the residential values held by members of the community, and the community power structure. Analyses of the socio-economic structure of residential areas have been handled largely by sociologists using the neighborhood concept or social area analysis as a framework. As originally conceived by Shevky and his associates (Shevky and Bell, 1955:68), social area analysis depended upon the somewhat arbitrary grouping of a series of census characteristics into three indexes: economic status (social rank), family status (urbanization), and ethnic status (segregation). Despite criticisms concerning the arbitrariness of this grouping, factor analytic studies of census tract data for a large number of large and medium-sized United States cities, using a wide range of socio-economic characteristics, have consistently identified these three basic factors of differentiation. Analysis of the spatial distribution of the index or factor scores of census tracts on these three dimensions may be used to test the concentric and sectorial models of urban structure and growth. (Results from the study of a limited number of cities suggest that economic status is primarily distributed sectorially, family status is a concentric phenomenon, and ethnic status is associated with the existence of ghettoes or similar clusterings of people with common cultural backgrounds.) This paper presents a very brief sketch of the theoretical and empirical background of comparative urban ecology and assumes the reader is familiar with both the classic descriptive models of urban ecology and also the classic studies of social area analysis. Following this review is a brief discussion of the general measurement problems of comparative urban ecology, the other general problems that are associated with the field, and, finally, the merits and drawbacks of factor analysis as they relate to this particular area of study.

THEORETICAL AND EMPIRICAL BACKGROUND

Although coming from a wide variety of subfields in the social sciences, ecological research has proved to be cumulative and complementary so that frequently work initiated in one field has been further developed by scholars in closely related fields. For example, although the social area analysts were originally concerned with describing the socio-economic structure of an urban population and disclaimed interest in traditional ecological preoccupations with urban spatial structure, one unintended but nevertheless highly significant consequence of their efforts has been a revitalization of the latter field (Abu-Lughod, 1969:168). A recent integration of this kind of work with that of social morphologists[1] such as Chombart deLauwe has been made by urban and social geographers. Chombart deLauwe (Dickinson, 1964) is responsible for the most fundamental conceptual contribution linking social space to the physical space of the city. In a study of the social morphology of Paris, he suggests that social space is made up of economic, demographic, cultural, and other kinds of space which, when superimposed on the physical space of the city, serve to isolate areas of social homogeneity. In this manner one is able to build up a comprehensive picture of urban social structure and to single out relatively uniform social areas for more detailed studies of social dynamics within the urban system. Chombart deLauwe's concept of social space can be quantified using modern factor analysis. In factor analysis, the dimensions that are derived are <u>independent</u> and <u>additive</u>. Each accounts for a separate portion of the total variance of the original observations (census tracts, in this case) as measured by the initial set of variables (socio-economic characteristics, in this case). In summation, the dimensions span the space of the original variables.

DESCRIPTIVE MODELS OF INTRA-URBAN LOCATION

The classic descriptive models of urban land use and social geography are zonal, sectorial, and multiple nuclei forms of urban growth and structure.

[1] Social morphology, following the Durkheimian tradition, is the study of relationships of population and environment to social structure. (Popenoe, 1969; 440).

1. The Concentric Zone Model

Concentric models of land use are not new. Early concepts were formulated by people such as Plato, Aristotle, and Marco Polo. The first person to formulate such a construct in the United States was E. W. Burgess. After a study of land use and social characteristics in Chicago, he indicated that urban patterns could be summarized in terms of five concentric zones: (1) the central business district, (2) the transition zones, (3) the zone of independent workingmen's homes, (4) the zone of better residences, and (5) the commuter's zone (Burgess, 1925). Or, in sum, he argued that socio-economic status varies directly with distance from the city center. As a generalized scheme the Burgess model has been criticized because it was developed from a study of only one city at one point in time, and, as a result, may not be applicable to other situations (Quinn, 1950; 116-137).

2. The Sector Model

The sector model was described originally by Richard Hurd (1903) in 1903 and formulated by Homer Hoyt (1939) following a pre-World War II study of the movement of rental neighborhoods in a number of United States cities. A more recent study by the same investigator using income data from the 1960 U. S. Census confirms the earlier findings (Hoyt, 1964). In Hoyt's model, the central business district remains as a circular form at the center of the city while residential areas of similar socio-economic status originating near the center tend to migrate in sectors toward the urban fringe. Socio-economic status, then, varies according to an angular measurement about the center of the city. Better quality residences spread out along major transportation routes and higher ground while the interstices fill in with lower quality residences.

3. The Multiple Nuclei Model

The multiple nuclei model as applied to urban areas was first suggested by R. M. Hurd and R. D. McKenzie and later elaborated upon by C. D. Harris and E. L. Ullman (McKenzie, 1933; Hurd, 1903; Harris and Ullman, 1945). The basic notion of this model is that urban land uses concentrate around several nuclei rather than a single core. In sum, this model suggests, unlike the Burgess and Hoyt models, that there is no one basic pattern of ecological structure common to many cities.

4. Empirical Verification

Since their inception all three models have been used with varied success to describe the spatial differentiation of land use patterns and population types in dozens of cities throughout the world. There are many investigators who feel that the individual city is so unique that idealized models can explain only a small proportion of the total spatial variations in ecological structure within the city. In a recent evaluation of the Burgess zonal model and his own sectorial model, Homer Hoyt (1964) discusses how these idealized patterns have been distorted to some extent by growth factors, especially the increased flexibility of location provided by widespread use of the automobile.

In many instances, as Berry and Simmons have pointed out, the three classical models of intra-urban location have been used simultaneously as conflicting descriptions of the internal structure of the city (Berry, 1964: 125-129; Berry, 1965: 111-119; Simmons, 1965: 170-174). Recent empirical evidence from the work of human ecologists such as Anderson and Egeland (1961) suggests strongly that the three models compliment one another with each describing a separate aspect of social differentiation within a city. (Also see Hurd (1903: 56-74) who recognized the additive characteristic of the three models as early as 1903.)

SOCIAL AREA ANALYSIS

Social area analysis was developed by Eshref Shevky and a group of sociological colleagues as a technique for classifying census tracts according to three indexes: economic status, family status, and ethnic status. The technique was first applied by Shevky and Williams (1949) to a study of Los Angeles and later elaborated upon by Shevky and Bell (1955) in a study of San Francisco. Since then the technique has been applied to a number of cities, primarily within the United States, often in conjunction with studies of such topics as crime, voting behavior, and the demand for intra-urban transportation. (See, for example, Polk (1958); Kaufman and Greer (1960); Oi and Shulderer (1962: 116-120).)

Three factors (dimensions) of differentiation which might be used to study a particular social system at one point in time are normally identified in social area analysis. These are the constructs of economic status (social rank), family status (urbanization), and ethnic status (segregation).

With three indexes available, census tracts can each be characterized by three scores. Those tracts which exhibit similar scores can be grouped into relatively uniform social areas. The authors divide what they call "social space" into sixteen cells or social areas by dividing social rank and urbanization each into four intervals. The result is a structural rather than a spatial representation of social space with each social area corresponding to a cell in a four-by-four table. Note is also taken of tracts with high indexes of ethnic segregation.

A study of the social structure of the San Francisco Bay Region in 1940 and 1950 demonstrates the use of the social area typology. Comparisons of the social area structure in these two years are made but as in most of the subsequent social area analyses very little mention is made of spatial differentiation and change. The authors explicitly leave this task to city planners, geographers, and human ecologists (Shevky and Bell, 1955: 43).

One idea that has been read into this theory is the one of increasing scale (e.g., McElrath, 1968). This aspect of the theory suggests that the pattern of social (and physical) differentiation in preindustrial societies (cities) would be relatively simple and essentially unidimensional, and that as the scale of society increases there would be a comparable increase in the complexity of differentiation and a separation of the axes or dimensions of differentiation.

EMPIRICAL VALIDITY

Emphasis has, in the last two decades, been placed on empirical testing of the social area typology and on more explicit analysis of the spatial distribution of the indexes. For the most part these studies have used some form of factor analytic model to verify the existence of the hypothesized patterns of urban ecological structure and in a few cases to examine their spatial distribution.

Analyses have suggested that all three indexes are necessary to describe socio-economic differentiation in an urban ecological system but do not mean that these indexes are sufficient to describe all socio-economic differentiation within such a system. However, the results give some reason to believe that the concepts are adequate to describe a good deal of differentiation in the published census characteristics.

MULTIVARIATE ANALYSIS

Aided by advancing computer technology, recent studies of the socio-economic structure of urban areas have been extended to include a much wider range of census characteristics. In most instances, characteristics are not chosen with the aim of specifically replicating the social area indexes but rather of isolating those dimensions which explain as much as possible of the socio-economic differentiation within urban areas. In some cases, the dimensions also serve as a basis for classifying urban areas for more specific studies. In each case, the desire is to eliminate redundancies within an inter-correlation matrix of census characteristics using multivariate statistical tools such as linkage analysis, component analysis, and factor analysis. The last two techniques also allow the researcher to investigate the spatial variations in urban ecological structure by mapping the scores of census tracts on the components or factors. The examples discussed below are somewhat representative of work in this field.

Frank L. Sweetser's (1961; 1962a; 1962b) study of ecological structure and change in metropolitan Boston analyzes both cross-sectional patterns in 1950 and 1960 and changes which have taken place during the decade. Sweetser applied the technique of elementary linkage analysis to matrices of inter-correlations for 1950 and 1960 data and then to a matrix of change, 1950-1960. Both cross-sectional analyses produced types of relationships closely associated with economic status and family status. On the basis of this evidence it is concluded that no fundamental change occurred in the ecological structure between 1950 and 1960. The change analysis corroborated these conclusions and although family status assumed greater significance than economic status, the basic importance of these two dimensions was once again underlined. Individual characteristics from the cross-sectional and change analysis were mapped and the resulting distributions showed generally concentric patterns, especially for variables measuring change. Sector patterns were of some significance, however, for variables closely associated with the economic status dimensions in 1950 and 1960. For example, in the cross-sectional analyses income was distributed sectorially outward from a tight concentric zone of low income at the center of the city.

In a more recent study, Sweetser (1965) compares the ecological structure of Boston and Helsinki using factor analysis and twenty comparable 1960 census characteristics. The results show a similar ecological structure in both cities with the same three major factors identified in each case. These are interpreted as socio-economic status, progeniture, and urbanism. Progeniture is associated with fertility and new housing while urbanism is closely related to women in the labor force. It will be noticed that this interpretation of urban ecological structure is similar to that of Anderson and Bean (1961) in their attempt to replicate the social area indexes in Toledo, Ohio. An analysis using the coefficient of congruence indicates that for each city factors one and two are markedly similar but factor three is only somewhat similar. No attempt was made to analyze the spatial structure of these dimensions in the two cities. The author concludes that factor analysis is an excellent tool for comparing urban ecological structure cross-nationally and intra-nationally and urges the inclusion of additional variables in factor analyses of urban ecological structure.

In a sequel to the study described above Sweetser (1965) analyzed the factorial structure of Helsinki's ecology using forty-two variables instead of the original twenty. Aside from an analysis of the substantive results, the purpose of the study was to test several hypotheses concerning the structural effect of adding variables to a factor analysis. Methodologically, the general invariance of factors under substitution, addition, and subtraction of variables was demonstrated. The substantive results are similar to those found in the study outlined above except that a factor related to home ownership and additional factors concerning specialized phases of familism are identified. As in the previous study, an ethnic status dimension does not appear as a meaningful factor in Helsinki.

A factor analysis of 1960 census characteristics for census tracts in Seattle has been completed by Schmid and Tagashira (1964). Although the Seattle study deals with only one point in time the variables selected for analysis are closely related to those analyzed in the present study. The forty-two variables, which were derived from the 1960 U. S. census, included measures of population change, sex, age, race and nativity, family relations, socio-economic status, education, employment, occupation, mobility, and housing. Four separate factor analyses were undertaken, each with a different number of variables ranging from a full set of 42 to a reduced set of 10. The purpose of the four analyses was to test the invariance of the factor structure at each stage.

The first-stage analysis included all forty-two variables and produced five interpretable factors. These were named: (1) family status, (2) socio-economic status, (3) maleness (high percentage of males, poor housing), (4) population stability, and (5) ethnic status. Three other factor analyses were undertaken using twenty-one, twelve, and ten variables respectively. At each stage a larger number of variables which showed a high degree of overlap on the basis of the correlation matrix were eliminated from the analysis. In all three analyses the three basic social area dimensions of family status, economic status, and ethnic status were reproduced thereby confirming the general invariance of the primary factors. This conclusion is similar to that reached by Sweetser in his study of Helsinki. Factor scores were derived for the forty-two variable and ten variable analyses and a composite map was drawn to show the spatial variation of the dimensions. However, the spatial distribution of the scores was not analyzed nor related to the classic spatial models of ecological structure and change. Finally, the factor scores from the forty-two variable and ten variable analyses and a selection of single variables were intercorrelated. The results were as expected: (1) the three social area dimensions were independent for each analysis, (2) the corresponding dimensions in the two different analyses were correlated, and (3) the selected single variables correlated highly with their respective factors.

Small area census data were provided in Britain for the first time in 1961 and a number of scholars at British universities have since been analy-

sing these results for urban subareas. The first study of this kind was
a component analysis of two contrasting urban areas, Merseyside and Hamp-
shire, by Elizabeth Gittus (1965). The inputs to the analysis included
a series of population and household characteristics for enumeration districts in the two areas. However, data on income, education, and occupation were not available for the analysis. The results were much the same
for the two areas and in each case four major components were identified
summarizing variations in family structure, household amenities, crowding,
and ethnic structure. A similar study of Cardiff and Swansea by D. T.
Herbert (1967) also produced components associated with housing conditions,
family status and less directly, ethnic structure and economic status.
Both of these studies reflect the increasing importance of the central government in Britain in the housing market.

A comparative study of the ecological structure of Copenhagen in 1950
and 1960 using factor analysis and fourteen census characteristics has been
undertaken by Pedersen (1967). The variables which were used in the analysis fell within the categories of age distribution, employment status, and
growth and mobility. The importance of these dimensions was not the same
in the two years. For example, family status, the least important of the
three factors in 1950, had become the most important by 1960. Pedersen also
investigated the spatial structure of these dimensions by mapping the factor
scores for each subarea. In each of the two years the family status dimension was found to be concentrically distributed, socio-economic status was
distributed sectorially, and growth and mobility was more complex with a
great deal of growth and change occurring at both the periphery and the
core. Changes in the geographic distribution of the factors between 1950
and 1960 were also investigated. Not unexpectedly, it was found that during this decade urbanization and high socio-economic status had moved outward from the city center in concentric and sectorial patterns respectively.
Finally, by means of regression analysis it was shown that the three factors
could be approximated by log population density, log average income, and
change in population density between 1950 and 1960 respectively.

An analysis of the ecological structure of Canberra, Australia using
census data for 1961 arrayed by district has been completed by Jones (1965).
A component analysis of twenty-four census characteristics produced three
major dimensions which the author entitled ethnicity, demographic structure,
and age of area. Although no direct measures of socio-economic status were
included in the analysis, an examination of component scores indicated that
these would likely be closely related to the ethnic component. Scores on
the first two components were graphed to determine neighborhood groupings
but no attempt was made to map the scores and relate the mapped distributions
to models of urban structure and growth. It is interesting to note that despite Canberra's position as Australia's national capital with its relatively
small size, large amounts of government housing, and large numbers of employees engaged in white-collar occupations the dimensions remain relatively invariant in comparison with analyses of the ecological structure of larger
and more diversified cities.

Berry and Tennant (1965) have recently used factor analysis as an aid
in understanding the retail structure of the Northeastern Illinois metropolitan area. Fifty social and economic characteristics were analysed for the
147 metropolitan municipalities in Northeastern Illinois with population
exceeding 2,500 in 1960. The ultimate aim of the analysis was to obtain

a socio-economic classification of the municipalities. Because the variables were examined in aggregate form the first and most important factor to be extracted from the analysis summarized size differentials. Six other significant factors including the three traditional social area indexes were also derived from the analysis. In order of importance these dimensions were social status, family structure, new suburbs, distance-density, housing vacancies and race.

Another recent study by Carey (1966) analyzes the interrelationships between population and housing patterns in Manhattan using 1960 census data. This is one of the first studies in which a geographer makes use of multivariate statistical techniques to investigate the ecological structure of a city. Because the author chose to study only the central core of the New York metropolitan area and included variables closely related to ethnic structure, employment characteristics, and housing structure, it is not surprising that a factor analysis separated out patterns related to ecological variations within the central city rather than urban-suburban dichotomies. Factors such as Puerto Rican subpopulation, Negro middle income, Negro live-in servant, low density transient resident, and west side rooming house are descriptive of these central city variations.

Few research efforts have assessed neighborhood changes over time on all of the societal dimensions, mainly because of the lack of data. However, Murdie (1969) was able to obtain data for fifty-six comparable variables in the 1951 and 1961 census data for tracts in Toronto. He produced a data matrix of relative change quotients which compared changes in each tract for each variable with the relative changes over the whole metropolitan area. Principle components analysis of this suggested the following six dimensions:

1. Suburbanization, a component isolating the peripheral areas of rapid population growth.
2. Ethnic change, identifying the areas of Italian and Roman Catholic invasion and succession.
3. Urbanization, a bi-polar component separating suburban areas of increasing familism from inner-zone tracts with more apartments and working women.
4. Changes in residential stability, which identified districts in which relatively more people had lived in the same house for more than four years than in the city as a whole, but for which other variables "do not produce consistent interpretations". (Murdie, 1969: 137)
5. Changes in employment characteristics, mainly due to a takeover of neighborhoods by high-occupation-status Jews.
6. Eastern European ethnic changes, another invasion and succession component.

Three model patterns - filtering, expansion of non-familism areas, and invasion and succession - were identified in the outward growth of Toronto. Analyses of variance for the component scores showed very strong zonal and sectorial elements in the distribution of most of the processes, with invasion and succession being mainly sectorial, filtering zonal and urbanism both. All six variance analyses produced statistically significant interaction effects, however, indicating that considerable proportions of the patterns were not accounted for by the zonal and sectorial framework (and perhaps suggesting growth around a number of nuclei).

PROBLEMS OF MEASUREMENT IN COMPARATIVE URBAN ECOLOGY

The single most important problem for sociologists in the field of urban ecology is that of the inadequacies of available data sources. It would seem to be imperative that research be coordinated more effectively, that efforts to standardize measures be increased, and that influence be exerted both in the area of data collection and data aggregation and in the way this is made available for scientific use. Unaggregated data needs to be made available, and yet not at the price of the respondent's loss of anonymity. At this time, the measurement processes are controlled in large by agencies such as the Census Bureau and may involve methods of aggregation which have not been given much study by sociologists. Unfortunately, sociologists and other ecologists in this area have tended to take no part in the data-collection and measurement-process and have tended to accept aggregation by proximity as an administrative convenience rather than as an aid to theoretical simplifications. Social area analysis is an attempt to apply theory to such aggregations, but even it must be accepted with caution, because it is, as Duncan and Hawley have pointed out, an ex post facto attempt.

Aggregation implies that linear models are being constructed. It also implies that there is homoscedasticity between variables within the aereal units. Thus, it seems important that the geographic aereal units chosen for study be homogeneous and this will be dependent on both the variables chosen and the size of the units. (A slightly more detailed discussion of this problem as it applies to factor analysis is discussed later in the paper.) Briefly, ecological units are modifiable in size, shape, etc., and thus can be chosen so that the aereal units are homogeneous. This assumption of homogeneity is of much importance in the relation of ecological correlations to the behavior of individuals. Of course the larger the area, the less inferences can be made concerning behavior within the community.

It would appear, then, that for comparative urban ecology, the most appropriate model seems to be one which lends itself to the technique of factor analysis. Factor analysis appears to be the most appropriate measurement technique for the theoretical model of ecological structure. Although most of them are well known points concerning factor analysis, the characteristics of factor analysis which make it so appropriate have been indicated in the next section of this paper.

CONSIDERATIONS ON THE USE OF FACTOR ANALYSIS TO EXPLAIN ECOLOGICAL STRUCTURE

Factor analysis is based on a set of mathematical principles which imply certain assumptions concerning the variables that are to be analyzed. The basic idea is that interdependence between variables can be evaluated statistically and a resulting set of factors obtained which is a combination of the original variables. Factor analysis, then, summarizes the data and in doing so causes the "focus of attention...[to be] transferred from the variables to the aspect, or dimensions, of which the variables serve as partial measures." (Carl-Gunnar Janson, 1969: 319)

Because the criteria for factoring and rotating are mathematical in nature, factor analysis is purely an inductive and empirical method. This not only assures that underlying factors which can be interpreted as ecological dimensions can be obtained, but it also assures that once the variables have been chosen, the extraction of these factors is completely free of any kind of bias by the researcher. Parsimony (which is normally a desirable goal) is also achieved with factor analysis. It reduces a large number of variables to a few basic dimensions and summarizes the way that each of the variables enters each dimension (factor loadings) as well as the total ecological structure (communalities). Of course, there are times when an ecologist may be interested in the individual variables and not in reduction of data to basic dimensions. Usually, however, with such an orientation one would not be concerned with a large set of variables simultaneously and so factor analysis would not be practical.

Careful attention should be given to the theoretical questions of "What variables do I select?" and also, more specifically for ecologists, "How do I delimit the territory that I am calling metropolitan, or urban?" If variables are selected carefully both for their content and for their "universe" then it is more likely that invariance of factors will be obtained, which, as will be discussed below, is a very important goal in comparative urban ecology. This is another measurement problem for this field of study.

Another assumption concerning the variables is that they are measured at the interval level at least (since each variable is considered to be a sum). Since many weighted linear variables in ecological theory are defined and measured at the ordinal level (this is, in part, because of the stage of development of the theory at the point and, in part, for convenience), there are options that may be made: (1) use the data, and make the assumption of robustness, (2) make a transformation on the data, (3) use an alternative--a nonmetric analysis, latent structure analysis, or a Guttman scale. Usually, however, the last two options are ignored and the data is used as is (which, in the case of ecological data, is quite often percentages which, in all likelihood, behave rather isomorphically to interval data).

From a theoretical standpoint, however, it would seem to be important to consider making a transformation on the data. One of the simplest of these is called the t-transformation (Cureton, 1970); however, Ahmavaara and Markkanen (1958: 88-89) have also recommended a transformation for noninterval data. Both of these also would change the ecological variables to a normal distribution before doing the correlation. It is still an open question as to whether normalizing is either necessary or advisable for ecological studies. At the very least it seems that a test for linearity should be made on the zero order correlations before the analysis is done. If the data is not linear, then one should remember that the model is linear and very seriously consider some transformation, either the ones recommended above or another transformation which would yield a linear model. It is suggested by Janson (1969: 332) that multinormal variables, while certainly not required by the model, may be the best kind to have since multinormal variables produce factors which are multinormal and, hence, independent. This would make interpretation simpler. However, if multinormal variables (which Janson points out are difficult to obtain) are not available, then unidimensionally normal variables would seem to be the best substitute for multinormal variables. Use of the t-transformation will also insure not only linearity, and normality of the individual variables, but will also produce bivariate normal regressions between each pair of variables and multivariate normal regressions between the set of variables. Again, there is no assumption of linear regression but if orthagonal rotation is used, it would seem a necessary assumption then.

As Fruchter (1954: 45) has pointed out, "one function of factor analysis is to analyze the common variance to determine the number and types of common variances which result in the correlations between variables."

Actually, the total variance is made up of three parts: the common variance, the specific variance, and the error variance. (The last two are also known as the unique variance of a variable.)

There are at least two problems in dealing with the components of the unique variance. The first of these is in trying to determine what part the specific variance is of the total variance, and later, how it might potentially be related to the other variables in the factor. By using unity for the communality estimate, it seems that an estimate of the reliability and therefore of the specific variance can be obtained. Principle components analysis, which uses unities in the pinciple diagonal, will yield eigenvalues which represent the amount of total variance accounted for by the factor and consequently, the importance of a component may be evaluated by examining what proportion of the total variance it accounts for. Knowing this might, of course, be of help both in realizing how much of the variance is error and also in attempting to "shift" specific variance into the common variance arena. Ideally, this would be a goal in any scientific investigation since it would improve the prediction value of the analysis.

Another problem that relates to the error variance has to do with "modifiable units." Obviously, the ecological units are modifiable in size and shape. The choice of units may influence the outcome of the analysis. The random error that is inherent has much to do with this problem. As the units become larger, the random component tends to have less weight and therefore is less of an influence on the outcome. Of course, the extreme values also tend to be averaged out as the units become larger. However, caution must be taken here. Once the units get too large, there is less tendency toward homogeneity and therefore the correlation will begin dropping because of this. It is necessary therefore to look for the balance between homogeneous units and unit size which will achieve the optimum correlations.

One of the most important theoretical considerations for factor analysis is whether orthogonal or oblique rotations are made. Many of the criticisms of factor analysis have been aimed at this--that orthogonal rather than oblique rotations have been made. It seems rather like the exception instead of the rule that factors would, in theory, be uncorrelated. However, in actual practice, it is likely that the type of rotation does not make much, if any, difference in the solution.

One of the major attractions of factor analysis rather than individual indicants in the analysis of urban structure is the assumption of invariance of factors. Factors should generally remain invariant under a whole barrage of variations in variables, techniques, etc., and these should be recognized.

First of all, factor analysis should be invariant regardless of the number and selection of theoretical variables. As mentioned earlier, as long as the variables are drawn from the universe of content, the factors are theoretically invariant under substitution of measures. In general, this has been demonstrated in factor analytic studies based on the theory of social area analysis. With a wide variety of cities and variables, three of four factors have consistently turned up. More specifically, invariance has been demonstrated for different sets of data (i.e., for different operational definitions of the variables) for the same community at the same point of time. The analyses by Schmid and Tagashira (1964) and Sweetser (1965) have given strong support for this assumption. As Sweetser (1965: 379) says "We are encouraged, therefore, in generalizing that ecological factors are invariant under substitution, addition, and subtraction of variables." Also, the theoretical definition and size and type of aereal units used do not seem to alter the assumption of invariance. Finally, the invariance also seems to stand up even with different methods of computation, and/or rotation.

The use of factor scores has not often been used to date in factor analysis but it seems that as the field progresses, this will be a necessary next step in order to discover distinctive patternings and to more fully utilize the factor model of ecological structure in the development of an ecological typology of urban communities.

Interpretation of results is a final, but perhaps the most important, consideration that must be made. Because it is normally used outside the context of rigorous testing and because most of the research thus far has lacked a hypothetical model, the results cannot be interpreted causally. Use of such exploratory information can, however, be used to formulate a tentative descriptive model.

Using the factor loadings as weights, the factors can be named according to those variables which correlated highest with them. This implies a kind of causal structure within a block of variables without implying the specific causal model. From here, a rough theoretical model might be hypothesized and an experiment designed. For example, in social area analysis, the three factors that consistently appear could be used in an experiment in controlled combinations, the experiment tested by factor analysis, and a measure obtained of the influence of each on the ecological structures of cities. From here, a more refined model could be developed, and so on, iteratively, until a linear causal model is substantiated.

It seems that any paper which makes recommendations for a field of study is incomplete without pointing out other variables or other types of studies in the area that should be made to improve knowledge about the field. It does seem important for social area analysts to begin thinking about incorporating a much wider variety of socio-cultural, temporal, and physical variables into their analyses of ecological structures in order to determine other ecological dimensions which exist and thus to add more clarification to the concept of residential area differentiation.

In sum, then, urban ecology is definitely in a developmental stage in most areas. Methodologically, factor analysis seems to be close to ideal both in the development of a theoretical model and in the analysis of a linear causal model if and when it is developed.

BIBLIOGRAPHY

Abu-Lughod, Janet
  1965 "The emergence of differential fertility in urban Egypt." Milbank Memorial Fund Quarterly 43:235-253.
  1969 "Testing the theory of social area analysis: The ecology of Cairo, Egypt." American Sociological Review 34:198-212.

Ahmavaara, Y. and T. Markkanen
  1958 The Unified Factor Model. Helsinki: The Finnish Foundation for Alcohol Studies.

Anderson, Theodore R. and Lee L. Bean
  1961 "The Shevky-Bell social areas: Confirmation of results and a reinterpretation." Social Forces 40 (December): 19-24.

Anderson, Theodore R. and Janice Egeland
  1961 "Spatial Aspects of social area analysis." American Sociological Review 26:392-9.

Berry, Brian J. L.
   1964 "Cities as systems within systems of cities," in John Friedmann
        and William Alonso (eds.) Regional Development and Planning.
        Cambridge: M.I.T. Press.
   1965 "Internal Structure of the city." Law and Contemporary Problems
        30: 111-19.

Berry, Brian and Philip Rees
   1968 The Factorial Ecology of Calcutta. Chicago: Department of
        Geography, University of Chicago.

Berry, Brian J. L. and Robert J. Tennant
      1965 Metropolitan Planning Guidelines: Commercial Structure. Chicago:
        Northeastern Illinois Planning Commission.

Burgess, Ernest W.
   1925 "The growth of the city," in R. E. Park, E. W. Burgess, and R. D.
        McKenzie (eds.) The City. Chicago: University of Chicago Press: 47-62.

Carey, George W.
   1966 "The regional interpretation of the Manhattan population and housing
        patterns through factor analysis." The Geographic Review 56:551-69.

Cureton, Edward E.
   1970 Transformations. Assorted mimeographed pages on normal standardizing
        techniques: 206-215.

Dickinson, Robert E.
   1964 City and Region. London: Routledge and Kegan Paul.

Fruchter, Benjamin
   1954 Introduction to Factor Analysis. Princeton: Van Nostrand.

Gittus, Elizabeth
   1964 "The structure of Urban areas." Town Planning Review 35:5-20.

Harris, Chauncey D. and Edward L. Ullman
   1945 "The nature of cities." The Annals of the American Academy of
        Political and Social Sciences 242:7-17.

Herbert, D. T.
   1967 "Social area analysis: A British study." Urban Studies 4:41-60.

Hoyt, Homer
   1939 The Structure and Growth of Residential Neighborhoods in American
        Cities. Washington: Federal Housing Administration.
   1964 "Recent distortions of the classical models of urban structure."
        Land Economics 40:199-212.

Hurd, Richard M.
   1903 Principles of City Land Values. New York: Real Estate Record
        Association.

Janson, Carl-Gunnar
  1969 "Some problems of ecological factor analysis," in Mattei Dogan
        and Stein Rokkan, Quantitative Ecological Analysis in the Social
        Sciences. Cambridge, Mass.: M.I.T. Press.

Jones, F. Lancaster
  1965 "A social profile of Canberra, 1961" The Australian and New
        Zealand Journal of Sociology 1:107-20.

Kaufman, W. C. and Scott Greer
  1960 "Voting in a metropolitan community: An application of social area
        analysis." Social Forces 38:196-204.

McElrath, Dennis C.
  1968 "Social differentiation and societal scale." Pp. 39-51 in Scott
        Greer et al (eds.) The New Urbanization. New York: St. Martin's Press.

McKenzie, R. D.
  1933 The Metropolitan Community. New York: McGraw-Hill.

Murdie, Robert
  1969 Factorial Ecology of Metropolitan Toronto. Chicago: Department of
        Chicago Research Paper No. 116.

Oi, Walter Y. and Paul W. Shuldiner
  1962 An Analysis of Urban Travel Demands. Evanston: Northwestern
        University Press: 116-20.

Pedersen, P. O.
  1967 "An empirical model of urban population structure: A factor analytic
        study of the population structure in Copenhagen." Proceedings of the
        First Scandanavian-Polish Regional Science Seminar. Warzawa: Polish
        Scientific Publishers.

Polk, Kenneth
  1958 "Juvenile delinquency and social areas." Social Problems 5:214-17.

Popenoe, David
  1969 Sociology. New York: Appleton-Century-Crofts.

Quinn, James A.
  1950 Human Ecology. New York: Prentice-Hall.

Schmid, Calvin and K. Tagashira
  1964 "Ecological and demographic indices: A methodological analysis."
        Demography 1:194-211.

Shevky, Eshref and Wendell Bell
  1955 Social area analysis: Theory, Illustrative Application and Computa-
        tional Procedures. Stanford: Stanford University Press.

Shevky, Eshref and Marilyn Williams
  1949 The Social Areas of Los Angeles: Analysis and Typology. Los Angeles
        and Berkeley: University of California Press.

Simmons, J. W.
    1965   "Descriptive models of urban land use." The Canadian Geographer
           9:170-74.

Sweetser, Frank L.
    1961   The Social Ecology of Metropolitan Boston: 1950. Boston, Mass.:
           Department of Mental Health.
    1961a The Social Ecology of Metropolitan Boston: 1960. Boston, Mass.:
           Department of Mental Health.
    1961b Patterns of Change in the Social Ecology of Metropolitan Boston,
           1950-1960. Boston, Mass.: Massachusetts Department of Mental Health.
    1965a "Factor structure as ecological structure in Helsinki and Boston."
           Acta Sociologica 8:205-25.
    1965b "Factorial ecology: Helsinki, 1960." Demography 2:372-85.

Udry, J. Richard
    1964   "Increasing scale and spatial differentiation: New tests of two
           theories from Shevky and Bell." Social Forces 42:403-413.

William C. Baer
Assistant Director
School of Urban and Regional Planning
University of Southern California
Los Angeles, California 90007

SOME POLICY QUESTIONS ABOUT
THE LOS ANGELES COMMUNITY ANALYSIS BUREAU'S
CHOICE OF HOUSING INDICATORS

ABSTRACT: A recent report for the City of Los
Angeles presented a careful analysis of housing need
as well as the probable costs in responding to those
needs under different policy options. But seemingly
slight changes in the criteria used in determining
need may have larger policy impacts than the proposed policy itself.
This paper examines the effect of altering the
criteria of need, as well as the underlying rationale
for adopting particular criteria in the first place.

INTRODUCTION

Recently, the Los Angeles Community Analysis Bureau (CAB)
published a report entitled The Los Angeles Housing Model [1] which
dealt with estimates of housing need and possible magnitudes of cost
to meet that need. The major focus was on renters. Of all renter
households in the county, 681,000 (about 54%) were shown to be in
"housing need". The approximate cost of a housing allowance to
meet this need was estimated to range between $9.1 million to
$169.6 million a year, depending upon the degree to which the renters
in need participated in the program. Thus social indicators and the
policy implications stemming from them were nicely integrated into
a single report.
The scope of the report is eminently realistic. No more is
attempted in the analysis than can be successfully accomplished.
Further, the report is useful for both operational policy analysis and

---

1 Community Analysis Bureau of the City of Los Angeles, The
  Technical Report, (July, 1974).

William C. Baer

for exploring some puzzling issues that have haunted housing analysis for years. The former I leave to City Hall; it is the latter I wish to pursue here.

The major purpose of the study is to test the costs of alternative participation rates in meeting the housing need. It demonstrates the potential impacts of these policies on one of three criteria of housing need: 1) the decrease in households paying excessive rent; 2) the decrease in overcrowded households; and 3) the decrease in occupancy of substandard units. In effect, it is a sensitivity analysis of the impact of different renter participation rates in a housing allowance program.

Such testing of policy is useful and to be commended. Overlooked in it all, however, is the opposite tack -- testing the impact on need of alternative social indicators. In other words, an equally large impact on housing need can be effected by changing the definition of that need. There may be very good reasons for more fully exploring this tack in housing policy. As I hope to demonstrate, the CAB's analysis may be unduly harsh in its estimation of need. Further, this excessive judgment may do great political damage in terms of convincing the public and politicians that something should be done. Finally, this whole aspect of social indicators and housing requires airing, even if one eventually agrees with CAB's approach. The study to be examined here provides a nice vehicle for doing all the above.

SELECTION OF THE SOCIAL INDICATORS IN THE CAB REPORT

As mentioned, the report uses three criteria to measure housing condition: excessive percent of income spent on rent; over crowding; and occupancy of substandard units. No explanation is given as to why these are the important criteria to use, but few practioners would argue that they are not. They are reported in the Census (a convenient rationale) and most other efforts at estimating housing need use them or some variant of them. [2] But the unquestioning lack of discussion and justification of the choice is disturbing. The Census Bureau is unhappy with the measures that they themselves report [3] and retreated to less meaningful but less misleading measures

---

2 David Birch, et. al., America's Housing Needs: 1970 to 1980, Joint Center for Urban Studies of the Massachusetts Institute of Technology and Harvard University (December, 1973).

3 U.S. Bureau of the Census, Measuring the Quality of Housing An Appraisal of Census Statistics and Methods, Working Paper No. 25 (Washington, D.C.: USGPO, 1967).

in 1970.[4]   Others have expressed even more dissatisfaction with current housing indicators.[5] Sources for housing indicator data other than the Census are hard to come by, hence there may be good reasons for the choices aside from theoretical perfection, but it would help if specific acknowledgement were made as to what the choice of indicators implies for subsequent policy analysis and decision.

Of more concern is the choice of demarcation on the indicator ratings as to what is a satisfactory or unsatisfactory condition. Here a normative judgment is registered about the meaning of a score. This judgment should not only be made explicit, but the ramifications should be explicit as well. The CAB report touched on this issue in passing but failed to stress its importance. By neglecting to emphasize its significance, it also failed to note its policy consequences which are considerable.

The CAB selected two sets of demarcations on the indicator scale to indicate need: "severe" and "moderate" the latter includes ("severe"). These are shown in Table 1.

Table 1

THE LOS ANGELES COMMUNITY ANALYSIS BUREAU'S
HOUSING NEED CRITERIA AND DEGREE OF NEED

Criteria	Degree of Need	
	"Moderate" (includes "Severe")	"Severe"
Persons/Room	$\geq$ 1.01	$\geq$ 1.51
Rent/Income Ratio	> 25%	> 35%
Lacking Complete Plumbing	X	X
SUMMARY EVALUATION OF NEED	Failing one or more of the criteria	Failing one or more of the criteria

4 George Sternlieb, "The Sociology of Statistics: Measuring Substandard Housing," Public Data Use 1 (July, 1973), pp. 1-6.
5 Peter Marcuse, "Social Indicators and Housing Policy," Urban Affairs Quarterly 7 (December, 1971) pp. 193-217.

William C. Baer

The choice of the cut-off point is critical for establishing the magnitude of need. For instance, according to the CAB study, if "moderate" needs is the criteria, 54% of renter households were in need. If "severe" is the criteria, only 9% were so situated. Establishing cut-off points that yield differences of this magnitude is not particularly helpful for policy analysis. A renter housing need of 54% of renter households is so enormous that its solution can be dismissed as being hopelessly beyond the realm of practical policy. Conversely, a need of only 9% can be responded to by a delaying action under the rationale that more serious problems in other areas demand immediate attention.

The question then arises as to why these particular cut-off points were chosen. There is not a clear answer. The CAB did not refer to the problem; they apparently just assumed the demarcations were reasonable. Indeed these are commonly accepted demarcations but no one has ever made clear why this should be so.

What should be obvious to persons familiar with social indicators is that the criteria used are all input measures, hence the meaningfulness of their choice is open to question.[6] It is not clear what improvement in any or several of them will accomplish in terms of people's housing well-being, for they assume cause-effect relationships which have subsequently been shown to be dubious at best. For instance, for a long time housing reformers have stressed that better housing will reduce illness, juvenile delinquency and crime, and will improve worker productivity and children's school performance. Rigorous analysis to date has questioned or disproved all of these assumptions.[7]

There are other issues associated with housing indicators, more amenable to resolution yet which have received even less attention. What policy purpose do we have in mind in selecting these measures? Are we attempting to measure a housing problem by the use of social indicators or to create one? Are the measures chosen indicators of housing quality or are they indicators of housing reformers' policy expectations? To examine this aspect requires a brief discussion of evolving measures of housing conditions.[8]

6 Ibid.

7 See Daniel Wilner, et. al., Housing Environment and Family Life (Baltimore: Johns Hopkins Press, 1962); and Leland Burns, Housing: Symbol and Shelter, International Housing Productivity Study, Graduate School of Business Administration, University of California Los Angeles (February, 1970).

8 For a more extensive discussion of this topic, see William C. Baer, "The Evolution of Housing Indicators and Housing Standards: Some Lessons for the Future," Public Policy, 24 (Summer, 1976) forthcoming.

William C. Baer

THE EVOLUTION OF HOUSING INDICATORS AND HOUSING STANDARDS

The measures of housing quality, used at the turn of the century reflected the provincial concern of only local governments that faced severe housing problems at the time, e.g., New York, Boston, Chicago, etc.

By the 1940's housing indicators had become largely standardized across the nation, as well as modified to reflect changing interests. For instance, susceptibility to fire was no longer considered, nor was ventilation and the adequacy of light. Apparently, these dangers to the populace were no longer perceived as major housing problems. Instead these problems were attacked through local fire protection services, through building codes, and through health indicators. Instead of counting the number of backyard privies ("school sinks") focus had shifted to whether a toilet was outside or inside the housing unit (not the housing structure or complex) and whether there was hot and cold running water.

From the turn of the century through the early 1920's, crowding was frequently expressed in terms of both persons per room and families per housing unit, the latter expressing a quite different facet of overcrowding. But overcrowding had so declined by 1940, that the latter measure was dropped completely. In the 1920's standards for designating overcrowding were set at either more than 1.5 or more than 2.0 persons per room. By the middle 1930's, accepted standards had dropped to 1.51 or more persons per room, and by 1960, the commonly accepted standard for overcrowding was 1.01 or more. In other words, the minimum standard for adequate housing conditions had been doubled in stringency from 1920 to 1960. The reason for change in these standards is probably accounted for by the drop in percentage of households living in overcrowded units. In 1940 some 9% of the U.S. households were living under these overcrowded conditons; by 1970 only 2% were so situated.

Criteria for determining the physical quality level and structural condition of housing have changed during the last 30 years. To the extent that a measure can be derived which is uniform during this period, it shows that the proportion of physically substandard units in the United States has dropped dramatically -- from 48.6% in 1940 to 7.4% by 1970. [9]

From these indices we can observe two trends: First, the "housing problem", as defined by traditional measures, had decreased substantially during the Twentieth Century. Second, the standards

---

[9] Executive Office of the President, Office of Management and Budget, Social Indicators 1973, (Washington, D.C.: USGPO, 1973).

applied to determine the adequacy of housing conditions have changed just as dramatically in becoming ever-more stringent. Thus, amelioration of the "housing problem" (as defined by the standards) has not occurred as rapidly as improvement in housing conditions, because the standards of adequacy have been shifted over time as well.

There has been a further change reinforcing the above points as well as adding another. With the decline of the housing problem as measured by physical quality and persons per room, a third criterion of housing condition began being stressed -- the percent of income that households were paying for housing. This indicator was first presented, by the Census in 1950 when 15% of the households were paying more than 30% of their income on rent. In 1960, the Census changed the categories so precise comparison is difficult, but the data shows that 19% were paying more than 35% of their income on rent. By 1970 some 22% of all renters were paying this ratio. Using slightly different criteria and in a somewhat different context, Birch et al. [10] showed that while the absolute number of households suffering from housing deprivation declined by about 2,000,000 from 1960 to 1970, the percent who suffered from a high rent burden increased from 24% in 1960, to 42% by 1970.

By the criterion of percentage of income devoted to rent, this facet of housing condition in the United States is getting worse. A cynic might suggest that it was a timely criterion to introduce, for otherwise the "housing problem" had largely disappeared, and what then would the housing reformers do? A more interesting conclusion, however, is that the new criterion of rent income ratio allows us to see that, for many, the housing problem has not disappeared; it has merely changed its form. Indeed, the very success of our housing policy and national prosperity in reducing overcrowding and substandard housing may have caused the increase in rent income ratio. Better housing stock and improved use of that stock may have driven up the rental rates to pay for it. The upshot is that marked success on some indicators may be offset by worsening on others.

THE IMPACT CAB'S ESTIMATES OF HOUSING NEEDS FROM REVISED STANDARDS

Thus CAB's selection of housing standards to determine housing need is in the mainstream of current practice, but that practice has never been well-defined or sharply articulated. It appears that selection of housing standards has been based on an unspoken or undeclared commitment by housing reformers to make these standards more stringent over the years (apparently to reflect national prosper-

---

10 Op. cit.

ity) and to introduce new measures of housing conditions when the old ones appeared less helpful in describing the current housing situation. The crux is the last part of that statement. If traditional measures of housing conditions were perceived as being increasingly less relevant, then the measures used not only measure housing condition, but also measure housing reformers' expectations about responses. The changing standards reveal an implicit expectation that we must do more and more as things get better and better. This might be an appropriate political strategy to attract more resources into the field of housing, but it is a poor way to report objectively on changing housing conditions. Furthermore, it tends to thwart evaluations of past policy impacts by making these impacts appear less than they are.

All of this is not to say that the CAB changed its standards or otherwise presented misleading estimates of need. The point is that failure to explain why the particular standards were chosen obscures some important issues with major implications for policy evaluation. These implications should be made clear.

To see the result of choosing somewhat different standards, we can examine two other recent efforts at determining housing needs for the Los Angeles area. HUD has published a special set of tabulations which show the number of households living in inadequate conditions.[11] The criteria used to determine "inadequate" are for the most part similar to those used by CAB, but in measuring overcrowding, HUD split the difference between the more traditional measures and used a standard of more than 1.25 persons per room. A rough estimate based on CAB data suggests that such a change would reduce the number of households deemed as "overcrowded" (by the 1.01 or more standard) by about 30%, but that overall the reduction in the number of households in need would only be reduced about 6%.

A more thorough examination of the issue was presented by Birch et al., in their estimate of housing deprivation for each SMSA in the U.S., including Los Angeles. Rather than adopt a uniform standard for a particular criterion, they adopted different standards for the same criterion based upon household characteristics and circumstance. Such an approach begins to address itself to the inherent variations in household housing need that one must expect with different household types, and poses an alternative to the traditional Procrustean standards.

For instance, Birch, et al., adopted different standards pertaining to overcrowding based upon household size: "... a household is over-crowded if it consists of at least three persons and has 1.5 persons or

---

11 U.S. Department of Housing and Urban Development, "Memorandum to all Area Offices," Transmittal of Special Tabulations of Owner and Renter Occupied Units by Living Conditions, 1970 (April 9, 1973).

more per room." [12] This is admittedly a conservative standard for the
1970's, but the authors present interesting evidence as to how crude,
across-the-board standards fail to acknowledge the subtleties of
households' own perceptions of what is overcrowding. Use of this
standard would drop the percent of renter households below even CAB's
"severe" category -- to less than 4%.

Similarly, Birch, et al., take issue with the simple criterion that
any rent income ratio over .25 is excessive. They suggest a more
subtle formulation:

> In establishing our definition of a high rent burden we
> have concentrated on lower-income households, on the as-
> sumption that a high-income family spending a large per-
> centage of its income for rent has, by choice, passed up
> opportunities for adequate housing at lower cost. On the
> other hand, a low-income family may have no way to obtain
> a "decent" home without paying 25 or 35 percent of its in-
> come. For purposes of this report, a household with a
> high rent burden is defined as one with an income under
> $10,000 which falls in one of the following three categories:
>
> 1. A two-or-more person household, with the head
>   less than age 65, paying more than 25 percent of
>   its income for rent.
> 2. A single-person household paying more than 35
>   percent of its income for rent.
> 3. A two-or-more-person household with the head
>   over age 65, paying more than 35 percent of its
>   income for rent.
>
> It has been assumed that households in the first two of
> these categories have fewer expenses beyond those for
> housing and thus can presumably afford somewhat higher
> rents. [13]

Using this modified standard of excessive rent/income ratio, they
found that only 18% of renter households in the Los Angeles SMSA paid
an excessive proportion of income on rent. This is a considerably
lower estimate than 43% for the City (using CAB's flat standard of
greater than .25 of income) or 28% (using its flat standard of greater
than .35 of income). It must be repeated that the geographic areas
of each study are not precisely the same, but the CAB stated that for
all intents and purposes the percentages were the same for the City

_____

12 Op. cit. p. 4-4.
13 Ibid., p. 4-5,6.

and for the County, and it is assumed that this holds approximately true for the SMSA as well. A figure of 18% suggests that a large number of households face serious problems in meeting their housing expenses from their incomes, but reduction in need from 43% of the renter households, or even from 28% to 18% is as large a reduction in the problem as any but the most ambitious housing policies could achieve.

So far, it has been shown that a substantial reduction in housing need can be made in two of the basic housing indicators by changing slightly the standard for determining need. Further, it has been shown that each of these changes is reasonable, and is based on as good evidence of what really constitutes an appropriate standard of need as any that have been presented as justification for CAB's standards. Finally, when taken collectively, it is clear that these changes reduce the magnitude of need by about half, with major implications for the amount of required expenditures to meet the housing problem for renters. But what of the needs of owner occupants?

ESTIMATES OF HOMEOWNER NEED

Complete estimates of housing need for homeowners have always proved more difficult to make than for renters. While the measures for physical condition and overcrowding are common to both renters and homeowners, the measures for housing expense are quite different. Renters pay rent, and perhaps utilities, but homeowners pay property taxes, maintenance costs, insurance, and usually a mortgage payment. These items are not reported by the Census for most geographic areas. Birch, et al., avoided this problem completely by focusing only upon renters. The HUD estimate of inadequate living conditions included the criterion of those owner-occupied units which were more than 30 years old and were valued at less than $10,000. This criterion would appear to overlap with that pertaining to physical condition. Accordingly, the aggregate HUD estimate must be treated with caution due to a possibility of double counting.

CAB addressed the issue more directly by attempting to equate house value with a rental equivalent, and then determining those households paying an excessive proportion of their income on housing. By their reckoning, the equivalent monthly rent of an owner-occupied housing unit is approximately .0075 of housing value. The common rule of thumb in the real estate market is between .0083 and .01. [14] I believe that the CAB has understated their estimate, or they are not comparing equivalent owner-occupied units to renter units in terms of quality. For one, they have apparently neglected an estimate for maintenance and depreciation, variously estimated at between .0017

---

14 Henry Aaron, Shelter and Subsidies (Washington, D.C.: Brookings, 1972).

and .0054 per month.[15] Furthermore, they have apparently failed to add in a factor for profit or opportunity cost were the homeowner's unit to rent on the market. These additions taken along would over-state the market rent. The value of deducting business expenses and taking accelerated depreciation should be deducted from this larger factor although the value of these deductions is in part dependent upon the owner's tax bracket. The net effect should be to raise CAB's factor, bringing it closer in line with the rule of thumb. While their factor is conservative, and raising it slightly would show more people paying excessive housing costs, owners also enjoy an unreported imputed income from the net rental value of the unit, which would serve to raise their income along with raising their homeownership costs.[16]

More serious, however, is an apparent failure to recognize dif-fering circumstances of homeowners. Calculations of house value to current income ratios conceal some important factors in homeowner-ship. First, some households own their units "free and clear" hence make no mortgage payments. This reduces their monthly housing costs substantially. National data show that approximately 39% of all owner occupants have no mortgage on their houses. The proportion is probably smaller for Los Angeles, assuming a higher propensity to move, but even so the percentage would be significant. Moreover, the lack of a mortgage is particularly true of the elderly. Nationally, some 85% of all elderly homeowners own their units free and clear. Since most of these elderly are retired, hence receive a reduced in-come, the standard income/value ratio may be   particularly ques-ionable. Birch et al., came to a similar conclusion with respect to the elderly renter as mentioned earlier. Adjustments of this sort would surely lower any estimate of the number of homeowners who pay excessive housing costs.

CONCLUSION

All of this is by way of demonstrating the CAB's estimate of "moderate" need is too high, and that an equally reasonable estimate of need would reduce the magnitude of the housing problem substan-tially. In fairness to the CAB report, which overall is excellent, it was not as oblivious of the consequence of selecting certain standards as might appear from the above. As the report stated:

1. The criteria cannot be used as sharp cut-offs, but
    rather as points within a range of possible cut-offs;

---

15 Ibid.
16 Ibid.

2. These criteria cannot be used, either singly or in combination, as final determinants of housing need; and;

3. The goal of any housing policy should not be reduction of the measured needs to a flat zero, since some households are apparently willing to incur higher housing costs for certain advantages.[17]

Despite these admirable caveats, however, the CAB report largely ignores them in employing their model, for the model is apparently based only on "moderate" need, and makes no mention of the impact were "severe" need used instead. Furthermore, while the caveats are good as far as they go, it would appear more germane for policy research to explicitly focus on the shortcomings of selecting one set of standards over another, and describing the background for the choice of the standards, rather than simply saying after the fact: "Be careful." Policy makers are better assisted if they are warned in what ways care should be exercised.

---

17 Community Analysis Bureau, op. cit., p. 16.

Peter G. Rowe
Dir., Env. Program
      and
Joel L. Gevirtz
Sen. Res. Assoc.

Southwest Center for
Urban Research
1200 Southmore
Houston, Texas, 77004

A NATURAL ENVIRONMENTAL INFORMATION
SYSTEM FOR LOCAL DECISION MAKERS

ABSTRACT: This paper describes aspects of a
natural environmental information system developed
to meet the operating conditions of decision makers
at local governmental levels (e.g. county and sub-
state regional). The relatively flexible structure
of the system allows a number of different types of
environmental management issues to be addressed.
This presentation will focus on one such issue,
namely the assessment of the natural environmental
impacts of land use acitivities. Two aspects of
this system function will be discussed. The first
concerns the approach taken to the theoretical problem of objectively representing the transactions
between land uses and their natural settings. The
second focuses on some of the considerations involved in translating this representation into an
automated user-oriented decision-assistance system
compatible with local needs and resource constraints.

INTRODUCTION

    With mounting concern over the effects on natural systems of land
use activity, it has become apparent that objective, analytical strategies are necessary to assess possible environmental impacts prior to
development. This concern has begun to manifest itself with the inclusion of natural environmental factors within the statutory requirements
for project evaluation that are becoming a part of the land management
and regulatory process.
    In order to respond to this concern it is not only essential to
have a functional understanding of the relationship between land uses
and their natural settings but to be able to present this understanding
in a manner that reflects many of the operating characteristics of the
public decision-making milieu. This is of particular importance to
local-government decision makers with jurisdictions on the fringes of
developing urban or industrial centers, who are often without the

planning resources of their more urban neighbours.

This paper describes part of an environmental information system developed to aid local government decision makers (county, sub-regional) in their environmental-management activities.[1] (see fig. 2) The presentation concentrates solely on the natural environmental impact assessment function of the system because, for the most part, the data base, storage-retrieval, and data display capabilities are similar to those already described in the literature[2] (Dangermond, 1975; Spann, 1975). Principally two aspects of this function will be discussed. The first concerns the approach taken to the theoretical problem of objectively representing the relationship between land uses and their natural settings, allowing impacts to be described, and facilitating transfer to other geographic settings. The second focuses on the translation of this representation into a user-oriented decision-assistance system compatible with local needs and resource constraints.

As a background for discussion of these two aspects, a brief description of the research and development context and the impact assessment system follows.

THE IMPACT ASSESSMENT SYSTEM

The study area for this project was Chambers County, Texas, until recently a sparsely populated predominantly rural county. The development of several large industrial plants in the western section of the county, on the outskirts of Houston, has started a trend towards increasing industrialization and urbanization. Chambers County is typical of the coastal environmental setting of east Texas and Louisiana including the extensive productive wetland and estuarine systems associated with Galveston and East Bays. The study area is a homogeneous political subdivision of the State of Texas and a member of a thirteen-county region council of governments, The Houston-Galveston Area Council (H-GAC). Essentially, the principal local governmental users and participants in this project are H-GAC and the Chambers County Commissioners Court.

1. This research was supported by the Rice Center for Community Design and Research under a grant to the Southwest Center for Urban Research from the National Science Foundation, Research Applied to National Needs, (Grant No. ERT-73-07880-A01).

2. The data base utilizes a fixed uniform geographic grid system of rectangular cells (3200 cells) referenced to the latitude-longitude co-ordinated system. Each grid cell currently contains information about 72 land use and natural environmental descriptors. Data display takes the form of numerical and gray-level maps and a CRT display capability. Spatial analysis routines include cluster Analysis and Ordination techniques.

The impact assessment system focuses most sharply on the potential natural environmental impact of waste disposal activities (residuals), impacts associated with development in encumbered areas, and impacts on the natural system due to the resource consumption. The approach does not explicitly address issues of visual amenity.

Briefly, in terms of information flow, the impact assessment system functions in the following manner. A proposed development, described in terms of its constituent land uses (single-family residential etc.) is first evaluated with respect to landscape features of the proposed site to determine the existence of possible constraints imposed by natural or man-made encumbrances. The presence of such conditions is immediately identified and becomes a part of the overall impact assessment. The land uses are then displayed in terms of the environmental inputs they introduce into the natural system: liquid effluent emmissions, solid waste and so on. This information is generated from a data base covering the typical occurrence of such inputs for some 40 land use types, including various densities of residential and commercial use. Depending upon the type of environmental input in question, a particular sequence of evaluations is made to estimate the magnitude of the impacts created within the natural system. This order is determined by the sequence of potential environmental effects associated with an input and established in the basic linkage structure of the system. For instance, the environmental input of groundwater withdrawal may lead to a reduction in the piezometric surface of the aquifer which in turn, under certain geologic conditions, can induce land surface subsidence, that in low-lying coastal areas can effect the biota by changing soil salinity. Of course, in common with other impact assessment systems, lack of a complete understanding of natural processes precludes the inclusion of every such sequence into the assessment process. However, within the study area, the present system does allow the direction and magnitude of a number of different types of impacts to be evaluated (see Rowe, 1976).

The impact assessment system itself[3] is made up of a series of subroutines (see fig. 2). Each subroutine is responsible for the calculation of an environmental input characteristic of land uses or for the evaluation of specific environmental effects. The linkage structure between the subroutines represents the calling sequence dictated by the potential sequence of environmental effects that may require evaluation for each input. However in practice this scheme has been streamlined to improve user-response time and general operating efficiencies of the system. As can be seen this portion of the information system does access a spatially-referenced data base as information is required by various impact evaluation sub-routines. So far, the impact assessment option has been kept fairly independent of other information system options dealing with data storage-retrieval, display, and spatial analysis.

----

3. The impact assessment system was developed on the IBM 370/155 (VS/TSO) facility at the I.C.S.A., Rice University using level G1 Fortran.

The user interface takes the form of an interactive time-sharing system inquiring first for a land use description of the proposed project and the location of the site within the study area. The user is then guided step-by-step through an evaluation, with the system prompting where further information is necessary. The system operates in essentially two modes: standard mode and expert mode. In expert mode much of the explanatory dialogue and fixed sequencing of the system subroutines can be suppressed.

REPRESENTING LAND USES AND THEIR NATURAL SETTINGS

Natural systems may be viewed as a set of interacting physical processes controlling flows of material and energy that in turn control the distribution of landscape features. Impacts upon this system may consist of man's removal of natural resources, or introduction of exotic materials and energy; either action results in some change occurring in the natural material-energy budget. Impact assessment thus requires, first, isolation of such changes, and, second, their evaluation in terms of the entire natural system.

The development of methodologies to determine and assess natural environmental impacts had relatively early beginnings. As early as the 1870's, the U.S. Army Corps of Engineers explicitly incorporated elements of present methodologies for assessing environmental impacts in isolated studies. Recent approaches, as described by several authors (Hopkins, 1973; Warner and Preston, 1974; Jameson, 1976), include overlay techniques, checklists, matrix approaches and network analyses. Only a few techniques purport to be complete methodologies for the preparation of natural environmental impact assessment. Rather, they represent a range of approaches for representing and evaluating various aspects of the interactions between land uses and the natural environment. Many suffer from the same inherent weaknesses: either they rely heavily on a priori judgements as to the nature of relationships between landscape features and their relative importance to the environmental framework; or they are designed to evaluate only the direct impacts resulting from a given development program, ignoring inevitable secondary and tertiary natural environmental consequences.

Discussion of the problem of representing the relationship of land uses and their natural settings for impact assessment purposes may be conducted in two parts: land use description and environmental description.

Land Use Description

Careful examination of processes involved in all phases of land development allows identification of several general categories of environmental inputs. These are: physical modifications to the land surface point and non-point discharge of liquid and solid effluent, and removal of material from its natural setting, i.e. resource consumption. Each major category can be further disaggregated into individual parameters; for example, point source liquid effluent inputs might include biochemical oxygen demand, chemical oxygen demand, nitrogen, phosphorus and

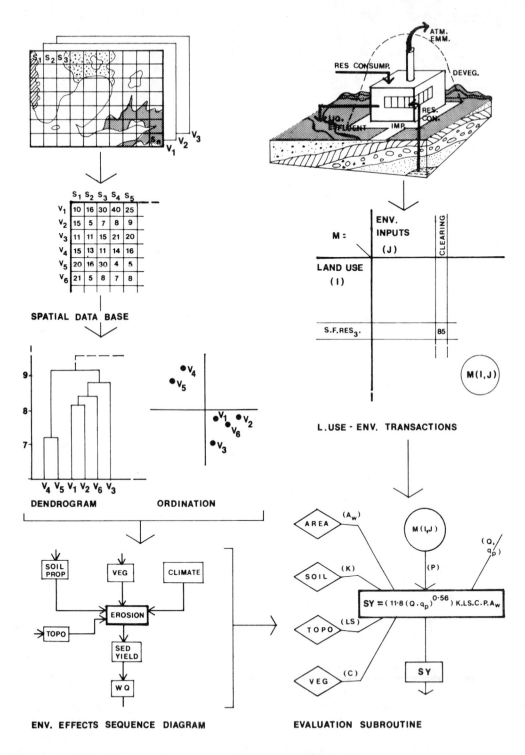

FIGURE 1: LAND-USE AND NATURAL ENVIRONMENTAL DESCRIPTION

suspended solids. Furthermore, most land-use categories must be considered as time-varying inputs, changing in relation to independent or successive stages of development activity: e.g., erosion is associated most with construction of a new facility, whereas wastewater effluent is associated most with its day-to-day operation.

For discussion purposes, environmental inputs and their temporal variation may be seen as being incorporated in successive sets of arrays showing their relationship to selected land uses (see fig. 1). The rows of each array represent land uses broadly classified according to appropriate Standard Industrial Classification system (S.I.C.) indices. This classification was adopted because it allows direct use of economic information describing changes in various industrial sectors as predicted by analytic techniques such as regional input/output models. Values shown in each array cell represent quantitative or semi-quantitative expressions of contributions made by each land use or activity to a particular environmental input parameter; for example, the expected level of B.O.D. point discharge of liquid effluent in lbs/day/unit of single family dwelling at a density of one dwelling unit per acre. Presently, all cell values are based on "typical" occurrences and do not account for any deviations due to specific design modifications. Ideally, each cell could contain a range of values to account for modifications and variation arising from differences in human habits. For instance, Linsley and Franzini (1972) found that concentrations of effluent discharge characteristics in residential developments was a function of interior water use; and interior water use for the same type of residential unit development often varies as a function of both household size and income group. If sufficient data is available, such factors can be incorporated into this concept as distribution functions rather than single values.

Important elements in any land use description are those processes that tend to mitigate environmental impact or reduce the contribution of certain inputs. For example, there are at least two ways to mitigate the amount of runoff associated with urban development. One is to create holding ponds to trap and store excess runoff, releasing it slowly into an existing stream or other receiving body of water; this timed release closely approximates the natural system, thus reducing the impact of increased runoff due to urbanization on the hydrologic regimen of the area. The other accepted method involves placement of structures and related impervious surfaces on soil types known to have the least capacity to absorb water, thereby minimizing the relative differences between the developed and undeveloped states and causing minimal change to the hydrologic regimen. These approaches are quite different; the first emphasizes a physical solution for controlling runoff, whereas the second depends on common sense in designing the facility in relationship to the natural system. The effects of strategies for mitigating environmental inputs may be expressed in the form of coefficients or modifying functions applicable to the initial land-use inputs displayed in the arrays.

Environmental Description

The natural system was defined above in terms of an underlaying material-energy budget; a totally objective environmental description, then, would ideally consist of a set of partial differential equations

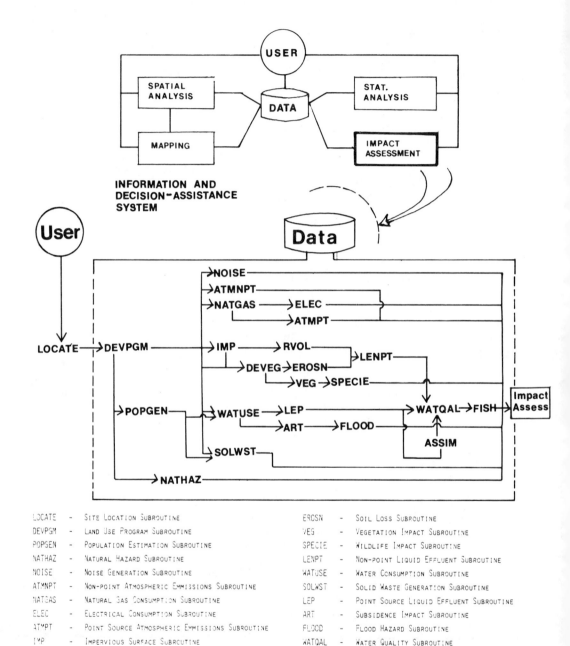

INFORMATION AND
DECISION-ASSISTANCE
SYSTEM

LOCATE	-	SITE LOCATION SUBROUTINE
DEVPGM	-	LAND USE PROGRAM SUBROUTINE
POPGEN	-	POPULATION ESTIMATION SUBROUTINE
NATHAZ	-	NATURAL HAZARD SUBROUTINE
NOISE	-	NOISE GENERATION SUBROUTINE
ATMNPT	-	NON-POINT ATMOSPHERIC EMMISSIONS SUBROUTINE
NATGAS	-	NATURAL GAS CONSUMPTION SUBROUTINE
ELEC	-	ELECTRICAL CONSUMPTION SUBROUTINE
ATMPT	-	POINT SOURCE ATMOSPHERIC EMMISSIONS SUBROUTINE
IMP	-	IMPERVIOUS SURFACE SUBROUTINE
RVOL	-	SURFACE RUN-OFF VOLUME SUBROUTINE
DEVEG	-	DEVEGETATION SUBROUTINE

EROSN	-	SOIL LOSS SUBROUTINE
VEG	-	VEGETATION IMPACT SUBROUTINE
SPECIE	-	WILDLIFE IMPACT SUBROUTINE
LENPT	-	NON-POINT LIQUID EFFLUENT SUBROUTINE
WATUSE	-	WATER CONSUMPTION SUBROUTINE
SOLWST	-	SOLID WASTE GENERATION SUBROUTINE
LEP	-	POINT SOURCE LIQUID EFFLUENT SUBROUTINE
ART	-	SUBSIDENCE IMPACT SUBROUTINE
FLOOD	-	FLOOD HAZARD SUBROUTINE
WATQAL	-	WATER QUALITY SUBROUTINE
ASSIM	-	STREAM ASSIMILATIVE CAPACITY SUBROUTINE
FISH	-	STREAM ORGANISM IMPACT SUBROUTINE

FIGURE 2: A NATURAL ENVIRONMENTAL IMPACT ASSESSMENT SYSTEM

representing thermodynamic relationships governing physical phenomena. This ideal mathematical model could ultimately be manipulated to predict any changes to the system resulting from proposed development activity. However, the present state of knowledge is not sufficiently advanced to permit all basic physical phenomena to be reduced to such well-defined mathematical statements, so a more practicable methodology for environmental description must be found.

A utilitarian approach that satisfies the requirement for objectivity is one that quantitatively analyzes spatial distributions of easily observable landscape features in order to elucidate the underlying physical framework. Because associations of landscape features are not random but are determined by the strength of regulating physical processes, distributional information may be used to isolate related groups of landscape features on the basis of similar occurrence. Environmental description can then be treated as a problem in multivariate polythetic classification.

A wide variety of objective techniques exist for the purposes of classifying multivariate data (Bray and Curtis, 1957; Sokal and Sneath, 1963; Ball and Hall, 1966; Anderberg, 1969; Sneath and Sokal, 1973). Selection of techniques appropriate for a given problem is based on the data at hand; mathematical assumptions from which the techniques are derived, as well as those defining their limiting conditions; and the purpose of the result.

With such considerations in mind, the environmental description of this approach is derived by means of an unweighted pair-group centroid method of cluster analysis (Sokal and Sneath, 1963; Sneath and Sokal, 1973; Anderberg, 1969) using Sorensen's index of pairwise similarity (Gevirtz, Park and Friedman, 1971; Park, 1974) and an ordination technique first described by Bray and Curtis (1957) and modified by Feldhausen (1970). Classification results are displayed in a dendrogram (Sokal and Sneath, 1963), a polynodal graph representing the structure of a symmetric matrix containing all pairwise similarities, or in a multidimensional scatter diagram displaying these relationships spatially (see fig. 1). The dendrogram allows groups occuring at 11 similarity levels to be evaluated; higher similarity levels exhibit groups composed of small numbers of items, while at lower similarity levels, groups include larger numbers of items. This arrangement is said to be hierarchical and nested (Sokal and Sneath, 1963). The scatter diagrams display the index relationships in a space defined by successive pairs of endpoint indices. Remaining indices are located in this space according to their relationship to all other indices. When displayed in this manner indices appear as chainlike fragments that may be used in conjunction with the dendrogram to aid in construction of a network (environmental effects sequence diagram) showing pathways of impact transmission through the system (see fig. 1).

Environmental description begins by developing an inventory of quantitative distributions of such easily observable indices as soils, vegetation, geologic features, animal distributions, and climatic variation.

These data ideally are gathered at carefully selected sampling stations in the field, to suit the purposes of the investigation; but in many cases, funding and/or contractual limitations force reliance on secondary data pre-gathered by various state, federal, and local agencies responsible for monitoring certain environmental variables. Such information, while readily available, is generally presented for public consumption in a wide variety of processed and interpreted forms, designed to serve numerous and often quite disparate needs. It is important for investigators to realize the limitations of secondary data. Unless adequate precautions are taken to ensure objectivity, environmental description based on such data thus may be lacking in resolution or biased by the original purposes the data were designed to serve.

To obtain meaningful results from these analytical procedures requires that index variation and relationships be initially examined to determine whether the indices are truly representative of the natural system under study. To some extent, each relationship reflects both natural and artificial influences. For example, soil scientists often base soil type boundaries on available vegetation data, and conversely, plant ecologists commonly depend on existing soil type information to delineate plant assemblages. In such cases, each discipline defines its boundaries on the basis of previously defined boundaries of the other; the complete similarity of occurrence of the two index sets thus results largely from overlapping methodology and cannot be said to accurately reflect any actual relationship. Unless such indices are mapped independently, they both must be considered as representative of a single soil-vegetational complex and, to avoid bias introduced by redundancy, their occurrence must be utilized as a single index set. On the other hand, if a given relationship does mirror an important natural process, all related indices should be reatined.

A more subtle form of interdependence any be introduced by measurement of a group of related indices, e.g., geologic formations, on maps indicating their occurrence in terms of percent presence. Because these percentages are based on a closed number system (0-100%), such indices may appear to be related on a purely numerical basis, irrespective of any actual relationship. Effects of this kind of artificially-induced dependency on multivariate procedures are much debated (Chayes, 1960); to date, no satisfactory solution to the problem seems to exist.

Invariance in data can similarly distort results by biasing index groupings. Sokal and Sneath (1963) and Sneath and Sokal (1973) have noted that inclusion of indices that are invariant throughout the study area tends to obscure subtle differences among their relationships. Invariance may be introduced artificailly, by use of data-smoothing techniques, or may reflect lack of natural variation among indices; in either case, indices displaying invariant properties should be considered inadmissable for analysis.

Once satisfactory data have been assembled, they can be analyzed to determine inherent relationships among indices by producing a hierarchical classification based on their distributions. The resultant dendrogram and scatter diagrams (fig. 1) indicated related groups of indices that are interpreted as having similar responses to existing physical gradients in the environment. Because of limitations inherent in the original data, the dendrogram and scatter diagrams used in this study were not directly integrated with land use inputs to predict development inpacts with any accuracy. However, they can be used in conjunction with additional environmental information withheld from classification to construct a causal chain of possible effects, termed here the "environmental effects sequence diagram."

The environmental effects sequence diagram and its associated computational procedures represent an attempt to develop a technique whereby the magnitudes of direct and indirect environmental effects of land use activities could be estimated and became the basic framework for the development of the impact evaluation subroutines of this system. It is a directed graph portraying natural material or energy flows as derived above. Each node in the diagram represents an index or group of indices that is altered by certain environmental inputs resulting from a given land-use activity. Links in the diagram indicate relationships between indices that demonstrate the direction of transmission of the impact through the system.

For each link in the diagram, relationships can be quantified using known engineering principles; e.g., the universal soil loss equation, runoff equations, stream assimilative capacity equations, etc. In some instances, equations may be derived entirely from information specific to the area in question. Equation constants, however, must always reflect local conditions.

It is important to realize that this approach to environmental description is of use for all areas, as long as the data from which the description is derived is both valid and extensive enough to adequately describe that locale.

THE USER AND THE INFORMATION SYSTEM

Several authors (Schultz, 1963; Meadows, 1970) have been quick to point out that the translation of an information processing technique into a user-compatible system often requires more of an orientation of technique to user than user to technique. In conducting several pilot case studies with local user-groups[4], several related issues became apparent.

First, there was a perceived need for the assessment system to be intelligible to the public decision-maker. It was felt that if the relationship between the various steps of the procedure were understandable to the decision-maker that many of the suspicions often associated with "black-box" approaches would be mitigated and the technique would gain a higher level of acceptance and application. Second, there was a perceived need for the assessment procedure to be easy to use in field operations and require a minimum of technical expertise. It was found that most local governments, particularly in more rural areas, could not afford large technical planning staffs or high operation and maintenance

---

4. Case studies include: an impact assessment of regional sewage treatment facilities under OMB A-95 Review for H-GAC; an impact assessment for the proposed extensions to the Texas Works for the U. S. Steel Corp.; and an impact assessment of a 500 d.u. planned unit development for Chambers County.

costs for decision-assistance technology. Third, there was a perceived need for the approach to be flexible enough to readily address different types of assessments ranging from consideration of a small number of impacts to more comprehensive analyses. Fourth, most applications of the approach would occur in the context of a preliminary examination of potential environmental impacts, prior to detailed study required by current permitting processes. Here a technique that would give good first approximation of the environmental effects of land use activities seemed appropriate.

Because final testing and implementation of the information system has not been completed it is difficult to be definitive about responses to these issues. However, several general comments can be made.

The need for the methodology of the assessment system to be intelligible to the decision maker argues for a fairly high level of structure within the conversational-mode interface. In fact by leading a user step-by-step through the evaluation procedure, rather than "black-boxing" the operation, the system can acquire a certain didactic capability. By operationally understanding the interrelationships between environmental factors and land use inputs the user gains a deeper appreciation of environmental management problems. Another argument for a fairly high level of structure, particularly in a technique that allows a certain amount of individual judgemental interpretation, is the tendency to minimize analyst bias. As several authors (Warner & Preston, 1974) have pointed out, absence of sufficient guiding structure in impact assessment methodologies tends to increase the occurrence of analyst bias. On the other hand some of the pragmatic considerations that seem necessary in order to adapt the system as improved evaluation techniques become available, suggest the need for considerable flexibility and perhaps a lower level of structure. The trade-off involved here led to the development of a modular approach to system design, in which the basic framework of environmental interactions is preserved, but within which actual assessment procedures could be tailored to the conditions of a particular locale or simply replaced.

The issue of low technological costs and ease of use with a minimum of technical expertise raises questions about the system's resource requirements. Many of the numerical techniques incorporated within the system for evaluating specific aspects of environmental impact, such as runoff and soil loss, are based upon procedures already widely used by various resource agencies. As a consequence the data generally required for the system is readily available at relatively low costs. In developing the system, resource constraints notwithstanding, an effort was made to try to avoid the necessity of developing complex and highly place-specific models for assessing particular environmental effects. While in some instances this obviously meant sacrifices in the reliability and validity of results, the principal intention, to indicate the natural environmental problem areas of proposed projects, seemed well served. In the limited case study testing, thus far undertaken, the results seem satisfactory.

Again, with only limited testing it has been found that operation and maintenance of the system requires a certain level of technical skill, well within the range of local staff planners and engineers. However, adaption of parts of the basic methodology to another geographic locale would seem to require relatively high levels of technical expertise. Applying and interpreting results of cluster analysis and ordination in developing the fundamental structure of the impact evaluation sequence requires special personnel. However, data base updates, including encoding, can be accomplished by moderately skilled personnel.

An original version of the impact assessment approach took the form of a "desk-top" procedure that could be applied with the aid of a hand calculator. For several, perhaps obvious reasons, the approach became further developed in the form of an interactive time-sharing system. First, many of the impact evaluation procedures often require large amounts of data from the natural environmental data base. Retrieval and manipulation of this information by hand becomes cumbersome, time consuming, and subject to error. Second, with available information, actual time taken to manually complete an impact assessment for a medium sized mixed-use development (e.g. 500 du. planned unit development) is in the order of 4-5 hrs. For regional-level use by agencies such as the local council of government (H-GAC) for the A-95 review purposes, this "turn-around-time" was found to be excessive.

Within the range of land uses selected, the basic methodology has been designed to be applicable to a wide range of project scales. Limitations of the system in Chambers County appear to relate more to the level of spatial resolution of the available natural environmental data than they do to the structure of the impact assessment system itself.

As indicated in the introductory comments, this aspect of the information system confines itself solely to the identification and measurement of natural environmental impacts. It does not purport to be a comprehensive impact assessment procedure taking into account socio-economic as well as natural environmental factors. In response to perceived user needs, other aspects of the information system are being broadened to encompass related socio-economic factors. The spatially referenced data base is being expanded and modified to include demographic characteristics, various economic development indicators and the results of a physical facilities' survey.

CONCLUSIONS AND FURTHER WORK

The impact assessment system allows direct and indirect natural environmental effects of a range of selected land uses to be identified and evaluated. Its basic structure permits a decision-maker to clearly understand the nature of all the land use natural environment interactions involved in a development project. In the context of a given sub-region, it provides the means by which a first approximation to the magnitude of a development's environmental effects can be determined. The approach seems generally applicable for field operations and will allow inclusion of alternative techniques for estimating the magnitude of specific types of environmental impact.

However, several issues are involved in the further development of the present system.

1. There is a need for more information describing the environmental inputs of land uses. Where appropriate, this data needs to reflect variations in the magnitude of certain types of environmental input as a consequence of modifications in specific site design. Some characteristics, such as: consumption of water and point source liquid effluent discharges were found to be very much a function of socio-economic characteristics. This aspect needs to be able to be reflected in the present framework.

2. The effects of project phasing on the types and relative magnitudes of environmental inputs requires further investigation. This concept seems to be the most promising method for developing a dynamic representation of the behaviour of the natural system with inputs from land-use construction and operation/maintenance activities.

3. For many of the interrelationships expressed in the impact evaluation sequence of the system there exist fairly standard techniques for estimating environmental effects. However, in several aspects, information for the study area was lacking. These were: estimation of the effect of subsidence on shoreline erosion, precise estimates of the effects of changes in soil properties on vegetation, and estimation of the effects of certain water qualty characteristics on freshwater and marine organisms. These aspects should become the subject of future scientific research.

4. Detailed calibration and/or validation of the current approach was beyond the scope of available monitoring data. Development of a monitoring program expressly designed to measure many of the types of land use-- natural environmental interactions suggested by the impact evaluation sequence would allow the approach to be calibrated.

5. Transferability of the overall assessment approach to other locales, is still open to question. Further development of the research does however include a detailed investigation of all the technical aspects of transfer feasibility.

6. The final development of the impact assessment approach in the form of an interactive time-sharing system would seem to enhance its useability and intelligibility to the local user. Without the benefit of having fully pursued the implementation of the system, it is still difficult to assess the degree to which it can become integrated into the environmental management process.

REFERENCES CITED

1. Anderberg, M.R., 1969, Cluster Analysis for Applications, Academic Press, New York.
2. Ball, G.H. and Hall, D.J., 1966, A Comparison of Some Cluster-Seeking Techniques, Stanford Res. Instit., Menlo Park.
3. Bray, R.R. and Curtis, J.T., 1957, An ordination of the upland forest communities of Southern Wisconsin, Ecol. Mono., V. 27, p.325.
4. Chayes, Felix, 1960, On correlation of variables of constant sum, Journal of Geophysical Research, V. 65, p.4185.
5. Dangermond, J., 1975, A summary description of the Maryland automated geographic information system, in Anochie, O.M. (editor), Computers, Local Government and Productivity, V. 1, (Proceedings Thirteenth Annual Conference of the Urban Regional Information Systems Association, 1975) p.167.
6. Feldhausen, P.H., 1970, Ordination of sediments from the Cape Hatteras continental margin, J. Math. Geol., V. 2, p.113.
7. Gevirtz, J.L., Park, R.A. and Friedman, G.M., 1971, Paraecology of benthonic foraminifera and associated micro-organisms of the continental shelf off Long Island, New York, Journal of Paleontology, V. 45, p.153.
8. Hopkins, L.D., 1973, Environmental Impact Statements, A Handbook for Writers and Reviewers, University of Illinois, Chanpaign, Illinois,
9. Jameson, D.L., 1976, Ecosystem Impacts of Urbanization Assessment Methodology, Env. Protection Agency, Washington, D.C.
10. Linsley, R.L. and Franzini, J.B., 1972, Water Resources Engineering, McGraw-Hill, New York, 2nd ed.
11. Meadows, C.T., 1970, Man-Machine Communication, Wiley, New York.
12. Park, R.A., 1974, A multivariate analytical strategy for classifying paleoenvironments, J. Math. Geol., V. 6.
13. Rowe, P.G. (editor), 1976, An Approach for Describing Natural Systems and for Assessing Natural Environmental Impacts, Rice Center for Community Design and Research, Houston, Texas.
14. Schultz, L., 1963, Digital Processing: A Systems Orientation, Prentice Hall, Englewood Cliffs, New Jersey.
15. Sokal, R.R. and Sneath, P.H.A., 1973, Principles of Numerical Taxonomy, W.H. Freeman, San Francisco, California.
16. Sneath, P.H.A. and Sokal, R.R., 1963, Numerical Taxonomy, W.H. Freeman, San Francisco, California.
17. Spann, G.W., 1975, A systems approach to land use inventories and information systems, in Anochie, O.M. (editor), Computers, Local Government and Productivity, V. 1, (Proceedings Thirteenth Annual Conference of the Urban Regional Information Systems Association, 1975), p.153.
18. Warner, M.L. and Preston, E.H., A Review of Environmental Impact Assessment Methodologies, Env. Protection Agency, Washington, D.C., 1974.

R.H. Harper, Manager
R.A. Murch, Senior Analyst
Management Systems Development Department
City of Calgary
P.O. Box 2100
Calgary, Alberta
T2P 2M5

CITY OF CALGARY
CITY-OWNED LAND INVENTORY SYSTEM

ABSTRACT.   In 1974, the City of Calgary began
the design and development of a computer supported
system to assist the Land Department in managing the
property and buildings owned by the City. *This paper
discusses the development approach used, the conceptual architecture adopted, and some of the problems
and benefits encountered.* Samples of the data items
maintained and the reports produced are also provided.
At present, Calgary owns some 6,000 parcels of
land comprising nearly 15% of the City's total surface area, which would cost over $280,000,000 to re-
place at current rates. After 2 years of a projected
3 - 5 year development period, the original approach
is still appropriate. The original objectives are, in
most cases, being surpassed or exceeded and the system
is successful.

INTRODUCTION

Calgary is one of the larger cities in Western Canada. It's population of over 470,000 people is dispersed over the 180 square mile area of
the City in a variety of commercial, residential, and industrial districts.
Because all the utilities and services (except telephone and natural gas)
are provided by the civic government, there is a very distinct requirement
for the City to own and manage land resources for parks, community centres,
parking lots, road allowances, firehalls, engineering depots, future road
development, police offices, etc. In fact, the 6,000 parcels of land currently owned by the City, comprise some 17,000 acres and would cost over
$280,000,000 to replace at current rates. It goes almost without saying
that City-owned land is perhaps the most valuable asset owned by the City
of Calgary. The Land Inventory System is designed to facilitate and support the responsible management of that asset.

DESIGN STRATEGY

The Land Department of the City of Calgary has three main responsibi-
ilities:
1.   The purchasing of properties and improvements for use by other
City departments in capital or operating budget programs.

-400-

2. The sale of properties owned by the City but not required for any current or future planned projects.
3. The renovation, maintenance, and leasing of City-owned properties and buildings to provide some revenue until the property is scheduled to be used.

In addition, one division of the Land Department is responsible for developing some industrial, commercial, and residential subdivisions - in much the same way that a private development company would operate. These developed areas are sold to the private sector on the open market at acceptable market rates. Properties which become City-owned through non-payment of taxes are also administered by the Land Department. Figure 1 illustrates the data flow within the Land Department's activities.

Understanding the scope of these responsibilities will be useful in reviewing the strategy followed in developing the Land Inventory System. Although the topic of computer support had been discussed previously, it wasn't really until 1974 that any concentrated systems development effort began. From the very beginning it was determined that the overall strategy and emphasis was to be on the quality of the result rather than the speed of implementation. *We wanted a useable system.* It was also necessary that the end result of the systems development effort provide information massaging and delivery at the *operating and management levels* of the entire Land Department.

Consequently, the basic approach was to create one base of data which would support all the functional requirements. This concept is illustrated in Figure 2. Because the land purchases or acquisitions are financed in several different ways (grants, debentures, donations, etc.) and other financial data are vital to valuing the land, it was important to provide a rather substantial interface with the City's centralized Financial Information System. The legislative requirements and the procedures for dealing with outside agencies made it necessary to provide interface support in those areas as well.

In addition, the overall strategy involved five major objectives:
1. Improvement of internal control over land transactions.
2. Satisfaction of reporting requests - particularly for summary and analytic data.
3. General improvement in the quality and integrity of the Land Department records.
4. Interface with other civic systems (Financial Information System, Budget Control, Insurance, etc.).
5. Development of improved support for City-owned land management planning.

These objectives provided a considerable degree of latitude for preparing the design approach used. The levels of technology, system structure, and implementation strategy were all left to be recommended by the project team.

DESIGN ARCHITECTURE

The project team included the accountant for the Land Department (as the project leader), a programmer-analyst from the Data Processing Services Department, and a senior management systems analyst from the Management

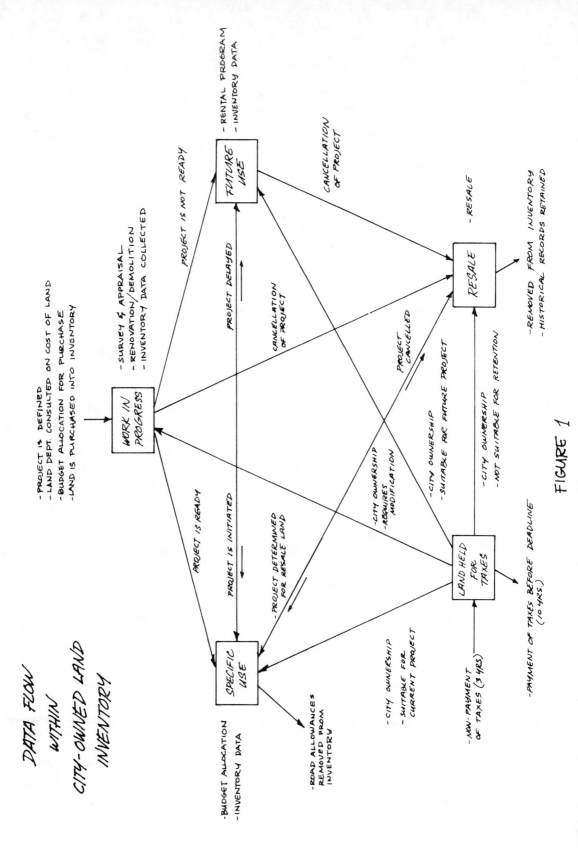

DATA FLOW
WITHIN
CITY-OWNED LAND INVENTORY

FIGURE 1

LAND INVENTORY / PROPERTY MANAGEMENT SYSTEM - FUNCTIONAL RELATIONSHIPS

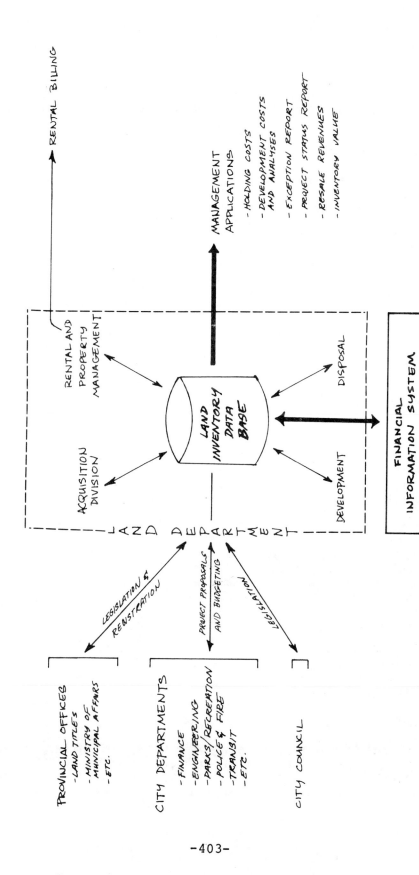

FIGURE 2

Systems Development Department. Additional expertise was added to the team as it was required throughout the project.

The proposal developed by this team recommended a 3 - 5 year development and implementation period and suggested that the effort be subdivided into a number of components to be developed in 5 phases:

Phase I   - Data Collection Component
Phase II   - Reporting Component
Phase III - Rentals Component
Phase IV   - Interface Components
Phase V   - Planning Support Components

This is illustrated in Figure 3. The proposal was submitted in August, 1974 and was accepted. Actual design and development for Phase I began in September, 1974. The initial approach was to provide mostly batch-oriented file processing and to allow the system to stabilize during Phases I and II. Then, as the Rentals Component was being addressed, during Phase III, conversion to on-line support and the use of a data base management system was to proceed. The ultimate goal was to provide as much on-line support as would be necessary to address the day-to-day information needs of the department.

PRESENT STATUS

We are now approximately 2 years into the development schedule, and the progress has been quite acceptable. The Data Collection Component has been in place since December, 1974, but it did take over a year to collect, enter, verify, and validate each of the data items for each of the 6,000 parcels of land. A sample data collection sheet, outlining all the data items maintained by the system, appears in the Appendix.

The Reporting Component was implemented in November, 1975 and currently produces 9 batch-oriented reports. Samples of these reports also appear in the Appendix. Also developed during this Phase, was an on-line register to record the location of the Duplicate Certificates of Title for the properties owned by the City. This facility was implemented in March, 1976.

The Rentals Component is presently in the detailed design stage and is scheduled for implementation during mid 1977.

The Interfaces and Planning Components are on-going throughout development of the complete system and the facilities provided to this time include the following:

- on-line access to city assessment and tax data
- inclusion of budget program analysis facilities
- financial source analysis facilities
- current replacement value data
- owner/user department coding
- diarized turnover date reporting

CONCLUSION

During the development process, two main problems arose. The most significant one was that none of the project team members was able to fully anticipate the magnitude (or potential magnitude) of the problems associated with reconstructing land transactions up to 80 years old. For

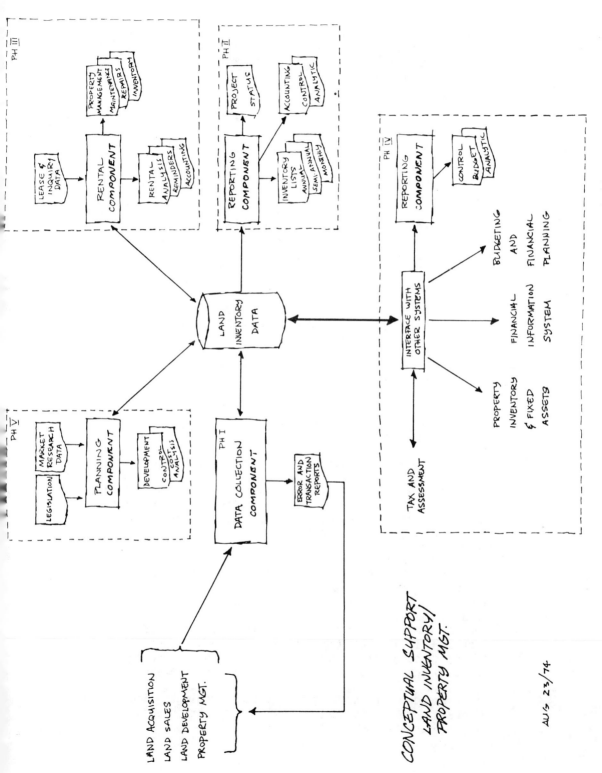

CONCEPTUAL SUPPORT
LAND INVENTORY/
PROPERTY MGT.

AUG 23/74

FIGURE 3

the more recent transactions, the problems were much fewer; however, for any transactions prior to 1950, many financial policies had to be formulated to provide proper valuations, title searches had to be performed, road plan registrations had to be made, etc. This was all in addition to the usual problems of missing or incomplete data.

The second basic problem was that we tried to complete the development and implementation of each component without hiring additional staff. This had several implications:

1. Special high priority tasks and departmental activities required attention. Such things as year-end accounting, urgent requests from city council or commissioners, expropriation proceedings, etc. all had to be addressed simultaneously with the system development.

2. Continuity problems arose when the first project leader (the Land Department Accountant) resigned from the City. This created a small hiatus in development until a new project leader was assigned from the Land Department.

3. Training new staff to work on development of the system was an on-going activity and took some time away from development activities.

4. The requirement for accuracy and detail made it necessary to utilize the senior and more experienced members of the Land Department. Consequently, they had priority conflicts with their own daily duties.

Despite these problem areas, the past 2 years have demonstrated some rather significant benefits for the Land Department:

1. There is now (possibly for the first time) a high level of confidence in the data. This means that the user population served by the Land Department (elected officials, senior city management, other departments, etc.) have much more credibility in the information provided.

2. There have been considerable improvements in the control procedures. The creation of the Land Inventory Team within the Land Department has provided the responsibility and authority for quality. The verification and validation procedures are well-defined. There is now good control over dissemination of information with the proper context.

3. There is greater flexibility and adaptability to information demands. New reporting formats have been accommodated relatively easily. New and additional data fields have been added with relatively few problems. Reports that were previously almost impossible to produce, can now be produced within a few hours or a few days.

4. Perhaps the most significant benefit is in the area of disaster back-up. If all the Land Department's records were to be destroyed through fire or vandalism, it would require only several hours to regenerate all the reports and information necessary to replace the Duplicate Certificates of Title and other official records. The cost of this process would be almost insignificant compared to what it would have cost in 1974 to completely replace these records.

After two years of effort, we feel we are being successful. Personnel throughout the City Service are using the system (and suggesting enhancements) and our initial objectives are being satisfied. In most cases, the expectations for analytic and management reporting are being exceeded. For us, this system is a success.

APPENDIX

Data Collection Document
  Land Inventory Data Sheet
Reports
  Property Detail Listing
  Cross References
  Listing by Owner/User Department
  Land under Lease
  List by Land Class
  List by Project
  Finance Source Codes
  Aging by Turnover Date
  Disposed Land

LAND DEPARTMENT
INVENTORY DATA SHEET

HOLDING NUMBER
6

T/C
7

1.- ADDITION
2.- CHANGE
3.- DELETION

8
1

SECTION PLAN
9 11|12 13|14

BLOCK
18|19

DESCRIPTION
22|23

52

PROVINCIAL TITLE NUMBER
53

CITY TITLE NUMBER
64 69

EASEMENTS
71

MINERAL RIGHTS
70

ENCUMBRANCES
72

CITY TAX ROLL NUMBER
9 17

TAX CLASS
18 21

ASSESSED VALUE
22 27

X
IF
CR.

ACREAGE
28 33

X
IF
CR.

8
2

LAND CLASS
9 11

FINANCE SOURCE
12

HOLDING COSTS
13 18

X
IF
CR.

REVENUE
19 24

X
IF
CR.

TURNOVER DATE
25 30

DAY MONTH YEAR

TURNOVER CODE
31 32

8
3

LR140 (REV. 03-76)
THE CITY OF CALGARY
LAND DEPARTMENT

SEC. _____

PREPARED BY:
INVENTORY APPROVAL:
DATE:

HOLDING NUMBER
1 6

T/C
7

1.- ADDITION
2.- CHANGE

8
4

LAND FILE No.
9 13

ACQUISITION DATE
14 19

DAY MONTH YEAR

LAND COST VALUE
34 43

X
IF
CR

ACQUISITION VOUCHER
20 25

OTHER ACQUISITION COSTS
44 50

X
IF
CR

DEPARTMENT
26 27

PROJECT / PROGRAM
28 33

REPLACEMENT VALUE
51 58

X
IF
CR.

DATE REPLACEMENT VALUE WAS ASSIGNED
59 64

DAY MONTH YEAR

ASSIGNED BY
65 66

8
5

LEASE No.
9 12

RENTAL VALUE
13 19

X
IF
CR.

DISPOSITION REFERENCE
36 45

DISPOSITION CODE
34

APPROVED SALES VALUE
20 27

X
IF
CR.

DISPOSITION DATE
46 51

DAY MONTH YEAR

DATE APPROVED
28 33

DAY MONTH YEAR

SEC. _____

PREPARED BY:
INVENTORY APPROVAL:
DATE:

LR140 (REV. 03-76)
THE CITY OF CALGARY
LAND DEPARTMENT

C I T Y   O F   C A L G A R Y
LAND INVENTORY – PROPERTY DETAIL LISTING   APRIL 12, 1976

TRANSACTION   HOLDING NUMBER   88 5

	SEC PLAN	BLOCK	DESCRIPTION		PROV TITLE	CITY TITLE	MIN EAS SPEC
1	069 A2	8	7		741004000	8185B	0 0 0

	ROLL NUMBER	TAX CLASS	ASSESSMENT	ACREAGE
2	069 00350 7	351	1,100.	0.15

	LAND CLASS	SC	HOLDING COSTS	REVENUE	TURNOVER DATE	TURNOVER CODE
3	220		0.00	0.00	01 01 76	01

	LND FLE	ACQ DATE	VOUCHR	D	PROJECT	LD COST VALUE	ACQ COSTS	REPLACE VALUE	REPLACE DATE	ASSIGNED BY
4	7 0889	03 12 73	108826	52	436502	11,025.00	0.00	900.	01 01 75	RW

	LEASE NO	RENTAL VALUE	APPROVED SALES VALUE	DATE APPROVED	DISP	DISPOSITION REF	DISP DATE
5		0.	0.		9	7510100	21 08 75

TRANSACTION   HOLDING NUMBER   89 3

	SEC PLAN	BLOCK	DESCRIPTION		PROV TITLE	CITY TITLE	MIN EAS SPEC
1	069 A2	6	8		741004000	8185B	0 0 0

	ROLL NUMBER	TAX CLASS	ASSESSMENT	ACREAGE
2		351	1,100.	0.13

	LAND CLASS	SC	HOLDING COSTS	REVENUE	TURNOVER DATE	TURNOVER CODE
3	220		0.00	0.00	01 01 76	01

	LND FLE	ACQ DATE	VOUCHR	D	PROJECT	LD COST VALUE	ACQ COSTS	REPLACE VALUE	REPLACE DATE	ASSIGNED BY
4	7 0889	03 12 73	108826	52	436502	11,025.00	0.00	780.	01 01 75	RW

	LEASE NO	RENTAL VALUE	APPROVED SALES VALUE	DATE APPROVED	DISP	DISPOSITION REF	DISP DATE
5		0.	0.		9	7510100	21 08 75

LAND INVENTORY CROSS REFERENCES FOR 12/ 3/76

LEGAL DESCRIPTION	HLD NO.	PROV. TITLE	ROLL NO.	CITY TITLE

FORM Z701-93   LAND INVENTORY SYSTEM - LISTING BY OWNER/USER DEPT. 52 FOR 20/ 7/76

HOLDING NUMBER	LEGAL DESCRIPTION	TURNOVER CODE	DATE	LAND CLASS	BOOK VALUE	PROJECT PROGRAM	ACREAGE
11320	116 AG 4895 21 A & H	01	010176	230	40,000.00	315299	2.84
11312	116 AG 4895 21 1-6	01	010176	230	10,000.00	315299	0.42
60574	116 A64895 T	01	010176	230	109,430.00	315299	19.30
64949	116 AK 2280 V	01	010176	230	87,205.00	315299	6.79
11239	116 AK 2280 W	01	010176	230	399,367.00	315299	71.07
60533	116 AK 2280 Z	01	010176	230	84,852.00	315299	15.10
11213	116 AK 2280 3	01	010176	230	20,454.00	315299	3.64
11221	116 AK 2280 32	01	010176	230	20,511.00	315299	3.64
67934	116 TR 116 29W4 UNREGISTED PLAN	24	080678	320	1.00	100000	25.56
11205	116 TR 116 29W4 PTN NE 1/4	01	010176	230	454,780.00	315299	154.64
11197	116 TR 116 29W4 SE 1/4	01	010176	230	469,953.00	315299	160.00
23564	118 AJ 5980 4 1	01	010176	240	60.00	325299	0.13
67942	119 AP 7500 A	01	010177	210	53,500.00	412603	2.03
67959	119 AP 7500 B	01	010177	210	53,500.00	412603	2.03
36012	120 AJ 1715 42 37-36	01	010176	240	107.38	325299	0.13
36004	120 AJ 1715 42 9-10	01	010176	240	124.05	325299	0.13
36038	120 AJ 1715 43 12-16	01	010176	210	9,000.00	412603	0.34
36020	120 AJ 1715 43 4	01	010176	240	20.40	325299	0.06
36046	120 AJ 1715 45 PNT19-26,SWOFR/W 566LK	01	010176	210	225.00	412699	0.02
36103	120 AJ 1715 45 27-28	01	010176	210	107.57	412699	0.08
35709	120 AM 375 W PAR A/316FS-& B/7308HE	01	010177	210	21,000.00	412603	1.71
67892	120 AM 375 26 29&30	60	010876	210	39,055.00	412603	0.14
64915	120 AM 375 26 40-41	01	010176	210	35,845.00	412603	0.14
35717	120 AM 375 27 18-19	01	010176	240	4,500.00	325299	0.14
35725	120 AM 375 27 23-24	01	010177	210	5,775.00	412603	0.14
66720	120 AM 375 27 42-43	01	010177	210	31,030.00	412603	0.14
65631	120 AM 375 27 5-8	01	010177	210	26,750.00	412603	0.28
65649	120 AM 375 27 9-10	01	010177	210	23,540.00	412603	0.14
65656	120 AM 375 28 1-3	01	010177	210	37,502.50	412603	0.21
64907	120 AM 375 28 39-40	01	010176	230	34,775.00	315299	0.14
35733	120 AM 375 28 4	01	010176	240	21.93	325299	0.07
65946	120 AM 375 28 43-44	01	010176	230	35,310.00	315299	0.14
35741	120 AM 375 28 9-10	01	010176	240	117.78	325299	0.16
35782	120 AM 375 29 PTN 38-41,42	01	010176	240	180.52	325299	0.12
35766	120 AM 375 29 11-18	01	010176	240	194.86	325299	0.56
60210	120 AM 375 29 19			410	139.93	0	0.06
35774	120 AM 375 29 20-23 PNTS	01	010176	240	194.80	325299	0.10

-412-

HOLDING NUMBER	LEGAL DESCRIPTION	TURNOVER CODE	DATE	PROJECT PROGRAM	LEASE NUMBER	ACREAGE	RENTAL VALUE	DEPT.
51003	034 JK 1838	0	01	010176	325299	816	0.73	0	52
48470	045 FO 5611	5 155	01	010177	422270	817	0.14	0	26
4929	093 S 1423	F PTN OF A(PCL1,8035FW)	01	010176	315299	818	0.28	0	52
28755	067 A1	20 37-38	01	010177	412612	823	0.15	0	52
29053	067 A1	26 15 W 1/2 2	01	010177	412612	825	0.11	0	52
5165	093 R 4724	E 31-32	01	010176	315299	827	0.14	0	52
10765	058 J 5600	F 1-4, W1/2 5	01	010176	412600	831	0.36	0	52
10158	060 FO 2563	4	01	010176	412614	838	0.15	0	52
53551	101 JK 390	E PTN	01	010176	325299	842	1.13	0	52
42440	067 P 4163	1 15,16	01	010176	260171	843	0.14	0	26
47613	045 P 5150	5 11,12	01	010176	422279	847	0.14	0	26
42537	067 FF 6505	20 6	01	010177	412612	848	0.15	0	52
28670	067 A1	20 5-6	01	010177	412612	852	0.15	0	52
28845	067 A1	21 32-33	01	010177	412612	853	0.15	0	52
28522	067 A1	11 6,7,8 N OF S25,ALL 9TO15	01	010176	412612	855	0.57	0	52
28530	067 A1	11 15-20	01	010177	412612	855	1.12	0	52
11858	059 AC 2112	E PTN BLK			325299	858	1.52	0	52
10272	077 JK 1335	PCL V	40	010177	0	859	2.42	0	65
47605	045 P 5150	5 4,10	01	010177	412610	863	0.14	0	20
52474	067 A	38 30-J FX 57' OF 30-33	51	010176	325299	864	0.50	0	52
27672	061 TR 61	240 PTN W1/2	41	010177	0	866	154.10	0	65
43463	079 TR 70	245 PNT SE1/4			0	868	57.65	0	65
19927	059 TR 56	145 PTN NE 1/4			0	870	1.00	0	81
42	060 TR 69	145 PTN SW 1/4 (12 AVE SE)			0	871	0.76	0	26
48293	045 R 3955	17 23-31			0	872	0.57	0	65
2923	082 GF 8598	1 19	01	010176	412614	875	0.14	0	52
6924	110 TR 110	145 PTN LS01,ALL OF 2			0	876	79.68	0	31
28757	067 A1	21 E 13-5' X 5 W 6.5'	01	010176	412612	877	0.07	0	52
42457	057 P 4163	1 37-40			260171	878	0.28	0	26
21048	056 JK 4118	2	01	010176	325299	885	0.40	0	52
4630	091 JK 5529	4	01	010176	325299	887	22.62	0	52
29140	067 A1	37 1 PTN	01	010177	412612	889	0.06	0	52
29157	067 A1	37 4 PTN	01	010177	416612	891	0.06	0	52
12716	090 GH 7703	LANE	01	010176	325299	895	1.24	0	52
28083	067 A1	24 13-19 S 70'	01	010177	412612	896	0.08	0	52
28543	067 A1	11 31 & PTN 32 & PTN 9 STREET	01	010177	412612	897	0.28	0	52
28589	067 A1	11 32-34	01	010177	412612	898	0.22	0	52

HOLDING NUMBER	LEGAL DESCRIPTION	LAND CLASS	BOOK VALUE	ACREAGE
44222 121 AN 7700	32 33-36	210	5,000.00	0.28
44230 121 AN 7700	32 37 AND 38	210	3,000.00	0.14
44248 121 AN 7700	32 39 & 40	210	70.52	0.14
44156 121 AN 7700	32 5 AND 6	210	13.80	0.14
65821 121 FN 8035	31 31	210	28,890.00	0.28
64717 121 FN 8035	31 32	210	16,050.00	0.21
13102 122 JK 1326	B	210	30,590.00	8.74
16774 123 AJ 3520	PTN OF 113&114	210	165,153.70	7.95
61283 123 AJ 3520	109 PTN	210	29,400.00	0.56
50476 124 HN 311	D	210	55,000.00	0.68
7575 128 GJ 8539	3 PIN	210	30,000.00	2.76
16139 129 JK 7110	13 15	210	1,346.35	0.19
15826 129 LK 1709	B	210	100,729.00	2.65
64493 124 TR 120	1W5 PTN SE 1/4	210	19,845.00	0.19
65862 130 HO 3766	1	210	200,000.00	0.95
65870 130 HO 3766	2 PTN	210	107,500.00	0.86
15388 130 HO 3766	7	210	4,050.00	0.09
63412 130 751:059	2 2	210	5,000.00	0.05
23705 131 JK 6514	X	210	49,120.00	4.28
8359 140 TR 140	1W5 PTN NE 1/4 IN RW57	210	923.45	0.23
8342 140 TR 140	1W5 PTN OF N100'IN NE1/4INKW113H-10	210	8,471.65	2.11
8600 140 741:261	D	210	28,240.00	3.55
8698 140 741:261	E	210	2,240.00	0.28
63719 142 GV 657	A	210	167,203.30	2.38
63720 142 GV 657	B	210	160,040.00	2.38
64642 142 GV 657	C	210	133,900.00	2.38
26492 162 AP 4990	3 PIN 1	210	25.00	0.14

TOTALS FOR 210

BOOK VALUE = 20,800,637.52   ACREAGE = 710.89

-414-

HOLDING NUMBER	LEGAL DESCRIPTION	TURNOVER CODE	DATE	LAND CLASS	BOOK VALUE	PROJECT PROGRAM	LEASE NUMBER	OTHER ACQ. COSTS
00675 041 AM 5140	C PTN OF BLOCK	01	010176	210	33,600.00	412602		0.00
30924 041 FK 3088	PTN 5	01	010176	210	4,500.00	412602		0.00
29538 042 AF 3898	Z	01	010176	210	30,000.00	412602		0.00
29546 042 AF 3898	1 PTN 1-4	01	010176	210	500.00	412602		0.00
29587 042 FN 7545	2 E1/2 OF 7	01	010176	210	9,000.00	412602		0.00
29611 042 FN 7545	2 PTN 9	01	010176	210	21,200.00	412602		0.00
29603 042 FN 7545	2 PTN 9	01	010176	210	26,250.00	412602	1205	0.00
29579 042 FN 7545	2 W 1/2 OF 7	01	010176	210	10,700.00	412602	967	0.00
29595 042 FN 7545	2 8	01	010176	210	22,500.00	412602	1010	0.00
29637 042 FN 7545	13 PTN 3 & ALL 4-6	01	010176	210	100,000.00	412602		0.00
29498 042 GJ 2176	A	01	010176	210	17,500.00	412602	1080	0.00
29504 042 GJ 2176	B	01	010176	210	13,500.00	412602	792	0.00
29512 042 GJ 2176	C	01	010176	210	16,300.00	412602		0.00
29421 042 JK 296	3 10	01	010176	210	8,500.00	412602		0.00
29415 042 JK 296	3 9,11,12	01	010176	210	21,500.00	412602		0.00
36384 057 P 791	26 E8°OF 35 ALL 36	01	010176	210	50,000.00	412602	1012	0.00
36368 057 P 791	26 16 & E 1/2 OF 17	01	010176	210	17,500.00	412602	1066	0.00
36376 057 P 791	26 29E0FW10° 30SW15°0F31	01	010176	210	27,500.00	412602	1013	0.00
30420 057 P 791	50 35&N101° OF 36	01	010176	210	22,500.00	412602	1024	0.00
22152 058 V 2187	3 21,22	01	010176	210	21,000.00	412602	1079	0.00
22173 058 V 2187	4 PTN21 S OF N4-5°,22	01	010176	210	20,000.00	412602		0.00
22160 058 V 2187	4 19,20	01	010176	210	41,500.00	412602		0.00
24594 058 V 2187	5 19-20	01	010176	210	50,825.00	412602		0.00
22186 058 V 2187	6 21,22	01	010176	210	19,500.00	412602	1011	0.00
22194 058 V 2187	6 23,24	01	010176	210	26,600.00	412602	1082	0.00
33835 101 AC 5454	13 11&12	01	010176	210	40,530.00	412602		0.00

TOTALS

ACTIVE LAND BOOK VALUE = 652,405.00
ACTIVE LAND OTHER ACQ. COSTS = 0.00

INACTIVE LAND BOOK VALUE = 0.00
INACTIVE LAND OTHER ACQ. COSTS = 652,405.00

HOLDING NUMBER	LEGAL DESCRIPTION	TURNOVER CODE DATE	LAND CLASS	BOOK VALUE	FIN. SOURCE
36129	957 TP 57 165 PTN SE SF 1/4		157	4,594.41	0
36135	057 TR 57 165 PTN SW 1/4		157	5,308.50	0
36152	057 TR 57 165 PTN SW 1/4		120	1,235.18	0
36157	057 TR 57 165 PTN SE 1/4		159	400.00	0
36160	057 TR 57 165 PTN SE SE 1/4		120	1,640.00	0
19025	058 F 1129 SP NOTS TL OF 13	01 010175	245	762.20	0
19784	058 J 5699 5 1-4, N1/C 5	01 010176	210	44,404.90	0
19802	058 J 5699 H PTN 65		120	75.60	0
19794	058 J 5699 4 PTN1		120	35.00	0
19517	058 J 5699 J 1/2 S 1/2 15	01 010176	211	44,500.00	0
19530	058 J 5699 J 40 PTN S S OF K		120	158.66	0
19744	058 J 5699 K		150	165.51	0
19800	058 J 5699 0		150	630.90	0
19515	058 C 2448 1 PTN 26		120	1.00	0
19521	058 0 2448 1 N 3. OF 6 x 42	01 010175	210	22,000.00	0
19530	058 0 2448 3 PTN OF 4TH OF S15' 3		120	1.00	0
19562	058 0 2448 6 19, 11	01 010176	210	20,450.00	0
19576	058 0 2448 8		120	275.28	0
19640	058 0 2448 15 N 55° OF 25 x 26	01 010175	210	1,500.50	0
19703	058 0 2448 15 STH 40 ARS PTN SW 1/4	01 010176	210	18,000.00	0
19883	058 0 2448 15 PTN 40 ARE PTN SW 1/4	01 010176	210	22,590.00	0
19711	058 0 2448 15 PTN26	01 010176	210	4.30	0
19633	058 0 2448 15 N 35° OF 25 X 20	01 010176	210	8,500.00	0
19512	058 0 2448 15 13	01 010176	210	11,550.00	0
19628	058 0 2448 15 12	01 010176	210	11,500.00	0
19553	058 0 2448 15 35, 37	01 010176	210	25,500.00	0
19661	058 0 2448 15 4	01 010176	210	14,500.00	0
19670	058 0 2448 15 43	01 010176	210	14,500.00	0
19687	058 0 2448 15 44	01 010176	210	25,900.00	0
19695	058 0 2448 15 45	01 010176	210	16,500.00	0
19245	058 0 5179 1 22, 23	01 010176	240	6,500.00	0
19752	058 0 5179 2 64, 65		120	1,500.00	0
19260	058 0 5179 3 N 33° OF 15 - 30		120	1.00	0
20955	058 P 1948 17 PTN29,LOT#25'		150	711.63	0
29441	058 P 1948 23 1,2	01 010176	240	74.04	0
29178	058 P 1948 25 20		310	139.71	0
29958	058 P 1948 25 30-32	01 010176	240	579.04	0

HOLDING NUMBER	LEGAL DESCRIPTION	TURNOVER CODE	TURNOVER DATE	PROJECT PROGRAM	LEASE NUMBER	LAND FILE NUMBER
15768	129 TR 129 1W5 PTN NE 1/4	01	010176	325299		71423
15479	130 JK 5541 27 PTN LANE BTWN66&67	01	010176	325299	725	
15487	130 73 1278 2 2	01	010176	325299		70334
15461	130 74 10294 6 ALL	01	010176	325299		
23648	131 JK 4325 10 PTN OF LANEWAY	01	010175	325299	924	61489
23739	131 JK 4826 10 LANE ADJ S OF LOT 148	01	010176	325299	1578	32051
13714	141 GK 4846 POPLAR RDS.E. W20°	01	010176	325299		91613
61663	148 TR 148 1W5 PTN RD ALL ADJ NW 1/4	01	010176	325299		82195
12864	148 TR 148 1W5 PTN RD 2182BM-NW 1/4	01	010176	325299		82166
12831	148 TR 148 1W5 PTN ROAD ADJ NW 1/4	01	010176	325299		82066
50690	100 TR 100 1W5 PTN NW 1/4	01	010176	412601		70065
53751	101 AC 5454 2 1-3	01	010176	412601		70707
53769	101 AC 5454 2 8&9	01	010176	412601		70727
53810	101 AC 5454 13 7&8	01	010176	412601		70727
53827	101 AC 5454 13 9&10	01	010176	412601		70727
64881	101 AJ 130 38 PTN 31-36 W OF 7&44H6	01	010176	412601		70727
53629	101 JK 2322 8 W OF E 167° OF 1	01	010176	412601	1009	70785
52571	102 GL 8573 4 7&8	01	010176	412601		70887
16659	103 AK 6120 32 21, 22, 23	01	010176	412601		70775
60673	041 AM 5140 C PTN OF BLOCK	01	010176	412602		70542
30924	041 FK 3088 PTN 5	01	010176	412602		70719
29538	042 AF 3898 7	01	010176	412602		
29546	042 AF 3898 1 PTN 1-4	01	010176	412602		70626
29587	042 FN 7545 2 E1/2 OF 7	01	010176	412602		70626
29603	042 FN 7545 2 PTN 9	01	010176	412602	1205	70719
29611	042 FN 7545 2 PTN 9	01	010176	412602		70467
29579	042 FN 7545 2 W 1/2 OF 7	01	010176	412602	967	70626
29595	042 FN 7545 2 8	01	010176	412602	1311	70719
29637	042 FN 7545 13 PTN 3 & ALL 4-6	01	010176	412602		70664
29496	042 GJ 2176 A	01	010176	412602	1030	70719
29504	042 GJ 2176 B	01	010176	412602	742	70624
29512	042 GJ 2176 C	01	010176	412602		70467
29421	042 JK 296 3 10	01	010176	412602		70585
29413	042 JK 296 3 9,11,12	01	010176	412602		70585
36384	057 P 791 26 E8°OF 35 ALL 36	01	010176	412602	1012	70699
36365	057 P 791 26 16 & E 1/2 OF 17	01	010176	412602	1060	70699
36376	057 P 791 26 29E0FW10° 30&W15°0F31	01	010176	412602	1013	70699

HOLDING NUMBER	LEGAL DESCRIPTION	LAND CLASS	BOOK VALUE	ACREAGE	PROJECT PROGRAM	OTHER ACQ. COSTS	SALES VALUE	DATE	CODE	DISPOSITION REFERENCE	DATE
51961 097 7410843	4 W60'OF8	320	5,089.00	0.96	72	0.00	38,400	071074	1	3-3441	140575
51946 097 7410843	4 6	320	11,450.00	2.29	72	0.00	87,020	071074	1	3-3474	080675
51953 097 7410843	4 7	320	11,450.00	2.29	72	0.00	87,020	071075	1	3-3474	080675
51979 097 7410843	4 9	320	44,950.00	8.99	72	0.00	359,600	071074	1	3-3441	140575
52100 097 7410843	6 N 1/2 1	320	6,300.00	1.25	72	0.00	50,000	071074	1	3-3482	220475
52118 097 7410843	6 2	320	12,650.00	2.53	72	0.00	101,200	071075	1	3-3498	171275
52126 097 7410843	6 3	320	13,300.00	2.66	72	0.00	106,400	071074	1	3-3498	171275
52134 097 7410843	6 4	320	13,100.00	2.62	72	0.00	104,800	071074	1	3-3499	171275
52142 097 7410843	6 5	320	13,350.00	2.67	72	0.00	106,800	071074	1	3-3499	171275
22574 098 LK 751	8 15	320	1,289.91	0.58	68	0.00	23,200	100674	1	3-3475	300975
22582 098 LK 751	8 16	320	1,289.81	0.58	68	0.00	23,200	100375	1	3-3476	020975
22590 098 LK 751	8 17	320	1,312.15	0.59	68	0.00	23,600	100375	1	3-3476	020975
22608 098 LK 751	8 18	320	18,240.00	0.57	68	0.00	22,800	100375	1	3-3476	020975
22491 098 LK 751	8 3	320	1,178.71	0.53	68	0.00	20,140	100674	1	3-3478	151075
22509 098 LK 751	8 4	320	1,245.43	0.56	68	0.00	21,280	100375	1	3-3479	071075
22632 098 LK 751	10 20	320	3,447.18	1.55	68	0.00	35,803	100674	1	3-3406	030275
22640 098 LK 751	10 21	320	4,336.78	1.95	68	0.00	45,045	100674	1	3-3360	080175
22657 098 LK 751	10 22	320	4,492.46	2.02	68	0.00	46,662	100674	1	3-3405	140575
22665 098 LK 751	10 23	320	4,336.78	1.95	68	0.00	45,045	100674	1	3-3405	140575
22673 098 LK 751	10 24	320	3,135.88	1.41	68	0.00	32,571	100674	1	3-3405	140575
22681 098 LK 751	10 25	320	5,448.78	2.45	68	0.00	53,900	100674	1	3-3392	090175
22699 098 LK 751	10 26	320	32,025.00	1.57	68	0.00	36,267	100674	1	3-3427	200875
22707 098 LK 751	10 27	320	12,943.70	5.82	68	0.00	120,980	100674	1	3-3442	130675
22715 098 LK 751	10 28	320	4,625.91	2.08	68	0.00	45,760	100674	1	3-3400	170175
22723 098 LK 751	10 29	320	3,602.87	1.62	68	0.00	35,640	100674	1	3-3400	170175
65045 098 7411095	A LOT 1	320	21,869.05	2.17	80	0.00	86,800	251174	1	3-3471	230875
61135 098 7411095	A LOT 2	320	20,357.36	2.02	80	0.00	80,800	251174	1	3-3471	230875

TOTALS

BOOK VALUE = 1,033,569.13   ACREAGE = 97.34   OTHER ACQ. COSTS = .00   SALES VALUE = 4,877,603

Gaybrielle E. Maxson
Planner
Ohio Department of Natural Resources
Fountain Square
Columbus, Ohio 43224

THE OHIO CAPABILITY ANALYSIS PROGRAM AND ITS APPLICATION
IN STARK COUNTY, OHIO

In response to the need of local and regional
planning agencies in Ohio for information about the
physical environment, the Ohio Department of Natural
Resources began a land capability analysis program in
October, 1972. The object of land capability analysis
is to gather information about the components of the
environment such as vegetation, soils, groundwater,
and slope and to analyze the ability of the components
to support various types of land use. Many planning
agencies lack the expertise to use uninterpreted resource data, such as a detailed map of soil types, but
increasingly they feel the need to consider this information when making land use decisions. For many
years, the Ohio Department of Natural Resources has
collected data on the physical environment and made it
available to interested persons. Through the capability analysis program the Department is able to provide
local planning agencies with help interpreting and
analyzing resource information.

Initially, the capability analysis was done
manually by overlaying base data maps and hand-drafting a capability map. It soon became apparent that if
large quantities of data were to be manipulated, analyzed, and stored efficiently, a computer system was
necessary. For this purpose OCAP (the Ohio Capability
Analysis Program) was developed. OCAP is a combination of computer programs which allows for mapping,
analyzing, overlaying, scaling, and retrieving detailed data. It has been used to complete capability
analyses for nine counties in Ohio and numerous
smaller studies.

Stark County was the third county in Ohio for
which a capability analysis was done. It was chosen
because of the complexity of the environment, because
much information was available, and because the county
is growing and development is spreading rapidly into
the suburban and rural areas. The Stark County land
capability study was completed in June 1975. The
Planning Commission received a series of computer maps
of the basic information on soils, slope, vegetation,
groundwater availability, land use, and mineral resources and maps in which the basic information was

combined and analyzed to point out problem areas for ten types of development, including single family homes, intermediate and large scale building, recreation, agriculture and local roads and streets. The Stark County Regional Planning Commission staff is using the analysis in several ways, including updating the county's general development plan, and considering the feasability of development proposals.

The Ohio Capability Analysis Program (OCAP) is a computer information and mapping system developed by the Ohio Department of Natural Resources to generate an environmental resource data base for the state. OCAP is used in conjunction with the Land Capability Analysis program through which the Department is attempting to encourage better land use decisions in Ohio. Planners and planning commissions have traditionally relied upon social, economic and population data when writing general development plans or zoning ordinances. When the physical environment is disregarded by the planner, the public may find industrial parks sinking because of unstable foundation material or septic tanks failing because of impermeable soils. Development alters run-off patterns, disrupts productive agricultural land, and costs taxpayers money when it occurs in a flood plain or other hazardous area.

In Ohio, land use decisions are made at the local level. There is, as yet, no state-wide land use plan or policy. One way for the state to influence development decisions and avert wasteful and costly forms of land use is to provide technical assistance to the local and regional planning agencies. The land capability analysis program was initiated in 1973 to provide information to these agencies on the physical environment which they can use with their traditional data to make more rational land use decisions. Environmental data should not replace social, economic, or population information, but supplement it and thereby add an important dimension to the planning process.

LAND CAPABILITY ANALYSIS AND THE OHIO CAPABILITY ANALYSIS PROGRAM

Land Capability Analysis is a methodology for assessing the components of the physical environment in terms of their ability to support or tolerate different types of land use. Data on soils, slope, groundwater, land cover, geology, and mineral resources are combined and analyzed to determine whether an area is suited for homes, industry, recreation, agriculture, all of these forms of development, or none of them. Quantities of environmental data have been collected within the Department of Natural Resources, but this information is not always easy to use, especially by people without a technical or scientific background. Through the land capability analysis program soils and geology maps can be translated into a form that local or regional decision makers can readily use to understand the problems and possibilities of the area with which they must deal.

There are several phases to the capability analysis process. The first involves defining the area to be included in a project, the data to be used, the types of development to be considered in the analysis, and how the final product will be presented. Extensive discussions are held with the county or regional decision makers regarding their problems and needs, and then data upon which the analyses will be based is gathered.

There is a heavy reliance on soils, slope, and land cover information, because these are mapped in great detail and more research has been done on their effect on development. Other resource data that may be used includes several geologic variables, mineral resources, and ground-water availability. Data supplied by the county may include political boundaries, watersheds, census tracts, traffic zones, land use, sewer and water service areas, or any other information considered important. Subsequent phases in the capability analysis process involve preparing basic data files, performing an analysis, and presenting the results.

In order to accomplish the latter phases of the capability study, a method for rapidly handling and storing large amounts of data had to be devised. The first capability analyses were done by overlaying the base data maps on a light table and hand-drafting a capability map from the overlay. This method may suffice for small areas with limited data, but for large areas with detailed information it is not feasible. Not only is it difficult to manipulate the information, but it is also time consuming, costly, and difficult to keep the information up to date. OCAP was developed to deal with these problems. It enables the user to process and store large quantities of detailed data, to map and update the data rapidly, and to analyze it in a variety of ways.

OCAP was initially developed by the Systems Research Group at Ohio State University as a research project. Subsequently, the Department of Natural Resources revised OCAP to meet the evolving demands of the land capability program. There were several reasons for developing a new system rather than using an existing one. In many systems, data is entered on a uniform grid-cell or polygon basis, but in OCAP, data is entered through a digitizing process on a line-by-line or polygon basis. The sequential line method is more accurate and preserves more detail; there are fewer scale and distortion problems; and irregularly shaped areas can be handled better. Apart from choosing a sequential line approach, it was desirable to incorporate diverse features from several systems; no one system had everything necessary to translate the capability analysis concept into a useful tool for local decision makers.

OCAP is written in PL1 and therefore requires an IBM computer with a PL1 compiler. The output consists of line printer maps and tabular listings; no interactive terminal capability or plotter graphics have been developed at this time. The department has three digitizers with which base data is encoded into the system, and a remote job entry terminal linked to the State Data Center's IBM 370-158 and 370-168.

There are twelve programs in the OCAP system through which data can be entered, edited, mapped, scaled, manipulated, and analyzed:

    1. Reformat - a program to reformat non-compatible data or to create several files from one. Soils and slope, for instance, are digitized simultaneously and then split into two files.

    2. Edit 1 - a program to run a format check on the data.

    3. Edit 2 - a program to create and to update the base data files.

    4. Polygon - a program for polygonal or point entry of relatively uniform data that does not require line-by-line digitizing.

5. Scale - a program to rescale the data which is usually entered at 1"=2000' to any other desired scale.

6. Boundary - a program to extract small areas such as watersheds, census tracts, or townships from larger files.

7. Merge - a program to combine data digitized in segments, often on the basis of USGS quadrangles. Data is generally merged into county files.

8. Search - a program to isolate areas within a given distance of a chosen variable category, such as areas within 2000 feet of water on a land use map.

9. Premod - a program to combine base data into a format that can be used for analysis.

10. List - a program to produce tabular summaries of the base data or capability data generated from an analysis. Summaries may be for one variable or for two. In the latter instance, the two are assessed simultaneously and the output lists such information as land use by traffic zone or degree of slope by watershed.

11. Matrix - a program through which an external attribute file (EAF) is created that can be linked to a base variable through the map program. There is a standard EAF for soils and the capability to generate user-defined EAF's to be used with other base data files, such as census tracts. For each soil type or census tract, auxilliary data such as permeability or population density can be stored, mapped, and used in the capability analysis.

12. Map - a program composed of nine electives to map and analyze the basic data. Built into the map program is a simple overlay routine and a more complex linear weighted model. The user may by-pass the linear model and supply an analysis program. Analysis generated through the overlay and modeling routines can be saved and used in further analyses.

Digitizing and editing are the most time consuming aspects of the capability process. Digitizing involves encoding all changes on a base map on a line-by-line basis. The number of lines depends upon the scale of the base map and the desired scale of the output. Most base maps are digitized in such a way that the output will be at 1:24000, the scale of the USGS topographic maps. At this scale, one computer character equals 1.15 acres. Frequently, the base maps do not conform to this scale and adjustments must be made. Once digitizing is completed, the cards with the codes and distances are fed through the reformat and editing programs as necessary to produce a computer file that can be mapped.

The computer map is then visually checked against the original map to ensure accuracy. The time involved in completing this phase of the capability analysis is directly related to the size of the study area and level of detail of the data. For an average county in Ohio of 465 square miles with a detailed soil survey, six months of work by two people would be required to complete this phase.

There are several reasons for preserving a high level of detail in the OCAP system. Most important is the variable nature of the soils, topography, and land use in most of the state. If a grid system were used where generalizations must be made over the entire cell, a great deal of information would be lost. By duplicating the base data maps through the digitizing process, little information is sacrificed and the subsequent analysis is that much more accurate.

An important aspect of the OCAP system is the ability to draw upon the external attributes file (EAF) for additional information. An EAF may be created in conjunction with any base file for which there is supplementary data. The most important EAF in terms of the ability to analyze development limitations is the one linked to the soils file. Numerous characteristics such as permeability, texture, and bearing strength can be associated with each soil type. These characteristics are more important in the analysis process than the soil type itself, yet maps of the characteristics do not exist. With an external attributes file in which information on the characteristics is stored, it is possible to map them and use them in the analytic process without digitizing more than the map of soil types. EAF's containing population and economic data have been created for census tracts and traffic zones, and ones showing site characteristics have been created for natural areas. All EAF's broaden the scope of the information that can be provided and allow the user to map information that is otherwise not readily available.

The overlay routine and the linear weighted model built into the mapping program provide the means for comparing variables and determining development limitations. It is at this stage of the capability analysis process that the local decision makers should take a particularly active role so that the output reflects their needs. There are a variety of ways in which the analysis can be done. No one method is absolutely correct or free of assumptions. The objective of the analysis is to delimit areas with few development limitations from those with severe limitations. The linear weighted model can evaluate up to 20 variables at a time through a system of weighting the variables and variable levels; the overlay routine is a comparison of two variables only. Files may be created from either procedure and used in further analysis.

The last step in the procedure is to present to the local or regional planning officials the final map and report. This is a very important aspect of the program, because the local decision makers must understand how to use the maps and other output or the project will be of little value to them. The educational process usually includes public meetings or seminars in which interested people are told about the information available to them. In addition, a report summarizing the study and explaining the analysis is published by the Department.

The Stark County Capability Analysis

The study completed for Stark County, Ohio is an excellent example of how the land capability analysis process operates through the use of OCAP. Stark County is located in northeastern Ohio, fifty miles south of Cleveland. Canton is the county seat and the largest city. Stark is the eleventh largest county in area in Ohio (371,840 acres) and seventh largest in population (372,210). The county's population is still predominantly urban, but the last census showed that the rural townships were gaining at the expense of the cities. In fact, Stark has the largest rural non-farm population in Ohio, but it also has the second largest rural-farm population. With such a population configuration, the possibilities for land use conflicts are very great.

The physical environment in Stark County is as diverse as the population. Stark is one of several counties that straddles the boundary of continental glaciation, a major force in shaping the county's physical character. Aside from the visible differences in topography, glaciers modified the drainage and left significant sand and gravel deposits. As a result of the terrain and the variety of parent materials, a large number of soil types can be found in the county and the soils can vary greatly over a small area. In addition to the significant effect of glaciation on the county, Stark has an abundance of mineral resources, including coal, limestone, fire clay, oil and gas. The first three are frequently strip mined.

Six trends in development were identified in Stark County:

1. Increased single-family residential development outside urban areas, putting a heavy reliance on septic systems and groundwater supplies,
2. Increased intermediate and large scale development (schools, churches, industry, etc.) outside the urban areas,
3. A need for more recreation space to serve the growing population
4. Increased reliance on the local street and highway system,
5. Conversion of valuable agricultural land to other uses, and
6. The need to redevelop urban areas and to reclaim strip mines.

The capability analysis done for the county dealt with the first five of these trends by assessing the capability for:

1. Small-scale development with water and sewer service;
2. Small-scale development without sewer and water service;
3. Intermediate-scale development;
4. Large-scale development;
5. Extensive recreation;
6. Intensive recreation without structures;
7. Intensive recreation with structures;
8. Local roads and Streets;
9. Pasture and dairy use; and
10. Row crop and speciality crop use.

The county planning commission staff, including a soil scientist, participated actively in the design of the capability analysis. It was decided that the capability maps would define the severe limitations rather than consolidating all severe problems into one severe category. The slight and moderate limitations were combined, which reduced the number of categories that would have resulted had they been defined as well. As an example, the capability categories for small scale development without sewer and water service are:

1. Insignificant Problems
2. Slight Problems
3. Moderate Problems
4. Severe Problems - Ground Water Difficult to Obtain
5. Severe Problems - Shallow Bedrock
6. Severe Problems - Poor Permeability and Excess Water
7. Severe Problems - Slope
8 Severe Problems - Flooding
9. Developed Land

This method of analysis involved a ranking of the severe problems. Developed land was given a very high rating and thus eliminated from further analysis. Next, areas subject to flooding were eliminated, followed by areas with severe slope, drainage problems, and shallow bedrock. The county determined which problems were most severe and established the ranking. This method may obscure some information. For instance, there may be a severe shallow bedrock problem and a severe slope problem in the same place, but only the slope problem would emerge because of the way the problems were ranked. It is possible to show both, but when many capability categories are displayed, the maps are difficult to read and interpret, because no clear patterns emerge.

After the ten land use analyses were completed for the county, they were combined into a composite analysis. This showed that 25% of the county is already developed and of the 75% remaining, 13% is capable of any type development, 33% can accomodate limited building, and 29% presents severe restrictions to any type of building. It should be noted that the severest restrictions can be overcome with sufficient money and proper design, as long as the limitations are understood and compensated for. With the capability maps the planning commission staff can better evaluate development proposals to be sure that severe limitations are being taken into account.

The Stark County study was completed in June 1975, after which the county planning commission office received a set of computer quadrangle maps of the basic data on soils, slope, land use, groundwater, etc. at scales of 1:24000 and whole county maps at 1:60000. They also received a set of capability maps at the same scales. They can request updates of their base files, such as land use which changes rapidly, or they can request revisions of the capability analysis because of the need for new information to evaluate development proposals. The computer maps are stored in the planning commission office, but they are available to anyone in the county who could benefit from the information, including developers, health department officials, home owners, or students.

In addition to the computer maps provided to the county, mylar overlays of the USGS quadrangles were supplied. These mylars help the user orient himself or herself with the computer map. One of the biggest problems with any computer map is that there are no immediate points of reference such as place names. Many local decision makers are baffled by a computer map alone, but have no difficulty with one overlaid by a transparency showing roads, towns, or other landmarks. Some display of the computer maps in which the road system or political boundaries is superimposed on the computer map is immensely useful in gaining acceptance of the analysis by local officials.

Stark County is using the analysis in several ways, but primarily to aid in updating their general development plan and to evaluate development proposals. The revised general plan will reflect the limitations indicated in the analysis as will the day-to-day evaluation of proposals. For instance, several school sites in the county were reviewed by the planning staff, and suggestions made for changes on the base data maps. Recent field checks of the basic data and the analysis maps have proven them to be very accurate. While it is not suggested that an OCAP map should be used in place of a site analysis, it can be used with confidence to provide an accurate assessment of significant problems in an area.

The capability analysis project for Stark County was done at no expense to the county. The computer costs were about 5¢ an acre for the entire project, and the total cost for the project was approximately $40,000. This cost will be significantly reduced for future projects, because of lower computer costs and the increasing efficiency of the operation.

Stark was the third county out of a total of nine for which a capability analysis has been done. Several smaller areas, such as townships and scenic river corridors, have also been completed. In addition, OCAP is being used for a NASA-sponsored land use inventory for the state using Landsat data, a 208 water quality planning project, a preferential tax assessment project, and the Coastal Zone Management Program for the Lake Erie shoreline. The capability analysis concept and OCAP lend themselves quite well to many programs where resource assessment is involved. Because OCAP is a flexible program, it can meet the wide variety of needs that have arisen. The goal of the program in the Department of Natural Resources is to complete the entire state. With such a data base, the state and local decision makers will be able to avert many future land use problems.

J. P. Dangermond
Director
Environmental Systems Research Institute (ESRI)
380 New York Street
Redlands, California 93273

H. W. Grinnell, Jr.
Urban/Regional Economist
Southern California Edison Company (SCE)
2244 Walnut Grove Avenue
Rosemead, California 91770[1]

LAND USE STUDIES AT SOUTHERN CALIFORNIA EDISON
THE DEVELOPMENT AND USE OF A LAND USE
ORIENTED PLANNING INFORMATION SYSTEM

ABSTRACT

Over the past four years the Southern
California Edison Company (SCE) has been
developing a land use-oriented planning
information system to assist in forecasting
future electrical load growth for general
facility planning and in the preparation of
environmental impact reports. The technical
elements of this program involve collection of
land use data from high altitude imagery,
automating this data using the PIOS system,
conducting various area overlay and mapping
studies, and incorporating this data into a
generalized methodology for forecasting land
use. In addition to a successful technical
program, SCE has worked closely with three
county agencies in definition of a mutually
usable data inventory and in establishing a
joint sponsorship program. As the SCE
program continues, there may be additional
areas of information system development
that become both possible and cost effective.
Some of these concepts are suggested herein.

---

1. Others involved in the program at SCE are R. G. Crouch,
   Manager of Urban/Regional Planning, R. E. LaPlante,
   Supervising Urban/Regional Planner, T. M. Aw, R. W. Day,
   and W. R. Ostrander, Urban/Regional Planners; and Mary
   C. Busch, Associate Urban/Regional Planner. Principal
   among contributors to the studies at ESRI were G. Huibregtse,
   Project Manager; Don Adams, Computer Programmer; and
   Darlene Brown, Project Assistant.

INTRODUCTION

In 1972, the Southern California Edison Company (SCE) initiated development of a planning information system which involves the collection automation, mapping and analysis of land use and selected environmental information for the urban and urbanizing areas of its Service Territory. This system is being developed incrementally as part of a ongoing series of land use studies used to support electric load growth forecasts and general facility planning for utility system development and the development of environmental impact analyses. The SCE land use studies also involve forecasting both land use and socio-economic change for ten and twenty year periods. The land use study program was initiated in Orange County and has subsequently been performed in San Bernardino and Riverside Counties as well as parts of Los Angeles, Kern, Tulare, Kings, Inyo, and Mono Counties.

This paper presents the technical approach and exper iences associated with the development of this system. This includes a description of the technical methodology employed in collection and automation of land use data, an explanation of ways in which the land use data was used in forecasting, a discussion concerning joint sponsor- ship for the data collection, and, finally, a series of concepts outlining possible improvements to the information processing aspects of the system.

The authors feel that the land use program presented in this report is very successful and that the technical methodology, as well as the formula for joint public/private sponsorship of data collection, can be expanded to encompass larger geographic areas. Therefore, while this paper deals only with land use in urban and urbanizing areas it represents a model for development of a geographic information system that could successfully be done on a much larger scale with a variety of other data types.

GEOGRAPHIC COVERAGE OF LAND USE PROGRAM

The SCE land use study program is designed to eventually develop land use information for its entire service territory. The sizeable costs involved in mapping urban areas for the entire territory has resulted in a staged program of imple- mentation. This implementation has involved a county-by- county data collection and analysis effort which will be followed by periodic updating and reanalysis of data.

For each county, projections are made within defined areas comprising the urban and urbanizing districts. The study area is broken down into smaller sub-areas that coincide approximately with the cities (or parts of cities) and major unincorporated areas. The study area is also subdivided into the SCE service districts that lie in the study area. Analyses and projections are made for the entire study area, the sub- areas, and SCE service districts.

TECHNICAL METHODOLOGY

The cornerstone of the SCE land use studies program is the development of land use inventory maps and statistics. To acquire this data, a survey program was designed involving two major categories of technical effort (i.e., photo interpretation of land use and automation of land use data). Each of these efforts is discussed below.

Land Use Interpretation and Mapping

The design of the land use classification scheme is a joint effort between the various cooperating county planning departments and SCE. Both groups have needs which required different classification levels. County agencies typically want 50-60 classes for land use, whereas the SCE needs required only fifteen classifications. The land use classification scheme developed is similar to the one currently being used on the 1970 CARETS Land Use Inventory developed by Anderson, et. al., 1971, but with considerably more detail in its Level III modifications. The classification scheme is designed for use with aerial photography, regional specificity, and collateral data on a mapping base of 1" = 2000' (1:24,000).

The minimum size specifications for land use categories are:

1. Urban categories are generally not delineated unless the unit is at least two and one-half (2.5) acres in area; non-urban categories must be at least four (4) acres in area to be delineated.

2. Linear units less than 210 feet wide in urban categories and 330 feet wide in non-urban categories are not shown, except as acute corners of larger features. Modification of this specification is contingent upon photographic quality, realization of professional standards, and product utility. Photo interpreters will endeavor to identify strip commercial linear units of less than 210 feet where it is deemed feasible and appropriate.

3. When more than one category occurs within a minimum size unit, photo interpreters shall determine the predominant category and classify the entire area corresponding to predominant land use occurrence.

The following are the land use classifications used in SCE studies:

A: Agriculture: orchards and vineyards, truck and field crops, specialty farms (horticulture), nursery, green houses, grazing, dairy, poultry and feed lots.

C: Commercial: business districts, regional shopping centers, office centers, neighborhood and roadside commercial development, hotels and motels, warehousing, building materials (hardware), farm machinery, lumber yards, etc., and miscellaneous retail trades (e.g., auto wrecking).

CE: Commercial Recreation: stadiums, race tracks, private cultural facilities, fairgrounds, amusement parks and drive-in theatres.

E: Extractive: sand and gravel pits, stone quarries, oil and gas wells, etc., associated storage and tailing areas associated facilities.

G: Open Space: parks, recreation areas and associated facilities, golf courses, cemeteries, campgrounds, wildlife preserves and greenbelts.

IH: Heavy Industry: foundaries, scrap yards, primary metals, mechanical processing, chemical processing, etc., and associated facilities.

IL: Light Industry: manufacturing and industrial areas including associated warehouses, storage yards, and parking areas.

M: Military Establishment: bases, camps, airports and support facilities.

P: Public Institutional: schools, government offices, fire stations, police stations, health care facilities, libraries, religious facilities, and public cultural and social facilities.

RM: Multiple Family Dwelling Units: attached dwellings including row housing, garden apartments and high-rise apartments; also mobile home parks.

RS: Single Family Dwelling Units: detached single family and duplex dwellings.

TCU: Transportation, Communications and Utilities: non-military airports, including runways, parking areas, hangers and associated facilities; railroads, including yards, terminals and rights-of-way; freeways and major arterials; electric utilities, including transmission line rights-of-way, substations and generating facilities; other utilities; gas, water sewerage, solid waste and sanitary land fill areas and facilities.

UD: <u>Vacant Developable Land</u>: vacant land less than 24% in slope and improved land not in National Forests.

UUD: <u>Undevelopable Land</u>: vacant land 24% in slope or greater and all land in National Forests.

W: <u>Water</u>: open water including lakes and reservoirs, streams and waterways, including associated floodplains and flood control facilities.

The basic process of photo interpretation is accomplished on U.S.G.S. 7-1/2 minute quad sheets. The following materials are used: photo imagery at two scales; a series of collateral data maps and books; and a base map series of cronoflex U.S.G.S. 7-1/2 minute quad sheets.

Polygon maps displaying outlines of land uses are made for each quad sheet. These maps are drawn as overlays on the U.S.G.S. quad sheets, and coordinate identification of these maps is made. Enlarged high altitude imagery (1:24,000 nominal scale) is used for a generalized interpretation base. These images are placed on cronoflex and registered with the U.S.G.S. maps for convenient interpretation. Low altitude color infrared aerial photographs are also used for detailed interpretations.

Collateral data used in the interpretation are also handled as mylar overlays. Two overlay sheets are drawn and registered to each quad. One sheet contains existing electric utility facilities, and the second sheet contains other public buildings, schools, health facilities, and park and recreation areas. Other non-map collateral data are used to clarify some of the questions with regard to the imagery.

This procedure results in a series of coordinated land use maps organized according to the U.S.G.S. 7-1/2' series. These maps are subsequently field checked. Unclear areas on the imagery are investigated and resolved. Upon completion of the final editing, blueprint manuscript copies of each quad are reviewed by SCE. They are subsequently digitized for computer map storage and retrieval. Because of the high quality of final computer map output, it is not necessary to redraft the final map products.

Discription of Automated Procedures

The second category of technical tasks involves automation and analysis of the land use subsequent to the basic mapping of land use. Four basic tasks are performed: 1) digitizing of input; 2) file creation and editing; 3) overlay processing; and 4) graphic output. These tasks are accomplished

using the Polygon Information Overlay System (PIOS) software system.[2]

The basic system for digitizing maps, according to the
PIOS layout, can best be understood by presenting the technical definition of "polygon": A polygon is an area which is
completely enclosed by a border of straight line segments.
These segments are defined by a series of discrete points
referred to as "vertices." The conversion of these vertices
to (X, Y) coordinate points is the basis for converting the
maps into machine readable files. The vertices do two things:
1) describe the area of each polygon; and 2) define the
spatial location of the polygon data relative to other geographic features. These coordinate vertex points are measured
for each polygon with the assistance of an electro-mechanical
device known as a digitizer. The digitizer converts horizontal
and vertical movements of a cursor into computer compatible
characters. The digitizer consists of 4 parts: a 32" x 60"
table similar to a drafting table; a 16K mini-computer; an
electronic digital display panel; and a paper tape device
which records the measurements of the digitizer. Mounted on
the table is a mechanical device which supports a movable
cursor or glass enclosed cross hair. The map to be digitized
is mounted on the table surface and each ploygon is recorded
as a series of points. The information is initially stored
in the mini-computer and transferred to tape for subsequent
processing.

File Creation and Editing

After a complete maps module has been digitized, data
contained on paper tape is processed into a general file for
permanent storage and use by the various programs. There are
three phases associated with this process.

Preliminary Edit: This phase of activity involves the transfer of all polygons for each variable (land use, census
tracts, etc.) onto single disc files. This data is written
onto disc storage from the digitizing operation. During this
phase an online edit of the data is made for checking of
basic accuracy. This edit step includes checking for format,
consistency of map number, polygon number, polygon type code,

---

2. The PIOS system was developed and is currently maintained
by Environmental Systems Research Institute of Redlands,
California, as a general purpose system of software programs for creation, storage, analysis, overlay, and
mapping of x,y coordinate information. The PIOS software
system and associated procedures has proved to be an
efficient structure for accomplishing these land use
studies and has also been successfully applied to numerous
other land use and environmental studies at Pacific Gas &
Electric, San Diego County, Pacific Telephone & Telegraph,
and the states of Maryland and Alabama.

alphanumeric code, missing or duplicate polygons, polygon closure, and digitized information. From this file, maps are plotted and used for the second edit involving graphic checking of the accuracy of the x,y coordinates that were digitized.

Graphic Edit: Graphic editing of polygons is the simplest and least costly method currently available. If the plot from the above file matches the original map within acceptable limits, then the file is assumed to be sufficiently accurate. The plotting edit is a two-step process. The first step is an overlay process whereby the outlines of the plotted information are visually compared with the outlines of the stable base (mylar) maps that were used for digitizing. The second step, verification, is done by comparing the two adjoining polygon perimeter lines to see that both lines follow the same path (within acceptable deviation standards). Data errors associated with characteristic identification of the polygon are relatively easy to correct. These include missing land use codes, misnumbered polygon numbers, misnumbered maps, etc. Edit software handles these alterations with minimum difficulty. In more complex cases the nature of the error is such that the entire polygon needs redigitizing. Subsequent to final correction of the various errors in the polygon file, the vertices are readjusted using the "MATCHVERT" program which averages the coordinates of points falling along common boundaries, thus eliminating the graphic and statistical problems that occur when common lines do not coincide exactly.

Final File Creation: After the necessary corrections are completed, a final file is created for each 7-1/2 minute base map, for each variable. This data is in a form which enables the overlay to take place. In its final form the PIOS polygons are defined in two records. The first record for each polygon contains six descriptions, whereas the second record contains all the horizontal and vertical coordinates orders to circumscribe the area.

Overlay Analysis

The first and, perhaps, most important analytic procedure resulting in usable output is the overlay analysis. This analysis involves the summary of land use areas by geographically defined zones (i.e., census tracts, SCE service districts, etc.) In order to aggregate land use by various boundaries, PIOS uses a computer program which performs an overlay of the polygon map files. This program determines the common areas of two sets of overlapping polygons for each quad sheet.

The overlay program is structured to process only two polygon sets at a given time. These are divided into a "major" polygon variable (i.e., the unit into which one desires the aggregation to take place, such as census tracts), and a "minor" polygon variable (i.e., the variable which one wishes to summarize, such as land use). The program processes only one major polygon at a time. It reads in the extreme points of this polygon and selects all minor polygons whose extreme points overlap those of the major polygon. In situations where there is known overlap, the program employs a line intersection routine which determines the locations of inter- secting lines from the two sets of polygons.

Having determined these intersections, the program re- structures the two previous polygon files into a single file of polygons which have common attributes (i.e., the same land use and census tract). The areas of these residual polygons are then calculated by the program and summarized according to the dominant polygon (e.g., census tract). Figure 1 is an example of land use acreages printed out by census tract.

As many as eight different printouts have been developed for each map module. They are:

1. Basic land use polygon listing showing polygon land use alpha code, polygon centroid and area.

2. Selected land use polygon listing showing polygon land use alpha code, polygon centroid and area.

3. Polygon listing by census tract showing polygon land use alpha code, polygon centroid and area.

4. Polygon listing by traffic analysis zone showing polygon land use alpha code, polygon centroid and area.

5. Polygon listing by corporate boundary showing the appropriate census tract and polygon land use alpha code, polygon centroid and area.

6. Summary printout by consolidated land use codes showing area by SCE service district.

7. Summary printout by consolidated land use codes showing area in each census tract for an SCE sub- region. The summary is broken down by area in National Forests and area not in National Forests.

8. Summary printout by consolidated land use codes showing area in each census tract for a County Planning District. The summary is broken down by area in National Forests and area not in National Forests.

```
LAND USE BY CENSUS TRACT                    RIVERSIDE COUNTY

  MAP MODULE    21
  OVERLAY BOUNDARY              460.000


                POLYGON
  POLYGON       CENTROID,              -------- POLYGON AREA --------
  LAND USE      NORTH-EAST   POLYGON                SQUARE        SQUARE
   CODE         (THOUS FT)   NUMBER     ACRES       MILES       KILOMETERS

    A           533-2501       15        34.7        0.05         0.14
    A           532-2503       33        14.5        0.02         0.06
    A           533-2505       34         2.8        0.00         0.01
    A           526-2506      137        29.4        0.05         0.12
 SUBTOTAL FOR LAND USE A                 81.4        0.13         0.33

   AC           534-2502       30         0.9        0.00         0.00
   AC           533-2504       30        93.8        0.15         0.38
   AC           535-2503       30       225.9        0.35         0.91
   AC           532-2503       31         4.0        0.01         0.02
   AC           533-2508       45       280.9        0.44         1.14
   AC           535-2508       45       247.9        0.39         1.00
   AC           536-2510       46        32.2        0.05         0.13
   AC           523-2505      129       366.8        0.57         1.48
   AC           526-2507      142         0.0        0.00         0.00
   AC           527-2511      143         0.3        0.00         0.00
   AC           523-2510      145       286.1        0.45         1.16
   AC           524-2509      152         2.8        0.00         0.01
 SUBTOTAL FOR LAND USE AC              1541.5        2.41         6.24

   AX           533-2502       20         5.2        0.01         0.02
 SUBTOTAL FOR LAND USE AX                 5.2        0.01         0.02

   AZ           536-2503       25        22.0        0.03         0.09
 SUBTOTAL FOR LAND USE AZ                22.0        0.03         0.09

                                      -------     -------      -------
 TOTAL FOR LAND USE CATEGORY A         1650.0        2.58         6.67

    C           531-2502       14         1.6        0.00         0.01
    C           532-2503       32         1.7        0.00         0.01
 SUBTOTAL FOR LAND USE C                  3.3        0.01         0.01

                                      -------     -------      -------
 TOTAL FOR LAND USE CATEGORY C            3.3        0.01         0.01
```

FIGURE 1 LISTING OF LAND USE POLYGONS BY CENSUS TRACT,
BLYTHE, CALIFORNIA

Graphic Output

High quality computer produced land use maps are the
second basic output of the PIOS system. These final computer
maps are produced on stable base mylar utilizing the PIOS
plot software and a large flatbed plotter (see Figure 2).
Maps were produced to each of the modulated land use polygon
files. These maps were drawn to various scales and referenced
to the State Plane Coordinate System and the U.S.G.S. quad
sheets by a series of plotted tic marks.

Update and Maintenance

In order to enhance the future utility of the data,
PIOS includes an update and maintenance software component.
The "update" package was included with the recognition that
geographic information, particularly land use, is seldom
static or complete. This update component permits SCE to
insert land use data changes (as they are monitored) into
the final data tapes. Updated land use maps, as well as
statistical summaries may then be produced periodically to
update facility need estimates.

USE OF LAND USE DATA IN THE FORECASTING PROCESS

Forecasting the time and location of need for future
electric utility facilities requires estimates of future growth
in demand for electric power. These demands can be estimated by forecasting of land use and other demographic changes
by small areas. The demographic variables include: population; dwelling units; and employment. The first step taken
in this process is the development of land use and socio-
economic statistics and their relationships for a base year
(e.g., the time when the high altitude photography is taken).
A study is then completed by projecting population, dwelling
units, and employment and land use into the future for ten
and twenty year periods.

The land use data collection and automation efforts
described in the previous section of this paper provide two
significant products which support the forecasting effort.
They are: 1) land use area listings as summarized by sub-
areas; and 2) land use polygon maps. Each of these is
described below in the context of ways in which they are
specifically employed. Color land use maps are developed
from these computer produced polygon line maps. This involves
manual application of colored zipatone cut to the shape of
land use polygons on quad maps. Special features such as
SCE facilities, freeways, and major arterials are also

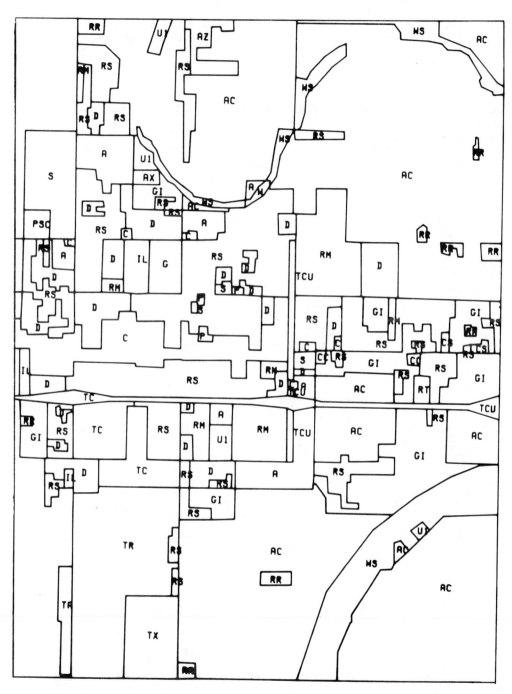

FIGURE 2 LAND USE PLOTTER MAP OF BLYTHE, CALIFORNIA

highlighted on the maps for purpose of orientation. These
color maps are used to produce working maps for the study
team, as well as final map graphics for the study report.[3]
The computer printouts of base year land use acreages by
census tract, sub-areas, and SCE service districts provide
land use for the base year. These are organized in tables
and presented in a study report along with copies of the
color-coded maps which show the location and masses of
base year land use.

However, the statistical land use data serves another
purpose and that is to permit the development of numerical
relationships between such socio-economic variables as population, dwelling units, and employment and the amount of land
in given uses by sub-area. A detailed description of how
socio-economic and land use projections are made in the land
use study is beyond the scope of this paper. The process can
be summarized, however, as follows. Projections of population,
dwelling units and employment are made for the entire study
area and for the sub-areas. Then, based on the relationships
developed between land use and socio-economic variables for
the base year, projections of socio-economic variables are
converted to projections of urbanized land uses to be added
to the land use inventory. The next step is to locate the
projected urbanized acreage added on the land use maps and
identify the projected land use transactions (i.e., how many
acres of vacant land and how many acres of agricultural land
are projected to become single family residential, etc.).
The color-coded working maps of the base year land use inventory
and the special polygon maps of developable land, together
with the computer printouts of data on developable land use
polygons, are used as visual and analytic aids in this part
of the forecasting methodology.

The forecast products of an SCE land use study are ten
and twenty-year projections of population, dwelling units, and
employment, and compatible projections of land use. Land use
projections are expressed both in terms of numerical projections
and maps of projected land use. Both of these land use projection forecasts are built from statistical printouts and
land use polygon maps developed from high altitude photography.

---

3. It is probable that on future efforts the zipatone process
    will be replaced with color computer maps produced on the
    DICOMED color processing unit. The software to perform
    color mapping for polygon files has recently been completed,
    and the preliminary results show considerable quality
    improvement at competitive costs. A pilot application
    of this process will be conducted on the land use study
    now in progress.

The quad scale land use maps provide the land use study
eam with a map base. The study team uses the maps to make
eographic allocations of land use based on their forecasts
or small areas. In this sense, the maps provide an immediate
omprehensible estimate of the remaining capacity for given
ypes of development when current land use is compared to an
rea's general plan and zoning designation. In other words,
he forecaster can see where vacant and agricultural land
re developable in the context of the current general plan
ind zoning constraints (which in California are mandated to be
consistent). In addition, these map comparisons help to understand and evaluate spatial conditions in land use where zoning
may not hold up to economic pressures for more productive
land uses.

JOINT COOPERATION IN DATA COLLECTION

When the feasibility of developing reasonably accurate
and up-to-date land use inventories was initially being examined
at SCE about four years ago, it became evident that land use
inventories were not generally being maintained by city and
county planning departments. In discussing this problem with
the various agencies involved, it became apparent that
there was a considerable interest in improving this situation
and that, if the opportunity was presented correctly, they
would be willing to jointly sponsor the development of new
inventories covering their jurisdictions.
    In response to this situation, SCE has, on four separate
occasions, taken a leadership role in proposing such joint
ventures. The consequence of them has been an expanded and
more comprehensive land use survey program. Four tasks are
typically required to make such a joint venture workable:

1.   Education of the local agency in the methodology of the
      project (e.g., photo interpretation, digitizing,
      computer cartography, overlay analysis, etc.).

2.   Specific discussion of ways in which the products
      of the land use project can be used successfully
      in an agency for ongoing planning studies.

3.   Working with the local agency in the development of
      a land use classification system that is appropriate
      to its needs.

4.   Agreeing to provide the cooperating agency with
      computer maps, data files, color maps, and most
      importantly, a working software system for general-
      ized geographic information handling.

FUTURE CONCEPTS FOR AN AUTOMATED LAND USE FORECASTING SYSTEM

The concepts for future land use analysis and forecasts at SCE, though not as yet translated into specific plans, center around development of a comprehensive land use/socio-economic information and forecasting system.

At this time a number of successful applications of automation have been instituted as part of the SCE land use program. There appears, however, to be a number of additional extensions that may have future benefit for making the forecasting methodology more efficient. These concepts are presented below in terms of general directions:

1. Expansion of land use data processing systems to enable interactive input, graphic and analytic capability. This would involve the development of a hardware capability to allow online updating of land use data polygons with projected land use and changes in land use.

2. Linked to the above system there could be a series of models for performing various functions. The most important of these would be a simple population-dwelling unit spatial allocation model which would permit machine allocation/updating of residential location projections, given updates in employment location, transportation characteristics, and other factors which affect residential choice locations. This model would also include an estimating system to update weighting factors indicating the relative influence of variables affecting residential location choices.

3. Based on these analysis models above, a system could be developed to convert land use forecasts directly into spatial electric load growth density forecasts. This system could, for example, indicate the peak load forecast for any arbitrarily defined service area. This would serve to test the adequacy of planned electrical facilities to service peak loads under simulations of planned and unplanned outages, for example. While a state, regional, or county system would probably not focus on this area per se (except for public utilities, perhaps), an analogous system can be envisioned for other services generally provided in the public domain.

4. Development of linkages between land use data and similar automated information associated with the environment (i.e., vegetation, slope, soils, geology, etc.).

5. Development of linkages with automated parcel information files. Opportunities exist for the establishment of such linkages: 1) an existing parcel coordinating digitizing effort within SCE, and 2) various parcel digitizing programs underway in local governments within the SCE service territory.

6. The final graphic output of the system is an area for possible improvement. The capability to produce computer generated colored land use maps printed directly from land use polygon data tapes has already been mentioned as an inexpensive capability that is technically feasible.

CONCLUSION

A land use information/forecasting system with capabilities such as those currently being used by SCE can serve as a guideline for the definition of comprehensive county, regional, or state land use information and planning systems. It should be noted that while some large cities are moving in this direction (e.g., Los Angeles with LUMIS (Land Use Management Information System) and other systems), land use information systems at the county, regional, and state levels have not come yet into a position of prominence. For its own purposes, SCE is developing a land use information system to support electric load growth forecasting, general facilities planning, and environmental impact studies. In the process, it is sharing land use data bases and data capture costs with county planning departments and providing land use data and forecasts to cities in its service territory as well as to regional jurisdictions on special projects.

REFERENCES

Eastern Division: Riverside County Land Use Study 1975-1995, Southern California Edison Company, February, 1976.

Crouch R. G. and Dangermond J. P., 1975, The Use of Remote Sensing Imagery and the PIOS System in Land Use Studies at the Southern California Edison Company, a paper presented at the Tenth International Symposium on Remote Sensing of Environment, October 1975.

Eastern Division: San Bernardino County Land Use Study, 1974-1995. Southern California Edison Company, April, 1975.

Southern Division and Orange County Land Use Study, 1973-1993. Southern California Edison Company, June, 1974.

Dangermond, J. P. 1972. A Classification and Review of Coordinate Identification and Computer Mapping Systems, a paper presented at the 1972 Urban and Regional Information Systems Association Conference.

David H. Lillie
Center for Applied Urban Research
Box 688 University of Nebraska
Omaha, Nebraska 68101

POPULATION ESTIMATION EMPLOYING LOW ALTITUDE PHOTOGRAPHY:
A CASE STUDY OF THE SOUTHWEST SUBAREA
OMAHA, NEBRASKA   1974-1976

ABSTRACT. The application of photogrammetry
as a valuable information system is but one, and
often overlooked facit of the myriad socioeconomic
data gathering processes.

This paper presents the need to identify and
monitor the physical arrangement of cultural
phenomena. A manual technique of interpretation
using sequential aerial photographs is described.
In addition, a change for the years 1974-1976 in
the number of households in Omaha's southwest subarea is detected. From these estimations a 1980
population projection is developed for this area.

INTRODUCTION

The development of aerial photography as a remote sensor can be
traced from the first known picture taken from a balloon over Paris in
the year 1858.[1] Since that time remote sensing and photographic interpretation have been greatly advanced by technology. Remote sensing
broadly defined is the study of objects from extended points in space.
Photographic interpretation as defined by the American Society of Photogrammetry is "The act of examining photographic images for the purpose
of identifying objects and judging their significance."[2] Such improvements have not only appeared in the form of interpretation techniques,
but also in the type of films employed. See footnote 3. Collectively,
their application can help solve many of the problems distressing today's
society. Each of these problems, whether it be population growth, urban
decay, substandard housing, transportation inefficiencies, pollution or
diminishing natural resources, has an interdependency to man's well-being
on this earth. But before any of man's problems may be solved, they must
be first recognized, second defined and third brought to the attention

1. Colwell, Robert N., Ed., "Development of Photographic Interpretation,"
    Manual of Photographic Interpretation (Massachusetts Avenue, N.W.
    Washington D.C.: American Society of Photogrammetry, 1960).
2. Olson, Charles E., Jr., "What is Photographic Interpretation?"
    The Surveillant Science Remote Sensing Of The Environment
    (Boston, Massachusetts: Houghton Mifflin Co., 1973), p. 95.
3. Several types of film employed are: panchromatic black and white,
    black and white infrared, color, color infrared-natural color,
    infrared-false color.

of the public. Thus, the application of photogrammetry as a valuable, public information system is but one, and often overlooked facit of the myriad socioeconomic data gathering processes. Consequently, with respect to this information system as a service to citizens, photogrammetry is of vital importance in discovering and defining the elements of urban spatial structure.

PHOTOGRAMMETRY AND SOCIAL INFORMATION SYSTEMS

Logically, the first questions to ask are: what is an information system? What is its purpose? An information system defined within the context of this paper is an arrangement of statistical data in a manner capable of supporting community decisions. Moreover, it has two purposes for improving decision making processes, viz, (1) to enlighten areas of past community programs and future public action; (2) to provide that vital link between an array of social and economic phenomena and their physical arrangement in an urban spatial structure.

The point of this second purpose is to suggest the need to focus upon a physical arrangement of cultural phenomena for a means of under-standing public issues and programs. Figure 1, "Spectrum of Human Interaction" contains many important elements of urban spatial structure. This figure of two intersecting circles shows the separation (right side) of those cultural characteristics capable of being monitored by photo-grammetry. They include the following elements: population densities, urbanized spatial pattern, housing number and quality, multiple dwelling units, deterioration, general land use inventory, vacant land, parcel identification, zoning pattern, open space, parks and recreation, Central Business District, shopping centers, neighborhood commercial districts, commercial ribbon developments, manufacturing, industrial parks, transportation routes, topography, vegetation, drainage and irri-gation patterns. However, it is the primary objective of this paper to specifically monitor the number of households between 1974 and 1976.

PURPOSE

An aerial photo-interpretation technique is presented in this paper whereby a physical arrangement of those cultural components by subarea may be identified and monitored. The primary objectives within this spectrum of human interaction are: (1) to detect a change between the years 1974 and 1976 in the number of households and the total number of persons in the southwest subarea of Omaha, Nebraska; (2) to develop a 1980 population projection for that same subarea.

Data collected by subarea will ultimately lead to a better under-standing of inter-city relationships. These may be subsequently compared to the subareas of other cities. The overall purpose, of course, is to improve the decision processes of public issues.

SPECIAL SAMPLING PROBLEMS

A first consideration in designing this study's objectives involved a decision of which of Omaha's subareas to use. For the purpose of clarification, Omaha is delineated into six subareas. Essentially, this is by the geographical location of Dodge Street, forming the north-south boundary and by the intersections of 42nd and 72nd Streets, constituting the east-west boundaries. See Figure 2. Although population changes within each of these subareas is of noteworthy significance to many agencies, planners and other individuals, the southwest subarea is chosen because of its recent population expansion. This area extends westward from 72nd Street to 168 Street and from the county line (Harrison Street) to West Dodge Road and Pacific Street.

Household estimates for this area as reported in the March issue, _Review of Applied Urban Research_, are shown below.[4]

TABLE 1

Omaha City Planning Department 1975	National Data Planning Corporation 1975	R.L. Polk Adjusted 1975	1970 Census
25,613	24,099	20,653	17,078

Furthermore, there is an intensifying concern over the westward population expansion in Omaha. In the same issue of the _Review_, Paul S. T. Lee, research associate, in his article, "Intra-Urban Migration and Omaha's Westward Expansion," states, "there remains a lack of information about the extent and speed of this outward expansion for the past several years and the socio-economic factors that might have caused it."[5]

This expansion and the numerous additional elements of urban spatial structure can be more efficiently monitored and measured through photogrammetry. See Figure 1 for an identification of these elements. However, in examining the elements of population change alone, there are several areas to be considered. They are (1) availability of imagery, (2) scale, (3) date flown, (4) sampling design, (5) sample size, (6) unbiased sampling techniques, (7) time and cost elements, (8) basis for checking results. A second area of considerations are found under the heading of interpretation precautions. They are (1) obscured detail, (2) office buildings, hotels and motels, (3) multistory dwellings, (4) group quarters, (5) manufacturing and warehousing.

METHODOLOGY

A manual technique is used for the accomplishment of this paper's objectives. This approach involves the use of sequential aerial photographs at a scale of 1:6000 and 1:12,000 for the years 1974 and 1976, respectively. The first stage in the sampling procedure consists of the development of a locationally stratified random sampling design. See Figure 3, "Sampling Design: Methodology For Southwest Subarea, A Locationally Stratified Random Section Sample." This stage is accomplished by subdividing the pre-selected area into 36, one-mile sections. Each section, then, is assigned in an East to West fashion (beginning with the NE top section) a number from a list of nonduplicated numbers, from a universe of 1-36 inclusively. These numbers are generated from a random numbers table. Refer to Figure 3. In a similar fashion, two sets of 9 numbers are generated from the random numbers table and subsequently identified by the corresponding section numbers on the sampling grid.

---

4. Todd, Ralph H., "Change in Family Income and Aggregate Income by Subarea, Omaha 1969-1975," _Review of Applied Urban Research_ (Omaha,
5. Ibid, p. 1.

The second stage concludes the sampling procedure. First, aerial photographs of the target area for each of the two time periods is covered with tracing paper. Second, the 9 randomly selected sections for each time period is outlined on the tracing paper.[6] Third, with the sampling design considerations and precautions in mind, a household unit enumeration for each time period is made. A total household unit estimation for the subarea as a whole is formulated for the years 1974 and 1976.[7] Finally, from these estimations, a 1980 population is projected for this subarea.

RESULTS

The results to this study's objectives are contained in Table 2.

TABLE 2

	1974	1976	1980
Households	29,462	33,307	39,968
Total Persons	89,859	101,586	121,903

Table 2 shows this continuing growth trend within the southwest subarea. The 1980 population estimation is projected by the following formula: $P_{b+n} = P_b + (q)P_b$, where P_b = base population, P_{b+n} = population n years following the base population, q = growth rate. A leveling-off effect of the growth rate is calculated as 1.5% per year.

CONCLUSION

Photogrammetry has been used for a great many different applications. A survey of current literature reveals its broad contribution to such areas as environmental analysis, land use identification, natural resource monitoring, mapping, charting, oceanography, agriculture and forestry. However, with respect to information systems in general, photogrammetry demonstrates its application in supporting community decisions. This study, furthermore, demonstrates its application of identifying and monitoring a physical arrangement of man's cultural urban elements. Moreover, this study should stand as an incentive to subsequent studies analyzing the numerous other component parts of man's urban spatial structure.

---

6. For the respective 1974 and 1976 imagery, these sections were randomly selected: 15, 09, 35, 20, 01, 29, 16, 12, 18; 34, 14, 05, 01, 31, 18, 16, 20, 23.

7. The calculating formula (from a 25% sample) is represented by: $\Sigma(\Sigma\bar{x}_r)(A/r)$, where $\bar{x}_r$ = row mean, A = total sample sections, r = total sample rows. For the 1976 calculation, row 4 had a zero mean, thus a mean of the row mean's summation was used.

Each household estimation for the years 1974, 1976 and 1980 was converted to total persons by a multiplying factor of 3.05. This represented the mean persons per household in the southwest subarea, according to 1970 Census, General Characteristics of the Population.

FIGURE 1

SPECTRUM OF HUMAN
INTERACTION

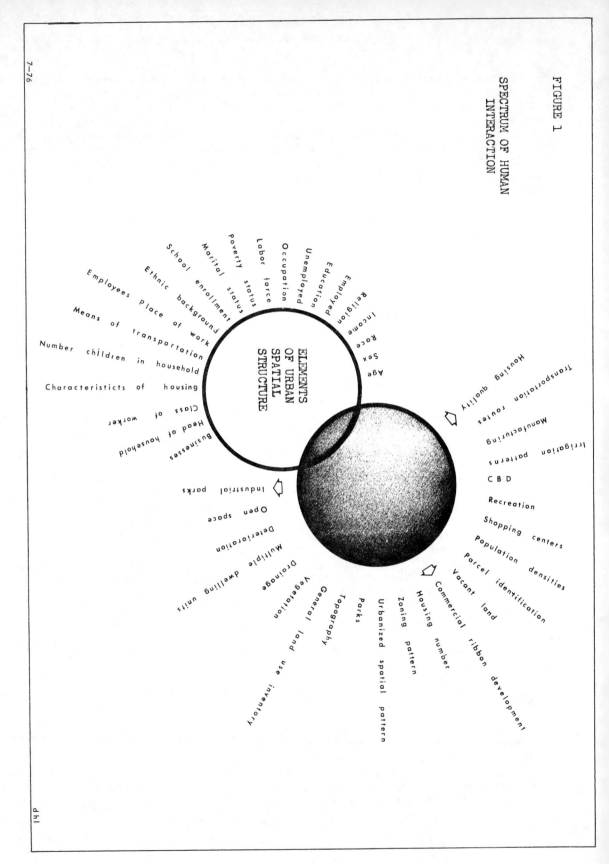

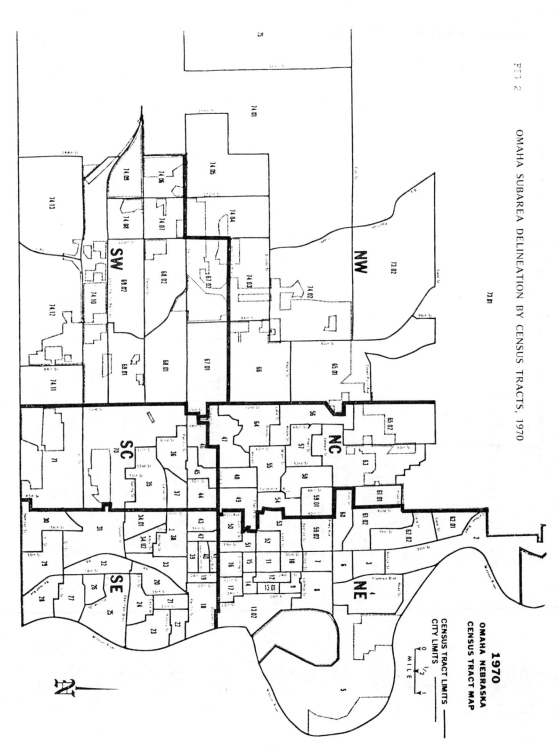

FIG 2   OMAHA SUBAREA DELINEATION BY CENSUS TRACTS, 1970

1970
OMAHA NEBRASKA
CENSUS TRACT MAP

CENSUS TRACT LIMITS ——
CITY LIMITS ——

0   ½   1
MILE

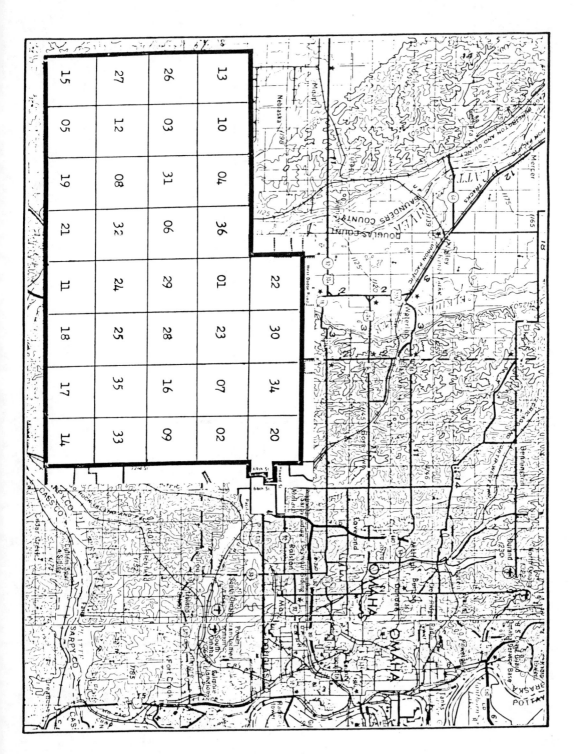

FIG. 3   SAMPLING DESIGN: METHODOLOGY FOR SOUTHWEST SUBAREA, A LOCATIONALLY
STRATIFIED RANDOM SECTION SAMPLE

William A. Howard
Director
Institute for Advanced Urban Studies
University of Colorado at Denver
Denver, Colorado 80202

   and

Charles F. Cortese
Assistant Professor
Department of Sociology
University of Denver
Denver, Colorado 80210

RESIDENTIAL ENVIRONMENTAL QUALITY ASSESSMENT
UTILIZING REMOTE SENSING TECHNIQUES:
AN EVALUATION OF METHODOLOGY

ABSTRACT: "Surrogates" or presumed socio-economic and physical indicators of the conditions of a population have been suggested rather forcefully by numerous authors as a way to extend the application of remote sensing techniques in urban areas. However, the soundness of the use of surrogates has not been fully evaluated. In this study, an attempt was made to ascertain the validity and the reliability of information derived from color infrared imagery using surrogates about residential areas in Denver, Colorado.

INTRODUCTION

As might be expected, the identification of objects represents the fundamental building block of making good use of remote sensing technology. Locating features, developing classification schemes to describe the features, and developing basic statistical assemblies are the main activities in this particular stage of study. Such efforts are necessary as a preparation for analysis.

The analysis phase of remote sensing applications, especially in urban areas, is concerned with the combinations of inventoried data pertinent to urban settings. From these data sets one illuminates the operations of inventory and analysis by using the findings for prescriptive instruments through the process of plan development.

In attempting to advance the scope of remote sensing technology and its applications from essentially physical applications to more socio-economic areas, the development of "surrogates" or presumed indicators of a population have been forcefully argued. (Green and Monier, 1955, Wellar, 1968, and Joyce, 1973). However, the soundness of the use of surrogates has not been fully substantiated. In this study, an attempt was made to evaluate the usefulness of remote sensing techniques as an information acquisition system specifically as regards residential environmental quality in an urban setting.

THE SETTING OF THE STUDY

The City and County of Denver, Colorado, was the setting of the study. There were a number of important reasons why Denver was selected. (1) Color infrared imagery at an appropriate scale was available on the entire City and County. In fact, sequential coverage was available providing the possibilities for comparison. (2) The Denver Planning Office has developed a data base on the city based essentially on the 1970 Census materials plus certain other data deriving from accessible records, most importantly, the assessors records. Access to these data was made available to the authors. (3) The City and County of Denver has one of the longer histories among Western American urban areas in terms of neighborhood planning. The City identified and delineated neighborhood planning units in 1958. These form spatial units and since one of the analytical requirements of this study was to treat the data spatially, such organization of the city, as well as the organization of the data in the Denver Planning Office's data base along spatial lines, made the analysis of the data more efficient. And, (4), the City and County of Denver has an active neighborhood planning program where environmental quality is one of the more important concerns. Reliable and current information is required if the neighborhood policies are to be effective.

Particular objectives of the neighborhood planning program, which related especially to this study are outlined below:

1. Attack the problem of deterioration and blight in terms of the physical conditions of neighborhoods and bring them to a sound physical condition.

2. Develop long-range neighborhood plans that will update, modify, and revise the Comprehensive Plan for Denver, and which will guide the growth and development of the respective neighborhoods.

3. Identify current physical problems of a manageable scale so that short-range planning may result in desired solutions.

4. Translate neighborhood needs into governmental programs directed toward meeting perceived needs.

5. Develop a high degree of dialogue, cooperation, and coordination between existing neighborhoods, the Denver Planning Office, and other city agencies.

6. Improve the social conditions of the neighborhood residents through physical planning methods and by assisting social agencies in the areas of education, employment, welfare, health and civil rights.

NATURE OF IMAGERY USED IN STUDY

In this study, Kodak Aerochrome Infrared 2443 imagery at a scale of 1:6,000 served as the primary data source. This imagery was originally part of a large scale effort in the metropolitan area of Denver to set up a management system utilizing remote sensing techniques to monitor the spread of the Dutch Elm Disease. To make it possible to make environmental quality assessments of conditions around individual houses or assemblages of dwellings, large scale imagery was essential. Either scales of 1:5,000 or 1:6,000 would have proven suitable. Anything smaller than 1:6,000 would have not permitted discrimination of individual trees or landscape objects. Certainly it is possible to extract a wide variety of information from CIR imagery at such large scales.

PROCEDURES FOR IMAGERY INTERPRETATION

The use of remote sensing has been, generally speaking, primarily associated with military reconnaissance and for the most part been concerned with object identification. In this study, concern was less on object identification and more on ascertaining general environmental conditions found from one part of a city to another. Such a focus required a different approach for acquiring information. "Surrogates" or presumed indicators of social and economic conditions of a population were used in the extraction of the data. The utilization of such surrogates and the information they presumably represented required a strong degree of judgment as to differences in value. Specific surrogates used in the study are shown in TABLE I.

TABLE I
Surrogates Used In Study

Vegetation
  1. Grass
  2. Trees and Landscaping
  3. Street trees
Litter
  4. Trash and junk
Vacant Lots
  5. Number of vacant lots
  6. Maintenance
Cemented Areas
  7. Sidewalks
  8. Curbs
  9. Street Maintenance
  10. Street width
Alley Conditions
  11. Pavement
  12. Litter
  13. Width

(Table I, cont'd)

       Residential Conditions
       14. Dwelling type
       15. Lot size
       16. House size

    To facilitate the imagery, interpretation necessitated the adoption of some kind of spatial unit. A spatial unit provides a starting or reference point for data extraction as opposed to a situation where the city has no form or character. Furthermore, sub-units provide convenient units for tabulation and analysis of data relating to portions of the urban mosaic.

    Four-block interpretation units were adopted for the study. It was determined that four city blocks represented an easy unit for the interpreter to manage. Beginning and ending points could be remembered easily, and the interpreter also could keep condition changes fairly well in mind as he or she moved across the imagery covering a unit and evaluating its environment. Ultimately, conditions by four-block units were composited to the census tract level. Thus, for analysis purposes in the study, the census tract becomes the primary unit.

DEVELOPMENT OF AN EVALUATION
SCORING PROCEDURE

    As a means of assessing changes in environmental conditions and putting the extracted data in a form suitable for quantitative analysis, it was necessary to adopt a rating or scoring procedure. In developing such an evaluation scheme, emphasis was put on adopting a scheme which could possibly be used at the operational level in a planning agency with a city. A three-point scoring scheme was adopted. Imagery, which contains thousands of bits of information, presents real difficulties for an interpreter in trying to differentiate a great number of values. To make the interpretor's task easier, a scoring scheme ranging from excellent environmental conditions through good to fair and ending with poor conditions was adopted. On the scale developed, the number 3 signified a high quality condition, which might be characterized as possessing well-maintained vegetation, little or no litter, few vacant parcels of land, and good street maintenance. An intermediate environmental condition represented by a score of 2 could be described as having well-maintained environmental conditions. But some problems are beginning to appear, e.g., overall quality is not the highest; vegetation is present but not luxuriant; few commercial structures are present within the territorial areas of neighborhoods; and streets, sidewalks, and curbs are present but require a minimum of maintenance. Finally, the poorest condition indicated by the score of 1 reflected a deteriorating to fully blighted environmental area. In other words, it possessed poorly maintained facilities, vacant lots, litter, dirty industries, and poorly maintained vegetation.

    The entire City and County of Denver was covered in the interpretation of the imagery. Each interpreter was equipped with a set of identifiable characteristics or "signatures" on each of the surrogates. Scoring sheets were used for each four-block interpretation unit.

DATA VALIDITY MEASUREMENT

Aerial sensing has been widely acclaimed as a potential method for acquiring timely and authoritative information about environments because it offers such advantages as flexibility of scheduling flights and rapidity of coverage, plus the fact that the data contained on imagery represent real time, i.e., it is current. Also, technological advances such as better cameras, programmed photographic scanners, and efficient and high-capacity data storage and retrieval systems combined with aerial photographs and signatures of accepted identificatory character suggest an almost unlimited source of information about environments (Wellar, 1967).

While the use of aerial sensing has been touted as a means of acquiring much information about urban environments, the "truthfulness" of the data collected has gone woefully unassessed. Through a variety of communications with people working in the area of remote sensing, the authors found that the usual tests of validity and reliability customary in social science seemed definitely lacking. Therefore, our study took as its primary focus this necessary requirement of testing for reliability and validity. Out process involved establishing or <u>measuring</u> the "truthfulness" of the data on three levels:

1. Are remotely-sensed data on environmental quality <u>reliable</u>, i.e., if a color infrared image of a particular areal unit is interpreted and thereby coded as showing poor environmental quality at one point in time or by one interpreter, will the same image be interpreted and scored as showing poor conditions at another point time or by another coder?

2. Are remotely-sensed data on environmental quality <u>valid</u>, i.e., is the remote sensing method measuring what <u>it is</u> supposed to measure? How sure can we be that we are actually measuring environmental quality and not something else?

3. Are remotely-sensed data on environmental quality useful as "surrogates" or alternative indicators of the other measures of environmental quality they are supposed to replace? Of course, the data must first be <u>reliable</u> and <u>valid</u> before they can be accurate surrogates.

IMAGERY CODER RELIABILITY MEASUREMENT

The reliability of quantitative remote sensing data is generally determined by measurement, with reliability becoming a function of accuracy.. Remotely-sensed data of a qualitative nature presents a different type of problem as regards reliabiltiy, i.e., judgment of the interpreter. Therefore, the problem which this section addresses concerns the reliability of qualitative remote sensing data: How reliable are such data when obtained from imagery interpretation?

In this study, a number of differing indicators were used which purport to show the "environmental quality" of urban residential areas. The quantitative characteristics of certain of these indicators are not difficult to obtain with a high degree of reliability. For example, determining the number of houses in a specified spatial unit merely involves the counting of the units and any error injected into the process results solely from inaccuracies in counting. However, the related indicator "lot size" introduces an entirely different problem of inter-pretation where reliability is concerned, namely that of judgment as to the probably dimensions of the lot.

While interpretation keys may be supplied the interpreter-coder, invariably he or she is faced with making judgments during the inter-pretation. By way of illustration, the key Lot Size was classified in this study into three categories -- small, average, large -- requiring judgment on numerous occasions. Rectangular or square lots in many areas of American cities may be easily categorized. But to which cate-gory are odd shaped lots assigned? In general, it involves the judgment of the individual interpreter and any error resulting form the use of judgment may be compounded with the use of more than one interpreter. Actual lot dimensions representative of the subject city can be developed for interpretation keys, however those permit little specificity as to conditions in particular locations unless one actually measures the dimensions of lots which in newer sections of cities where front lawns, and occasionally back ones merge one into the other. No "territorial" references are available.

For data derived by remote sensing techniques to be useful it should be possible to reduce reliability related to errors to the point of being at least statistically acceptable. When only one interpreter is coding data which requires qualitative judgment, reliability of interpretation may be assured through the test-retest method. This method requires the interpretation of the same set of imagery on two different occasions by the same interpreter. The result may then be statistically evaluated to determine whether or not the interpretation is consistent and reliable.

Qualitative interpretation involving two or more persons may be examined for reliability using the method of inter-coder reliability. It is possible by using this procedure to determine the amount of agree-ment between several interpreters. It is also possible that error in reliability can be reduced to the point where it is statistically accept-able when used in conjunction with the test-retest method.

Inter-Coder Reliability

The evaluation of inter-coder reliability involved the use of per-sons with no previous experience with remote sensing techniques. Through-out the research design of the study a deliberate effort was made to couch the study in potential city agency user terms, and the authors thought the probability low that such a city agency as the Denver Planning Office would have on its staff highly trained and experienced "expert" remote sensing interpreters for acquiring data. Therefore, this aspect of the evaluation of inter-coder reliability involved the use of persons with no previous experience with remote sensing techniques. Four individuals (graduate students) were given an orientation as to what the general study was about. A series of training sessions followed involving instructions in basic imagery interpretation as well as an explanation of the type of imagery used in the study. The signature characteristics of each of the surrogates were reviewed for each individual.

Two sets of imagery were selected for interpretation by the trainees. The first set consisted of selected areas from three census tracts. Each tract exhibited differing environmental characteristics as determined by criteria set by the study. Within each tract, six four-block aggregates were delineated for interpretation giving a total of 24 sample units. The second set of imagery consisted of the same 24 frames used by the experienced staff interpreters in their reliability tests. This provided the opportunity for comparison between the trainees and the experienced interpreters.

As much control as was feasible was placed on the actual interpretation by the trainees. Two light tables were set up isolated from each other. Two trainees could interpret simultaneously with no discussion between them. Furthermore, no help has afforded any individual nor were questions related to interpretation answered so that all of the trainees had to rely or make decisions solely on the basis of the surrogate signatures provided to them. Once scores were recorded on the coding sheets they were then statistically analyzed to determine the amount of agreement between the trainees.

Reliability Measurement Findings

There are a number of statistical techniques available for measuring reliability. The technique used in this study was developed by W.S. Robinson and provides a means for measuring "the agreement (rather than the correlation) between two or more variables" (Robinson, 1957). With this method, perfect agreement (A value of 1.00) is achieved when the paired scores are identical. Table II provides Robinson's measurement of Agreement (A) as well as the Pearson Product Moment Correlation Coefficient (r) for the four coders on each of the sixteen surrogates.

The results in Table II indicate that the degree of reliability is statistically unacceptable on each of the variables. Using a conventional "rule-of-thumb" of a score on Robinson's measure of Agreement (a) of .90 or higher and a standard of a correlation (r) of .80 or higher (explaining at least 64% of the variance), we find that some of the variables approach an acceptable level of reliability. Therefore, it was determined that the "truthfulness" of data acquired in this way, at least by inexperienced and minimally trained interpreters, is sufficiently in doubt that further analysis of such data is meaningless.

The actual remotely-sensed data covering the entire City and County of Denver, however, were not acquired by such inexperienced interpreters but were developed by experienced and relatively well-trained professional planner-geographers. The "expert" interpreters were given a different set of 24 frames as a test of the degree of reliability between them. Essentially the same controls were placed upon this experiment as were used with the four inexperienced coders. Table III provides the results of this test of inter-coder reliability.

TABLE II

INTER-CODER RELIABILITY TEST WITH PREVIOUSLY INEXPERIENCED INTERPRETERS

	A=	r=
Grass	.640	.521
Trees, Landscaping	.462	.283
Street Trees	.671	.561
Litter	.547	.397
No. of Vacant Lots	.438	.250
Maintenance	.586	.448
Sidewalks	.539	.386
Curbs	.419	.226
Street Maintenance	.290	.053
Street Width	.438	.251
Alley Pavement	.630	.507
Alley Litter	.308	.077
Alley Width	.218	-.042
Dwelling Type	.473	.298
Lot Size	.647	.530
House Size	.287	.050

TABLE III

INTER-CODER RELIABILITY TEST WITH EXPERIENCED STAFF INTERPRETERS

Variable	Agreement
Grass	.750
Trees, Landscaping	.775
Street Trees	.571
Litter	.620
No. of Vacant Lots	.847
Maintenance	.385
Sidewalks	.863
Curbs	.846
Street Maintenance	.682
Street Width	.264
Alley Pavement	.798
Alley Litter	.510
Alley Width	.404
Dwelling Type	.944
Lot Size	.928
House Size	.700

The results in Table III demonstrate that the agreement between the experienced staff coders was considerably higher than that for the inexperienced coders. Nevertheless, only on two variables ("house type" and "lot size") does the reliability between the two staff interpreters reach a statistically acceptable level. On two other variables ("maintenance" and "street width"), the agreement between the "expert" interpreters is lower than that between the four inexperienced coders. As a whole, the reliability test between the two staff interpreters indicates insufficient reason to doubt the "truthfulness" and reliability of such data.

Reliability Over Time: Test-Retest

To measure the extent to which a given coder interprets the same imagery in the same way at two or more points in time, the experienced interpreters were required to re-code the same twenty-four sample units two weeks following the initial effort. The results of this "test-retest" reliability check are presented in Table IV.

TABLE IV

TEST-RETEST RELIABILITY WITH EXPERIENCED STAFF CODERS

Variable	Coder # 1		Coder # 2	
	A=	r=	A=	r=
Grass	.933	.865	.880	.760
Trees, Landscaping	.820	.641	.967	.933
Street Trees	.842	.684	.956	.913
Litter	.821	.642	.979	.957
No. of Vacant Lots	.914	.827	1.000	1.000
Maintenance	.750	.500	*	*
Sidewalks	.857	.714	.914	.828
Curbs	.890	.781	.979	.958
Street Maintenance	.898	.797	.743	.486
Street Width	.884	.768	*	*
Alley Pavement	.850	.699	.795	.590
Alley Litter	.750	.500	.953	.906
Alley Width	.636	.273	.904	.809
Dwelling Type	.882	.765	.847	.693
Lot Size	.911	.821	.976	.952
House Size	.642	.283	.937	.874

*Interpreter did not code a sufficient number of units to allow for statistical comparison.

Coder # 1 exhibits acceptable reliability of interpretation over time on only three of the sixteen variables. Coder # 2, however, was within the range of acceptable reliability on ten of the sixteen variables. While both of the staff coders were experienced in imagery interpretation, Coder # 2 had considerably more experience than Coder # 1. This probably accounts for the greater reliability of Coder # 2. Nevertheless, there was still a considerable amount of variation in the way that Coder # 2 interpreted at least four images at two different times. These were the variables of "condition of grass", "street maintenance," "alley pavement," and "dwelling type."

The conclusion could tentatively be offered regarding the reliability of imagery interpretation that over time such efforts will generally fall within acceptable limits given a certain and rather high level of experience in remote sensing imagery interpretation. An individual, through a great deal of experience and training, might develop a high degree of consistency in his or her interpretation. A computer ultimately may be programmed to interpret imagery with even a higher level of reliability. While either of these approaches could arrive at a point where we could be relatively assured of the same thing in the same way time after time, the question would still remain as to whether we were measuring what we wanted to measure, i.e., environmental quality.

DETERMINING VALIDITY OF REMOTE SENSING MEASURES

The method of validating the measures of environmental quality derived from the interpretation of aerial imagery was to test the degree of correspondence between the environmental quality scores given to areal units by the imagery interpreters with environment quality scores for the same areal units taken from independent sources.

The outside source selected for this test was the Denver Planning Office's rankings of neighborhood "conditions" as of 1970 (Denver Planning Office, 1972). In this report, neighborhoods were scored by rank according to an index of "overall condition", which included such measures as housing lacking plumbing; age of housing; housing rent; housing value; housing with over-crowding; accessibility; voter registration; education level; crime rate; infectious disease rate; unemployment; median family income; family welfare; child welfare; and old age assistance.

A Pearson Zero order correlation was performed between the average (mean) score of the sixteen imagery surrogates for each areal unit and rank score of "overall condition" assigned for that unit by the Denver Planning Office. This test yielded a correlation coefficient (r) of 0.375 and an $r^2 = 0.14$. Clearly, such a low correlation does not validate the use of remotely sensed data to measure environmental quality. The correlations between the outside measures of environmental quality and each of the sixteen imagery surrogates are provided in Table V.

While all coefficients in Table V are in the proper direction (indicated by negative sign), several are quite low (-.02, -.10, -.11) and even the highest coefficients obtained (-.53, -.52, -.51) indicate very little correspondence between the two methods of measuring environmental quality.

TABLE V

CORRELATION OF AERIAL VARIABLES WITH OUTSIDE MEASURE
OF ENVIRONMENTAL QUALITY

Aerial Variable	Correlation
Grass	-.516
Trees	-.386
Street Trees	-.364
Litter	-.414
No. Vacant Lots	-.332
Maintenance Vacant Lots	-.393
Sidewalks	-.449
Curbs	-.466
Street Maintenance	-.379
Street Width	-.348
Alley Pavement	-.024
Alley Litter	-.118
Alley Width	-.105
Dwelling Type	-.252
Lot Size	-.522
House Size	-.537

There are several reasons for this lack of correlation. One is that rather than the two measures being different operational definitions of the same concept (i.e., environmental quality), there were actually two different conceptual definitions at work. That is, if the respective researchers meant different things by the terms environmental quality or "condition," then one would expect to find a low correlation.

This, however, is not likely. The text of the Denver Planning Office report indicates that the author's concept of "condition" dealt primarily with "patterns of blight and deterioration" and such a definition is in large agreement with the author's conceptualization of "environmental quality" as attempted to measure through remote sensing techniques.

While it is entirely possible that the Denver Planning Office scores do not adequately reflect the actual environmental conditions of the areal units, the authors must conclude that no evidence has resulted from this test to validate our measures. To be on the safe side, we must interpret these findings as at least tentative evidence that such use of presently available remote sensing techniques to measure environmental quality in residential areas of cities is inappropriate.

The author's final concern in the study was whether the data "were useful as 'surrogates' or alternative indicators of the other measures of environmental quality which they supposedly reflected or replaced."

It is obvious that it should first be established that such data are reliable and valid before they can be considered accurate surrogates. Since such reliability and validity were not indicated by the procedures employed in this study, further investigations in relation to surrogates as indicators of environmental quality proved unwarranted.

CONCLUSIONS

Out of this study emerges a singular important point. Before remote sensing can serve as an important means of acquiring data for quality determinations about residential areas of cities, much more evaluation is needed. While this observation could be taken as a researcher's lament for taking such study further before a final judgement relating to conclusions is given, it has been clearly established as a result of this study that there are some fundamental problem areas that must be addressed before a method can be developed that carries with it operational usefulness.

The principle findings from this study relate to validity and reliability of the data extracted from remote sensing imagery. In the hands of reasonably proficient interpreters, a relatively high level of reliability and validity is possible. However, the same task put in the hands of uninitiated individuals proves hopelessly wanting. Inconsistencies and lack of agreement in interpretation can easily occur with trained interpreters. High validity is a function not only of skills in interpretation, but also in the knowledge of the subject inquiry. High levels of agreement among differing interpretors require consistent clarity of appropriate guidelines and signatures for interpretation.

In both instances, reliability and validity are areas within the remote sensing community that have gone unexamined. Among the many workers queried as a result of this study, there was little recognition of the procedural difficulties that these two areas present. One suspects that there is an underlying concern regarding these problem areas because one quite frequently hears the expression used by researchers in the remote sensing community that "interpretation is still more art than science."

At the risk of appearing too negative as a result of this study, the authors would like to point out that the logic of the procedures utilized in the study are intuitively sound in their opinion. And, suggestions can be offered to where the results could be much improved and quite possibly elevated in terms of soundness of findings to where they could have partial, if not complete, operational importance.

Within the research design, the imagery used was at a single scale and of a single variety. For many of the surrogates employed, differing scales would have made interpretation more valid. A good illustration in this regard relates to occurrence of trash. At a scale of 1:6,000, it is extremely difficult to ascertain whether what is thought to be trash is in fact just that. A larger scale would have aided in assuring that trash was indeed present. Furthermore, for some of the surrogates, possibly an entirely different sensor altogether would have proven more appropriate to interpretation. As a case in point, alley conditions could have probably been much better established as to surface materials through the use of a thermal scanner, where a definite signature of concrete or gravel or dirt could have been more easily isolated.

Another area where the validity of the data could have been improved is through the use of sequential imagery where seasonal effects, such as differences in colors, could have served as interpretation keys. A particular slice in time yields little information about the dynamic characteristics of an environment. For certain surrogates, winter may be a more appropriate time for looking for a particular feature, such as trash accumulated below trees, whereas summer is a more appropriate period for evaluating vegation and its condition. Only through sequential imagery can seasonal effects be accounted for.

In the final analysis, it is highly possible that with an appropriate assessment of seasons, much higher validity levels could be brought about assuming the use of a single interpreter. However, in the area of reliability, much work is required where more than one interpretor is used. Within the context of this study, appropriate measures have been identified for measuring reliability of interpretation among interpreters. The needed improvement of this area of investigation is the outstanding recommendation which emerges from this study.

SOURCES

Green, Norman E. and Robert B. Monier, Reliability and Validity of Air Reconnaissance as a Collector Method for Urban Demographic and Sociological Information, Technical Report No. 11, Air University Human Resources Research Institute, Maxwell A.F.B., Alabama, 1955.

Joyce, Robert E., "A Practical Method for the Collection and Analysis of Housing and Urban Environment Data: An Application of Color Infrared Photography" in Aerial Photography as a Planning Tool, Eastman Kodak Co., 1974, pp. 15-20.

Wellar, Barry S., Generation of Housing Quality Data from Multiband Aerial Photographs, Contract 14-08-001-10654, Geographic Applications Program, U.S. Geological Survey, Evanston, Ill. (Department of Geography, Northwestern University), April 1967.

Robinson, W.S., "The Statistical Measure of Agreement," American Sociological Review, Vol. 22, 1957, pp. 17-25

Community Renewal Program, Denver: Condition of the City, City and County of Denver Planning Office, March, 1973.

J. R. Wilson, C. Blackmon
Atlanta Regional Commission
100 Peachtree Street, N.W.
Atlanta, Georgia 30303

G.W. Spann
Metrics, Inc.
290 Interstate North
Atlanta, Georgia 30339

LAND USE CHANGE DETECTION
FROM COMPUTER PROCESSED LANDSAT DATA

ABSTRACT. The Atlanta Regional Commission and the
EROS Data Center participated in a demonstration of the use of
computer processed Landsat data to detect land use change in
the Atlanta Region. Using the GE Image 100 system, temporal
overlays were made by combining Landsat Band-5 data from
October 1972 and 1974. The data were ratioed, dividing 1972
data by 1974. Areas where land use changed have low ratio
values. These areas were assigned to a land use change
theme. A classification based on the use of the four bands of
the 1974 multispectral scanner data yielded six land use categories: commercial/industrial/apartment, single-family
residential, cleared land, open space, forested land, and
water. The 1974 land use categories and the change theme
were then combined to determine types of changes between
1972 and 1974.

INTRODUCTION

The U.S. Geological Survey (USGS) in cooperation with the Georgia
Department of Natural Resources (DNR) has completed a 1° x $1\frac{1}{2}^{\circ}$ Atlanta
topographic quadrangle map at a scale of 1:100,000. The map covers the
same area as 96 seven and one-half minute USGS topographic quadrangles
and includes the seven counties in the Atlanta Region. As part of an extensive program of derivative map products at this scale, USGS/Geography
Program is preparing a land use overlay for the Greater Atlanta Region
quadrangle. The map will present land use and land cover at levels I and
II of a land use classification system proposed by USGS for use with remote
sensing data.[1]

The DNR-sponsored land use map will not meet precisely the criteria of the Atlanta Regional Commission (ARC) for a development patterns map. However, USGS/Geography Program has agreed to prepare additional overlays showing the following level III land uses: (1) high density residential areas from USGS photointerpretation, (2) institutions, and (3) parks and other developed open spaces from maps prepared by ARC. After slight modifications by ARC, these overlays will be used by ARC to print a development patterns map of the seven-county Atlanta Region which will be distributed to serve multiple planning purposes where land use/land cover data are important inputs.

PURPOSE, SCOPE, OBJECTIVES

The ARC comprehensive regional planning process requires that the initial development patterns map be updated at frequent intervals, if possible on an annual basis. Automatic processing of Landsat (formerly ERTS) data is the most promising alternative for updating the 1974 map annually (or even more frequently), as these data provide the only systematic imagery readily available to ARC on a continuing basis. Cloudfree Landsat imagery is available for the Atlanta Region about once every three months. In contrast, aerial photography (low, medium, or high altitude) of the entire region is not available on a regular basis, and it would be quite expensive for ARC to contract with an aerial survey firm for regular photographic coverage of the region.

In November 1974, the ARC Data Center staff visited the Kennedy Space Center to use the General Electric Image 100 system to test the feasibility of automatic interpretation of land use data from Landsat computer compatible tapes (CCT's) and NASA high-altitude aerial photography. The Image 100 was selected as the most appropriate system for completing the tests in the limited time available. A complete report of the test is included in an ARC staff paper.[2] Results of the test were not sufficient for use as direct input to a current map of urban land use. However, the results indicated that automated processing of Landsat data would be a promising method for monitoring changes in land use.

Further tests on the Image 100 were conducted to determine the best techniques for detecting changes in urban land use. For this purpose, ARC and the Applications Assistance Branch of the EROS Data Center (EDC) entered into a joint demonstration test of advanced urban land use change detection techniques.

The study covered the majority of the seven-county ARC planning area, and included an area of approximately 5,180 square kilometers divided into six 29.3 x 29.3 kilometer subscenes at a cathode ray tube (CRT) scale of 1:100,000. In preparation for the tests, ARC obtained Landsat computer compatible tapes from October 1972 and October 1974, and EDC personnel prepared the appropriate Image 100 video files.

METHODOLOGY

Change detection has as its objective the detection of changes in land use that have occurred during a specified time interval. Change detection using Landsat data is essentially a process of comparing data from two different dates on a pixel by pixel basis. (A pixel is one Landsat picture element, an area on the ground which measures approximately 57 by 79 meters, or .45 hectares.)

At least three methods may be used to detect changes in land use by processing Landsat data on the Image 100. All three techniques rely on the same basic premise--that different types of land use reflect energy differently in one or more of the four Landsat bands. The technique for implementing each, however, is somewhat different. Three methods of change detection are: (1) ratioing, (2) classification and comparison of different dates, and (3) split screen classification.[3] Each of these types of change detection is described briefly in the following paragraphs. Also included is an evaluation of the strengths and weaknesses of each technique in light of the limitations of the Image 100 analysis system.

Ratioing is the simplest and quickest method of change detection on the Image 100. However, ratioing will not identify the types of changes. The intensity of reflected electromagnetic radiation (EMR) in one band of one Landsat scene is divided by the intensity of reflected EMR in the same band of a different Landsat scene on a pixel by pixel basis. In all areas where the reflected EMR is approximately the same in each scene (i.e., the same type of land cover in each scene), the result of the division is nearly 1. In other areas of the scene--where land cover changes from one scene to the next--the result of the division is significantly different from 1. By a procedure similar to density slicing, the latter areas are separated from other areas, assigned a theme color, and displayed over the background imagery. The theme represents areas of change from one Landsat scene to the next.

Classification and comparison of two different dates requires that training and 4-dimensional classification of land use/cover types be performed twice, using Landsat data of different dates. The results from the two efforts are compared to provide detection and identification of types of land use changes. The quality of the change detection results, however, are highly dependent on the classification results which are, in turn, often subject to considerable error.

Split screen classification involves the simultaneous side-by-side display on the CRT monitor of the same geographic area from two different scenes. The two displays are then classified as though they were part of the same scene. Split screen classification is the most time consuming of the three methods because it requires visual analysis to detect changes and because smaller, and thus more, subscenes must be analyzed. Again, the quality of the change detection results are dependent upon the accuracy level of the classification.

Ratioing was selected to be tested first because it is the simplest and quickest method and because detection of land use changes is not dependent upon an accurate classification of land use types. During the tests of ratioing, it became evident that the change detection results were good. Based upon the ground truth information available at the time of analysis, all major changes were detected when using the ratio of the band 5 data.

Ratioing was tested using each of the four bands of data. Ratioing of the two infrared bands--6 and 7--did not detect areas of significant land use change. Because band 4 and band 5 data were contained in separate video files and time was a major constraint during the tests, it was arbitrarily decided to use only the band 5 data for remaining subscenes.

After ratioing band 5 data for the entire study area, the 1974 Landsat data were classified into six types of land use. This classification was then compared with the land use change areas in order to determine the types of changes which had occurred from 1972 to 1974. This procedure gives similar information as the classification/comparison methodology, but requires considerably less time. Moreover, the quality of the change detection results is not dependent upon an accurate classification of land use types.

CHANGE DETECTION PROCEDURES

Video files with band 5, 1972 overlayed with band 5, 1974 data were used for the ratio processing. After ratioing band 5, 1972 divided by band 5, 1974 data, a histogram of the band 5 ratio was displayed on the Tektronix terminal. The histogram of the ratioed data is bellshaped (Gaussian) with a large number of points in the center and a lesser number of data points at the extremes. The problem of analyzing ratioed data centered on determining what portion of the area represented by the histogram indicated changes in land use.

For the purpose of detecting change, the data represented by the upper and lower portions of the histograms were examined. By successively eliminating data (working from the center toward the lower bound) we were able to determine those areas which represented change for the lower portion of the histogram. When satisfactory data were obtained, they were saved on a theme. The determination of satisfactory change detection was made by visually observing the results as displayed over the background and over the ratioed data and by comparison of the ratioed data with available ground truth information.

The data represented by the upper portion of the histogram were then examined. However, these data seemed to reflect bad data lines or points, changes in water quality, or perhaps slight misregistrations along linear features rather than changes in land use. Thus it was decided that all urban change of interest was contained in the land areas represented by the lower portion of the histogram of ratioed data. These areas were stored on a theme track. The ratio theme and raw data were stored on tape for later comparison with the classification results.

Instead of classifying both 1972 and 1974 Landsat scenes and then comparing the two resulting thematic maps to determine changes in land use, only the 1974 scene was classified. The categories decided upon were: single-family residential, open space, cleared land, forest, water, and commercial/industrial/apartment. These categories were determined on the basis of past experience, trial classification at EDC, and analysis of these results.

After classification of the 1974 subscenes into the above categories, the area of intersection of each theme (i.e., each land use category) with the areas of change in that subscene was determined. During the ratioing tests all areas of "change" were established and stored for future use. The area classified "residential", for example, was then compared with the area classified as "change". The areas which were classified as both "residential" and "change" represented new residential construction which had occurred since 1972. This area of overlap was then assigned a theme color and stored for future use.

By following the above steps for other categories of land use, such as commercial, cleared land, etc., it was possible to locate the areas of change by the type of final land use. This in turn should theoretically enable ARC to update the 1974 development patterns map with minimum field checking.

ACCURACY

An intensive accuracy evaluation of one portion of the ARC test region was performed, covering an area of approximately 136 square kilometers. The total change theme in this test area consisted of 2549 pixels (1147 hectares) in 438 separate areas. Those areas containing three or fewer pixels (1.4 hectares) were determined to be "noise" - misregistration, changes too minor to be of significance, etc. Eliminating the noise left 106 areas consisting of a total pixel count of 2108 (949 hectares).

Two dates of aerial photography were used in making the accuracy evaluations--October 1972 and February 1975. The October 1972 photography was taken within two weeks of the Landsat overflight. The February 1975 photography was taken four months after the corresponding Landsat data.

The overwhelming majority of categorized change areas did, in fact, represent true changes although the exact area of change was sometimes off by 1-2 hectares. A small percentage of the categorized areas had not changed, thus leading to an erroneous indication of change. Nineteen of these 24 areas, however, contained less than 10 pixels (4.5 hectares). The overall evaluation shows that 91.4 percent of the change theme was accurate to within about 1.4 hectares.

The total number of change areas may be broken down into four subcategories to evaluate the classification accuracy in detail. Of the 106 change areas:

1. Twenty-one areas, representing 19.6 percent of the total number of change areas, contained 299 pixels (135 hectares)--14.2 percent of the total area of change--and were correctly classified and of the proper size when compared to ground information.
2. Fifty areas, representing 47.0 percent of the total number of change areas, contained 1316 pixels (592 hectares)--62.4 percent of the total area of change--and were correctly classified but were found to be too large in size when compared to ground information. The aggregate should contain 1134 pixels (510 hectareas); the mean decrease needed per change area is 3.2 pixels (1.4 hectares).
3. Eleven areas, representing 10.3 percent of the total number of change areas, contained 311 pixels (140 hectares)--14.8 percent of the total area of change--and were correctly classified but were found to be too small in size when compared to ground information. The aggregate should contain 427 pixels (192 hectares); the mean increase needed per area is 4.6 pixels (2.1 hectares).
4. Twenty-four areas, representing 22.4 percent of the total number of change areas, contained 182 pixels (82 hectares)--8.6 percent of the total area of change--and were found to be incorrectly classified when compared to ground information. The mean size of these areas is 7.6 pixels (3.4 hectares).

A test was also made of the accuracy with which the change theme was classified. For the category residential, 10 of 19 areas of change were classified correctly. For the category commercial/industrial, 53 of 63 areas of change were classified correctly. While the accuracy achieved by automatic classification is relatively good, it is probably not good enough for the data to be used without additional field checks.

Overall the accuracy evaluation was highly promising. Some additional processing of the data after change detection and (or) classification will eliminate many of the errors discussed above.

CONCLUSION AND RECOMMENDATIONS

The results of the change detection and land use classification tests were not entirely satisfactory to meet ARC's operational needs. Major problem areas included the "noise" inherent in the data, and the identification of some areas as change when, in fact, they had not changed. The results were extremely encouraging, however, and slight procedural modifications are expected to increase greatly the utility of this technique.

A part of the 1976 ARC land use program is to update the 1974 development patterns map. This map was prepared from 1974-75 aerial photography by USGS/Geography Program in cooperation with ARC and the Georgia Department of Natural Resources. Computerized land use data files will also be available as a result of the USGS/Geography Program. It is recommended that computer processing of Landsat data be employed to try to obtain the data necessary to update both the 1974 map and the associated digital data bases. However, it is recognized that substantial manual interaction with the data will be required both during and after Landsat processing.

The following procedural changes are recommended to allow for the maximum utilization of computer processed Landsat data even though some analysis may need to be accomplished manually.

1. Computer processing of Landsat data should be employed as a first step in obtaining the data necessary to update the 1974 development patterns map.

2. Use mid-winter scenes, if possible. Lack of foliage on hardwoods may improve change detection and classification accuracy.

3. Screen the computer processed data with a "noise-reduction" program to eliminate all categorized areas of change which are less than four hectares in size. This may remove isolated true changes along with the noise but all major changes should be preserved. An on-line noise reduction program would be desirable but not necessary.

4. Attempt to produce a 1:100,000 scale map overlay by use of an output film recorder. The data should be as geometrically correct as possible. This overlay could be used with the 1974 development patterns map as a visual indication of change.

5. Try to update the digital data base associated with the 1974 Atlanta Region land use maps using the results of the 1976 Landsat change detection and land cover classification work. Substantial manual interaction may be required for this task.

The use of computer processing of Landsat data is favored by:

1. Data that are available fairly regularly and cover the entire ARC region simultaneously. Reliance on aerial photography means that available data must be used unless routine aerial surveys of the entire region are commissioned.

2. Areal measurements that are automatically available. Manual methods of determining areas are slow and often contain significant commission and omission errors.

3. Results that are stored on computer tapes so that map overlays can be prepared directly from the machine-processed results. Preparation of map overlays by this method should be more timely and cost effective.

4. Actual change detection process that can be accomplished in less than one week. Manual methods would take several months to complete.

Conditions favoring the use of manual methods (aerial photography/ photo interpretation) include:

1. In some years complete, simultaneous aerial coverage of the ARC region may exist.
2. Photo interpreters could be more accurate than the computer in detecting changes. However, it is not known that the accuracy might be using entirely manual methods.
3. Determination of the type of change might be more accurate by manual methods.

Given no wide disparity in costs, the computer processing of Landsat data is favored by data availability, speed and consistency, and versatility of both analysis and display capabilities.

References

1

Anderson, James R. Hardy, Ernest E., and Roach, John T., A Land Use and Land Cover Classification System for Use with Remote Sensor Data, U.S. Geological Survey Professional Paper 964, Washington, U.S. Geological Survey, 1976.

2

Atlanta Regional Commission, Land Use Study Design, Atlanta Regional Commission, 1974.

3

Spann, G. William, Land Use Change Detection Using Landsat Data, prepared under contract with the Atlanta Regional Commission, 1975.

Jerry C. Coiner
Senior Research Associate, Department of Geography
Columbia University
New York, New York 10027

GEOGRAPHIC INFORMATION SYSTEMS IN DEVELOPMENT PLANNING

ABSTRACT A geographic information system,
designed specifically for a Third World site, Marinduque Island, Republic of the Philippines, is
presented to give an example of how geographic data
sensing can be used to monitor development. The
system is intended to enhance development planners'
ability to identify spatial dynamics inherent in the
development process and to monitor relationships
between infrastructure changes and other landscape
components such as land use. These capabilities
were demonstrated with Marinduque data and are
reported in brief here. Future research will
address methodologies available to incorporate satellite sensed data into the system.

INTRODUCTION

Traditional static methods of displaying spatial relationships may
be limited as tools to analyze economic development and social modernization. This is particularly true when planning, policy formulation
and program implementation are all considered links in the series of
governing functions concerned with development. To formulate coherent
policy, the planning function requires base line data, while the policy
making function relies on data synthesis either by planners or outside
sources, and the implementation function requires precise environmental
and social data of an engineering nature. As the work of the
simulation modelers has shown, actions which implement the functions
impact each other through feedback loops changing the objective reality
on which the planning rests. In such a dynamic situation, it is
obvious that a static data base, of the type represented by a single
land cover map, cannot provide all the data necessary for successful
planning. From this inadequacy emerges the requirement for large scale
geographic information systems to support governmental functions that
provide the impetus for development.[1]
Researchers of geographic information systems tend to view their
work in terms of planning integration over large areas, but they are
somewhat ambiguous about how this might be employed in the development

1 Tomlinson, R. F., Geographical Data Handling, Vol. 1 (Ottawa: IGU
   Commission for Geographical Data Sensing and Processing, 1972).

process.[2] It is proposed that if geographic information systems were
coupled with replicative data sensing, the consequences of feedback
loops inherent in the development process could be monitored. To
illustrate this monitoring capability, a Third World site was selected,
and a combined human settlement-environmental data base was constructed
for use as part of a geographic information system.

As is becoming widely recognized, planners must concurrently
address the condition of human settlement and the state of human
induced changes in the physical environment, thereby creating height-
ened demands for large numbers of data elements to describe these
phenomena.[3] One source of data, which encompasses both human infrastructure and numerous aspects of the physical environment while
retaining spatial orientation, is aerial photography and more recently,
remotely sensed data from satellites such as LANDSAT I and II.[4] However, in its raw form, remotely sensed imagery, whether from aerial
cameras or satellite scanners, does not represent a planning base. It
must be subjected to a systematic approach that includes collection,
analysis, storage, retrieval and display, i.e., it must be formulated
and processed into a geographic information system. Such a system was
designed to address development in a Third World area, Marinduque
Island, Republic of the Philippines.

MARINDUQUE CASE STUDY

The experimental information system for Marinduque Island allows
the collection and maintenance of spatial relationships inherent in the
landscape through generalization of a preselected number of data
elements into a uniform grid cell (25 hectares or 60.25 acres). Storage
is achieved by arraying the data elements as records, based on the grid
cell's location within the predefined Universal Transverse Mercator
(UTM) geographic reference system.[5] Either aggregated data, categorized and combined into tables, or spatially displayed data in the form
of computer maps, can be recalled for analysis and planning support.
Programming allows presentation of discrete symbology or choropleth
categories in the computer generated maps (Fig. 1). Display of either
symbols or patterns can be accomplished in multiple colors. In the
initial tests, an IBM 370/145 was the basic computer hardware and was
supplemented by an off-line CALCOMP drum-type plotter for automated
cartographic products.

---

2 Billingsley, Frederic C. and Bryant, Nevin A., "Design Criteria for
   a Multiple Input Land Use System" (Pasadena: Jet Propulsion
   Laboratory, 1975, Xerox).
3 United Nations, Human Settlements: The Environmental Challenge
   (United Nations: Department of Economic and Social Affairs, 1974);
   Vann, Anthony and Rogers, Paul, eds., Human Ecology and World
   Development (London: Plenum Press, 1974).
4 Steiner, Dieter, "Remote Sensing and Spatial Information Systems,"
   in Earth Survey Problems (Berlin: Academie Verlag, 1974).
5 U.S. Department of the Army, Map Reading, FM 21-26 (Washington,
   D.C.: Government Printing Office, 1969).

The Marinduque data set consisted of three time series, 1948, 1967, and 1972, taken from aerial photographs. Each of the data series were divided into two parts, 1) a land use classification, and 2) selected point data related to development, particularly human settlement infrastructure. Data elements were assigned to three categories by spatial type, a point (e.g., house), a line (e.g., road) or area (e.g., mangrove swamp). Each spatial type was then analyzed relative to changes over time within types and between types.

Land use categories interpreted from aerial photographs of Marinduque Island were originally developed as part of an effort to support agrarian reform throughout the Philippines, particularly Central Luzon.[6] Because of its original purpose, the classification required slight modification and supplementary land use categories to describe the Marinduque landscape. Of the land reform project categories, twenty-one were identified as area extensive on Marinduque (Table 1). A numeric code was assigned to aid in storing the land use data on computers. The classification logic used in the three-digit computer code was as follows: hundredths digit--general land use type; tenths and lower digits--specific land cover. To mark areas that had similar land uses, a photo symbol code was applied to the photographs, a necessary step when data takeoff was a separate operation from photo interpretation.

Studies of land use dynamics indicate that area extensive land cover categories, seen in Table 1, can have large cyclic components which do not reflect change wrought by development. These cyclic components may be induced by such environmental factors as long term climatic variations and competition between plant communities. In an effort to retain cyclic components in the data and to overcome intrinsic generalization of land use within a grid system, data were acquired not only on the most area extensive land use but also on the second and third most extensive in each cell. Also, certain types of land uses were not treated as area extensive and were recorded separately. The latter were considered part of the selected development data in Table 2.

Selected development data were collected to determine infrastructure changes thought to be associated with development, i.e., changes in the number of dwelling units, schools, churches, industrial and governmental facilities, the condition of transport facilities, and the numbers and location of alternate sources of food, such as fish ponds and fishing boats. These additional data elements were thought important to avoid distortions created by employing land use data alone to measure development change.

For planning purposes, the information system was operationalized in the following way. Each of the 4,008 twenty-five hectare cells, which when combined represent a virtual map of Marinduque Island in the data base, were studied for changes in and between various development variables. These changes were measured and tested using

6 Veracion, J. G. and Bruce, R. C., "A Study and Evaluation on the Use of Photo Interpretation Techniques for Land Capability of Rizal Province," Philippine Journal of Geodesy and Photogrammetry, Vol. 2 (1967), pp. 49-61; Veracion, J. G. and Bruce, Romeo C., "Keys for Photo Interpretation in Philippine Agriculture Surveys," Philippine Journal of Geodesy and Photogrammetry, Vol. 1 (1966), pp. 165-174.

nonparametric statistics to determine the effect of specific infrastructure additions or deletions (e.g., roads, school buildings,
industrial facilities, etc.), on other infrastructure components and
proximate land use. Since the grid was spatially registered through
time, change occurring within the cell could be positionally related,
allowing assessment of the change's impact. Also, negative impacts,
such as Myrdal's postulated peripheral backwash effects, were measurable.[7] In the Marinduque case, initial use of the system demonstrated
the high degree to which emplacement of infrastructure focused
development into either poles or corridors depending upon the type of
government or private investment. Also revealed was the tendency for
backwash effects to be primarily peripheral to poles and corridors.

Studies now underway are intended to develop methods for more
continuous updating of the Marinduque data base with LANDSAT data.
The primary effort will be to develop for each twenty-five hectare
cell a single indicator of change as derived from UTM preregistered and
aggregated LANDSAT data. Anomalous or unique changes over time could
thus be detected and corroborated either with ground reconnaissance or
high resolution aircraft imagery.

CONCLUSIONS

Employing an experimentally designed geographic information system
that used remotely sensed data from Marinduque Island, Philippines in
the form predominantly of aerial photography, it has been shown that
changes associated with development can be monitored. The system
allowed the identification of change and its location, and through
analysis of this change, development was measured in a spatial context.
If this system can be used by development planners to observe implementation of planning efforts, it may be possible to introduce
corrective mechanisms early in the development cycle so that undue time
does not pass between the implementation of programs and the identification of their weaknesses and strengths.

ACKNOWLEDGEMENT

Programming of the system and design of the data base-plotter
interfaces were originated by Ronald Domsch, Wyandotte County Planning
Commission, Kansas City, Kansas. Research concerning LANDSAT updating
is supported by NASA Grant NSG-5080.

---

7 Myrdal, Gunnar, "Regional Economic Inequalities," in George Dalton
   (ed.), Economic Development and Social Change (Garden City, N.Y.:
   The Natural History Press, 1971), pp. 386-400.

TABLE 1. LAND USE CLASSIFICATION FOR MARINDUQUE ISLAND, PHILIPPINES

Computer Coding No.	Photo Symbol	Land Use
101[a]	Ar	Land intensively used for rice
102	Ac	Corn, beans, forage crops, upland croplands
104	Aom	Mixed orchard (backyard orchards around homesites)
105	Aoc	Coconut orchard
108	Ai	Fallow lands
109	Aq	Aquatic lands (commercial fish ponds, salt beds, moss production, oyster beds)
112[b]	Am	Mangrove swamps (to include nipa palm areas)
201[c]	Fr	Natural forest stands
202	Fb	Forest brushland (go-back, *parang*) and grassland (*cogon*)
203[b]	Fg	Natural bamboo (include all riverine tree vegetation)
301[d]	Rh	High density greater than 10 houses per centimeter on 1:15,000 air photo
302	Rm	Medium density 5 to 10 houses per centimeter on 1:15,000 air photo
303	Rc	Road strip and cross road community
503[be]	Es	Strip mining
605[f]	Pm	Military base and governmental centers
706[g]	Ta	Airport
901[h]	Ns	Sand/beach
902	Nr	Rock, exposed bare earth
903	Wn	Fresh water lakes and ponds greater than 7.5 hectares
904	Wr	Permanent streams and river (to include the entire width of river courses)
906[b]	Wn	Open salt water

[a]100 series, agriculture
[b]Added land use category for Marinduque study
[c]200 series, forest land
[d]300 series, residential land use
[e]500 series, extractive industry land use
[f]600 series, public and semi-public land use
[g]700 series, transportation land use
[h]900 series, non-productive land use

TABLE 2.   SELECTED DEVELOPMENT DATA ELEMENTS COLLECTED PER 25 HA. CELL

Number of occupied houses (dwelling units)

Number of schools

Number of churches

Number of government buildings

Number of buildings associated with industrial activity, including oil
  tanks and storage areas

Number of commercial buildings, including *sari-sari* store front houses
  where identifiable

Number of market places

Type of roads/trails
  0 = no road or trail
  1 = all-weather road
  2 = seasonal road, usually passable to wheeled vehicles
  3 = trail, not normally usable by wheeled vehicles

Number of bridges

Number of boats

Number of piers or boat landings, beaches

Number of concrete drying platforms or basketball courts

Number of fish ponds

Number of fish traps

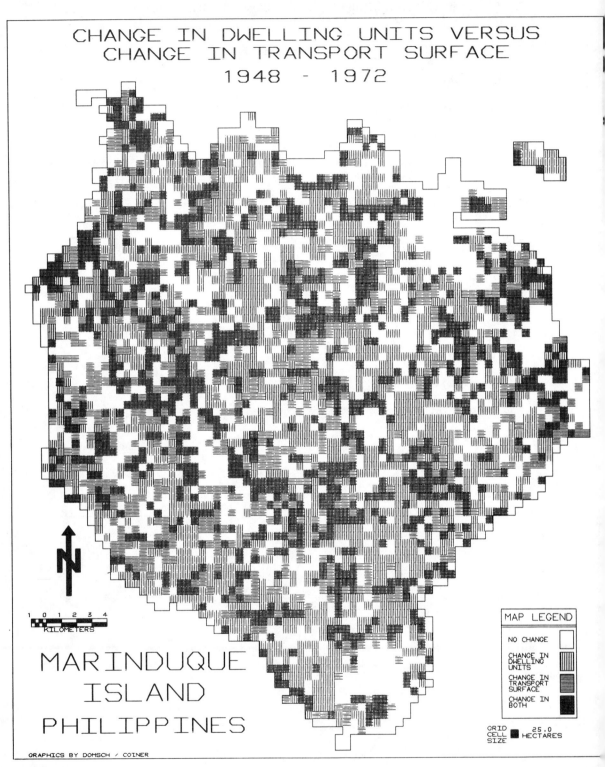

CHANGE IN DWELLING UNITS VERSUS
CHANGE IN TRANSPORT SURFACE
1948 - 1972

MAP LEGEND

NO CHANGE

CHANGE IN
DWELLING
UNITS

CHANGE IN
TRANSPORT
SURFACE

CHANGE IN
BOTH

GRID
CELL   25.0
SIZE   HECTARES

1 0 1 2 3 4
KILOMETERS

MARINDUQUE
ISLAND
PHILIPPINES

GRAPHICS BY DOMSCH / COINER

Charles M. Williams
Information Systems Department
Georgia State University
Atlanta, Georgia   30303

INFORMATION RETRIEVAL FROM COMPUTER DATA BASES
USING AUTOMATICALLY DIGITIZED MAPS

A method currently under development is described for
the almost totally automatic retrieval of information from
spatially keyed data bases. The system uses an automatic
digitizer-scanner to transduce maps into computers. Manual
labeling of enclosed areas is then required to correlate
map features with previously coded keyed information in a
computer data base. Subsequent retrieval of this data may
then proceed by using other automatically digitized maps
with the manual insertion of their registration points only.
The system will permit the virtually automatic formation
of one spatially oriented data base from another with a
resolution largely dependent upon the accuracy of the maps
involved and the degree of mismatch of their areal boundaries. In most instances boundaries may be demarcated by
either dashed or solid lines.

INTRODUCTION

The practicability of geographically organized computer based information systems can be severely limited by the difficulty of entering
cartographic information into the computer. The manual digitization
of maps can be a time consuming, tedious and error-prone process [1]
even when accomplished by semi-automatic methods. This report describes a system currently under development for totally automating
many of the tasks required to prepare a cartographic data base.

AUTOMATIC SYSTEM COMPONENTS

The first key component of the system is a totally automatic digitizer-scanner [2] which can convert an 11x17 inch hard-copy map into
digital form in roughly two minutes. This devices has an accuracy of
0.005 inches and records points at 200 samples per linear inch. It
can also work at 400 samples per inch (0.0025 inch accuracy) with a
recording time of approximately four minutes.
The second key component of the system is computer software which
processes the digitized data in three stages:
1.   The Graphic Collation software organizes the digitizer infor-
     mation into lists of coordinate points describing the lines,
     curves, and black areas on the map.

2. These lists of coordinates are then processed by vectorizing software which derives "thinned" line coordinates ready for replotting. This stage also determines line widths which can be used in replotting or for line description purposes. Concurrently a node list is prepared which gives the coordinates of the end points and intersection points of these thinned lines.
3. Finally this node list is used to prepare a table of the lines and nodal points which encompass closed areas on the map.

MANUAL SYSTEM COMPONENTS

These automatic components of the system can thereby generate a mathematical description of both the geometric and the topological (network) features of a map. What remains to be done is the identification in human terms of these features.

This labeling of lines, nodal points, and areas can be accomplished by manual methods which employ graphic data tablets, light pens, manual digitizers, or the like. This step does require human interaction, but the drudgery of accurately digitizing lines has been eliminated. Moreover, the accuracy required for labeling previously isolated map features is dependent solely upon the relative spacing of those features. (Software can use closest distance criteria to avoid most of the problems usually associated with coordinate point inaccuracies.)

INFORMATION RETRIEVAL

This system will permit a map to directly control information retrieval from a normal computer data base provided entries can be keyed by enclosed areas on the map. The process proceeds as follows:
1. As described in previous sections a base map is automatically digitized, converted into mathematical form, and correlated with entries in the data base.
2. The retrieval map is then automatically digitized and converted into mathematical form.
3. Manual digitizing methods are then used to identify reference points common to the retrieval map and the base map. This step establishes the scale and orientation of the new map relative to the old.
4. The computer then mathematically superimposes the two maps and determines the relationship of closed areas on the retrieval map to those on the base map.
5. These relationships will then permit closed areas on the new map to retrieve data keyed by closed areas on the base map. The retrieval will be perfect provided an area on the base map lies totally within an area on the new. In other cases the computer can determine the degree of mismatch and act according to rules to be established by experience.

This system will initially require reasonably uncluttered maps as extraneous lines, symbology, lettering, and marks are potential sources of misinformation. This type of cleanup can be performed with such standard desk supplies and typists' correction fluid and pencil. The system is capable of bridging short gaps in lines, and in most instances boundaries may be demarcated by either dashed or solid lines.

SUMMARY

The primary design objective of this project has been to create a mechanism which is both easily used and easily interfaced with existing information retrieval systems. It is modularly constructed and will operate largely independent of specific computer idiosyncrasies. It is hoped that its use will remove most of the drudgery and inaccuracies usually associated with obtaining a cartographic data base by manual methods. It should be easy to use for information retrieval of areal data as the process will be controlled by means of drawings (maps) rather than by seemingly endless streams of commands entered by keyboard.

REFERENCES

1. Williams, C.M., 'The Automatic Transduction of Drawings into Data Bases,' Proceedings of AFIPS 1973 National Computer Conference (June 1973), pp. 635-637.

2. Broomall Industries, Inc.
   700 Abbott Drive, Broomall,
   Pennsylvania, 19008.

Allen F. Downard
Research Supervisor,
Polk County, Florida
3008 Redwood Avenue
Lakeland, Florida   33803

HOW TO DEAL WITH A GEOGRAPHIC BASE SYSTEM WITHOUT A COMPUTER

ABSTRACT: The use of a geographic data base has been approached in many different ways. As sophistication has grown, so too have costs. The data is usually stored and manipulated either on paper or in electronic form. The data starts as an image and is then reduced in some manner, manipulated, and then redisplayed as an image.

This paper deals with manipulating geographic data while it stays in image form. This transfer is usually expensive when done with air photography and conventional cartography or through the use of data processing procedures. The use of a Bausch & Lomb Zoom Transfer Scope can reduce the cost, time and energy needed in dealing with geographic data.

The machine is described here and examples are given of how it has been used along with suggestions for future projects. Advantages and disadvantages are discussed.

The information in this paper was originally prepared for publication to persons who know little about the field of geographic base files or the means available to manipulate them. I assume here that the general knowledge of how computers make use of geographically related social, economic, and other data has been absorbed, and the fantastic costs that go with them have been examined.

Recent estimates for a computerized system will run from $25,000 up to a quarter million dollars. That is just for the hardware; the software to make the thing go is extra. The subject of this paper, a Bausch & Lomb Zoom Transfer Scope (ZTS), is far cheaper and comes ready to plug in.

A normal geographic base file starts with a source document and then goes through a number of steps before it is ready to be used. With the ZTS, the source document is

a set of air photos for the area needed to be studied.
Armed with the photography, there are no other steps needed
to use the source document as a geographic data base.

The ZTS will reduce the air photo data to whatever
scale is needed and allow the particular data to be transferred to another medium, either for analysis or presentation.

The data that is transferred from the air photo may be
of any type that is identifiable on the photo. This can
include urban remote sensing data from a low level at a
scale of one inch to one hundred feet to LANDSAT regional
land use data at a scale of one inch to 16 miles.

If all that the ZTS did was to reduce data in a mechanical means, then it would have no more versatility than a
reducing Xerox machine. In fact, the data and not the image
is reduced, with an intelligent operator doing the work of
the interface. Through an intelligent operator, those areas
which have importance can be studied while unimportant areas
are ignored. The decisions as to what is important can be
made while the work is going on and not in a review stage.
These decisions are made during actual operation since the
ZTS is an active device that is always "on line" and working
with the user.

The machine works by optically superimposing two images
into one in the same manner as the toys which advertise that
"you can draw anything." Through the use of lights, it is
possible to view either the map or photo or both. With the
zoom feature, it is possible to bring two maps with very
different scales into agreement and study them together. I
have found that it takes less than an hour to learn how to
fully use the device, and that mastery can be had in a day
or so of work. In my office, there are five people using
the machine on a regular basis in their work.

In Polk County, Florida we have used the ZTS on three
major projects in the last two years, and we have found that
we would have been unable to accomplish what we did without
the ZTS.

The first use of the machine was in updating our Metropolitan Map Series (MMS) for the Bureau of the Census. The
MMS that Polk County received from the Bureau for the Lakeland-
Winter Haven SMSA were based on the available USGS maps. Some
of these maps had not been changed since World War II days,
while others were updated as recently as 1970. We naturally
thought that bringing these maps up to date would take a
considerable amount of time. The Lakeland-Winter Haven SMSA
covers all of Polk County and contains over 2000 square miles
of land and lakes. There were a total of 62 maps at scales
of one inch equalling either 1600 feet or 3200 feet. Our
sources to update the maps were air photography at scales of
one inch equalling either 400 feet or 2000 feet.

The Census Bureau provided us with the MMS maps long before we started working on them. Our delay came while attempting to determine a method of easily doing the work. At the time, we had only two persons available, myself and my assistant, Linda Fairbanks. We attempted modifying the maps by using scales and standard drafting methods. This was quickly abandoned since the changes that were needed were massive and the accuracy desired simply would not be achieved. Our second thought was to use a pantograph, but this too failed the test, since it would have taken far too long to use.

When we purchased and received the ZTS, we found that the work could be done rapidly and accurately through use of the 2000-foot photos. I originally estimated that doing all of the county would take nearly a year. The entire project actually took about four months with two people working on the project part time.

The changes we made in the maps consisted of adding new streets not shown on the maps and deleting streets which were only cow trails or orange grove roads. For some maps, it seemed as if we would have been better off starting with blank paper.

The second major project that we became involved in required the estimation of the number of dwelling units which were thought to be exposed to high levels of radiation. This radiation is the result of high concentrations of phosphate, radium, and uranium deposited near the surface of the ground in one quarter of Polk County. The Environmental Protection Agency believed that this posed a health hazard to residents of the county. The local Health Department came to us with the results of a fly-over by a gamma ray detecting airplane. This data was displayed on USGS Quad sheets. Our job was to determine the number of dwellings in the high radiation area and the number of dwellings in close proximity to the radiation areas.

By superimposing the available air photos onto the Quad sheets and magnifying them, it was possible to complete 15 sheets in 15 days. I would estimate that even using the most advanced computerized procedures, it would be impossible for one person to complete this work in twice the time. When we finished, we had covered over 534 square miles and had counted over 9,594 dwelling units. All these units were located in rural and semi-rural areas of the county. Two cities were not counted using the ZTS as they were completely covered by indications of high radiation, and therefore, Census figures were used.

Our third use of the ZTS has been the update and correction of the HUD flood maps for Polk County which are a part of the National Flood Insurance Program. While the floods which occur in other parts of the country are related to the overflow of streams and rivers, the majority of the flood area in Polk County is associated with ponding wetlands that extend beyond their normal limits. The rest of the nation is working on the statistical assumption of a 100-year flood. Polk County has a flood every year. Since the areas which have been delineated on our flood maps correspond to the ponded wetlands, it is very easy to see these flood areas in air photos. Because of our annual wet-dry cycle in Central Florida, these areas flood every year. Through the use of our ZTS, we can superimpose the data interpreted from air photos onto the flood maps and obtain a more accurate flood map.

In the future, there are a number of different ways that we will use the ZTS. As part of our continuing zoning program, we use the ZTS to impose information such as flood-prone and environmentally sensitive areas onto zoning maps for study in each case. It is also possible to use the ZTS to do land use work. When land use change studies are done, the changes almost jump out at you when viewed through the ZTS. Areas as small as a city block can be mapped through the ZTS; although I believe the most productive use of the ZTS is in analysis of photos at a much smaller scale. LANDSAT photos are a continuing inexpensive source of land use data. We have used LANDSAT photos to check land use mapping done by other agencies. We have found that the use of LANDSAT on a regional scale can provide a rapid and very cost effective means to develop land use data. Since LANDSAT produces a photo every 18 days or so, it is possible to obtain an historic view of an area and compare current data with past data and even compare data created in different seasons.

The advantages of the ZTS make it a useful alternative for the agency that must deal with geographic data. It is low cost, running between $4,800 and $5,600. It requires little specialized training to use, although knowledge of air photo interpretation certainly helps. It is always on line, never needs a programmer or systems analyst, and never gets backed up in keypunch. The ZTS works best on data that computers have difficulty with.

The ZTS does have drawbacks where a computer far surpasses it. It is basically useless in dealing with social data such as police reports, poverty status, or quality of life. While computers can take massive data files, such as the Census, and summarize them, the ZTS has no such capability. The final limiting factor is that it is only useful for observable data. If an event occurred, such as a heavy rain, snowfall, or spring plowing, and the air photo plane missed it, there is no way to study it.

The ZTS has helped bridge a gap for Polk County. We cannot afford a high-priced geographic data system that is computer based. Such systems are too specialized for our needs and for our abilities to use them. However, Polk County must make use of geographic data in some form in our land-related work. We believe that the ZTS fits into this gap very nicely. We are able to use the expertise that we have been able to develop and use the best available data source to provide a means to manage and manipulate geographic data.

F. M. Weaver
Executive Director
F. M. Weaver Associates, Inc.
301 S. McDowell Street, Suite 915
Charlotte, North Carolina 28204

GEOPROCESSING CAPABILITY TRANSFER

Proven geoprocessing technology, available
from several local government agencies, presents
an attractive alternative to independent development by an agency interested in establishing a
geoprocessing capability in-house. The City of
Charlotte geo-system has been transferred to the
City of Newark in support of police computer-
assisted dispatching and to the City of Shreveport
to serve as the principal base for a geographic
information system. This paper reviews the results
of these transfers and presents specific comments
on the state-of-the-art in technology transfer.
Costs associated with transfers, benefits to the
transferee, technical considerations and local
issues controlling technology transfer are discussed. The role of the transfer agent as a
catalyst is identified.

Background

Federal, regional and local government investment in information system technology during the past decade totals many
millions of dollars. The USAC program alone invested twenty-one
million dollars over a five-year period. Add to this the HUD 701
grants, LEAA support and Census CUE program funding and the aggregate dollars are quite significant. As part of this major investment, several geoprocessing "systems" have been developed.

Given the experience base of local agencies which have worked
with geographic information systems, many entry level geoprocessing
applications have been pioneered and are available for transfer.
Any search today by local agencies for a geoprocessing system
should start with a careful review of this technology base. The
assumption that every local area is unique in its requirements is
very erroneous, can result in wasted funds, delays in the benefits
to the users, and invites unnecessary risk. Indeed, in the transfer cases presented here--the Newark NC-4 CAD GBF Subsystem and
the Shreveport GIS System--ninety percent of the user's requirements were met by the transfer modules with the final costs less
than ten percent of the original development cost.

The City of Newark, New Jersey, Police Department required a complete description of the city streets and intersections for the NC-4 Computer-Assisted Dispatch (CAD) System. Recognizing the benefits of the Bureau of the Census Geographic Base File (GBF) in terms of availability and long-term maintenance, the City of Newark decided to use the GBF for police department needs and, at the same time, to make the GBF available to other city departments. Since the data necessary for computer-assisted dispatching is a subset of the GBF data with added local police codes, a series of computer programs were needed to add local police codes, and reorganize and format the street segment and intersection pairs data. The solution selected by the City of Newark was the transfer of the Geographic Data Index Maintenance (GDIM) Module from the City of Charlotte. Based on the Bureau of the Census GBF, the GDIM module had already been applied to the police dispatching requirements of the City of Charlotte.

The City of Shreveport, Louisiana, Data Processing Department had established the objective of developing and implementing a Geographic Information System (GIS) which initially would be based on the GBF/DIME file and would later be expanded to the address level. What was required was an integrated set of files and indexes for segments, nodes, intersection pairs, and various feature name, place and alternate spelling indexes. The solution selected by the City of Shreveport was the transfer of the City of Charlotte GDIM module enhanced by the City of Anaheim version of the ADMATCH system.

These two transfer projects offer an important experience base from which other local agencies may learn prior to development or transfer of a geoprocessing capability. In the following sections, the decision-making process involved in a transfer project is discussed first, followed by a definition of the geosystem capabilities transferred to Newark and Shreveport. Technical issues are next discussed such as computer environment, host operating systems and unique system conditions encountered during the transfer. The final section presents key points observed during the original module development and the subsequent transfers.

THE DECISION TO TRANSFER

The justification of a technology by a local agency and
the subsequent decision to either develop or transfer may be
as ordered as the process suggested in a previous paper[1] or
may follow any of a number of less involved processes. When
dealing with a basic geoprocessing capability, the proposed
system will serve one or more of the following needs of the
local agency:[2] 1) Location Verification, 2) Location Correlation, 3) Locational Relationships, 4) District Coding, 5) Route
Analysis, 6) Areal Analysis, and/or 7) Mapping. The key factor
in determining the costs, and the benefits, of a proposed geoprocessing system is the level of detail. For example, a data
base may be developed which can verify an address location to
the blockface accuracy (such as is possible with the GBF/DIME
file) or the data base may contain an entry for each known
address thus permitting individual address comparisons. The
difference between the lower cost GBF/DIME file and the higher
cost address data base is significant (between 8 to 10 times
more costly to build and maintain). While this basic subject
of justification of a geoprocessing capability is greatly in
need of documentation, the focus of this paper is not justification of the application but rather it is assumed that a need
has been identified and the question is whether to develop or
to transfer. Given the cost advantages alone, some agencies
will find the decision to transfer brings the costs within
reach and therefore makes the geoprocessing system possible.

A manager who recognizes a requirement for a geographic
data base must define the management, planning and/or operational application data needs and identify the level of required
detail. From this initial definition, or statement of need, a
preliminary review of the costs to develop the capability is
made in terms of man-months of analysts and programmers. With
time and related costs initially documented, a search is made
of currently operational geoprocessing systems to identify the
availability of similar systems. Identification of one or more
such systems provides the information base to compare with the
initial estimates. Unless the initial process was guided by
outside support, these estimates will generally be two to three
times lower than that experienced by agencies with operational
systems. That is, if the initial estimates called for 12 man-
months over six calendar months, it is reasonable to expect the
user with a similar system in operation to have expended 36 man-
months over a period of 18 months to develop the capability.

A simple reason exists for this difference in resource
estimates: In almost any development of a computer program,
the problem is never understood by the user or developing group
until it is operational and all the details made visible to the
user. At that time the user begins to understand what he really

wanted in the first place and expects the developers to make it work "right." This process is not necessarily aided by detailed system analysis since the experience base of the person analyzing the problem cannot be totally communicated to the programming team in writing in the form of a design document. Where the analyst is also the development team manager, the communication problems are eliminated and only the fundamental issues of trying to understand what the user wants and what is really needed surface clearly. Thus, when initially estimating geoprocessing system resource requirements, make the best estimate during the initial phase and multiply by three to arrive at a working number.

After the desired system has been designed and a real-world estimate developed as to cost, the manager desiring to have a geoprocessing capability has three basic alternatives: 1) give up, 2) seek a large Federal "pouch" of dollars, or 3) locate a system which provides most of the local requirements and then transfer this capability. A fourth alternative of scaling down the capabilities and attempting to develop the resultant capability with local agency funds may be attempted. This approach, however, carries the highest risk of failure if the project is estimated to take over six months.

Since giving up is avoided by most managers and the pot of Federal dollars for new system development is shrinking rapidly, the selection of the transfer approach to meeting the objectives is the logical alternative to pursue. The author admits he has treated the decision-making process lightly but with good purpose. Simply stated, unless there is a large block of development funds with a management team at the highest levels giving nearly blind faith, any project covering more than one funding year runs the highest chances of failure by abandonment of top management when the proposed development falls behind schedule. Recognition of this fact is the single strongest supporting factor favoring transfer technology. The transfer approach offers the highest chance of success, at the least cost, of any alternative. When dealing with the geo-system as part of a larger, complex operational system, such as a computer-assisted dispatch system, the reduction of the chance of failure of a key component in and of itself is a reason to elect to transfer rather than develop.

The author has experienced the full development cycle for several significant geo-systems including the Charlotte GDIM module. The above remarks should not be dismissed lightly regarding initial cost/time estimates, degree of complexity of geo-systems, problems with analyst/programmer interfaces, or problems in general with the development of geo-systems. Likewise, the author states without reservation that the use of a geo-system by a local agency to serve operational and planning requirements can be achieved in a cost effective manner with minimum risk to the agency. The author further states that benefits from such effective transfers can exceed the costs to the agency for the transfer and the long-term benefits of a geo-system to a data processing operation can be demonstrated.

Having addressed the subject of transfer versus development of a geo-system, the primary focus of this paper may now be developed. The following section defines the computer programs and processes transferred to Newark and Shreveport.

TRANSFERABLE GEOPROCESSING MODULES

The factors favoring transfers of the Charlotte GDIM module, the CUE programs and the Anaheim ADMATCH module are: 1) each module is a series of stand-alone batch programs which process data in a serial job stream, 2) each program is in standard COBOL or FORTRAN language and does not utilize system-unique features, 3) all modules are well documented in operational, training, system and computer program description areas, and 4) there is an experienced user base for this technology. The above technology is based on the GBF/DIME file computer map concept[3] and utilizes the standard 300-character "DIME" file. Thus, any of the nearly 300 major metropolitan areas in the United States may take advantage of the technology to meet local needs. Figure 1 illustrates the transfer "links."

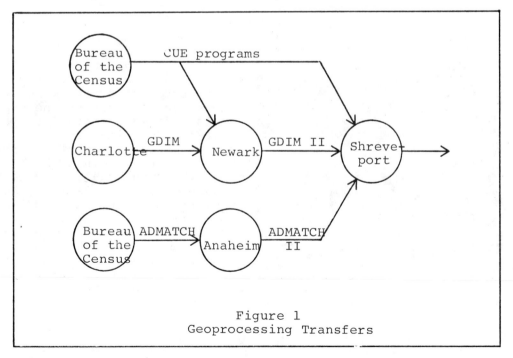

Figure 1
Geoprocessing Transfers

The GDIM module transferred to the City of Shreveport is not the original Charlotte GDIM module transferred to the City of Newark but rather an enhanced version. The "current" version is significantly improved due to the two transfers because the same agent directed the development of the Charlotte module and performed both transfers. Any geo-system technician would welcome three chances to "get it right," to benefit from past experience and to have the advantage of 20-20 hindsight going into a project. The primary point here is that when technology is transferred by a knowledgeable transfer agent, experienced with the system, the delivered product is more than a simple transfer but an enhanced version of the module tailored to meet local requirements.

The CUE Program

The GBF/DIME file is created and maintained using the Bureau of the Census Correction, Update and Extension (CUE) Program. The CUE Program is a well-defined set of procedures, based on standard maps for all major metropolitan areas in the United States and computer programs to process and edit the GBF/DIME file. The Bureau's administrative, technical and financial support to local areas is based upon their past use of the GBF/DIME files in 1970 for the decennial census and the upcoming 1980 activities which again will utilize the technology to meet their internal processing requirements.

Figure 2 is a sample map with a minimum of detail for clarity. Figure 3 illustrates the computer programs which make up the automated portion of the CUE Program. The GBF/DIME file is simply a map that the computer can understand and work with because each feature on the paper maps is defined in detail to the computer. Contained in each record for a street segment are the from and to node points which define the straight-line segment, the name of the map feature, low/high left and right side address ranges, X-Y coordinates, and several area identifiers such as census tract and block numbers. Questions about the availability of the file should be directed to the Geography Division of the Bureau of the Census (301/763-5636).

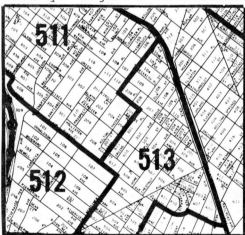

Figure 2
Sample GBF/DIME Map

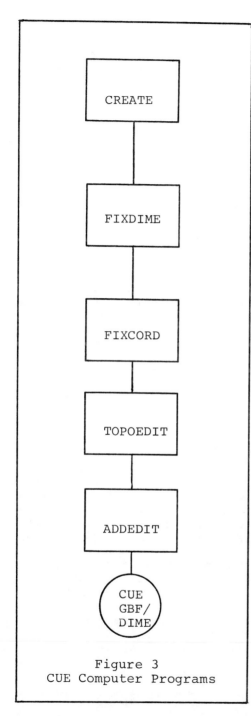

Figure 3
CUE Computer Programs

The CREATE program is used when the GBF/DIME file is first established or when major parts to the file are being added. It edits the input data and assigns record identifiers to each segment for future reference.

The FIXDIME program permits changes to be made to the GBF/DIME file to keep the computer map current with the paper-map version. As time passes, new segments must be added, old street segments deleted and with these changes go changes in associated records.

FIXCORD permits the addition of X-Y coordinate data to the GBF/DIME file on a node-by-node point basis. Originally the X-Y coordinate data was placed on the GBF/DIME file by the Bureau of the Census but as limited nodes are added to the file, it is simpler to add the coordinate values locally.

TOPOEDIT processes the file to detect missing segments or segments which are coded incorrectly. The program works with individual city blocks and chains around each block using the common node numbers of the bounding segments.

ADDEDIT processes each street feature as a contiguous chain and edits the address ranges looking for breaks in adjoining segment address ranges and for segments with other logical errors.

Generally TOPOEDIT and ADDEDIT are processed less often than FIXDIME and FIXCORD. A current GBF/DIME file actually changes little in a short time period. Given this computer map describing the land area, a wide variety of program applications may be undertaken.

The GDIM Modules

The GDIM processing has two major functions. First is to take the segment GBF/DIME file and process and reformat it into a set of interrelated files and indexes. These files may be used to work with a wide variety of both geographic and non-geographic data. For example, data collected in the field is often located by the intersection of two street features rather than by the address. To integrate data input in this manner with street segment or address data requires a skeleton network of files linked to the intersection data. The GDIM module creates both node point and intersection pairs data structures. The GBF/DIME derived files and indexes form the basic definition for a geographic information system. Support files within the GDIM module include a map feature name-to-number file, landmark or place name file, and an alternate spelling file.

The second major function performed by the GDIM module is the addition of local user codes to the GBF/DIME file. This is accomplished using a polygon processing technique with a simple user interface to aid in district definition. An example of this function is when the Newark Police Department added patrol sector numbers to the GBF/DIME file. The sector values for both sides of each segment were then carried through the GDIM file processing programs using an option to generate a computer-assisted dispatching load file for their mini-computer system. A similar area encoding process in the City of Shreveport added Planning District codes to the file to support the ADMATCH process.

Figure 4 presents the primary computer programs which together are called the GDIM module. The GBF/DIME file is first "preprocessed" to add to the file certain binary values for use by succeeding FORTRAN programs and to edit the file for feature names which are not in the name-to-number directory maintained by the GDIM module. The preprocessed file is then "split" to form a node-segment file. This file is sorted and processed to build a direct access file based on the node points. Using this working file, user defined area codes are input. The GDIM module first verifies all defined area code node input and then, if necessary, fills in missing points between the given node points. The result of this processing activity is a set of polygons (police sectors, planning districts, etc.) defined in terms of X-Y coordinates (from the GBF/DIME file) for use by the polygon processing program. The GDIM module next processes the GBF/DIME file and by testing each segment against the polygon set selected for encoding, left and right side local codes are added to the GBF/DIME file. After all sets of district codes have been added to the file, a final program produces special area-coded node and intersection pairs files.

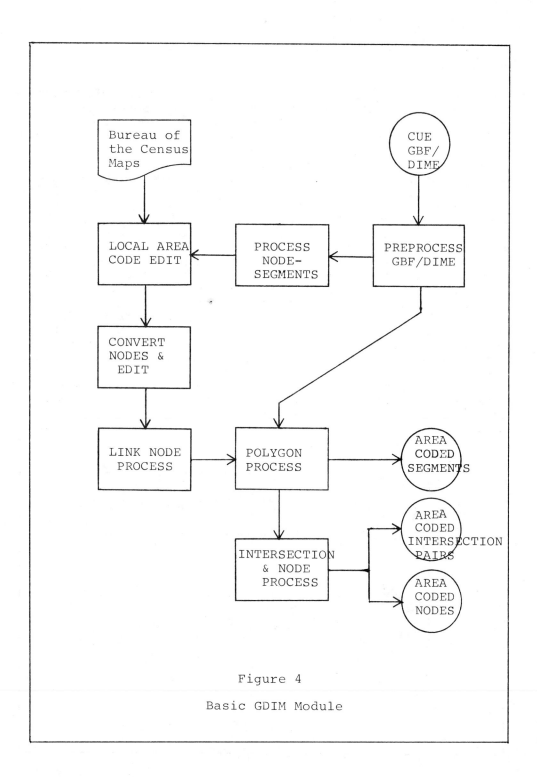

Figure 4

Basic GDIM Module

The ADMATCH System

    The ADMATCH system functions to relate meaningful identi-
fiers (census tract/block numbers, X-Y coordinates, local
district codes) to user address files. As summarized in
Figure 5 below, it is first necessary to take the CUE GBF/DIME
file and preprocess it into a special matching format. This
is done only once for each time the GBF/DIME is updated by the
local agency. The same preprocessed GBF/DIME, or reference
file, is used for all matching activities. The user data file
containing the address identifiers is likewise preprocessed
into a special matching format. Given the two input files are
formatted correctly and subsequently sorted in the same key
sequence, the matcher program processes the two files using
the reference file as the source of geographic data. The file
output by the matcher is the same as the input data file with
the addition of selected geocodes to the user records where
matches with the reference file were possible.
    The City of Shreveport is utilizing the ADMATCH system to
add Planning Districts to individual water utility accounts.
Grouping the accounts by district and totaling the number of
net gains or losses by district (measured in terms of new hook-
ups and disconnects) over a selected period of time has provided
an operational measure of change within the City of Shreveport.
This is the first of a series of applications of the ADMATCH
system in the City of Shreveport.

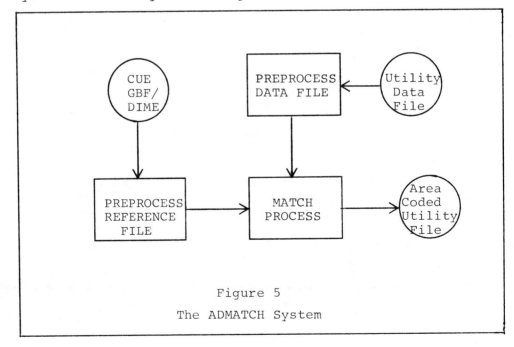

Figure 5

The ADMATCH System

The ADMATCH system selected for transfer to Shreveport was an enhanced version of the standard Bureau of the Census COBOL ADMATCH. The City of Anaheim, in cooperation with Garden Grove, Huntington Beach and Santa Ana, California, installed the ADMATCH system with the support of HUD 701 funds in the Four City Consortium project.

TECHNICAL ENVIRONMENT

The GDIM module was initially developed for the RCA Spectra 70 system (similar to the IBM 360 series) but was converted by the City of Charlotte to the Burroughs 6700 during an equipment upgrade. The original development was completed over a period of twelve months by a four-man project team. One false start prior to actual development consumed twelve months with a varying number of technical personnel involved.

While the programs are written in standard COBOL and FORTRAN, different vendors have slightly different "standards" with which to implement the languages. Add to this the differences in the B-6700 paging approach to processing compared with the RCA core-resident approach and it is possible to understand the significant investment in time and resources by the City of Charlotte (and HUD through the USAC project funding).

The City of Newark has twin IBM 370/145's under DOS with a background partition size of 100k bytes. At the time of the transfer, the systems had just been placed under control of a facilities management firm. The DOS had not been maintained to current status and utilities (e.g., Clear disk could not clear areas on the 3330 drives) presented some difficulties. By far the single greatest problem with the DOS was the limitation to 256 characters for record length of files. Since the GBF/DIME file is 300 characters, it was necessary to split the GBF/DIME with a COBOL program and to perform double reads and writes with the polygon FORTRAN program. The transfer of the GDIM module involved the expansion of the basic GDIM module to format special CAD load files and to support the feature names files (i.e., name, place and misspelling files). This was accomplished over a proposed six-month period which actually required ten months for final delivery. Parallel to the technology transfer, a GBF/DIME file was created and area-coded with Police Districts. A significant portion of the transfer process was invested in documentation of operations, training procedures, computer program descriptions, and overall system description.

The City of Shreveport has an IBM 370/115 with one tape and four 3340 disk units. The 370 is a virtual system with 192k of real memory. The FORTRAN on the 370 has the Option I feature which permits the processing of records greater than 256 characters. The Geographic Information System (GIS) was provided with one spindle for processing with an additional spindle available for ADMATCH processing activities. The confinement to one tape and one disk unit was a limiting factor. Given this constraint, however, the transfer modules were enhanced to take advantage of the situation. For example, the Newark system utilized four tape units and a disk spindle. Each polygon area definition set (X-Y coordinates) was stored on a separate reel of tape (Police, Planning, etc.). To overcome the limitations of processing devices in Shreveport, all polygon sets are stored in a special disk index with control card selection of the desired set. Likewise, the processor speed of the 370/115 was of concern so rather than going tape-to-tape as in Newark, the Shreveport utilizes an in-place disk approach which can, under certain circumstances, approach the 370/145 processing speed for polygon processing of GBF/DIME files.

The important point in the above discussion is that the core technology was quite transferable and since the project resources were not consumed with basic development work, each local situation was addressed successfully within the available budget and close to schedule. In both cases the final system cost significantly less and was installed in a fraction of the original development time.

Both Newark and Shreveport required the local installation of the CUE system to support maintenance activities for the GBF/DIME files. Since the transfers were COBOL from an IBM 360/40 DOS to IBM 370 DOS no problems were encountered. Both sites did have internal sort verbs added to eliminate card handling activities by operational personnel which has eliminated job execution problems due to card sequence errors.

The ADMATCH system is a series of COBOL programs which are operational on an IBM 370/145 in the City of Anaheim. Transfer in this case involved simple SELECT statement changes. The JCL, however, did require serious review to permit breaking the job steps into acceptable "chunks" of time. The reference file processes at approximately 8,000 records per hour. To match the 65,000 record utility file requires a full shift be dedicated. This will be improved when the 370/115 is upgraded to a two channel (Model 2) system. Even with the commitment of large blocks of time for ADMATCHing, the process is executed only upon demand and thus is not an over-riding factor in DP operations. All GDIM processing is of short duration with most runs less than thirty minutes.

Hands-on-Transfer

It has been observed that there are two ways to thread a needle: 1) with boxing gloves and 2) without. Most would choose the second alternative when possible. The same is true in technology transfer. The computer is partially protected from errors by the language compilers (COBOL and FORTRAN). When an occasional keypunch error causes a syntax problem, the compilers will so indicate. Successful implementation of a

computer program on a "new" system is a direct function of the
number of times the program is processed through the computer
for compiles and tests. If the lag time between submission and
return of results is one hour and twenty passes through the computer are needed, then if the programmer can stay awake, twenty
hours plus "thinking" time is the full program implementation
period. Should, however, the lag time be one day, then twenty
interactions with the computer, assuming weekends and operations
goof-ups, will take a month.

In both the Newark and Shreveport transfers, the primary
processing was accomplished over weekend periods with total
system dedication to the transfer. In practice during the
Shreveport transfer, the 4-11 pm shift Saturday and a double
shift from 7 am until 11 pm on Sunday proved very successful.
The quantity of valid data processing during a hands-on weekend
is difficult to understand unless experienced.

As programs became operational, operators were involved
both for training purposes and to permit a greater degree of
efficiency during the hands-on sessions. The GDIM preprocessor
permits the selection of any census tracts from the GBF/DIME
for the "internal" GBF/DIME file further processing. By selecting a test area of limited size, full program execution would
only take a short period of time. The combination of full access
to the computer, operator support and finite data base made for
a very efficient transfer environment.

Working with ideal conditions as in Shreveport, in two weekends the twenty-plus thousand source statements were installed
and initial testing began. Problems which arose were in JCL
changes and in the special enhancements for each local area.
Again it must be noted that, by having this base of technology
as the starting point, full attention was given to local enhancements, and later, to full documentation of the resultant system.

Cost Comparisons

The original GDIM system was developed at an expense in
excess of two hundred thousand dollars. The cost of the CUE
and ADMATCH systems are not known to the author but given the
degree of documentation and support by the Bureau of the Census,
the cost certainly exceeds the investment by the Charlotte IMIS
Project for GDIM. For discussion purposes the author will use
the aggregate software investment for the transfer modules of
four hundred thousand dollars.

The Newark transfer project was funded for $67,814 by LEAA
as part of the total NC-4 CAD Project. Since this project also
involved the creation of a GBF/DIME file and significant user
documentation in addition to the basic transfer, it is difficult
to identify a transfer cost alone. For the purpose of this paper,
the author believes that a figure of $45,000 is realistic.

The Shreveport transfer project was funded at $40,000 by HUD under the 701 program. No GBF/DIME file work was included as part of the GIS Project. Subsequent CUE support was requested under separate agreement.

Each of the two transfer projects was executed for ten percent of the conservative cost identified above for the development of the original technology. Given the local enhancements, the "value" of the present package is somewhat greater than the original.

In addition, these figures do not include a factor for inflation in man-power cost over the last four years, nor has an attempt been made to place a value on the learning curve experienced.

OBSERVATIONS ON TECHNOLOGY TRANSFER

The preceding discussion of two specific transfers of the same base technology have defined the working environment and related details in a monologue form. Here the author will summarize key points seen to be of value to local agencies considering technology transfer for in-house geoprocessing system capabilities. They are:

o   Most "wheels" have been invented and it is only necessary to locate the one with the proper configurations to meet local requirements.

o   The alternative to finding a usable "wheel" is to undertake a task whose size and proportion is little understood and even less likely to succeed without significant dollar and management commitment.

o   The most successful transfers will take place when the transfer agent is fully aware of available technology and invests time in learning local needs. Even then, a great deal of flexibility is necessary by both parties to ensure final system success.

o   Local cooperation will determine the degree of long-term success of the in-house transfer system. This includes system and programming personnel involvement, availability of computer resources as needed, and data processing management support.

o   Documentation of the system must be extensive and complete to ensure the system's survival when the trained personnel leave and, as important, to ensure long-term independence from the transfer agent.

o   Local training of personnel must include hands-on
    work with the system and the products produced by
    the system. Geoprocessing is a technology with its
    own unique areas of detail. It must be learned or
    hard lessons will be experienced by the local user.

o   The host computer system, in this case, must support
    both COBOL and FORTRAN languages and be capable of
    processing GBF/DIME files (300-character records
    with several thousands of records defining the com-
    puter map).

Further project specific documentation is available from
the author upon written request. The state-of-the-art in technology transfer in local government areas is rapidly growing.
Based on the nationally available GBF/DIME file, the geoprocessing
technology discussed above has wide applicability and is within
financial justification of most local agencies.

References

[1]Weaver, F. M., "Triad Analysis: A Decision Making Technique for Determining the Transferability of USAC End Products,"
URISA Ninth Annual Conference, 1971, pp. 137-165.

[2]City of Long Beach, Geographic Indexing Support System,
"Conceptualization," GIS-STR-002, October 1973.

[3]"Description of Operations," Bureau of the Census,
GEO-FC-100, September 1974.

Victor M. Davis, Jr.
Project Leader, Graphics Project
Systems and Programming Division
City Hall
Atlanta, Georgia 30303

GEORGIA COMPUTER MAPPING PROGRAM

ABSTRACT: This paper is an outline of the joint
efforts of the City of Atlanta, the Georgia Power Company, the Atlanta Gas Light Company, the Southern Bell
Telephone and Telegraph Company and the Georgia Department of Transportation in a computerized mapping program. The program utilizes the techniques of photogrammetry, the computer, line plotters, and graphic
video terminals. The use of a common grid (State Plane
Coordinate) and common scale (1:1200) are in themselves
an important departure from the norm. Previously each
of the parties involved had several scales, and most
had different grids for different mapping applications.
In addition to the advantages of a common grid and
scale, the parties received the economic benefit of
shared costs. Provisions were also made within the
program for computer update of the data base which
produces the maps.

The Georgia Computer Mapping Program is a coordinated joint
mapping effort involving the City of Atlanta, the Georgia Power
Company, the Atlanta Gas Light Company, the Southern Bell Telephone and Telegraph Company, and the Georgia Department of Transportation. It involves aerial photography into computer-readable
data, and the subsequent plotter drawing of planimetric maps
from this computer data base.

An additional involvement is the agreement in the jointly-
executed contract for the City of Atlanta to continually update
this computer data base. The City has also contracted with its
partners in this project to furnish them with updated planimetric
maps from its data base at the cost of reproduction.

The beginning of the involvement of the City of Atlanta in
this project was a study by the Systems and Programming Division
of the City as to what way interactive and batch processing
graphics might be useful to the City of Atlanta.

The initial results of this study indicated that graphical
representation on a map sheet of crime statistics might have
great value in police beat assignments, street lighting patterns,
accident analysis, etc.

As an addendum to this, it was determined after several
natural gas line ruptures and explosions, a location of utility
transmission systems might very well pay off for all concerned.

From this point, the City began studying the various types of hardware and software available for a system that would answer its needs.

At approximately this point in time, it became obvious that several interests were involved in this area. One of these interests was the Georgia Power Company, who had been for some time attempting to find a way of accurately updating its maps. In this enterprise, Georgia Power had been working on involving other utuilities who might have a similar need to locate underground plant facilities. The consensus of the utilities, other than the City of Atlanta (which provides water and sewer service for a large area of Metropolitan Atlanta) was that the State Plane Coordinate grid was the system they desired.

The most significant thing which was accomplished in the early stages of the City's and the utilities' efforts (before the entry of the State into the project) was the establishment of a responsible representative for each interested potential participant. The primary problem which was encountered earlier was that committee meetings such as the one held with NOAA were attended by twenty-eight to forty supposedly interested individual paticipants, but there was no one who could speak with any degree of authority for any particular potential participant organization. When we agreed to have each interested organization designate one specific individual who could speak for his company or group, we began to make progress. Once this significant step was achieved, the parties involved could discuss on a one-to-one basis the potential compromises they might make on behalf of their individual participating companies or governments.

After that we were able to make several significant compromises. For example, all parties were able to agree on the use of the State Plane Coordinate grid system. Significant compromises were also made having to do with the acceptance of the scale to which the original photographs were to be made. The final decision was to use a scale of one to twelve hundred. Once this decision was made, it appeared that work would rapidly proceed toward the production of the photography and the digitizing.

There were further compromises on color versus black and white photography, whether to digitize directly from the stereo model or the finished orthophotograph, and who was to keep the system updated after it had been computerized to a data base, etc.

The Georgia State Department of Transportation became involved due to the fact that all of the concerned parties were being bombarded with various allegations by photogrammetrists engaged in the commercial production of orthophotgraphs. Of the whole group, the State had the only qualified photogrammetrists available. Consequently, the parties attached to this group decided to request the assistance of the State Department of Transportation in giving some background in photogrammetry and evaluating some of the proposals. As a result of this request the State became interested in the joint project and requested that they be allowed to enter it as an equal partner.

In referece to the scope of the project, we have several ways in which this can be defined. One of these is the number of map sheets to be produced. The initial agreement was that the map sheets would be 20 X 30 inches at the previously mentioned scale. Under the arrangements proposed by one of the participants, the initial project size would have included 4700 map sheets. Another proposal, which included only 813 map sheets was finally agrred upon.

This area includes only the incorporated city limit boundaries of the City of Atlanta. However, all of the partners involved, including the City of Atlanta, have interests which extend beyond this area. The City, for example, furnishes sewage services·within the Peachtree basin and the unincorporated area of Fulton and DeKalb Counties. It also furnishes Fire services to the unincorporated areas of Fulton County. The Georgia Power Company and the Atlanta Gas Light Company serve the entire state of Georgia. The Georgia Department of Transportation also is interested in the entire state. The Southern Bell Telephone and Telegraph Comapny encompasses four southeastern states. Therefore, the area encompassed by the present contracts is considered as a pilot project for the overall program.

This line of thought leads directly into the follow-on projects which are predicted. The first is the sncompassment of the entire metro area in the program within the next three to five years. We believe that this will be accomplished by a county-by-county cooperative year-to-year enlargement of the original project. Future projects are contemplated which will probably encompass the entire State of Georgia, although not necessarily at the same scale agreed to in the contracts which set up this particular project.

The funding of this program was accomplished in various ways by the different partners. In the case of the utility companies involved and the Georgia Depatment of Transportation, the funds were diverted from existing funds for various mapping projects. In the case of the City government, the project was established as a one-time special project including the purchase of the computer hardware necessary to keep the data base updated and to plot the planimetric maps from the data base.

A particularly interestin feature of this system is that centroids of adresses and intersections are also being contracted. this will permit the City or any other participants to relate any file which they may presently hold in a computerized format to the geographic location involved by an interplay between the address in the existing file and the relationship of the geographic centroid of the building or intersection of the location involved.

One of the things which has become apparent to those involved with the Georgia Computer Mapping Program is the absolute necessity of local government involvement. This is due to the requirement of keeping maps accurately updated in as near a "real-time" fashion as possible. All of the records necessary to perform this update are a matter of public record and could theoretically be obtained from a service bureau operation directly interfaced with the local government involved. However, the accuracy of these computer updated records is liable to be considerably greater if the local government has a vested interest in the accuracy of these records.

In view of the foregoing remarks, it is also of interest to take a look at what the desirability of maintaining these records in an accurate fashion might be to a local government. Of primary interest to most governments is the fact that they are all involved in some utility-type operation (i.e., sewer, water, electric and/or telephone utility). In view of these operations, it is of extreme interest to them to obtain the updated maps. Also, all local governments are engaged in the abandonment and dedication of streets or roads which comprise the majority of the travel-ways upon which this program is based.

Also of local government interest is the field of traffic engineering. The participating organizations may input to the system the geographic coordinates of projected five year plans of maintenance and/or construction. The obvious areas of conflict may then be graphically presented for all to see.

By undertaking an operation like this, a local government can afford to work out with the utilities the underground plant maintenance and construction requirements for some significant period of time, such as five years. The plans of the participating parties to request the local government to close down streets, reroute traffic, and redesign one-way throughfares may now be coordinated to occur only once during the planning period.

There are also certain "fall-out" capabilities which are derived from a local government's having the hardware and software facilities which the City of Atlanta contemplates having in place this year. The first of the capabilities is that of performing automated drafting on as-built water, sewer, or other utility-type functions which the local government may be involved with. The second is the ability to automatically plot charts and graphs which will be of help in presentations to governing bodies. The third immediately apparent capability is to be able to access by a geocoded location any computerized central file which has an address associated with recorded events. The final "fall-out" capability which we see at this time is the possibility for automatic vehicle monitoring for law enforcement vehicles, emergency medical service vehicles, rapid transit vehicles, school buses, sanitation vehicles, etc. All in all, this presents a considerable advantage to participants and a thinking local government.

Stephen W. Kinzy
Chief, Municipal Information Division
Omaha City Planning Department
1819 Farnam Street - Civic Center
Omaha, NE 68102

ODIS - AN ON-LINE DIME IMPLEMENTATION SYSTEM

ABSTRACT An On-line DIME Maintenance
System has been designed and successfully
implemented in Omaha. The system integrates
the three DIME implementation procedures of
correction, update and extension into a unified program. ODIS has allowed DIME maintenance
to become a simple, efficient operation and has
helped refine DIME technology into a more useful product for local government. Due to the
success of ODIS, a transfer program has recently been established, that has resulted in
the transfer of ODIS to various SMSA's in the
United States. This paper describes ODIS in
terms of its DP and management environments,
its systems design and Transfer Program.

ODIS an Alternative DIME Maintenance Program

The creation of ODIS (On-line DIME Implementation System)
during 1975 as an alternative DIME maintenance program grew out
of the frustrations of local agencies to implement the DIME
Program in Omaha between 1970 and 1974 (Kinzy, 1975), and the
existence of a highly successful data processing environment
for local government in Omaha. In order to better understand
the reasons behind the creation of ODIS in Omaha, a description
of the data processing environment and the ODIS Technical Committee is required.

The Douglas County Systems and Data Processing Center

(Schoettger, 1973 - Carpenter, 1975 - Kinzy, 1975)

The Douglas County Systems and Data Processing Center (DCSDP)
is a cooperative city-county venture serving the needs of both
jurisdictions (the City of Omaha and Douglas County). The Center
was first established in 1967 for the purpose of:

1. Developing a computer center offering the latest
    technology to departments in batch and telepro-
    cessing modes;
2. Organizing a professional staff offering systems
    and programming capabilities to maximize computer
    usage;
3. Encouraging the concept of sharing common data
    bases with each county and city department, adding
    to and retrieving from data based at the computer
    center.

DCSDP is an IBM shop containing two computers: an IBM System 370, Model 155 with 2000K available memory, and an IBM System 360, Model 40 with 256K available memory. The shop also contains 12 tape drives and a disk storage system consisting of 24 IBM 2314 disk spindles and 10 IBM 3330 disk spindles. The center operates under OS/MFT. DSCDP has a full time staff of over 80 and operates 24 hours a day, 365 days a year. Financing of the data processing center has been accomplished through approximately 95% local, county, or city funding. The annual budget of the center is over two million dollars and is paid for by 42 governmental departments and user agencies within Douglas County.

One of the major functions of the center has been teleprocessing inquiry begun in 1969. Today the teleprocessing network of DCSDP consists of over 150 remote CRT and typewriter terminals, answering between 25,000 and 30,000 daily user inquiries. The principal teleprocessing applications maintained by the center include:

1. Douglas County Real Property System (Ownership, assessment, tax and permit information are available by owner's name, legal description, property address and account number.)

2. Criminal Justice System (Municipal, District Courts and Police records are available by name, ticket and warrant number, address, driver's license and record bureau number.)

3. Douglas County Auto Title/Registration/Tax File System (Automobile records are available by owner, license, title and registration number.)

4. Douglas County Government Accounting System (Inventory and purchase orders are available.)

5. Douglas County Hospital System (Admissions, laboratory and accounting records are available.)

6. Omaha Street Inventory System (Street characteristics/conditions, traffic accidents and volumes are available.)

7. Omaha Sanitation Inventory System (Sewer location, type, condition, and sewer plant maintenance data are available.)

8. Industrial Waste Water Sampling System (Industrial water quality condition data are available.)

9. Public Works Cost Accounting System (Manpower and machinery accounting are available.)

10. Building Structural Condition and Content System (A classification system of commercial and industrial buildings maintained by the Omaha Fire Division.)

In addition to the above teleprocessing systems, DCSDP maintains a larger number of data files and software for city-county departments and agencies. The center is a recognized census summary tape shop, and maintains a majority of the 1970 census summary tapes for the SMSA. DCSDP also maintains a library of statistical/engineering programs, computer mapping packages (SYMAP, SYMUV, SAMPS, GRIDS, and C-Map are among the mapping programs available. The center also operates a 30-inch Cal-Comp drum plotter.), and two powerful software systems; IBM's Information Management System (IMS) and the Informatics Mark IV File Management System, in addition to the traditional data processing lauguages (COBOL, ASSEMBLER, FORTRAN, etc.). This user oriented software has provided important data management tools for city-county government.

The Douglas County Systems and Data Processing Center is one of the major reasons for the development of ODIS in Omaha, for without the necessary data processing technology available at DCSDP, the system could not have been created. The data processing environment in Omaha is fortunate to consist of only one computer installation for local government because this has allowed us to avoid the problems of competing computer centers with diverse hardware and software configurations. Additionally, the center has allowed governmental users to maximize the effectiveness of their data processing budgets through the consolidation of systems development and data requests. In recognition of the quality and efficiency of the Douglas County Systems and Data Processing Center, the National Association of Counties distinguished the center in 1973 with a county achievement award.

The ODIS Technical Committee

The second major reason for the creation of ODIS in Omaha was that a decision was made to broaden the participant base of the DIME Program. Since the start of the ACG/DIME Program in 1968 until 1974, the program was entirely operated by MAPA (Omaha-Council Bluffs Metropolitan Area Planning Agency). In 1974 with the creation of the ODIS Technical Committee, the DIME Program was expanded to include not only MAPA but the City of Omaha and DCSDP. The purpose of the committee was initially to provide the specifications for the on-line computer system. Today the committee's role has been expanded to serve as the management mechanism for the DIME/ODIS Program. This new role of the ODIS Technical Committee has been carefully delineated in the DIME/ODIS Joint Agreement between MAPA and the City of Omaha, signed February 3, 1976.

In addition to defining the role of the ODIS Technical Committee, the DIME/ODIS Joint Agreement formalizes the areas of responsibility between the City of Omaha and MAPA regarding the DIME file and related activities. The Agreement sets overall policies, delineates local usage of the DIME file, defines geographic areas of responsibility and financial obligations.

The ODIS Technical Committee consists of five permanent member organizations, each with a specific responsibility:

1. <u>Metropolitan Area Planning Agency (MAPA)</u> - serves as a policy organization for DIME because of Census Bureau requirements. MAPA is responsible for the ODIS Program in rural Douglas, Sarpy and Pottawattamie Counties, as local governments in these areas are not now directly involved in the program. MAPA has also supplied 50% of the data processing funds for the creation of the ODIS system.
2. <u>Omaha City Planning Department</u> - serves as the City of Omaha's coordinating organization and is responsible for the maintenance of the ODIS Program in urban Douglas County (the City of Omaha). City Planning also provides the computer terminal for ODIS and most of the source materials for Omaha.
3. <u>Omaha Public Works Department</u> - is providing the DIME geocoding staff and has supplied a portion of the data processing funds for the creation of ODIS.
4. <u>Omaha Police Division</u> - provides the technical day-to-day supervision over the geocoding work (The coding supervisor for the ACG Improvement Program in 1970 is now working for the Omaha Police Division and has fortunately been allowed to participate as the clerical supervisor for ODIS). The Police Division has also funded part of the ODIS system.
5. <u>Douglas County Systems and Data Processing Center</u> - while not a part of the DIME/ODIS Joint Agreement, the Center serves as an advisory capacity providing the technical systems analysis, programming and data processing services required for ODIS.

The ODIS Technical Committee structure has worked extremely well and is excellent proof that inner-governmental cooperation can solve DIME problems. The creation and function of the Committee has been predicated on the need for DIME in local government and the inability of any one agency within the Omaha area to adequately upgrade and maintain DIME because of financial, staff, and data requirements.

<u>ODIS System Design</u>

The Douglas County Systems and Data Processing Center and the ODIS Technical Committee have largely been responsible for the design and creation of a DIME maintenance system that has eliminated many of the problems inherent with the CUE System. ODIS has been made highly efficient with the integration of the three DIME implementation procedures of correction, update, and extension into a simply unified program. ODIS has subsequently reduced the number of manual and computer operations and yet is comprehensive in its review of the MMS maps and DIME file. Due to this reduction in the number of operations, the error potential of ODIS has subsequently been diminished. Because ODIS has been designed as a teleprocessing system, response times are extremely fast (overall response times are between 3 to 5 sec.) with no accumulation of updates required. This teleprocessing capability also allows for immediate operator response and interaction with the computer for problem solving. The system utilizes the computer topological and address edit programs not as a primary correction mechanism, but rather as a final refinement and check of the DIME file. Finally and most importantly, ODIS requires substantially fewer local resources than CUE because the system can operate successfully with the skills of as few as one person, thus maximizing productivity and reducing costs.

ODIS does not totally abandon the Census Bureau's guidelines and procedures; on the contrary, the system has been designed to utilize Census Bureau standards and most of the technical procedures concerning MMS map revisions, interim block renumbering, node numbering, addressing, etc. It is extremely important that a national geographic base file standard be maintained in order to maximize applications, the use of computer software, and to minimize cost. DIME has been a major breakthrough in standardizing GBF use and application nationally, to deviate from that program would be counter productive. This does not mean that applications or maintenance oriented software should not be refined and enhanced or that DIME should not be modified to meet local requirements, but the potential for resurrecting a standardized DIME file should always be maintained. One of the big advantages of the DIME system is its flexibility in meeting local needs, without sacrificing its theoretical structure. ODIS capitalizes on this flexibility and provides a mechanism for total DIME implementation.

ODIS is designed as a two phased operation; development and maintenance. The development phase consists of correction, update and extension operations required to bring the GBF/DIME file and MMS to a current (1976) status. The maintenance phase continues updates to the GBF/DIME file and MMS once the file has reached current (1976) status. (MAPA/City of Omaha, 1976). Both phases utilize the same basic work elements, although there is some variation in the identification of file changes and in the use of the Census Bureau's computer edits. The following outline identifies the work elements and activities within both phases (see ODIS flow diagrams Example No. 1):

I.   ODIS Development Phase
     A.   ODIS Geocoding
          1.   Identification of Sources and Conversion of
               1970 DIME File into ODIS Format
          2.   DIME Segment Name Standardization
          3.   Creation of Block, Node, and Tract Reports
          4.   MMS Map Revision
          5.   DIME Record Revision
     B.   ODIS Teleprocessing and Editing
          1.   Creation of IMS Data Base
          2.   On-line DIME Record Update
          3.   Audit Report Review
          4.   Topological and Address Edit

II. ODIS Maintenance Phase
      A.   ODIS Geocoding
            1.   Identification of Updates
            2.   MMS Map Revision
            3.   DIME Record Revision
      B.   ODIS Teleprocessing
            1.   On-line DIME Record Update
            2.   Audit Report Review

ODIS Geocoding is the manual portion of the program basically involving the revision of the MMS maps and the 1970 DIME file. ODIS does not make the assumption that the 1970 MMS or DIME file are accurate, thus the program involves a comprehensive review of both the MMS and DIME file against local sources. Upon completion of the manual work, the second work element, ODIS Teleprocessing begins. Revisions identified in the geocoding activity are made directly to the file via the on-line entry system on a CRT (Cathode Ray Tube) terminal. As part of this process, changes, deletions, or additions are edited for accuracy and if any problem arises, the operator is immediatley informed and the problem is solved. The last portion of the ODIS development phase requires the use of the Census Bureau's edit programs as a final logical check of the DIME file.

Census tracts are used as the basic correction/update unit for ODIS with individual tracts assigned to local personnel for review. ODIS is designed so that total continuity can be maintained between the individual and his or her area of responsibility throughout both work elements. This allows the staff member to review and revise the maps, code the corrections or updates, and enter them into the terminal, all in one continuous efficient operation.

The DIME file for the Omaha, Nebraska-Iowa SMSA consists of approximately 30,000 records. For the purpose of the ODIS Program, only the higher level DIME elements are maintained, these elements consist of basic segment, address, topological and coordinate descriptors (see the ODIS display screens). The coordinate information on the DIME file is not being corrected or updated locally as part of the ODIS Program, because digitizing hardware is unavailable. Under current conditions, it is planned that the Census Bureau shall upgrade the coordinate values on the file. Upon completion of the development phase of ODIS, a revised copy of the MMS maps and DIME file shall be sent to the Census Bureau. From these materials the Bureau shall digitize the new, missing, and incorrect coordinates and return a copy of this corrected file to Omaha for local use. This indirect coordinate maintenance activity, admittedly is not the most efficient means of maintaining this portion of the file, thus a local on-line coordinate entry system (modeled after the FIXCORD Program) is currently being designed. It is anticipated that this sytem will enable the coordinate information on the file to be maintained locally without digitizing equipment, although any major coordinate related application of DIME will probably require the purchase or lease of a digitizor which shall provide a better long-range solution to coordinate maintenance.

ODIS operations on the Douglas County Systems and Data Processing Center's IBM 370 Model 155 Computer with OS/MFT and has been designed solely for use with IBM's Information Management System/360, Version 2 (IMS). The ODIS Teleprocessing Programs (TP) are written in IBM OS full American National Standard Cobol, Version 4, Release 1.2. Maximum main storage required for execution of the ODIS TP programs is a 32K region. Reports generated by ODIS are prepared under the Mark IV File Management System. (Carpenter, 1975).

ODIS Transfer

Due to the success of ODIS in Omaha, various requests for ODIS software from other SMSA's throughout the United States have been received. Thus in November of 1975, the ODIS Technical Committee formulated a "transfer policy" (see Example No. 2) to provide ODIS software to other agencies involved with the DIME Program, thus enabling them to benefit from the Omaha experience. At the time of this writing, four transfers have been successfully completed.

1. The Kentuckiana Regional Planning and Development Agency - Louisville, Kentucky.
2. The Environmental Improvement Agency - County of San Bernardino, California.
3. U.S. Postal Service - Washington, D. C.
4. City of Fort Worth - Fort Worth, Texas.

The creation of ODIS as an alternative DIME maintenance program has definitely not been an overnight development, but rather has been the evolution of the hard work of many people and organizations. The system is proof that inter-governmental cooperation can and does work effectively to get things done. ODIS or CUE in the final analysis are not the only or maybe the best systems for DIME maintenance, but they are two distinctively different systems, both of which should have potential applications in many SMSA's throughout the United States. Whichever system is used, the goal of operational DIME files will hopefully be achieved.

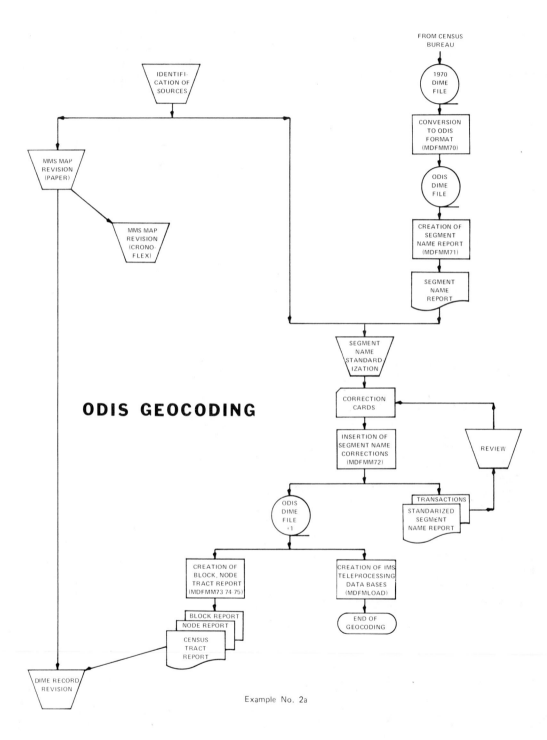

ODIS GEOCODING

Example No. 2a

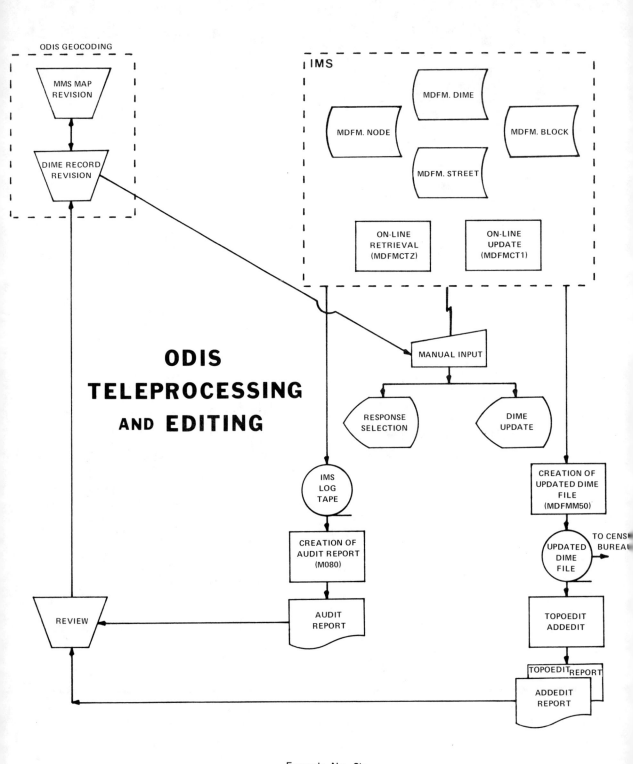

ODIS
TELEPROCESSING
AND EDITING

Example No. 2b

odis technical committee bulletin nov 75

Omaha-Council Bluffs Metropolitan Area Planning Agency · Omaha City Planning Department
Omaha Public Works Department · Omaha Police Division
Douglas County Systems and Data Processing Center

ODIS TRANSFER POLICY

Since 1973 the City of Omaha and the Omaha-Council Bluffs Metropolitan Area Planning Agency (MAPA) have been involved in the development of an on-line DIME maintenance System which has culiminated in the creation of ODIS (On-line DIME Implementation System). ODIS integrates the three DIME implementation procedures of correction, update and extension into a unified maintenance program (the system is described in detail within the enclosed publication, "ODIS vs. CUE: A Look at DIME File Maintenance"). ODIS is maintained and managed by a technical committee consisting of five (5) local agencies, MAPA, Omaha City Planning Department, Omaha Public Works Department, Omaha Police Division and Douglas County Systems and Data Processing.

Due to the success of ODIS in the Omaha area and the various requests for ODIS software from other SMSA-s throughout the United States, the ODIS Technical Committee has decided to make ODIS software available to other agencies involved with DIME development. The software has been designed to operate as a tele-processing system under IBM's IMS (Information Management System), on an IBM system 370 Model 155 (operating under OS/MFT) Computer, thus ODIS currently will only be compatible with data processing shops with similar hardware/software configurations.

It is the philosophy of the ODIS Technical Committee to provide ODIS software to other agencies involved with the DIME program to enable them to benefit from our experience and work. Thus, ODIS software shall be made available to agencies requesting it under the following conditions:

1. ODIS software will only be made available to those agencies or their sub-contractors directly involved with DIME Maintenance.

2. ODIS software will be made available at a cost of $100.00, to cover the cost of an ODIS program tape (9 track tape: 1600 BPI, or 800 BPI), and ODIS program documentation.

It should be understood that ODIS software should not be sold or distributed by the recipient agency to any other party without the consent of the ODIS Technical Committee.

3. The ODIS Technical Committee in providing the software does not make any commitments to support or debug the programs, although the Committee does hope to provide a clearinghouse function between recipient agencies and itself for the purpose of refining ODIS and adding additional capabilities. Thus it will be expected that recipient agencies keep the ODIS Technical Committee advised of any improvements to the system. The Committee shall then advise other users of the improvement and the appropriate contact for information.

4. Finally, it is the recommendation of the ODIS Technical Committee that any agency wishing to obtain ODIS software visit Omaha to view the system in operation, and to participate in an individualized one day educational seminar. Based on previous experience, this visit could eliminate any potential misunderstandings or technical problems involved in the transfer. There will not be any charge for this service.

The ODIS Technical Committee has found that ODIS allows DIME Maintenance to become a simple and efficient operation and has helped refine DIME technology into a more useable product for local government. We sincerely hope that ODIS can be used by other agencies with similar results.

For more information, please contact:

ODIS Technical Committee
c/o Stephen Kinzy
Omaha City Planning Department
Civic Center
1819 Farnam Street
Omaha, NE 68102

Phone 402-444-5211

Bill Harrison
MAPA
7000 West Center Road
Omaha, NE 68106

Phone 402-444-6864

EXAMPLE NO. 2

The ODIS Teleprocessing System

The ODIS Teleprocessing System consists of eight DIME record display formats, on-line to a CRT terminal, with one add-update display format for on-line transactions (see request and response No. 1). The add-update display is the most complete, with all primary segment, topological, coordinate, and local code information available from it. The add-update display for this geo-coding activity is accessed by record identification number. The system's update capabilities allow for changes to be made in any record on the file by simply entering the proper action code (C for change, D for delete, and A for add) and then entering the revised information in the proper field. The computer then performs over 50 logical edits on the revised data to verify the proper entry of valid information. If the edits locate any errors within the revised data, the display indicates the error for correction. When the display is correct, the new record revises the master DIME file and acknowledges the successful transaction. Additionally, the ODIS update capabilities allow for either deletion or creation of records. In addition to the add-update feature of ODIS, a data retrieval system has been created with eight specific DIME information displays. The displays are available from a "request menu" (see Appendix 1-2) which indicates both the fields necessary for a response and the special function key required for the display. This system also allows for any record identification number appearing on a response screen to be activated to return to the add-update display format for that record. The eight displays are as follows (display No. 1 is the add-update screen access by record identification number).

2. Inquiry by address - The fields necessary for a response are address, street, and area code, if different from Omaha; the response is the add-update screen with the requested record. (Inquiry by address allows us to have limited ADMATCH ability on-line.)

3. Boundary Nodes within a Map - The field necessary for response is map number; the response is a series of display screens with a list of all census tract boundary nodes within a map and the associated map-set-mile coordinates for the nodes.

4. Internal Nodes within a Tract - The field necessary for a response is census tract number; the response is a series of display screens with a list of all internal nodes within a tract and the associated map-set-mile coordinates for the nodes.

5. Blocks within a Tract - The field necessary for response is tract number; the response is a series of display screens with a list of all census blocks within a tract and the associated place and MCD code, additional room is available for transportation zone and police cruiser district.

6. <u>Block Face Chaining</u> - The fields necessary for response are tract number and block number; the response is a display screen showing all records associated with the block number requested. (This display and the following two displays allows us to easily check the topological structure of any block within the file.)
7. <u>Internal Node Chaining</u> - The fields necessary for a response are map number, tract number and node number; the response is a display screen showing all records associated with the node number requested.
8. <u>Boundary Node Chaining</u> - (Same as internal node chaining, but for census tract boundary nodes.)
9. <u>Street Name Chaining</u> - The fields necessary for a response are street and area code; the response is a series of display screens with a list of all records associated with the street requested. The request has the flexibility of selecting all records within the file with different area codes (as shown in Appendix 1-6) or with the same area code.

Carpenter, Michael (1975), "ODIS Technical Summary"; unpublished.
Kinzy, Stephen (1975), "ODIS vs. CUE: A Look at DIME File Maintenance"; <u>Proceedings of the International Symposium on Computer-Assisted Cartography</u>.
MAPA/City of Omaha (1976), "DIME/ODIS Joint Agreement"; unpublished.
Schoettger, Richard (1973), "The Douglas County Systems and Data Processing Center"; unpublished.

REQUEST 1

```
                        D I M E   F I L E   R E C O R D   U P D A T E
RECORD NUMBER 021315                                    ACTION CODE
      PREX          STREET NAME        TYPE    SUF    NON-ST    COD LIM

_ _ _ _ _ _ _ _ _ _ _ _ F R O M   N O D E _ _ _ _ _ _ _ _ _ _ _ _ _
        NODE          MAP                      STATE PLANE CODE
        MAP SET MILES              STATE PLANE          LAT. / LONG.
        X-COORD  Y-COORD       X-COORD  Y-COORD      X-COORD  Y-COORD

_ _ _ _ _ _ _ _ _ _ _ _ T O   N O D E _ _ _ _ _ _ _ _ _ _ _ _ _
        NODE          MAP                      STATE PLANE CODE
        MAP SET MILES              STATE PLANE          LAT. / LONG.
        X-COORD  Y-COORD       X-COORD  Y-COORD      X-COORD  Y-COORD

_ _ _ _ _ _ _ _ _ _ L E F T   B L O C K   F A C E _ _ _ _ _ _ _ _ _
    ADDRESS              TRACT    AREA    STR          PLACE    ZIP     TRANS    CRUZ
LOW      HIGH    BLOCK BASIC SUF CODE    JUR    MCD    CODE     CODE    ZONE     DIST

_ _ _ _ _ _ _ _ _ _ R I G H T   B L O C K   F A C E _ _ _ _ _ _ _ _ _
    ADDRESS              TRACT    AREA    STR          PLACE    ZIP     TRANS    CRUZ
LOW      HIGH    BLOCK BASIC SUF CODE    JUR    MCD    CODE     CODE    ZONE     DIST
```

RESPONSE 1

```
                        D I M E   F I L E   R E C O R D   U P D A T E
RECORD NUMBER 021315                                    ACTION CODE
      PREX          STREET NAME        TYPE    SUF    NON-ST    COD LIM
                 MADISON                ST
_ _ _ _ _ _ _ _ _ _ _ F R O M   N O D E _ _ _ _ _ _ _ _ _ _ _ _ _
        NODE    73    MAP   7                  STATE PLANE CODE 55
        MAP SET MILES              STATE PLANE          LAT. / LONG.
        X-COORD  Y-COORD       X-COORD  Y-COORD      X-COORD  Y-COORD
        015523   007337        2980677  0576650      0959357  411947
_ _ _ _ _ _ _ _ _ _ _ T O   N O D E _ _ _ _ _ _ _ _ _ _ _ _ _
        NODE    72    MAP   7                  STATE PLANE CODE 55
        MAP SET MILES              STATE PLANE          LAT. / LONG.
        X-COORD  Y-COORD       X-COORD  Y-COORD      X-COORD  Y-COORD
        015395   007332        2980000  0576595      0959381  411946
_ _ _ _ _ _ _ _ _ _ L E F T   B L O C K   F A C E _ _ _ _ _ _ _ _ _
    ADDRESS              TRACT    AREA    STR          PLACE    ZIP     TRANS    CRUZ
LOW      HIGH    BLOCK BASIC SUF CODE    JUR    MCD    CODE     CODE    ZONE     DIST.
1501     1699    403    28       OMA     OMA    075    1825     68107
_ _ _ _ _ _ _ _ _ _ R I G H T   B L O C K   F A C E _ _ _ _ _ _ _ _ _
    ADDRESS              TRACT    AREA    STR          PLACE    ZIP     TRANS    CRUZ
LOW      HIGH    BLOCK BASIC SUF CODE    JUR    MCD    CODE     CODE    ZONE     DIST.
1500     1698    315    28       OMA     OMA    075    1825     68107
```

REQUEST MENU

```
            D I M E   R E S P O N S E   S C R E E N   S E L E C T I O N

ADDRESS ------------ S T R E E T ------------   AREA  MAP  TRACT  NODE  BLOCK
   NO.   PREFIX        NAME        TYPE SUFFIX   CODE  NO.   NO.   NO.    NO

     COMPLETE THE NECESSARY FIELDS AS INDICATED BELOW FOR THE DESIRED SCREEN
     AND DEPRESS THE APPROPRIATE KEY
AVAILABLE RESPONSE SCREENS           FIELDS NECESSARY FOR RESPONSE      DEPRESS:
INQUIRY BY ADDRESS                   ADDRESS, STREET, (AREA CODE)       PF 1 KEY

BOUNDARY NODES WITHIN MAP            MAP NO                             PF 2 KEY

INTERNAL NODES WITHIN TRACT          TRACT NO.                          PF 3 KEY

BLOCKS WITHIN A TRACT                TRACT NO.                          PF 4 KEY

BLOCK FACE CHAINING                  TRACT NO, BLOCK NO                 PF 5 KEY

INTERNAL NODE CHAINING               TRACT NO, NODE NO.                 PF 6 KEY

BOUNDARY NODE CHAINING               MAP NO NODE NO.                    PF 7 KEY

STREET NAME CHAINING                 STREET, (AREA CODE)                PF 8 KEY
     AREA CODE IS OPTIONAL DEFAULT IS OMA
```

REQUEST 2

```
            D I M E   R E S P O N S E   S C R E E N   S E L E C T I O N

ADDRESS ------------ S T R E E T ------------   AREA  MAP  TRACT  NODE  BLOCK
   NO.   PREFIX        NAME        TYPE SUFFIX   CODE  NO.   NO.   NO.    NO.
  1520            MADISON           ST
     COMPLETE THE NECESSARY FIELDS AS INDICATED BELOW FOR THE DESIRED SCREEN
     AND DEPRESS THE APPROPRIATE KEY
AVAILABLE RESPONSE SCREENS           FIELDS NECESSARY FOR RESPONSE      DEPRESS:
INQUIRY BY ADDRESS                   ADDRESS, STREET, (AREA CODE)       PF 1 KEY
```

RESPONSE 2

```
                    D I M E   F I L E   R E C O R D   U P D A T E
  RECORD NUMBER 021315                              ACTION CODE
       PREFX        STREET NAME        TYPE   SUF   NON-ST   COD LIM
              MADISON                  ST
  - - - - - - - - - - - - - F R O M   N O D E  - - - - - - - - - - - - -
            NODE   73   MAP   7              STATE PLANE CODE 55
            MAP SET MILES         STATE PLANE           LAT. / LONG.
            X-COORD  Y-COORD      X-COORD  Y-COORD      X-COORD  Y-COORD
            015523   007337       2980677  0576650      0959357  411947
  - - - - - - - - - - - - - T O   N O D E  - - - - - - - - - - - - -
            NODE   72   MAP   7              STATE PLANE CODE 55
            MAP SET MILES         STATE PLANE           LAT. / LONG.
            X-COORD  Y-COORD      X-COORD  Y-COORD      X-COORD  Y-COORD
            015395   007332       2980000  0576595      0959381  411946
  - - - - - - - - - - - L E F T   B L O C K   F A C E  - - - - - - - -
    ADDRESS            TRACT   AREA   STR           PLACE   ZIP    TRANS   CRUZ
  LOW    HIGH   BLOCK BASIC SUF CODE   JUR   MCD    CODE    CODE   ZONE    DIST.
  1501   1699   403    28       OMA   OMA   075     1825    68107
  - - - - - - - - - - R I G H T   B L O C K   F A C E  - - - - - - - -
    ADDRESS            TRACT   AREA   STR           PLACE   ZIP    TRANS   CRUZ
  LOW    HIGH   BLOCK BASIC SUF CODE   JUR   MCD    CODE    CODE   ZONE    DIST.
  1500   1698   315    28       OMA   OMA   075     1825    68107
```

APPENDIX   1-2

REQUEST 3

```
        D I M E   R E S P O N S E   S C R E E N   S E L E C T I O N

ADDRESS ----------- S T R E E T ------------    AREA   MAP   TRACT   NODE   BLOCK
  NO.    PREFIX       NAME        TYPE SUFFIX    CODE   NO.    NO.    NO.     NO.
                                                         7
     COMPLETE THE NECESSARY FIELDS AS INDICATED BELOW FOR THE DESIRED SCREEN
     AND DEPRESS THE APPROPRIATE KEY.
AVAILABLE RESPONSE SCREENS          FIELDS NECESSARY FOR RESPONSE      DEPRESS:
BOUNDARY NODES WITHIN MAP           MAP NO.                            PF 2 KEY
```

RESPONSE 3

NODE	MAP	X-COORD	Y-COORD	NODE	MAP	X-COORD	Y-COORD	NODE	MAP	X-COORD	Y-COORD
701	7	015153	010725	702	7	015196	010780	703	7	015217	010808
704	7	015455	010834	705	7	015453	010729	706	7	015449	010649
707	7	015450	010548	708	7	015447	010415	709	7	015453	010330
710	7	015451	010250	711	7	015452	010075	712	7	015385	010040
713	7	015333	010013	714	7	015303	009997	715	7	015287	009976
716	7	015272	009976	717	7	015201	009971	718	7	015093	009975
719	7	015021	009977	720	7	015523	010248	721	7	015594	010246
722	7	015662	010246	723	7	015734	010246	724	7	015799	010245
725	7	015802	010330	726	7	015804	010416	727	7	015803	010549
728	7	015800	010651	729	7	015802	010834	730	7	015804	010909
731	7	015870	010649	732	7	016004	010649	733	7	016072	010648
734	7	016141	010646	735	7	016202	010648	736	7	016203	010671
737	7	016302	010669	738	7	016347	010673	739	7	016397	010671
740	7	016414	010671	741	7	019227	009977	742	7	016414	010618
743	7	016474	010621	744	7	016574	010626	745	7	016689	010621
746	7	015869	010245	747	7	015935	010243	748	7	015934	010185
749	7	015932	010057	750	7	015992	010055	751	7	016052	010054

REQUEST 4

```
        D I M E   R E S P O N S E   S C R E E N   S E L E C T I O N

ADDRESS ----------- S T R E E T ------------    AREA   MAP   TRACT   NODE   BLOCK
  NO.    PREFIX       NAME        TYPE SUFFIX    CODE   NO.    NO.    NO.     NO.
                                                               28
     COMPLETE THE NECESSARY FIELDS AS INDICATED BELOW FOR THE DESIRED SCREEN
     AND DEPRESS THE APPROPRIATE KEY
AVAILABLE RESPONSE SCREENS          FIELDS NECESSARY FOR RESPONSE      DEPRESS:
INTERNAL NODES WITHIN TRACT         TRACT NO.                          PF 3 KEY
```

RESPONSE 4

NODE	MAP	X-COORD	Y-COORD	NODE	MAP	X-COORD	Y-COORD	NODE	MAP	X-COORD	Y-COORD
1	7	015009	007961	2	7	015076	007959	3	7	015015	007839
4	7	015078	007844	5	7	015149	007843	6	7	015216	007841
7	7	015279	007846	8	7	015342	007845	9	7	015406	007868
10	7	015420	007824	11	7	015466	007887	13	7	015008	007716
14	7	015076	007714	15	7	015153	007719	16	7	015218	007718
17	7	015289	007716	18	7	015344	007715	19	7	015407	007720
20	7	015512	007717	21	7	015589	007724	22	7	015637	007723
23	7	015776	007694	24	7	015858	007729	25	7	015080	007583
26	7	015150	007581	27	7	015188	007587	28	7	015213	007586
29	7	015283	007591	30	7	015346	007590	31	7	015388	007589
32	7	015411	007588	33	7	015413	007653	34	7	015458	007594
35	7	015512	007656	36	7	015511	007591	37	7	015594	007595
38	7	015642	007596	39	7	015145	007525	40	7	015193	007523
41	7	015240	007524	42	7	015285	007530	43	7	015343	007525
44	7	015391	007524	45	7	015460	007527	46	7	015518	007531
47	7	015643	007534	48	7	015197	007468	49	7	015240	007466
50	7	015283	007465	51	7	015347	007463	52	7	015390	007462

APPENDIX   1-3

REQUEST 5

```
           D I M E   R E S P O N S E   S C R E E N   S E L E C T I O N

ADDRESS ------------ S T R E E T ------------   AREA   MAP   TRACT   NODE   BLOCK
  NO.    PREFIX         NAME        TYPE SUFFIX  CODE   NO.    NO.    NO.    NO.
                                                              28
      COMPLETE THE NECESSARY FIELDS AS INDICATED BELOW FOR THE DESIRED SCREEN
      AND DEPRESS THE APPROPRIATE KEY
AVAILABLE RESPONSE SCREENS          FIELDS NECESSARY FOR RESPONSE      DEPRESS:

BLOCKS WITHIN A TRACT               TRACT NO.                          PF 4 KEY
```

RESPONSE 5

BLOCK	PLACE	MCD	TRANS	PCD	BLOCK	PLACE	MCD	TRANS	PCD
001	182	075			101	182	075		
102	182	075			103	182	075		
104	182	075			105	182	075		
106	182	075			107	182	075		
108	182	075			109	182	075		
110	182	075			111	182	075		
112	182	075			113	182	075		
114	182	075			115	182	075		
116	182	075			117	182	075		
118	182	075			119	182	075		
120	182	075			201	182	075		
202	182	075			203	182	075		
204	182	075			205	182	075		
206	182	075			207	182	075		
208	182	075			209	182	075		
210	182	075			211	182	075		
212	182	075			213	182	075		
214	182	075			215	182	075		
216	182	075			217	182	075		
218	182	075			301	182	075		
302	182	075			303	182	075		
304	182	075			305	182	075		

REQUEST 6

```
           D I M E   R E S P O N S E   S C R E E N   S E L E C T I O N

ADDRESS ------------ S T R E E T ------------   AREA   MAP   TRACT   NODE   BLOCK
  NO.    PREFIX         NAME        TYPE SUFFIX  CODE   NO.    NO.    NO.    NO.
                                                              28            403
      COMPLETE THE NECESSARY FIELDS AS INDICATED BELOW FOR THE DESIRED SCREEN
      AND DEPRESS THE APPROPRIATE KEY
AVAILABLE RESPONSE SCREENS          FIELDS NECESSARY FOR RESPONSE      DEPRESS

BLOCK FACE CHAINING                 TRACT NO. BLOCK NO                 PF 5 KEY
```

RESPONSE 6

```
           B L O C K   N U M B E R   C H A I N   R E S P O N S E

TRACT =   28     BLOCK =403     MCD =075    TRANS ZONE =       CRUZ DIST.
```

PRE	S T R E E T NAME	TYPE	SF	NODES FROM	TO	MAP FM	TO	ADDRESS LOW	HIGH	AREA CODE	SIDE R/L	NON ST	REC. ID.
S	015	ST		73	76	7	7	6500	6598	OMA	R		001653
S	017	ST		72	75	7	7	6501	6599	OMA	L		002000
	MADISON	ST		73	72	7	7	1501	1699	OMA	L		021315
	MONROE	ST		76	75	7	7	1500	1698	OMA	R		022331

END OF INQUIRY RESPONSE

APPENDIX 1-4

REQUEST 7

```
            D I M E   R E S P O N S E   S C R E E N   S E L E C T I O N

ADDRESS ------------ S T R E E T ------------    AREA   MAP   TRACT   NODE   BLOCK
   NO.    PREFIX         NAME         TYPE SUFFIX  CODE   NO.    NO.    NO.     NO.
                                                           7     28     73
       COMPLETE THE NECESSARY FIELDS AS INDICATED BELOW FOR THE DESIRED SCREEN
       AND DEPRESS THE APPROPRIATE KEY.
AVAILABLE RESPONSE SCREENS           FIELDS NECESSARY FOR RESPONSE        DEPRESS:

INTERNAL NODE CHAINING               TRACT NO, NODE NO.                   PF 6 KEY
```

RESPONSE 7

```
 NODE =   73   N O D E   N U M B E R   C H A I N   R E S P O N S E
STATE = 55     STATE PLANE    X-COORD = 2980677  Y-COORD = 0576650
               MAP SET MILES  X-COORD = 015523   Y-COORD = 007338
               LAT. / LONG.   X-COORD = 0959357  Y-COORD = 411947
---------- S T R E E T --------- N O D E S   M A P   ADDRESS  AREA SIDE NON   REC
PRE         NAME          TYPE SF FROM   TO  FM TO  LOW  HIGH CODE R/L  ST    ID.
 S  015                   ST        62   73   7  7  6499 6498                001652
 S  015                   ST        73   76   7  7  6501 6500                001653
    MADISON               ST        74   73   7  7  1499 1498                021310
    MADISON               ST        73   72   7  7  1501 1500                021315
END OF INQUIRY RESPONSE
```

REQUEST 8

```
            D I M E   R E S P O N S E   S C R E E N   S E L E C T I O N

ADDRESS ------------ S T R E E T ------------    AREA   MAP   TRACT   NODE   BLOCK
   NO.    PREFIX         NAME         TYPE SUFFIX  CODE   NO.    NO.    NO.     NO.
                                                           7            0837
       COMPLETE THE NECESSARY FIELDS AS INDICATED BELOW FOR THE DESIRED SCREEN
       AND DEPRESS THE APPROPRIATE KEY.
AVAILABLE RESPONSE SCREENS           FIELDS NECESSARY FOR RESPONSE        DEPRESS:

BOUNDARY NODE CHAINING               MAP NO, NODE NO.                     PF 7 KEY
```

RESPONSE 8

```
 NODE =  837   N O D E   N U M B E R   C H A I N   R E S P O N S E
STATE = 55     STATE PLANE    X-COORD = 2979349  Y-COORD = 0576602
               MAP SET MILES  X-COORD = 015272   Y-COORD = 007338
               LAT. / LONG.   X-COORD = 0959405  Y-COORD = 411947
---------- S T R E E T --------- N O D E S   M A P   ADDRESS  AREA SIDE NON   REC.
PRE         NAME          TYPE SF FROM   TO  FM TO  LOW  HIGH CODE R/L  ST    ID
    MADISON               ST        71  837   7  7  1899 1898                021320
    MADISON               ST       837   11   7  7  1901 1900                021322
    RAILROAD              AV       836  837   7  7  6499 6498                024799
    RAILROAD              AV       837  838   7  7  6501 6500                024800
END OF INQUIRY RESPONSE
```

APPENDIX 1-5

REQUEST 9

```
┌─────────────────────────────────────────────────────────────────────────┐
│            D I M E   R E S P O N S E   S C R E E N   S E L E C T I O N    │
│                                                                           │
│ ADDRESS ------------ S T R E E T ------------   AREA  MAP  TRACT   NODE  BLOCK │
│  NO.    PREFIX        NAME          TYPE SUFFIX  CODE  NO.   NO.    NO.   NO. │
│                 MADISON             ST                                     │
│     COMPLETE THE NECESSARY FIELDS AS INDICATED BELOW FOR THE DESIRED SCREEN │
│     AND DEPRESS THE APPROPRIATE KEY.                                       │
│ AVAILABLE RESPONSE SCREENS            FIELDS NECESSARY FOR RESPONSE    DEPRESS: │
│ STREET NAME CHAINING                  STREET, (AREA CODE)             PF 8 KEY │
│     AREA CODE IS OPTIONAL. DEFAULT IS OMA                                  │
└─────────────────────────────────────────────────────────────────────────┘
```

RESPONSE 9

```
┌─────────────────────────────────────────────────────────────────────────┐
│          S T R E E T   N A M E   C H A I N   R E S P O N S E              │
│                                                                           │
│ STREET NAME      MADISON              ST                                   │
│                  ---------- L E F T ---------   --------- R I G H T ------- │
│    NODE      MAP      ADDRESS            AREA     ADDRESS            AREA  REC │
│  FROM  TO  FM TO   LOW   HIGH  TRACT BLOCK CODE   LOW   HIGH  TRACT BLOCK COD  ID. │
└─────────────────────────────────────────────────────────────────────────┘
```

FROM	TO	FM	TO	LOW	HIGH	TRACT	BLOCK	CODE	LOW	HIGH	TRACT	BLOCK	COD	ID.
323	305	5	5	201	299	7413	138	MIL	200	298	7413	136	MIL	010430
1264	98	3	3	601	699	310	206	COB	600	698	310	101	COB	021308
70	74	7	7	1201	1299	28	401	OMA	1200	1298	28	317	OMA	021309
495	496	8	8	1351	1399	10102	705	BEL	1350	1398	10102	705	BEL	021312
494	495	8	8	1301	1349	10102	705	BEL	1300	1348	10102	705	BEL	021311
74	73	7	7	1301	1499	28	402	OMA	1300	1498	28	316	OMA	021310
497	516	8	8	1451	1503	10102	705	BEL	1406	1522	10102	709	BEL	021314
496	497	8	8	1401	1449	10102	705	BEL	1400	1404	10102	706	BEL	021313
73	72	7	7	1501	1699	28	403	OMA	1500	1698	28	315	OMA	021315
516	520	8	8	1505	1599	10102	710	BEL	1524	1640	10102	709	BEL	021316
520	521	8	8	1601	1731	10102	711	BEL	1642	1758	10102	709	BEL	021317
521	561	8	8	1733	1863	10102	711	BEL	1760	1876	10102	709	BEL	021318
72	71	7	7	1801	1849	28	404	OMA	1700	1798	28	314	OMA	021319
71	837	7	7	1851	1899	28	404	OMA	1800	1898	28	313	OMA	021320
561	563	8	8	1865	1999	10102	711	BEL	1878	1998	10102	709	BEL	021321
837	11	7	7	1901	1999	29	225	OMA	1900	1998	29	10899	OMA	021322
837	11	7	7	1901	1999	29	225	OMA	1900	1998	29	10899	OMA	021322
10	9	7	7	2101	2299	29	209	OMA	2100	2298	29	10899	OMA	021324

APPENDIX   1-6

Gary A. Gezann
Regional Analyst
NOUS Research Corporation
820 Huron Road
Cleveland, Ohio 44115

A GEOCODED MUNICIPALITY-UTILITY PLANNING SYSTEM

ABSTRACT: This computerized system combines data from
municipalities and utilities to facilitate better planning of
construction within the street right-of-way. Planning data
is combined with information on existing municipal and utility
facilities for each census street segment. Because the data
is geocoded, it will add an additional set of data to a
regional information system which is presently being developed.
The purpose of the municipal-utility data system is to coordinate construction, when possible, in order to prevent
unnecessary cutting and resurfacing by utilities of new
municipally installed pavement, sidewalks, curbs and lawns.
This will save the public money both as municipal taxpayers
and utility consumers. It also demonstrates the willingness
of utilities and municipalities to work together.

INTRODUCTION

The computerized municipality-utility information system developed
by Northern Ohio Urban System Research Corporation (NOUS)* focused on
solving a problem which faces many utilities and municipal governments.
Construction and maintenance projects within the rights-of-way are not
always coordinated because each is not fully aware of all projects
planned by the other for the same area. Because one of the primary
goals of NOUS is to promote regional cooperation at all levels of public
and private planning, the computerized system had to be applicable to a
very heterogenous region of thirty-five counties in Ohio and Pennsylvania.
A pilot-study approach was used to expedite the development of a working
model. NOUS is now using the model to demonstrate the concepts of the
system to municipalities throughout its study region.

_____

*The Northern Ohio Urban System Research Corporation is a privately
sponsored, non-profit, non-governmental organization which is attempting to assist in the public planning process by examining the regional
and long-term consequences of urbanization in the area, and by making
suggestions for improving the region. Funds for this and all NOUS
research projects are provided by the sponsors: The Higbee Company,
Ohio Bell Telephone Company, and The East Ohio Gas Company.

THE PROBLEM

The scenario for the problem which led to the development of this information system is repeated on streets in many places: A street is paved or resurfaced. New sidewalks, curbs or treelawns are put in. The utility company arrives a week later to make repairs or new installations. Although the curbs, walks and treelawns are adequately replaced, additional time and money is expended - and the patched surface is never quite the same. The inconvenience and occasional access interruption caused by municipal construction is repeated soon after by the utility company. A citizen who has just paid for the municipal project in taxes realizes that the utility project costs are included somewhere in his monthly bill. Phones ring in the mayor's office and the utilities' consumer relations office. These redundant costs and inconveniences are unacceptable to the public - and rightly so.

THE SOLUTION

The proposed solution to this problem is a computerized project-planning information system which is standardized enough to make the system usable throughout the service area of any utility. The pilot-study approach has allowed NOUS to develop a working system for two dissimilar communities. The purpose of the system is to quickly provide accurate and current data on the construction plan within the right-of-way of each street segment in the region. Several objectives were used as guidelines when formulating the system.

Objectives of the System

1. Encourage cooperation among communities and utilities throughout the region in the construction and maintenance of their physical plants within the various rights-of-way in each community.

2. Be able to demonstrate to the taxpayer-customer-constituent that an attempt is being made to hold down utility and tax costs.

3. Use a common standardized data code and format which encourages regional cooperation, yet is versatile enough to answer the specific needs of each community.

4. Include information on the existing physical plant of the municipality and the utility in the right-of-way for each block segment.

5. Add a geographic code to each segment which will allow for cross-referencing the right-of-way information with census and other important planning data.

The fifth objective was an important consideration for making the right-of-way data compatible with a broader regional planning information system. When combined with information about land use within each block, the street segment data will help to complete a land use data base.

THE PILOT-STUDY APPROACH

Because of the non-governmental, multi-jurisdictional nature of the NOUS organization, a pilot-study approach was considered the best way to develop and test the system concepts in the shortest possible time. Two communities were selected for the test study. One is an older, almost completely developed city, while the other is a more rural community which is presently undergoing rapid construction and growth. Although these two places do not contain the entire range of possible system variability, they do offer a great variety of the more common situations which can be expected in the NOUS region. The costs of testing different alternatives are obviously reduced using this approach. Feedback from presentations to potential users has allowed us to make changes to the system as part of the development process. Costs of system development and maintenance are also being tabulated.

SYSTEM DEVELOPMENT
Development of the pilot model system has progressed in three stages:
1. Investigation
2. Implementation
3. Promotion and Revision

The NOUS staff is currently active in the third stage of promotion and revision.

Stage 1 - Investigation
Both community and utility personnel were interviewed in order to identify the data which would be the most useful to them, keeping in mind the primary purpose of coordinating construction projects when possible. An important consideration during this initial phase was to identify only basic data which would be most useful, relatively easy to collect, code and store in order to have the system operating as quickly as possible. Utilities serving the region were questioned to determine if such a system already existed or was under development. The utilities usually work together during major construction projects. An advisory system is in operation in Ohio to notify others of any intentions to do excavation. It, however, is only used when digging is imminent. Municipalities and utilities do work together in planning the larger construction in the right-of-way. No system exists by which municipalities or utilities regularly notify each other of planned construction projects of all types. This fact alone prompted the continuation of the project to the implementation stage. It was also found that some municipalities do not have a current inventory of all improvements within the right-of-way. This influenced the selection of data. Information on geographic identifiers used by the Census Bureau was also collected at this time.

Stage 2 - Implementation
All of the necessary data was gathered from the utilities and the two municipalities. A data management system was selected and appropriate programs were written. The data was then coded and entered into the system. Several designs were tested before the present system was adopted.

Data - The data collected from each community was a listing of all planned improvements. Also included was information on the size and condition of sidewalks, curbs, treelawns and pavement. Measurements recorded for a typical surface profile are shown in Figure 1. The utilities also provided data on planned construction, but pointed out that emergency repairs requiring excavation are never planned. Location of the utilities was only a generalized indication of odd or even street side.

Computer System - The computer facilities of NOUS are limited to a high speed telephone terminal through which commercial venders are

FIGURE 1

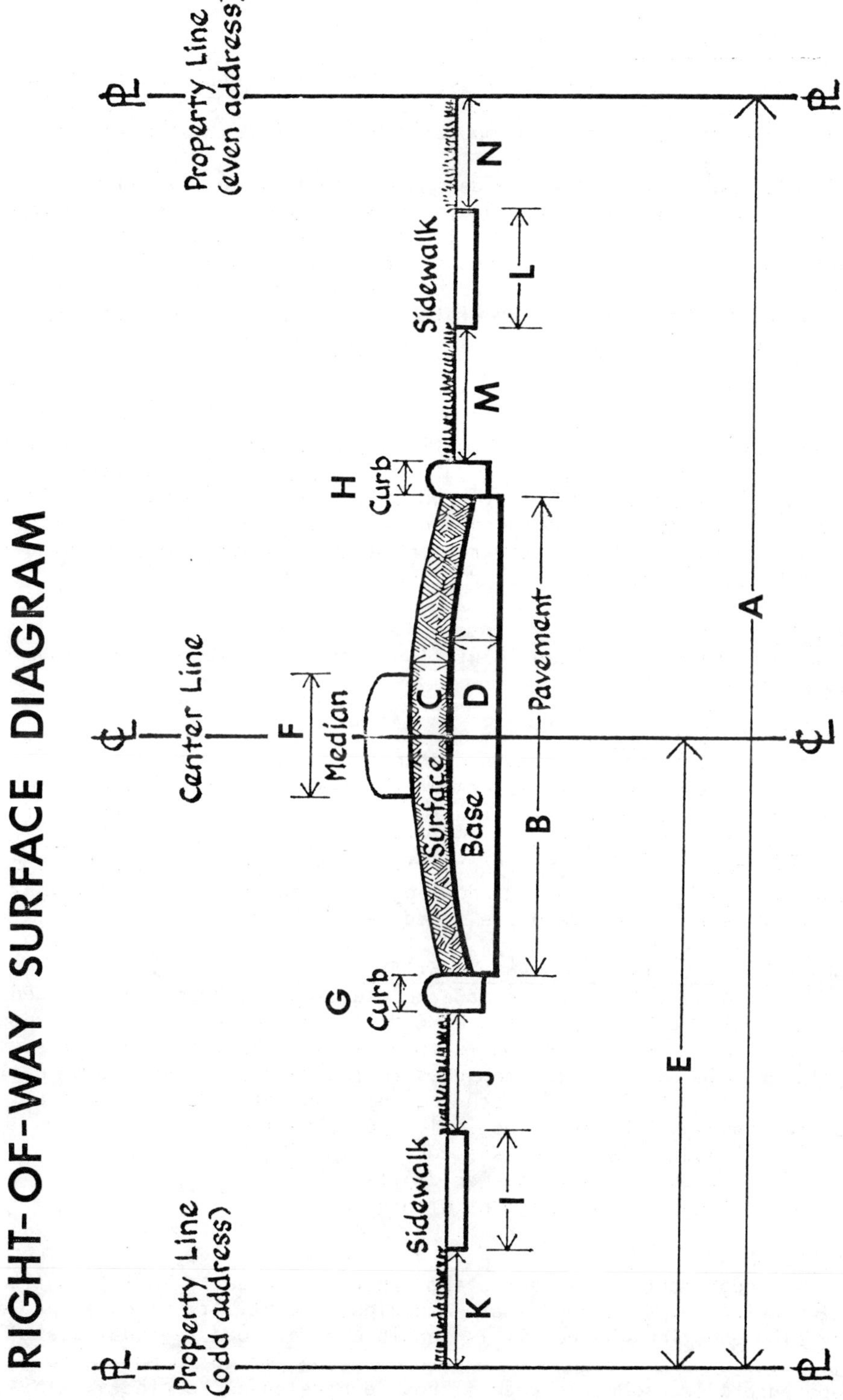
RIGHT-OF-WAY SURFACE DIAGRAM
Property Line (odd address)
Property Line (even address)
Center Line
Sidewalk
Sidewalk
Curb
Curb
Median
Surface
Base
Pavement
A
B
C
D
E
F
G
H
I
J
K
L
M
N

accessed. The data handling system of General Electric best fit the needs of this project. This commercially available data management routine allowed us to quickly operationalize the demonstration at minimal programming costs.

Data Coding - Arbitrary codes were used to identify features located in the right-of-way. Distance measurements are coded in feet and tenths. Street segments are identified by a seven-digit code consisting of the five-digit Census Bureau street code and a two digit number. The two digit number was derived by consecutively numbering each segment along a given street from the western or southernmost end of the street. Numbering increased by fives to allow for possible new segments.

Stage 3 - Promotion

Presentations on the construction planning concept and demonstrations of the system are being given to utility company and municipality personnel in order to promote the concept throughout the NOUS Region. Response to the project has been generally positive. Most encouraging was the favorable response toward linking the construction coordination and right-of-way data to a broader geocoded information system.

PROBLEMS

Two problems have been identified during the promotional stage of this project.

Problem - Data Integrity

Misuse of the planned date of construction information was a fear expressed by some potential users of the system. The primary concern was that once a proposed construction date is released to others, it would be difficult to change. The utility or municipality might face some resistance in altering construction schedules and would loose some planning flexibility. Public knowledge of planning schedules may bring public pressure to maintain the schedules.

Problem - Standardized Segment Identifier

An effort is still being made to use existing Bureau of the Census geographic identifiers from the DIME file to identify street segments where possible. The intention is to eliminate the last two arbitrary digits we have added to the census street code and use some combination of census codes to identify each segment. No satisfactory combination has been found which meets the following criteria:
1. Already existing census code
2. Sixteen or fewer integer digits
3. Unique for each segment within each SMSA

CONCLUSION

Although most people agree that there is value to an information system which helps to coordinate municipal and utility planning projects, many also question whether it is feasible on a broad regional scale. A major hindrance has been the concern of being forced to adhere to a proposed project schedule once it has been released to others. This concern may result in NOUS taking a new approach to the structuring of the system.

Rosemary Horwood
Senior Planner/Supervising Environmental Specialist
City of Seattle, Department of Community Development
306 Cherry Street
Seattle, Washington 98104

CORRELATION OF VIEW AND HOUSING VALUES
USING GEOCODED BUILDING PERMIT DATA

This study was designed to measure the significance of view in housing decisions. One of a package of CZM Act, Section 305 studies, its purpose was to aid in the development of Seattle's Shoreline Master Program to manage its water shorelines.

In the Washington State Shorelines Management Act and the local shorelines management program, much emphasis has been placed on preserving views of water in addition to increasing public access to the waters of the State. However, there has been no quantification of the economic significance of view, as a support to the regulations.

This study provided proof that view is a major component of housing investment decisions for upper income groups, and that housing values are influenced very heavily by view.

The findings were striking, in that for the five-year period studies, only one high-value residence out of 2700 constructed in Seattle did not have a water and/or mountain view.

PURPOSE

The study was one of a package of studies in a Coastal Zone Management Section 305 grant to the City of Seattle.

The purpose of this study was to determine the degree of correlation between view, price/expenditure decisions, and new single and multiple residential construction, as well as owner-reported housing values, and to work toward developing a quantitative economic value for view.

DATA SOURCES

Two data sources were used. One was 1970 Census Block data on residential value as reported by owners, hand colored onto a map of the city. This map shows by inspection a high correlation of residential value to view but provides no quantitative data, although a computer run could be made from Census Block data.

The other source was geocoded computer-generated maps from building permit data, 1965-1969 inclusive. These show actual location of new single-family construction permits, new multi-family permits, and permits for remodeling, additions, etc. issued from 1965 to 1969.

METHODOLOGY

A computer-generated map was produced for each of the three types of residential building permits. The single-family permit covers five years of permit records and contains nearly 2,700 permits. The multi-family permits also cover five years. The remodeling/renovation permits were plotted for 1965, 1967 and 1969 separately. Due to the large number of such permits, all permits for the period could not be printed on one map without over-printing excessively. The number of residential repair permits by year is shown below:

Number of Permits for Repairs by Year

Year	Permits
1965	1,005
1966	985
1967	1,102
1968	1,307
1969	1,073

The permit printout maps were overlaid by a transparency of the city identifying the street pattern outlining areas with major views of water and mountains. The degree of correlation of housing values with view, and the converse, was determined by examination. The computer maps identify the location of each permit, and each symbol shows one of four categories of value, the year the permit was granted, and the actual permit amount, except that the multi-family map identifies number of units instead of permit value. The printouts were designed to fit the U.S.G.S. 1" = 2,000' topographic maps. View areas were determined from the U.S.G.S. maps and were drawn onto the transparent mylar view overlay.

The view area map was prepared by a three-step process of (1) delineating known view areas, (2) checking topographic cross sections for view potential, and (3) field checking areas in question. Numerous photographs were taken to document the field check.

NEW SINGLE FAMILY RESIDENTIAL CONSTRUCTION

Findings:

View areas contained virtually all of the top value permits for the five-year period for which data were available. Only one of the high value permit locations could be considered as not having a major water/mountain view, or an offsetting amenity value, such as private beach rights or special locational factors, as in six other cases. The total number of permits plotted for the five-year period was 2,692. The high value permits follow topography so accurately that even without the view overlay, major topographical features can be identified.

Most of the housing in the second highest value category tended to be located in view areas as well. View areas also contained some of each of the other price categories, including the lowest. However, these were very few compared to the general non-view location of most of the low-value permits.

Having shown that view is a major characteristic generally in common between high value residential properties, it is fair to conclude that view has added value to such properties. Although view is not the only variable affecting property value (other variables are discussed below), it is clear that view both directly and indirectly affects the location of housing and has a strong bearing on other variables affecting housing location.

In addition, certain distinctions can be made with respect to quality of view vis-a-vis housing value. For example, properties overlooking a heavy industrial area have wide (up to 180°) views of the Olympic Mountain Range and Elliott Bay. (Both water and mountains are essential components of "view" as used here.)

The reported values of housing and the building permits in such areas suggest that these views apparently do not have perceived view quality of similar water view areas not overlooking an industrial area.

Obviously, many other demographic variables such as race and age of housing, location with respect to other land uses, location of freeways, transition areas, transportation, schools, and the like enter into private housing investment decisions.

Inspection indicates that in Seattle, with perhaps one possible exception, no area with major view can be described as declining, or as a "transition area." Striking changes in housing patterns do occur in view areas with greatly increased density. But few other symptoms of social changes are visible in "Gold Coast" view areas.

View thus can be, and in fact is, perceived not only as an amenity but also as a factor adding long-range economic value, a built-in "neighborhood-insurance." One reason is, of course, that the affluent can best afford both the amenity and the insurance, and the economically disadvantaged are forced into less desirable residential locations, which thereby are rendered even less desirable in the market.

MULTI-FAMILY CONSTRUCTION

Findings:

The computer-generated map locating new multi-family con- struction from 1965 through 1969 shows that in general, multi- family units, including apartments, condominiums, and housing for the elderly follow the zoning pattern closely with less relation to view. Most apartment structures tend to have a small number of units and thus represent smaller investors. Renters thus have less access to view than owners. Because most of multi-family zoning is located along certain major ar- terials, the location of multi-family units tends to be more independent of view than single-family residences, with the ex- ception of a few significant areas.

Several groupings of large apartments with 15 units or more occur on the west side of Capitol Hill and the south and east sides of Queen Anne Hill. In these cases, there are excellent, often spectacular, views of the mountains and water, combined with easy access to the Central Business District. Many of these structures are condominiums, for which view is an important selling point. Nearly all Seattle condominiums have good views.

Concentrations of small numbers of units per apartment occur in Fremont, Central Ballard, Wallingford, California Avenue S.W., Rainier Avenue S.E., and South Lake City, to name illustrative locations. Other clusters of small to medium large numbers of units (up to 15) occur in the S.W. Roxbury, Rainier Avenue S.E., and Madison Park areas. Good views are quite limited in these areas.

Much smaller multi-family construction appears to repre- sent conversion from older single-family residential use in many cases, particularly where the zoning or conditional use provisions permit such increases in density.

Thus, the lower easterly face of the Magnolia district, the Wallingford area, and Central Ballard contain clusters of such permits. View does not appear to have been a factor in these investment decisions.

It appears that the amount and location of what may be a relatively scarce resource of land zoned for multi-family units (and therefore not requiring the time and expense of a rezone) has been a major determining factor in where smaller apartment structures have been built.

However, it is also clear from the location of the largest (and most expensive) multi-family structures that, in order to obtain top rentals or condominium sales, view is essential. None of the largest permits were located in non-view areas.

REPAIRS AND REMODELING

Findings:

Three maps, for 1965, 1967 and 1969, were generated. At first glance the scattering of repair permits for any year appeared to be completely random. However, aside from the great likelihood of underreporting both as to estimated cost of the remodeling and as to unknown amounts of actual remodeling without permits compared with permit-authorized remodeling, which also would affect the distribution and location, close inspection showed that higher value permits are generally located along the shoreline fringes in view areas, although the pattern is less obvious than for single-family or multi-family units.

Factors other than view seem to be more significant in this type of investment decision, although the existence of view correlates well with higher values in remodeling. Since the data at hand did not provide immediate clues, no further analysis was undertaken.

CONCLUSIONS

For Seattle, view is the major consideration in investment decisions related to higher value housing construction. In marked contrast to most other cities, no one district or community contains a major percentage of top value housing in Seattle. Instead, the distribution of views, primarily around the fringes of the city, related to the water, is the major determinant of high value residential location.

Therefore, the emphasis on view preservation, both in the State Act and the Seattle Master Program, appears to be well founded economically and in the general value system of the public.

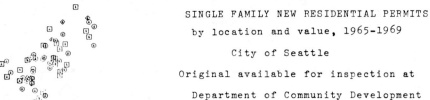

SINGLE FAMILY NEW RESIDENTIAL PERMITS
by location and value, 1965-1969
City of Seattle
Original available for inspection at
Department of Community Development

Multi-Family, New and Added Units/Building Permits,
by location and value, City of Seattle,
1965-1969

Original available for inspection at

Department of Community Development

Building Permits for Repairs, by location
and value, 1965, City of Seattle

Original available for inspection at
Department of Community Development

Building Permits for Repairs, by location and
value, 1967, CITY OF SEATTLE

Original available for inspection at
DEPARTMENT OF COMMUNITY DEVELOPMENT

Building Permits for Repairs
City of Seattle, 1969
by location and value.

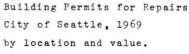

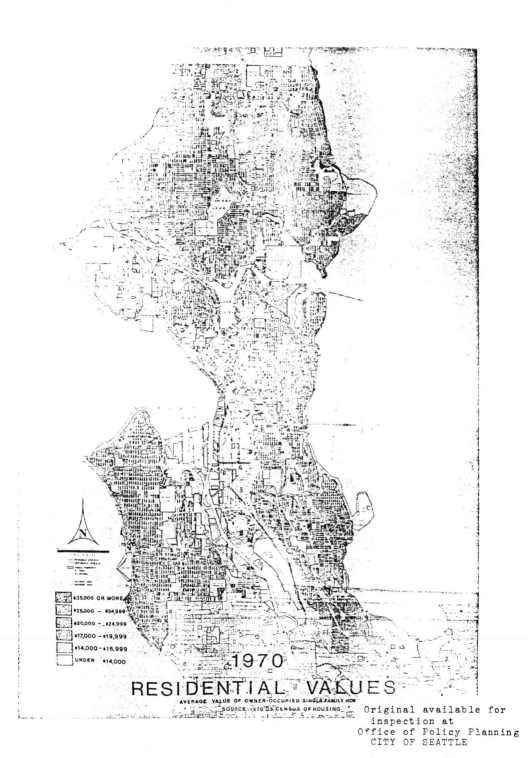

1970

RESIDENTIAL VALUES

AVERAGE VALUE OF OWNER-OCCUPIED SINGLE FAMILY HOM
SOURCE 1970 US CENSUS OF HOUSING

Dr. Forrest B. Williams
Research Analyst
Battelle-Columbus Laboratories
505 King Avenue
Columbus, OH 43201

DEVELOPMENT OF A GEOGRAPHIC INFORMATION
SYSTEM FOR AUTOMATED REAL ESTATE ASSESSMENT

The design of a geographic information system (land
records system) for computerized real estate assessment
presents problems unique to this application. The
objective of using this system for other land data applications adds other considerations to the design. This
paper discusses land records systems (as related to this
research), describes the chief functions of the system -
followed by comments on the GBF design - and summarizes
special considerations that are required of an information system that supports real estate assessment and
meets the requirements of a Comprehensive, Unified,
Land-Data System.

INTRODUCTION

Over the past year and a half, Battelle's Columbus Laboratories
has participted in Phase I of a NSF project conducted by the Kentucky
Department of Revenue to design a Computerized Real Estate Assessment
and Land Records System (CREAL). This author contributed to the
design of the geographic information system (the land records portion)
of CREAL, and it is this area to which this paper is limited. Readers
interested in other aspects of this comprehensive project are referred
to the Phase I Final Report and to a URISA paper presented last year
by David Moyer.[1]

The paper is divided into four major sections. First, a brief
summary of land records research as it relates to this project is
provided. This is followed by a concise discussion of the major
functions of the system, followed by some comments on GBF design. The
paper is concluded with a summary of special considerations that are
required of an information system that supports real estate assessment.
The reader is assumed to be knowledgeable in geographic information
systems and census geography and terminology.[2]

---

[1] Kentucky Department of Revenue Real Estate Assessment and Land Records
System Research Project Phase I Final Report, Kentucky Department of
Revenue, Frankfort, Kentucky, 1976.
Moyer, D. David, "Real Estate Assessment and Land Records System",
Papers from the Thirteenth Annual Conference of Urban and Regional
Information Systems Association, URISA, 1313 East 60th Street,
Chicago, 1976.

[2] For additional background in these areas see:
Tomlinson, R. F., (Editor), Geographic Data Handling, Volumes 1 and 2
(UNESCO/IGU Second Symposium on Geographical Information Systems,
Ottawa, 1972), IGU Commission on Geographical Data Sensing and
Processing, 1972.
U.S. Bureau of the Census, 1970 Census Users' Guide, U.S. Government
Printing Office, Washington, D.C., 1970.

One of the first tasks of the Kentucky project was an extensive literature review of systems and literature in the land records area. Several important considerations were obtained from this process.

1. The concept of a land records system is still evolving. The term "land records system" does seem to imply that a computerized file of land parcels is being used for property descriptions, for example, by the county deed recorders office. At the time, however, there was no existing model of a land records system.

2. A considerable amount of literature and professional activity has been associated with the development of a model of a land data system to support a number of applications.[3] This material provides a number of useful guidelines for the design of any data system dealing with land parcels.

3. To design an integrated land records system to support a number of applications would be difficult because the variety of data entities that are required are not reconcilable. For example, the land use planner works with land use zones that have boundaries that do not correspond to parcel boundaries. To fully support this application, basic entities smaller than parcels (the least common geographic until LGCU) would have to be used.[4]

These realities led us to believe that a land records system that would fully support a number of applications was beyond the scope of the project. We decided instead to utilize the model of a Comprehensive Unified Land-Data System to design a geographic information system to support real estate assessment.

The existing work in land data systems gave us some useful guidelines for system design, particularly with regard to basic data entities (LCGU) and parcel identifiers. The system designed meets the CULDATA criteria and its parcel identifier meets the CLIPPP criteria[5] (see Tables 1 and 2).

---

3   Proceedings of the North American Conference on Modernization of Land Data Systems [A Multi-Purpose Approach], North American Institute for MOLDS, Woodward Building, Room 430, 733 15th Street, N.W., Washington, D.C., 1975.
    Moyer, D. David, and Kenneth P. Fisher, Land Parcel Identifiers for Information Systems, American Bar Foundation, 1155 East 60th Street Chicago, Illinois.

4   This type of problem has been previously identified by Crhisman. See Chrisman, Nichola, "Topological Information System for Geographic Representation", Papers from the Thirteenth Annual Conference and the Urban and Regional Information Systems Association, URISA, 1313 East 60th Street, Chicago,1976.

5   See Moyer and Fisher, op. cit.

TABLE 1.   CRITERIA FOR COMPATIBLE IDENTIFIER (CLIPPP)

1. Simplicity

    a.   Ease of Understanding

    b.   Reasonable Permanence

2. Uniqueness

    a.   Ease of Maintenance

3. Accuracy

    a.   Statistical Sampling

    b.   Point Location and Relocation

4. Flexibility

    a.   Data/Coordination

    b.   Selection of Relevant Data

    c.   Capability of Defining an Area or a Point

5. Economy

    a.   Efficient Use of ADP Equipment

    b.   Compatibility with X-Y Digitizers and Plotters for
       Determining Grid Coordinates

6. Accessibility

    a.   Availability on Current Map

    b.   Facilitation of Graphic Computer Output

    c.   Worldwise System

TABLE 2.   CRITERIA FOR A COMPREHENSIVE,
UNIFIED LAND-DATA SYSTEM (CULDATA)

1. The system will be automated by use of computers and suitable peripheral equipment.

2. The basic building block is the individual land-ownership parcel.

3. Each parcel should have a unique identification number that indicates its location on the earth.

4. A system of large-scale, accurate maps should be maintained for both urban and rural areas.

5. Each parcel should be described using a system of coordinates that are tied into a national or international grid system.

6. A parcel index, based on location, should be available.

7. When the parcel number and parcel index are established, all land and land-related data should be coded by parcel number.

8. If data on persons is added to CULDATA, a file should be developed containing a code number for each individual, business, and organization.

9. The data collection and data use activities at the various levels of government should be coordinated.

Major Functions of the GIS

The overriding objective of the system is to efficiently provide and maintain geographic information for the CREAL system. The most important physical components of the system are the geographic base file (GBF) and the assessor's maps. The geographic base file is a data set containing all geographic information on a particular locality and is the basis of the function. A good base file should be built with land parcels (see Table 2) as the basic entity, although a "proxy" file could be built using street addresses from the Census Bureau GBF/DIME files. Mapped information is provided by the assessor's maps, and the system must be able to cross-reference or duplicate these.

The six main functions of the geographic information system are:

- Provide Geographic Information System I/O
- Maintain and Retrieve Geographic Data
- Perform Geographic Calculations
- Display Geographic Data
- Provide Chain-of-Title Information
- Provide Census Bureau GBF/DIME File Interface

Providing I/O for the system entails inputting transactions and retrieval requests from assessment, inputting digitized data, and inputting area indexes (for update). "Maintain and Retrieve Geographic Data" encompasses the ability to update and retrieve information from the GBF. Geographic calculations include calculating areas and distances from coordinate data. The display of geographic data means the generation of computer maps and the generation of summary area listings. Chain-of-Title information consists mainly of ownership data (history) by parcel ID. The function "Provide GBF/DIME File Interface" recognizes the importance of the capability of using this system in conjunction with the GBF/DIME Files. Its task is to reconcile differences between the two files with regard to basic orientation.[6]

The system is designed to support non-assessment applications. They interface by providing (in digitized DIME format) the summary areas for which data items from the assessor's file are to be tabulated. These summary areas are termed Polygon Defined Summary Areas (PDSA) and are utilized by the "Display Geographic Data" function. This particular organization means that the GBF does not have to contain information for every possible application, only the geography that needs to be maintained for the assessor. It also means that the information system is virtually limitless in the number of different types of tabulations (i.e., summary areas) that it can produce.

---

6 The GBF/DIME Files are segment-oriented while the CREAL GBF is parcel-oriented. See Chrisman, op. cit.

The geographic base file was designed to provide the maximum amount of flexibility while providing an efficient means of accessing geographic data. For purposes of explanation, the GBF can be seen as having two formats. In the first (static format), the GBF record would contain all indexes and keys for a particular parcel. Retrieving geographic information means simply accessing the GBF by parcel ID and extracting desired indexes.

In the second (dynamic format), the record contains the parcel ID and the visual parcel centroid of the GBF. In addition, the GBF maintains polygon definitions of all summary areas. Retrieving information from the GBF requires performing a point-in-polygon routine for every parcel using the polygon definitions of summary areas. The indexes extracted are those of the polygons in which the parcel lies.

Each format has its own advantage. The first allows efficient processing but requires storing and maintaining every usable index for every parcel. If a useful index is discovered after the GBF is built, then every record (parcel) in the file must be updated.

The second format requires more overhead processing since a point-in-polygon routine is required rather than a simple table reference. Storage is more efficient since every record contains only a parcel ID and parcel visual center (polygon definitions must also be stored). More importantly, it is more flexible since additional indexes are easily added to the GBF by coding their polygon definitions. [7]

The GBF designed for the system takes advantage of both of these formats. It contains indexes for important area indexes and a parcel visual center which is used with polygon definitions for additional, less frequently used indexes. The user defines the GBF and he can select which indexes will be handled in the different formats. It is anticipated that the assessor will include most of "his" indexes in the static format while hoping to support other applications with the dynamic format.

---

7   This concept has been more adequately discussed by other authors. See Dueker, Kenneth J., Richard Talcott, Michael Goodchild, and John Milligan, Final Report 11 - Land Resource Information System: A Development and Demonstration for the State of Iowa, Institute of Urban and Regional Research, The University of Iowa, Iowa City, Iowa, 1974.
Blumberg, Maurice H., "A Generalized Geographic Information System for Managing a Non-Redundant Demographic and Resource Data Base", Papers from the Thirteenth Annual Conference of the Urban and Regional Information Systems Association, URISA, 1313 East 60th Street, Chicago, 1976.

The real estate assessment application required several special considerations in design of the geographic information system. Probably the most important of these is in the basic data entity of the system. The assessor works with a single taxable entity termed a tax parcel. It often does not correspond directly with ownership parcels as filed in the deed recorder's office. In some cases, it may not even be contiguous. A CULDATA system requires that the basic entity be land parcels. "The land parcel should, in most cases, be isolated on the basis of ownership. If a finer breakdown is needed, such as in the case of an apartment building or condominium, appropriate subsystems can be introduced."[8] Although the land parcel concept helps in cross-referencing tax parcels and ownership parcels, the correspondence is far from exact. When building a GBF of land or ownership parcels, special consideration should be given in the static portion of the file to tax parcels.

Another problem is dictated by the manner in which taxes are levied. Tax districts are defined in most jurisdictions without respect for parcel boundaries and, as a result, a parcel may exist only partially in a given tax district. In most cases, the assessor handles such a case by weighting his assessment depending on the portion of the property in each tax district. This type of geographic referencing could also be handled in the static portion of the GBF.

The problems of resolution and scale are critical to the system because of the need of locational integrity. If the objective of the system is to provide geographic information to tax assessment and other similar applications, then parcel visual centroids located within an accuracy of ten feet were deemed sufficient to describe parcel locations. Other applications, such as the deed recorder's office, might require digitized parcel boundaries with accuracies sufficient for legal parcel description. Such an application was beyond the scope of this project and interested readers are referred to the Forsyth County land records system.[9]

---

8   Moyer, D. David, "An Economic Analysis of the Land Title Records System", unpublished manuscript.

9   Papers from the FIRST Workshop, Public Information Office, Forsyth County, North Carolina, March, 1976.

CONCLUSION

The design of a geographic information system for CREAL draws
heavily from the CULDATA conceptual model of land data systems.
This design primarily supports the six functions of the CREAL system
but also can support any number of secondary applications.

The GBF for the system is parcel-oriented and consists of both
a static and dynamic portion. This format helps to circumvent some
of the special problems of an assessment data base and also provides
a flexible geographical retrieval capability with Polygon Defined
Summary Areas. This flexibility, plus the adoption of the CULDATA
and CLIPPP criteria, insures that the system can adequately support
a number of land data applications.

Edward J. Spar
President, Market Statistics
633 3rd Avenue
New York, New York 10017
August 1976

ANNUAL UPDATING OF SOCIO-ECONOMIC DATA

ABSTRACT. Market Statistics annually produces Sales
Management's Survey of Buying Power. This publication
contains updated population, households, income and retail sales data for every county in the United States.
In order to generate this information, data such as
births, deaths, school enrollment, Chamber of Commerce
information, Census Bureau data, local sales tax data,
etc. are collected.
Many techniques are used in order to update this
series of information. At the same time, each series is
demographically and socio-economically tied to each other.
The purpose of this paper is to show how this series of
data is updated and how the private sector of the economy makes use of it.

Introduction

In order to give you a rounded picture of what the private sector is
producing in the way of socio-economic and demographic updates, I think
it is necessary to first state why we make these estimates. Basically,
we are asked three questions. First, where are the potential customers
geographically for a specific product? Second, how much money do they
have to spend for retail trade? And finally, how much money do they have
to spend for on various merchandise or in certain types of stores?
Since a business organization is rarely, or should I say, tries not
to be an eleemosynary entity, the three questions just raised are posed
for the purpose of evaluating the sales strength of the organization. In
fact, the data are used to help answer three basic marketing questions.
First, am I getting the most that I can out of my sales force? Since the
answer to this question is never a total yes, the data can be used to pinpoint those salespeople who are below potential - and those above. Second,
am I marketing in the right areas? Many times the answer to this question
helps answer the first. The final question as you could guess is related
to the first two. Am I allocating my resources, such as advertising dollars and distribution facilities properly in order to maximize potential?
The answers to these questions lie at the heart of a successful business.
The techniques used to answer them range from simple descriptive printouts
to multivariate statistical analyses. I do not think, however, that a discussion of these analytical approaches are in the scope of this paper.

My company anually updates three major sets of data for the 3142 counties and independent cities in the United States. The first series is population. We produce updated estimates annually for: total population, total households, age of head of household, size of household, each individual age for both sexes for the total population, for the black population and Spanish language population. The second series is income related. We produce estimates, again on a county basis for: disposable income, the number of households in $1,000 income groups, and the amount of income in each of these groups. The third and final segment is retail trade. We estimate the annual volume in major store categories such as department stores, food stores, apparel stores, drug stores, automotive dealers, and about fifteen others. We also estimate the sales volume of specific merchandise such as furniture, apparel, floor coverings in department stores and specialty shops. We publish the data in July of every year. The population estimates are dated as of the 31st of December of the previous year. Income and retail trade data are for the full previous year. For example, our present estimates are for the year 1975; either for December 31 or for the full year.

We look at the concepts of fertility and much more important, migration, as dynamic processes. The decisions to have children or to move are a function of the availability of jobs, space, and goods and services. Population cannot be measured as an isolated entity. In our analyses, we are continually crossing over categories. Changes in per capita disposable income from year to year have to make sense. The amount of disposable dollars being allocated to retail trade must have consistency. Per capita expenditures for durable and non-durable goods should follow fairly regular patterns. As you can see, by looking at a geographic unit such as a county in this manner. we can derive a powerful picture of the dynamics of that area. This enables us to refine our estimates so that the interrelationships are logical. Bearing in mind that we do not cross over the three major categories in our estimating procedures, I will now cover each section separately - discussing the methodologies used for each.

Population

The starting point and the one from which all other figures stem is total population; even though we may change a population figure due to information found relevant to retail sales or income. In order to estimate each county's population we utilize the following data bases: Births, Deaths, Federal State Cooperative Program Estimates, Current Population Report Data, Public School and College Enrollment figures, Military Installation data, Special and Local Census figures, Vital Statistics reports, special studies conducted by Universities and Local Governments, Chambers of Commerce figures, and data collected by local newspapers.

First, we break population change into its two component parts; those being migration, and natural increase or decrease. Our first step is to estimate the current fertility rate adjustment factors based upon the latest census estimates. These adjustments are applied to the previous year's actual fertility rates which are derived using the known births and the estimated female 15-44 age cohort. Births are then calculated by multiplying the fertility rate by the 15-44 female age cohort. This circuitous approach has to be used since actual birth data collected from state agencies is always one year behind. Death rates by county are then applied to the previous year's population estimates. The difference between births and deaths yields our natural increase or decrease. This, of course, is the easy part. The migration segment is much more complex. Utilizing the Bureau of the Census Federal State Cooperative Program, we estimate the amount of migration in each county by subtracting out our natural increase or decrease data from their estimates. Since we feel the Bureau's figures are subject to fluctuations due to sensitive equations, we set up a migration trend over time for each county; correcting for overly large changes in their figures by averaging. A current estimate from this trend is then developed. Once we have derived our first estimate of migration for the county, we check our Chamber of Commerce, Military, Newspapers and all other files for indications of any special population movements into or out of a county. About twenty percent of the figures are changed by hand using this "live" data. Once we are satisfied with the migration component of population change, it is combined with natural increase or decrease to yield a total population figure for the county. The counties in each state are then summed up and compared to Census Bureau estimates of the state's population. If there are wide divergencies, we look further into each individual county in the state. We do not proportionally allocate differences.

As an aside, we find this approach more accurate than using a school enrollment age cohort technique. Such an approach was feasible in the 1960's when the proportion of of expected enrolled students was fairly constant. With the vast changes in the school age cohort, this type of estimating procedure is no longer stable. As I mentioned, we utilize the Federal State Cooperation data in our estimates. This data is a year and a half old when we use it. Therefore, our current estimates come out before the latest updated Federal estimates are made. A problem we have is trying to validate our own estimates. One way is to compare our estimates adjusted for the different dates, to the Federal State data. This analysis was performed using our 1973 Survey of Buying Power for counties of 250,000 or more. You can see the results in the handout which is broken down by county size. Overall, we are quite pleased with the results.

The next statistic estimated is the number of households per county. We are given only two sets of information. First, we have the 1970 Census of Population counts, and second, the updated estimates for states from the Current Population Reports. Using the year to year state changes, we estimate the rate of change in the size of households. These factors, on a state by state basis, are applies to our previous year's household size estimates. These adjusted size factors are in turn divided into our current population estimate to yield an updated estimate of households. This type of estimating procedure sometimes leaves us all a little nervous. Obviously, with precipitous decline in household size, we might conceivably generate a set of estimates for a county where the population is declining and the number of households increasing. Needless to say, we do flag these potential problems. Since our estimate of households come out three months before the one the one published by the Census Bureau, we have no control total to check against. We are pleased that our estimate of the total households in the United States has never been off by more than two tenths of one percent from the Census estimate.

At this point I would mention that we, Market Statistics, produce Sales and Management's Survey of Buying Power. Through them, we send our figures out to the media, mostly newspapers, around the United States. If there is some reason that they feel an estimate is too low they will contact us. If they can produce valid data that we might have missed, we will revise our estimates. As could be expected, we do not have on record one complaint of over estimation.

The next series of data generated is age by sex for each individual age. We produce these data for total population, black population and Spanish language population. We have gone back to the 1960 Census and the 1970 Census, breaking the data into single year groups - up to 85 years of age and over by sex. Our data files contain birth and death data for the intervening years by county. What we have done is create annualized ratios of change for each segment by county. In other words, we have calculated the proportion of a specific age group that will be in the county as the age group goes, let us say, from age eleven to age twelve. By applying these ratios of change each year to the previous year's estimates, we develop the number of people in each age group. The base year, of course, is 1970. We have made one major assumption, that is, the rate of change between the years 1960 and 1970 will be the same as the rate of change from 1970 to 1980. Since we know there have been counter migrational trends, especially from the north back to the south, we change some of the calculated ratios to account for this. Also, since we do control the sum of the ages to our overall county total population, this phenomenon is partially self corrected. The methodology might break down in the case of military bases and university counties where the rates are not the same over ten years. In these cases, we do not try and age the military cohort, These and the college group are adjusted by hand. However, where the rates of change are constant, the procedure properly accounts for military and college group populations. The same age factors are used for black and Spanish language groups. In the case of Spanish language, we have developed a consistent definition for all counties. As you may or may not know, the Bureau of the Census has a number of Spanish definitions. In New York, New Jersey and Pennsylvania we added black in the non-Puerto Rican stock. In the Southwest, we adjusted for the Spanish surname additions. Our algorithm for migration of Spanish and black utilizes data supplied by the United States Department of Health, Education and Welfare on Public Elementary and Secondary Enrollment by Racial and Ethnic Groups. These data are suplemented by studies conducted by the media. Once control totals for black and Spanish are estimated and the rates of change applied, we then check the relationship of these groups to the total population, by age, for consistency. Gross deviations are corrected by hand.

We now return to households. The next step is an updating of head of household and size of household distributions. Utilizing the Current Population Report data on a national basis, we apply ratios of change to each group in order to estimate the number of households in each group. In the case of age of head of household, we also track the relationship between the number of heads in an age group to the total number of people in that group. By doing so, we can immediately spot where we are incorrectly aging the distribution. For size of household, we multiply the number oh households in each group by the size and derive - in a

backwards way - an independent population total. By comparing this to
our basic estimate, we can adjust the size distribution up or down in
order to make them match. This basically covers our population estimating procedures. The next series is income.

Income

As I mentioned, population and income are closely related. We annually develop estimates of disposable, or after tax income. Using the
data from the 1970 Census and the Bureau of Economic Analysis, we have
detaxed and created a county by county distribution. This distribution
is updated annually, utilizing covered employment statistics supplied by
each state, on a county basis. By calculating the change in the per
household covered earnings and applying this to the previous year's disposable income we can update the series. Thanks to tabulations from the
Bureau of Economic Analysis, we are also able to adjust to our growth
factors by the difference between place of residence and place of work.
The final figures are then analyzed on a per household and per capita
basis for logical growth, and our state totals are compared to the Survey of Current Business Estimates for disposable income. At this point
we might have to revise a population estimate if there is undue change in
disposable income.

Once disposable income has been established, we estimate the number
of households in thousand dollar income groups. This is accomplished by
using a combination of the analysis of mean densities and Pareto Curves.
Each interval is taxed in order to estimate the number of households in
what became disposable income groups. Internal Revenue Service data is
utilized in order to accomplish this. The bases for the distribution are
the 1970 Census fourth count household, unrelated individual, and family
income distributions. Working with the detaxed class intervals, new groups
are again formed based upon the growth in per household income. As in
the case of disposable income, state and local data are utilized here.
Since we have shifted the income classes, we must interpolate to find how
many households now fall within the original $1,000 income intervals.
Up to this point, the previous year's income distribution has been re-
distributed based upon the change in the economy. We then proportionally
allocate the overall annual change of households in the county to each income class.

Retail Sales

The final set of estimating procedures I would like to describe is
for retail trade. The flow of durable and non-durable goods in a local
market is crucial in fine tuning the demographic and socio-economic profile of the area. Utilizing the Census of Retail Trade as a base, we
annually update those store groups mentioned earlier. Our approach
makes use of retail sales tax data collected on a county basis. The
growth in tax collected applied to the previous year's sales gives us a
measure of retail growth. At the same time we use the County Business
Pattern Data base and shopping center directories to spot the openings
or closings of stores. Also, the local Chamber of Commerce information

collected is crucial here. Once total retail sales is updated, we allocate the growth to each store group. Now obviously, food stores don't
grow in sales in the same proportion as automobile dealers sales, especially these days. Therefore, the allocation of growth is weighted by the
specific store growth for each state. This data is available from the
U.S. Department of Commerce and the various state departments. The overall matrix of retail sales is then controlled by the national growth. At
each step, we check the relationship between disposable income and retail
sales. In ninety percent of the cases, this relationship is fairly constant. In some counties, the phenomenon can exist where the retail sales
is greater than the disposable income. In these cases, the county is obviously drawing its sales from the surrounding areas. This often happens
in rural counties, On the average, however, fifty-seven cents of every
possible spendable dollar goes to retail sales. We also track the growth
in per capita retail sales. In doing so, this also provides us with another means to check our population estimates. To repeat, population,
income and retail sales are so interweaved that they must be looked at as
a single entity.

The final phase of retail sales updating deals with the merchandise
sold in the retail outlets. By estimating these sales, we now have the
entire picture of retail trade in balance. Also, from a user point of
view, let us say a furniture manufacturer, he is totally disinterested in
the sales of television sets in department stores. Therefore, this type
of data is much more usable for our clients. The techniques for estimating these sales are similar to our retail store methodology. The key
to developing good estimates for merchandise lines is the proper tracking of the percentage of any store's sales for the specific line. Most
goods, such as furniture, apparel, and shoes, remain fairly consistent.
We would expect department stores to sell each year, about the same proportion of various merchandise. One contradicting example is in drug
stores. In the 1960's drugs represented a large percentage of a drug
store's sales. In the last six years, drug stores have become mini super
markets, thereby reducing this percentage drastically.

Summary

By collecting as much local data as we can, we have found ways to develop
updated statistics that are usable in the private sector. We are continually refining our techniques and looking for new sources of information.
You can readily see that we are aware of the fact that this is a very inexact science - at best. And perhaps even more of an art. At each step
we have to look at the data. Nothing ever comes out of the computer
neatly wrapped up and ready for consumption. Not only does this not bother
us, we feel that a hands on approach to demography is a much more realistic way of dealing with data that continually tries to defy generalities
and logic. After all, demography deals with people.

As I mentioned earlier, I believe the business community's uses and
the techniques developed for them are outside the scope of this paper.
If you have any questions on the applications of the data, I will be happy
to go into details later.

MARKET STATISTICS

ANALYSIS OF POPULATION ACCURACY

COUNTIES 250,000 - 500,000 POPULATION

COUNTY	MARKET STATISTICS 7/1/72 (INTERPOLATED)	FEDERAL/STATE ESTIMATES 7/1/72	% DIFFERENCE
Mobile, Ala.	326.6	323.8	less than 1
Pima, Ariz.	388.7	387.0	less than 1
Pulaski, Ark.	299.5	297.8	less than 1
Santa Barbara, Cal.	271.0	271.8	less than 1
San Joaquin, Cal.	295.3	297.2	less than 1
Kern, Cal.	339.9	336.0	1-2
Ventura, Cal.	406.5	404.7	less than 1
Fresno, Cal.	425.1	430.5	1-2
Riverside, Cal.	481.8	486.5	1-2
New Castle, Del.	402.5	393.8	2-3
Orange, Fla.	375.0	373.8	less than 1
Palm Beach, Fla.	375.7	378.0	less than 1
Hillsborough, Fla.	533.3	511.5	3-4
De Kalb, Ga.	437.5	449.2	2-3
Madison, Ill.	254.6	253.2	less than 1
Kane, Ill.	251.8	260.9	3-4
St. Clair, Ill.	288.6	283.6	1-2
Lake, Ill.	387.5	389.6	less than 1
Du Page, Ill.	508.4	515.1	1-2
Allen, Ind.	288.1	289.6	less than 1
Polk, Iowa	299.6	295.1	1-2
Sedgwick, Kans.	338.9	337.8	less than 1
East Baton Rouge, La.	294.1	292.4	less than 1
Jefferson, La.	351.4	367.6	4-5
Anne Arundel, Md.	309.5	314.2	1-2
Plymouth, Mass.	356.3	350.2	1-2
Bristol, Mass.	466.7	457.2	2-3
Hampden, Mass.	469.0	462.8	1-2
Ingham, Mich.	275.5	266.6	3-4
Kent, Mich.	420.3	415.6	1-2
Genesee, Mich.	461.4	454.4	1-2
Ramsey, Minn.	488.4	471.8	3-4
Douglas, Neb.	399.1	407.7	2-3
Clark, Nev.	297.5	295.8	less than 1
Mercer, N.J.	314.4	315.3	less than 1
Burlington, N.J.	327.6	341.3	4-5
Morris, N.J.	401.2	393.7	1-2
Camden, N.J.	468.9	478.6	2-3
Passaic, N.J.	478.9	464.3	3-4
Monmouth, N.J.	472.6	478.6	1-2

COUNTY	MARKET STATISTICS 7/1/72 (INTERPOLATED)	FEDERAL/STATE ESTIMATES 7/1/72	% DIFFERENCE
Bernalillo, N.M.	330.5	337.5	2 - 3
Oneida, N.Y.	276.3	274.5	less than 1
Albany, N.Y.	286.9	287.8	less than 1
Richmond, N.Y.	314.7	308.2	2 - 3
Onondaga, N.Y.	474.7	473.9	less than 1
Guilford, N.C.	300.5	296.2	1 - 2
Mecklenburg, N.C.	368.3	361.5	1 - 2
Lorain, Ohio	260.5	261.1	less than 1
Mahoning, Ohio	305.8	306.7	less than 1
Stark, Ohio	381.6	375.6	1 - 2
Lucas, Ohio	501.1	490.0	2 - 3
Tulsa, Okla.	414.3	406.5	1 - 2
Lehigh, Pa.	261.5	261.3	less than 1
Erie, Pa.	264.4	271.0	2 - 3
York, Pa.	282.6	279.4	1 - 2
Chester, Pa.	286.7	287.8	less than 1
Berks, Pa.	307.1	301.4	1 - 2
Lancaster, Pa.	324.3	330.0	1 - 2
Luzerne, Pa.	345.4	346.9	less than 1
Westmoreland, Pa.	384.1	382.2	less than 1
Bucks, Pa.	431.3	439.1	1 - 2
Hamilton, Tenn.	257.7	260.9	1 - 2
Knox, Tenn.	286.8	285.1	less than 1
Davidson, Tenn.	456.4	447.6	2 - 3
Travis, Tex.	325.7	318.4	2 - 3
El Paso, Tex.	370.2	373.9	less than 1
Salt Lake, Utah	480.8	482.3	less than 1
Norfolk, Va.	312.7	283.0	10
Fairfax, Va.	482.7	482.1	less than 1
Snohomish, Wash.	272.8	264.8	3 - 4
Spokane, Wash.	296.0	301.8	1 - 2
Pierce, Wash.	414.5	405.3	2 - 3
Dane, Wis.	299.9	300.2	less than 1

SUMMARY

Total Counties	Less than 1%	1-2%	2-3%	3-4%	4-5%	More than 5%
73	29	23	12	6	2	1

MARKET STATISTICS

COUNTY	7/1/72 (INTERPOLATED)	FEDERAL/STATE ESTIMATES 7/1/72	% DIFFERENCE
Jefferson, Ala.	638.4	646.3	1-2
Maricopa, Ariz.	1057.3	1053.0	less than 1
Contra Costa, Calif.	578.5	572.7	1-2
San Mateo, Calif.	557.0	562.9	less than 1
Sacramento, Calif.	658.4	669.4	1-2
San Bernardino, Calif.	703.3	692.0	1-2
San Francisco, Calif.	692.2	690.3	less than 1
Denver, Colo.	533.2	511.9	4-5
New Haven, Conn.	756.0	760.8	less than 1
Fairfield, Conn.	801.5	793.9	less than 1
Hartford, Conn.	829.5	833.8	less than 1
District of Columbia	740.0	752.0	1-2
Pinellas, Fla.	577.1	580.1	less than 1
Duval, Fla.	540.1	535.3	less than 1
Broward, Fla.	689.0	684.9	less than 1
Fulton, Ga.	616.7	596.8	3-4
Lake, Ind.	562.5	552.8	1-2
Marion, Ind.	809.0	798.3	1-2
Jefferson, Ky.	708.6	707.6	less than 1
Orleans, La.	594.9	589.0	less than 1
Montgomery, Md.	554.9	545.1	1-2
Baltimore, Md.	637.7	640.4	less than 1
Prince Georges, Md.	687.7	694.5	less than 1
Baltimore City, Md.	907.2	896.9	1-2
Norfolk, Mass.	629.4	609.7	3-4
Worcester, Mass.	659.4	644.7	2-3
Essex, Mass.	663.4	649.4	2-3
Suffolk, Mass.	717.4	739.5	3-4
Macomb. Mich.	634.6	645.9	1-2
Oakland, Mich.	920.0	933.8	1-2
Hennepin, Minn.	966.9	954.8	1-2
St. Louis City, Mo.	605.7	586.4	3-4
Jackson, Mo.	668.7	660.3	1-2
St. Louis, Mo.	956.7	957.1	less than 1
Union, N.J.	558.1	547.6	1-2
Middlesex, N.J.	598.8	595.6	less than 1
Hudson, N.J.	623.5	610.7	2-3
Bergen, N.J.	910.3	896.8	1-2
Essex, N.J.	951.7	938.8	1-2
Monroe, N.Y.	729.3	714.6	2-3
Westchester, N.Y.	904.2	897.4	less than 1
Summit, Ohio	562.4	551.9	1-2
Montgomery, Ohio	618.5	606.2	2-3
Franklin, Ohio	854.3	864.5	1-2

Hamilton, Ohio	938.5	921.8	1-2
Oklahoma, Okla.	548.6	547.6	less than 1
Multnomah, Ore.	573.2	550.4	4-5
Delaware, Pa.	595.6	601.9	1-2
Montgomery, Pa.	640.1	633.0	1-2
Providence, R.I.	587.7	590.4	less than 1
Shelby, Tenn.	746.4	736.0	1-2
Tarrant, Tex.	751.8	724.9	3-4
Bexar, Tex.	869.6	874.3	less than 1
Honolulu, Hawaii	661.4	660.1	less than 1

SUMMARY

Total Counties	Less than 1%	1-2%	2-3%	3-4%	4-5%	More than 5%
54	20	22	5	5	2	-

COUNTY	MARKET STATISTICS 7/1/72 (INTERPOLATED)	FEDERAL/STATE ESTIMATES 7/1/72	% DIFFERENCE
Santa Clara, Calif.	1123.7	1126.7	less than 1
Alameda, Calif.	1108.4	1097.2	1-2
San Diego, Calif.	1426.9	1443.1	1-2
Orange, Calif.	1532.4	1527.3	less than 1
Los Angeles, Calif.	7023.0	6999.6	less than 1
Dade, Fla.	1346.1	1331.2	1-2
Cook, Ill.	5561.6	5542.4	less than 1
Middlesex, Mass.	1371.6	1418.4	3-4
Wayne, Mich.	2712.8	2660.5	1-2
Erie, N.Y.	1119.5	1117.8	less than 1
Suffolk, N.Y.	1191.0	1180.5	less than 1
Nassau, N.Y.	1440.9	1416.8	1-2
Bronx, N.Y.	1506.7	1478.8	1-2
New York, N.Y.	1516.5	1495.0	1-2
Queens, N.Y.	1965.8	1998.0	1-2
Kings, N.Y.	2631.6	2567.1	3-4
Cuyahoga, Ohio	1764.1	1693.1	4-5
Allegheny, Pa.	1595.9	1588.5	less than 1
Philadelphia, Pa.	1929.3	1916.0	less than 1
Dallas, Tex.	1404.4	1361.3	3-4
Harris, Tex.	1855.0	1835.8	1-2
King, Wash.	1151.2	1134.8	1-2
Milwaukee, Wis.	1065.5	1060.1	less than 1

SUMMARY

Total Counties	Less than 1%	1-2%	2-3%	3-4%	4-5%	More than 5%
23	9	10	-	3	1	-

MORE POPULATION

Total Counties	Less than 1%	1-2%	2-3%	3-4%	4-5%	More than 5%
150	58	55	17	14	5	1

Kay Eileen Sari
Geoprocessing Services Planner
Urban Data Center (FX-10)
University of Washington
Seattle, Washington 98195

USE OF SCHOOL ENROLLMENT IN POPULATION ESTIMATION:
THE SEATTLE CASE STUDY

This paper is designed to accomplish two objectives:
first, to present a methodology for the use of school
enrollment data in estimating intercensal population change;
and second, to apply the methodology to the subject city and
make observations on what is actually happening. The estimating model presented is not overly sophisticated but offers
some ready and easy procedures for small area forecasting, as
well as setting some reasonable limits on forecasts published
by local agencies.

The estimation process is based on two reasonable assumptions: (1) the relationship of current school enrollment to
the total population; and (2) school in- and outmigration and
its likely extrapolation to the total population. For example,
between 1970 and 1975, Seattle's total school enrollment
dropped approximately 25,000, a 25% loss. This drop is one
which started, according to census statistics, in 1960, and
the 1960 to 1970 student loss was similar to the decline in
the total population for the same period. Therefore, a large
population decline has in all probability occurred between
1970 and 1975 in Seattle.

Traditionally, municipal populations have been estimated by monitoring building permits, demolitions, utility hook-ups, vacancies and
other information that relates to the housing unit itself. In a number
of states, including the State of Washington, state tax conventions are
based on population estimates updated annually under the supervision of
some branch of the state government. Under these circumstances bargain-
ing goes on between the various local jurisdictions and the supervising
agency because generally the overall state population totals must be
allocated to the various jurisdictions each year, and those jurisdictions
that gain may do so at the expense of jurisdictions that will necessarily have to lose. As a consequence, a fair amount of politics are
involved in municipal population estimation.

Added to the above are considerations of cities based on population.
Constitutional prohibitions in most states prevent special legislation
for particular cities, and as a result classifications have taken place
in most of the states which nominally preclude special legislation for
particular cities. This raises the interesting specter of cities dropping below their class levels and becoming legally ineligible for certain privileges or procedures based upon their membership in a population

class. Here again, the City of Seattle is vulnerable to losing its legal status if it drops below 500,000 people.

The traditional methods of municipal population projection based upon the housing unit as the entity are subject to various non-linear impacts as cities grow or diminish in population. For one thing, water meters and electrical outlets are often shared by groups of housing units in apartments or other group housing arrangements. For another, as cities age a measure of their housing stock becomes undesirable and actually falls below reasonable standards of occupancy. In southern and western cities as an example, where the housing built in the first two or three decades of the twentieth century was of wooden construction, large numbers of homes have become obsolete in the past decade. As a consequence, the traditional vacancy rates obtained from real estate listings may not accurately measure housing that is not in the market, including everything from derelict buildings without occupants to those verging on dereliction which have only a few of their units occupied.

As a consequence of the above, the following analysis introduces a different concept of population estimation based on school attendance data and the ratio of school population to total population. It is reasoned that this ratio has limits of change constrained by the reproduction mores which should help in differentiating between natural population increase and migration in and out of cities. Another factor of importance is that records may be available in many areas of inmigrants and outmigrants to and from the school population, as is the case to a limited extent for the Seattle urban area. (Unfortunately, complete records are unavailable but sufficient data is available upon which to base some reasonable analysis.) In any event, the use of school enrollment data including its migration trends might be an interesting check on population estimation from traditional means. With this in mind, the following analysis is presented.

This part discusses changes in the relationship between school enrollment and total population over time and investigates the utility of estimating intercensal population based on school enrollment data. The first section inspects trends of school enrollment to total population ratios at the national, state and local levels. The second section employs two approaches to estimate Seattle's total population in 1975. The first is based on recent information about Seattle with respect to changing public school enrollments by neighborhood, and the second on migrations of students in and out of the city. The last section summarizes the findings and draws conclusions about the utilities and limits of school enrollment data for population estimations.

1.0 Historical Trends

The population enrolled in school, grades Kindergarten through 12, has been generally increasing over the past several decades in the United States, Washington State, King County and Seattle (Figure 1.1). Each of the graphs in Figure 1.1, except for Washington State, showed a decrease in enrollment during the 1930's, a result of the great economic depression during that time. From 1940 to 1950, the total school enrollment in the United States continued in a slight decline from 1930, but resumed its upward trend after that. Only Seattle and King County have shown a

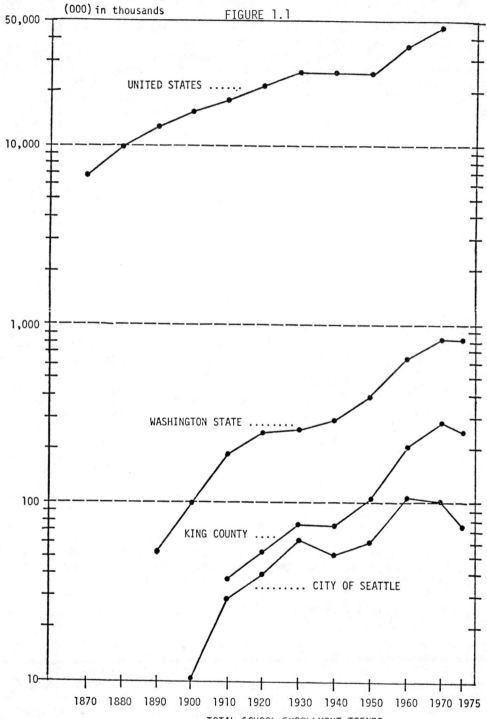

FIGURE 1.1

TOTAL SCHOOL ENROLLMENT TRENDS
SOURCE: U.S. CENSUS STATISTICS (SEMI-LOG SCALE)

decrease in student enrollment in recent years. King County lost a few thousand students since 1970, and Seattle started its downward trend in student enrollment in 1960 with a gradual drop-off to 1970, followed by a very large decline since 1970.

Of interest in Figure 1.1 is the way in which greater relative changes occur as the area of investigation becomes smaller. As an example, for the United States as a whole, the slopes of the lines representing intercensal change are all relatively modest compared to those for the City of Seattle. This is a natural phenomenon based on the fact that as the area of analysis becomes smaller the population is less representative of the nation as a whole and more subject to local economic factors that create in- and outmigration at a greater rate than for the nation as a whole. Figure 1.1 is also presented to show that unlike the nation as a whole, the State of Washington's school enrollment is decreasing slightly, and that of the metropolitan County of King has decreased even more between 1970 and 1975 based on the school enrollment data collected by the State of Washington. This is of particular interest in viewing Seattle's population change wherein it would be difficult to make a case that the County was gaining substantially as a result of the outmigration of families with school-age children from the city. This must represent both a change in the reproduction mores of some time preceding 1970 or an outmigration from the metropolitan County including the City of Seattle. We do know for a fact that the State of Washington has estimated a population loss of 8,633 in King County between 1970 and 1975[1] and that the Bureau of the Census estimated a County population loss of 7,433 in studies made in 1975.[2]

The next set of four figures displays the changing relationship between the ratios of students to the total population and the census defined school-age population, or 5 to 17 year olds, to the total population as well as the ratio of the school enrollment totals to the 5 to 17 year olds.[3] The first graph, displaying the ratios for the United States (Figure 1.2), shows the 5 to 17 year olds ratio on a general downward trend from 1890 to 1950, which probably indicates that even though the population and the 5 to 17 year olds were increasing over time, the increase of the 5 to 17 year olds was not keeping up with the growth of the population, probably due to large adult inmigration during that time and due to the population generally becoming older. The school enrollment ratio did not completely follow the 5 to 17 year old decline from 1890 to 1950, but the overall trend was the same: each hit a low in 1950, and then each became larger proportions of the total population. From 1890 to 1940, the ratio of school enrollment to the school age population became larger, meaning larger proportions of the school age population were enrolled in school. Between 1940 and 1960, the two became more discrepant, but by 1970 the ratio of the enrolled children to the school age children were more similar than in previous years.

Washington State displayed a different character than the United States in its ratios of students and 5 to 17 year olds to the total population. At any one time the ratio of the students to the 5 to 17 year old population was greater than the similar ratio of the United States. Washington State has traditionally had more students per school-age population enrolled in school than the country as a whole. The two ratios of the 5 to 17 year olds to the total population and the enrolled

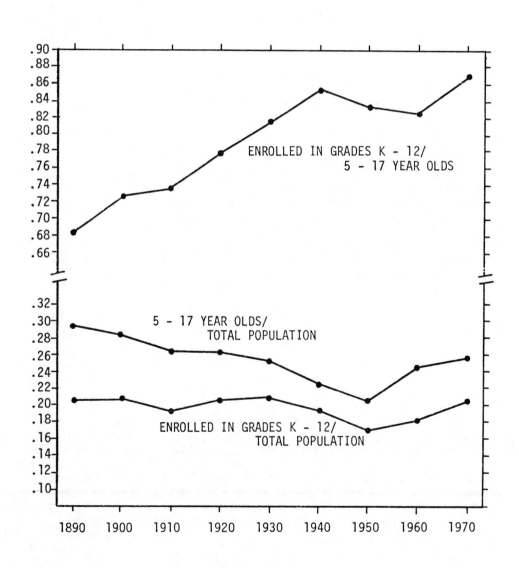

FIGURE 1.2

SCHOOL AGE AND SCHOOL ENROLLMENT RATIOS
FOR THE UNITED STATES

SOURCE: U.S. CENSUS STATISTICS

ENROLLED IN GRADES K - 12/
5 - 17 YEAR OLDS

5 - 17 YEAR OLDS/
TOTAL POPULATION

ENROLLED IN GRADES K - 12/
TOTAL POPULATION

students to the total population follow each other much more closely than the same ratios for the United States. Each ratio follows a snake-like pattern, with the two becoming more closely aligned over time. (Figure 1.3)

King County's ratios of 5 to 17 year olds to the total population and of the enrolled students to the total population were generally smaller than the same ratios for Washington State, meaning the population in King County has been older than the State's population. Also, the value of the ratio of school enrollment to school age population in King County has always been higher than the same ratio at the State level. The ratio of the students to the 5 to 17 year olds has never, at any one time, had a value less than the State's value. King County experienced a large increase of the proportion of enrolled students to the 5 to 17 year olds between 1920 and 1930, but in 1940 the ratio had dropped to within four percentage points of the 1920 level. In 1970, the ratio of the enrolled students to the 5 to 17 year olds was 0.99 indicating that virtually all of the school age children were enrolled in school. (Figure 1.4)

Seattle's ratios fluctuated in patterns similar to King County. The 5 to 17 year olds to the total population and the enrolled students to the total population followed similar paths from 1920 to the present, with the two ratios becoming more similar over time. In fact, the ratio of the enrolled students to the 5 to 17 year olds was 1.00 in 1970. (Figure 1.5)

In summary, the four figures have shown that while the ratios of the enrolled students to the total population and the school age children to the total population have fluctuated over time, the two ratios are becoming more similar. Probable limits can be set on the changes in the values of the ratios between decades because we would expect future changes in the ratios not to exceed changes found historically. Possible ratio value changes from the last known value to the present can be estimated on historical trends of the ratios and on known changes in local enrollment tabulations, consequently these data are well suited to this type of analysis following.

2.0 Estimation of Seattle's 1975 Population

The total population in Seattle has probably declined steadily from 1970, when by U. S. Census count there were 520,161 persons in the city. Several reasons for the decline and estimations of the actual population in 1975 are presented here. Each of the ideas are tied to school enrollment as an aid to determining their reasonableness.

In the Seattle area since 1950, the average number of persons per household has declined, and a recent survey of households in Seattle[4] indicated the downward trend extended through 1974. (See Figure 2.1) This trend is supported by both the decrease of Seattle's school enrollment of grades K through 12 from 1960 to 1975 (See Figure 1.1), and by Seattle's declining ratio of enrolled students to the population between 1960 and 1975. (See Figure 1.5) If both the persons per household and the number of students have declined, then the total population must have declined.

Figure 2.2 graphically depicts three estimations of Seattle's 1975 population based on their relationship to the known student enrollment

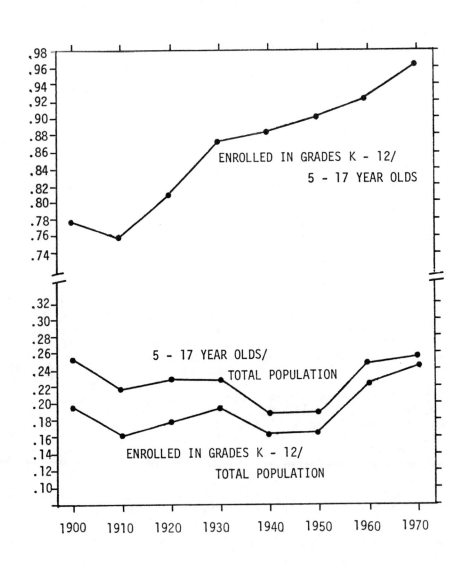

FIGURE 1.3

SCHOOL AGE AND SCHOOL ENROLLMENT RATIOS
FOR THE STATE OF WASHINGTON

SOURCE: U.S. CENSUS STATISTICS

ENROLLED IN GRADES K - 12/
5 - 17 YEAR OLDS

5 - 17 YEAR OLDS/
TOTAL POPULATION

ENROLLED IN GRADES K - 12/
TOTAL POPULATION

FIGURE 1.4

SCHOOL AGE AND SCHOOL ENROLLMENT RATIOS
FOR THE COUNTY OF KING

SOURCE: U.S. CENSUS STATISTICS

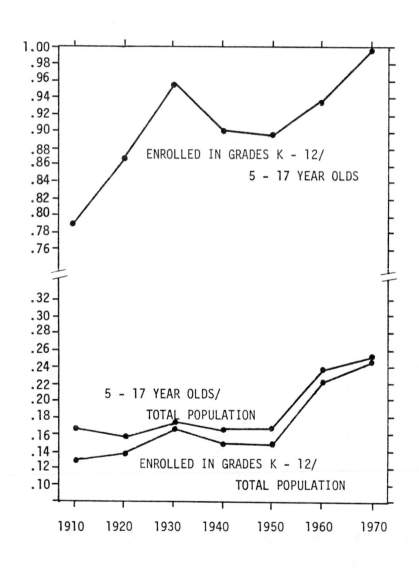

FIGURE 1.5

SCHOOL AGE AND SCHOOL ENROLLMENT RATIOS
FOR THE CITY OF SEATTLE

SOURCE: U.S. CENSUS STATISTICS

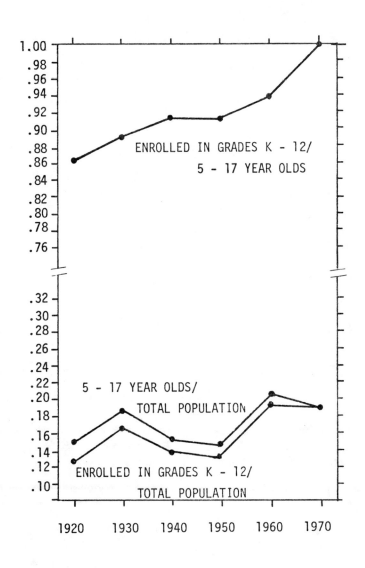

FIGURE 2.1

AVERAGE HOUSEHOLD SIZE
IN SEATTLE AND KING COUNTY

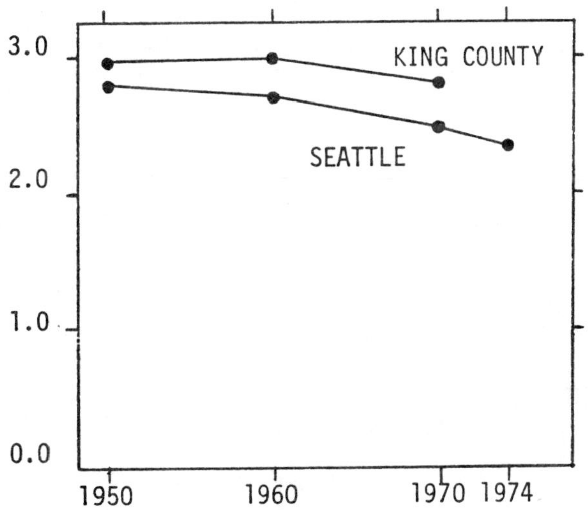

SOURCES: U.S. CENSUS TRACT STATISTICS
AND R.L. POLK, 1974

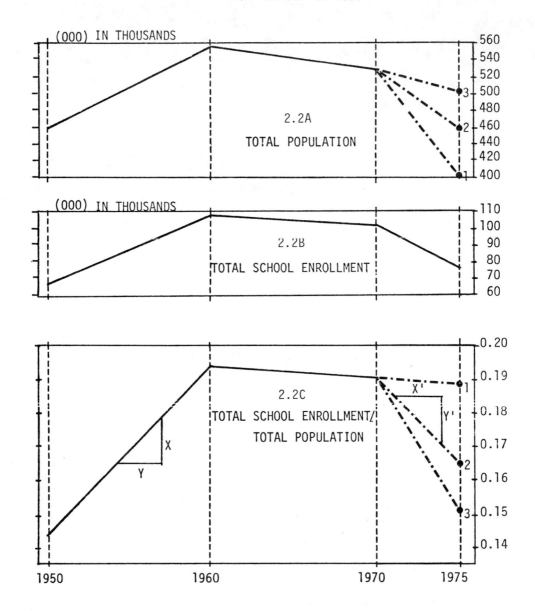

FIGURE 2.2

POPULATION ESTIMATES BASED ON TOTAL SCHOOL ENROLLMENT
FOR SEATTLE IN 1975

1. City population estimate of total enrollment/total population
   trend continues.

2. City population estimate if ratio of 1970 - 1975 falls at same rate as
   1950 - 1960 gain, i.e., X/Y = X'/Y'.

3. Official 1975 city population estimate and the resulting ratio of
   students to the population.

-568-

in 1975, shown with an historical perspective from 1950 to 1970. The
first estimate (Figure 2.2A, point 1) is based on a ratio derived from
projecting a straight line from the 1960 total student enrollment to the
total population ratio through 1970 to 1975. (Figure 2.2C, point 1) The
resulting 1975 population is estimated at 400,833. The second estimate
(Figure 2.2A, point 2) reflects a 1975 ratio of students to population
(Figure 2.2C, point 2) deflated the same relative amount from 1970 as
the 1960 ratio was inflated over the 1950 value (i.e., x/y = x'y' in
Figure 2.8C). The absolute change in ratio values from 1950 to 1960
displayed the greatest amplitude between any two consecutive decades in
Seattle from 1920 to 1970. (See Figure 1.5) This second 1975 population
estimate is 458,890. The third estimate (Figure 2.2C, point 3) of
503,500 is the published estimate released by the State of Washington.[5]
The resulting decline necessary in the student to population ratio to
achieve the estimate (Figure 2.2C, point 3) is even lower, by 1.5 percentage points, than the second estimate. See Table 2.1 for the values
represented in Figure 2.2.

The first and third estimates presented above set reasonably logical
limits on Seattle's 1975 population. If the first estimate of the population were true, then a decrease of approximately 130,000 people in the
city would have occurred, implying a very large outmigration of the population. If the third estimate were true, then the decline of 26,551
people, from 530,161 to 503,500, would be explained mainly by the
decrease of 25,277 students from 1970 to 1975. This seems unlikely
because parents usually leave with their children. (A large portion of
the loss of students was probably due to outmigration and not a natural
decrease.) Table 2.1 provides the numbers of each estimate.

Additional factors must be taken into account to estimate the actual
loss of students due to either outmigration or natural decline. A
recently conducted migration study of students in school districts in
King County[6] determined Seattle School District has been experiencing a
net outmigration of students. The study found that the 1974 to 1975
school year in Seattle Public Schools there was an inmigration of 5,900
students and an outmigration of 9,900 students, resulting in a net outmigration of 4,000 students for that year. We extended these migration
figures for the years 1970 through 1975 by normalizing the in- and outmigrations to the total population estimates by the State of Washington.
This was accomplished by assuming an average decline of 5,000 persons
per year in Seattle. This estimated rate of decline in the total population, which is more conservative than the third estimate discussed
above, allows us to estimate the migrations of the students for each
year. As a check on the migration figures, we estimated each year's
student enrollment based on the past year's total students, plus those
added to the system and minus those leaving the system. The added students include natural increase due to births five years prior to the
school year, discounted 10 per cent for outmigrants, and inmigration.
The students leaving the system include those graduating, drop-outs,
and outmigration.[7] Table 2.2 shows the year-by-year estimations based
on the above values. Each of the estimations of the following year are
very close to the actual enrollment figures. Because of this, the estimations of in- and outmigrations of students are probably fairly accurate. The total inmigration of students for the five year span is

TABLE 2.1

POPULATION ESTIMATES BASED ON TOTAL SCHOOL ENROLLMENT
FOR SEATTLE IN 1975

YEAR	TOTAL POPULATION	TOTAL ENROLLMENT	TOTAL POPULATION/ TOTAL ENROLLMENT
1950	467,591	66,912	0.1431
1960	556,008	107,812	0.1939
1970	530,161	101,315	0.1911
1975	---	76,038	---
1975-1	400,833	76,038	0.1897
1975-2	458,890	76,038	0.1657
1975-3	503,500	76,038	0.1510

TABLE 2.2

ANNUAL ESTIMATES OF SEATTLE'S PUBLIC SCHOOL ENROLLMENT
BASED ON STUDENTS ENTERING AND EXITING THE SYSTEM

SCHOOL YEAR	INTO SYSTEM			OUT OF SYSTEM				OCTOBER ENROLLMENT	ESTIMATED ENROLLMENT
	ESTIMATED IN-MIGRATION	NATURAL INCREASE*	TOTAL IN	ESTIMATED OUT-MIGRATION	GRADUATES	DROP OUTS	TOTAL		
69-70	6,190	7,500	13,690	10,390	6,020	2,804	19,214	87,137	
70-71	6,130	7,800	13,930	10,290	5,134	3,413	18,837	82,094	81,613
71-72	6,080	7,700	13,780	10,190	5,439	1,768	17,397	76,598	77,185
72-73	6,020	7,500	13,520	10,100	5,242	1,771	17,113	72,079	72,981
73-74	5,960	7,600	13,560	10,000	5,683	2,763	18,446	68,637	68,483
74-75	5,900	7,100	13,000	9,900	4,657	2,356	16,913	65,632	63,751
TOTAL	36,280	45,200	81,480	60,870	32,175	14,875	107,920		

Estimated net student migration from 1970 to 1975 is 36,280 -60,870 = -24,590

*Natural Increase is the next year's five year olds, based on births and discounted by approximately 10 percent for outmigration of children prior to reaching school age.

approximately 36,280, and the outmigration of students was 60,870, resulting in a net outmigration of approximately 24,590 students over the five years. By factoring up the student net outmigration by a value representing the average number of people leaving with each student, we will obtain a population value for Seattle reflecting the impact of the net outmigrations of the students. For example, if the average number of persons leaving the city per student were 2.33, the household size determined by the 1974 survey,[8] the resulting 1975 Seattle population would be 472,866. A value of 2.5 would yield a population of 468,686; and a value of 3.0 would result in a population of 456,391. The net outmigrations of the students probably do not fully explain the net migration of the city's population. Most likely, the net outmigrations of the students is partially balanced by an inmigration of persons without school-age children. Table 2.3 shows the student migration values and the resultant effect on the total population.

3.0 Summary and Conclusions

To adequately inspect the extent of the inmigration of young childless adults, as well as other demographic shifts, an accounting of several changes in the city would have to be made. For example, changes in the housing stock would affect the types of persons likely to move into the city, and changes in the economic conditions of the region would affect the growth potential of the whole area. The 1974 survey[9] reported a modest increase in numbers of young adults, both single and married without children, but not nearly enough to compensate for outmigration. Close inspection of these and other exciting facts about Seattle extend beyond the immediate scope of this study.

In summary, school enrollment data appear very useful for developing alternative estimates of the population which may in fact be as good or better than housing unit data. However, the data cannot be utilized easily to obtain population estimates in small areas. Improvements and refinements of this type of analysis will be possible as data collection by local agencies continues. One of the more important pieces of information regarding school enrollment information is the annual in- and out-migration studies. If this information were continually collected over time, a more reliable population monitor could be developed.

TABLE 2.3

POPULATION ESTIMATES BASED ON

ESTIMATED NET STUDENT MIGRATION

FOR SEATTLE IN 1975

STUDENT NET MIGRATION	MULTIPLICATION FACTOR	ESTIMATED MIGRATION 1970 - 1975	ESTIMATED 1975 POPULATION
-24,590	2.33	-57,295	472,866
-24,590	2.50	-61,475	468,686
-24,590	3.00	-73,770	456,391

NOTES

1. Office of Program Planning and Fiscal Management Population Studies
    Division, State of Washington Population Trends 1975. Olympia:
    State of Washington Publication, July, 1975.

2. U.S. Bureau of the Census, Population Estimations and Projections.
    Series P25, No. 624. Washington, D.C.: U.S. Government Printing
    Office, May, 1976.

3. The values for computing the ratios for the United States are
    derived from the U.S. Bureau of the Census, Statistical Abstract
    of the United States in years 1915, 1925, 1935, 1945, 1955, 1965,
    and 1975; for Washington State, King County and Seattle, the values
    are from the U.S. Bureau of the Census, population and housing sta-
    tistics for the years 1910, 1920, 1930, 1940, 1950, 1960 and 1970.

4. R. L. Polk and Co., Profile of Change: Seattle, Washington.
    Financed through a grant from the Department of Housing and Urban
    Development, Section 701 of Housing Act of 1954 as amended. Detroit,
    Michigan: R. L. Polk and Co., 1974.

5. Office of Program Planning and Fiscal Management Population Studies
    Division, 1975.

6. Jack Trowbridge, Student Migration. Olympia: joint production by
    Educational Service District #110, King County, and the Office of
    the Superintendent of Public Instruction, State of Washington, 1975.

7. Statistics provided by Alan Metcalf, Office of Superintendent of
    Public Instruction, Statistical Information Services Section, State
    of Washington, Olympia, Washington, in a telephone interview, June,
    1976.

8. R. L. Polk and Co., 1974.

9. R. L. Polk and Co., 1974.

Dan Moravec
John R. Wilson
Atlanta Regional Commission
100 Peachtree Street, N.W.
Atlanta, Georgia 30303

"ATLANTA REGIONAL COMMISSION: SMALL-AREA AGE, RACE AND SEX ESTIMATES"

ABSTRACT. The Atlanta Regional Commission's (ARC) age, race, and sex estimating system was designed to complement ARC's Annual Population and Housing (P&H) estimating program and, in fact, was designed to become part of the annual program. The methodology consists of two main parts. The first part develops annual county-level age, race, sex (ARS) population estimates controlled to P&H estimates. The technique employed was the well documented cohort migration-survival approach which simulates population growth by accounting for births, death, and migration. The second part develops census tract age, race, sex estimates also controlled to P&H estimates. The method used assumed that the 1975 ARS distributions by tract have not significantly changed from the 1970 distributions reported by the U. S. Bureau of the Census. Consequently, tract distributions were factored to both P&H tract totals and cohort county totals. This paper summarizes the work accomplished on the age, race, sex estimating system including problem framework, methodologies and an evaluation.

NEED

Functional planning in areas such as health, aging, and criminal justice are generally the result of particular problems impacting a selective age, race, sex portion of the total population (Dever, 1975). Thus specific target populations which are subject to specific problems must be identified, measured, and located as part of program planning and evaluation. Health planners concerned with eradicating lead poisioning, for example, need to know where children ages 0-6 live so that programs can be implemented to reach the target population. Aging planners and recently transportation planners need to know where the elderly (aged 60 and over) reside so that they can be provided better transportation service. Similarly criminal justice planners concerned with juvenile delinquency need to know how many juvenile (ages 10-18) there are and how they are spatially located. To assist planners, ARC has implemented a detailed, small-area age, race, sex estimating procedure designed to identify the magnitude and location of target populations which are concern to functional planners.

OBJECTIVES

The primary study objective was to develop an annual census tract age, race, sex (ARS) estimating methodology compatible with ARC's annual population and housing estimates. A secondary objective was to produce tabulations of 1975 ARS estimates for counties and census tracts within the Atlanta region.

The work program was structured into four phases:

1. Literature search - designed to uncover existing, pertinent methodologies and data sources.
2. Data inventory - designed to assess the availability, timeliness, and format of data which potentially could be utilized.
3. Methodology evaluation - designed to determine the best methodology given data constraints identified by the literature search and data inventory.
4. Methodology implementation - designed to establish a formal age, race, sex estimating system and to estimate 1975 population by age, race, and sex.

Specific end products which were developed as part of this study include 1975 census tract and county ARS estimates, narrative and flow chart description of the methodology used, and computer program and system documentation.

LITERATURE REVIEW

A literature review was conducted to identify those demographic principles, procedures, and methodologies which are applicable to producing both county and census tract ARC estimates. Most references however addressed the problem of estimating total county population. Most notably the U. S. Bureau of the Census's federal-state cooperative program for local population estimates has resulted in two summary reports.

In general the authors found that little literature exists in county-level or census tract ARS estimating procedures. The Georgia Department of Human Resources (DHR) has published 1975 and 1980 Georgia county ARS projections based upon the cohort migration survival method (DHR, State of Georgia 1975). At the sub-county level, two studies utilized regression techniques. One related the change in population to the number of births and deaths over the period. (Morrison and Relles 1974). The other regressed total population and population by age against various demographic characteristics including school enrollment and drivers license information (PMM & Co. 1974).

A second objective of the literature review was to determine the data required to make ARS estimates. It was found that both cohort and regression methodologies commonly utilized five types of data; they are:

1. Base year population stratified by ARS,
2. Number of births by age and race of mother,
3. Number of deaths stratified by ARS,
4. School enrollment data,
5. Driver's licenses by age, sex.

The primary sources of data are the U. S. Census of Population and state or county vital statistics. School enrollment obtained from school districts has been used to estimate migration rates as in the census's Component Method II and as independent regression variables. Driver's license data have only been used in the Albuquerque study (PMM & Co. 1974). The data, derived from state's Public Safety Department, represents a potentially rich secondary data source because of the strong, logical correlation between population by age and licensed drivers by age.

In addition to methods and data, the literature review revealed several estimating principles which were invaluable in shaping ARC's approach. Shyrock and Siegel point out six estimating principles (Shyrock and Siegel, Vol. 2, 1973). Most important they stress (a) the use of direct data e.g. births and deaths, and (b) the use of cohort methodology because of its logic and reasonableness.

DATA INVENTORY

Given the five general data categories identified in the literature, a data inventory was conducted to determine what data are available, their geographic level of detail, their coverage, and their timeliness. Among the data inventoried were the 1970 U. S. Census of Population as the source of base year population broken down by age, race and sex. Current year population data are provided by the ARC Population and Housing estimating system. Birth and death data are assembled and made available by the Georgia Department of Education. Total enrollment by school and school district are also available for private schools. Drivers license records represent a logical source of age and sex information for the adult population, but unfortunately the release of any information from these records other than total number of drivers by county is prohibited by Georgia confidentiality regulations. The DIME file, a geographic base data information system, has the potential for use in geocoding large volumes of small area data through address matching. It is not fully operational at this time in Atlanta but may be come so when current update and expansion efforts are completed.

The ARC Population and Housing (P&H) estimating system provides current year estimates of total population by race, as well as estimates of housing units and group quarters population. This system uses the housing unit method of population estimation. On an annual basis building permit data are collected, which when coded to Census Tract and supplemented by field checks, are used to provide a basis for the estimates. This system plays an essential role in the ARS system since its estimates provide population control totals at tract level.

METHODOLOGY EVALUATION

After the literature had been reviewed and the available data inventoried, applicable methodologies were evaluated and the ARS methodology defined. Basically there were four methodologies to evaluate--cohort migration-survival, regression, factoring, and sample surveys.

Cohort Migration-Survival Method

The cohort migration-survival method is a simulation of the process by which a population ages. Typically a base year population is broken into groups by age, race, and sex. A cohort is a particular age group identified by race and sex such as white males ages 30 through 34. An estimate of population five years from the base year is obtained by aging the 30-34 cohort so that it then becomes the 35-39 cohort. In the aging process, a certain portion of the initial cohort can be expected to die; therefore, deaths are subtracted from the base year cohort's population. This general process is repeated for each cohort within the total population.

During this five year simulation period, people can also be expected to move into or out of an area, and births can be expected. Thus after each cohort is aged, net migration is added to the surviving population. Next newborns are birthed based upon the age of mother; however, because some newborns can be expected to die (infant mortality) the newborn population is converted into surviving population.

The above cohort migration-survival method is strongly recommended by Shyrock and Siegel (Shyrock and Siegel, 1973) because of its logical structure and because of its reliance upon primary source data.

Regression Method

Regression approaches generally attempt to explain an unknown variable such as future year cohort population using known variables such as the number of births, deaths, and school enrollment. The mathematical relationship between the unknown (dependent) variables and the known (independent) variables is established for points in time when both the dependent and independent variables can be measured. This relationship is then used to estimate the dependent variable at a future date.

In the past, regression methods have successfully been used, most notably in St. Louis by Morrison and in Albuquerque by PMM & Co. In addition, ARC has also used regression models to forecast future age groups.

Experience has shown that there are three main problems with regression:

1. Significant data development is required;
2. Statistical aberrations inherent in any regression approach reduces user confidence in the results; and
3. Statistically significant relationships generally require collapsing categories resulting in information loss.

Because of the lack of census tract data, the lack of a workable DIME file, and the lack of detailed age categories, the regression approach was not chosen. At the county level data problems are even worse because the number of counties in the region (seven) is not adequate to calibrate statistical relationships.

Factoring Method

The term factoring is used to describe the method of assuring that a future year distribution of ARS population will be proportional to a base year distribution and then applying these proportions to future total population to obtain the required distribution.

Over a five to ten year period, one may assume that the best estimate of the current year's ARS estimates is the base year 1970 distribution reported by the U. S. Bureau of the Census. Regression and/or cohort migration-survival may or may not yield better results; however, the primary advantage of the factoring approach is that its biases are crystal clear and the data may be used in that light.

The case in which simple factoring as a method fail are those in which census tracts with very small base year population by race grow dramatically by the current year. In this case the base year distribution is too small to represent the current year. In addition the migrating population's characteristics are simply different from the base year resident population's.

Survey Method

Sample surveys which directly measure ARS characteristics would significantly improve the quality of the estimates. The cost of such surveys required to estimate tract level ARS however prohibited this approach from being considered.

Limited surveys of group quarters population are made annually as part of P&H. These surveys could be expanded to include ARS information. No more than one man-week would be required for this task.

METHODOLOGY DEFINITION

Based upon evaluation of available data and methodologies, a twofold ARS estimating procedure was defined. First, county ARS estimates were computed using the cohort migration-survival approach. Second, census tract estimates were made by factoring 1970 ARS census tract distributions to P&H census tract estimates by race and then factoring the resultant distribution for each county to county estimates developed in step one. This two-way, row and column factoring defines a factoring iteration which is repeated until tract data for each county converges to county totals while equaling P&H census tract totals. In this way, 1970 census tract ARS distributions were aged to reflect 1975 county ARS distributions. Prior to factoring, however, 1970 base year tract distributions, which were determined to be inadequate because of significant in-migration or racial transition, were replaced by more reasonable ARS distributions.

Initially the methodology was designed to estimate total population by age, race, and sex. Because group quarters population is relatively stable and discrete a revised methodology was developed which estimated the household and group quarters' segments of the total population independently and then summed these to estimate total population. In this way the major portion of error is in household population estimates; but because household population is less than total population, the error in total population by ARS should be reduced by the revised methodology. Household ARS estimates were computed using the two-step cohort migration-survival and factoring method described above. Group quarters were estimated by updating the 1970 census figures utilizing an ARC nursing home survey along with limited telephone surveying.

The cohort migration-survival program used was originally found in Keyfitz and Flieger's Population Facts and Methods of Demography. The actual computer program used, however, was received from the Georgia Department of Human Resources (DHR) and modified by both DHR and ARC staff.

The factoring approach used is a simple row and column matrix factoring method described in Kriklewicz (Kriklewicz, 1975). The census tract ARS distributions for each county define a county ARS matrix which is relatively first row factored to census tract P&H estimates by race. Next the matrix is column factored to cohort migration-survival county estimates which have been controlled by county P&H estimates. The combination row and column factoring defines one iteration. Generally, the process converges in three iterations with an error of at most ± 10 in any one ARS county cohort value.

The overall ARS approach can be summarized in five steps:

1. Develop county level ARS control totals controlled to P&H totals.
2. Estimate current year group quarters population by ARS by tract and sum to county.
3. Subtract county group quarters estimates from county total population estimates to yield county household population estimates. (Step 1 minus Step 2).
4. Make tract level estimates of household population by ARS, controlling to P&H household population estimates by race.

5.   Add household and group quarters population to obtain final
     estimates. (Step 2 plus Step 4).

ASSUMPTIONS

Inherent in the ARS methodology are several critical assumptions concerning such factors as fertility and migration. In all there are four major
assumptions made; they are:

1.   P&H estimates are a good source of population by race for
     census tracts and hence for counties. There are several
     known sources of error in the P&H estimates. Assumptions are
     made on vacancy rates and household sizes by race which have
     a significant impact on the resulting population estimates.
     Nevertheless, these are the best available and are sufficiently
     accurate to provide a basis for further refining them by age and
     sex.

2.   The 1975 ARS census tract distributions are approximately
     the same as the 1970 distributions obtained from the U. S.
     Bureau of the Census except where determined to be inap-
     propriate because of significant in-migration or racial
     transition. Initially, the system assumed that 1970 distributions
     were reasonable in all census tracts. However, analysis of the
     initial results of the system indicated that the ARS methodology
     is faulty when the ARS distributions are seriously altered by
     migration either into or out of the tract. For those identified
     tracts, the appropriate distributions of the migrating popula-
     tion were substituted from the 1970 distribution. The tracts
     having net out-migration were not altered because: (a) the
     losses were relatively small and few when compared to in-
     creases, and (b) no data are readily available to substitute for
     the 1970 data. In this way, the ARS methodology was im-
     proved.
     Tracts whose 1970 ARS distribution does not adequately reflect
     1975 conditions were identified based upon growth from 1965-
     70 and 1970-75. Tracts experiencing constant growth over the
     period 1965-75 were not altered because it was assumed that the
     1970-75 migrants have the same characteristics as the 1965-1970
     migrants, and that the 1965-70 migrants distribution is reflected
     in the 1970 census data. Thus, only tracts experiencing major
     growth over the 1965-70 period are identified. A total of 28 out
     of 242 census tracts were considered in need of this special
     procedure.

3.   1970 county fertility rates will decline in proportion to
     Georgia's fertility rate decline. Since there is a several year
     lag in the publication of county level fertility rate levels, State
     wide trends are used to make estimates of county level rates.

4. Demographic ARS profiles of net migrants will be similar to the profile of migrants during the 1960's. Consequently available migration data can be used to estimate current net in-migration. Assumptions on net migration profiles by age, race and sex have a powerful impact on the resulting estimates. The P&H System makes a current estimate of net total population by race; the ARS system then uses two basic components to estimate the age, sex, distribution of total population at county level. First the base year (1970) population is allowed to grow through simulation of births and deaths -- natural increase. The results are compared to the P&H estimate. Migration is assumed to make up the difference. Test applications of the cohort survival method revealed a problem with the formulation of the migration data. As found in Keyfitz and Flieger's Population Facts and Methods of Demography, the migration data was formulated as a rate of ARS cohort migrants to the base ARS cohort population. Thus the base year cohort may be small compared to migration effects, and generate a very large and unreasonable rate. A second problem with the rate method was the influence of "humps" in the base year population (i.e. Post-War Babies). To control these problems a profile of migration was adopted and the computer program modified. In this approach, the percentage of total migrants in each cohort was input to the estimating program. A final point worthy of note, is that migration data, like other data is subject to errors in collection. Graphing and comparing the ARS migration profiles revealed several cases where obvious problems existed with the data. By using a net profile over several counties, a reasonable estimator was obtained.

SYSTEM DESIGN

The ARS system consists of two primary computer programs along with supporting report and utility programs. The first main program is the cohort migration-survival program ARSGO which simulates the dynamics of household population (HHPOP) change for each county. County population estimates are reported using the report program POPSUM. Intermediate life table results are optimally reported by program LIFTAB.

The second main program is MATFAC which performs the matrix factoring function to estimate census tract ARS estimates. The three inputs into this program are (a) current year (1975) P&H household population by race for census tracts, (b) 1970 census household population by race modified to reflect significant changes due to in-migration or racial transition, and (c) county level household population estimates. This last input is computed by subtracting current year group quarters population by county from total population estimates created by ARSGO. Census tract household population estimates are then added to current year group quarters estimates to yield total population estimates by census tract. These results are then tabulated by the report program CTSUM.

This methodology is visually represented by the flow charts in figures 1 through 3. Figure 1 describes the general flow and order to executing programs while figures 2 and 3, respectively represent the group quarters and household population update procedures. For both updates, the program SDIST was created to modify census tract distributions. It should be noted that both the 1975 group quarters and household population estimates can subsequently be used as SDIST input whenever new updates are identified. In general it is anticipated that group quarters population will be updated annually; however, because the current year is so far removed from 1970, the year of the last census, it is not anticipated that household population will have to be updated every year.

ANNUAL PROCEDURES

Annual ARS update procedures consist of three main steps. First group quarters population must be examined and selected census tract distributions updated, if necessary. Second household population growths since 1970 must be examined and updated if necessary. Third ARSGO control cards must be changed to reflect current year, county total population estimates.

RESULTS

This section documents the results of ARC's 1975 age, race, and sex estimating system. Figure 4 summarizes county and regional population changes from 1970 to 1975 by race in terms of estimated net migration and natural increase.

Figure 5 presents 1970 and 1975 age, race, sex population pyramids for the Atlanta region. In general, these pyramids reflect three continuing trends which impact the regional population. First, reduced fertility rates result in a lower percentage of children aged 1-4. Second, continued in-migration in the 25-34 age category causes a bulge in the pyramids. Third, lower death rates in the elderly age group coupled with limited in-migration in the same group result in a greater percentage of elderly population.

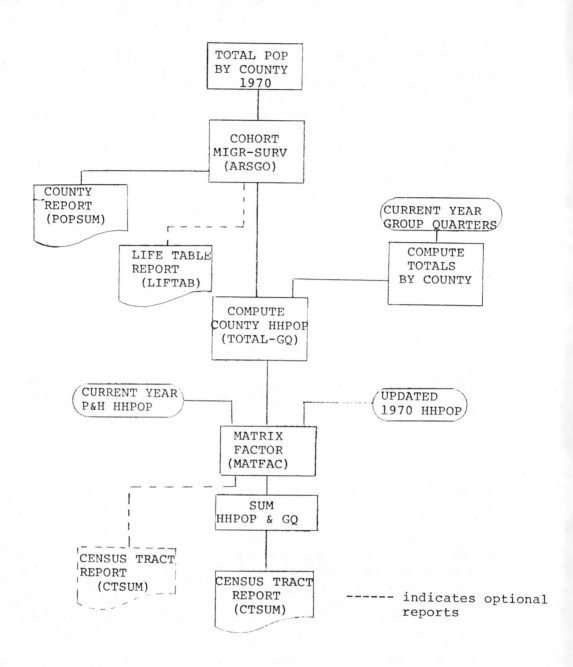

FIGURE 1:   ARS Methodology

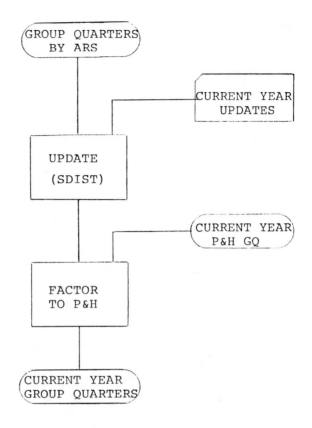

FIGURE 2:   Group Quarters Update

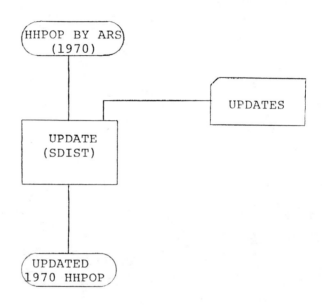

FIGURE 3:   Household Population Update

FIGURE 4: Population Changes 1970-1975

		Population 1970	Natural Increase 1970-75	Net Migration[1] 1970-75	Population[2] 1975
FULTON:	White	366,946	9,331	-35,877	340,400
	Non-White	238,369	18,928	20,403	277,700
	Total	605,315	28,259	-15,474	618,100
DEKALB:	White	357,514	16,884	12,002	386,400
	Non-White	57,873	5,895	13,432	77,200
	Total	415,387	22,779	25,434	463,600
COBB:	White	188,160	11,122	41,718	241,000
	Non-White	8,633	739	-572	8,800
	Total	196,793	11,861	41,146	249,800
CLAYTON:	White	93,394	6,438	26,168	126,000
	Non-White	4,649	382	169	5,200
	Total	98,043	6,820	26,337	131,200
GWINNETT:	White	68,551	4,386	38,763	111,700
	Non-White	3,798	374	-472	3,700
	Total	72,349	4,760	38,291	115,400
ROCKDALE:	White	14,998	819	9,383	25,200
	Non-White	3,154	262	-316	3,100
	Total	18,152	1,081	9,067	28,300
DOUGLAS:	White	25,985	1,403	15,812	43,200
	Non-White	2,674	205	-479	2,400
	Total	28,659	1,608	15,333	45,600
REGION:	White	1,115,548	50,383	107,969	1,273,900
	Non-White	319,150	26,785	32,165	378,100
	Total	1,434,698	77,168	140,134	1,652,000

1. Number of persons moving into the region minus number of persons moving out of the region.
2. Total population as estimated in the 1975 ARC Population and Housing Report; Natural increase and net migration as estimated by ARS system.

ATLANTA REGION

1970 AND 1975

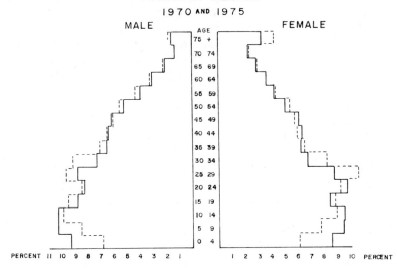

WHITE POPULATION

---- 1975
—— 1970

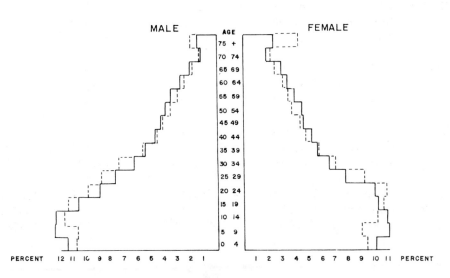

NON-WHITE POPULATION

FIGURE 5

References

Atchley, Robert C.
1970   <u>Population Projections and Estimates for Local Areas</u>.
Oxford, Ohio: Scripps Foundation.

Bogue, Donald J.
1974   <u>Techniques for Making Population Projections: How to
Make Age-Sex Projections by Electronic Computer</u>.
Chicago: University of Chicago Community and Family
Study Center.

Dever, G.E. Alan
1975   "Small Area Population Forecasts for State Planning and
Development: Needs, Problems, and Prospects,"
Paper presented at Oakridge National Laboratory.

Keyfitz, N. and Flieger, W.
1971   <u>Population Facts and Methods of Demography</u>.
San Francisco: W. H. Freeman and Company.

Kriklewicz, E.
1973   <u>The Michigan Housing Market System: Purpose and
Structural Characteristics</u>. Lansing: Michigan State
Housing Development Authority.

Lowry, Ira S.
1966   <u>Migration and Metropolitan Growth: Two Analytic Models</u>.
San Francisco: Chandler Publishing Company.

Morrison, Peter and Relles, Daniel
1975   "Recent Research Insights Into Local Migration Flows,"
Rand Paper Series. Santa Monica: Rand Corporation.

Office of Planning and Budget
State of Georgia

1972a   <u>Net Geographic Migration in Georgia: 1960-1970</u>.
Atlanta

1972b   <u>Georgia County Migration Patterns: 1960-1970</u>.
Atlanta

Peat, Marwick, Mitchell & Company
    1974   Albuquerque Area Urban Transportation Planning
                    Information System. Prepared for U. S. DOT, FHWA.
                    Report No. FHWA-RD-74. Washington.

Rasmussen, W. Nelson
    1975   "The Use of Driver License Address Change Records for
                    Estimating Interstate and Intercounty Migration," Inter-
                    censal Estimates for Small Areas and Public Data Files
                    for Research, Small-Area Statistics Papers Series GE-41,
                    No. 1. Washington: U. S. Department of Commerce,
                    Bureau of the Census.

Ritchey, P. N. and Bishop, B. L.
    1974   Components of Change for the Adult Populations of Cities
                    by Age, Sex, and Color, Vol. VII.
                    Prepared for U. S. Department of Housing and Urban
                    Development by Oakridge National Laboratory. Oakridge,
                    Tennessee.

Shyrock and Siegel
    1973   The Methods and Materials of Demography.
                    Washington: U. S. Bureau of the Census.

U. S. Department of Commerce,
Bureau of the Census
    1973   Mobility for Metropolitan Areas. Washington:
                    U. S. Bureau of the Census.

Barry S. Wellar
Chief, Urban Management
Ministry of State for Urban Affairs
Ottawa, Canada K1A 0P6

FUNCTIONAL ROLES IN THE EVOLUTION OF INFORMATION SYSTEMS

ABSTRACT. Institutions with an information
systems component continually face this question:
  What are the roles of the management (executive),
  planning, operations, and information technology
  functions in ensuring that the information
  system capability best meets the needs of the
  institution, and hence the needs and aspirations
  of the citizens and community served by those
  institutions?
During a recent Symposium this topic was explored
in depth. A number of opinions and practical
examples of what is, and what should be, were
offered for consideration.
    This paper summarizes and analyzes the view-
points offered, and relates them to ways and
means for improving the delivery of goods and
services to citizens and the larger community.

INTRODUCTION

There are two powerful sides to the argument of what is
done in a particular post: what the incumbent thinks he
should be doing, and what everyone else thinks he should be
doing. Due to the simple fact that most institutions are
continually undergoing change, it is small wonder that the
two trains of thought are rarely running side by side on
parallel rails. More often than not they are on the same
rail, and running headlong at each other, repeatedly!
    This problem was the basis of a series of Track Sessions
at a recent Symposium on Information Technology and Urban
Governance.[1] That the topic is perceived to be of importance
by others in the field is testified to by the presentations
made, and papers submitted for a Symposium Proceedings.[2]

---

1 The Symposium was held at the Conference Centre, Ottawa,
   Canada, February 24-26, 1976.

2 Proceedings of the Symposium on Information Technology
   and Urban Governance, B. Wellar, Editor. (Ottawa, Canada:
   Ministry of State for Urban Affairs, 1976).

As noted in the Abstract, four functions of institutions in general, and urban and regional governments in particular are specified: management, planning, operations, and information technology.[3] The information technology (IT) component is separated from the other three functions primarily for the reason that it is essentially a service rather than line function. Secondly, in most institutions the IT capability is the responsibility of a distinct data processing, organization and methods, management systems, etc. department. These four functions then, are the organizing foci of discussion.

The structure of the paper follows the theme of the Symposium, and builds directly upon the opening sentence in the Introduction. That there are many different perceptions about the roles of the functions is amply demonstrated by the Symposium. Further, one need only consult previous URISA Proceedings to come to the same conclusion.

Assuming that there are indeed established differences in the perceived (as well as actual) roles of the various actors of the IT game, it is appropriate to pose the question, "So what?". Hopefully the remaining sections of this report will demonstrate that while benefits to be derived from attaining preferred functional roles will be hard come by, costs will accrue with great ease if modifications are not achieved.

---

3 Although there may be a general, implicit appreciation of the four terms, they are defined briefly to ensure that their usage in this paper is explicitly understood:
Management represents the activities of setting priorities, defining goals, allocating resources, etc. for the planning and operations (and IT) functions;
Planning represents physical and social planning in the sense of comprehensively linking management and planning inputs and outputs with those of operations, the private sector, and citizens in a manner which renders them all compatible over time and space;
Operations represents such line agencies as engineering, finance, transportation, personnel, utilities, assessment, policy, fire, etc.;
Information Technology (IT) is used broadly here to include computer hardware and software, telecommunications, remote sensing devices, and management science and systems analysis techniques, ie., instruments and ways and means used to specify, acquire, process, disseminate and use (apply) data and/or information in conjuction with such functions and activities of, for example, management, planning, operations, etc., in the public (private, university, etc.) sector(s).

In this brief paper it will not be possible to relate the mechanical aspects of IT to the non-mechanical component. However, one other item should also become clear: if we do not improve on the non-mechanical factor, any improvements in governance which could arise as a result of IT-induced modifications will be seriously offset by failings of that factor.

The Set of Perceptions

In an earlier paper, a comprehensive set of IT interest groups (governments, private sector, university, and research institutions, citizenry) were defined and discussed in considerable detail.[4] This paper deals with but one aspect of that larger set, governments, and attempts to both refine and advance arguments in the context of that umbrella. The entities comprising this paper, and the perceptions or points of view to be explored are presented in Figure I.

From \ To	Management	Planning	Operations	Information Technology
Management	↻	↓	↓	↓
Planning	↑	↻	→	→
Operations	↑	→	↻	→
Information Technology	↑	→	→	↻

Figure I. Functional Communication/Interaction Flows in Urban Institutions

Where:
↻ Intra-functional communication

↓ Vertical (top down) communication

↑ Vertical (bottom up) communication

→ Horizontal communication

---

4 A. Saumier and B. Wellar, "Results Accruing from Information Systems in Urban and Regional Governments: Contexts, Identification and Measurement, Appreciation", Proceedings of the 1974 URISA Conference, pages 7-22. Also published as Discussion Paper B.74.27 (Ottawa, Canada: Ministry of State for Urban Affairs, 1974).

As shown in Figure 1, there are four points of view concerning the role of each of the functions in terms of effecting an information system capability which best meets the needs of an institution, and the citizens and community served by that institution. By way of illustration, referring to column 3, the points of view to be expressed about the role of the operations function would emanate from the management, planning, operations, and information technology functions.

The Symposium presentations numbered two for each point of view, for a total of eight presentations per TRACK, and thirty-two overall. In addition, Rapporteurs reported on further expressions of opinion during each of the Sessions. This statement attempts to summarize the positions taken or advanced, and to provide the occasional interpretive remark. It is suggested that the interested reader examine the Symposium Proceedings[5] for more detailed arguments.

FUNCTIONAL ROLES: SELF PERCEPTIONS

The following sections in this part of the paper treat perceptions in the following order: management on management; planning on planning; operations on operations; and information technology on information technology.

Management on Management

The generic responsibility of management was seen in the first instance to be that of managing; that is, to be in charge, to make final decisions about the overall level and share of resources to be devoted to achieving a set of objectives which management defines within a given political context. When coupled with an IT responsibility, it was observed that management know-how and application in addition to some knowledge of the why's and wherefore's of IT are required for effective, efficient, and politically sensitive management to occur.

Some attendees expected that with a 15-20 year history, management should be more heavily involved in determining the ways, extent, and purposes of IT in local government. That is, management should exercise more interest and control over such fundamentally important, continuing decision areas as priorities of applications development and implementation. It was observed, in this vein, that management seldom extended its interest beyond the hardware stage, and then only in terms of whether to buy or rent.

---

5 Proceedings of the Symposium on Information Technology and Urban Governance, op. cit.

The counter-argument was that with so many avenues opening up management simply could not make the time to acquire an in-depth knowledge of IT or its roles in local government. Hence, while it was conceded that management should get more heavily into IT, no area or field of endeavour was identified as the preferred one(s) to be sacrificed in favour of IT.

Planning on Planning

It was observed during the Symposium that the perceived cost-effectiveness ratio for words spoken or written about planning (cost) vis-a-vis modifications to or understanding of the planning process as a consequence of those words (effectiveness) is pitiful. Further, it was often argued that it didn't matter whether the spokesperson was for or against planning!
A case for the planning problem is appreciated if one recalls that:

1. planning involves preparing comprehensive plans before the fact of social or physical change, incorporating citizen, operations, management, political (recall citizen) and private sector input in those plans as the inputs arise (planning is dynamic) so as to achieve a whole which is somewhat greater than the sum of its parts, and

2. for reasons of mandate, political power, public apathy, public involvement, sectoral thrusts (of line departments), institutional inertia, private sector pulls and tugs, etc., planning is often relatively weaker than any of the parts which comprise the planning process (as opposed to planning products, which come in for their own share of criticism).

With the above as context, planning saw its role in the evolution of IT as follows:

1. Planning should take a lead role in the development of outputs which marry at least some of the many thrusts of operating departments; in particular, graphics packages for demonstration, evaluation, etc., purposes, and incorporating a variety of socio-economic data, structures data, assessment data, etc., should evolve under the lead of planning.

2. Planning, with its heavy citizen interface and involvement responsibility, must become much more active in the exploitation of IT as a means for

communicating (informing, hearing) with the public. This requires that planners become much more aware of the powers of IT, and the fact that IT is more than simply a toy of the number crunchers.

3. Planners must begin to perceived the parabiosis of information systems and flows and government systems and flows. That done, they can take on an advocates role in bringing about critical mass improvements of a comprehensive nature in the methodological, problem, and institutional arenas. If that does not happen then planning, more than any other function, does not get beyond square one.

Operations on Operations

Discussions on this topic made it abundantly clear that while other functions described in this paper may have inter-functional relations/rivalries, operations has them on an intra-functional basis as well. That local authorities may have 15 to 50 IT-user departments/agencies points up the problematic dimensions of this local government function. It was also frequently noted that the operations function finds its outputs and activities consumed in two different ways, ie., as part of the day-to-day functioning of government in a line operation context, and as input to program modification, quality control, and planning activities, ie., as staff service.

Operations perceives three modes of activity: a) re-active and preactive, with management setting the pace in the former case, and operations doing that in the latter case, or b) a mix of the two. Since the mix-mode was accepted as the more popular candidate in terms of how the universe unfolds, it is described here.

In the view of operations, the preferred role of the operations function is seen to be as follows:

1. Within the set of constraints imposed by management (priorities, budgets, target populations, etc.) operations with its line responsibilities should serve as the interpreter/translator of IT-related management directives.

2. While operations should be the originator of applications to be accommodated by the IT function, there is a place for IT initiatives. However, these initiatives should be addressed to operations, or via operations as the interpreter to management.

3. Single-purpose systems or applications should be designed, developed, etc. jointly by the involved operating department and the IT component.

4. Multi-purpose systems should be a joint operations/ IT function effort, eg., as a task force, but over- all systems responsibilities should reside with the IT function.

Information Technology on Information Technology

Two distinctive modes of IT performance were defined by the IT function:

1. IT as a strictly responsive service, with functional responsibilities defined by management and users evaluating IT outputs, users providing feedback to management and management re-instructing IT, ad repetitio;

2. IT as a skill bureaucracy, with its own perspectives on the preferred ways, extent, and purposes of IT use and extension.

The third IT mode, as with operations, was a mix of the two, and depends upon the IT environments. Hence, while IT is self-perceived as a servicing unit in all instances, it assumes a reactive stance in one mode, a preactive stance in an other, and a mix in the third mode.

In the reactive mode, the IT on IT view suggested that the IT function gets along by going along. That is, it is incumbent upon management and users (operations, planning, research, etc.) to provide the ways and means and applications environment for the IT function to do its job as best it can, under an exogenously defined and constrained set of operating conditions.

As a preactive agent of local government, however, the IT function guides users as to appropriate treatment of current activities by IT, informs management of new organizational thrusts to be accommodated by IT etc.; in short, the IT function carves out a lead role for itself with respect to the defining and carrying out of tasks of the management, planning, operations, and information technology functions.

The third mode, and the more popular IT position, involved doing a bit of both of the above. In this way there would be some respite from what could be a humdrum, automaton existence (respond when asked), and opportunities for some innovative R & D or applications work. On the other hand, IT spokespersons preferred not to tread too heavily upon the directive domain of the users of its methods, techniques, and outputs.

FUNCTIONAL ROLES: EXTRA-FUNCTION PERCEPTIONS

In this section of the paper, each function is discussed
in terms of views held by the other functions in the following
order: planning, operations, and IT on management; management, planning, and IT on planning; management, planning
and IT on operations; and management, planning, and operations
on IT.

Planning, Operations, and IT on Management

While being more or less empathetic to management in
terms of the generic responsibilities of management, speakers
in this TRACK were not particularly sympathetic. In these
regards, the following shortcomings of management were noted:

1. a tendency to be input-oriented to the virtual
   exclusion of concerns about outputs;

2. a crisis orientation, so that information and other
   demands arise at the point of crisis, and rather
   than being planned for;

3. an unwillingness (or inability) to engage in for-
   malized, systematic evaluation;

4. a tendency to be pre-occupied with statistical
   reports (not prepared at management request or by
   those genuinely familiar with management issues)
   instead of specifying key questions it needs/wants
   answered.

These observations, among others, were common to all three
functional points of view.
    In terms of what management should be doing vis-a-vis
evolution of information technology at the local (or other)
level, the follow arguments were advanced:

1. Management must ensure that operations, planning
   and IT functions are more fully apprised of
   management issues and concerns. This done, then
   the latter three functions can relate to management
   thrusts when developing and implementing ways and
   means of problem anticipation, resolution, and
   evaluation (pre-and post-impact). This holds in
   general, and with respect to information technology
   in particular;

2. Management must actively encourage and support
   evaluation of programs, operations, etc. as a basis

to finding out what is going on. This includes recognition by management that:

> (a) information (specification, acquisition, processing, dissemination, application) is not costless, and
>
> (b) the quality and quantity of information available and accessible is a direct function of ways and means in place to generate it in the first instance and process it in the second;

3. Management has to focus on outputs as well as inputs, including a continuing assessment of the role of the IT component as a contributor to outputs;

4. Management must get its hands dirty and introduce such accountability mechanisms as utilizing more sensitive IT charging procedures (to regulate nature and level of use), and instituting service contracts for IT applications and verification of acceptable performance. Further, it is management's role to explore and resolve the pros and cons of decentralizing programmers and analysts, in a context which satisfies management, key users (operations, planning, public), and the IT function.

5. Management, while it must be appreciative of planning, operations, and IT function information, must play a lead role in specifying the content and intent of management function information, including determination of the market or target population to which programs are directed.

The three functions were in agreement that just as they evolve via information inputs and outputs, so should management. In this regard, management must "get off its hands", and begin to more fully appreciate the significance of information and IT as a key ingredient to effective and efficient execution within the management function. As part of this rigorous look at IT, management must also examine carefully the place of IT within an overall institutional context, and ways and means to render IT and IT users accountable.

Management, Operations and IT on Planning

Possibly because of the planners predisposition with what should be, representatives of other functions were on occasion somewhat harsh in pointing out the reality of what is, at least as they see it:

1. Planners have no grasp of analytical methods and techniques;

2. The computer is beyond the comprehension of planners and cannot be used by them;

3. Data file comparability is not an issue with planners as they either do not employ data, or use them erroneously;

4. Planners deal in generalities and hand-waving, have no fix on objectives or goals, and hence cannot take advantage of IT as an analytical tool, idea source, or communications medium.

These put downs of planning actually included, simultaneously, suggested avenues for planning to pursue in the evolution of IT. Some of these are:

1. Planning must assume overall responsibility for ensuring comparability of data (data elements/ items/formats) which constitute the basis of draft or official local area plans. Discrepancies in maps, for example, which are used at public meetings, was mentioned as a glaring illustration of a planning function shortcoming.

2. Planning cannot afford to sit back and wait for information technology "specialists" to set up courses, manuals, etc. for their benefit, but must participate in the process. It was noted, for example, that planners tend to have little appreciation for the fiscal implications of their plans, problems associated with developing and maintaining geo-information systems, testing and calibrating urban development models, etc. Hence, numerous suggestions of a curriculum and real world situation nature were made to help get planners (existing and future) "up to speed".

3. Planners, in order to better get out the message of management and operations to the public and its elected officials, must up-date its communication/ display capability. In this vein it was observed that planners unduly reply upon hand-drawn, limited- flexibility, crayon-coloured maps when the target population has long been ready for IT-based outputs, and the opportunity to electronically interact with planners and their products.

The first two of these points are not new by any means, and serve in many respects to draw attention to the third point. The three commenting functions were in large agreement that planning should get into IT soon, and well, for the benefit of planning and on behalf of the other functions, as planning is in many respects their window to the world.

Management, Planning and IT on Operations

Articles, municipal reports, URISA Proceedings, etc., suggest/contend/point out that in terms of quantity of use of IT, operations far surpasses management and planning combined. It is becoming increasingly popular, and sometimes painfully appropriate, however, to inquire of the ways, extent, and purposes of these usages.[6] As the perceived primary customer of IT, operations' usage of IT is being subjected to considerable scrutiny, therefore, by management, planning, and IT (and the larger public). Pertinent questions along this line include the following:

1. As the prime generator of urban data, including administrative and survey data, what efforts are being made to reduce or at least hold the line on data base build-ups in general, and demands upon the public for data in particular?

2. As the determiner in the first instance of confidential data, what are operating departments doing to ensure data security?

3. As the primary users of IT, what evidence does operations have at hand or plan to obtain to justify IT-related expenditures on behalf of operations?

4. In terms of sectoral thrusts by individual operating units, what is being done to ensure that the well-being of the whole (of urban and regional government) is not being jeopardized for the sake of the parts which comprise that whole? This larger institutional question becomes IT-relevant when specialized data bases, special purpose IT systems, etc. are brought into the discussion.

This TRACK SESSION was especially noteworthy in that representations from the three commenting functions were more inclined to pose questions than raise assertions or contentions about the role of operations. Clearly, operations

---

6 For further discussion see B. Wellar, "Impressions on the Status of Computer-Assisted Information Systems in Urban Governance". Discussion Paper B.76.2 (Ottawa, Canada: Ministry of State for Urban Affairs, January, 1976).

holds the pre-eminent position among IT users, and even management seems to have little to offer, whether as re-enforcement of this status or challenge to it. Hence, other than to re-state that all functions must work more closely together, and appreciate each others' needs and constraints, little direction was provided to operations in terms of its preferred role re evolution of a desired IT capability.

Management, Planning and Operations on Information Technology

The IT role as seen by representatives of the three commenting functions is essentially of the three types noted earlier: reactive, preactive and a mix of the two. Since a "mix of the two" was perceived by IT and other functions as how IT does and should proceed for the most part, that mode is discussed here.

Management, which is into IT in only a very limited way, perceived IT as a check and balance vis-a-vis some of the more industrious users of the computer and associated applications. Similarly, management held the notion that IT may help "bring along" planning and some of the softer departments in the adoption of quantitative methods and subsequent generation of hard facts. Hence, IT is seen by management as both a dampener or control agent, and as a catalyst.

Planning is more inclined to incorporate IT processes, products, and personnel in its activities (whereas manage-ment simply "uses" them), possibly in the hope of gaining a footing more equal to that of the stronger operating units. Planning, then, perceives IT as a supplier of goods, services, and expertise, and is not adverse to IT offering them up voluntarily.

It is from the operations function that the role of IT is most seriously challenged, or subject to shaping. While operations perceives the need for some flexibility, in terms of what analysts and programmers do, operations appears to be strongly advocating decentralization of the hardware-software configuration, and farming out of programmers and analysts the users' shops; that is, a return of control to users (operators in this case). It was frequently argued that the IT function has become removed from operations, and that IT was coming to be sustained by its own juices. To combat this (perceived) deleterious state of affairs, opera-tions is endorsing an IT role which, while distinctly IT in character, is much more closely aligned with, associated with, and attuned to operations in a logistical as well as accountability/directive sense.

CONCLUSION

The primary purpose of this paper is to provide bench-
mark treatment of an important topic: the preferred roles
of different governance functions in the evolution of an
information technology capability which best meets the needs
and aspirations of the citizens and communities served by
urban, regional, etc. government and agencies.

This topic is a long-standing one in a generic sense,
in that the functions of management, planning and operations
have been subjected to role discussions for years. It
appears, however, that IT has added a new wrinkle in that
it can be a bias-free mirror for reflecting upon institutional processes and relationships. Further, because of the
interactive nature of IT, some of it realized and much more
waiting in the wings, and its capacity for more closely
linking government with the public than was possible with
manual methods, the IT dimension is injecting new and
different streams of perceptions, expectations, etc. in
government and society.

Clearly, then, and as illustrated in the paper, the
traditional functions and IT are impacting upon each other.
What we have at this stage is a series of first-cut,
explicit impressions about functional roles in the evolution
of information systems, and a substantial body of opinion and
information to the effect that roles taken on markedly affect
an institution's ability to deliver. Now that the topic
has surfaced, and has been subjected to an "in full view"
discussion, it is urged that it be pursued. We cannot
afford not to do so.

John A. Kaiser
Program Manager, U.S.-U.S.S.R. Program for
Scientific and Technical Cooperation on the
Management of Large Cities
Center for Government Studies
Columbia University
New York, New York 10027

THE USE OF COMPUTER SYSTEMS BY LOCAL GOVERNMENTS IN THE SOVIET UNION

ABSTRACT   The status of computer applications by municipal governments in the U.S.S.R. is discussed. Soviet cities
have been directed to adopt large integrated automated management systems in order to better control their development
and improve the efficiency of their governments. Since Moscow and Leningrad lead other cities of the U.S.S.R. in this
effort, examples of operational systems in these cities are
examined and potential benefits and problems discussed.

INTRODUCTION

The aim of this paper is to provide a brief overview of the status
of computer usage by the municipal governments of major cities in the
Soviet Union. Specific data will refer to Moscow and to a lesser extent
Leningrad. Resources are made available to these cities by the central
government on a priority basis for all forms of municipal management
and service requirements, and thus they are generally foremost in the
application of computers to urban administration.

It is assumed that the reader knows little about either the management structure of Soviet cities or the characteristics of Soviet computers. The latter is easily overcome by references to similar American
machines, but the former will require a bit of background information.
In the course of the paper, first the administrative framework of Soviet
cities will be outlined, using Moscow as an example, then highlights of
the major current activities under way in Moscow and Leningrad in the
area of municipal computer usage will be given, and finally, some potential benefits and problems generated by the introduction of broad computer usage within these city governments will be touched upon.

The information upon which this paper is drawn has been acquired
through the activities of the U.S-U.S.S.R. Program for Scientific and
Technical Cooperation on the Management of Large Cities. Funded by the
National Science Foundation and carried out by the Center for Government
Studies at the Columbia University Graduate School of Business, this program is just one of the many facets of bilateral cooperation currently
functioning under the auspices of the U.S. - U.S.S.R. Agreement on

Scientific and Technological Cooperation signed in Moscow in May of 1972. It represents an attempt to establish closer and more regular cooperation between scientific and technical organizations and specialists of both countries on a basis of mutual benefit, equality and reciprocity.

In the area of computer applications to large city management, we have, with our Soviet counterparts, developed a program of joint research covering such subjects as productivity and efficiency in urban service delivery, computer support of urban freight and passenger transportation services, and the special problems involved in the development of large-scale urban management information systems. Cooperative activities include joint seminars, the development of joint reports, reciprocal visits by urban and computer specialists, and team visits of moderate length for purposes of concentrated research. After one and one half years of effort specific areas of mutual interest and potential benefit have been identified, and considerable progress is being made towards providing municipal computer systems designers, managers and administrators in this country with new sources of information and ideas related to the improvement of urban service quality and efficiency through the use of computers.

THE ADMINISTRATIVE STRUCTURE OF THE CITY OF MOSCOW

In theory, Moscow is governed by the City Soviet or City Council, consisting of 1600 deputies representing individual small constituencies within the city. In fact, administrative power is in the hands of the twenty-five member Executive Committee of the City Soviet which meets every two weeks. Foremost in this body is the Chairman of The Executive Committee (informally known as the mayor), his nine Deputy Chairmen and The Committee Secretary. These eleven individuals are responsible for the day-to-day administration of the city. Each oversees an interrelated group of the city's sixty agencies. Thirteen agencies, those concerned with the most essential services, and generally having the greatest size are termed Main Administrations. In decreasing order of importance, the remaining organizations are termed Administrations, Departments and Bureaus.

The range of operations and services provided by the municipal government is much wider in the Soviet Union than we are accustomed to in the United States. For example, the city constructs and maintains 90% of the housing in the city, and operates almost all food and retail stores. In addition, it runs most hotels, theaters, restaurants, repair shops and personal service shops. Consequently, although New York and Moscow have comparable populations, New York City employs approximately 300,000 people, while Moscow has 1.4 million city workers. It is important to bear this in mind when we discuss Moscow's design of an integrated automated management system for the entire municipal government. This is for them an even more complex task than it would be for most western cities.

A further important point concerns the status of Moscow and Leningrad within the governmental framework of the Soviet Union. Almost all cities in the U.S.S.R. are legally subordinate to the Republic or Autonomous Republic in which they are located. Moscow and Leningrad, however, are directly subordinate to the Union government although they are located in the Russian Republic. Such special status is translated into significant power and privilege in terms of budget allocations and priorities for computers and support equipment. This factor, together with the role of these two municipalities as showcase cities for Soviet society, helps to explain the lead they exhibit over other cities of the U.S.S.R. in broad municipal computer application.

Finally, it should be mentioned that parallel to the administrative structure of the city is the corresponding structure of the Communist Party. The Party has patterned its organization in the city to mirror the city's governmental organization. Thus, within each sub-division of municipal government there exists a cohesive sub-unit of the city Party organization whose role is stated to be one of advice and inspiration. In most cases the administrative sub-division leaders are also active members if not leaders of the corresponding Party units. This is usually more the case the higher up one goes in the administrative hierarchy. Thus, in a very real sense, there is a pervasiveness of Party influence throughout the municipal government, with major appointments and policy decisions being made inevitably and at the very least, with Party concurrence. With this in mind, however, one can then proceed to examine the municipal governmental agencies and their functional operations as one would those of any western city.

THE AVAILABILITY OF COMPUTERS TO MUNICIPALITIES

It is a widely held feeling among U. S. experts who have studied the subject that the Soviet Union is five to ten years behind the U.S. in the overall field of computers and their applications. The operative word here, however, is overall. In the areas of technological know-how, the existence of advanced Soviet military and space systems provides ample evidence of their ability to produce the up-to-date computer equipment necessary to support such activities. Similarly, in the area of applications theory, Soviet literature on the subject is voluminous and conceptually advanced.

The crux of the Soviet problem appears to be the lack of depth in their electronics industry, without which, broad production and widespread application of computers has not been possible. For example, the U.S.S.R. began mass production of integrated circuits in the late 1960's at a time when there were already four firms doing so in Western Europe and Japan and over thirty in the U.S. So too, the highest level of integration currently used by the Soviets is several logic gates per chip, while the U.S. uses chips containing several thousand interconnected logic elements.[1]

As a consequence of the delayed production of large numbers of computers, and of the priorities followed in the central allocation of computers, Soviet municipal agencies have only recently begun to acquire and utilize significant numbers of these machines. Relevant figures for mid 1973 are as follows:[2]

City	Population	Operational Computers
Moscow	7.5 million	13
Leningrad	4.0 million	17
Kiev	1.8 million	1
Novosibirsk	1.2 million	0

In 1971, by decree of the Twenty-Fourth Congress of the Communist Party of the Soviet Union, local governments and their subsidiary organizations were charged with improving the efficiency of their operations through the adoption of modern management techniques and tools, including the use of Automatic (computerized) Systems of Management, referred to as ASU in Russian. ASU is a catch-all term, covering any computer application which contributes to the administration of an organization, quite analagous in usage to our term, "MIS". Soon after the decree, ASU's began to sprout, at least in design form, in agencies throughout the local governmental structure of most moderate and large cities. In 1973, the first Soviet complex of upward-compatible, third-generation computers, complete with peripherals and fully developed software, was unveiled in Moscow. Developed jointly by the U.S.S.R., Bulgaria, Hungary, East Germany, Poland, and Czechoslovakia, the RYAD computers (ES-1010, ES-1020, ES-1021, ES-1030, ES-1040, ES-1050, ES-1060) are close equivalents to the small and moderate sized members of the IBM 360 series of machines and said to be program compatible with them.[3]

1. Turn, R. and Nimitz, A. E., "Computers and Strategic Advantage: 1. Computer Technology in the United States and the Soviet Union." The Rand Corporation, R-1642-PR (May 1975)

2. Savas, E. S., "Municipal Data Systems in the Soviet Union," Government Data Systems Nov/Dec 1973, p. 16

3. Turn, R. and Nimitz, A. E., op. cit.

The increasing availability of these machines has begun to make possible the realization of the ASU designs stemming from the 1971 Party Congress decree. At the present time, most large agencies in Moscow and Leningrad are in the midst of converting their procedures from manual to automated modes, and, at the same time, providing for the integration of their operational and control data into more comprehensive systems covering the management of whole sectors of the local economy. All of these sectional or branch management systems are, in turn, to contribute to an enormous integrated ASU governing the entire municipal administration of the city. This is indeed an extremely active time in the evolution of municipal government in the Soviet Union.

CURRENT APPLICATIONS IN MOSCOW

The key organization in the expansion of computer usage in Moscow is the Main Scientific-Research Computing Center which is subordinate directly to the Executive Committee of the City Soviet. The Center has some 500 employees at three locations in the city. The role of the Center is threefold:

It coordinates and plans the work of all computing centers of departments and enterprises directly subordinate to the Moscow City Soviet;

It acts as a service bureau for those agencies which do not themselves have a computer capability;

It undertakes original and self-initated research including the development of ASU's for individual organizations and branches of the municipal economy, and of the overall integrated city management system 'MOSKVA' mentioned below.

As an indication of the powerful role played by this Center, in addition to handling approximately 60% of the computing requirements of the city government, all requests for new and replacement computers computers from those agencies having their own computer capability must be screened and evaluated by the Center before being passed on to the State Committee for Science and Technology and the State Planning Commission for funding.

The service bureau activities of the Center appear to be primarily routine data processing tasks at this time, including the support of a job-matching or employment agency activity for municipal agencies, the automated billing of utilities, fees and rents for the apartments controlled by the city, and a form of purchasing system.

By far the most interesting activity of the Center is its role in the development of the all-city automated system of management 'MOSKVA',

and its component subsystems. The goal of this complex system is to insure the optimal orderly development of the city through a general improvement of the quantity and quality of relevant information supporting
and influencing municipal management decision making. It is felt by the
Soviets that in a centrally planned entity such as Moscow, it is scientifically possible to quantify the interrelationships and dynamics of
the city organism so that given certain annual quotas of material, labor
and financial resources, decisions can be made which will optimize the
desired output. This output is defined as the improvement of conditions
under which residents and visitors live, conduct business, and obtain
services in Moscow.

In order to realize this ambitious goal, four levels of automation
have been incorporated into the overall design. At the most basic level,
local ASU's are being implemented which address management problems of
individual enterprises within the municipal service economy. Primarily
systems of an informational, accounting and routine data processing nature, city officials feel that the number of such ASU's may eventually
reach several tens of thousands. The second level ASU's are called
'Branch'Automated Management Systems. Such systems are concerned with
problems and tasks of all enterprises linked either organizationally
within the structural framework of the city, or geographically within the 30 district scheme utilized for the administration of service
delivery. With some 55 to 60 service agencies and 30 districts currently
in Moscow, it is felt that the number of Branch ASU's will eventually
approach 100.

The third level of automation, the "Interbranch Complex" ASU's
must handle the key problem of the optimal development and functional
coordination of complexes of closely interrelated branches. An example
of such a group, characteristically unified by a common goal, is the
interbranch complex and ASU 'CONSTRUCTION'. It encompasses all or part
of eight branches, including the Main Administrations for Architecture,
Housing Construction, Industrial Construction, Engineering Construction,
Construction Materials, Housing Management, the Administration for Production Enterprises, and the Construction Transportation Division of
the Main Administration for Auto Transport. Some eleven such 'Interbranch
Complex' ASU's are planned.

Finally, we have the all-city ASU 'MOSKVA'. Feeding upon information passed up from the subordinate ASU's, MOSKVA attempts to solve
problems involving development goals for municipal services, possible
local compositional variants in these development goals, and the need
for balance among the development plans of the interbranch complexes.
Among the subsystems of MOSKVA are those dealing with city service planning, operational control and management, various resource needs and
availabilities (financial, material, technical, population, labor),
social programs, and management science progress.

Having produced a model for this system, a plan was developed for
the introduction of computers and the development of component ASU's
through 1990. Within this framework a total of 36 ASU's at all four

levels have been developed to date and implemented to some degree. These systems are supported at approximately 24 computing centers employing 3500 people. By 1990 the introduction of 87 ASU's is planned, serving 115 client organizations at various levels. A total of 135 computers (primarily those of the RYAD type) will be utilized at that time with a general productivity of 15×10^6 operations per second. The planners in Moscow estimate that their 1990 data processing volume will be 167×10^9 bytes per year.

Some examples of ASU's already developed and at least partly operational in Moscow are listed below.

1. 'GORPLAN' - a system developed for the City Planning Commission which is centered around a complex of planning algorithms intended for the development of the 20 year, 5 year and annual plans for municipal services, for interbranch complexes and for districts of the city.

2. 'FINANCES' - developed for the Finance Administration, to monitor and control the execution of the municipal budget.

3. 'MATERIAL TECHNICAL SUPPLY' - developed for the administration of the same name to manage the supply and purchasing functions of the Moscow City Soviet Executive Committee.

4. 'POPULATION AND LABOR RESOURCES' - The job-matching system mentioned above.

5. 'KURS' - A system developed to automate the distribution and management of all housing subordinate to the City Soviet.

6. 'SIGNAL' - An interesting system developed to monitor and control the execution of all orders from administrative agencies as well as decisions of the Executive Committee itself. The authors of the system claim that its implementation has resulted in:

   A. higher quality directive documentation (due to informational requirements of the system);

   B. better quality control of execution deadlines;

   C. increased effectiveness of information output for the Executive Committee;

   D. increased reliability and clarity of control results.[4]

7. 'MOSSOVIET' - The goal of this system is the improvement of the

4. Tkachenko, P.N., Naumov, S.I., Loginov, A.A., Andreev, E. V."A Control System for the Implementation of Decisions of the Moscow City Soviet Executive Committee" Gorodskoe Khozyaistvo Moskvi No. 10, 1974; Translated at Center for Government Studies, Columbia University, Feb. 1975

operational administration of municipal services by the Moscow
City Soviet through the use of econo-metric and management science techniques.

The above seven ASU's were developed by and are run at the Main
Scientific-Research Computing Center of the Moscow City Soviet Executive Committee. They are run on the Center's Minsk 32, (second generation) and ES-1020 computers, and were developed at a stated cost of
11.2 million rubles, or 15.7 million dollars at the arbitrary but
official exchange rate. One of our research goals is to take a closer
look at several of these systems, as well as at the derivation of the
stated development costs.

Among the Branch and Interbranch ASU's are:

8. ASU GLAVMOSSTROI - for the automated development of five year
and annual programs of municipal construction, and for the coordination of the member organizations of the interbranch construction complex. Developed at a cost of 8.8 million rubles, it
utilizes six second generation computers, four of the URAL type,
and two MINSK 32's. The system supports a complex of branches
which constructs more than 5 million square meters of general
housing area in Moscow each year, in addition to schools, hospitals,
theaters, commercial buildings, etc. Typical tasks of the system
are:

   A. development of hourly assembly and transport schedules for
   such items as mortar, concrete, asphalt and other materials
   and equipment;

   B. monitoring the actual execution of hourly and daily assembly schedules;

   C. calculating yearly plans for resource requirements and
   work programs for construction trucks;

   D. preparing management summaries and reports for top administration of the various construction agencies.

Each day this system processes 3.6×10^5 characters of information,
much of it gathered by means of 140 radio transmitters and 200 teletypes
in direct communication with construction organizations and construction
sites. As was mentioned above, it is the heart of an enormous operation
involving eight of the largest agencies in the Moscow City Government.

9. ASU 'GLAVMOSAVTOTRANS' - This system was developed for the centralized management of urban freight flow, including the optimization of truck routes, inventory control, and maintenance operations;
the system utilizes two URAL 14 and one ES-1030 computers, and was

developed at a cost of 6.13 million rubles.

10. ASU 'START' - An automatic traffic control system developed at
a cost of 2.5 million rubles, and utilizing an M-6000 mini-computer.

Additional ASU's exist for such services and organizations as the
food and retail trade network, the municipal taxi system, the METRO
(subway) operation, the emergency ambulance service, the epidemic forecasting and control service, the Police department, the bread baking
and distribution industry, the tailoring industry, the municipal laundry
and hotel operation, the water supply and disposal system and the management of social welfare services.

These systems are in various stages of implementation and are constantly being expanded. During recent visits to the Soviet Union we were
frequently told that such expansion awaits only the delivery of a new
ES-1020 or ES-1030. There is no doubt that the city officials are committed to an extended period of growth in computer utilization.

CURRENT APPLICATIONS IN LENINGRAD

The situation in Leningrad is quite similar to that we see in Moscow. The same motivations are causing the city officials there to
rapidly develop and adopt computer based management systems, and at the
same time, the same constraints and shortages are somewhat retarding
progress. An all-city ASU called 'LENINGRAD' is being developed by Lensystemotechnica, a scientific research and development center subordinate to the Leningrad City Soviet. It was founded in 1970 and has some
1500 employees. In addition to the task of developing ASU's for the
Leningrad municipal government, Lensystemotechnica conducts a sizable
program of training in the utilization of computer systems for municipal
technical and managerial employees.

Leningrad has over 700,000 employees to serve its population of
4 million. Its municipal government exhibits a breadth of responsibilities similar to that of Moscow's. Officials at Lensystemotechnica, however, have taken a somewhat simpler approach to the development of the
all-city ASU. They have defined only two levels of organizational
structure in ASU 'LENINGRAD', functional and territorial, as opposed to
the four in ASU 'MOSKVA'. There appears to have been less emphasis
placed in Leningrad upon the creation of a massive system into which
every element of municipal government and its related ASU must be fitted.
Considerable study has been centered on the appropriateness of automation
for each of the various municipal departments. Thus it was decided to
create the ASU 'LENINGRAD CLOTHING' to serve the management of a group of
21 fashion houses, but a proposal for a similar system for the network of
over 100 tailoring establishments was rejected since it was estimated that
such a system would increase overall expenditures by 20 to 30 percent.

First priority is being given to the development of a number of basic subsystems to ASU 'LENINGRAD';

1. ASU 'CONSTRUCTION' - with well over 100,000 employees, the complex of Leningrad construction agencies builds over 2.2 million square meters of living space per year in addition to commercial and engineering structures. They are also responsible for building repairs. ASU 'CONSTRUCTION' has been under development by Lensystemotechnica in collaboration with the Leningrad Institute for Civil Engineering since 1973. When fully operational, it will support the planning, scheduling, monitoring of all construction performed by the municipal government. Segments of the system are currently in the testing stage.

2. ASU 'HOUSING' - for the management of the housing stock controlled by the City Soviet.

3. ASU 'PUBLIC TRANSPORTATION' - for the administration of surface mass transit in the city, including such functions as bus scheduling and taxi fleet management.

4. ASU 'TRADE' - for the management of the network of retail stores in Leningrad.

Systems are also under development which automate certain functions of the City Planning Commission, the Bread Industry, the Clothing Industry, the Police Department, the Department of Supply and the Pharmacy Network.

All these systems are in the early implementation stage. By the end of 1975, there were to have been 12 such branch systems at various stages of implementation, applied to some 140 specific urban management problems. On the whole, most of the more ambitious plans for systems applications appear to remain on paper, awaiting the availability of both machines and trained programmers. Moscow, because of its central role in the nation, has first claim among municipalities in the USSR on computers and thus exhibits a significant lead in terms of operational automated management systems.

PROBLEMS AND BENEFITS

It is inevitable that such a rapid surge towards the adoption of computer-based management systems, with the corresponding transitions from manual to computer oriented procedures would cause considerable churning within as bulky and established a bureaucracy as that of the Soviet Union. Initial problems caused by local shortages of everything from print-out paper, to canned programs, to peripherals seem to be gradually working themselves out. A potentially more serious problem,

sensed perhaps by skeptical American experts more than by the confident
Soviet analysts, lies in the danger of placing too much reliance on
mathematical models of urban management. Based upon admittedly limited
observations and conversations by U.S. municipal management and computer
specialists, there appears to be excessive confidence on the part of the
Soviets that the enormously complex elemental interrelationships which
together constitute the dynamic of a large city's progress, can be faith-
fully represented and controlled by a hierarchy of integrated, computerized, management systems. In this most centrally planned of economies,
the consequences of erroneous algorithms in such a system could be quite
serious. On the other hand, if designed with subtlety and built-in flexibility and if used with sufficient circumspection the ASU's 'MOSKVA'
and 'LENINGRAD' could prove to be of enormous aid in managing bureaucracies of 1.4 million and 700,000 employees respectfully, and valuable
examples to the rest of the world.

An interesting by-product to the advance in computer usage in the
Soviet Union is the opening up of new paths for the advance of young
bright Soviet technicians. This is not an unusual phenomenon in and of
itself. We have seen such rapid career advances in the United States
in similar circumstances. In the U.S., however, there exist a large
number of means to rapid progress for bright and ambitious young people.
Our observations in the Soviet Union, on the other hand, appear to indicate a management structure securely in the hands of middle aged or
older men. With the Soviet Union placing new emphasis on computer usage
in management, we are beginning to see the emergence in that country of
a class of young technical experts who are influencing decision making
at levels heretofore reserved for the older, established bureaucrats.
It will be interesting to see whether this becomes a truly significant
trend, and whether real power passes into the hands of this group as a
consequence of the expanded role they are coming to play in municipal
management.

Soviet cities are now going through a period of experimentation,
exploring the limits to which computer oriented management systems may
be utilized to produce more rational urban development. This can be a
valuable object of study for the U.S. regardless of the eventual results in the USSR. We should follow their progress, noting the causes
for specific successes and failures. Some of these will be related to
their political system, but I suspect a number will not. From these
especially, American urban managers can gain useful information for
the better planning and servicing of their cities.

Sheila and Wilbur Steger
CONSAD Research Corporation
121 North Highland Avenue
Pittsburgh, Pennsylvania 15206

THE INFORMATION ECONOMY AND
THE URBANIZED REGION: A PROGRESS REPORT

This is a progress report on a project CONSAD is undertaking for the U.S. Office of Telecommunications Policy. The purpose of the project is to raise and examine a number of policy issues flowing out of the growth of the "information sector" of the U.S. economy. While the purpose of the project is not specifically focussed on small-area or urban economies, per se, we wish to take this opportunity to speculate on certain facets of the study which bear upon the policy interests of URISA's members. Such interests include certain national information policy issues -- such as privacy, economic productivity, and the information role of the public sector, generally -- the continual resolution of which impacts upon each and every subnational unit of government in the nation. These also bear upon similar investigations which subnational units of government -- state, county, and city -- might wish to undertake relative to issues specific to their constituencies and geographical areas.

INTRODUCTION AND STUDY BACKGROUND

The Office of Telecommunications Policy (OTP) is not alone in recognizing the possibly pervasive changes in our national economic and social institutions brought about by the growing role of information in every facet of our lives. However, given its designated overview role and responsibility for informing the Office of the President on government- and economy-wide issues either affecting the flow of information and/or affected by the flow of information, OTP has observed two "trends". Combined, these trends have led to substantially increased concern that information-related public policy may be seriously deficient and in need of substantial revision.

The first of these is the increasing awareness that, in the post-war period, the United States economy has gradually, but nonetheless certainly, experienced fundamental changes in the structure of aggregate output and in the composition of labor and other inputs. The evolution has been described variously as a movement toward a "Post-Industrial Society" (Bell), an "Information Economy" (Porat, Parker), and one specializing in the production and distribution of "knowledge" (Machlup). * In national income terms, estimates have ranged from Machlup's 1962 estimate that approximately 30% was directly related to "informational" inputs and outputs (in the 1950's) to more recent estimates and projections that, by 1980, considerably more than 50% are directly so related. Many others have noted (albeit less rigorously) similar trends. At least, in part, the general trend is corroborated by the steady growth of the nation's communications requirements over time. This trend, though often noticed and remarked, is not sufficiently identified in character nor understood in implication.

During the same period, developments in welfare economics and public policy analysis has reflected increased awareness of and concern for the roles of information, knowledge and communication in the efficient utilization of scarce national resources. These developments include identification of specific attributes of some goods or services, which attributes collectively define a class of "public" or "quasi-public" goods. ** These goods are characterized notably by the presence of economies of scale, externalities and indivisibility; and by the difficulties of excluding users, appropriating the product, and pricing it. The explicit controversy in the literature concerns the efficacy of markets and market processes in providing for the efficient and equitable production and distribution of "public" or "quasi-public" goods.

---

*Machlup, Fritz, The Production and Distribution of Knowledge in the United States, Princeton University Press, 1962; P. Drucker, The Age of Discontinuity, London Handbooks Limited, 1969; Marc U. Porat, The Information Economy, Ph. D. Dissertation, Stanford University, 1976; Ben Bagdikian, The Information Machines, Harper and Row, 1971, and Edwin B. Parker, Information and Society, Annual Review of Information and Technology, V. 8, 1973.

**Arrow, Kenneth, "Limited Knowledge and Economic Analysis," American Economic Review, March 1974; Michael Rothschild, "Models of Market Organization with Imperfect Information," Journal of Political Economy, November/December, 1973; Jack Hirschleiffer, "The Private and Social Value of Information and the Return to Inventive Activity," American Economic Review, September, 1971; and Harold Demetz, "Information and Efficiency: Another Viewpoint," Journal of Law and Economics, 1969.

OTP has viewed with great interest the combination of the "public good" characteristics of many kinds of information goods, coupled with the apparent growth of what can be termed an "information sector" in industrialized nations. The general purposes of the present inquiry flowing from this concern are: (a) to examine the structure of post-war growth in the United States economy with respect to its information/knowledge component; (b) to ascertain the extent to which the growth path is biased toward information output with "public" or "quasi-public" goods characteristics; (c) to define the public policy issues emerging from this pattern of growth; and, (d) to identify and evaluate the full range of national policy options for dealing with those issues.

The objectives of this study are severalfold:

(1)   To identify various types or classes of information goods or services; develop a taxonomy which illustrates the extent to which each type or class displays "public" goods characteristics; and, estimate the relative importance of the growth of "public" information goods.

(2)   To identify and explicate major policy issues arising from the growth and changing structure of the information sector. For each of these issues, a set of available policy options are to be identified and critically assessed. This set is to include legislative changes in the specification of private property rights, changes in methods of financing and/or pricing the availability of information, programs and policies designed to alter the growth path of the information sector, and emphasis or de-emphasis on markets and market processes in the efficient and equitable allocation of resources.

(3)   Based on the results from the preceding tasks, the study is to propose: (a) topics for further research, (b) issues deserving current action, and (c) ongoing developments which may require monitoring by the Executive Office.

This paper represents a progress report on this project and a brief explanation of how it might be of special interest to URISA members.

APPROACH

A literature search in the fields of economics and information science, as well as other relevant literature (e. g., from the "Futures" field) has been conducted, to identify growth rates in the information sector of the economy, as well as key policy issues relating to information. A critique of the "information sector" estimates -- Machlup, Porat, and Parker -- has served as validity and reliability checks to the original projections. These have been used to ascertain rough measures of the information sector component of the U.S. economy. These types of analysis have been broadened to other functional areas (e. g., transportation, health, environment). Information systems components (subsystems) have been specified, and the functional areas (above) analyzed, over time periods, to determine the subsystem cause/effect relationships to/from previously identified information policies.

The project is entering its next phase. A "dialectic debate" is planned. The data from the analyses, the inferences drawn from the analyses, and the information policy issues will constitute the data base for this debate. An experts/panel will develop probability estimates and assessments concerning policy questions and generate, in turn, suggestions for the implementation of policies that will increase productivity in the desired directions (as dictated by those identified policies).

The final results should include an estimate of the growth rate of the information sector (in general), and by subsystem and social functional areas in particular instances. The enumeration of information policy issues, as they currently exist, will be ranked in order of importance, and the implications of this ranking assessed. Further, suggestions as to the feasibility of implementing these policies which will foster increased productivity in the information sector will be made.

The limitation will be the exactness of the quantification estimates. These will be well-informed ("best estimate") assessments, and the range of the estimates will be given. The variance between the minority and majority opinions of the panel of experts will be stated. The use of a dialectic debate, it is anticipated, will provide a mechanism whereby the interdisciplinary nature of the subject can be fully exploited, and the policy suggestions that result from this exercise will be realistic, as well as varied.

SOME IMPLICATIONS FOR URISA MEMBERS

Empirical Issues

URISA members are familiar with the truism that the last quarter of the 20th Century is characterized as the "post-industrial society," distinguished by the "information explosion," "knowledge revolution," and other similar terms. These terms indicate the trend away from that "product" produced as a result of mechanical energies applied to resources, to those "products" produced as a result of human intellectual processing capabilities, extended by the use of electronic calculating and computing machines, and telecommunication devices, technologies which help record, encode, reproduce, and disseminate information, sometimes modifying and reprocessing data (e.g., analyzing, aggregating them) for specified purposes. The generation, reorganization, storage and distribution of information is ubiquitous, elevating the concept of information more explicitly to the status of a resource, to be studied and analyzed as are the natural resources of matter and energy, with the differences being that information is not degraded nor destroyed with use. "Data banks" therefore represent a commodity (such as other natural resources) which can (theoretically) be, for example, measured, used, priced, exchanged, transformed; there are markets for information. There are also public sector budgets for information not typically developed through the market mechanism. URISA members are familiar with the increasing pressures -- legitimately needed, in many cases -- for policies regarding its "control." Public policy questions vis a vis equity, privacy, distribution need to be addressed.

Peter Drucker has estimated that as of 1975, 40-odd million "knowledge workers" hold more than half the jobs in our economy.

"Knowledge, like electricity or money, is a form of energy that exists only when it does work ... the substitution of knowledge for manual skill as the productive resource in work is completely changing our society ... in the past 20 years we have created a brand new resource, namely knowledge. From an economy of goods -- which America had as recently as World War II -- we have changed into a knowledge economy. By the late 1970s, the knowledge sector, concerned with ideas and information rather than goods and services, will account for one half of total national product."*

---

*Britannica Year Book, 1974, page 16.

From the standpoint of both the professionals in the field, as well
as EVERYPERSON, who is impacted every day in hundreds of ways by
the information economy, what is needed is the definition, description,
and analysis (both macro- and micro-economic) of the information industry and segments of government (i.e., private and public domains)
devoted to the various phases of information and information processing in the United States (e.g., generators, transformers, acquirers,
analyzers, processors, distributors, to name several).

Information and its handling is an identified, key resource, and
the techniques by which it is handled, the legal and institutional limitations and the values that are placed upon it, as well as the demands
and costs for it, are all worthy of analysis. National information
policy issues, as raised by Lamberton,* need to be explicitly stated
and examined. Examples of other issues that might be raised in this
domain are:

.   Do some information processing segments (e.g.,
    generation vs. distribution) have a possibly misallo-
    cated share of resources devoted to them (through
    public and/or private sector actions) than others?

.   Is this the result of implicit social or fiscal policies?

.   Is this the cause of implicit social or fiscal policies?

.   Is this allocation beneficial, in a national income
    sense? In a quality of life sense?

An interesting question here concerns the differential rate of
growth among the structural components of an information system, as
these are implemented through planning, programming and budgeting
decisions in the "real world." If one can "decompose" an information
system into the following subsystems or components:**

---

*"National Information Policy," by Donald M. Lamberton, in
Information Revolution, Annals of the American Academy of Political
and Social Science, v. 412, March 1974.

**This model is one proposed and utilized for design, research,
and development of information systems by Anthony Debons, Co-
Chairman, Interdisciplinary Doctoral Program in Information Science,
University of Pittsburgh.

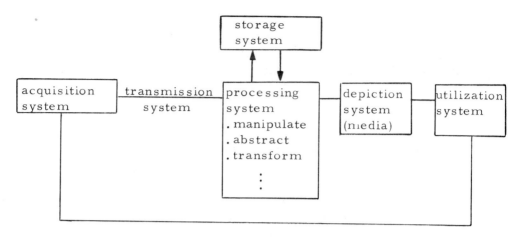

feedback

one can then ask the following questions. Is the <u>rate</u> of growth among
these subsystems in any one functional area (e. g., health), or across
functional areas by subsystems (e. g., storage function <u>vis a vis</u> education, welfare and health, for example) different? If there is a differential rate of growth, is this an <u>effect</u>, for example, of technology,
information policies (implicit in priorities and concomitant allocation
of resources), or pricing systems? Or, conversely, does this <u>cause</u>,
for example, a re-allocation of resources, larger incentives to newer
(or greater diffusion of) technology, changes in national information
policies, redistribution of income shares? In other words, is this
differential rate of growth an effect of "public" goods characteristics,
or is this the cause of "public" goods characteristics. Or both? Is
there a bias for/against this, or not?

We are also investigating the utility of an analysis of expenditures,
by functional area(s), across these sub-systems, in yielding gross
proportional measures, as well as growth rates. For instance:

Functional Areas

subsystems	Health			Education			...
	t_1	t_2	t_n	t_1	t_2	t_n	...
S_1							...
S_2							...
⋮	⋮	⋮	⋮	⋮	⋮	⋮	...
S_j							...

While our empirical analyses are intended to result in crude approximations, they are also designed to learn more about how these types of analyses can be done, what data exists to implement these analyses, and what do not. Some of the information policies, in fact, will arise from what we learn in the doing of these analyses.

Policy Analysis Issues

In the current stage of the study, national information policy issues are to be made explicit (identified qualitatively, and quantitatively, where possible). At the least, these are to be ordinally ranked. A panel of experts are to be convened for this task. A dialectic exercise is being developed that is to elicit not only the issues involved in information policy, but also which (if any) specific subsystems impact, or are impacted upon, by the previously identified equal/differential rates of growth of information sectoral input and output. *

The issues to be debated include, but are not limited to the following:

.   The uses to which information is put in a market economy (e.g., consumer preference, decision-making);

.   The users of this information (the "haves" and "have-nots" question);

.   The efficiency and equitability questions of property rights (vis a vis patents, copyrights);

---

*Briefly, a dialectic debate is a methodology which employs the use of the strongest possible opponents on an issue. A data base (information base) has been developed (the same one for each side of the issue) and areas for debate are specified. Each antagonist then develops arguments for his side of the issue using this common data set. The purpose of the exercise is to marshall the evidence to elicit the hidden assumptions behind the arguments, to develop areas where there is agreement (a consensus on some points is reached) and the problem area is re-defined in the light of the now-explicit assumptions; this is subject to a restructuring of the common data base, and a further debate (i.e., it is, or could be, reiterative).

.   Freedom of access to information;

.   Privacy issues;

.   Structural changes (e.g., institutional, organi-
    zational, legal, regulatory);

.   Equality of access to information (motivational
    questions);

.   Equal access vs. differential access;

.   Efficiency/effectiveness questions (re: science
    and technology information services); and

.   Improvement in social welfare.

This dialectically-based analysis is to yield not only the identification and enumeration of growth segments of the information sector,
but also insights into the reasons for, and implications of, this growth.
The relative efficiency of different allocations of resources to information systems (and subsystems) can be enumerated and analyzed here.
An insight into where investment should be made to increase the productivity of this sector can be addressed. Possible investment areas
include: research and development; marketing and property rights;
promotion; legislation; reallocation of resources; and information
management.

Specific Subnational Statistics Issues

URISA members may note a specific set of subnational statistics
issues, raised in recent national-level forums:

.   The President's Commission on Federal Statistics
    (1972-1973) questioning the "degree of public inter-
    est" and worthwhileness of collecting and making
    available detailed small-area (i.e., subnational)
    demographic, economic, and social statistics;

.   The President's Commission on Federal Paperwork
    (1975-current) questioning the public interest of
    County Business Patterns and county-aggregations
    of Federal income tax data; and

. Continual OMB-Agency debates over the "public
interest" in specific local efforts, mid-decade
censuses, etc.

The degree to which matters of privacy, access to information,
the primacy of the market economy, the merger of public and private
data bases, the use of information as power, and a host of other
national-level policy issues: these impact on the availability of data,
budgets, and laws concerning the use of data. No user of state, county,
and/or urban data can ignore the seriousness of these national-level
debates.

CONCLUDING REMARKS

Roles of information, according to Marschak,* have been specified as inquiring, communicating and deciding. Information is not a
free good -- as determined by the above analyses, a large (how large
should be able to be estimated, at this point in our study) proportion
of our GNP is devoted to the production of information (included here
is not only the production per se, but also the analysis, dissemination,
communication, transformation, etc.). By our investigation of national
information policies we have arrived at some assessment as to what
does, in fact, currently determine the allocation of our national
resources to science, technology, and information activities generally.
Parker, in "Information and Science,"** summarizes Arrow's
arguments succinctly. He states:

"In a classic paper, Nobel prize-winning economist
Kenneth Arrow argues that a free-enterprise economy
can be expected to underinvest in information production
for three reasons. One is the "indivisibility" of information; a second is inappropriability (the discoverer
or inventor cannot obtain all the economic benefits from
his discovery); and the third is uncertainty. His arguments are made in the context of technical invention,
but they can be broadened to include investment in information production generally. "

*Jacob Marschak, Economics of Inquiring, Communicating,
Deciding, Los Angeles: Western Management Science Institute,
University of California, 1968. Working Paper No. 134.
*Chapter 11, in Annual Review of Information Science and Tech-
nology, Vol. 8, 1973.

We do not know if these observations will be confirmed by the policy analysis dialectic we are currently initiating. Either way, we anticipate that URISA members will find the results stimulating, useful to them as professionals, and hopefully help point the way to analogous investigations into policy issues related to their concerns and constituencies.

Richard E. Horne
Assistant Superintendent, Business and Financial Services
Office of the Los Angeles County Superintendent of Schools
Downey, California 90242

Reese C. Wilson
Assistant Director, Urban and Regional Studies
and
Blair C. Burgess
Senior Systems Specialist
Urban and Social Systems Division
Stanford Research Institute
Menlo Park, California 94025

LOS ANGELES COUNTY EDUCATION AND
BUSINESS SYSTEMS IMPROVEMENT PROGRAM[*]

ABSTRACT: A program to improve education and
business systems within the Los Angeles County
Superintendent's office has been initiated to better
support the 95 school districts operating within the
county. The overall program relies on increased
organization effectiveness in the use of electronic
data processing (EDP) resources and the resulting
provision of needed services to districts. EDP support services are currently under development for
seven interrelated systems: educational planning
and management; student information; educational
research and analysis; computer-related instruction;
financial planning and management; payroll/personnel;
and operations support.

INTRODUCTION

The Need for Improved Services and Systems

The Office of the Los Angeles County Superintendent of Schools provides leadership and coordination for the improvement of local educational programs and contributes to regional and statewide educational
efforts. The activities of the County Superintendent's office extend
throughout the 4,060 square mile area of Los Angeles County to each of
the 95 constituent school districts.

---

[*] The authors gratefully achknowledge the technical assistance provided
by Jerry FitzGerald, Phil Sorensen, Stephen Oura, and Allen Vejar of
SRI and Lester Simpson, George Oshiro, and Wes Williams of the County
Superintendent's office.

The Office employs approximately 2,600 persons, over 1,700 of whom work in schools and classes operated by the LA County School Superintendent's Office. The staff operates under general policies and procedures prescribed by the laws of the State of California, by Federal laws, and by regulations promulgated by the Los Angeles County Board of Education.

Although the political, administrative, and educational leadership within the County of Los Angeles has managed to guide the public education programs and resources through a period of unprecedented growth, increased planning and management capacity will be needed in the next decade. As the cost of energy rises, more and new forms must be found. The declining U.S. birth rate means a decreasing number of students in some school districts while others have an increasing load of non-English-speaking students. Also, older channels of fiscal support for the schools no longer work as they once did. Planning and management of educational resources have become increasingly important in developing an adequate response to changing employee, student, legislative, and public finance patterns.

In 1975, the Office of the LA County Superintendent of Schools set up a program to improve the effectiveness of education and business services offered to county school districts and those needed by the staff of the County Superintendent's Office. Although some of these services already rely on electronic data processing (EDP) technology, the quality and economy of many other services can be enhanced through increased EDP use. The planning and management of EDP resources to better satisfy priority needs of the County Superintendent's Office and the school districts will become increasingly important as employee wages and facility operating costs increase over the next decade, as the level of automation increases, and as computer hardware and software systems become more complex.

The purpose of this paper is to describe the EDP system capabilities that the LA County School Superintendent's Office plans to realize over the next decade.

Potential User Profile

Planning for a future that appears highly uncertain over both the short and the long term demands a detailed and reliable knowledge of the present so that needs can be seen in time to make an efficient response, trends can be identified, and undesirable changes can be prevented. Management of a large educational system in transition requires access to data in sufficient detail to permit the efficient allocation of scarce resources and prevent misuse or correct errors. However, in order to set up a system that can provide all of the needed data, it is necessary to delineate the users and their specific needs.

According to reports for fiscal year 1974-75, the 95 school districts in LA County serve an enrollment of over 2 million children, young people, and adults with an annual expenditure of over $2 billion. Summary statistics are shown below:

ESTIMATED EXPENSE OF EDUCATION (1974-75)

Districts	Number of Districts	Schools	Average Daily Attendance	Expense Amount (millions of dollars)	Dollars per ADA
Elementary	33	237	122,872	$ 139	$1,130
High School	7.	48	71,754	92	1,280
Unified	42	1,500	1,318,452	1,720	1,305
Community College	13	20	181,185	233	1,288
Total	95	1,850	1,694,263	$2,184	$1,289

The Average Daily Attendance (ADA) ranges from 678,276 for the Los Angeles Unified School District down to 36 for the Gorman Elementary School District, suggesting a wide range of potential service requirements. Many of the districts depend on the County Superintendent's Office for satisfying Federal and State mandates, and for the providing of essential services. Some districts are almost completely self-sufficient (e.g., Los Angeles and Long Beach Unified School Districts) and provide their own EDP support. Other districts are too small to need or afford anything but the basic State-mandated services provided by the County Superintendent's Office (e.g., payroll, special education). The current and potential user base for services to be provided by the County Superintendent's Office lies somewhere between these two extremes.

Although the County Superintendent's Office will continue to provide selected support to all 95 school districts, most of its resources should be directed towards satisfying priority service support needs of users. A ten-year planning horizon, subdivided into three sequential time periods, was adopted:

· Near-term period covered by the three fiscal years 1976 through 1978 (FY 1975-76, FY 1976-77, FY 1977-78).

· Mid-range period covered by the four fiscal years 1979 through 1982 (FY 1978-79, FY 1980-81, FY 1981-82).

· Long-range period covered by the three fiscal years 1983 through 1985 (FY 1982-83, FY 1983-84, FY 1984-85).

Goals for EDP Systems in the County Superintendent's Office

The primary EDP-related goal of the County Superintendent's Office is to offer and provide essential support services to staff and to school districts. This goal includes achieving a balance between education and business support systems that is commensurate with school district needs and priorities, and with available resources.

The realization of this general EDP goal is subordinate to the planning, management, and teaching capabilities of those persons holding responsible positions in the County Superintendent's Office and school districts. Electronic data processing, by itself, is no panacea. Rational planning and use of EDP resources can provide vital assistance, but only if those concerned express their requirements in a realistic context, considering the availability of resources, and agree to operate and maintain systems once they are installed.

Generalized EDP goals of the County Superintendent's Office reflect a recent user survey and personal interviews undertaken by SRI, and are listed below:

- Provide effective and economical EDP support services for mandated functions, such as payroll, in a manner that reconciles school district needs with sound EDP policies such as the recommended configuration control and standards policy.

- Provide effective and economical EDP support services for essential functions such as student information.

- Provide computer capability, through remote job entry.

- Provide consultant assistance to districts for critical functions where the development or operation of the EDP capability should not be undertaken by the County Superintendent's Office for practical reasons.

- Provide for an ongoing users group to conduct needs assessment, evaluations, and modifications, and to carry out planning for future user needs.

The system described in this paper is consistent with these broad goals.

PRIORITY SYSTEM REQUIREMENTS

total computerized information system is visualized as a group of interrelated and integrated subsystems, with each subsystem performing several related EDP functions. Although the organization of functions under subsystem categories has a sound rationale, the placement of some functions may be arbitrary. Ultimately each function is supported by a group of applied programs, some of which supply or update the data base while others generate output and are commonly referred to as applications.

The placement of each function and its attendant applications into a specific subsystem will not detract from the overall effectiveness of the total system, the subsystem, or other functions. This approach, usually called a total information systems approach, recognizes and accommodates important interdependencies among all the

A list of functions organized within subsystems is presented in Table 1. The list reflects the user requirements of the County Superintendent's Office and the school districts. Priorities necessarily represent a compromise between user perceptions and system development realities. The final priority ratings reflect the recommendations of a senior management panel, two user advisory panels, and the users who were surveyed. The priority rating for each function, coupled with the amount of resources needed to develop and perform the function, suggests the development estimates shown in Table 1.

The subsystems, functions, and the main attendant applications are described below in general terms to provide a base for later discussion of system design alternatives.

Student Information System

The Student Information System is designed to support the information needs of students, their parents, teachers and counselors, service personnel, and management or administrative personnel at all levels. The system contains three main categories of student-related data: (1) basic student data, (2) counseling/guidance, progress assessment, and any other appropriate historical data, (3) course or master schedule data pertinent to secondary schools.

This system generates the basic information needed by students, parents, and staff as well as special information desired by teachers and counselors, supporting service staff, and management. The system must be flexible enough to satisfy a reasonable assortment of school-district options and must be responsive to changing user needs over time.

Educational Planning and Management System

This system is intended to provide support to staff at all levels of district and County Superintendent's Office management. The success of this sytem is dependent on the ability of potential users to define their systems requirements--a task that still remains to be done. The complexity of the task suggests that the various functions will not be served until the midrange or perhaps the long-range time period, except for the school district master data function, which will use data extracted from other systems and subsystems.

Educational Research and Analysis System

This system is intended to support the preparation of standard and custom district and school program profiles, and the performance of standard and custom research and analysis studies. The functions and attendant applications associated with this system generally rely on the data base and supporting files maintained in the other systems, or on data available, in manual or machine-readable form, now located at user sites or other governmental agencies.

Computer-Related Instruction

This set of functions is designed to facilitate learning and instructional processes through the use of computers, remote minicomputers, and strategically located terminals. In concept, it includes the use of the computer (1) as a tool to assist with problem solving, drill and practice, and diagnostic testing; (2) as a resource offering simulations, games, decision-making, and extended instruction in a variety of

Table 1

DEVELOPMENT OF SUBSYSTEMS AND FUNCTIONS WITHIN THE OVERALL SYSTEM

	Priority Ranking by Survey Respondents	Development Priority Ranking by SRI*	Earliest Period in Which Initial Development Could Be Completed		
			Near Term	Mid-range	Long Range
Student Information System	2				
Student master data		1	x		
Student attendance accounting		1	x		
Student mark reporting		1	x		
Student scheduling		2	x		
Miscellaneous student reporting		1	x		
Master course directory		2	x		
Counseling and guidance	7	3		x	
Student assessment		3	x		
Educational Planning and Management System	5				
Management information reporting		2		x	
Program planning and evaluation		3			x
Instructional strategies	9	2		x	
Instructional materials information		2		x	
School district master data		1	x		
Text editing system		3			x
Planning and management statistics and history		2	x		
Educational Research and Analysis System	4				
District and school analysis		2		x	
Program analysis		3		x	
Statistical analysis		1	x		
Geographic base file		2		x	
Forecasting and simulation		3		x	
Socioeconomic and demographic analysis		3			x
Educational statistics and history		2			x
Computer-Related Instruction System	8				
Drill and practice		2		x	
Tutorial		2		x	
Simulation and games		2		x	
On-line diagnostic testing		2		x	
Problem solving		2		x	
Computer-managed instruction		2		x	
Payroll/Personnel System	1				
Payroll master data		1	x		
Pay function		1	x		
Retirement function		1	x		
Benefits function		1	x		
Labor distribution		1	x		
Personnel master data	3	1	x		
Skills inventory		2			x
Personnel statistics and history		2	x		
Position control		2	x		
Credentials		2			x
Career development		2			x
Financial Planning and Management System	1				
Program budgeting and accounting		1	x		
Tax rate computation		1	x		
Budget simulation		3			x
Accounts payable		1	x		
Financial statistics and history		2		x	
Operations Support System	6				
Operations planning and management		2		x	
Fixed assets		2		x	
Stores inventory		2		x	
Audiovisual support		2		x	
Transportation optimization		3		x	
Operation support and statistics and history		3		x	

*
SRI's priority ranking for development takes into account technological constraints, sequential constraints, and time constraints as well as expressed needs.

disciplines; (3) as a tutor to interactively teach new curriculum, explore career choices, and teach programming languages; (4) as an object of instruction to provide the technology for students and staff interested in computer science; and (5) as a manager to support prescriptive or individualized instruction. These uses do not constitute an exhaustive list of the ways in which computers may be used to support instruction.

Payroll/Personnel System

The payroll function is a required service that must be provided to the users at no cost. If the relative autonomy in school districts is to be maintained, the Payroll/Personnel System must support a variety of demands, which in turn implies that the system must have available numerous options for timing, turnaround, report type, report content, and rules or specifications for processing. An additional complexity is imposed by the dissimilar requirements of the State and the County retirement system.

Financial Planning and Management System

This system, designed to serve the school districts and the Los Angeles County Superintendent of Schools, supports the functions of budgeting, accounting, financial reports, commercial warrant processing, and historical reporting. It interfaces with the Payroll/Personnel System, with the evaluative portion of the Educational Planning and Management System, and with the Student Information System.

Operations Support System

This system is designed to support planning and management activities relating to facilities, equipment, material, supplies, and other physical entities that support the operation of the educational complex in Los Angeles County. The data base contains inventory data predominantly controlled by personnel of the County Superintendent's Office. However, this system is also available to school districts.

SYSTEM DESIGN ALTERNATIVES AND CONCEPTS

The EDP systems requirements, functions, and applications described above can be realized through a range of system design alternatives within the identifiable economic, social, political, and technological constraints. Since the constraints are dynamic, however, the utility of any given alternative will change over time, suggesting that the EDP systems developed by the County Superintendent's Office must be flexible, and must be capable of change to accommodate new situations. Current capabilities must gradually be expanded from the present level to a level that better satisfies priority user and systems requirements. It is important that the extent and rate of expansion be planned in terms of what is feasible within the political, financial, and developmental environment of the County Superintendent's Office. Technology, per se, is not viewed as the limiting factor. System design alternatives must be selected that will take advantage of the benefits of available technology, but technology must not outweigh practical considerations.

Basic design decisions must be made regarding the degree of centralization and decentralization of functions and controls, equipment and facilities, and developmental and operational staff. Other decisions must be made regarding trade-offs between large central computers and decentralized minicomputers. Many combinations of these basic factors are technically possible, but most are not practical. Other technically feasible concepts to be considered in the development of preferred alternatives include: remote user access to centralized EDP files and applications; distributed processing and network computing; remote job entry and intelligent terminals; on-line, timesharing operations with attendant security provisions; data base management systems; and computer utility operations.

The selection of alternatives that foster effective and economical provision of EDP support services to users in school districts and in the County Superintendent's Office is also dependent on the factors suggested below:

(1) The County Superintendent's Office must be relatively
     certain that an EDP function and its applications will
     meet the needs of a continuing collection of users
     prior to committing resources to its development. This
     means that sufficient users must indicate their inten-
     tions to use the capability.

(2) The development and subsequent operation of an EDP
     function and its applications must be attained within
     a reasonable time frame and for reasonable cost. This
     means that sufficient developmental resources must be
     available or obtainable.

(3) Specific design alternatives must be selected to be
     compatible with user needs and their level of sophistica-
     tion as well as with the EDP systems development capacity of
     the County Superintendent's Office. This means that the
     scope of the data entry and report output demands must
     be established and sustained to meet the desired level
     of operations.

The user requirements, subsystems, EDP functions, and applications described in this paper can be realized through a wide range of design alternatives that cover the spectrum from simple centralized batch operations up to highly sophisticated decentralized on-line operations. The system design alternatives most appropriate for serious considera-tion lie between these two extremes, with the near-term posture closer to the batch end of the spectrum and with the total system evolving towards on-line operation over the decade.

The design approach employed recognizes that today's technology is usually not the limiting factor in system operations—it is the people who must sustain the system (e.g., keep the files up to date). The first step in the identification and selection of design alternatives is a functional analysis to highlight potential areas of commonality among applications and subsystems. Each subsystem is then analyzed with regard to potential volume and turnaround parameters. Various alternatives are examined in a context of system responsiveness and cost. Finally, the preferred alternatives are discussed in greater detail to provide the basis for the basic system concept.

Functional Analysis

Most EDP functions and applications rely to some extent on the following generalized information processing functions:

- Data acquisition, transmission, and entry, to include the various manual or automated processes needed to collect data and enter them into files. Data and files should be accessible to other processes, as appropriate, to effect the needed data communications, message switching, edit and validation, and so on.

- Information storage, update and retrieval, to include the various processes needed to establish and maintain data base files and to extract information for system processes and users (while maintaining data base integrity and security). This function overlaps somewhat the data acquisition, transmission, and entry function as well as with the information processing and analysis function. It represents the interface with master data base files and, often, with temporary transaction or special analysis files that may be associated with major EDP functions.

- Information processing and analysis, to include higher-order manipulation of data such as scheduling, arithmetic or statistical operations, and logical operations. Simple extraction operations and all report generation operations are normally considered to be performed by other functions.

- Information display and reporting, to include the preparation of output reports based on the data supplied by the information storage update, and retrieval, and information processing and analysis functions.

Major reliance is placed on these four generalized information processing functions by all education and business subsystems. The commonality among subsystems allows a new perspective to be considered in the design process in that subsystems could be developed along the dimensions suggested by the four generalized information processing functions as well as the dimensions established by the grouping of similar EDP functions and their applications into logical subsystem categories. A data acquisition, transmission, and entry subsystem, for example, has the potential to support data collection activities for all data files and all subsystems.

Preferred System Alternatives

The concept for the basic education and business system should accommodate a modern data-base management system (DBMS). Several of the available DBMS provide most of the needed information storage and retrieval processes (e.g., file generation, file maintenance), and a few include many of the data acquisition, transmission, and entry processes (e.g., on-line data entry, edit and validation). In addition, many DBMS have password and access control features needed to preclude unauthorized access to data files. The data management concept is compatible with the need to establish and maintain an integrated set of data base files, with several EDP functions and their applications having access to each needed data element no matter which file it is stored in.

The successful development and operation of an integrated set of files under the control of a DBMS is not a trivial task. However, the data management concept cannot be ignored throughout the next decade-- it must be faced now.

Other techniques and technologies merit serious consideration as well:

- Remote data entry--The County Superintendent's Office serves a geographically dispersed user base, suggesting that most data entry operations cannot be centralized in a single regional data processing center. The basic system concept should be compatible with a variety of remote data entry options (e.g., on-line display terminals, teletypes, remote job entry stations, minicomputer operations, other computers). Data entry activities must be gradually decentralized, beginning soon.

- Remote information reporting--In many cases, information needed by users, can and should be displayed or printed at the user site, rather than in a single regional data processing center. Most data entry devices allow output as well as input operations. Most, however, do not provide for high-speed printing, and this capability will ultimately be needed to satisfy some users.

- Distributed processing--This concept, which can be employed within a single physical center or within a geographical region through interconnected processors, assigns various system functions to various devices. A decentralized data entry and information reporting network connected to a centralized computer could represent the near-term initiation of such a concept. Long-range implementation, technically but not politically or operationally feasible now, could result in a computer network covering Los Angeles County, with each computer in the network assigned specific functions and specific user bases.

- Computer utility--This concept allows remote users having systems analysis and computer programming skills to use a centralized computer to develop and operate specially tailored systems for their own use, without having to operate and maintain computer hardware. This concept can be realized in the near term if users in the County Superintendent's Office or districts desire it (some users have expressed such a desire).

- Time-sharing operations--The various concepts and techniques expressed above suggest that a time-sharing capability of some sort will be needed in the near term. Time-sharing allows a number of users to access a single central processor at essentially the same time. The number of users who can be simultaneously supported by a single central computer or a network of computers depends on several factors, most notably the design of the central processor.

The extent to which the various concepts above can be realized is dependent on a number of factors, such as cost and implementation time.

The process of selecting preferred system alternatives and incorporating them into a basic system concept and supporting development plan must be based on cost-performance determinations. Does the expected (or actual) performance of a system or system component justify its cost?

Many system configuration alternatives fail to meet important design considerations, at least in the near term. For example, separate computers in major school districts with a centralized systems analysis and programming staff would require a significant investment, although this posture could prove cost-justifiable for instructional functions such as computer-related instruction in the midrange time period. Decentralized staff for each installation is even more difficult to cost justify. This is not to say that extremely large school districts should not have their own EDP capability. They should, pending realization of a county-wide educational computer network.

Extensive decentralization would require significant investment in personnel, hardware and physical sites. It would also increase overall costs in areas such as development of software, and maintenance of software, hardware and physical sites. From the point of view of the County Superintendent's Office, decentralization would also increase the span of control, and therefore increase the possibility of miscommunication. Under these circumstances it would be difficult to cost justify a decentralized computer system configuration.

A centralized computer system configuration is less expensive in terms of initial and continuing costs and can satisfy many priority user requirements and the EDP goals of the County Superintendent's Office. The considerations shown in Table 2 indicate that alternatives involving high centralization represent the best near-term course of action.

Considering the implications of the factors in Table 2 and the stated goals of the County Superintendent's Office, the initial design configuration definitely tends toward a centralized computer facility that would evolve into decentralized functions beginning with data entry and printing of reports. This degree of decentralization is needed to efficiently handle the volume and turnaround requirements associated with many of the education and business systems.

Table 2

CONSIDERATIONS FOR CENTRALIZATION VERSUS DECENTRALIZATION

Design Considerations	Comments Regarding	
	Centralization	Decentralization
Technical Feasibility		
Practical	Yes	No
Reliable	Yes	Yes
Cost		
Personnel	Medium	High
Hardware	Medium	High
Software	Medium	High
Maintenance	Medium	High
Education & Training	Medium	High
Future Growth	Good	Good
Implementation	Easy	Difficult
Technical Competence Required	Medium	High
Management Control	Excellent	Fair
County Auditor Function	Excellent	Fair

Within the framework of a centralized computer system, the County Superintendent's Office can offer services to the districts, as well as internally, through the following options, all of which are needed in the near-term:

(1) Batch operations, where each user submits input documents for keypunching (or key-disk, key-tape), processing, and manual return of the output.

(2) Remote data entry, where each user enters data through his own input terminal, for processing and subsequent manual return of related outputs. Remote data entry will ease the current centralized keypunch/keytape bottleneck as well as speed up the turnaround time for batch-processed jobs. This option could be expanded to include a terminal that can receive the output directly from the computer, and that can query on-line files.

(3) Remote job entry, where each user submits data/programs through his own input/output terminal and receives the output on his terminal (computer utility concept). The computer utility aspect appears especially desirable for some financially pressed districts that want to maintain

their own systems/programs and, at the same time, cannot afford a larger computer facility (or even the one they are currently using). Remote job entry assumes that each user is responsible for the following: data entry and updating of his own files, writing and maintaining his own programs, conducting his own system design activities, and complying with the Regional Data Processing Center standing operating procedures.

The Regional Data Processing Center is responsible for providing computer time, communications facilities, remote terminals, and technical assistance, all at reimbursement costs.

(4) On-line data base maintenance, where each user's files are integrated into a centralized data base that can be accessed from batch programs/remote terminals. This concept will be pilot-tested in the near term and introduced in the midrange period.

In addition to these four immediate system options, the County Superintendent's Office could consider selected minicomputer installations for computer-related instruction.

Table 3 illustrates the major considerations involved for each of the four options preferred for early implementation. These alternatives, coupled with midrange and long-range alternatives, provide the basis for the basic system concept.

Table 3

CONSIDERATIONS FOR PREFERRED OPTIONS

Design Criteria	Near Term System Options			
	Batch Opera- tions	Remote Data Entry	Remote Job Entry	Pilot Test On-Line Data Base
Technical Feasibility				
Practical	Yes	Yes	Yes	Yes
Reliable	Yes	Yes	Yes	Yes
Cost				
Personnel	Low	Medium	High	High
Hardware	Low	Medium	High	High
Software	Low	Medium	High	High
Maintenance	Low	Medium	High	High
Education and training	Low	High	High	High
Future growth	Poor	Good	Excellent	Excellent
Implementation	Easy	Easy	Difficult	Difficult
Technical competence required	Low	Medium	High	High
Management control	Excellent	Excellent	Fair	Good
County auditor function	Excellent	Good	Fair	Good

Basic System Concept

The best course of action is to formulate a basic system concept that is reasonably certain to meet all near-term and most midrange possibilities, and flexible enough to accommodate a reasonable number of long-range scenarios. This approach postulates three stages of system sophistication:

- System Level 1--Centralized computer and staff in the Regional Data Processing Center provide services for extremely high priority EDP functions such as payroll, accounts payable, and selected student information system applications. The data management concept is introduced on a pilot test basis. Data entry activities are decentralized where feasible. This level includes: (1) batch operations, (2) remote data entry, (3) remote job entry, and (4) on-line data base pilot testing. Instructional support to districts would be maintained by the current minicomputer system with minimal enhancements, unless special funding can be obtained.

- System Level 2--Centralized computers and staff in the Regional Data Processing Center would interact with relatively sophisticated remote input/output processing satellites. A large integrated data base would be established and maintained--primarily for business and administrative functions, with district instructional requirements satisfied through remotely located minicomputers. Instructional requirements of the County Superintendent's Office would probably be placed on the centralized computers. A high level of user access to stored data and information processes is envisioned for Level 2.

- System Level 3--Network computing through two or more large sub-regional centers is envisioned, under the control of the County Superintendent's Office, but incorporating large-district capabilities when politically and economically feasible. Level 3 could include a number of technically advanced options, such as functional as well as geographical decentralization, in various combinations depending on the specific EDP application and user demands. Level 3 is intended to represent the most sophisticated posture that could reasonably be attained in the next decade.

If sufficient EDP resources can be applied to the education and business systems improvement program, and if the potential user demand materializes, it is reasonable to correlate the three system levels with the three time periods as indicated in Table 4. Incorporation of some of the more advanced techniques could take over a decade. Nevertheless it is legitimate to consider them in the basic system concept. System Level 2 is depicted in Figure 1 as the conceptual framework for the basic system.

The centralized part of the configuration highlights the seven user subsystems linked to various files through a data management subsystem that, in turn, is shown providing the interface with four types of

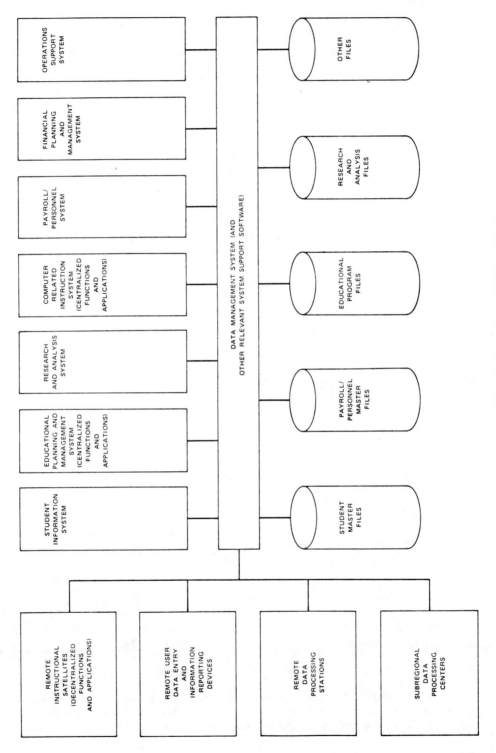

FIGURE 1 CONCEPTUAL FRAMEWORK FOR SYSTEM DESIGN

Table 4

POSSIBLE COMPUTER SYSTEMS CAPABILITY SCHEDULE

EDP Technique	Time Periods*		
	Near Term	Midrange	Long Range
Batch operation	X		
Remote data entry (input entry and validation)	X		
Remote job entry (pilot test) utilizing on-line input, processing, and output	X		
Data base management system (DBMS) pilot test	X		
Remote data entry (input and output)		X	X
DBMS on-line		X	X
Interface on-line processing		X	X
Remote input/output processing		X	X
Subregional center(s)		X	X
Network computing			X

*Near term--fiscal years, 1975-76 to 1977-78.
 Midrange--fiscal years, 1978-79 to 1981-82.
 Long range--fiscal years, 1982-83 to 1984-85.

decentralized activities: instructional satellites, user devices, input/output processing stations and subregional data processing centers.

The full realization of such a concept is dependent primarily on the extent of user requirements and the ability of the County Superintendent's Office to satisfy them cost-effectively. Although most of the EDP resources of the County Superintendent's Office--staff, software, computers--will be centralized in a single regional center under a single individual, acquisition and effective utilization of these resources is the responsibility of the Board, the Superintendent, Assistant Superintendent, and selected division directors. Unless these persons carry out the responsibilities their roles imply in relation to the Regional Data Processing Center, the person assigned formal responsibility for the Center has no chance of succeeding in his role of providing needed services.

Dr. E. R. Callahan, Jr.
Dr. R. Wayne Gober
Dr. Jack Y. Pursifull
School of Business
Middle Tennessee State University
Murfreesboro, TN 37132

ACCUMULATION PATTERNS FOR SELECTED CONSUMER DURABLE
GOODS FOR THE EAST SOUTH CENTRAL REGION:
A CONDITIONAL PROBABILITY APPROACH

Econometricians and marketing strategists have
directed attention to the problems of explaining and
predicting consumer demands for household durable
goods. The accelerating demand and the importance
of durable goods in a growing advanced economy, both
as items of supply and demand, have created a need
for knowledge of the growth rates and the determinants of the household's accumulation pattern of
household durable goods.

By definition, durable goods are characterized
by ownership and use for relatively long periods of
time. These goods are generally of relatively high
cost, and the process by which they are accumulated
extends over a significantly long period of time.
Consequently, it appears that this process of
accumulation may be planned and that some order of
preference for the next good may be established.

If a household desires a set of three goods
(S = A, B, C,), it does not necessarily select from
the set randomly. The household plans for the
accumulation of the set in the order that appears
to be most rational, given the restraints operating
on the household. The relative frequency of the
purchase of good B can be more **formally stated as**
R (B next good purchased | A, S)
in which R is the relative frequency of occurrence
derived from the accumulation patterns, given that
the household owns good A of the set S.

Using relative frequencies in conjunction with
the 1970 Public Use Sample data, conditional probabilities and accumulation patterns for purchasing
specific durable goods are synthesized for the East
South Central region--Alabama, Kentucky, Mississippi,
and Tennessee.

INTRODUCTION

Econometricians and marketing strategists have directed attention
to the problems of explaining and predicting consumer demands for
household durable goods. The accelerating demand and the importance

of durable goods in a growing advanced economy, both as items of supply and demand, have created a need for knowledge of the growth rates and the determinants of the household's accumulation pattern of household durable goods.

By definition, durable goods are characterized by ownership and use for relatively long periods of time. These goods are generally of relatively high cost and the process by which they are accumulated extends over a significantly long period of time. Consequently, it appears that this process of accumulation may be planned and that some order of preference for the next good may be established.

GENERAL PRIORITY PATTERNS

Pyatt divides domestic household durable goods into two groups.[1] The first group is composed of those goods which are sufficiently inexpensive so that anyone who desires ownership of an item can achieve it. The goods comprising the second group are sufficiently more expensive so as to be excluded from the first group. In the inexpensive group, ownership of such items as an electric knife, electric skillet, and other small durable goods may come about in various ways; their purchase may be planned or unplanned, or ownership may be achieved through gift-giving. Generally, the problem facing the consumer is not a saving-purchase decision, but rather a decision concerned with the quality level he should buy. Furthermore, most consumers are not troubled by doubts of being able to afford items from the inexpensive group. However, this attitude is not the same for the expensive group, as the items contained in the expensive group require greater purchasing power.

McFall combines the two groups and contends that products are bought in sets over life-cycle periods.[2] McFall identifies several sets of goods and suggests that these sets are acquired over a period of time, as evidenced by empirical observations.

THEORETICAL ANALYSIS

Intuitively, if a household desires a set of three goods (S = A, B, C,), it does not necessarily select from the set randomly. Furthermore, the household plans for the accumulation of the set in the order that appears to be most rational, given the restraints

---

[1]F. Graham Pyatt, Priority Patterns and the Demand for Household Durable Goods (Great Britain: Cambridge University Press, 1964), 3-4.

[2]John McFall, "Priority Patterns and Consumer Behavior," Journal of Marketing 33 (October, 1969), 51.

operating on the household. Differing accumulation patterns exist because all households will not accumulate goods in the same order. Table I illustrates six possible accumulation patterns for a set of three hypothetical goods. In general, there will be n-factorial (n!) accumulation patterns from a set having n household goods.

TABLE I

POSSIBLE ACCUMULATION PATTERNS FROM A SET OF
THREE HOUSEHOLD DURABLE GOODS

A, B, C	B, A, C	C, A, B
A, C, B	B, C, A	C, B, A

Observing the accumulation patterns of consumers owning household durable goods can reveal interesting decision-making information. Employing the set of three hypothetical goods in Table I, additional observations can be made regarding consumer acquisition patterns. For example, if consumers with a given set of characteristics (the vector ē) each own either good A or good B, the inference can be made that those consumers who own good A and decide to purchase a second good will select good B before good C. The inference derives from subtle peer influences and pressures which tend to produce similar behavior among individuals. Continuing with the example, if the household's choices are limited to the set (S = A, B, D) and the household possesses the characteristic vector ē, the relative frequency of the purchase of B can be more formally stated as

$$R \text{ (B next good purchased } | \text{ A, S, ē)}$$

in which R is the relative frequency of occurrence derived from the accumulation patterns, given that the household owns good A of the set S and also possesses the list of socioeconomic characteristics in the vector ē. It is also assumed implicitly that most of the people at the point of selection will imitate people with similar characteristics who have already made their selections. Couched in Bayesian terminology, posterior knowledge of those possessing k household goods can help establish prior priorities of those possessing k-1 goods.

SOURCE OF EXPERIMENTAL DATA

The data for this research are taken from the 1970 Public Use Samples (PUS) created by the Census Bureau. The PUS is a one-in-a-

hundred sample of all households in the United States, representing
one-fifth of the records in the Census Bureau's file containing
records from the 5-percent basic records. The PUS is self-weighting,
in that a count from the sample multiplied by one-hundred estimates a
state's total. Three options of geographic information are available:
(1) County groups, (2) States, and (3) Geographic divisions with
neighborhood characteristics. Any one sample contains only one of the
three types of information. This study presents statistics derived
from the geographic information of the states comprising the East
South Central Region (ESC)--Tennessee, Kentucky, Alabama, Mississippi.

The 1970 ESC Region PUS is composed of 42,295 households. For
the study, 6,333 of these households were omitted because they were
either vacant, or were occupied by a group of people comprising more
than a family unit. A net sample size of 35,962 occupied households
are included in the analysis.

All of the tables presented are tabulated from the 1970 ESC Region
PUS. The frequency of occurrence describes only the 35,962 households
of the sample, whereas the percent distributions derived from this
sample are also appropriate in describing the regional distribution.

HOUSEHOLD DURABLE GOOD OWNERSHIP

Tabulation of the 1970 ESC Region PUS indicates the number of
household durable goods owned by the individuals included in the PUS.
The distribution of household durable goods accumulated is shown in
Table II.

All five durables are sufficiently expensive to assure that
decisions to purchase them will be made only after some deliberation.
Subject to technology and quality variation, they have all been
available for several years and are generally accepted as being
desirable assets.

TABLE II

DISTRIBUTION OF HOUSEHOLD DURABLE GOODS
IN EAST SOUTH CENTRAL REGION: 1970

Item	Households owning durable goods					
	Tenn.	Ky.	Ala.	Miss.	Region	Percent
Television	10,786	8,592	9,001	5,357	33,756	93.87
Washing machine	8,368	6,917	7,091	3,973	26,349	73.28
Clothes dryer	4,421	3,138	3,067	1,475	12,101	33.65
Food freezer	4,218	2,756	3,830	2,666	13,470	37.46
Dishwasher	1,764	973	1,330	694	4,761	13.24

SOURCE: Data are a resultant of computer tabulation of the 1970
East South Central Public Use Sample.

Physical restraints explain why some of the households have not accumulated a particular good. The tabulation of the 35,962 households included indicate there are: (1) 2,985 households without piped water, (2) 2,464 households without gas, and (3) 91 households without electricity. Since all the goods are electrically operated, this would be the most limiting utility. However, the data reveal this to be only a nominal limitation in the ESC Region.

The household durable good that could be classified as yielding "entertainment" as opposed to "labor-saving" is the good that has the greatest proliferation. At least one television set is owned by approximately 94 percent of the population. This will also be very evident in later analysis.

The washing machine is the durable good with the second highest distribution. Traditionally, the washing machine has been the most desirable labor saving device for a household. The washing machine is owned more than twice as frequently as the next most frequently owned labor saving good, the clothes dryer.

Less than 40 percent of the population own one of the other three durable goods. The dishwasher is the least owned good, with only 13 percent of the population owning one. The dishwasher is the most recent of the goods on the market and, obviously, is considered by most households to be a luxury good.

RELATIVE FREQUENCY OF DURABLE GOODS ACCUMULATED

The households are limited to the selection of durable goods from the set, S, which is composed of the household durable goods shown in Table III. The number of goods that a household owns from the set is represented by k. The distribution displayed in Table III does not indicate which of the goods the household owns but indicates the number of goods accumulated from the set.

The relative frequency distribution shown in Table III indicates that more households own three goods than two, more households own one good than four, and more households own five goods than none. If the number of household durable goods owned, k, is rank ordered, the ranking would be 3, 2, 1, 4, 5, 0, indicating the ordered quantity of accumulation of the goods.

Cumulative frequencies also can be derived from the relative frequencies. The data indicate approximately 50 percent (49.71) of the households own three or more goods and that 70.78 percent own from two to four of the goods in the set.

The data in Table III do not indicate the order in which the goods are accumulated or which goods are owned. However, in the next section the number of goods owned, k, is given and the priority of the particular goods accumulated is developed.

TABLE III

THE RELATIVE FREQUENCY DISTRIBUTION OF HOUSEHOLDS
OWNING k DURABLE GOODS OF THE SET, S

Durable goods owned	Households owning k durable goods					R(k|S)
k			Number			Percent
	Tenn.	Ky.	Ala.	Miss.	Region	
0	300	261	360	337	1,258	3.50
1	2,204	1,870	1,774	1,195	7,043	19.58
2	2,910	2,678	2,649	1,550	9,787	27.21
3	2,986	2,621	2,639	1,653	9,899	27.53
4	2,125	1,318	1,540	789	5,772	16.05
5	815	403	634	351	2,203	6.13
	11,340	9,151	9,596	5,875	35,962	100.00

SOURCE: Data are a resultant of computer tabulation of the 1970 East South Central Region Public Use Sample.

RELATIVE FREQUENCY OF THE DURABLE GOODS ACCUMULATED GIVEN THE NUMBER OF GOODS ACCUMULATED

If the number of durable goods accumulated, k, is zero or five, obviously, the household would have none or all of the goods in the set, S. Since k is given in this section, there would not be a relative frequency distribution of those owning zero or five, rather it would be certain the households had none or all of the goods in the set. However, this would not be the case for the households owning one through four goods of the set. Tables IV through VII show the relative frequency distribution of the households owning one through four goods of the set, respectively. The five durable goods included in the set are symbolized as follows: Television set--TV, Washing machine--WM, Clothes dryer--CD, Food freezer--FF, Dishwasher--DW.

The data in Table IV indicate that over 91 percent (91.24) of the households select the TV as their first good to accumulate. This is sufficiently greater than all of the others combined to infer that the TV will be the first good accumulated by the households making the first purchase. The data in Table V show that 80 percent of the households that have accumulated two household durable goods have a TV and a WM. Again, a sufficient majority is present to infer that most of the households selecting the second durable good will choose a WM.

However, the selection of the third good is not dominated by a single good. The data in Table VI indicate that the CD and the FF are candidates for the third good to be accumulated.

TABLE IV

THE RELATIVE FREQUENCY DISTRIBUTION OF HOUSEHOLDS
OWNING ONE DURABLE GOOD OF THE SET, S

Durable good owned	Households that own D					$R(D\|k=1,S)$
		Number				Percent
D	Tenn.	Ky.	Ala.	Miss.	Region	of Region
TV	2,062	1,665	1,619	1,080	6,426	91.24
WM	115	192	125	73	505	7.17
CD	2	0	0	0	2	0.03
FF	19	13	24	42	98	1.39
DW	6	0	6	0	12	0.17
	2,204	1,870	1,774	1,195	7,043	100.00

SOURCE: Data are a resultant of computer tabulation of the 1970 East South Central Region Public Use Sample.

TABLE V

THE RELATIVE FREQUENCY DISTRIBUTION OF HOUSEHOLDS
OWNING TWO DURABLE GOODS OF THE SET, S

Durable goods owned	Households that own D_1, D_2					$R(D_1,D_2\|k=2,S)$
		Number				Percent
D_1, D_2	Tenn.	Ky.	Ala.	Miss.	Region	of Region
TV, WM	2,296	2,328	2,102	1,076	7,802	79.72
TV, CD	19	14	5	4	42	0.43
TV, FF	325	198	396	375	1,294	13.23
WM, CD	189	66	81	45	381	3.89
WM, FF	24	14	16	8	62	0.63
WM, DW	56	57	48	41	202	2.06
CD, FF	1	1	0	1	3	0.03
CD, DW	0	0	0	0	0	0.00
FF, DW	0	0	1	0	1	0.01
	2,910	2,678	2,649	1,550	9,787	100.00

SOURCE: Data are a resultant of computer tabulation of the 1970 East South Central Region Public Use Sample.

TABLE VI

THE RELATIVE FREQUENCY DISTRIBUTION OF HOUSEHOLDS
OWNING THREE DURABLE GOODS OF THE SET, S

| Durable goods owned | Households that own D_1, D_2, D_3 | | | | | $R(D_1,D_2,D_3 \mid k=3,S)$ |
| | Number | | | | | |
D_1, D_2, D_3	Tenn.	Ky.	Ala.	Miss.	Region	Percent of Region
TV, WM, CD	1,456	1,410	938	364	4,168	42.11
TV, WM, FF	1,369	1,110	1,601	1,216	5.299	53.50
TV, WM, DW	86	65	73	40	264	2.67
TV, CD, FF	12	7	2	3	24	0.24
TV, CD, DW	2	0	1	1	4	0.04
TV, FF, DW	35	10	10	15	70	0.71
WM, CD, FF	23	13	9	11	56	0.57
WM, CD, DW	3	4	5	3	15	0.15
WM, FF, DW	0	2	0	0	2	0.02
CD, FF, DW	0	0	0	0	0	0.00
	2,986	2,621	2,639	1,659	9,899	100.00

SOURCE: Data are a resultant of computer tabulation of the 1970 East South Central Region.

TABLE VII

THE RELATIVE FREQUENCY DISTRIBUTION OF HOUSEHOLDS
OWNING FOUR DURABLE GOODS OF THE SET, S

Durable goods owned	Households that own D_1, D_2, D_3, D_4					$R(D_1,D_2,D_3,D_4\|k=4,S)$
D_1, D_2, D_3, D_4	Number					Percent of Region
	Tenn.	Ky.	Ala.	Miss.	Region	
TV, WM, CD, FF	1,498	896	1,021	551	3,966	68.71
TV, WM, CD, DW	561	375	435	177	1,548	26.82
TV, WM, FF, DW	60	45	83	59	247	4.28
TV, CD, FF, DW	1	0	0	0	1	0.02
WM, FF, DW, CD	5	2	1	2	10	0.17
	2,125	1,318	1,540	789	5,772	100.00

SOURCE: Data are a resultant of computer tabulation of the 1970 East South Central Region Public Use Sample.

TABLE VII

MOST LIKELY ACCUMULATION PATTERNS OF FOUR
HOUSEHOLD DURABLE GOODS IN THE SET, S

Priority of accumulation	Household durable good
First	TV
Second	WM
Third	FF CD
Fourth	CD FF DW

SOURCE: Compiled from Tables IV through VII.

Although Table VII shows that the fourth good selected most often is the good, CD or FF, that was not selected third. Also the DW enters as a viable candidate to be accumulated fourth.

The three most likely accumulation patterns are shown in Table VIII. The patterns TV, WM, CD, FF and TV, WM, FF, CD account for 69 percent of the households that have accumulated four of the household durable goods, while the pattern TV, WM, CD, DW accounts for 27 percent, these percentages are taken from Table VII.

SUMMARY AND CONCLUSION

To the extent that relative frequencies and conditional relative frequencies may be interpreted as probabilities, the relative frequencies developed in this paper have potentially significant marketing implications. Based on the analysis of the data and the interpretations of the findings, it seems apparent that all newly formed households are potential customers for a television set. Furthermore, the marketing effort should be directed toward a washing machine after the television set is acquired. A clothes dryer or a food freezer then becomes the candidate for the next good to be acquired. The final good to be acquired in the pattern is the dishwasher.

Different patterns of acquisition may develop with changing socioeconomic characteristics, goods sets of varying size and composition, and shifts in tastes and preferences of consumers.

TRACKS AND SESSIONS	NUMBER OF PAPERS			
	A	B	C	TOTAL[*]
General Administration Track:				
Information for the Citizen Planner	1	1	1	3
Management and Administration	–	5	–	5
Citizen Information	2	2	2	6
Development of Information Systems	2	–	2	4
Intercensal Estimates	3	2	–	5
Applications Track:				
Natural Resources Management	2	–	2	4
State/Regional Land and Natural Resources Information Systems	1	1	–	2
Transit Planning Applications	1	1	1	3
Housing Applications	1	–	3	4
Fire and Emergency Services	1	2	1	4
Human Services System	5	1	2	8
Planning and Census Applications	1	2	1	4
Fiscal/Budgetary Systems	5	3	–	8
Urban Planning and Analysis	2	2	1	5
Special Interest Group Track:				
Social Indicators	4	1	4	9
Criminal Justice	5	1	5	11
Remote Sensing	4	1	–	5
Geoprocessing	3	6	2	11
Evaluation	1	4	–	5
Minicomputer	–	–	10	10
International	1	2	2	5
Technology Transfer	1	2	3	6
Poster Sessions	8	4	5	17
Plenary Sessions	–	2	3	5
CONFERENCE TOTAL	54 36.2%	45 30.2%	50 33.6%	149 100 0%

A = Papers included in this conference Proceedings (i.e. papers received by August 1, 197

B = Papers received after August 1, 1976 (not included in this Proceedings)

C = Papers which were not submitted to the Papers Committee or were not passed on to the Proceedings editor.

[*]Does not include several panel discussions for which formal papers had not been prepared

Ashkenas, Ron and Grundstein, Nathan D., "The Campaign Organization
    as a Structure for the Management of Meaning" (12 pp)

Carter, James R., "An Address Matching - Line Printer Mapping
    System In Cobol C for Small Cities" (8 pp)

Carter, Jim R. and Barb, Charles E., "Adaptation of the Public
    Technology, Inc. Fire Station Locator: The Oklahoma City
    Experience" (13 pp)

Craig, William James, "Accessibility Measurement and Use in Land
    Use Planning" (13 pp)

Barb, Charles E., "Initial Experience in Information System
    Technology Transfer in the Urban Technology System (UTS)
    Experiment" (13 pp)

Berlin, Geoffrey N., "Assign: An Interactive Pupil Assignment
    Model" (11 pp)

Bohl, Frederick L., "The Development of an Urban Information System:
    The Ann Arbor Experiment" (19 pp)

Burroughs, Kendall, "Information Technologies For Development -
    The Minicomputer: A Rational Alternative" (3 pp)

Dangermond, Jack, "Integrated Terrain Unit Mapping (ITUM) - An
    Approach for Automation of Polygon Natural Resource
    Information" (11 pp)

Davies, James J., "Q - Methodology as an Approach to Creation of
    Social Indicators" (15 pp)

Delahanty, Dolores, "Overview of Human Services Coordination
    Alliance" (9 pp)

Diuguid, William H., "A Computerized Land Use Evaluation System
    for Medium-sized Cities" (12 pp)

Dooley, J. E., Maas, R. B., Keir, A. and Pisarzowski, G., "A
    Systems Study For Retail Policy Planning" (16 pp)

Engels, Richard A., "Local Area Population Research and Federal
    Programs" (12 pp)

Ferguson, J. F. and Herman, F. D., "An Operating System for the Intergovernmental Sharing of Data" (11 pp)

Furino, Antonio, "Construction Information System: San Antonio" (16 pp)

Furino, Antonio and Stevens, James W., "A Preliminary Report on the Status of Regional Information Systems: A National Survey" (15 pp)

Grier, George and Grier, Eunice S., "Using Movership Data to Improve Intercensal Estimation of Population and Housing Market" (14 pp)

Griffiths, Daniel W., Miller, Mitchell and Ungar, Bruce D., "Government Contractors and Academic Research: A Case Study of Conflict and Cooperation in the Creation of a Management Information and Evaluation System" (11 pp)

Hanson, Perry O., "Information Systems Considerations for Urban Crime Analysis" (7 pp)

Hewey, Dell May and Barb, Charles E., "Document and Expert Advisory Support Sub-systems: Overlooked Dimensions in Urban and Regional Information Systems" (10 pp)

Holm, Nils, "The Danish Road Data Bank and Its Use in Traffic Accident Analysis and Prevention" (7 pp)

Icove, David J. and Carter, James R., "Computer-assisted Arson Investigation" (8 pp)

Johnson, James C. and Ruch, David A., "An Information System for Fiscal Analysis" (14 pp)

Kelly, Fred L., "Property Tax System: DeKalb County" (11 pp)

Kraemer, Kenneth L., "Lassiez Innover: A Critique of Federal Involvement in Development of State and Local Government Information Systems" (14 pp)

Krause, Hank and Johnson, Gary, "Maximization of Resources in the Development of a Low Cost Geographic Base Information System for Small Communities" (9 pp)

Marcus, Morton J. and McCoskey, C. Lowell, "INDIRS: The Indiana Information Retrieval System" (6 pp)

Moore, J. R., "The Urban Dweller as Information Seeker: Citizen Information as a Private Game" (7 pp)

Norris, David A. and Heath, Walter D., "The North Carolina Title XX Contract Services Evaluation System" (11 pp)

Renshaw, Richard W., "Utilizing the Intersection File: A Local Perspective of GBF/DIME" (16 pp)

Rogers, Everett M., Eveland, J. D. and Klepper, Constance A., "The Diffusion and Adoption of GBF/DIME Among Regional and Local Governments" (14 pp)

Schweitzer, Richard H., "Defining Urbanized Areas With the Aid of Landsat Imagery" (11 pp)

Shawcroft, Robert G., Marshment, Richard S. and Horwood, Edgar M., "Experimental Interactive Urban Analysis Using Geoprocessed Data" (12 pp)

Sherr, David M., Hersh, Harvey and Jones, Lester, "Some Notes on the User Oriented Development of a Client Tracking System for Information and Referral" (5 pp)

Sherr, David M. and Masciocchi, Carla, "A Perspective on Simulation Models as Decision Aids" (11 pp)

Silver, Jacob, "GBF/DIME - Status 1976" (6 pp)

Strahan, Bruce, "A Case for Delivering Police Services Using the GBF/DIME File" (8 pp)

Thune, Gene E., Marshment, Richard S. and Sari, Allan O., "Integrating Transit Planning Needs With Geographic Basefile Systems" (12 pp)

Travers, John K. and Bratakos, Petros, "Major Features of the New Automated Earnings Tax System - City of St. Louis" (17 pp)

Turner, Jerry E., "Time Sharing for Local Government" (7 pp)

Williams, Thomas D., "The Development of a Needs-oriented Reporting System for Assessment of a Community-based Outreach Program" (14 pp)

Wood, Peter M., "Interactive Thematic Mapping - A Report" (10 pp)

Woodie, Paul R. and Riordan, Timothy H., "Program Strategies: Translating Philosophy Into Daily Decisions" (15 pp)

Zobrist, Albert L., Bryant, Nevin A. and Landini, Albert J., "IBIS: A Geographic Information System that can Use Satellite Data for Urban Analysis" (16 pp)

URISA CONFERENCE PROCEEDINGS: ORDER FORM

I am interested in purchasing the following Conference proceedings:

☐ PROCEEDINGS OF THE FOURTH ANNUAL URISA CONFERENCE ON URBAN PLANNING
INFORMATION SYSTEMS AND PROGRAMS, 1966 ....$ 5.00

☐ URBAN AND REGIONAL INFORMATION SYSTEMS FOR SOCIAL PROGRAMS: Papers
from the Fifth Annual URISA Conference, 1967 ....$ 6.50

☐ URBAN AND REGIONAL iNFORMATION SYSTEMS: FEDERAL ACTIVITIES AND
SPECIALIZED SYSTEMS: Papers from the Sixth Annual URISA Conference, 1968...$ 6.50

☐ URBAN AND REGIONAL INFORMATION SYSTEMS: SERVICE SYSTEMS FOR CITIES.
Papers from the Seventh Annual URISA Conference, 1969 ....$10.00

☐ URBAN AND REGIONAL INFORMATION SYSTEMS: PAST, PRESENT AND FUTURE.
Papers from the Eighth Annual URISA Conference, 1970 ....$10.00

☐ URBAN AND REGIONAL INFORMATION SYSTEMS: INFORMATION SYSTEMS AND
POLITICAL SYSTEMS. Papers from the Ninth Annual URISA Conference, 1971....$10.00

☐ URBAN AND REGIONAL INFORMATION SYSTEMS: INFORMATION RESEARCH FOR AN
URBAN SOCIETY, VOLUME I. Selected Papers from the Tenth Annual URISA
Conference, 1972 ....$10.00

☐ URBAN AND REGIONAL INFORMATION SYSTEMS: INFORMATION RESEARCH FOR
AN URBAN SOCIETY, VOLUME II. Selected Papers from the Tenth Annual
URISA Conference, 1972.. ....$10.00

☐ URBAN AND REGIONAL INFORMATION SYSTEMS: PRESPECTIVES ON INFORMATION
SYSTEMS, Papers from the Eleventh Annual URISA Conference, 1973............$10.00

☐ URBAN AND REGIONAL INFORMATION SYSTEMS: RESOURCES AND RESULTS, VOLUME I.
Selected Papers from the Twelfth Annual URISA Conference, 1974.............$10.00

☐ URBAN AND REGIONAL INFORMATION SYSTEMS: RESOURCES AND RESULTS, VOLUME II.
Selected Papers from the Twelfth Annual URISA Conference, 1974.............$10.00

☐ URBAN AND REGIONAL INFORMATION SYSTEMS: COMPUTERS, LOCAL GOVERNMENT AND
PRODUCTIVITY, VOLUME I. Selected Papers from the Thirteenth Annual
URISA Conference, 1975...$10.00

☐ URBAN AND REGIONAL INFORMATION SYSTEMS: COMPUTERS, LOCAL GOVERNMENT AND
PRODUCTIVITY, VOLUME II. Selected Papers from the Thirteenth Annual
URISA Conference, 1975...$10.00

ORDERS FOR THE ABOVE PROCEEDINGS SHOULD BE SENT TO:

URBAN AND REGIONAL INFORMATION SYSTEMS ASSOCIATION
1313 East 60th Street
Chicago, Illinois   60637

When ordering from outside the continental United States, add $0.75
for surface mail or $6.50 for airmail.

Name: _____

Title and Dept.: _____

Employer: _____

Address: _____ Zip: ____